TO

LAW

This book reflects the wide range of current scholarship on Roman law. The essays, newly commissioned for this volume, cover the sources of evidence for classical Roman law; the elements of private law, as well as criminal and public law; and the second life of Roman law in Byzantium, in civil and canon law, and in political discourse from AD 1100 to the present. Roman law nowadays is studied in many different ways, which are reflected in the diversity of approaches in the essays. Some focus on how the law evolved in ancient Rome, others on its place in the daily life of the Roman citizen, still others on how Roman legal concepts and doctrines have been deployed through the ages. All of them are responses to one and the same thing: the sheer intellectual vitality of Roman law, which has secured its place as a central element in the intellectual tradition and history of the West.

David Johnston is a Queen's Counsel who practises at the Bar in Scotland, mainly in the fields of public and commercial law. He holds MA, PhD, and LLD degrees from the University of Cambridge. From 1993 to 1999 he was Regius Professor of Civil Law at the University of Cambridge and a Fellow of Christ's College. He is currently an honorary professor at Edinburgh Law School. Johnston is the author of many publications, including *The Roman Law of Trusts* (1988), *Roman Law in Context* (1999), and *Prescription and Limitation* (second edition, 2012).

THE CAMBRIDGE COMPANION TO

ROMAN LAW

Edited by

DAVID JOHNSTON

Faculty of Advocates, Edinburgh

CAMBRIDGE
UNIVERSITY PRESS

CAMBRIDGE
UNIVERSITY PRESS

32 Avenue of the Americas, New York NY 10013-2473, USA

Cambridge University Press is part of the University of Cambridge.

It furthers the University's mission by disseminating knowledge in the pursuit of education, learning and research at the highest international levels of excellence.

www.cambridge.org
Information on this title: www.cambridge.org/9780521719940

First published 2015

A catalogue record for this publication is available from the British Library

Library of Congress Cataloguing in Publication data
The Cambridge companion to Roman law / [edited by] David Johnston, Edinburgh Law School.
pages cm
ISBN 978-0-521-89564-4 (hardback)
1. Roman law. I. Johnston, David, 1961– editor.
KJA147.C335 2015
340.5′4–dc23 2014038626

ISBN 978-0-521-71994-0 Paperback

Contents

Contributors

JEAN-JACQUES AUBERT is Professor of Classical Philology and Ancient History at the University of Neuchâtel.

R. H. HELMHOLZ is Ruth Wyatt Rosenson Professor of Law at the University of Chicago.

CAROLINE HUMFRESS is Reader in History at Birkbeck College, London.

DAVID IBBETSON is Regius Professor of Civil Law at the University of Cambridge.

DAVID JOHNSTON is a QC and Honorary Professor at the University of Edinburgh.

WOLFGANG KAISER is Professor at the Institute for Legal History and Historical Comparative Law at the University of Freiburg im Breisgau.

ANDREW LEWIS is emeritus Professor of Comparative Legal History, University College London.

ANDREW LINTOTT is a Fellow of Worcester College, Oxford.

LAURENT MAYALI is Lloyd M. Robbins Professor of Law and Director of the Robbins Religious and Civil Law Collection, University of California at Berkeley.

ERNEST METZGER is Douglas Professor of Civil Law at the University of Glasgow.

ELIZABETH A. MEYER is Professor in the Department of History at the University of Virginia.

PAUL DU PLESSIS is Senior Lecturer in Civil Law and Legal History at the University of Edinburgh.

JOHN RICHARDSON is emeritus Professor of Classics at the University of Edinburgh

MAGNUS RYAN is a Fellow of Peterhouse, Cambridge.

A. J. B. SIRKS is emeritus Regius Professor of Civil Law at the University of Oxford.

BERNARD H. STOLTE is Professor of Byzantine Law at the University of Groningen.

LAURENS WINKEL is Professor at the Erasmus School of Law, Erasmus University Rotterdam.

JOSEPH GEORG WOLF is emeritus Professor at the Institute for Legal History and Historical Comparative Law at the University of Freiburg im Breisgau.

REINHARD ZIMMERMANN is Professor and Director at the Max-Planck-Institut für ausländisches und internationales Privatrecht, Hamburg.

Abbreviations

1. General

AARC	Atti dell'Accademia Romanistica Costantiniana
AE	*L'Année Épigraphique*
AJP	*American Journal of Philology*
ANRW	*Aufstieg und Niedergang der römischen Welt*, edited by H. Temporini (Berlin, 1972–)
BIDR	*Bulletino dell'Istituto di Diritto Romano*
c.	caput (i.e., chapter)
C.	Code of Justinian (*Corpus iuris civilis* vol. 2, edited by P. Krueger)
C. 1 q. 1 c. 1	*Decretum Gratiani*, Causa 1, quaestio 1, canon 1
CAH	*Cambridge Ancient History*, 2nd edn. (Cambridge, 1970–2005)
CCG	Cahiers du Centre Glotz
CGL	*Corpus Glossariorum Latinorum*, edited by G. Goetz, 7 vols. (Leipzig, 1893–1901)
CIL	*Corpus Inscriptionum Latinarum* (Berlin)
Collatio	*Mosaicarum et Romanarum Legum Collatio* (in *FIRA* vol. 2, 541–89)
CPL	*Corpus Papyrorum Latinarum*, edited by R. Cavenaile (Wiesbaden, 1958)
CQ	*Classical Quarterly*
C.Th.	Theodosian Code
D.	Digest (*Corpus iuris civilis* vol. 1, edited by T. Mommsen and P. Krueger)
DD	*Doctores* (authoritative jurists on the *ius commune*)
Dist. 1 c. 1	*Decretum Gratiani*, Distinctio 1, canon 1
D. p.	Dictum post (in the *Decretum Gratiani*)
Ed. Just.	Edict of Justinian

FIR	*Fontes Iuris Romani*, edited by C. G. Bruns, 7th edn. by O. Gradenwitz (Tübingen, 1909)
FIRA	*Fontes Iuris Romani Anteiustiniani*, edited by S. Riccobono, J. Baviera, C. Ferrini, J. Furlani, and V. Arangio-Ruiz, 3 vols., 2nd edn. (Florence, 1968)
fo.	folio
FV	*Fragmenta Vaticana* (in *FIRA* vol. 2, 463–540)
Gaius	*Institutes* of Gaius
gl.	gloss
gl. ord.	*glossa ordinaria*
ILS	Inscriptiones Latinae Selectae
Inst.	*Institutes* of Justinian (*Corpus iuris civilis* vol. 1, edited by P. Krueger)
JJP	*Journal of Juristic Papyrology*
JRS	*Journal of Roman Studies*
lex Irn.	*lex Irnitana*
lib.	liber (i.e., book)
ms	manuscript
Nov.	Novels (*Corpus iuris civilis* vol. 3, edited by R Schoell and G. Kroll)
PS	*Pauli sententiae* (in *FIRA* vol. 2, 317–417)
PSI	Pubblicazioni della Società italiana per la ricerca dei papyri greci e latini in Egitto
RAAN	Rendiconti dell'Accademia di Archeologia Lettere e Belle Arti di Napoli
RAC	Reallexikon für Antike und Christentum (Stuttgart, 1950–2012)
RE	*Paulys Realencyclopädie der classichen Altertumswissenschaft*, edited by G. Wissowa et al. (Stuttgart, 1894–1978)
RHDFE	*Revue Historique de Droit Français et Étranger*
RIDA	*Revue Internationale des Droits de l'Antiquité*
Roman Statutes	Roman Statutes, edited by M. H. Crawford, 2 vols. (London, 1996)
SB	Sammelbuch Griechischer Urkunden aus Ägypten
SDHI	*Studia et Documenta Historiae et Iuris*
SEG	Supplementum Epigraphicum Graecum
Sext 1.1.1	*Liber Sextus*, Lib. 1, tit. 1, cap. 1
TH	Herculaneum tablet

TP	Pompeian tablet
TPN	New Pompeian tablet (in edition by Wolf, 2010)
TPSulp	New Pompeian Tablet (in edition by Camodeca, 1999)
TR	*Tijdschrift voor Rechtsgeschiedenis*
TUI	Tractatus universi iuris (Rome, 1584–86)
UE	*Ulpiani Epitome* (in *FIRA* vol. 2, 259–301)
X 1.1.1	*Decretales Gregorii IX*, Lib. 1, tit. 1, cap. 1
ZSS	*Zeitschrift der Savigny-Stiftung für Rechtsgeschichte* (unless otherwise stated, all references are to the Romanistische Abteilung)

2. Classical Authors

App. *Iber.*	Appian, *Iberica*
Apul. *Apol.*	Apuleius, *Apologia*
Ar. *Pol.*	Aristotle, *Politica*
Asc. *Corn.*	Asconius, *in Cornelianam*
Mil.	*in Milonianam*
Scaur.	*in Scaurianam*
Aug. *Ep.*	Augustine, *Epistulae*
Caes. *Gall.*	Caesar, *De bello Gallico*
Call.	Callistratus
Cels.	Celsus
Cic. *Att.*	Cicero, *Epistulae ad Atticum*
ad Brut.	*Epistulae ad Brutum*
Brut.	*Brutus*
Caec.	*pro Caecina*
Cat.	*in Catilinam*
Clu.	*pro Cluentio*
Deiot.	*pro rege Deiotaro*
Dom.	*de Domo sua*
Fam.	*Epistulae ad familiares*
Flacc.	*pro Flacco*
Inv.	*de Inventione*
Leg.	*De Legibus*
Mur.	*pro Murena*
Off.	*de officiis*

de Orat.	*de Oratore*
Part.	*Partitiones Oratoriae*
Phil.	*Philippicae*
Q. Rosc.	*pro Q. Roscio comoedo*
Quinct.	*pro Quinctio*
Quint. frat.	*Epistulae ad Quintum fratrem*
Rab. perd.	*pro Rabirio perduellionis reo*
Rosc. Am.	*pro Roscio Amerino*
Sest.	*pro Sestio*
Sull.	*pro Sulla*
Top.	*Topica*
1 Verr. /2 Verr.	*in Verrem (actio prima/secunda)*
Dio	Cassius Dio, *Historia romana*
Diod.	Diodorus Siculus, *Bibliotheke*
Dion. *Ant.*	Dionysius Hallicarnassensis, *Antiquitates Romanae*
Eutropius	Eutropius, *Breviarium Historiae Romanae*
Front. *de aq.*	Frontinus, *de aquis urbis Romae*
Gai.	Gaius
Gell. *NA.*	Aulus Gellius, *Noctes Atticae*
Isid. *Etym.*	Isidore, *Etymologiae*
Jul.	Julian
Lact. *Mort.*	Lactantius, *De mortibus persecutorum*
Livy	Livy, *ab Urbe Condita*
Marcel.	Marcellus
Marci.	Marcian
Mod.	Modestinus
Ov. *Trist.*	Ovid, *Tristia*
Pap.	Papinian
Paul	Paul
Petr. *Sat.*	Petronius, *Satyrica*
Plin. *Ep.*	Pliny (Caecilius Secundus), *Epistulae*
Plin. *NH.*	Pliny (Secundus), *Naturalis Historia*
Plin. *Pan.*	Pliny (Caecilius Secundus), *Panegyricus*
Plut. *Cato*	Plutarch, *Cato maior*
Cic.	*Cicero*
Pomp.	*Pompey*

Quaest. rom.	*Quaestiones romanae*
Sull.	*Sulla*
Polyb.	Polybius, *Histories*
Pomp.	Pomponius
Quint. *Inst.*	Quintilian, *Institutio Oratoria*
Sall. *Cat.*	Sallust, *Catilina*
Hist.	*Historiae*
Jug.	*Jugurtha*
Scaev.	Q.Cervidius Scaevola
Sen. *Apoc.*	Seneca, *Apocolocyntosis*
Ira.	*de Ira*
SHA	Scriptores Historiae Augustae
Stat. *Silv.*	Statius, *Silvae*
Strabo	Strabo, *Geographia*
Suet. *Aug.*	Suetonius, *Augustus*
Calig.	*Caligula*
Claud.	*Claudius*
Galb.	*Galba*
Jul.	*Julius*
Ner.	*Nero*
Tib.	*Tiberius*
Tac. *Ann.*	Tacitus, *Annales*
Dial.	*Dialogus*
Hist.	*Historiae*
Ulp.	Ulpian
Val. Max.	Valerius Maximus, *Facta et Dicta Memorabilia*
Varr. LL.	Varro, *de Lingua Latina*
Vitr.	Vitruvius, *de Architectura*

Part I

INTRODUCTION

1 Introduction

David Johnston

This *Companion* brings together in a single volume essays that reflect the wide range of modern scholarship on Roman law. A conventional textbook on Roman private law would explain in turn the law of persons (family, slavery, citizenship); property (ownership and possession and how they are acquired and transferred, subsidiary real rights, testate and intestate succession); obligations (contract, delict, unjustified enrichment); and actions (the courts and civil procedure). This is the scheme pioneered by the second-century Roman jurist Gaius, whose *Institutes* is still perhaps the best introductory textbook ever written on Roman law.

This *Companion* is not a textbook of that kind. It does cover the traditional institutional topics, but it seeks to range much more widely. Before examining *how*, we should ask *why*? Why is it, in the twenty-first century, that Roman law is still studied and is still important? Here are several possible answers, although this is by no means an exhaustive list.

First, Roman law provides what might be called a vocabulary of rights and obligations. The institutional scheme just described provides the analytical structure for most modern systems of private law. Even nowadays a good grasp of that essential structure and vocabulary is a powerful tool in the hands of a lawyer wrestling with the correct analysis of a legal problem. That is why in some universities Roman law is still a compulsory subject for first-year law students: nothing else conveys the vocabulary of rights and obligations so clearly and economically, without an untidy accretion of case law.

Second, even beyond the field of private law, the contribution of Roman law to the western legal and political tradition has been enormous. Roman law was the foundation for the law of the church – canon law. And within political discourse it was the source of central ideas about empire – doctrines drawn from Roman private law were deployed in order to elaborate concepts of public law, as well as in argument about the relationship between rulers and those they ruled.

Third, it is no accident that Roman law has had such influence. The surviving sources, especially as transmitted in Justinian's *Digest* and *Code*, present a legal system of extraordinary sophistication. The sheer intellectual challenge involved in seeking to understand Roman law does much to explain why for centuries it has attracted the attention of scholars. Since about 1100 Justinian's *Digest* and *Code* have been subjected to a process of minute textual interpretation and criticism in a way paralleled in the western tradition only by the attention given to the Bible. It is therefore safe to say that all surviving Roman legal works have been interpreted, reinterpreted, and re-reinterpreted. That being so, one might reasonably ask: is it possible nowadays to say anything new and interesting about Roman law?

The answer (as is to be expected in a companion to Roman law) is 'yes'. The foci and approaches adopted by scholars have of course varied over the centuries. Initially, the main concern was to understand the legal doctrines set out in the Roman texts, especially Justinian's *Digest* and *Code*. Only much later did the focus shift from viewing the *Digest* as a unified body of law to a body containing the work of numerous different Roman jurists of different periods. That was a decisive shift from viewing Roman law as a source of doctrine to viewing it as a product of history. The shift made it possible to consider what differences of opinion could be discerned between early and late jurists, or between jurists of different schools of thought, and more generally to examine the evolution of legal rules and doctrines over the centuries. More recently still, legal historians have begun to focus on wider contexts. Some have been concerned to locate Roman law in its intellectual context, by reference to philosophy, rhetoric, or literature. Others have attempted to understand how Roman law worked in Roman society, how it influenced particular kinds of economic activity; or, conversely, how it was itself shaped by the demand to be able to engage in certain economic activities within a legal framework.

This *Companion* aims to explain how Roman law was formed, especially from the late Republic onwards; how it was applied in practice in Rome and its empire; the various ancient sources of information about Roman law; the main institutions of Roman law, private, public, and criminal; and the later life of Roman law in Byzantium and beyond, in civil society, in the church, and in political discourse.

Chapter 2 considers the Roman jurists within the wider intellectual and cultural context of their times. The chapter identifies three different schools in modern scholarship on Roman law. At one extreme is a close but somewhat ahistorical focus on legal doctrine; at the other an emphasis on law in context, whether the context is intellectual, social, or economic.

The third school adopts an intermediate position. The editor of this *Companion* has made no attempt to impose uniformity of approach (even if such a thing were possible), so the various essays reflect these diverse perspectives.

It may be helpful to add a few words on the remaining chapters. Chapter 3 deals with the ways in which the law was made in Roman antiquity, from the Republic through to the late empire. There are important elements of continuity in the development of the law under changing political structures, but the differences are equally striking. As a result of Roman imperialism, Roman law came to be the law not just of the city of Rome but also of the territories into which Rome had expanded. Chapter 4 looks at how far Roman and how far local law applied within various provincial communities.

Part III contains four chapters on the sources of evidence for Roman law. The most important source remains Justinian's compilation, discussed in Chapter 8. The excerpts from classical writings contained in the *Digest* and the legal pronouncements of emperors brought together in the *Code* reflect the law as it stood at different times. Studying how the Justinianic compilations were put together is an important part of recreating a picture of the evolution of Roman law over the preceding centuries. Yet there is also much Roman law to be found outside the *Corpus iuris civilis*. Much can be found, for instance, in literary works such as those of Cicero. Documentary sources are also a vital resource for understanding Roman law in practice. Chapter 5 discusses the documents preserved as a result of the eruption of Vesuvius in AD 79. They illustrate everyday legal transactions such as borrowing and granting securities. It is also important to understand the changing role that writing played in legal documents, so Chapter 6 explores the apparent shift towards greater dependence on legal documents. One very rich vein of material on Roman law, little explored so far, is to be found in the patristic sources, the subject of Chapter 7. Not only do they attest forensic activity and settlement of disputes, they also provide a wealth of information about Roman law as social practice. Conversely, they illustrate how Roman law served as a natural reservoir of metaphors for late Roman theologians.

Part IV explores the main areas of Roman private law. Chapter 9 on slavery, family, and status considers the key legal institutions that governed the lives of Roman citizens. The central question is how a person could become a legitimate Roman citizen; interlinked with this is the unique Roman institution of paternal power. The chapter also deals with the place occupied by slaves and freedmen. Chapter 10, 'Property', first surveys the structure of the Roman law of property in the schemes presented in the *Institutes* of Gaius and of Justinian and argues for the need to pay more attention to the concepts and categories that underpin these schemes. It goes on to give a brief historical survey of the law of property, emphasizing that an adequate survey, especially where land is concerned, needs not just to consider the law but also to include a social, economic, and political perspective. Chapter 11, 'Succession', is concerned with how property was transferred on death. There were detailed rules about the formal validity of wills, but the emphasis in the chapter is on what could be done in a Roman will and by what means. It attempts to understand the legal rules in the context of the society in which they operated. Chapter 12, 'Commerce', reviews how the various sources of Roman law contributed to the legal aspects of business life. It surveys the Roman law of contracts and such topics as sale, hire, lending, banking, securities, organization of businesses, use of slaves, partnership, and insolvency. Chapter 13 is concerned with delicts. Its main topics are the broad scope of the law of theft; *iniuria*, a delict which covered a wide range of violations of what we might call the right to respect for one's person and personality; and the *lex Aquilia*, which provided remedies for damage to certain kinds of property. In all of them close attention is paid to the interpretative techniques elaborated by the jurists. Litigation, the subject of Chapter 14, is the final topic in this part. Rules in law books cannot be understood in context except against the framework of civil procedure. This chapter considers the various types of court procedure; judges; evidence; representation in court; rhetoric; and advocacy. It also gives an outline of the rules and, where possible, the working practices under the various procedures.

Part V deals with criminal and public law. Chapter 15 on crime and punishment traces the law from the Republican period through to the Dominate. Among the themes pursued are the centrality of revenge and compensation in Roman thought, and the belief that communities have a necessity to reward virtue and punish vice; the relatively limited field of criminal law under the Republic, its extension in the late Republic through the system of jury-courts, and reforms under the emperor Augustus; and the introduction of imperial jurisdiction and trials in the senate. Chapter 16 considers public law, one of the more neglected areas of the work of the Roman jurists: while they devoted most of their energies to work on private law, they also produced significant work on constitutional and administrative law. Even before the emergence of an imperial bureaucracy, the jurists had elaborated public-law concepts such as *imperium* and *iurisdictio*, and the late classical jurists had written treatises on various public offices and other aspects of public law and life.

Part VI, 'Byzantium and Beyond', deals with the afterlife of Roman law. Chapter 17 concerns Byzantine law. It began as Roman law but followed its own course, in a different language and a different cultural environment; nonetheless, it never lost sight of its Roman origins. This chapter points out that it sometimes seems that an ever-greater divide separates scholars of East and West and emphasizes the importance of looking across the divide. Chapter 18, 'The Legacy of Roman Law', traces the development of a European *ius commune* from its starting point in northern Italy in the eleventh and twelfth centuries. Bologna was the centre for the study of the newly rediscovered *Corpus iuris civilis* of Justinian, and Irnerius the leading figure there in the early twelfth century. A line of scholars became established in Bologna who based their instruction on close study and annotation of the Justinianic texts. This method gradually spread beyond Italy. In the second half of the thirteenth century attention turned to writing commentaries and treatises as well as giving advice (*consilia*) on specific legal questions. These writings laid the foundation for a *ius commune* which by the end of the middle ages had spread into Germanic lands too. Canon law, the subject of Chapter 19, is concerned with the place occupied by Roman law in the law of the church. It examines in turn three historical periods and the differing role played by Roman law in solving the legal and administrative problems faced by the church at those times. It shows how Roman law played a part in the formulation of the *Corpus iuris canonici*, the basic source collection of law for the church in the West, by filling in gaps, supplying legal principles, and adding scholarly weight to the canons. It also considers the developed *ius commune* and how this amalgam of the canon and Roman laws was the foundation for the church's law, taught in the European universities, long served as a standard for interpretation and a source of law in both church and secular courts, and was developed by a host of learned commentators. Chapter 20, 'Political Thought', introduces the main ideas about empire which were current in the law schools and looks at how concepts of private law were applied by medieval jurists to the relationships between the rulers and the ruled. Legal education changed significantly in the late thirteenth century as lawyers embraced the political problems of their day in their teaching; the corollary was that political debate took on legal characteristics.

Chapter 21, on Roman law in the modern world, asks what it means to say that the modern continental civil codes are based on Roman law. While there are usually Roman foundations, often a very un-Roman edifice has been built on them. Even where modern rules in various codes are based on Roman law, they are hardly ever identical; there is considerable diversity within a fundamental intellectual unity. The chapter considers in what sense Roman law became the basis of a *ius commune* or civilian tradition, and explores the extent to which it is possible to speak of a European tradition. That raises the question of the influence of Roman law in England and elsewhere.

The chapters of this *Companion* show that Roman law can be – and actually is – studied in many different ways and for many different purposes. Among them are: understanding how the law grew and evolved in ancient Rome; investigating how it worked in the daily life of the Roman citizen; studying the crystallization and development by the Roman jurists of key legal concepts and doctrines; and pursuing the deployment of those concepts and doctrines through the ages and to the present day, in contexts variously civil, ecclesiastical, and political. There is room for all of these approaches. Diverse as they are, they represent responses to one and the same thing: the sheer intellectual vitality of Roman law. It is that vitality that has secured the position of Roman law as a central element in the intellectual tradition and history of the West.

2 Roman Law and Its Intellectual Context

Laurens Winkel

Roman law in the form of the legislation of the emperor Justinian has been studied in Western Europe since the end of the eleventh century in Bologna.[1] It has had enormous authority – mostly on an informal basis, but bolstered by a strong ideology.[2] Since 1900, the year in which the German civil code came into force, hardly anywhere in Europe has it been possible to speak of Roman law as a direct source of current private law.[3] Nevertheless, it was – and still is – a 'common frame of reference' long before this expression was coined in the framework of European private law of the future.[4]

1. The Study of Roman Law in Its Intellectual Context

It is possible to distinguish at least three different ways of studying Roman law today. A first approach starts with actual legal problems. One can certainly ask about the historical background of these problems, but the actual problems remain the centre of attention. So Roman law is a kind of auxiliary tool for the understanding of modern private law. It is a treasury of legal ideas that can be put to use in solving today's legal problems. Institutions of Roman law are detached from their original context and so take on an air of timelessness. Examples are the clauses that accompany the contract of personal security: the *beneficium divisionis* or the *beneficium excussionis*. The *lex commissoria* in the law of sale and of pledge is another example. This is the timeless and the 'infallible' part of private law, useful for understanding modern private law.[5] This approach has its roots in the Historical School of German jurisprudence of the nineteenth century and appears to be totally ahistorical. But that is not necessarily so: see, for example, the impressive book by Reinhard Zimmermann.[6] He deals with the general structure of the law of obligations and explains clearly its historical roots, starting with the elliptical texts of the Roman jurists and going on to the legal scholars of the nineteenth century, the German Pandectists, who built complex dogmatic structures on the basis of Roman legal texts. For real rights there is now a comparable work by Willem Zwalve.[7] It explains the law of ownership and other real rights using examples from historical sources and comparative law.

There is a second approach to Roman law.[8] In it the emphasis is also on matters of private law, but there is a far greater sensibility to legal evolution within Roman law itself. This approach began as early as the nineteenth century, when Roman law gradually ceased to be a direct source of current (private) law. Early representatives of the approach are Alfred Pernice (1841–1901)[9] and Otto Lenel (1849–1935).[10]

We owe to Lenel two of the most important modern tools for the study of classical Roman law: first, the reconstruction of the writings of classical jurists in the so-called *Palingenesia*[11] by using the inscriptions at the beginning of each fragment of the *Digest*. These are carefully preserved in the most important manuscript of the *Digest*, the *Littera Florentina*, which is the point of reference for all modern editions.[12] The second tool is in a sense a continuation of the *Palingenesia*. Here Lenel collected quotations from the *Edictum Perpetuum* set out in the commentaries written by the classical Roman jurists and rearranged them so far as possible in their original order.[13]

This neo-humanistic approach only had its true breakthrough in the seventies of the last century. In the initial period of historical studies of Roman law, the trend was to identify massive changes to the classical texts ('interpolations') attributed to the law-making process in the time of Justinian.[14] That trend began in the second half of the nineteenth century.[15] Only a century later was this approach at last fundamentally questioned; in retrospect the assumption of interpolations was found to be totally unfounded. With some justification, these first attempts at a historical approach to Roman law were criticized, on the grounds that they dealt in legal phenomena which were a construction and which never existed in reality. That was to a certain degree true in the heyday of interpolationism: Romanists[16] developed all kinds of ideal concepts, such as the notion that the jurists wrote Ciceronian Latin, which is nowadays regarded as untenable. Today the approach to interpolations is far more prudent. The great majority of Romanists think that the only unquestionable interpolations are to be found in the substitution of words referring to institutions abolished by Justinian (for example, the informal transfer of ownership by way of *traditio* replaces the references to the formal *mancipatio*; *fiducia* as an older form of security is replaced by *pignus*). For other interpolations one has to look first at the Justinianic constitutions in the *Code*, which contain much information on Justinian's legal policy. This source of evidence had long been neglected, as Lokin has rightly argued.[17] The definitive turning point came in 1967 at the conference 'La critica del testo' organized by the Società Italiana di Storia del Diritto. There the leading Austro-German Romanist Max Kaser developed for the first time an explicit, coherent, and modern methodology for the study of the texts of the *Corpus iuris civilis*.[18]

Scholars adhering to this approach distinguish between earlier and later generations of Roman jurists; they take the individual qualities and opinions of the Roman jurists into account; and they are aware (far more than the earlier group of Romanists was) that Roman law had its roots in legal practice and concrete cases. They do not aim to diminish the differences within the *Digest*. On the contrary, these differences are discussed at length and explained by identifying differences between individual Roman jurists, generations of jurists, or schools of jurists. Classical Roman law rather than Justinianic law is the main focus. The reason for this is the fascinating diversity of legal opinions in the period before Justinian, to which only Justinian himself put an end.[19]

This is the approach of Franz Wieacker (1908–94),[20] Max Kaser (1906–97), and many other Romanists. Together they form the neo-humanistic school which had its roots in late nineteenth-century Germany. This does not mean that in their works there are no surviving signs of the Pandectism which prevailed earlier. In student textbooks in particular, but also in the structure of Kaser's *Handbuch*, it is a systematic rather than historical approach that prevails. So, there would still be room for distancing this approach further from nineteenth-century Pandectism ('Entpandektisierung').[21] It might be wise in the future to follow the example of J. C. van Oven, who in his post-war student manual of Roman law (1945/1948) closely followed the structure of Gaius's *Institutes*.[22]

Now there is a third approach to Roman law. This approach agrees in many respects with the second, neo-humanistic one, but it has a much wider scope. I propose to call it the contextual approach to Roman law. Scholars adhering to this approach are not only concerned with legal sources but also consider these sources as a part of intellectual history. They try to understand Roman law not only as a legal phenomenon but also as a part of the history of ideas in general. They are interested in how far the Roman jurists, when searching for solutions to the legal problems they encountered, made use of concepts derived from other non-legal domains like philosophy, rhetoric,[23] physics, or theology. This approach is practised by scholars such as Dieter Nörr,[24] Wolfgang Waldstein,[25] and – somewhat differently – by Okko Behrends.[26] In Italy it is favoured by Mario Talamanca,[27] Aldo Schiavone,[28] and Antonio Mantello.[29] Other adherents are Alfons Bürge,[30] Giuliano Crifò,[31] David Johnston,[32] and Ulrike Babusiaux.[33] This new approach, however, is not entirely without its dangers: most Romanists are only jurists and they are not necessarily familiar with philosophy, rhetoric, or theology. They may also lack expertise in the difficult domain of the history of textual transmission of the writings of antiquity.[34] In other words, a prerequisite for this group of scholars is a preliminary, thorough study of non-legal primary sources and reliable secondary literature. Otherwise there are new threats of unprofessionalism, just as in the period prior to 1970 when Romanists without a sound philological knowledge criticized what they regarded as the non-Ciceronian Latin of the Roman jurists of the first centuries AD.

Nevertheless, it is possible to develop modest, effective strategies.[35] One of the main questions here might be, considering the history of the textual transmission of a non-legal text, is it possible that a particular Roman jurist would have been aware of the text? And is there any circumstantial evidence of such knowledge elsewhere in his work?

Within these three schools the relationship between the historical and the systematic approach to Roman legal texts differs greatly. The school which is primarily interested in legal doctrine considers the texts of the Roman jurists as containing traces of legal dogmatic principles which have yet to be clearly formulated, while the second group of scholars is more concerned with the inscription of the text and with its palingenetic context. The third group goes still further in the contextual approach and considers the jurists as intellectuals amongst other contemporary intellectuals in Roman society. The 'dogmatic' and the 'contextual' approaches can be found in earlier periods of legal history. In the sixteenth century, for instance, we find, on the one hand, jurists who continued the medieval, mostly ahistorical tradition of Bartolus and, on the other, legal humanists like Hugo Donellus (1527–91),[36] who chose a systematic approach, and still others, such as Franciscus Connanus (1508–51)[37] and Jacobus Cujacius (1522–90),[38] who took a historical, antiquarian approach.[39] This last group of humanists, in explaining texts of the *Corpus iuris civilis*, quoted extensively from the non-legal literature of antiquity. Much work could still be done to investigate these quotations.

2. ROMAN LAW IN ITS HISTORICAL INTELLECTUAL CONTEXT

It goes without saying that for the third group of modern scholars – those who follow the contextual approach – Roman law can only be fully understood when non-legal literature is taken into consideration. This does not imply, however, that the other groups of modern Romanists never look at non-legal literature. For example, in his *De officiis* and other works Cicero gives very important information about the introduction of *bona fides*, the *exceptio doli*, and the contract of sale.[40] This material has formed part of Romanist scholarship at least since the humanists; it was also employed by the Pandectists and neo-humanistic Romanists. For the early period of Roman law the comedies of Plautus, who wrote in the second half of the third century BC (he died in 184 BC), contain indispensable information, especially because epigraphic sources are scarce for that period, as are the writings of jurists earlier than Quintus Mucius Scaevola (±100 BC).[41]

The third approach to Roman law is in a way related to what in modern legal theory is called the Law and Literature Movement. In modern legal theory this movement aims not only at a better understanding of the law through literary texts, but also at understanding law in its cultural and social context. Here the emphasis is on the element 'law in literature' rather than 'law as literature'.[42] It was in this sense that Leopold Wenger (1874–1953) wrote:[43] he was indeed a forerunner of the third group of scholars of Roman law and an advocate for a comparative approach to the different legal orders of antiquity. An important Dutch Romanist who devoted attention towards the social and ideological background of Roman law was Henk (H. R.) Hoetink, a generation younger than Wenger.[44] In his inaugural lecture as a professor of Roman law at Amsterdam University (1935) he devoted attention to the background of Roman law and emphasized its social, ideological, and economic aspects.[45]

As an illustration of this contextual neo-humanist approach let us consider some problems which may be encountered in the use of non-legal literature as a means of acquiring a better understanding of the intellectual background of Roman law. In the first and third titles of the *Digest* (*De iustitia et iure; de legibus senatusque consultis et longa consuetudine*) we find quotations from Greek philosophers such as Chrysippos, founder of the Stoa (±300 BC). One of these quotations contains the famous Greek expression νόμος βασιλεύς ('the law as king'), which is the origin of all theories about the rule of law (Marcianus, D. 1.3.2).[46] Theophrastos (±300 BC), successor of Aristotle as the head of the Peripatos, is quoted twice (Pomponius, D. 1. 3.3; Paulus, D. 1.3.6). In the Greek context these quotations deal with the distinction between νόμος and ψηφίσμα – that is, the field of application of a statute. Another example comes from Ulpian, who in D. 1.1.6.1 quotes the well-known opposition between ἔγγραφοι and ἄγραφοι νόμοι (written and unwritten law). Ulpian's definitions of *ius naturale* and *ius gentium* (D. 1.1.1.3 and 4) are also certainly influenced by Greek philosophical ideas, although direct Greek quotations cannot be found in the actual text.[47] Moreover, it is probable that the definition of justice (Ulpian, D. 1.1.10) in its turn depends on Greek philosophical ideas as well.[48]

As such, Greek influence on Roman law cannot be easily denied. Occasionally, however, the significance of the first titles of Book 1 of the *Digest* is played down, and they are regarded as containing only popular – even vulgar – philosophy. I do not share this view and think it necessary to give a thorough overview of the philosophical ideas behind these texts, a task which has not been carried out in recent times.

Since the beginning of Legal Humanism in the sixteenth century, scholars have speculated on the relation between parallel ideas in Greek philosophy and Roman law. Franciscus Connanus and – even more so – Jacobus Cujacius are important in this respect. Since that time the relation between Greek philosophy and Roman law has been a bone of contention in legal scholarship. Nowadays, the majority of modern scholars of Roman law remain firmly convinced that there was hardly any influence of Greek philosophy on Roman law.[49] I am inclined to think that the current opinion lacks balance and has a rather exaggerated notion of the 'independence' of legal scholarship in the Roman Republic and Principate. It could well be that current opinion still reflects nineteenth-century ideas about the special position of the jurist, advocated first by Friedrich Carl von Savigny (1779–1861) and his followers in the German Historical School. Savigny and the Historical School regarded the jurist as the sole interpreter of the *Volksgeist*. This view led to emphasis on the independence of legal scholarship from external influences. Behind the scenes it still plays a role in current debate on the position of jurists, as well as in the debate between the Romanists of the three different schools mentioned earlier.

One might suppose that the prevailing view of the relative independence of Roman jurisprudence might deny that non-legal literature could contain information on the content of legal norms in Roman society; in fact, that is not entirely the case. As early as the second half of the nineteenth century, numerous books were devoted to legal passages in non-legal Latin literature; not coincidentally this was in countries where a codification of private law had taken place (France) or was about to take place (Italy). For Cicero we have books by Gaston de Caqueray[50] and Emilio Costa,[51] who was also the author of comparable books on Plautus and Terence.[52] Plautus himself stressed the importance of the role of the law in education.[53]

Cicero in his turn tells us that in schools it was compulsory in the old days to learn the Law of the XII Tables by heart (as a *carmen necessarium*), and he regrets that this custom has lapsed.[54] Henriot quotes Horace, who laments ignorance of the laws, and speaks of *sanctarum inscitia legum*.[55] Finally, we have the testimony of the jurist Pomponius, who refers to a conversation between Quintus Mucius Scaevola and Servius Sulpicius Rufus in which the former reproaches the latter for his lack of knowledge of the law.[56] Henriot[57] gave an interesting explanation for the high esteem attached to the law in Rome. According to him, in modern times there has been a decline in the sanctity attached to jurisprudence: it no longer belongs to the skills one has to learn as an intellectual in society. In the Roman past that was still the case. In recent times Dieter Nörr, one of the most prominent adherents of the contextual approach to Roman law, has given a full account of the position of the jurist in Roman intellectual society.[58]

3. Three Examples and Dilemmas of the Contextual Approach

To illustrate the problems that can be encountered in the contextual approach to Roman law, here are three examples and dilemmas.

1. In the Verrine Orations Cicero successfully blamed Verres as much as he could for his fraudulent administration of justice in Sicily. Here, however, we have no other source than the necessarily biased testimony of Cicero himself in his role as prosecutor (*accusator*). Cicero blamed Verres for the abusive use in procedural formulae of the fiction of citizenship, with a view to extracting additional taxation. Fernand de Visscher even wrote of Verres' 'fantasies with formulae' ('fantaisies formulaires').[59] The question is, how can we find an objective standard to judge this claim? How can we reliably survey the actual administration of justice in the first century BC in Sicily? The whole question becomes even more debatable when in the *Tabula Contrebiensis* of 87 BC we find a similar formula with a fiction of citizenship.[60] Ultimately it appears that Cicero used as an instrument to blame Verres a practice that was actually recognized in the administration of justice in the Roman provinces.

A general methodological question may be asked here: is non-legal Roman literature a reliable source for information about the historical reality of Roman law? A universal answer cannot be given. The Romanian Romanist Tomulescu took up this question in an article on the reliability of legal information in Livy.[61] Another scholar, J. W. Tellegen, has studied the law of succession in Pliny the Younger[62] and concluded that Pliny was a reliable source of information for Roman law. Other examples have been given already.

2. A second example of the difficulties with the contextual approach concerns the controversy on the existence of a domestic court (*iudicium domesticum*) at the end of the Roman republic. As a source we have here a passage from Dio of Halicarnassus, written in Greek, that the kinsmen (σύγγενεις) are to give their verdict (ἐδίκαζον). There was a dispute between Volterra and Kunkel on whether a *iudicium domesticum* really existed, and this has recently been revived by Donadio.[63] Kunkel took the wording *iudicium domesticum* in a technical sense, while Volterra considered it to have only a figurative sense. Who are we to believe? Is there a standard of technicality in the language used by non-jurists?

3. A third dilemma on the origins of the notion of the will[64] has an immediate impact on several topics of Roman law, such as the standard of liability and the doctrine of error in contracts such as *stipulatio* and sale. It is the well-known problem of the interpretation of intent (*animus*),[65] evil intent (*dolus*),[66] and volition (*voluntas*). Albrecht Dihle,[67] a well-known German historian of philosophy, maintains that the theory of the will as developed by St Augustine, which is the origin of the modern concept of intention, was derived from the *voluntas testatoris* ('will of the testator') used in interpreting the testator's will in classical Roman law. Throughout the history of philosophy from the early Greeks, Dihle does not identify a coherent theory of the will before St Augustine, and certainly not in Aristotle.[68] So far this view has not been taken into consideration by scholars of Roman law, although its consequences could be quite far-reaching. Dihle is not the only historian of philosophy who has studied the history of the will. Anthony Kenny, and R.A. Gauthier in his well-known commentary on Aristotle's *Nicomachean Ethics*,[69] are even more radical. Kenny starts his book rather surprisingly: 'There is no theory of the will in Aristotle.' According to Gauthier there is no theory of the will in classical antiquity, in Aristotle, or in the deterministic Stoic philosophy. Indeed, there is none until Johannes Damascenus,[70] a Byzantine scholar of the eighth century AD, who interpreted Aristotle's account of necessity and free will. Later, according to Gauthier, this view reached the Latin West and was integrated into Latin medieval philosophy. Gauthier implicitly leaves out the influence of St Augustine here, although Thomas Aquinas, important for the transmission of the ideas of Aristotle in the Western world, quotes St Augustine frequently.

These opinions leave us with a lot of questions. One example: are these views on the origin of the will compatible with those of Romanists who say that the subjective will (*animus*, etc.) was increasingly taken into account in postclassical Roman law? I am inclined to reject that view, although it is not possible here to give an extended analysis of the evolution of the notion of volition in legal and non-legal sources.

4. CONCLUSIONS

What will be the future of these three approaches to the Roman legal sources? The first will retain its importance, perhaps not as a part of legal history in the strict sense, but as a theoretical method of constructing the concepts of a common European private law. The second approach too will have a future, albeit only within the framework of legal studies. Not all the implications of the casuistic texts of the Roman legal tradition have yet been exhausted, even after a millennium of advancing different interpretations, starting with the early days of the University of Bologna. The individuality of the Roman jurists could still be studied in further detail. The same applies to study of the controversies between the jurists and their schools. Palingenetic research could also be refined.[71] The third, contextual approach to the Roman legal sources is perhaps the most promising for the future. It implies intensive inter-disciplinary collaboration within the various fields of study of antiquity. The third – most difficult – example of the notion of volition in antiquity illustrates that the problems here do not differ from those encountered in the study of the history of ideas in general. One is the old problem of nominalism versus realism, already known in the Middle Ages: continuity in the use of words does not necessarily imply the continuity of an idea.[72]

What can be illustrated with the three examples of this third approach is that, beyond the strict legal analysis of Roman juristic texts, there remain enormous numbers of intriguing problems and questions open for generations of scholars willing to study Roman law in its intellectual context.[73]

NOTES

1. H. Coing, *Handbuch der Quellen zur neueren europäischen Privatrechtsgeschichte, vol. I: Mittelalter* (Munich, 1973), 25.
2. Koschaker called it the 'political idea of Rome': see P. Koschaker, *Europa und das römische Recht* (4th edn., Munich, Berlin, 1966), 38.
3. For exceptions, see J. Chorus, 'Romeins recht op de Zuidpool en elders', in *Coniectanea iuris Romani*, ed. J. E. Spruit (Zwolle, 1974), 139–49.

4. This is also a reason why so many Romanists and legal historians are involved in the various projects to generate a unified European private law; for example, the Accademia dei Giusprivatisti Europei founded by Giuseppe Gandolfi, which has produced a series of proposals regarding the unification of European private law.
5. E. M. Meijers, 'Het feilloze deel van ons Burgerlijk Wetboek [The Infallible part of the Civil Code]', *Weekblad voor Privaatrecht, Notariaat en Registratie* 3031 (1928); also in E. M. Meijers, *Verzamelde Privaatrechtelijke Opstellen* I (Leiden, 1954), 93–98. There was undoubtedly an irony in the title of the article: Meijers was challenging the idea that the codification of private law was coherent, without serious mistakes, and adequate to cope with juridical situations that might arise in the future. He advocated here for the first time a recodification of Dutch private law. That eventually came about only in the second half of the last century; in 2015 it is still not complete.
6. R. Zimmermann, *The Law of Obligations: Roman Foundations of the Civilian Tradition* (Cape Town, 1990).
7. W. J. Zwalve, *Hoofdstukken uit de geschiedenis van het Europees Privaatrecht I: Inleiding en zakenrecht* (Deventer, 2006), reviewed by L. Winkel in *Zeitschrift für europäisches Privatrecht* 16 (2008): 435–37. German edition: W. J. Zwalve and A. J. B. Sirks, *Grundzüge der europäischen Privatrechtsgeschichte, Einführung und Sachenrecht* (Cologne – Weimar – Vienna, 2012).
8. For an interesting polemic between the first and second school, especially concerning the teaching of Roman law, see W. J. Zwalve, 'De toekomst van het Romeinse recht', *Ars Aequi* 42 (1993): 455–59; J. A. Ankum, 'Stenen voor brood', *Ars Aequi* 42 (1993): 459–63; R. Zimmermann, 'Rechtsvergelijking, rechtsgeschiedenis en *ius commune*', *Ars Aequi* 43 (1994): 276–83.
9. A. Wacke, 'Lothar Anton Alfred Pernice', in *Neue Deutsche Biographie*, vol. 20 (Berlin, 2001), 194–95 (also available online: http://www.deutsche-biographie.de/sfz94665.html). Pernice wrote an unfinished series of books on Roman law in the time of Marcus Antistius Labeo, a contemporary of the first Emperor, Augustus.
10. E. Bund, 'Otto Lenel', in *Deutsche Biographie*, vol. 14 (Munich, 1985), 204–5 (also available online: http://www.deutsche-biographie.de/sfz50210.html).
11. O. Lenel, *Palingenesia iuris Civilis: Juris consultorum reliquae quae Justiniani Digestis continentur ceteraque juris prudentiae civilis fragmenta minora secundum auctores et libros* (Leipzig, 1889, repr. Graz 1955).
12. Cf. Chapter 8 by Kaiser in this volume, 130–1.
13. O. Lenel, *Das Edictum Perpetuum, Ein Versuch zu seiner Wiederherstellung* (3rd edn., Leipzig, 1927).
14. Cf. Chapter 8 by Kaiser, 128-30.
15. O. Gradenwitz, *Interpolationen in den Pandekten* (Berlin, 1887). In legal humanism there was an earlier attempt at this kind of textual criticism: see L. Palazzini Finetti, *Storia della ricerca delle interpolazioni nel Corpus Iuris Giustinianeo* (Milan, 1953). For a comparison between these two periods, see M. Kaser 'Gradenwitz, Otto', in *Neue Deutsche Biographie*, vol. 6 (1964), 702–3 and http://www.deutsche-biographie.de/pnd116807229.html.
16. One of the most radical representatives of this tendency was Gerhard von Beseler, professor in Kiel. See K. S. Bader, 'Beseler, Gerhard Friedrich von', in *Neue Deutsche Biographie*, vol. 2 (1955), 175 and http://www.deutsche-biographie.de/pnd116154012.html.

17. J. H. A. Lokin, 'The End of an Epoch, Epilegomena to a Century of Interpolation Criticism', in *Collatio Iuris Romani: Etudes dédiées à Hans Ankum*, ed. R. Feenstra et al. (Amsterdam, 1995), 261–73.
18. Later published separately with the title *Zur Methodologie der römischen Rechtsquellenforschung* (Vienna, 1972), and sometimes criticized on the grounds that Kaser puts (too?) much emphasis on the intuition of the Roman jurists. See also M. Kaser, 'Ein Jahrhundert Interpolationenforschung an den römischen Rechtsquellen', in M. Kaser, *Römische Rechtsquellen und angewandte Juristenmethode* (Vienna – Cologne, 1986), 112–54.
19. K.-H. Schindler, *Justinians Haltung zur Klassik: Versuch einer Darstellung an Hand seiner Kontroversen entscheidenden Konstitutionen* (Cologne, Graz, 1966). See also Lokin, 'The End of an Epoch', (n 17).
20. Wieacker initially argued for the need to distinguish different textual layers in the transmission of the texts of the classical jurists: F. Wieacker, *Textstufen klassischer Juristen* (Göttingen, 1959, repr. 1975). This depended on comparing different versions of the same fragment of the Roman jurists in pre-Justinianic and Justinianic sources and postulating that the differences were due to postclassical changes in the texts. In *Römische Rechtsgeschichte* vol. I (Munich, 1988), 88, Wieacker also dealt with Roman law in non-legal Roman texts – without, however, mentioning the methodological difficulties discussed in this chapter.
21. See R. Knütel, '"Nicht leichter, aber um so reizvoller": Zum methodologischen Vermächtnis von Max Kaser', *ZSS* 115 (1998): 52; 64–65. Knütel clearly assumes – with Kaser – a specific dogmatic structure, even in classical Roman law. J. A. Ankum, in his review of M. Kaser, *Das römische Privatrecht* I (2nd edn. Munich, 1971) in *Nederlands Juristenblad* (1972): 138, suggests that Kaser still presents classical Roman law according to a dogmatic structure derived from nineteenth-century Pandectism.
22. J. C. van Oven, *Leerboek van Romeinsch Privaatrecht* (3rd edn., Leiden, 1948).
23. See the debate following publication of J. Stroux, *Summum ius summa iniuria* (Leipzig, 1926). Stroux's opinion on the considerable influence of rhetorical theory was followed by the Italian Romanist Salvatore Riccobono but strenuously contested by nearly all other Romanists at the time. See also F. Lanfranchi, *Il diritto nei retori romani* (Milan, 1938); and, for a recent survey of the relation between law and rhetoric, O. Tellegen-Couperus, ed., *Quintilian and the Law* (Leuven, 2003).
24. D. Nörr, *Historiae Iuris Antiqui: Gesammelte Schriften*, ed. T. J. Chiusi, W. Kaiser, and H.-D. Spengler, 3 vols., (Goldbach, 2003). D. Nörr, *Schriften 2001–2010* (Madrid, Barcelona, Buenos Aires, 2012).
25. See *Ars boni et aequi: Festschrift für Wolfgang Waldstein*, ed. M. J. Schermaier and Z. Végh (Stuttgart, 1993), xi–xiv, with a bibliography of Waldstein's publications to that date.
26. O. Behrends, *Institut und Prinzip: Siedlungsgeschichtliche Grundlagen, philosophische Einflüsse und das Fortwirken der beiden republikanischen Konzeptionen in den kaiserzeitlichen Rechtsschulen. Ausgewählte Aufsätze*, ed. M. Avenarius et al., 2 vols. (Göttingen, 2004).
27. See especially M. Talamanca, 'Lo schema genus – species nelle sistematiche dei giuristi romani', in *La filosofia greca e il diritto romano*, vol. 2, (Rome, 1977), 1–319.
28. A. Schiavone, *Nascita della giurisprudenza: cultura aristocratica e pensiero giuridico nella Roma tardo-repubblicana* (Rome, 1976); A. Schiavone, *The Invention of Law in the West* (Cambridge, Mass., 2012).

29. A. Mantello, '*De iurisconsultorum philosophia*, spunti e riflessioni sulla giurisprudenza nel primo principato', *SDHI* 67 (2001): 1–57.
30. A. Bürge, *Römisches Privatrecht, Rechtsdenken und gesellschaftliche Verankerung* (Darmstadt, 1999); A. Bürge, 'Der Text als Problem des Kontextes', *ZSS* 105 (1998): 150–60.
31. See n. 42, this chapter.
32. D. Johnston, *Roman Law in Context* (Cambridge, 1999).
33. U. Babusiaux, *Papinians Quaestiones, Zur rhetorischen Methode eines spätklassischen Juristen* (Munich, 2011).
34. See, in general, *Die Textüberlieferung der antiken Literatur und der Bibel*, ed. H. Hunger et al., 2nd edn. (Munich, 1988).
35. See L. Winkel, 'Le droit romain et la philosophie grecque, quelques problèmes de méthode', *TR* 65 (1997): 373–84.
36. L. Pfister, 'Doneau (Donellus), Hugues', in *Dictionnaire historique des juristes français, XIIe–XXe siècle*, ed. P. Arabeyre et al. (Paris, 2007), 256–58.
37. L. Pfister, '*Connan (Connanus), François*', in *Dictionnaire historique des juristes français*, 199–200.
38. L. Winkel, '*Cujas (Cujacius), Jacques*', in *Dictionnaire historique des juristes français*, 220–22.
39. For a survey of Legal Humanism, see H. E. Troje, *Graeca leguntur, Die Aneignung des byzantinischen Rechts und die Entstehung eines humanistischen Corpus Iuris Civilis in der Jurisprudenz des 16. Jahrhunderts* (Frankfurt, 1970), concentrating on humanistic textual criticism. See X. Prévost, *Jacques Cujas* (Paris – Geneva, 2014). Elsewhere I have tried to explain why the historical approach and the systematic approach necessarily go together: 'Rechtsgeschiedenis en integratie van de rechtswetenschap', in *Geïntegreerde rechtswetenschap*, ed. R. Foqué et al. (Arnhem, 1994), 211.
40. E.g. on the *exceptio doli*: Cic. *Off.* 3.69–71, quoted already by Cujas in his commentary on D. 4.3 *De dolo malo* (see Cujas, *Opera Omnia* (Frankfurt, 1623), vol. 2, 148).
41. See P. Leitner, 'Die plautinischen Komödien als Quellen des römischen Rechts', in *Diritto e teatro in Grecia e a Roma*, ed. E. Cantarella and L. Gagliardi (Milan, 2007), 69–92 with further references.
42. The expression 'Law and Literature' was coined by US Supreme Court judge Benjamin Cardozo (1870–1938) and further developed by James Boyd White. For an echo in Italy, see G. Crifò, 'Isolierung e valutazione giuridica', in *Diritto e letteratura*, ed. F. Spantigati (Milan, 2006), 30–36. Cf. U. Mölk (ed.), *Literatur und Recht: Literarische Rechtsfälle von der Antike bis in die Gegenwart* (Göttingen, 1996).
43. See, e.g., L. Wenger, 'Um die Zukunft des römischen Rechts', in *Festschrift Fritz Schulz* (Weimar, 1951), vol. 2, 364–86.
44. P. B. M. Blaas, *Henk Hoetink 1900–1963, een intellectuele bibliografie* (Hilversum, 2010), 66–70.
45. H. R. Hoetink, *De achtergrond van het Romeinse recht* (Haarlem, 1935); French translation: 'L'arrière-plan du droit romain', in: H. R. Hoetink, *Opera Selecta* (Zutphen, 1986), 73–108.
46. Marcello Gigante, *Νόμος Βασιλεύς* (Naples, 1993).
47. L. Winkel, 'Einige Bemerkungen über *ius naturale* und *ius gentium*', in *Ars boni et aequi: Festschrift für Wolfgang Waldstein*, ed. M. J. Schermaier and Z. Végh, (Stuttgart, 1993), 443–49.
48. L. Winkel, 'Die stoische οἰκείωσις-Lehre und Ulpians Definition der Gerechtigkeit', *ZSS* 105 (1988): 669–79.

49. Although in his later days a scholar such as Max Kaser was more impressed by the contribution of philosophy to Roman law: cf. R. Knütel (n. 21), 61, with references to the second edition of Kaser's famous 'Handbuch', *Das römische Privatrecht* (Munich, 1971–75), vol. 1, 179, 182, 194; vol. 2, 7–8.
50. G. F. M. de Caqueray, *Explications des passages de droit privé contenus dans l'œuvre de Cicéron* (Paris, 1857; repr. Aalen, 1969).
51. E. Costa, *Cicerone giureconsulto* (Bologna, 1927; repr. Rome, 1964).
52. *Il diritto privato romano nelle comedie di Plauto* (Turin, 1890; repr. Rome, 1968); for Plautus, cf. P. Romeijn, *Specimen juridicum inaugurale exhibens loca nonnulla ex Plautii comoediis jure civili illustrata* (Deventer, 1836); C. Tomulescu, 'Observations sur la terminologie juridique de Plaute', in *Sodalitas: Scritti in onore di Antonio Guarino*, ed. V. Giuffrè (Naples, 1984), vol. 6, 2771–81; E. Costa, *Il diritto privato romano nelle comedie di Terenzio* (Turin, 1890; repr. Rome, 1970); E. Henriot, *Les poètes juristes* (Paris, 1858; repr. Aalen, 1970); A. F. Murison, 'The Law in the Latin poets', in *Atti del Congresso Internazionale di Diritto Romano Roma* (Pavia, 1935), vol. 2, 609–39.
53. Plautus, *Mostellaria* 126: *Liberos parentes expoliunt, docent litteras, iura et leges.*
54. Cic. *Leg.* 2.59; cf. J. Triantaphyllopoulos, 'Cantar le leggi', *Atti dell'Accademia Mediterranea delle Scienze*, Anno I, Vol. I, Supplemento I (Catania, 1983), 27–34.
55. *Satire* 2.80. For further studies of legal aspects in Horace, see O. Diliberto, 'La satira e il diritto, una nuova lettura di Horat., *sat.* 1.3.115–117', in *Annali del Seminario Giuridico dell'Università di Palermo* 55 (2012): 385–402.
56. D. 1.2.2.43: *turpe est patricio et nobili, ius in quo versatur ignorare.* See L. Wenger, *Die Quellen des römischen Rechts* (Vienna, 1953), 483, n. 100, with further references.
57. E. Henriot, *Moeurs juridiques et judiciaires de l'ancienne Rome d'après les poètes latins* (Paris, 1858 ; repr. Aalen, 1970), 2.
58. D. Nörr, 'Der Jurist im Kreis der Intellektuellen: Mitspieler oder Außenseiter?' in *Festschrift Max Kaser*, ed. D. Medicus and H. H. Seiler (Munich, 1976), 57–90; also in D. Nörr, *Historiae Iuris Antiqui* (Goldbach, 2003), 951–84.
59. F. de Visscher, 'Les fantaisies formulaires de Verres', *Revue d'Etudes Latines*, 33 (1956): 136–39, reprinted in F. de Visscher, *Etudes de Droit romain* (Milan, 1966), vol. 3, 425–28.
60. L. Winkel, 'Some thoughts on the *formulae ficticiae* of citizenship in Gaius, 4,37: a form of reception?' in *Judge and Jurist: Essays in Memory of Lord Rodger of Earlsferry*, ed. A Burrows et al. (Oxford, 2013), 299–308.
61. C. St. Tomulescu, 'La valeur juridique de l'Histoire de Tite-Live', *Labeo* 21 (1975): 295–321.
62. J. W. Tellegen, *The Roman Law of Succession in the Letters of Pliny the Younger* (Zutphen, 1982).
63. N. Donadio, '*Iudicium domesticum – riprovazione sociale e persecuzione pubblica di atti commessi da sottoposti alla patria potestas*', *Index* 40 (2012): 175–95.
64. For an introduction to the wide range of problems of volition, cf. V. Aucouturier, *Qu'est-ce que l'intentionalité?* (Paris, 2012), who rightly distinguishes between ontological and epistemological aspects of volition.
65. Knütel, 'Nicht leichter, aber um so reizvoller' (n. 21), 37; cf. also D. Simon, 'Die animusbesessene Spätzeit', *Rechtshistorisches Journal* 14 (1995): 253–80.
66. Cf. D. Daube, *Roman Law, Linguistic, Social and Philosophical Aspects* (Edinburgh, 1969), 131; L. Winkel, 'Inst. Iust. 4,4 pr.: Kübler et Daube sur les mots ἀδικία (adikia) et ἀδίκημα (adikèma), ἁμαρτία (hamartia) et ἁμαρτήμα (hamartèma)', in *Fides, humanitas, ius: Studi in onore di Luigi Labruna* (Naples, 2007), vol. 8, 5927–34.

67. A. Dihle, *The Theory of the Will in Classical Antiquity* (Berkeley, 1981), 135.
68. A. Kenny, *Aristotle's Theory of the Will* (Oxford, 1980), 2: 'It is a commonplace that there is no theory of the will in Aristotle.' The difficulty is that the notion of volition in Aristotle is based on lack of knowledge; the psychological element in our modern notion of the will is still lacking. This has to do with so-called ethical intellectualism in antiquity; see F. J. C. J. Nuyens, *Ontwikkelingsmomenten in de zielkunde van Aristoteles* (Nijmegen, Utrecht, 1939); French version: *L'evolution de la psychologie d'Aristote* (Louvain, 1948); cf. L. Winkel, 'Das sokratische Paradoxon "οὐδεὶς ἑκὼν ἐξαμαρτάνει" und strafrechtliche Zurechnung im Lichte der neueren Literatur', in *Symposion VI: Beiträge zur griechischen und hellenistischen Rechtsgeschichte* (Vienna, Cologne, 1989), 109–17.
69. R. Gauthier, 'Introduction', in R. A. Gauthier and J. Y. Jolif, *L'Ethique à Nicomaque*. 2nd edn., (Louvain, Paris, 1970), vol. I–1, 266.
70. See M. Frede, 'John of Damascus on Human Action, the Will and Human Freedom', in *Byzantine Philosophy and its Ancient Sources*, ed. K. Ierodiakonou (Oxford, 2006), 63–96.
71. A project to improve and correct details in Lenel's *Palingenesia* is being coordinated in the University of Oxford.
72. Cf. M. M. Adams, 'Universals in the early fourteenth century', in *The Cambridge History of Later Medieval Philosophy*, ed. N. Kretzmann et al. (Cambridge, 1982), 411–39.
73. I thank Javier Rodriguez Diez for his help and for critical remarks on an earlier version.

Part II

LAW MAKING

3 Sources of Law from the Republic to the Dominate

David Ibbetson

The term 'sources of law' can be used in two distinct ways – historically and analytically. A historical treatment involves looking at where the law at any particular time and place could be said to have come from, as English Common law might be said to have its source in the customs of English people or of English lawyers, British colonial laws to have their main source in the English Common law, or much of modern European private law to have its source in the Roman law of Justinian. An analytical treatment, by contrast, looks to the places to which a lawyer at some particular time or place should go in order to identify the proper rules to apply to some legal situation. It is with the latter, analytical sense that this chapter is concerned.

It needs to be emphasized at the start that the analysis of law in this way leads almost inexorably to (or stems almost inexorably from) a model of law consisting of rules whose validity can be determined by reference to their sources. Even in modern, highly developed societies such a model of law would be contested by some on the basis that moral values or political sentiments play a dominant role in determining the outcome of legal disputes; in societies which are not so highly developed it is hardly meaningful to distinguish between legal and other rules of conduct. So far as Roman law is concerned, we can use such a source-based model without substantial qualification when dealing with the late Republic onwards, but the further before that we go, the more important it is to be aware that the distinction between legal rules and social rules might hardly have been meaningful.

Over the course of the millennium between the beginning of the Republic and the reign of Justinian there were inevitably very substantial changes in the way in which the law was perceived and operated in Rome. Although there was never any radical break with the past there were two major caesuras, the first occurring around 150 BC and the second around AD 200. In the first period the law was in what might be called a pre-scientific stage, largely based on custom and with very little in the way of distinctively legal sources apart from scattered pieces of legislation; it can most usefully be thought of as a prologue to the second period. The three or four centuries between about 150 BC and AD 200 mark the mature period of Roman law, characterized most notably by the work of the jurists; it was an age of legal science, when highly able lawyers used their reason to identify ever more complex legal rules. Finally, after the deaths of Papinian, Paul, and Ulpian, the three great jurists of the late second and early third centuries, imperial power came to dominate all aspects of the law; if the second period was an age of science, the third was an age of authority.

1. The Pre-Scientific Stage

Examination of the extant sources of law before the end of the second century BC does not reveal a great deal. There is a certain amount of legislation, but little more than that. These legislative sources are undoubtedly important, but they need to be put in the context of the nature of law and the legal process of the period.

The first Roman legislation about which we have any real information is the XII Tables.[1] This is attributed by Livy to the years 451–450 BC,[2] and there is no strong reason to doubt this dating. No text of the XII Tables survives, but later writers, both lay and legal, refer to many of the provisions found in it; scholars from the sixteenth century onwards have consequently been able to reconstruct a plausible version of the original, though not its original language. As its name suggests, it would have been a substantial text; but with under 100 clauses (as reconstructed in the modern editions) it would probably have been only about one-third of the size of the so-called Code of Hammurabi promulgated over a millennium earlier in Babylon. The traditional account of the creation of the XII Tables, given by Pomponius and written around the middle of the second century AD, treats it as having been enacted in response to demands for greater certainty than could be provided by mere custom, and based on materials collected from Greece and other places.[3] It is impossible to be sure of this, although similarities of form to Greek (and perhaps also Mesopotamian) texts together with a number of substantive parallels make it possible, if not probable, that there was some foreign influence at work.[4] But one thing is clear: it would be a mistake to see the XII Tables as a code in the modern sense of being a complete statement of legal rules; its provisions are far too piecemeal to allow for any such conclusion. Its importance lay in the fact that henceforth some rules would be in a fixed form and therefore resistant to the gradual shifts that are characteristic of customary law, and in the way in which many centuries later it could be seen as the foundational text of Roman law.

From the early Republic there were two representative assemblies with legislative power, the *comitia centuriata* and the *comitia tributa*, with the former being by far the more important; a third assembly, the *comitia curiata*, was concerned only with formal business such as the election of magistrates and the ratification of wills. Although authority was vested in the *comitia* the real power lay with the magistrates and the Senate, since the role of the *comitia* was limited to approving or rejecting proposals put before it by a magistrate. After 287 BC – though some sources put it as early as 449 BC– enactments of the plebeian assembly, the *concilium plebis*, were also given fully binding force.[5] The most important pieces of private law legislation of the Republic – perhaps all of them – were plebiscites.

We have references to an average of approximately one piece of legislation per year in the 350 years after the XII Tables,[6] although the earliest epigraphically attested *lex* dates only from a few years before 110 BC.[7] The vast majority of these are one-off determinations – to make war or peace, for example, or to allow a triumph or impose a fine – or are what we would regard as matters of constitutional importance or things which relate to the legal process. Very few deal with crimes, and only a tiny handful deal with private law – the legal relations between individuals.

Most substantive law at this time, therefore, would have been custom; or, more precisely, little distinction could have been drawn between legal and social rules. This is not surprising. Legal process at this time was based on the so-called *legis actiones*, a highly ritualized set of oral formulae within which any legal claim had to be framed.[8] There were only five types of these, shaped by reference to the remedy sought by the plaintiff rather than by the basis of his or her claim, sometimes supported by an oath or wager, with the decision falling to a single judge or a group of judges. But these judges were laymen, and their decisions would rarely have been based on any externally identifiable legal rules. Moreover, there was nothing in the *legis actio* system to upset this: provided the appropriate forms were gone through, all depended on the judges' sense of what was right and wrong. This is not to say that there was no room for legal expertise or innovation; but legal expertise was largely knowledge of the ritual forms and, aside from new acts of legislation, legal innovation could involve little more than the manipulation of the rules of the XII Tables. In all of this the College of Pontiffs was dominant, underscoring the lack of any specifically legal science at this time.[9] The College of Pontiffs would similarly have been the body which had knowledge of other ritual forms, such as the proper way to transfer ownership in the most important items of property or the proper way to enter into a formal marriage. Individual pontiffs provided answers (*responsa*) to questions from individuals, initiating a practice which was to be of great importance in the following period of Roman law.

2. The Age of Science

The great flowering of Roman law occurred between the second half of the second century BC and the first quarter of the third century AD.[10] The change from the pre-scientific stage was triggered by two factors: the development of a different type of legal procedure, known as the formulary system, a remedial framework which gave sharper definition to the basis of claims; and the emergence of a class of jurists who applied a more sophisticated type of reasoning to the law than had previously been the case.

In all probability the formulary system emerged in the third century BC as a substitute for the *legis actio* procedure to deal with cases involving foreigners who could not swear the necessary oaths, but after the *lex Aebutia* (about 140 BC) it could be freely used by Roman citizens.[11] The plaintiff's claim still had to be framed in a predetermined form, but here – unlike in the *legis actio* procedure – the available forms were shaped by the cause of action: why the plaintiff was entitled to a remedy rather than what remedy was requested. These remedies were provided by the praetors, the officials responsible for the administration of the legal system in Rome.[12] New remedies could at first be invented relatively freely, but in practice they were largely settled by the end of the Republic. The edict, a list of remedies issued at the start of each praetor's year of office but increasingly building on his predecessor's edict, provided a framework for the beginnings of analysis of private law.

The second factor triggering the change was the application of more sophisticated types of reasoning to the law, very possibly under Greek influence. The earliest protagonists of this thinking, men such as P. Mucius Scaevola, were themselves pontiffs, but those of the first century BC were not. We can trace a degree of continuity from the pontiffs to them, as they continued the earlier practice of giving *responsa*, but there were two major differences. First, they began to produce written texts; and second, they did not speak with the pure authority that the status of pontiff had afforded their predecessors. Cicero recounts a dinner-time discussion of a legal point, comparing the opinions of Sextus Aelius, Manius Manilius, and Marcus Brutus on the one hand, and Scaevola and Testa on the other.[13] That such a discussion could take place at all shows that judgments on matters of law by that time depended on criteria of reason which allowed the conclusions of different jurists to be evaluated. Elsewhere Cicero says that jurists had expertise in matters of written law (*lex*) and custom.[14] So far as the former was concerned, their skill lay in the interpretation of the texts. As for custom, their expertise lay both in the identification of general social practices and in the use of such techniques as reasoning by analogy to reach conclusions that went beyond what would generally have been recognized by citizens.

The best starting point for any study of the sources of Roman law in this period is the *Institutes* of Gaius, an introductory manual written in the middle of the second century AD and not superseded until the production of the *Institutes* of Justinian four centuries later. The *Institutes* begin with a list of the sources of law:

> The laws [*iura*] of the Roman people consist of *leges*, plebiscites, *senatusconsulta*, imperial constitutions, edicts of those possessing the right to issue them, and answers of the learned.[15]

We can usefully sub-divide this into three types: legislative sources, procedural sources, and juristic sources. Notably, for Gaius, there was no place for custom as an independent source of law, but we cannot completely ignore it.

Legislative Sources

Gaius launches into his treatment of the sources with *leges* and plebiscites:

> A *lex* is a command and ordinance of the *populus*. A plebiscite is a command or ordinance of the *plebs*. The *plebs* differs from the *populus* in that the term *populus* designates all citizens including patricians, while the term *plebs* designates all citizens excepting patricians. Hence in former times the patricians used to maintain that they were not bound by plebiscites, these having been made without their authorization. But later a *lex Hortensia* was passed, which provided that plebiscites should bind the entire *populus*. Thereby plebiscites were equated to *leges*.[16]

That *lex* took pride of place is very revealing, in two ways – all the more so given the relatively small number of legislative enactments in Rome. First, it shows that Gaius's conception of law (*ius*) had at its heart rules which had been consciously laid down after deliberation. Law was not principally something immanent, waiting to be discovered; it was something that could be, and in its paradigm form was, created by human act. Secondly, it was the *leges* of the three representative *comitia* that came first, with plebiscites coming after them. Not only was their authority chronologically later, but Gaius's language points to their being, in his eyes, a second-class form of legislation: it was only the *lex Hortensia* that had raised them up to the status of true *leges*. The reason for this is transparent in his text: *leges* were enacted by the whole of the citizenry, whereas plebiscites were enacted only by a subset of them – the plebeians. It was not just the fact that *leges* and plebiscites had been enacted in accordance with certain recognized procedures that was important, therefore, but that in their ideal form they articulated choices which had been made by the whole of the Roman people. Perhaps more than anything else this reveals the continuity of legal thinking across the political caesura of the transformation from Republic to Empire.

It is worth emphasizing just how few *leges* and plebiscites are referred to in Gaius's text: a total of around 35 in his 4 books. Of these, just under half regulated wills, personal status, and family relations, and about the same number regulated legal procedure. In the field of private law (the relations between free individuals), there are only 8. Moreover, by the time at which he was writing, the creation of law by *lex* or plebiscite was completely moribund; however, this did not prevent their appearance as the primary source in his list:

After *leges* and plebiscites in Gaius's list, there come *senatusconsulta*:

> A *senatusconsultum* is a command and ordinance of the senate; it has the force of *lex*, though this has been questioned.[17]

Again we see the binding force expressed in terms of *lex*. It is not simply that *senatusconsulta* are binding on the Roman people, but that in this respect they are equivalent to *lex* itself.

The doubt expressed at the end of Gaius's text demands some exploration. We may be sure that Gaius did not share it, since elsewhere in the *Institutes* he makes references to rules stemming from *senatusconsulta* without any qualification, but clearly there was at the time an element of ambiguity about their status. It seems clear that in the Republic the Senate, for all its political power, was not seen as having the ability to legislate for Rome (legislation for the provinces was a different matter). It could make proposals to other bodies in the strong expectation that they would be adopted, but no more than that. However, in the early Empire, we find resolutions of the Senate being referred to as such, even though effect was given to them by clauses in the praetor's edict: the Augustan *senatusconsultum Silianum*, for example, or the *senatusconsultum Macedonianum* passed under Vespasian. Whether we treat the *senatusconsultum* or the edictal provision as the true source of the rule is largely a matter of semantics – hence, we can surmise, the doubt referred to by Gaius. From about the time of Hadrian, however, there are self-standing *senatusconsulta*, the first unequivocal one being the *senatusconsultum Tertullianum* (attributed to Hadrian by Justinian[18]). Very probably the shift can be attributed to the fact that by this time the text of the edict had been fixed,[19] so that it would not have been possible to engineer change in the law through this formal route. Gaius's text therefore probably represents the reality at the time when he was writing in the AD 150s and early 160s. It was not to be the end of the matter. Already the Senate was in practice doing little more than ratifying proposals made by or on behalf of the emperor, and before the end of the second century it could be said that the true source of authority lay in the emperor's *oratio* rather than in the Senate's resolution.[20] This fitted more easily with the political and juridical situation of the later Principate, and the notion of the *senatusconsultum* as an independent source of law faded away.

Gaius's final legislative source is in many ways the most problematic:

> An imperial constitution is what the emperor by decree, edict or letter ordains; it has never been doubted that this has the force of *lex*, seeing that the emperor himself receives his *imperium* [sovereign power] through a *lex*.[21]

That imperial constitutions were binding could hardly have been denied in the middle of the second century, but there are two elements of Gaius's statement which give grounds for pause. First, as with the other legislative sources he enumerates, their force is described by reference to *lex*, the ordinances of the whole of the Roman people. The belief that it is *lex* that represents the ideal source of law is unmistakable. Second, it is not merely stated that imperial constitutions have the force of *lex*, a reason is given for this: the emperor's power is given by *lex*. Even more strongly than in the first statement, then, Gaius here roots the emperor's law-making power in the resolution by the people to recognize him as emperor, the so-called *lex regia*. It is appealing to see this as a reflection of a perhaps outmoded republicanism in Gaius's own beliefs, but exactly the same reason is given by Ulpian half a century later.[22] More probably it reflects the complex ideology playing through the law, and indeed elsewhere, stressing the continuity between the republican constitution and that of the Empire, at the same time as accepting the reality that imperial constitutions were indeed sources of law in their own right. A version of this principle ascribed to Ulpian was destined to become one of the most explosive statements in western political theory: *quod principi placuit legis habet vigorem* – 'what pleases the prince has the force of law'.[23]

Gaius enumerates three distinct forms of imperial constitution – decrees (*decreta*), edicts (*edicta*), and letters (*epistulae*). There was no magic in the ordering of the different forms; they simply reflect different ways in which imperial power might generate legal rules.

Imperial edicts were a type of legislation in its strictest form: rules deliberately introduced to make new law or amend the old.[24] Provincial governors and similar magistrates had the right to issue such edicts in the Republic, and the emperor, vested with magistral powers, was doing no more than exercising the same right. Most of the earliest imperial edicts of which we have evidence were of limited application, restricted either to particular localities or particular individuals or groups. There was nothing to prevent the making of edicts introducing general rules, such as that of AD 212 giving Roman citizenship to all free people in the Empire,[25] but it was not until the end of the third century that this practice became widespread. Analogous to these were *mandata*: administrative instructions to officials.

Decrees were rules derived from the decisions of the emperor sitting as a judge.[26] From the time of Augustus, the emperor might make decisions outside the normal course of legal procedure, by taking cognizance of a lawsuit; the procedure was therefore known as the *cognitio extraordinaria*. Although he would sit with an advisory *consilium*, it was the emperor who made the decisions. We have, for example, a report of his being on one occasion persuaded by the jurist Paul (a member of the *consilium*) to change his mind, and another of his following a view of Papinian contrary to the advice of Paul.[27] The decisions of the emperor were, of course, binding on the parties, but they might also go beyond this and allow the formulation of a general rule. Hadrian ruled, for example, that a child born to a woman eleven months after her husband's death might be legitimate, and Marcus Aurelius that violence did not necessarily involve any wounding.[28] Around the start of the third century

Paul collected three books of such decrees, extracts of which survive in Justinian's *Digest*.

Gaius's final category, letters (*epistulae*), is a composite term referring to all communications from the emperor.[29] Some of these were addressed to officials, but more important and apparently more numerous were those addressed to private individuals. These took the form of rescripts, answers to petitions (*libelli*), with the imperial response written below the request. Julius Caesar is known to have dealt with such petitions, and it is likely that the imperial practice was a continuation of this. By the reign of Tiberius at the latest these petitions might concern matters of law: Papinian cites a rescript of his on the subject of adultery by public officials.[30] The surviving evidence points to there having been a massive increase in the number of rescripts issued during the reign of Hadrian, probably associated with the increasing legalization of government at this time,[31] after which they became an increasingly important source of law. The rescripts were always given in the name of the emperor, and there is strong evidence that until the end of the second century the emperor's part in making them was not merely nominal, although he would presumably have taken advice from members of his *consilium*. A text of Ulpian records a rescript of Marcus and Verus (and hence of the AD 160s) making reference to what they had learned from 'those skilled in giving legal opinions' and to discussion with the jurist Volusius Maecianus and others, leading ultimately to the emperors favouring the view of Julian and others over that of Proculus.[32] From the start of the third century, however, the personal input of the emperor began to wane, as responsibility for the drafting of rescripts was delegated to jurists in the imperial service, in particular to the principal secretary *a libellis*.

While the first of Gaius's categories of imperial constitutions was unequivocally legislative, the second and third were far more ambiguous. On the one hand they purported simply to apply or state the law as it was, not to create anything new, and the recourse they had to legal experts emphasizes that this was taken seriously. On the other hand, since they were determinations of the emperor they were by definition authoritative statements of the law which took effect just as if they were genuinely legislative acts. As if to underscore this, by the time of Hadrian and probably earlier, rescripts were copied and recorded in the imperial archives, where they were available for consultation and hence came to be integrated into the legal fabric; the fact that at the beginning of the third century Paul could collect three books of decrees suggests that they too were recorded in some way, even if they might not have been so easy to consult.

Procedural Sources

After describing the various types of legislation, Gaius turned to what we might regard as procedural sources, the edicts of those possessing the right to issue them:

> The right of issuing edicts is possessed by magistrates of the Roman people. Very extensive law [*ius*] is contained in the edicts of the two praetors, the urban and the peregrine, whose jurisdiction is possessed in the provinces by the provincial governors; also in the edicts of the curule aediles, whose jurisdiction is possessed in the provinces of the Roman people by quaestors; no quaestors are sent to the provinces of Caesar, and consequently the aedilician edict is not published there.[33]

We need not concern ourselves with the elements of provincial administration, nor with the aedilician edict (although it was important, especially for the regulation of sales in the market place), but should focus on the praetor's edict.

As has been seen, from the third century BC the praetors had provided formulae structuring lawsuits.[34] These formulae were collected together in their edict by the first century BC, and constituted a catalogue of available civil law remedies and defences. Although change was still possible, the edict had ceased to be a creative force by the end of the Republic. A century and a half later Hadrian commissioned the leading jurist of the time, Julian, to produce a definitive text, after which no further changes were possible unless they were made by the emperor.[35]

Gaius's description of these procedural sources is telling: nowhere does he mirror his previous texts and say that they had the force of *lex*. Nor could he, since they did not create legal rules in the same way as *leges*, plebiscites, *senatusconsulta*, or imperial constitutions. They did not really create rules at all, but in so far as they constituted the categorical list of remedies and defences – most were articulations of custom or derived from legislation, while some had been invented by praetors themselves[36] – it was impossible for lawyers to ignore them. In reality, a knowledge of the edict was far more fundamental than a knowledge of legislation. Its inclusion in Gaius's list brings home the point that the separation between substantive law and procedure, explicit in his statement that all the law relates to persons, things, or actions,[37] is largely artificial, and that procedural law can have a direct effect on substantive legal rules.

The Jurists

The late second and early first centuries BC had seen the rise of a cadre of secular jurists, whose role, according to Cicero, was to know and advise on *lex* and custom.[38] In the early part of the Empire they developed a formidable expertise, with a range of techniques to identify what was the correct result to any legal question, so that at the time Gaius was writing a substantial part of Roman law would have been seen as jurists' law.

Gaius's brief description raises as many questions as it answers:

> The answers of the learned are the decisions and opinions of those who are permitted to establish the laws. If the decisions of all of them agree, what they so hold has the force of *lex*, but if they disagree, the judge is free to follow whichever decision he pleases. This is declared by a rescript of the divine Hadrian.[39]

The first point to note is that juristic opinion, provided it was unanimous, created a rule on a par with *lex*. This may seem surprising since jurists were not formally appointed in any way, and were no more than men who claimed to have the appropriate expertise and were recognized as having it. However, the way in which Roman law had developed over the previous two or three centuries meant that it was almost inevitable that such force should have been given to at least some juristic opinion. At the core of this was that a major task of the jurists had been to identify and formulate custom. Whilst it might be said that here the binding force of the jurists' statements lay not in their articulation of the custom but in the very fact that it was the custom of the Roman people, this would have been unsatisfactory in so far as it would have laid the way open for anyone – however unlearned – to deny that the custom was as it had been stated. For the purpose of identifying legal rules, which is the concern of any study of the sources of law, the unanimous view of the jurists was to be treated as conclusive.

On the other hand, if there was disagreement among the jurists the judge was free to decide as he pleased, and since there was room for a good deal of disagreement it would seem to follow that there was a very considerable area in which there was no law. We have no reason to doubt Gaius's statement, nor the existence of Hadrian's rescript on which he bases it, but it is nonetheless impossible to believe that the jurists of the second and third centuries would have accepted any conclusion of this sort without some qualification. Very much the reverse: their activity from the late Republic onwards implicitly assumed that it was possible, by the exercise of reason, to identify accurately what the law was in any situation.[40] Gaius's statement needs to be understood in a more nuanced way. It was not that there was no law when there was juristic disagreement, but that the law was (as yet) indeterminate. There was no clear law that the judge had to follow, but he should take advice and use his own reason to discover what was the 'true' rule and to apply it.

It is this seeking after legal 'truth' (and the assumption that it exists) that characterizes much of the work of the jurists. Sometimes this involved the identification of the essence of some legal concept. The first-century jurist Labeo, for example, identified the idea of contract with exchange, the Greek *synallagma*; a century later Pedius identified it with agreement, an analysis that was adopted by Gaius in distinguishing between the claim for the repayment of a loan and the claim for the recovery of money paid by mistake.[41] Sale came to be recognized as an agreement to exchange a thing for money, thereby excluding agreements to exchange things.[42] Paul defined possession as having a mental and a physical aspect – *animus* and *corpus* – thereby framing a way to address the question of whether one still possessed one's home when away at the market.[43] But not all jurists were so happy with definitions. In the second century Javolenus is recorded to have said that 'All definitions in the civil law are dangerous, for there is hardly any that cannot be subverted.'[44] More commonly we see the sharpening up of the scope of a rule or legal institution by applying it to variant sets of fact. Thus it was said that ownership could be transferred by *traditio*, whose core meaning was delivery, without a physical handing over – for example, by pointing to a statue or other large object, or by climbing a tower and indicating the boundaries of land to be conveyed.[45] In the same vein, Ulpian explored the meaning of *corrumpere* (spoil), under the third chapter of the *lex Aquilia*, by examining a whole series of fact situations.[46] Equally, a rule might simply have been applied to facts without there necessarily having been any sharpening of its scope.

In doing this the jurists used a variety of techniques. Greek dialectic had brought about the division into *genus* and *species* in the late Republic, allowing the systematization achieved by Quintus Mucius Scaevola and later Sabinus, whose three books on civil law (his *Iuris Civilis Libri Tres*) were regularly commented on by the later classical jurists. Principles (*regulae*) were identified. Building on this, much argument proceeded by making analogies, together with its corollaries, the drawing of distinctions between different cases and the *reductio ad absurdum*. Etymology, sometimes fanciful, could be used to explore the meaning of words. Problems of the interpretation of legal acts – contracts, conveyances of property, wills, and the like – might be elucidated by reference to the actual or presumed intentions of the makers, or by literally construing the terms in which they were couched. Arguments could be made from equity or fairness; Ulpian in particular may have been fond of these. Alternatively, reasoning might be based on *utilitas* – perhaps close to a modern idea of public policy.

With the notable exception of the *Institutes* of Gaius, which exists in a near-complete text probably dating from the fifth century, practically all of our knowledge of the work of the jurists comes from the extracts from their writings that appear in Justinian's *Digest*.[47] From this we can see that they composed a variety of types of works: commentaries on the praetor's edict (especially after Julian's consolidation) and Sabinus's *Ius Civile*; collections of real or hypothetical cases; and monographs on a wide range of subjects, including some like criminal law, military law, and testamentary trusts (*fideicommissa*) which did not fall within the edict. Within this literature they frequently refer to each others' works: sometimes they approve; sometimes they disagree, occasionally vigorously, as, for example, where Paul refers to an opinion of the great Quintus Mucius Scaevola as most inept;[48] and very often they simply cite without comment. Tellingly, they commonly use the present tense when referring to other jurists, even where the earlier writer might have died centuries previously: the common endeavour in which they were all engaged was one which transcended time and was fundamentally anti-historical, however much they were aware that their law had a long history.

It is, therefore, a serious error to suppose that there was a single, uncontroversial Roman law whose content can be discovered from the juristic texts. Its essentially controversial nature, except for the core on which everyone agreed, is brought out by the existence of two distinct schools of jurists in the first century and a half of the Empire: the Sabinians and Proculians. In the brief historical section at the beginning of the *Digest*, Pomponius, writing about the middle of the second century, describes these schools and allocates the principal jurists of the previous generations to one or other of them. We do not know whether these were educational establishments, although, since the individual jurists undoubtedly engaged in teaching, whether they did so as members of a particular school or not may be an empty question. Clearly, though, there were points of law on which they disagreed, as schools and not just as individual jurists, and substantial traces of these disagreements can be identified in both Gaius's *Institutes* and Justinian's *Digest*. Whether there was any consistent philosophical basis to their differences is uncertain, and there need not have been any, but their continuity over a century and a half is ample testimony to the way in which Roman law at this time was able to tolerate and incorporate opposing points of view. The schools died out after the middle of the second century – Gaius, a Sabinian, is the last jurist whose allegiance to a school is recorded – but this did not mark an end to juristic disagreement; it was just that it took place at the level of the individual jurist and not by adherence to a group.

Although it is through their writings that the jurists are primarily known to us, an important part of their work was the giving of advice – *responsa*. Already in the early Republic the pontiffs had done this, and in the third century BC a *pontifex maximus*, Tiberius Coruncanius, began to give *responsa* in public,[49] a practice which continued on the part of the secular jurists from the latter part of the second century. According to Pomponius, a change occurred under Augustus, who granted to some the power to give *responsa* under the authority of the emperor – the *ius publice respondendi*.[50] What exactly this meant is desperately unclear,[51] but since Pomponius tells us that its purpose was to give greater authority to the law it is probable that it was a response to the uncertainty caused by (self-styled) jurists giving contradictory opinions to litigants and judges and thereby bringing the law into disrepute. Jurists need not seek the privilege – we only know of two who had it – so it is unlikely that it was a prerequisite to giving a *responsum* which could be cited to a judge, though we might guess that added weight would attach to the opinion of one of these patented jurists: an attractive parallel can be drawn with the appointment of a Queen's Counsel in the modern world.[52] It is not clear whether the institution continued in practice after Tiberius, nor whether it changed its function if it did; but in any event Pomponius's description of it makes it clear that it was abolished by Hadrian, by which time it might already have become moribund.

According to Pomponius, the *ius publice respondendi* allowed the favoured jurist to give *responsa* with the authority of the emperor, and the purpose of the institution was to enhance the authority of the law. But nowhere is it suggested that these *responsa* would have binding authority in the modern sense. In Gaius's terms, they did not have the force of *lex*. This was all the more the case with juristic writings, except where all the jurists agreed. Herein lay the fundamental difficulty of the scientific approach which characterized the jurists' work: any piece of analysis was provisional and at risk of being countered by another jurist with better, or perhaps just different, reasoning. And, paradoxically, the more sophisticated the jurists, the more likely it was that conflicting results might be reached.

The high point of Roman legal science was reached in the late second and early third centuries, with the three greatest of the jurists:

Papinian, Paul, and Ulpian. Extracts from the works of these make up a large proportion of Justinian's *Digest*, testifying to their reputation in the Byzantine world. While they had different approaches to the law – Papinian was perhaps more prone to draw fine distinctions, Paul to seek the essence of legal concepts, Ulpian to favour the pursuit of equity – all three of them were analytically flexible and imaginative in adapting the law to different circumstances. At the same time, *responsa* to specific questions became more concrete as those who needed to know what the law was in some particular case took advantage of the system of imperial rescripts[53] – what one scholar has referred to as a free legal advice service.[54] Both Papinian and Ulpian were probably secretaries *a libellis* with responsibility for the drafting of these rescripts, so there need be no doubt about their quality at this time. Nonetheless, there was an inevitable tension between authoritative rescripts, which determined the legal point once and for all since they were in theory decisions of the emperor, and the private works of jurists, which were true only to the extent that their reasoning was persuasive. Moreover, as the number of rescripts increased, the more problematic was the scientific approach, since each rescript marked a fixed rule which had to be incorporated into the legal system, however difficult was its fit.

The scientific period of Roman law – what is generally known as the classical period – came to an end in the decade or so after the murder of Ulpian in AD 223. The writing of reflective legal works died out. In part, this was no doubt because political unrest at this time stood in the way of devoting time to it, and the rescript system must have raised questions about the value of attempting to discover the law purely by the exercise of reason. This does not, of course, mean that jurists – legal experts – died out; it was simply that the energies of the best of them were focused on the production of rescripts.

Custom

Although Gaius does not include custom in his list of sources of law, elsewhere in the *Institutes* he does refer to a form of succession to property as not being introduced by the XII Tables or the praetor's edict but as 'law [*ius*] received by common consent'.[55] Julian – perhaps Gaius's teacher – also referred to custom as the basis of law in this context, but his thought is framed in language which was susceptible of a more general application.[56] In so far as *lex* gained its binding force from the consent of the people expressed in their representative assemblies,[57] all the more should long-standing practices create binding rules even though they were not put into writing. In reality, there was probably little difference between Julian's position and Gaius's ascription of binding force to the unanimous opinion of jurists, except that Julian's treatment provided an intellectual justification for his conclusion whereas Gaius's did not.

3. The Post-Scientific Stage

Somewhere around AD 230 there was a major watershed in the functioning of Roman law. In particular, the scientific work of jurists seems to come to a very sudden halt, with the *Digest* preserving only a small number of texts extracted from the works of half a dozen jurists post-dating Paul and Ulpian. That said, just as the transition from Republic to Empire was achieved without the appearance of radical change, so the transition across this watershed retained the formal features of the earlier period. The treatment of the sources of law in Justinian's *Institutes*[58] is substantially derived from that of Gaius.

Against this background of substantial similitude, we should note three changes: first, a shift of juristic activity away from the production of scientific literature and towards the giving of rescripts as members of the imperial bureaucracy; second, a change in the way in which juristic literature (largely from earlier periods, of course) was treated; and third, a sharper focus on custom.

The sharp decline of juristic writing is immediately visible from Justinian's *Digest*. By contrast with the 2,000 extracts from Paul and approximately 3,000 from Ulpian, only one of the five or six post-Severan jurists is responsible for more than a tiny handful. This sole exception was Hermogenianus, probably writing in the fourth century: around 100 extracts from his *Iuris Epitomarum Libri* are found. But the title of his work is revealing: it was not a work of independent thinking, but a collection culled together from the writings of Paul and Ulpian and other major writers of a century or more earlier. Another work of the same kind is the so-called *Sentences* attributed (probably fancifully) to Paul, whose origins probably date from shortly before AD 300: a brief collection of texts constituting a conveniently accessible handbook for practitioners. What we lack, so far as our evidence goes, are juristic works revealing any real originality of thought.

This does not mean that jurists suddenly ceased to exist, nor that legal thinking disappeared. The successors of men like Papinian and Ulpian still worked in the imperial bureaucracy and prepared rescripts in the name of the emperor just as their predecessors had done,[59] and through the work of these men which survives in the *Code* of Justinian we can see the continuity of legal thinking from the private writings of Papinian, Paul, and Ulpian. It was only after the reign of Diocletian, at the beginning of the fourth century, that this system died away, and with it the constructive work of the jurists.

A corollary of this decline in juristic science was an intellectual shift, as jurists' opinions took on a greater degree of authority. Rescripts, by their nature, created binding rules of law since they were in form determinations by the emperor himself. Collections of these imperial constitutions were made from the end of the third century – the *Codex Gregorianus* and the *Codex Hermogenianus*[60] – and hence formed a corpus of fixed legal rules. The works of earlier jurists could not be binding in this way, but they were cited in courts as evidence of what the law was, and even a mean work like the popular *Sentences* was used in this way. This tendency reached its peak with the Law of Citations of AD 426,[61] which limited citation in court to five named jurists – Gaius, Papinian, Paul, Ulpian, and Modestinus – and provided that the view of the majority should prevail, with Papinian to be followed if opinion was evenly split; only if there was no majority and Papinian was silent was the judge to exercise his own discretion. No longer was reason any test of legal validity.

From the beginning of the third century, greater weight was also put on custom as a formal source of law. The trigger for this, almost certainly, was the greater use of Roman law in the provinces after the extension of Roman citizenship to all free people in the Empire in AD 212. In so far as there was a theory grounding legal rules in popular consent, as Julian had argued,[62] where different practices had become established in different places it would have been difficult to argue that Roman law in its entirety should be applied. Hence Ulpian was able to contemplate the application of local custom even when it was contrary to Roman law, and Paul to argue that the customary interpretation of a *lex* in some particular place ought to be respected in that place.[63] Julian might well have agreed with this, since his text suggested that a *lex* could be impliedly repealed simply by being ignored by the people. However, the problem for Gaius and other jurists of the middle of the second century was that there was no easy way to identify custom, and the writings of the jurists had to serve as a proxy for this.[64] Yet half a century later legal process was changing, as the formulary system was being superseded by the *cognitio* procedure. Instead of a lay judge deciding a case within the terms of a formula approved by the praetor, there was a trial before a professional judge in which law and fact were intermingled. This allowed an alternative mechanism for the identification of custom: regularity of judicial decision. For Ulpian, local custom would be recognized if it was embodied in a decision, and his contemporary Callistratus referred to a rescript of the emperor Severus to the effect that a stream of decisions would determine the interpretation of an ambiguous *lex*.[65] Custom, identified through decisions, was therefore able to replace the opinion of jurists as a source of law. This was confirmed, but also limited, by a constitution of Constantine of the early fourth century, providing that custom was of 'no mean authority' (the Latin word is *auctoritas*), unless it was contrary to *lex* or reason (*ratio*).[66] As a consequence, the risk that observing custom would degenerate into the mindless following of previous decisions was neutralized.

This recognition of custom as a formal source of law is reflected in the treatment of the sources of law in Justinian's *Institutes*.[67] The basic division here is between written and unwritten law. The elements of written law are the same as those dealt with in Gaius's *Institutes*: *lex*, plebiscites, *senatusconsulta*, imperial constitutions, magisterial edicts, and the opinions of jurists. Apart from the removal of the doubt expressed by Gaius as to the force of *senatusconsulta*,[68] the main differences visible in Justinian's treatment are that greater weight is given to the force of imperial constitutions (strengthened by the opening of the text with Ulpian's statement that what pleases the prince has the force of *lex*[69]), and that the weight given to juristic opinion is reduced by changing the tense of the text from the present to the imperfect, thereby giving it more of a flavour of historical reminiscence.[70] Offset against this is the unwritten law – custom – whose force derived from the tacit consent of the people.[71]

Notes

1. *Roman Statutes*, 555–721.
2. Livy 3.34; the final two tables were probably added later.
3. D. 1.2.4.
4. R. Westbrook, 'The Nature and Origin of the Twelve Tables', *ZSS* 105 (1988): 74.
5. The *lex Hortensia*; this chapter, 29–30.
6. G. Rotondi, *Leges Publicae Populi Romani* (Milan, 1912).
7. *Roman Statutes*, 39.
8. See the chapter by Metzger, 281–3.
9. A. Schiavone, *The Invention of Law in the West*, trans. J. Carden and A. Shugaar (Cambridge, Mass., 2012), 74–84.
10. Schiavone (n. 9), 131–306. Still useful, if dated, is F. Schulz, *History of Roman Legal Science* (Oxford, 1946).
11. See the chapter by Metzger, 282.
12. See the chapter by Metzger, 283.
13. Cic. *Fam.* 7.22.
14. Cic. *de Orat.* 1.212.
15. Gaius 1.2.

16. Gaius 1.3.
17. Gaius 1.4. For *senatusconsulta*, see R. J. A. Talbert, *The Senate of Imperial Rome* (Princeton, 1984).
18. Inst. 3.3.2.
19. 34, this chapter.
20. D. 2.15.8 pr.
21. Gaius 1.5; F. Millar, *The Emperor in the Roman World* (London, 1977), 228–259. With particular reference to the later Principate, see J.-P. Coriat, *Le Prince Législateur* (Rome, 1997).
22. D. 1.4 pr.
23. D. 1.4.1.
24. Millar (n. 21), 252–259.
25. D. 1.5.17; cf. the chapter by Lewis, 172.
26. Millar (n. 21), 228–240; T. Honoré, *Emperors and Lawyers*, 2nd edn. (Oxford, 1994), 28.
27. D. 36.1.76.1; D. 29.2.97.
28. Gell. *NA* 3.16; D. 4.2.13 (= D. 48.7.7).
29. Honoré (n. 26); Millar (n. 21), 240–252.
30. D. 48.5.39.10.
31. Honoré (n. 26), 14, based on G. Gualandi, *Legislazione Imperiale e Giurisprudenza* (Milan, 1963).
32. D. 37.14.17 pr.
33. Gaius 1.6.
34. 28, this chapter; O. Lenel, *Das Edictum Perpetuum*, 3rd edn. (Leipzig, 1927).
35. C. *Tanta* 18.
36. See the chapter by Metzger, 284.
37. Gaius 1.8.
38. 28–9, this chapter.
39. Gaius 1.7.
40. Schiavone (n. 9), especially at 285–306.
41. D. 50.16.19; D. 2.14.1.3.
42. D. 18.1.1.
43. D. 41.2.3.1.
44. D. 50.17.202.
45. D. 41.2.1.21.
46. D. 9.2.27.13–27.28.
47. See the chapter by Kaiser, 127–33.
48. D. 41.2.3.23.
49. D. 1.2.2.35, 38.
50. D. 1.2.2.49.
51. R. Bauman, *Lawyers and Politics in the Early Roman Empire* (Munich, 1989), 1–24, discussing earlier views; T. Leesen, *Gaius Meets Cicero: Law and Rhetoric in the School Controversies* (Leiden, 2010), 20–29, with further references at 22 note 51.
52. Bauman (n. 51), 17.
53. 33, this chapter.
54. Honoré (n. 26), 33.
55. Gaius 3.82.
56. D. 1.3.32.

57. 30, this chapter.
58. Inst. 1.2.3–10.
59. Honoré (n. 26), 71–185.
60. See the chapter by Kaiser, 120.
61. C.Th. 1 4 3.
62. D. 1.3.32; 39, this chapter.
63. D. 1.3.34; D. 1.3.37.
64. 35, this chapter.
65. D. 1.3.34; D. 1.3.38.
66. C. 8.52.2.
67. Inst. 1.2.3–9.
68. Inst. 1.2.5; 30, this chapter.
69. Inst.1.2.6; 32, this chapter.
70. Inst.1.2.8.
71. Inst.1.2.9.

4 Roman Law in the Provinces

John Richardson

For centuries the academic study of Roman law has centred, with some notable exceptions, on the courts in the city of Rome itself, and especially on the jurisdiction of the urban praetor. Given the richness of the sources preserved in the *Digest* and the *Institutes* of Gaius and Justinian and their importance for the development of subsequent legal scholarship and systems, that is scarcely surprising. But in the historical context of the Roman Republic and Empire it is misleading. From the second century BC onwards Roman military power and Roman administrative control came to dominate the Mediterranean basin, eventually encompassing north-western Europe, the lands on the southern bank of the Danube, Egypt, and the modern Middle East. With this power and control came the necessity of making legal decisions, demanded not least by the local inhabitants of the areas subject to that control, who recognized the value of judgments which carried the weight of Rome's military dominance. The context within which such cases were decided was not, juridically speaking, Roman, and the cases themselves might not involve Roman citizens at all, but those to whom it fell to oversee them belonged to the class from which the urban praetors were drawn, and in some cases had themselves held that office earlier in their careers. It was inevitable that when they needed structures and patterns to manage their own jurisdiction they turned to those of the *ius civile*, even though the parties to the cases were not Roman citizens. It is the interplay of Roman procedure and local, non-Roman legal rights and individuals which gives the legal work of provincial governors its particular flavour and interest, especially in the earlier centuries.

1. *Provinciae* and Provinces: The Basis of Provincial Jurisdiction

The *provinciae* (provinces) which made up the Roman Empire had not begun as territorial areas of administration or government, still less as areas of jurisdiction. In the third century BC, when Roman expansion beyond Italy began, *provincia* was a task assigned to a holder of *imperium* (the power and authority held by an elected magistrate of the city), or a pro-magistrate (holding the power without the office). This task might be administrative or juridical (thus the *provincia* of the *praetor urbanus*, first elected in 367 BC, was the hearing of legal cases in the city of Rome), but was for most magistrates the command of an army. This was normally the case for the two consuls, as the senior executives of the city, and for the increasing number of praetors who were elected through the third, second, and first centuries BC, as Roman military activity expanded into the Mediterranean world. These praetors held an *imperium* described as 'lesser' than that of the consuls. By the time of the reforms of the dictator L. Cornelius Sulla in 81 BC, the number of praetors had grown to eight, and by this stage most of the *provinciae* held by consuls and praetors had geographical names and had increasingly become areas with determined boundaries.

While the responsibilities of *imperium*-holders within their *provinciae* remained essentially military, they had inevitably grown through the second century BC to include other relationships between the Roman military presence and the inhabitants of the areas concerned, including taxation and jurisdiction. These responsibilities formed the origins of Roman provincial government. From the reign of the first emperor, Augustus (31 BC to AD 14), the provinces were divided between those to which the senate continued to send former magistrates as proconsuls (called the '*provinciae* of the people') and those more military areas (which were 'Caesar's *provinciae*') to which the emperor sent his own nominees: senior men drawn from the senatorial order but holding propraetorian *imperium*, who were designated as the emperor's legates (*legati Augusti pro praetore*). In some areas (most importantly Egypt) the emperor appointed non-senators as *praefecti* (prefects) or as *procuratores*, a title which derived from the civil law term for an agent. The responsibilities which had developed under the Republic devolved onto these provincial governors; and by this stage the term *provincia* (although retaining its formal meaning of a task given to an *imperium*-holder) normally meant an area of the Roman Empire, organized in terms of the structures of Roman provincial government.[1] Under the Republic a governor was able to appoint a *legatus* to assist him in various parts of his work, including jurisdiction, and this continued in the people's provinces; but in Caesar's provinces the *legatus Augusti* did not have this power of delegation, and in some cases, such as Hispania Tarraconensis or Britannia, the governor was assisted in the work of jurisdiction by a *legatus iuridicus*, appointed by the emperor.

This was also the case in Egypt, where the *praefectus Aegypti* was assisted by a *iuridicus*, an official drawn from the equestrian order.[2] There also developed a parallel jurisdiction undertaken by other *procuratores* of the emperor, who were not in charge of provinces but who were responsible for the collection of taxes in the provinces of the emperor and for the management of imperial estates. These men are recorded as conducting trials concerning public finances and with having local jurisdiction in the case of imperial properties; this power was formally established in AD 53 when the emperor Claudius secured a decree to this effect from the senate.[3] Appeal against decisions in procuratorial courts was usually only to the emperor, on whose behalf the procurator was acting.

In this context, it is not surprising that the basis of jurisdiction within the provinces through the period of the Republic, and to a great extent under the empire too, depended directly on the *imperium* of the governor. The only statutory provision relating to the administration of the provinces was concerned with the behaviour of the governor himself, in particular the series of laws *de rebus repetundis*, which set up a permanent commission of investigation (*quaestio*) as early as 149 BC under the *lex Calpurnia de rebus reptundis*. It could be convened on demand to deal with accusations of improper seizure of money by holders of *imperium*. By 122 BC at the latest this process was available to non-Romans in the provinces, who could accuse a governor to a specified praetor. This statute, proposed by the radical tribune of the plebs, C. Gracchus, has survived in large part on a bronze inscription which has been known since the sixteenth century.[4] The statute provides for a holder of *imperium* who is charged with wrongly seizing monies to be accused by his victim (or a Roman *patronus* acting on his behalf) to the praetor in the charge of the court, the case being heard by a *quaestio* made up of 50 men, who could not be senators or relations of senators, which first determined the guilt or innocence of the accused and then (in the case of a guilty verdict) the amount due to the plaintiffs. The level of restitution was double the amount wrongly taken. The importance of this court is clear from the fact that over the next hundred years there was a continuous political struggle over the composition of the *quaestio* (particularly with regard to membership of senators on the jury); the scope of the wrongs which were covered by the legislation was subsequently widened and refined, especially by laws passed by Sulla in 81 BC and by Julius Caesar, when consul in 59 BC.[5]

These courts could be used against governors who had misused their juridical power to their own benefit, as can be seen in Cicero's speeches in the trial of C. Verres in 70 BC under Sulla's law, following his governorship of Sicily from 73 to 71 BC. In his first speech (the only one actually delivered, because Verres went into exile as a result of it) Cicero undertakes to show how Verres systematically abused his control of the courts and the legal process to enrich himself; and, of the five speeches which he was unable to give but which he published subsequently, the first two are devoted to Verres' jurisdiction – one to his time as praetor in charge of the court of the *praetor urbanus* in Rome in 74 BC and the second to his time in Sicily.[6] However, accusations could only be brought once the governor had laid down his *imperium* at the end of his period of office. Before that, the governor's decisions were not open to challenge, and no appeal could be made against his judgments, not even by Roman citizens. Moreover, it was only to Roman citizens that the Roman *ius civile* applied. In cases solely concerning local inhabitants, who were, in Roman terms, peregrines (*peregrini*: foreigners), the governor had a much freer hand in determining not only the judgment but also the basis on which it was made. In either case, the governor was in a strong position with regard to jurisdiction: Cicero wrote a lengthy letter to his brother Quintus in late 60 or early 59 BC, which was in effect a commendation of Quintus' governorship of the province of Asia, which he had held since his praetorship in 62 BC, combined with an essay on how to govern, in which he recommended a mild and courteous approach in conducting trials; this, he says, is appreciated in the courts in Rome, where the praetor is surrounded by other magistrates, appeal courts, and the power of popular assemblies and the senate, and is to be praised still more in a governor whose nod is awaited by all the Roman citizens in the province and all the cities and communities, and who is inhibited by no appeal, no protest, no popular assembly.[7]

2. Limits to the Governor's Jurisdiction

Given the essentially military and unlimited nature of the *imperium* of the magistrate and pro-magistrate while in his province, the nature of provincial jurisdiction is best seen in the constraints which delimited it. It used to be believed that each province had a statute of its own, known as the *lex provinciae*, which laid down the basic patterns by which the governor had to abide. It is now generally agreed that, although such *leges provinciae* existed for some provinces, they were usually decrees issued by individual commanders and subsequently ratified by the senate, and certainly were not laws passed by the Roman popular assemblies.[8] In the Republican period, Cicero mentions a law which the Sicilians called the *lex Rupilia.*[9] The younger Pliny, in his correspondence with the emperor Trajan in the early second century AD, refers to a *lex Pompeia* 'given to the Bithynians', presumably by Pompey in the late 60s BC, which regulated the age at which magistracies in the cities of the province of Bithynia could be taken up.[10] A passing reference in a letter of Cicero's mentions a law for Cyprus, given by P. Lentulus Spinther, who was the first governor there from 57 to 53 BC.[11] A *lex Cornelia* which appears on an inscription from the Augustan period, and that regulated the date on which priesthoods were to be taken up in the province of Asia, may be part of a more general set of regulations given by Sulla.[12] However, most provinces do not seem to have had such 'laws', and, so far as juridical matters are concerned, even these seem to have been limited in scope. The *lex Rupilia* in Sicily is perhaps the best known because of Cicero's references to it in his prosecution of Verres in 70 BC. It specified the circumstances in which a governor could hear cases brought to him by non-Roman inhabitants, and in particular the nationality (whether Roman or local Sicilian) of the *iudices* whom he could appoint to make decisions.[13] It was the work of the consul P. Rupilius, who in 132 BC was responsible for putting down a slave revolt in Sicily. By that date there had been praetors governing the province for nearly a century, and although Cicero several times mentions a *lex Hieronica* – named for the ruler of Syracuse in the third century BC, and which regulated the collection of tithes on grain – there is no indication of any more general law on the judicial powers of the governor before the last third of the second century. It is clear that a *lex provinciae* was not an essential part of the structure of a province under the Republic, and there is no indication that, even where they existed, they covered the whole of the juridical work of the governor.

The main external factors which constrained the jurisdiction of a governor were related to the statuses held by the various communities within the boundaries of his province. These consisted of three groups: those constituted by the senate and people of Rome as *coloniae* or *municipia*; those peregrine communities which had been given privileges which established them as free (*civitates liberae*), some of which had these privileges granted by a formal treaty (a *foedus*; hence their name, *civitates foederatae*); and those which had no special status (*civitates peregrinae*), which are sometimes referred to as *civitates stipendiariae* because they were liable to pay a regular contribution to the Romans (*stipendium*). The substantive law in these communities was different in each case, as was the *locus standi* of the governor. Of the first group, those which consisted of Roman citizens (*coloniae civium Romanorum*, which were usually settlements of Roman veteran soldiers, often based on pre-existing towns; and *municipia civium Romanorum*, which were already existing communities, granted municipal status) had access to the Roman civil law, while those of Latin status (*coloniae Latinae* and *municipia Latina*) had laws set out in their own charters. By the end of the first century AD, at least in the case of the Latin *municipia* of southern Spain, these charters prescribed that the substantive law to be used was to be based by default on the civil law as used in the civil courts in Rome.[14] The peregrine communities of the other two categories would each have their own legal systems, but differed in that free communities and those with a treaty had a guarantee that they were not to be interfered with by the governor (in the case of the *civitates foederatae*, secured by formal treaty); the others had no such guarantee, and consequently the extent of Roman intervention depended entirely on the attitude of the governor.

The provincial governor was also constrained by the edict that he himself had issued before leaving Rome to go to his province. It set out the matters on which he was prepared to hear cases and the principles on which he would make his judgments, in the same fashion as did the *praetor urbanus* and the *praetor peregrinus* in Rome (though it is not clear whether he was bound by the *lex Cornelia* of 67 BC, which required the city praetors to abide by their own edicts). The best evidence for a provincial edict under the Republic comes from a famous letter of Cicero to his friend Atticus, written while he was governor in Cilicia in 51 BC.[15] Cicero explains that the specifically provincial parts of his edicts covered administrative topics (including municipal finances, debts, interest, bonds, and relations with the *publicani*, who were representatives of private companies which had won the contracts to collect taxes), and matters concerned with property and inheritance, which it was convenient to collect together in the governor's edict. For the rest, he kept his edict short by stating that he would follow the edicts of the city praetors. He is writing here about the content rather than the structure of his edict.[16] He also mentions that he took several provisions from the edict of the famous lawyer, Q. Mucius Scaevola (governor of the province of Asia [western Asia Minor] in the 90s BC), including one which stated that cases between Greeks should be tried under their own laws. Scaevola's governorship is said to have been so admirable that the senate decreed that his edict should be used as a norm for subsequent governors of that province.[17] It appears, however, that Cicero, like other governors, constructed his edict as he himself saw fit, rather than using a standard form taken over from previous governors. In Cicero's case that led to an acrimonious correspondence with his predecessor. In this respect, as in others, the governor had more freedom than the praetors in Rome.

In the imperial period, the provincial edict appears to have become more standardized, as might be expected when so many provinces were under the control of legates of the emperor. When in AD 131 (in the reign of the emperor Hadrian), Salvius Julianus fixed the content and structure of the edict of the *praetor urbanus*, he did the same for the provincial edict; and when some twenty years later Gaius wrote a commentary on the provincial edict in 30 books, it is clear that the edict was in many respects identical to that of the city praetor. Additional material relating to circumstances in particular provinces is likely to have been added as an appendix.

3. Roman Law in Practice: The Governor, The *Conventus*, and Local Courts

As the source of Roman jurisdiction, the governor, both in the later Republican period and under the empire (whether as a proconsul in the people's *provinciae* or as *legatus Augusti* in Caesar's), presided at courts within his province. Cicero's correspondence while he was proconsul in Cilicia in 51–50 BC shows that jurisdiction took up much of his attention; even Julius Caesar, in the midst of his military campaigns against the Gauls through the 50s BC, crossed the Alps at the end of each season to hear cases in Illyricum and Cisalpine Gaul.[18] Strabo, writing about the province of Hispania Tarraconensis at the end of Augustus' reign, states that the *legatus Augusti* spent the whole of the winter on such cases.[19] Already in the Republican period, at least in more settled areas, a pattern had emerged of governors travelling to various parts of the province for the purpose of hearing cases, a process which, as appears from Cicero's experience, was arranged by the governor himself. At least by the end of the first century AD, this had become formalized into an assize system, with annual visits to a number of designated centres, and in the eastern parts of the empire there was considerable competition among cities for this designation.[20] Even so, the conduct of these assizes was very much in the hands of the governor: the day on which a particular case was to be heard might not be set until after the assize had begun, and although Ulpian recommended that proconsuls should pay attention to the order in which petitioners' cases were heard in order to avoid problems of bias or corruption, this in itself indicated the freedom of the governor in the conduct of the hearings.[21] The importance of the assizes was that it was only through the governor (or his or the emperor's *legatus iuridicus*) that access could be gained to a Roman court, although in Egypt, where a more complex system was in place, there existed lower courts at a more local level, from which cases could be passed to the assize of the prefect of Egypt.[22] Under the Republic there was no appeal from the governor's court, but under the emperors there was always the possibility of an appeal to Caesar, whether from a *legatus Augusti* or from a proconsul. Suetonius, in his biography of Augustus, states that the emperor delegated appeals from litigants from Rome to the praetor and appointed a number of former consuls, one for each province, to hear those from provincials.[23] In any case, it was to the emperor that appeals were made, even when the governor was not involved: in 6 BC the free city of Cnidos sent an embassy to Augustus to present an accusation concerning the alleged murder of one of its citizens by another and his wife. Since the accused man was dead and his widow was resident in Rome, in response the emperor appointed one of his 'friends' (*amici*), Asinius Gallus, to investigate the matter. When Gallus concluded that the accused had suffered harassment from the dead man and were innocent of his murder, Augustus ordered that this verdict should be entered in the public records of the city of Cnidos.[24] This was not an appeal as such, as there was no prior judgment by a Roman official, but it illustrates the way in which even from the beginning of the imperial period the emperor acted in a judicial capacity when cases were referred to him from those in the provinces.

In practice, in civil cases which involved the members of one community, governors seem to have left much jurisdiction in the hands of that community, although they could intervene at any time. Cicero, writing from his province to his friend Atticus in 50 BC, reported with a certain smug self-satisfaction that he had allowed the Greek cities the autonomy which enabled them to use their own laws and law-courts.[25] In cases where such intervention took place, it seems to have been structured in terms of the processes of Roman law, even when the substantive law was not Roman. An interesting early example of this may be found in the *Tabula Contrebiensis*, inscribed on a bronze tablet dated to 87 BC, which records the case of a water dispute between two peregrine communities in the Ebro valley in northern Spain, the Salluienses and the Allavonenses, about the purchase of land by the former despite the objections of the latter, from a third group, the Sosinestani. The case is embodied on the inscription in a *formula* such as would be issued by a praetor in Rome, which was given by the governor in the province and which appoints the senate of a fourth local community, Contrebia Belaisca, to act as judges. The *formula* is of considerable legal sophistication – the governor concerned, C. Valerius Flaccus, had been *praetor urbanus* in 96 BC – and includes a *fictio* which assumes the existence of the Sosinestani as a *civitas*, a community capable of taking legal decisions. It is by no means clear that the Contrebian judges understood the significance of all these sophistications, since the *formula* presented two separate issues to be decided, but the judgment is presented simply in the form of agreement with the arguments of the Salluienses. They can be expected, however, to have understood the legal basis of the case since it is to be judged according to local law as it applied to the Salluvienses (*iure suo*), rather than according to Roman law (*iure Quiritium*), as would have been the case if the dispute had been between Roman citizens.[26] Valerius Flaccus is using the process of the Roman courts to apply the local law of the area in a dispute between peregrine communities.

Similar blendings of Roman and local law are frequent in evidence from Egypt in the imperial period, notably from the recently discovered dossier of a Nabataean Jewish woman named Babatha in the province of Arabia, which was found near the Dead Sea and had been deposited in the first half of the second century AD. Babatha was involved in a dispute with the guardians of her son, Jesus, after the death of the boy's father. The documents include three copies of an outline of a *formula*, two in the same hand, which were presumably intended to be used by Babatha in presenting her case to the provincial governor.[27] Although there is no way of knowing whether the governor used this *formula*, and indeed it is not at all clear that it was directly relevant to the case, it is interesting to see its inclusion in Babatha's papers: although none of the individuals involved in the matter was a Roman citizen, she apparently believed (or was advised) that this part of the Roman process might be relevant to her case. The expectation was that the Roman official would act as Valerius Flaccus had done in Spain, using the structures of the Roman civil law as the basis for a judgment in a non-Roman, peregrine context.

The clearest picture of the way in which law was administered in a province of the Roman Empire in the early imperial period comes from the charters issued to towns in southern Spain under the Flavian emperors. These resulted from the grant to many Spanish communities of the Latin right (*ius Latii*) by the emperor Vespasian, probably in AD 73–74.[28] They follow a standard form and seem to be based on a uniform model, lightly adapted for the individual communities to which they were granted. The most complete, discovered in 1981, relates to the hitherto unknown town of Irni, or, as it now became, the *municipium Flavium Irnitanum*. This small settlement, some 30 km south of Osuna in Andalucia, received its charter in the reign of Domitian in or shortly after AD 91.[29] The document, originally on ten bronze tablets each approximately 57 cm by 90 cm, presents details on the ordering of the life of the *municipium*, its council of 63 *decuriones* and its magistrates, of whom the most important were 2 *duoviri*. A long section just before the end (chapters 84 to 93) provides for the jurisdiction that may be undertaken by the officials of the *municipium*.

The scope of the jurisdiction of the municipal magistrates was limited to those cases which did not concern a sum of more than 1,000 sesterces and which did not involve violence, the loss of freedom, or a breach of faith to someone to whom a special duty of trust was demanded under Roman law, such as a ward or a person to whom an explicit promise had been made.[30] Such cases were to be referred to the provincial governor unless both parties to the dispute agreed that they might be heard locally. In any case, the conduct of cases took place in the context of the overall juridical oversight of the governor. The edict which the governor issued on his entry into his province covered legal matters, including information about which cases could be heard and how proceedings should be handled. It was to be posted, written on a whitened board, at a place in the *municipium* from which it could be read with ease.[31] However, within that general context, the *duoviri* (and to a lesser extent, the *aediles*) had a considerable amount of juridical work to do. Each year the *duoviri* had to select the people who were to act as judges (*iudices*) in private law cases, and to preside over the selection and assignment of a judge when cases arose; they had comparable responsibilities for those cases which were to be dealt with by the alternative process of reference to a group of *recuperatores*.[32] Similarly, the grant of an adjournment in a case was within their competence.[33] In all these matters, however, in addition to observance of the governor's edict, there was another general requirement of which those responsible for jurisdiction had to take account. In these clauses of the statute, the local magistrates were enjoined to do everything just as it would be done in a similar case tried in Rome – that is to say, in the court of the urban praetor, who had jurisdiction between Roman citizens in private law cases. Most remarkable of all, the section on local jurisdiction ends with a catch-all clause, which states that for all matters about which members of the *municipium* shall go to law with one another and which are not specifically dealt with in the provisions of the statute, they should proceed as though the process was being carried on under Roman law and between Roman citizens.[34] What the local magistrates are doing is applying the provisions of Roman private law to the members of the *municipium*, the majority of whom are not Roman citizens at all, but Latins – that is to say, *peregrini*. The form of the *ius Latii* which Vespasian had given to the Spanish towns provided for the grant of Roman citizenship to those who had held the senior magistracies in the *municipium*, but this did not apply to the population as a whole.

4. THE RECEPTION OF ROMAN LAW AND THE ACTIVITY OF THE GOVERNOR

The evidence of the *lex Irnitana* is, of course, about what the Romans *intended* should happen in the Latin *municipia* in Spain, and not what *actually* did happen. The picture it gives, however, is coherent with that which emerges from the other material already examined. The governor has overall supervision of the judicial process in the *muncipium*, and justice is to be administered there according to the terms of the governor's edict, but he is only directly involved when the matter concerned is sufficiently important to merit it. Nonetheless, there is a fundamental difference between what was to happen at Irni and the activity of Valerius Flaccus or Cicero. In the earlier period the law that the local communities applied under the supervision of the Republican governors was the local law of the communities themselves. In the *lex Irnitana* the law to be applied was that which Roman citizens used under *ius civile*.[35] This too seems to be what Babatha expected in taking her dispute to the governor of the province, given that the copies of the *formula* which she kept in her dossier were of the Roman *actio tutelae*, even though she was not a Roman citizen with access to rights under the *ius civile*. The change here is one of substantive law rather than of legal process: both the parties involved in the case recorded on the *Tabula Contrebiensis* and the Latin citizens of Irni had their disputes settled through processes which were essentially Roman in character. It is true that, properly speaking, in neither case was the substantive law Roman: the citizens of Irni were not for the most part *cives Romani*, and thus could not avail themselves of the *ius civile* any more than Babatha could.

The clause in the *lex Irnitana* which deals with the law applicable to the citizens of Irni (the *ius municipum*) specifies that any matters not explicitly covered by the charter should be dealt with between the *municipes* in the way in which Roman citizens dealt with it under the *ius civile*. This careful wording makes clear that the Irnitani, although they were not *cives Romani* and their legal actions were under the *ius* of their own *municipium*, were to act as though the *ius civile* applied to them. The distinction between the *lex Irnitana* and the dispute settled at Contrebia is not between the use of Roman law and local law, but that in the later case the local law itself is to be based on the law that the Romans used, even though it was not that law. In effect, the change that has taken place is the suppression of whatever laws the community at Irni used before it became a Latin *municipium* and their replacement by another set of laws which was, so to speak, a mirage of the *ius civile*.

It must be said that the contrast between the *Tabula Contrebiensis* and the *lex Irnitana* presents almost too clear a shift towards the establishment of Roman law in the provinces. In other parts of the empire, particularly in Egypt and the Hellenized provinces of the eastern Mediterranean, the substantive law of the local cities (or, in the case of Egypt, the Greek and Egyptian law that had been in place in the period of the Ptolemaic kings down to 31 BC) remained in place alongside the Roman law.[36] It is probable, however, that even here the drift was towards increasing use of Roman legal patterns, if only because the oversight of jurisdiction was the business of the Roman governor and, beyond him, of the emperor and his legal advisers. Even when attempts were made to retain the laws of an area, the decisions were made by men trained in Roman law.[37] The spread of Roman citizenship will also have promoted the use of Roman law, although even after the declaration by the emperor Caracalla in AD 212 that all free persons in the empire were to be Roman citizens there is evidence that elements of local law continued to be used, especially in Egypt.

The history of the development of Roman law in the provinces is not one of systematic exportation of one pattern of law to replace others, undertaken by an imperial power anxious to impose uniformity on its subjects. Still less does it seem to be the adoption by non-Romans of a set of laws seen as intrinsically superior to their own. Roman law travelled with the men who conquered and subsequently governed the provinces of what became the Roman Empire, and the judicial responsibility that these men acquired must be seen in the first instance as the result of their military predominance. It is worth remembering that C. Valerius Flaccus, who issued the complex and sophisticated *formula* found on the *Tabula Contrebiensis*, had not only held the post of *praetor urbanus* before taking up his post in Spain, but was also responsible as governor of Hispania Citerior for the slaughter of 20,000 Celtiberians and the capture and killing of a group of rebels in Belgeda (a town not far from Contrebia), who had burnt their councillors in their own council-house because they were hesitant about opposing the Romans.[38] It is perhaps not surprising that it was to him that the Salluienses, seeking confirmation of the legitimacy of their purchase of land for an aqueduct, came for judgment.

It is to be expected, then, that when provincial jurisdiction was so firmly in the hands of the governor and subsequently of the emperor, the patterns of its development, and in particular the tendency of governors to use the processes of the law administered by the praetors in the courts of

Rome, were strongly influenced by the intellectual background of those who came to control and govern the provinces. As the judicial work of the governors expanded, and especially once military control began to take second place to civil administration, they were faced with questions, brought to their courts by non-Roman provincials as well as by those who had obtained Roman citizenship, whose resolution involved the application of local law. The governors do not seem to have been unwilling to allow this, nor is there any reason why they should have been; but, especially in the earlier period, the decision about how they should handle particular matters was entirely their own. Roman law in the provinces changed as the notion of a province changed. The various forms it took were the product of the nature of each individual province and the governors who were responsible for it.

Notes

1. For this development, see J. S. Richardson, *The Language of Empire: Rome and the Idea of Empire from the Third Century BC to the Second Century AD* (Cambridge, 2008).
2. On *iuridici* in Tarraconensis, see G. Alföldy, *Fasti Hispanienses* (Wiesbaden, 1969), 230–259; for Britain, see *ILS* 1011, 1015, 1123 and 1151; for Egypt, see Strabo 17.1.12 and Ulpian, D. 1.20; for instances, see *ILS* 1434, 1452 and 2691.
3. Tac. *Ann.* 12.60. See P. A. Brunt, 'Procuratorial jurisdiction', in P. A. Brunt, *Roman Imperial Themes* (Oxford, 1990), 163–187.
4. For text, translation and commentary, see *Roman Statutes*, no. 1.
5. A. Lintott, 'The *leges de repetundis* and associate measures under the Republic', *ZSS* 98 (1981): 162–212.
6. Cic. 1 *Verr.* 5.13–15, 2 *Verr.* 1 (*de praetura urbana*), and 2 *Verr.* 2 (*de praetura Siciliensi*).
7. Cic. *Quint. frat.* 1.1.22.
8. A. Lintott, *Imperium Romanum: Politics and Administration* (London, 1993), 28–32.
9. Cic. 2 *Verr.* 2.32.
10. Plin. *Ep.* 10.79, 80.
11. Cic. *Fam.* 13.48.
12. R. Sherk, *Roman Documents from the Greek East* (Baltimore, 1969), no. 65 D, lines 82–84.
13. Cic. 2 *Verr.* 2.32–34 and 90.
14. See 55–6, this chapter.
15. Cic. *Att.* 6.1.15.
16. As observed by A. J. Marshall, 'The structure of Cicero's edict', *American Journal of Philology* 85 (1964): 185–189.
17. Val. Max. 8.15.6.
18. Caes. *Gall.* 1.54.3; 5.1.5; 5.2.1; 6.44.3. See A. J. Marshall, 'Governors on the move', *Phoenix* 20 (1966): 231–246.
19. Strabo 3.4.20.
20. Cic. *Att.* 5.21.9; 6.2.4. For the development of the system, see G. P. Burton, 'Proconsuls, assizes and the administration of justice under the empire', *JRS* 65 (1975): 92–106.

21. Ulp. D. 1.16.9.4.
22. See the comparison drawn by Burton (n. 20) 99–102.
23. Suet. *Aug.* 33.3. On appeals to the emperor, see F. Millar, *The Emperor in the Roman World* (London, 1977), 507–516.
24. Sherk (n. 12), no. 67.
25. Cic. *Att.* 6.2.4.
26. P. B. H. Birks, A. Rodger, and J. S. Richardson, 'Further aspects of the *Tabula Contrebiensis*', *JRS* 74 (1984): 45–73.
27. N. Lewis, Y. Yadin, and J. C. Greenfield, *The Documents from the Bar Kochba Perod in the Cave of Letters. Greek Papyri, Aramaic and Nabataean Signatures and Subscriptions.* (Jerusalem, 1989), nos. 28–30. On the case in general, see H. Cotton, 'The guardianship of Jesus, son of Babatha: Roman and local law in the province of Arabia', *JRS* 83 (1993): 94–108.
28. See J. S. Richardson, *The Romans in Spain* (Oxford, 1996), 188–210.
29. For the text, an English translation, and a brief commentary, see J. González, 'The Lex Irnitana: a new Flavian municipal law', *JRS* 76 (1986): 147–243.
30. *Lex Irn.* ch. 84.
31. *Lex Irn.* ch. 85.
32. *Lex Irn.* chs. 86–88; on *recuperatores*, see B. Frier, *The Rise of the Roman Jurists* (Princeton, 1985), 197–234, and A. Lintott, 'Le procès devant les recuperatores d'après les données épigraphiques jusqu'au règne d'Auguste', *RHDFE* 68 (1990): 1–11.
33. *Lex Irn.* chs. 90–92.
34. *Lex Irn.* ch. 93. See D. Johnston, 'Three thoughts on Roman private law and the lex Irnitana', *JRS* 77 (1987): 62, 63.
35. *Lex Irn.* ch. 93.
36. See Lintott (n. 8), 154–160. The classic case for the survival of local law was made by L. Mitteis, *Reichsrecht und Volksrecht in den östlichen Provinzen des römischen Kaiserreichs* (Leipzig, 1891).
37. For an example of the problems facing a governor and an emperor in attempting to reconcile different legal solutions to a situation occurring in different areas with different laws, see Plin. *Ep.* 10.65–66.
38. App. *Iber.* 100.436–467.

Part III

ROMAN LAW: THE EVIDENCE

5 Documents in Roman Practice

Joseph Georg Wolf

1. Introduction

Our knowledge of ancient Roman law is based primarily on fragments of legal literature from the first and second centuries AD and the first few decades of the third century. It is transmitted in the *Digest*, as well as in a number of earlier works preserved independently.[1] The literature of this period, the classical period of Roman law, was a scholarly literature, written by jurists for jurists; even when they drew their material from practice, as in their collections of opinions (*responsa*), this does not enable us to draw conclusions about the practical application of Roman law or about its effectiveness in everyday life. The same is true of postclassical writings: although they were not addressed to jurists, they were addressed to those with at least some legal knowledge. Roman law developed into an extraordinarily complex and difficult system, so much so that this has sometimes led to the suspicion that its practical utility took second place.

This suspicion is strikingly contradicted by documents dealing with transactions and acts which were of legal significance, of which we now have a large number. I am not referring to the countless papyri from Roman Egypt: prior to the edict of Caracalla of AD 212 these were almost without exception created by and for foreigners (*peregrini*) and reflect the peculiarities of the traditional systems of land registration and execution of judgments in Egypt.[2] Epigraphic documents, whether on stone (such as the sale of fiscal land, the will of Lucius Dasumius, or rights of way and aqueduct) or on copper (such as documents of conveyance or establishing foundations, or military diplomas), also need separate discussion. This chapter is confined to wax tablets: this is the type of document that the Romans actually used.[3] We can limit ourselves to the four most important collections, which are typical of the whole:

(i) The first wax tablets were found in Romania between 1786 and 1855, in gold mines near the Transylvanian town of Verespatak (the ancient Alburnus maior, which lay north west of Apulum). Only a few of the 25 documents that were found in the mines at this time are complete; in most cases only parts are preserved.[4] In 1840 Hans Ferdinand Massmann first succeeded in deciphering their cursive Latin script.[5]

(ii) On 3 and 5 July 1875 some of the business papers of Lucius Caecilius Iucundus were found in his house in Pompeii – 127 extremely charred documents were found tightly packed in a locked wooden chest:[6] these were receipts for sums the banker had paid out, with few exceptions in connection with auctions. Most of these documents were edited by Giulio di Petra as early as 1876.[7]

(iii) The Tabulae Herculanenses introduced us to a wide range of legal transactions: between 1946 and 1961 they were edited by Giovianni Pugliese Carratelli with a commentary by Vincenzo Arangio-Ruiz;[8] Giuseppe Camodeca is working on a new edition. Only parts of most of these tablets are preserved; the editors assign them to 102 different documents, but that number is clearly too high.[9]

(iv) The most important find of Roman procedural and business documents took place in 1959 in Murecine, a southerly suburb of Pompeii which had hardly been explored; this occurred in the course of construction of the motorway from Pompeii to Salerno. The most striking features are the large number of documents, their unusually good state of preservation, and the variety of the transactions attested. They were first edited in nine instalments by Carlo Giordano[10] and Francesco Sbordone[11] between 1967 and 1980, and were newly edited by Giuseppe Camodeca in 1999 in an exhaustive and clearly improved edition.[12] The first edition contained 148 documents; Camodeca's edition contains 127 documents as well as fragments of documents.

2. The Technique of the Documents

The Roman documents are made up of small rectangular wooden tablets (*tabulae*), roughly the size of a hand. On one or both sides they have a small slightly raised edge, and the surfaces within the edge were covered with a kind of wax: hence, they were known as wax tablets (*tabulae ceratae*).[13] The writing was inscribed on the wax with a metal stylus. On one of the longer sides there were usually two holes through which strings were drawn, making it possible to combine two or three tablets into a *codex* which could be handled like a book. The prepared surfaces were inscribed parallel to the spine of the book: the writing on the second side ended at the spine, while the writing on the third side began at the spine: the holes were therefore at the bottom of the second side but at the top of the third (and, for a triptych, the fifth).[14]

A diptych (as the name suggests) consisted of two tablets. In this case, the (outer) sides of the cover were not prepared: only the inner sides, sides 2 and 3, were inscribed; they could then be laid together, and the raised edges would prevent the writing from becoming smeared. The document was then closed in order to protect the writing and secure the text against forgery. A string was wound over the spine and around the tablets. It was secured in a groove of about a finger's breadth on the back of the second tablet (side 4), and it was in this groove (*sulcus*) that the witnesses placed their seals on the string, so that the seals were within the indentation rather than standing proud of the surface. The string would need to be cut or the seals broken if the document was to be opened again, for example to lead evidence before a court. As a reminder of the contents of the document, the text within was repeated on the unprepared 'cover' sides of the diptych (the *scriptura exterior*).

A triptych consisted of three tablets and therefore had six sides. Sides 2 and 3 were inscribed in the same way as with a diptych and sealed in the same way. The external text was written on side 5 and remained accessible. In order to make the document easier to find, an indication of its contents was often also written in ink on the first or last side. Occasionally, in the case of both diptychs and triptychs, an indication of this kind is also found on the edges of the tablets opposite its spine.

Under Nero, a senatusconsultum of AD 61 provided further protection for the internal text: it provided that the edge of the tablets should also be perforated and a string should be drawn through this perforation three times.[15]

3. TWO TYPES OF DOCUMENT

The Romans used two types of document: the *testatio* and the *chirographum*. The *testatio* was a record: it was objective, expressed in the third person, and attested that something had taken place. Its evidential value rested solely on the participation of the witnesses: their seals on the string not only secured the integrity of the text on the closed sides 2 and 3 but also, more importantly, their seals attested that what the writing stated had taken place before their very eyes. (The names of the witnesses appeared in the genitive next to their seals, usually on the right of side 4, written in ink and parallel to the long side of the tablet.) The witness did not need to remember the contents of the document: as long as he recognized the seal as his own, he supplied the evidence that what the text of the document reported had actually taken place. So the *testatio* was a combination of proof by means of document and by means of witnesses.[16]

The chirograph was quite different. It was a declaration made by the author of the document and was intended to provide proof – to be used against him – that he had made the declaration in question. The declaration was subjective, in the first person, and had to be written by the person making it in his own hand. The probative value of the chirograph resided in the fact that it guaranteed that the writing was a declaration made by its author. To strengthen this guarantee, the author of the document often added his seal below the writing as well. Witnesses were not needed in order to give the chirograph probative value, but usually they were used in any case. But while in the case of a *testatio* seven or more witnesses were involved in sealing the internal text, for a chirograph it was unusual to have more than three. The author of the document always put his own seal on the string, often twice. If he was a slave, his owner usually added his seal too. For the chirograph the primary function of the seal was to secure the internal text and especially to protect it from forgery at the hand of the recipient of the document. Beyond that the seals could not in fact guarantee anything more than did the writing in the author's own hand and his own seal, namely that he really had written the internal text.

A person who was illiterate could have a trusted person or a slave write for him. Generally the writer of the document recorded that he had prepared it on request or following an order. The writer was then the author of the document, but, if the illiterate person added his seal under the internal text or on the string that bound it, it was still evidence against him. Women generally had their chirographs written by others.

We know nothing about the procedure for creating these documents. Almost without exception the Transylvanian and the new Pompeian documents appear not to have been created *ad hoc*; instead they usually follow tried and tested formulae in which every word was fixed. The formulae did have to be completed with variables such as date and place, names, amounts, and time-limits, and they could also be adjusted to fit individual requirements. Probably the actual text for the document was drafted before the document was itself prepared. A *testatio* could clearly be written in advance, and then what it recorded could be witnessed and the document read out and sealed. In the case of a chirograph, the author of the document could write a pre-prepared text on the tablets in front of witnesses. He could copy that from a draft or it could be dictated to him either from a draft or from the external text that had already been prepared: sometimes we do find that the writing of the external text is in a different hand from that of the internal text.

4. The Transylvanian Documents

The 25 documents found in the Transylvanian goldmines are all triptychs or part of triptychs: 5 are complete; in 4 cases there are 2 surviving tablets, and in 16 there is 1. It is hardly possible to tell what the subject-matter of 12 of the documents was. They were created between AD 131 and AD 167; the earliest which is completely preserved dates from 17 March 139 and the last from 9 February 167. The documents were prepared in various different places, the majority in Alburnus maior, which was a settlement of the Pirustae, an Illyrian people; others in Densaris, in the settlement next to the base of the 13th legion Gemina,[17] in Katus or Immenosus maior.

Four of the documents which are completely preserved attest sales and their completion. They come from AD 139, 142, 159, and 160 and relate to the sale of a slave-girl, a slave-boy, a house, and a slave-woman.[18] They follow the same formula,[19] and they document the sale, conveyance of the object sold, and a warranty that it is free from defects (these are listed individually in the case of the slave-girl and slave-boy, but for the slave-woman are confined to a statement that she is in good health). In the case of the slave sales this warranty is incorporated in the warranty against eviction. In the two earlier documents that warranty is for double the value; and in the two later ones simply for the amount of the buyer's interest. The warranty in the case of the house covers its fencing, various ancillary items, and its freedom from servitudes. Then comes a declaration by the seller that he has received the price and, in the cases of the slave-boy and slave-woman,[20] the appointment of a surety. Conveyance is by means of the formal conveyance of *mancipatio*, although in the case of provincial land this was unnecessary, as *traditio* would have sufficed. And *mancipatio* would have been unnecessary in all four cases if the contracting parties were foreigners, as most of the names[21] and the choice of words in the *stipulatio* (*fide rogavit* or *fide promisit*) suggest.[22] The documents are formulated as records in the third person,[23] and in each case are sealed by seven people, including the seller and, where there is a guarantor, by the guarantor too. There are six witnesses (in two documents only five). These various anomalies give rise to the suspicion that in creating the documents the parties did not receive expert advice.

The two completely preserved documents of loan also have their peculiarities. One,[24] dated 20 June 162, first sets out a *stipulatio*, by means of which the debtor promises repayment of the amount of the loan together with interest; it then provides that the debtor is bound to repay the loan and the interest on the date of demand by the creditor; finally, it again sets out the promise made at the outset. The other document,[25] a diptych dated 19 October 162, first sets out the promise to repay the amount of the loan on the date of demand by the creditor; next there is a declaration by the debtor that he has received the loan in cash and owes it; then a specific promise relating to interest; and finally a guarantee obligation by a third party for repayment of the loan and the interest. Apart from this last declaration, which was not sufficient to prove a guarantee obligation before a Roman court,[26] the contents of the two documents do provide evidence for the transaction that had occurred. Compared with the formulae in use in the new Pompeian documents of the first century AD, the formulation in these documents – such as the repetition of the stipulation or the omission of a declaration that the loan has been received – is rather imprecise and amateurish, even unpredictable. Here too the names and the form of the promise (*fide rogavit* or *fide promisit*) suggest that at least the creditor in the first case (Anduenna Batonis) and the debtor in the second (Alexander Caricci) were foreigners.[27]

A triptych of 28 May 167[28] documents clearly and simply a declaration by Lupus Carentis that he has received by way of loan 50 denarii from Iulius Alexander,[29] as well as the transfer of the 50 denarii, and declares that Lupius Carentis owes their repayment without any dispute. This document is professionally drafted and unremarkable.

Two contracts for work from AD 164 and a third which is undated are formulated as chirographs.[30] They follow the same formula: the hirers (Memmius Asclepis; Restitutus Senior; and possibly Lucius Ulpius Valerius) bind themselves to work in the goldmines for a year, in each case until 13 November 165. The agreed wage is probably to be paid at the end of the contract. These chirographs were written not by the hirers themselves, who are stated not to be literate, but at their request, in the case of the dated documents by Flavius Secundinus and an assistant called

Macari. The employers are Aurelius Adiutor, probably a slave who worked for an employee of the state administration of mines, and Socrationis Socates, probably the tenant of a mine.[31] All of these documents are clearly structured, and their drafting is precise and legally correct.

Finally, mention should be made of a contract of partnership (*societas*) of 28 March 167. It too is clearly structured, legally correct, and precise.[32] Cassius Frontinus and Iulius Alexander agreed to carry out banking transactions in partnership for the period from 23 December 166 to 12 April 167.[33] The date of the contract, shortly before it was due to terminate, was no doubt only the date of execution rather than of the conclusion of the contract. It provided that the partners would share profits and losses, as well as setting out the contributions that each must make: Alexander was to provide 500 denarii in cash or kind; for Frontinus, his agent Secundus was to provide 267 denarii. There was also provision for a fine to be paid by one to the other if he were found to have done anything fraudulently or in bad faith. At the end of the contract each was to have his contribution returned to him, and the remainder was to be divided. At the end of the document Frontinus obtains a promise from Alexander that all of this should be done and observed. Here the wording of the promise (*stipulatus est/spopondit*) suggests that the two were Roman citizens. We should also take it that Alexander obtained the same promise from Frontinus and that it was evidenced in an identical document.

These documents do not provide a single view of legal or documentary practice in Dacia Superior. Clearly Roman law applied. Whether Roman succession, family, and property law with all their institutions also applied, or just the law of commerce attested in these documents, can remain an open question. But even the applicability of this part of the law is remarkable: it was only in 105 and 106, during the second Dacian war, that the emperor Trajan conquered the northern part of Dacia, including the gold mines around Apulum, and only in 106 that the whole of the conquered land was made a Roman province.[34] The application of the law of commerce shows the romanization of the new province, one of whose principal means was imposing the obligation to make use of the Roman legal order. This may perhaps have been made easier as a result of the depopulation of the area owing to the bloody wars of the 80s, followed by the settlement of colonists from all over the empire and from neighbouring Asiatic states;[35] in the mining region this applied above all to the Pirustae, who came from Dalmatia and were known for their experience in mining.[36]

But Roman law was not always applied with adequate knowledge or practical experience. The sales of the slaves and the house, as well as the two loans, were evidently conducted by private individuals without the assistance of experts: they probably just followed standard documentary formulae as a guide. The contracts for work and the partnership agreement are quite different: in every respect they are correct; the drafting would have been no different in Italy, the centre of Roman law. So far as the contracts for work are concerned, this is probably because the employer was ultimately the state administration of mines and in the other probably a tenant of mines, so in each case the contract would be just one of many identical contracts, which would have been drafted by experts for the use of the mining enterprise. In the case of the partnership, it is likely that bankers would have secured legal advice in this as in all their transactions.

5. The Pompeian Receipts

A find in 1875 in Pompeii in the house of the banker and auctioneer Lucius Caecilius Iucundus brought 153 documents, mostly triptychs, to light.[37] With the exception of two documents from AD 15 and 27 respectively, the documents all date from the years AD 53 to 62. The ruinous state of the documents – largely caused by extensive charring – restricts their legibility considerably.[38] All of the documents are receipts: the vast majority[39] relate to payment of the proceeds of auctions; these were made through the banker to the seller and principal in the auction.[40] There are also 16 receipts[41] from the town of Pompeii for payments the banker made to it.

In two respects, these documents have their own peculiarities. Even in external appearance they differ from the Transylvanian and the new Pompeian documents. In the case of the triptychs only sides 2, 3, and 5 were prepared for writing, while the cover sides 1 and 6 and side 4 were smooth wood surfaces, side 4 having a groove through which the string closure ran where the seals were placed. The internal text was on sides 2 and 3 as usual, and the external text on side 5. On side 4 next to the seals the names of the witnesses were written in the genitive in ink (these are better preserved than the text itself). For the few diptychs, sides 1, 2, and 3 correspond precisely to these sides of the triptychs, while side 4 was intended for the names of those signing and the external text. The narrow edges of the triptychs on the opposite side from the spine seem generally to have given an indication in ink of the content of the document, so that it could easily be found.

The second peculiarity is, for most of the documents, a difference between the internal and external texts. The true purpose of the external text was to repeat verbatim the words of the internal text, to show the content of the sealed internal text. Most of the receipts of Caecilius Iucundus are different: the internal text of most triptychs (on sides 2 and 3) is a *testatio*, while the external text on side 5 is a chirograph.[42] The *testationes* are written by the same hand, presumably that of Caecilius Iucundus, and they record a declaration by the creditor that he has received a sum of money from Caecilius Iucundus. In the chirographs, on the other hand, the creditors acknowledge receipt of a sum of money from Caecilius Iucundus either at their own hand or (in the case of those unable to write) at the hand of a person who could write. In a few cases the internal and external texts do match, both being either *testationes*[43] or chirographs.[44]

The *testationes* attest a declaration by the creditor (the seller and principal) that he has received a specific sum of money, less a fee for conduct of the auction, from Lucius Caecilius Iucundus. This sum was promised in a verbal contract (*stipulatio*) which Lucius Caecilius Iucundus had made in relation to the principal's auction. An example is a document from 23 December 57.[45] Here Tullia Lampyris agreed with Caecilius Iucundus that he should auction for her an item which is not identified in the document: the contract was one of letting work to be done (*locatio conductio operis*). In terms of the contract Tullia Lampyris owed a fee (payment for the work done), while Caecilius Iucundus was obliged to carry out the auction and pay her the price realized. But the parties did not limit themselves to the obligation under a contract of letting: as usual, Caecilius Iucundus also promised by means of a *stipulatio* that he would pay the sale price realized: Tullia Lampyris's claim under the contract of let may have been novated by this means. The *testatio* speaks only of the *stipulatio*. The deduction of the fee for work done was based on Tullia Lampyris's contractual obligation. The auction was regarded as hers, since the goods for sale were hers, and she was the principal and seller. All the *testationes* are sealed by at least seven and sometimes more seals placed on the string in the groove on side 4. Where there are more than seven, among their number are the author of the document and the creditor.[46]

The external text was in the form of a chirograph, which Tullia Lampyris did not write herself. Instead Sextus Pompeius Axiochus wrote it at her request; women generally let others write on their behalf. The chirograph ends with a final clause referring to her having been asked questions about the sealed tablets (*ex interrogatione facta tabellarum signatarum*). This can refer only to the sealed *testatio* and to the declaration by Tullia that she had obtained the money that was due. The declaration was the answer to a corresponding question,[47] but that does not alter the fact that it is a receipt. The probative value of the chirograph receipt rested on the declaration by the creditor at her own hand that she had received the specified sum of money – and it was against the creditor that the document needed to supply proof. Chirographs were also sealed:[48] generally the creditor granting the receipt placed his or her seal on the string, often twice,[49] while Marcus Alleius Carpus sealed his chirograph of 24 June 56 four times.[50] Third parties were also involved as witnesses: sometimes just one,[51] frequently two or three.[52] Seven witnesses, such as used for *testationes*, are not found.

The receipts granted by the town of Pompeii for payments made by Caecilius Iucundus are all chirographs, with regard to both the internal and the external text. In most cases the external text repeats the internal text with minor, insignificant differences, although sometimes it is just an extract from the internal text.[53] The authors of these documents were slaves of the town, the chirograph of 14 March 53 being by a Secundus,[54] while so far as can be seen the others are by a Privatus: both are described as slaves of the town of Pompeii (or, to be precise, the *coloni* of the *colonia Veneriae Corneliae Pompeianorum*). The documents whose dates are preserved come from the years 53, 55, 58, 59, 60, and 62. In each case the slave placed his seal twice on the string closure,[55] and, in order to show their authority to do so,[56] so did both of the duumviri[57] – or else only one of them did so,[58] in which case he sealed twice.[59] In addition there are regularly seals of one or two independent third parties.[60] An example is a document from 19 February 58,[61] according to which Lucius Caecilius Iucundus paid 1,652 sesterces to the town of Pompeii in respect of a fuller's workshop (*ob fullonicam*). In the same year he went on to pay a further 1,652 sesterces;[62] the following year, on 10 July 59, he paid 1,651.5 sesterces;[63] and on 8 May 60 once again 1,652 sesterces.[64] All the payments were made in respect of the fuller's workshop. Caecilius Iucundus did not rent the shop himself; instead he farmed the tax that the fullers had to pay the town of Pompeii for their use of the workshop.[65] Caecilius Iucundus took the rent paid by the fullers and paid the town the tax due to it; the difference was his profit or loss. Tax-farming contracts were entered into for five years, and the payments were made annually. On the first side of each of these four documents there is reference to the year in respect of which the payment was made; the reason for the slight difference in the payment for the third year is unclear. There is no doubt that these payments relate to tax farming; the first three payments were paid when they fell due, on 1 July, while the fourth was paid before it fell due.[66]

Three receipts – from 5 January and 13 June 58, and 18 June 59[67] – relate to a tax-farming contract for taxes due by the tenant of a pasture owned by the town; and a document of 14 March 53 as well as a damaged chirograph[68] attest payments by Caecilius Iucundus probably in relation to a tax-farming contract for taxes due under a long lease.[69]

In spite of their uniformity, these receipts provide a direct view of two of the lines of business of an evidently successful banker and auctioneer; a glimpse of everyday life and the administrative arrangements of Pompeii; and, not least, an insight into just how precise and how rich in information these documents are.

6. The Herculaneum Tablets

These tablets were discovered in the 1930s in the ruins of Herculaneum, a small coastal town at the foot of Vesuvius. The town had already suffered from an earthquake on 3 February 63, but the damage had evidently been repaired when, with the eruption of Vesuvius on 24 August 79, the town was overwhelmed by mud and lava. The places where wax tablets were discovered are well-known: the majority were found in the Case del Bicentenario, others in the Casa di Lucius Cominius Primus, and quite a few in the Casa di Venedius Ennychus.[70] Between 1946 and 1961 Giovanni Pugliese Carratelli edited them and, in 6 instalments, published a total of 102 documents. In a great number of them only a few words are legible; many are damaged and their texts need extensive reconstruction. There are only a few that are complete or sufficiently complete that their reconstruction is not in doubt. The date is preserved in only about twenty documents: the oldest are from 52, 55, and 59;[71] and the latest from 70, 75, and 76,[72] while the majority date from the 60s. If these dates are representative of the whole, then by far the greatest number of documents belongs in the reign of Nero, and a few in that of Vespasian.

Giuseppe Camodeca is preparing a second edition, and the many publications he has produced in the course of his work show just how much it is needed. For example, he has established that tablets TH 77, 78, 80, 53, and 9 are parts of one and the same document,[73] and that the same is true of TH 44 and 45; TH 70 and 71; and TH 52 and 90.[74] He has also put forward new and convincing readings,[75] and by combining previously neglected fragments has discovered new parts of these documents.

In spite of their fragmentary condition, the Herculaneum tablets too give a lively impression of everyday life in the town. The large number of well-preserved[76] names of witnesses and the order in which they placed their seals; the *cognomina* (surnames) which often show that their bearers were freedmen; and, not least, the business carried on by the protagonists, such as L. Cominius Primus and C. Vibius Eurynus: all of this material provides an insight into the social structure of the town.[77]

L. Cominius Primus borrowed and lent money. He was probably a banker (*argentarius*). In two documents slaves of Ulpia Plotina acknowledge receipt from L. Cominius Primus of sums paid in settlement of an obligation, probably arising out of a stipulation: in the first case Venustus, probably on 6 November 61,[78] acknowledged 1,000 denarii; in the second, Felix, in June 70,[79] acknowledged an unknown sum of denarii. From other documents we discover that on 31 January 65 Cominius Primus borrowed 20,000 sesterces from M. Messenius;[80] in 68 (or earlier)[81] he borrowed a further 6,000 sesterces;[82] he made a loan to Laelius Euphrosymus of 20,000 sesterces;[83] and probably also a loan to Venustus of 19,000 sesterces.[84] A *testatio*[85] probably of 20 January 69 records that M. Nonius Fuscus conveyed his slave-woman Nais to L. Cominius Primus in security by way of *fiducia*, after first swearing that she belonged to him. This was done in relation to a debt of 600 sesterces. On 12 May 59 C. Vinius Eurytus became surety for a debt of 1,000 sesterces owed by Pompeia Anthis to L. Cominius Primus.[86] Ten year later, in early 69, L. Cominius Primus was involved in a boundary dispute with L. Appuleius Proculus, which they brought before Tiberius Crassius Firmus as arbiter.[87] A further document shows us L. Cominius Primus in January 70, after his divorce from Paullina, in a dispute about return of her dowry.[88]

From the archive of Lucius Venidius Ennychus there is a *testatio* of 24 July 60 which has no parallel – it attests his declaration that his wife Livia Acte has given birth to a daughter: it was no doubt intended for the register of births and to enable the daughter to secure her legal position, freedom, citizenship, and membership of his family.[89] A fragment of a *testatio* of May 52,[90] only part of whose external text can be read, documents an agreement that Venidius made with his opponent to interrupt or bring to an end legal proceedings before a judge.[91] Another *testatio* records a declaration by Venidius Ennychus to the effect that L. Annius Rufus meets the requirements for standing as a candidate for public office;[92] unfortunately the date of the *testatio* is not preserved – only the external text on side 4, which was written in ink on wood, is preserved and is barely legible.

A series of documents deals with preparations for a civil case.[93] We do not know how the case ended – or even whether it actually took place. The litigants were two women, Petronia Iusta and Calatoria Themis, and the case concerned the status of Iusta. She maintained that she had been born as a free person (*ingenua*), while Calatoria claimed to be her patron, since Iusta had been her slave and she had freed her. Iusta wanted to bring the dispute to court. Three documents about *vadimonia* are preserved; two are identical.[94] They were executed on 7 September 75 and show, first, that Iusta and Calatoria agreed that Calatoria would appear before the tribunal of the urban praetor in the forum Augustum in Rome at the second hour on 3 December. There Iusta could have summoned her to appear before the praetor (*in ius vocatio*). In the event that she did not appear, Calatoria had, with the consent of her tutor, C. Petronius Telephorus, promised to pay 1,000 sesterces. Second, the documents also attest a further *vadimonium* with the same content, this time agreed with the tutor, Petronius. We do not know whether they observed their *vadimonia*, but as far as we can tell the litigation did not take place. According to a third document,[95] Marcus Calatorius bound himself to Petronia Iusta to appear, again in Rome in the forum Augustum, in front of the temple of Mars Ultor at the third hour. (According to the editors, the document was executed on the same day as he was to appear, which seems rather unlikely.) It is not clear what part Calatorius played, but it may well be that he intended to conduct the case on behalf of Calatoria Themis. It is unclear whether Calatorius observed his obligation and appeared, or appeared but was not summoned by Petronia before the praetor. These uncertainties are not resolved by any of six further documents, all chirographs, whose authors make declarations on behalf of the parties, either Iusta[96] or Calatoria.[97] They all give reasons for their statements and end with the formula that she was 'born a free girl/woman' or 'is or was a freedwoman of Calatoria Themis'.

Finally, mention should be made of tablets which follow a formula that was previously unknown. Their written form is itself distinctive: the first line is evidently a superscript which consists of the word tablets (*tabellae*) and a name in the genitive: *tabellae L. Comini Primi*. In Herculaneum only fragments of these documents have been found; the best preserved is an internal text of 12 May 59, the two parts of which have been separated and separately edited.[98] The first part is an extract from *tabellae*, probably the account book of L. Cominius Primus: the extract duplicates the payment of a loan of 1,000 sesterces in cash (*ex arca*) to Pompeia Anthis; the second part records that C. Vibius Eurytus stood surety for repayment of the loan.

The documents from Murecine are more numerous and much better preserved, and we will turn to them now.

7. The New Pompeian Documents

In the course of construction of a motorway from Pompeii to Salerno in April 1959, the remains of an ancient house were discovered outside

Murecine, to the south of Pompeii.[99] Since construction was well advanced, the excavation, which was undertaken as an emergency, was able to reveal only a small part of the expansive buildings, in particular part of the courtyard and five dining rooms. The courtyard was on an unusual scale, although its design and furnishings were not untypical; the number of dining rooms, however, was most remarkable. The villa was neither a guest house nor an inn; it was fitted out as a private house, although its many dining rooms can hardly have served private purposes. This unusual feature, as well as the striking scale of the building, its elaborate furnishing, its location beyond the gates of the town near the coast and harbour, and, above all, its similarity to the Casa del Triclini in Ostia suggest that the villa was owned by a *collegium*.[100]

On 24 and 25 July 1959, in the middle of the three dining rooms at the front of the courtyard, archaeologists found a wicker basket which was full to the brim with documents, namely the legal records of a bank. The bank was based not at Pompeii but at Puteoli (the present-day Pozzuoli) on the north coast of the gulf to the west of Naples. The formal elements of these documents include the place and date of their execution; insofar as the place of execution is preserved and legible, it is with few exceptions[101] Puteoli.

There was scarcely a better location for a banking business. With the growth of the Roman economy after the Carthaginian wars Puteoli swiftly became one of the leading trading places of the ancient world. So began a period of particular wealth for the town. This is reflected in the new documents in ways that are striking as well as unexpected. The many public buildings which are mentioned and whose existence we discover here for the first time were, to judge from their names, without exception foundations and thus notable evidence not just for the history of architecture but also of the wealth of the citizens of the town.

According to a report by Olga Elia,[102] an archaeologist, the tablets were found in excellent condition, with the wood well-preserved. The then superintendent of antiquities for the provinces of Naples and Caserta had never experienced a find in such remarkable condition. What they did was the best they could possibly have done: they documented the find and recorded it in 302 excellent photographs.[103] This documentation was, however, incomplete: even their photographs show that not all of the tablets were systematically photographed on both sides.[104]

Olga Elia reported the total number of tablets in 1960 as 300; the conservator Selim Augusti reported in 1966 that it was 200. According to Camodeca the documents preserved in whole or in part in the find must originally have been around 350, of which barely more than half survived the catastrophe and the centuries in their wicker basket and can be referred to today.[105]

The documents come, as already mentioned, from a banker's archive. They are evidently a selection. Few of the selected documents are complete and most are preserved only in part, so the diptychs and triptychs must have been taken apart in Puteoli or Pompeii – being by then no longer required for purposes of proof – and many disposed of before the remainder were carefully stored in the wicker basket. The selection may have depended on factors such as the size of the basket, although there may have been other criteria.

The edition of the new documents took some time. It was entrusted to Oscar Onorato, who wanted to publish the documents not in instalments but as a whole, but he died in 1965 before he had completed his work. Owing to these unfortunate circumstances editing began in 1967 and was completed in 1980. The editors were Carlo Giordano, one of the directors of the Pompeii excavations, and Francesco Sbordone, professor of classical philology at the University of Naples. They published most of the tablets in nine instalments in the *Rendiconti dell'Accademia di Archeologia Lettere e Belle Arti di Napoli.*[106] Addolarata Landi published a supplement in the *Atti dell'Accademia Pontaniana.*[107] The first edition comprised 148 documents and parts of documents. Camodeca has described its deficiencies in minute detail.[108] His own *Edizione critica dell'archivio puteolano dei Sulpicii* appeared in 1999, contains 127 documents, and meets the highest standards.[109] My recent edition, *Neue Rechtsurkunden aus Pompeji. Tabulae Pompeianae Novae*, of 2010 contains 117 documents.[110]

In 55 of the 117 documents the date is preserved with year, month, and the consular year. Three can be only roughly dated as the consular year is unclear.[111] In six other cases the date of execution is not preserved, but the consular year allows the year and period within which the document was executed to be identified.[112] And for a further five at least the year is preserved.[113]

The documents fall into three decades: the last, TPN 74, was executed on 22 February 61; the earliest on 14 July 29.[114] The bulk, consisting of 34 dated documents, was executed in the 40s. This shows us that the majority of the dated documents come from the 20 years between AD 35 and 55, in the reigns of the emperors Caligula and Claudius, and so they were 25 to 45 years old when they were submerged in mud and preserved until the present day.

The precise dates on the documents are important for the chronology of the time; and, precisely because of the increasing number of suffect consulships in this period, they are no less important for political history, in making possible confirmation, correction, and amplification of the consular Fasti for these years.

The protagonists of the events attested in the documents are members of the Caii Sulpicii: Faustus Maior, Faustus, Cinnamus, and Onirus. C. Sulpicius Faustus Maior appears in the earliest documents and makes his final appearance in January or February 35; C. Sulpicius Faustus appears from March 34.[115] The third, who appears the most often, is Cinnamus, who enters the scene in March 42.[116] We see Faustus in the business for 17 years and Cinnamus for 14, while Onirus appears only briefly. Faustus appears for the last time in May 52,[117] Cinnamus in March 56, and Onirus first appears – for the only time – in February 61.[118]

These Sulpicii were freedmen.[119] As Cinnamus stated himself, he was a freedman of Faustus. Faustus was probably freeborn but the son of a freedman called C. Sulpicius Heraclida. These bankers could, given their status and their business, have sat at the table of Trimalchio, their contemporary and fellow citizen – although their business certainly did not allow them to accumulate the great riches that he did.

The representatives of the bank are typical of the society that we encounter in the documents. It is largely a society of freedmen. Admittedly, of the well over 100 Roman citizens who appear in the documents, few are expressly described as freedmen. But often the *cognomen* is an indication of status which is just as reliable: Attimetus, Agathopus or Epaphroditus, Isochrysus, Onesimus or Plistus, Anthus, Thallus, Agathemer or Hermeros – only a freedman could have a name such as this. They were, it seems, the middle, often unobserved stratum of Roman society, or perhaps its foundation. Even the imperial household (*familia Caesaris*) is repeatedly attested and the style of names of its slaves and freedmen allows us to draw conclusions about its inner structure.

The internal texts of these chirographs show the prevalence of literacy: of the 30 chirographs among these documents, only 4 are not written in the hand of the person against whom they were intended to serve as proof. Of these, one was written for a woman: L. Patulcius Epaphroditus wrote it 'on the request and on the instruction' of his freedwoman, Patulcia Erotis, and in her presence.[120] Women generally made use of someone else to write their chirographs.

Almost without exception, the documents follow established formulae and so are generally written in proper standard Latin. Departures from that are rare. Nonetheless we do read 'Putolis' in the chirographs of C. Novius Eunus. Eunus[121] and Diognetus,[122] the first a freedman and the second a slave of C. Novius Cypaerus, wrote as they spoke: a robust vulgar Latin. Their chirographs date from 28 June and 2 July 37, 29 August

38, and 15 September 39. They provide new and detailed indications of vulgar Latin word formation. Only the inner text of a document had to be written in one's own hand since, as already mentioned, only it had probative value. In three instances the external texts of the chirographs are preserved, and they are indeed not in the hand of Novius Eunus or Diognetus; nor are they written in vulgar, but in standard, Latin. These three chirographs, with their internal and external texts,[123] just like inscriptions written in two languages, record the same text in two contemporary versions, one vulgar and one standard. There is no parallel to this in surviving Latin literature.

Almost 40 of the documents are concerned with procedure in court or before an arbiter: there are numerous promises to appear in Puteoli or in Rome for citation before the magistrate;[124] various *testationes* dealing with appearing there in time; administering and swearing oaths,[125] as well as examination before the magistrate in relation to institution as heir or the power of a master over his slave. The highlights are documents dealing with an agreement on the appointment of a judge,[126] a draft court decree,[127] and the settlement of a dispute.[128]

Most of these documents deal with contracts and other commercial acts of legal significance. The commonest is loan. This is often accompanied by security, whether in the form of surety or a pledge.[129] Pledges are accompanied by contracts for letting storage rooms, where the goods pledged (grain and pulses) are stored.[130] Alongside these contracts of loan, sureties, pledges, and letting of storage, are acknowledgments of obligations and of outstanding balances,[131] receipts, and guarantees. Thirteen documents are concerned with auctioning securities that have become forfeit: these relate to pledges or conveyances in security of purple material, land, and slaves.

The bank of the Sulpicii was not a large one. In AD 48, apart from C. Sulpicius Faustus and C. Sulpicius Cinnamus, there were four slaves at work. The penalties provided in the *vadimonia* for the event that a person bound to appear did not do so amount to a few hundred or a few thousand[132] (in three cases[133] it was admittedly 50,000 sesterces, which perhaps corresponded to the sum sued for). For 25 loans, acknowledgments of debt, and receipts we know the sums that were lent, acknowledged, or received: only rarely do they exceed 20,000 sesterces; mostly they are concerned with appreciably smaller sums.

In the documents, Faustus and Cinnamus each lend 20,000 sesterces on one occasion: Faustus on 13 March 40 to L. Marius Iucundus,[134] and Cinnamus on 3 October 45 to M. Lollius Philippus;[135] on 1 May 46 one or other of them lent 30,000 sesterces in cash to Magia Pulchra.[136] On

28 June 37 C. Novius Eunus acknowledged receipt of a loan of 10,000 sesterces from Evenus Primianus, a freedman of the emperor Tiberius, through his slave Hesychus. On 3 March 49 P. Vergilius Ampliatus acknowledged 5,000 sesterces, likewise by way of loan, from Sex. Granius Numenius. On 31 December 44 Cinnamus issued a receipt that on 4 December 44 he had received from Alcimus, a slave of C. Eprius Valgus, 30,000 sesterces against a claim by his patron Faustus of 50,000 sesterces.[137] On 14 October 51 six slaves whom M. Egnatius Suavis had conveyed to Cinnamus in security of a claim for 27,000 sesterces were to be auctioned. A chirograph of 11 January 49 deals with 120,000 sesterces:[138] if we interpret it correctly, Purgias, a foreigner, had requested and mandated Cinnamus to convey, no doubt in security, a slave named Aprilis to Cerinthus, who was a slave of the emperor. This was in security against a claim of 120,000 sesterces. In 51 we find the bank on the debtor side: on 2 May 51 Cinnamus declared that he owed 94,000 sesterces to Phosphorus Lepidianus, a slave of the emperor Claudius, and promised to repay it by 13 June.[139]

As this sketch shows, the main business of the bank of the Sulpicii was the provision of credit. The bank, of course, did not lend money interest-free. For loans (*mutua*) interest had to be promised in a separate *stipulatio*, although no documents of this kind were found in the wicker basket. They evidently did not survive the selection process, since there can be no doubt that they must have existed. The amount of the loans was not always modest, but the return on them will not have made the Sulpicii rich. The maximum rate of interest was fixed at 12 per cent per annum, and it is not likely that they would have been able regularly to exceed this maximum.[140]

Notes

1. See the chapter by Kaiser, 119, 128.
2. See H.J. Wolff, *Das Recht der griechischen Papyri Ägyptens*, vol. 1 (Munich, 2002), 1–8, 15, 213ff.
3. There is a selection in FIR 283–422 and FIRA vol. 3.
4. T. Mommsen in *CIL* III 921–59; III Suppl.; and T. Mommsen, *Ephemeris epigraphica* II 467; IV 187.
5. H. F. Massmann, *Libellus aurarius* (Leipzig, 1840).
6. D. 33.64: 'a chest containing documents and debtors' undertakings' (*arca in qua instrumenta et cautiones debitorum erant*).
7. G. de Petra, *Le tavolette cerate di Pompei* (Naples, 1876); C. Zangemeister, 'Tabulae ceratae Pompeis repertae annis MDCCCLXXV et MDCCCLXXXVII', in CIL IV Suppl. I (1898), no. 3340 I–CLIII (including a detailed introduction at 275–80); T. Mommsen, 'Die pompeianischen Quittungstafeln des L. Caecilius Iucundus', in T. Mommsen, *Gesammelte Schriften* (Berlin, 1907, repr. 1965), vol. 3, 221–74.

8. V. Arangio-Ruiz and G. Pugliese Carratelli, 'Tabulae Herculanenses', instalments I–VI in *La Parola del Passato* 1 (1946): 379–85; 3 (1948): 165–84; 8 (1953): 455–63; 9 (1954): 54–74; 10 (1955): 448–77; 16 (1961): 66–73.
9. See, e.g., G. Camodeca, 'Riedizione del trittico ercolanense TH 77+78+80+53+92 del 26 gennaio 69', *Cronache Ercolanensi* 24 (1994): 137–46; J. G. Wolf, *Aus dem neuen pompeianischen Urkundenfund: Gesammelte Aufsätze* (Berlin, 2010), 209.
10. *RAAN* 41 (1966): 107–21; 45 (1970): 211–25; 46 (1971): 183–95; 47 (1972): 311–16.
11. *RAAN* 46 (1971): 173–82; 47 (1972): 307–10; 51 (1976): 145–67; 53 (1978): 248–69, as well as F. Sbordone and C. Giordano, *RAAN* 43 (1968): 3–12; A. Landi, 'Ricerche sull'onomastica delle tabelle dell'agro Murecine', *Atti dell'Accademia Pontaniana* 29 (1980): 193–97.
12. *Tabulae Pompeianae Sulpiciorum: Edizione critica dell'archivio puteolano dei Sulpicii*, 2 vols. (1999); J. G. Wolf, *Neue Rechtsurkunden aus Pompeji: Tabulae Pompeianae Novae* (Darmstadt, 2010).
13. The material in the new Pompeian tablets was in fact not wax but shellac: S. Augusti, *RAAN* 37 (1962): 127; cf. also R. Büll and E. Moser, 'Wachs', in *RE* Suppl. 13 (1973), cols. 1366–72.
14. This is a key criterion for placing the sides of the tablets in the correct order.
15. Suet. *Ner.* 17; *PS* 5.25.6.
16. Denying one's own seal was punishable.
17. Its base was in Apulum, a defensive centre and junction of the Dacian road network.
18. FIR nos. 131, 130, 133, 132.
19. This was drafted in terms of a male slave, which is how Bruns accounts in FIR no. 131 line 9 for the use of the male pronoun.
20. FIR no. 130 line 14; 331 no. 132 line 14.
21. Most of the names point towards peregrine status: they have one name, to which is added the name of the father in the genitive (e.g., Alexander Antipatri). See W. Schulze, *Zur Geschichte Lateinischer Eigennamen*, 2nd edn. (Berlin, 1966) on Bellicus Alexandri (FIR no. 130) at 42 n. 4, 292 n. 1, 428; on Maximus Batonis and Anduena Batonis (FIR nos. 131 and 133) at 31 n. 3; on Dasius Verzonis (FIR no. 131) at 39 n. 3; on Vibius Longus (FIR no. 130) at 102, 425; and on Dasius Breucus (FIR no. 130) at 19 n. 1, 39 n. 1, 44 n. 5.
22. Gaius 3.93.
23. P. Krüger, *Geschichte der Quellen und Litteratur des römischen Rechts*, 2nd edn. (Munich – Leipzig, 1912), 269, states that documents such as chirographs were written by the debtors themselves.
24. FIR no. 153, 1; FIRA 3 no. 123.
25. FIR no. 153, 2; FIRA 3 no. 122.
26. Cf. J. G. Wolf, 'Die Naulotike des Menelaos – Seedarlehen oder Seefrachtvertrag?' in *Iuris Vincula: Studi in onore di Mario Talamanca* (Naples, 2001): 456 (repr. in Wolf (n. 9), 181).
27. Possibly also the surety in the second document, if the name Primitius is a mistake for Primitivus: cf. FIRA 3.394 n. 5.
28. FIR no. 155; FIRA 3 no. 120.
29. Iulius Alexander is the debtor in the first loan document, the creditor in the second, and one of the partners in the partnership agreement. It seems likely that this is one and the same person. The form of *stipulatio* in the partnership agreement suggests that he was a Roman citizen.

30. Bruns no. 165, 1–3; different and clearly better readings in FIRA 3 no. 150.
31. On the state properties in Dacia, see C. Brandis, 'Dacia', in RE IV (1901) cols. 1973–74.
32. FIR no. 171; FIRA 3 no. 157.
33. The document was therefore executed after the event, shortly before the termination of the contract.
34. Brandis (n. 31), cols. 1967ff.
35. Eutropius 8.6.2.
36. In the case of the sale of the slave-girl (FIR no. 131), the seller Dasius Verzonis was a *Pirusta ex Kavieretio*. Another triptych (FIR no. 133) attests the sale of half of a house in *Alburnio maiori vico Pirustarum*. Cf. also O. Hirschfeld, *Die kaiserlichen Verwaltungsbeamten*, 4th edn. (Berlin, 1975), 154–55. Breucus, the name of the seller in FIR no. 130, is evidently Illyrian: C. Patsch, 'Breuci', in RE III (1897), col. 831.
37. For 153 documents: Zangemeister (n. 7), no. 3340 I-CLIII; also Krüger (n. 23), 279; FIRA 3.401. For 127 documents: Mommsen (n. 7), 222; FIR 354; B. Kübler, *Geschichte des römischen Rechts* (2nd ed., 1925), 302; for 132 documents: O. Karlowa, *Römische Rechtsgeschichte* (Leipzig, 1885), vol. 1, 132.
38. See the very detailed edition by Zangemeister with illustrations (n. 7). According to Mommsen (n. 7), 222, the 127 documents are legible wholly or in part.
39. 137 documents, according to Zangemeister.
40. In the document of 28 May 15 the auctioneer is Lucius Caecilius Felix, probably a relative of Iucundus and possibly his father: FIR no. 157; FIRA 3.4 n. 5 and no. 128a.
41. Zangemeister (n. 7), no. 3340, 138–53.
42. See, e.g., FIRA 3 no. 129.
43. FIRA 3 no. 128.
44. FIRA 3 no. 130.
45. Zangemeister (n. 7), no. 3340 XL; Mommsen (n. 7), 267 n. 34; FIRA 3 no. 129b.
46. Mommsen (n. 7), 240.
47. Mommsen (n. 7), 241ff. therefore took the *testatio* to record an *acceptilatio*. Karlowa (n. 37) 799 followed him and also sought to counter the successful contrary arguments advanced against Mommsen by C. G. Bruns, *Zeitschrift für Rechtsgeschichte* 13 (1878): 360ff. cf. FIRA 3.404.
48. Mommsen (n. 7), 238f.
49. Zangemeister (n. 7), no. 3340 L, LXII, and XCVII; FIR.357.
50. Zangemeister (n. 7), no. 3340 XXI; FIR.356; FIRA 3 no. 130b.
51. Zangemeister (n. 7), no. 3340 XLV; FIR.356. P. Alfenus Pollio was the principal in whose name the auction took place.
52. Zangemeister (n. 7), no. 3340 XXIV.
53. Mommsen (n. 7), 270–71, nos. 118 and 119; FIR.359; FIRA 3 no. 131c.
54. Mommsen (n. 7), 274 no. 125; FIR.360; FIRA 3 no. 131a.
55. Whether he had to seal the document twice in order to give it probative value is an open question.
56. C. 11.40 (AD 222–35).
57. Mommsen (n. 7), 273f., nos. 124–25; cf. no. 123.
58. Mommsen (n. 7), 272 no. 121.
59. Mommsen (n. 7), 270 no. 117.
60. Mommsen (n. 7), 251–52.

61. Mommsen (n. 7), 270 no. 117: the text (followed by seals) runs: *Sex Pompeio Proculo/ C Cornelio Macro IIvir i d/ Xi k Mart/Privatus coloniae ser/scripsi me accepisse ab/L Caecilio Iucundo sest/ertios mille sescentos/quinquaginta duo num/mos ob fullonicam/ex reliquis anni unius/Act Pom/Nerone Aug III/ M Mesalla cos.*
62. Mommsen (n. 7), no. 118. Payment was made on 14 July: cf. also no. 124, where payment was made on 6 June and the receipt prepared on 18 June 59.
63. Mommsen (n. 7), 119.
64. Mommsen (n. 7), 120.
65. Karlowa (n. 37), 805; Mommsen (n. 7), 255. For farming of taxes due in relation to a public pasture, see the document of 18 June 59, no. 124 in Mommsen.
66. The chirograph of 18 June 59 notes that on 6 June 1,000 sesterces had already been paid towards the sum of 1,675 sesterces evidenced by the document.
67. Mommsen (n. 7), nos. 121, 122, 124; Zangemeister (n. 7), no. 3340 CXLV, CXLVI, CXLVII; FIRA 3 no. 131d.
68. Mommsen (n. 7), nos. 125, 126; Zangemeister (n. 7), no. 3340 CXXXVIII, CXL; FIRA 3 no. 131a.
69. Mommsen (n. 7), 256ff.
70. See V. Arangio-Ruiz, 'Lo "status" di Venidio Ennico ercolanense', in *Droits de l'antiquité et sociologie juridique. Mélanges Lévy-Bruhl* (Paris, 1959), 9–24; G. Camodeca, 'Per una reedizione dell'archivio ercolanense di L. Venidius Ennychus', *Cronache ercolanensi* 32 (2002): 257–80 and 36 (2006): 189–211.
71. See Arangio-Ruiz and Pugliese Carratelli (n. 8), III no. 44; I no. 1; IV no. 71.
72. See Arangio-Ruiz and Pugliese Carratelli (n. 8), III no. 43; V no. 87; II nos. 13–15; possibly also VI no. 88 (from AD 77).
73. Arangio-Ruiz and Pugliese Carratelli (n. 8), V, 451ff. VI, 70; III, 462; Camodeca (n. 9); J. A. Crook, 'Three Hundred and Six Stakes', in *Quaestiones iuris*, ed. U. Manthe and C. Krampe (Berlin, 2000), 77–81; J. G. Wolf, 'Eine Empfangserklärung aus Herculaneum', in *Studi in onore di Antonio Metro* (2010), 491–501 (repr. in Wolf (n. 9), 209–217).
74. Camodeca (n. 70), 266; G. Camodeca, 'Per una riedizione delle *Tabulae Herculanenses*', *Rivista di antichità* II – n. 2 (1993); G. Camodeca, 'Per una riedizione delle *Tabulae Herculanenses* I', *Cronache ercolanensi* 23 (1993): 115–16.
75. For TH 89 see G. Camodeca, 'La ricostruzione dell'élite municipale ercolanese degli anni 50 – 70', *CCG* 7 (1996): 172; G. Camodeca, 'Per una riedizione dell'archivio Ercolanese di L. Venidius Ennychus II', *Cronache ercolanensi* 36 (2006): 191–93; for TH 85 see G. Camodeca, 'Nuovi dati dalla riedizione delle Tabulae ceratae della Campania', *Atti del XI Congresso Internazionale di Epigrafia Greca e Latina* (Rome, 1999), 530–31.
76. Because they were written in ink on the wood of side 4.
77. Camodeca (n. 75, *CCG*), 167–78.
78. TH 8: Arangio-Ruiz and Pugliese Carratelli (n. 8), I, 383 (sealed twice by Venustus).
79. TH 43: Arangio-Ruiz and Pugliese Carratelli (n. 8), III, 459 (sealed twice by Felix).
80. TH 39: Arangio-Ruiz and Pugliese Carratelli (n. 8), III, 457: so the external text on side 4; whereas on side 1 an index notes that the sum was the sale price paid by L. Catulus Sabinus for wine.
81. A. Degrassi, *I fasti consolari dell'impero romano* (Rome, 1952), 18; V. Arangio-Ruiz *BIDR* 61 (1958): 297.

82. TH 35: Arangio-Ruiz and Pugliese Carratelli (n. 8), III, 456–57 (sealed twice by Cominus).
83. TH 42: Arangio-Ruiz and Pugliese Carratelli (n. 8), III, 459 (sealed twice by Laelius; additionally he promised repayment of the sum in a stipulation). According to Camodeca (n. 74, *Cronache* 23), 115–16, the document was executed on 4 November 67.
84. TH 90: Arangio-Ruiz and Pugliese Carratelli (n. 8), VI, 68–69.
85. TH 65: Arangio-Ruiz and Pugliese Carratelli (n. 8), IV, 64.
86. TH 70 + 71: Arangio-Ruiz and Pugliese Carratelli (n. 8), IV, 68; Camodeca (n. 74, *Rivista*), 201–2.
87. TH 76: Arangio-Ruiz and Pugliese Carratelli (n. 8), V, 449; cf. Wolf (n. 73).
88. TH 87: Arangio-Ruiz and Pugliese Carratelli (n. 8), V, 91–92, with discussion.
89. TH 5: Arangio-Ruiz and Pugliese Carratelli (n. 8), I, 382–83; Camodeca (n. 75, *Cronache*), 206–9.
90. Camodeca (n. 70, 2002), 262.
91. TH 82: Arangio-Ruiz and Pugliese Carratelli (n. 8), V, 459. The reading seems to me to be wrong.
92. TH 5.
93. See V. Arangio-Ruiz, 'Il processo di Iusta', *La Parola del Passato* 3 (1948): 129–51; V. Arangio-Ruiz, 'Nuove osservazioni sul processo di Giusta', *La Parola del Passato* (1951) 116–23; V. Arangio-Ruiz, 'Nuovi aspetti del processo romano in un "fascicolo" ercolanense', in *Atti del Congresso Internazionale del Diritto Processuale Civile* (1953): 166–204. These discussions are vitiated by an understanding of *vadimonium* that has since been superseded.
94. TH 13 and TH 14: Arangio-Ruiz and Pugliese Carratelli (n. 8), II, 168–70.
95. TH 15: Arangio-Ruiz and Pugliese Carratelli (n. 8), II, 170–71.
96. TH 16, 17, 19, 20: Arangio-Ruiz and Pugliese Carratelli (n. 8), II, 171–76.
97. TH 23, 24: Arangio-Ruiz and Pugliese Carratelli (n. 8), II, 177–80.
98. TH 70 + 71 Arangio-Ruiz and Pugliese Carratelli (n. 8), II, 68; Camodeca (n. 74, *Rivista*), 203.
99. M. Pagano, 'L'edificio dell'agro Murecine a Pompeii', *RAAN* 58 (1983): 325–61 (with plans and further bibliography); G. Camodeca, 'Per un primo aggiornamento all'edizione dell'archivio dei Sulpicii', *CCG* 11 (2000): 175–79; Camodeca (n. 12), 12, 14; G. Camodeca, 'Altri considerazioni sull'archivio dei Sulpicii e sull'edificio pompeiano di Moregine', in *Moregine*, ed. V. Scarano Ussani (Naples, 2005), 23–41; O. Elia, 'La domus marittima delle tabulae ceratae nel suburbio di Pompei', *Bolletino d'Arte* 46 (1961): 200–11; K. Schauenburg, 'Zur ' "Porticus der Triklinen" am Pagus maritimus bei Pompeji', *Gymnasium* 69 (1962): 521–29.
100. Pagano (n. 98), 347–52. On the basis of the themes in the frescoes, M. Mastroroberto considered it possible that the villa was a lodging (*taberna deversoria*) of the emperor Nero; Camodeca (n. 98, *Moregine*), 35ff., disagrees.
101. TPN 12 and 27 were executed in Capua; TPN 85 in Volturnum.
102. Elia (n. 99), 211 n. 5.
103. The negatives are numbered A. 13510–13726 and 14670–14754 and are now under the charge of the Soprintendenza Archeologica di Pompeii, where a new inventory has been prepared. Camodeca (n. 12) provides a concordance of the numbers.
104. Camodeca (n. 12), vol. 1, 31–36, and tables at 41–43; reviewed by J. G. Wolf, *ZSS* 118 (2010): 77–78.

105. Camodeca (n. 12), 19–20.
106. TP 1–12 in *RAAN* 41 (1966): 107–21 (Giordano); TP 13 in *RAAN* 43 (1968): 3–12 (Sbordone); TP 14–22 in *RAAN* 45 (1970): 211–25 (Giordano); TP 23–28 in *RAAN* 46 (1971): 173–82 (Sbordone); TP 29–44 in *RAAN* 46 (1971): 183–95 (Giordano); TP 45 in *RAAN* 47 (1972): 307–10 (Sbordone); TP 46–54 in *RAAN* 47 (1972): 311–16 (Giordano); TP 55–69 in *RAAN* 51 (1976): 145–67 (Sbordone); TP 70–134 in *RAAN* 53 (1978): 249–69 (Sbordone).
107. Landi (n. 11).
108. Camodeca (n. 12), 17, and in discussion of the individual documents.
109. Reviewed by Wolf (n. 104); U. Manthe, *Gnomon* 76 (2004): 685–90. Camodeca also examines the re-editions of various documents which have appeared in recent years.
110. Wolf (n. 12).
111. TPN 12 and 27, dated 27 and 29 August and under the previously unknown consuls T. Axius and T. Mussidius Pollianus. AD 38 is a possible year (41, 42, and probably 44 are not). TPN 82, dated 5 December and under the also previously unknown consuls P. Fabius Fyrmanus and L. Tampius Flavianus.
112. TPN 16: November/December 51; TPN 23: January/March 49; TPN 28: 14 January/13 February 35; TPN 111: June/July 44; TPN 118: July/December 48.
113. TPN 52, 75, 87, 88, 108, 113.
114. Camodeca (n. 12), vol. 1, 116 believes the sale document TPN 83 to have been executed on 18 March 26 (cf. Wolf (n. 104), 79).
115. TPN 103.
116. TPN 50.
117. TPN 65.
118. TPN 73, 74, 75.
119. J. H. D'Arms, *Commerce and Social Standing in Ancient Rome* (Cambridge, Mass., 1981), 121–48.
120. The slave Pyramus did not write TPN 48 for his owner, Caesia Priscilla; rather, he concluded a contract of loan with C. Sulpicius Faustus in his own name.
121. TPN 43, 44, 58, 59.
122. TPN 86.
123. TPN 43, 39, 86.
124. J. G. Wolf, 'Das sogenannte Ladungsvadimonium', *Satura Roberto Feenstra oblata*, ed. J. A. Ankum et al. (Fribourg, 1985), 59–69.
125. TPN 22, 23; see J. G. Wolf, 'Eine Eidesdelation und eine Eidesleistung', *Festschrift für Rolf Knütel*, ed. H. Altmeppen et al. (Heidelberg, 2010), 1459–68.
126. TPN 28.
127. TPN 29; see J. G. Wolf, 'Die Kondiktionen des C. Sulpicius Cinnamus', *SDHI* 45 (1979): 142–77.
128. TPN 32; see J. G. Wolf, 'Die Streitbeilegung zwischen L. Faenius Eumenes und C. Sulpicius Faustus', *Studi in onore di Cesare Sanfilippo* (Milan, 1985), vol. 6, 769–88.
129. E.g. TPN 43, 44; see J. G. Wolf and J. A. Crook, *Rechtsurkunden in Vulgärlatein* (Heidelberg, 1989), 17–19.
130. TPN 86; Wolf and Crook (n. 129), 20–21.
131. TPN 58; Wolf and Crook (n. 129), 21–22.
132. Amounts in sesterces: TPN 4: 840 and 660; TPN 15: 1,000; TPN 3: 1,200; TPN 12: 2,000; TPN 13: 3,000; TPN 9: 3,333.
133. TPN 2, 5, 10.

134. TPN 45.
135. TPN 39.
136. TPN 52.
137. TPN 62.
138. TPN 101.
139. TPN 60; cf. M. Rostovtzeff, *Gesellschaft und Wirtschaft im römischen Kaiserreich* (1929, repr. Aalen, 1985), vol. 1, 150.
140. The limit did not apply to interest due for late payment. In TPN 59 the promise is of a daily penalty of 20 sesterces for late payment; on a debt of 1,250 sesterces this amounts to an interest rate of 600%; cf. Wolf and Crook (n. 129), 23.

6 Writing in Roman Legal Contexts

Elizabeth A. Meyer

Modern legal experiences in Europe and the United States immerse their participants and observers in an ocean of paper. Most legal acts involve paper and signatures, and in litigation, from the written summons through written evidence, written verdicts, and a written transcript of the trial, paper is ubiquitous and unremarkable – unless, in a moment of drama, handwriting experts need to be called in or the record needs to be read back. Writing on paper is a tool and a technology, a neutral facilitator of the procedural and probative goals of the law and of the courts. By contrast, writing in Roman legal acts was not consistently ubiquitous, and Roman trials incorporated writing far less until the late-antique period. Before then, therefore, different questions about writing used in Roman legal contexts should dominate the discussion. What physical forms did such writing take? How were different types of written document valued when they were used? And what could these forms of writing have meant to those who used them? For centuries these were not, for Romans, legal questions at all. Instead, the legal documents of Roman citizens were, through the classical period, generated with the help of all-purpose scribes, not official notaries; their ultimate legal weight was determined not by any 'law of evidence' but by their impact in court, in which traditional assumptions about their authority as well as rhetorical deftness in circumventing those assumptions played a role. It is a modern assumption that writing is functional, and a similarly modern verdict that legal documents, even Roman ones, almost always serve only as proof.[1] The Romans, their legal world imbued from an early date with religiosity and scrupulous ritual, saw writing both in documents and in procedure as powerful in different and (to the modern reader) unexpected ways.[2]

Legal documents of Roman citizens, written in Latin, survive only by chance, and as a consequence the more than 1,000 preserved documents tell only a stop-motion story of developments well underway by the time they can be studied. No documents from the Republican era survive, although we know from Cicero that they existed;[3] from the imperial period there are substantial collections from Pompeii and Herculaneum, Britain, Germany, Vindonissa in Switzerland, Dacia (Romania north of the Danube), and Egypt, with a smattering coming from other locations.[4] Physical circumstances had to be favourable, since these collections make clear that wood was the preferred medium for such documents, and the survival of wood depends on very specific climactic conditions. Indeed, it appears that Roman legal documents were almost always written on wood-and-wax tablets; even in the late Empire, when the formal requirements of (unspecified) materials and language were officially relaxed, wooden tablets were still used, as a cache from fifth-century North Africa demonstrates: the form was chosen even when not apparently required.[5] This legal use of wooden tablets was therefore significant and special, and distinguished Roman legal documents from their Greek contemporaries, which were of papyrus and on scrolls.

The physical form of this wooden tablet, and the treatment of the text on a wooden tablet, changed over time. The two earliest known examples show two different forms. The simpler form belongs to the second oldest,[6] which seems to have had merely a single copy of its text written horizontally, parallel to the long side, into the wax on the interior faces of two tablets hinged together. These were then closed face-to-face as a form of protection, with a string wound around both together. By contrast, the very earliest so far found, from 8 BC and published only very recently,[7] already had its string fixed in place by seals, with the names of the eight sealers (three partially preserved) written next to their seals. A copy of the interior text was (simultaneously with this development) written on the exterior of the tablet, in ink and parallel to the short sides, making this what is called a doubled diptych. To protect the seals better, in the next phase a wide groove called a *sulcus* was built into an exterior side of the second tablet, and the seals were placed in this channel over the string. Gradually, for some documents a third tablet was then added to the two that were sealed shut. The third carried the exterior copy (instead of, or sometimes in addition to, the text being copied on the exterior of the first two tablets)[8] while also, when shut, giving added protection to the seals in the *sulcus* on the back of the second tablet.[9] This is a triptych. This general format – two or three tablets, two copies (interior and exterior) of the text, the seals in a *sulcus* – is the one most commonly found (although not always or even usually with all tablets intact). Polyptychs, with more than three tablets, also existed, and were used for especially lengthy documents like wills. In AD 61 a *senatusconsultum Neronianum*[10] required that tablets (of the will of a Roman citizen) be pierced and that the string be threaded three times through the holes, thereafter to be sealed in place by seals in a *sulcus*. Soon most documents on tablets followed this practice (a late-antique text actually claimed that the *senatusconsultum* applied to all legal documents).[11] It is thus deducible that, at and after this point in time, four physical aspects of a legal document had come to be thought important: the use of wooden tablets; the existence and protection of a written original text (the sealed interior version); an accessible copy of the text (the exterior version); and the attestation of presence and weight of social standing provided by the sealers whose names were written next to their seals. Sealers were listed in order of social prominence and were lending their authority and their *fides* (trustworthiness) to the document so sealed.[12] For Pliny the Younger, the performance of this vital social task of sealing (especially for wills) was one of the ways he spent his time when in the city of Rome.[13]

As these changes in the physical format of the tablet suggest, this is a story of increasing protection of both interior text and of seals, but also of a development caught at a particular moment in time and with an earlier history all but invisible to us. The axis provided by the types of legal acts found on first-century tablets similarly suggests change and development caught in mid-stride. Those tablets specifically from the area of Campania (before AD 79) permit some assessment of the relationship between physical form, date, and type of act. There are, on the one hand, tablets of the older formal, ceremonial acts of Roman law, especially those based on the acts of mancipation and (as I have argued) stipulation[14] and those related to the formalities of Roman legal procedure, all only accessible to Roman citizens: these are written in the third person in careful and often archaic legal language, have between seven and eleven sealers, and consistently use the older diptych form through the middle of the first century AD. But then there are also tablets of informal or *bona fides* ('good-faith') acts: these are written in the first person in freer if also mostly formulaic language (and often called chirographs – 'handwrittens'), have between three and five sealers (including the author of the act himself, who sometimes seals twice), and consistently use the triptych form as early as AD 35.[15] Formality and *bona fides* are, in a sense, two different tracks in Roman private law, and the legal acts based on them differ not only in who can use them, but also in the origins of their powers (formal acts from the efficacy of their correctly performed ritual, informal acts through enforcement by the praetor). The different rate of adoption of the triptych form for the two categories of act, along with the differing number of sealers, suggest that tablet-documents and their sealers initially played different roles depending on the type of act, even though they were on track to become much more similar by the 70s AD. Some documents that combined individual legal acts of the two different types (like a formal mancipation and an informal pact,[16] or a formal *acceptilatio* [release from obligation] and an informal chirograph[17]) suggest a similar trajectory towards amalgamation of traditions formerly (and in the law) treated separately. For neither type of act, formal or informal, was the prevention of forgery the first or only *raison d'être* for the complex physical form, since all tablets would otherwise have been constructed and sealed in the same way from the very beginning. The *senatusconsultum* of AD 61 is the first and last official indication before the late-antique period of an interest in the techniques of preventing forgery and can help to explain why many tablet-documents came to look much more similar after that date; before that date, however, tablets in the two traditions were different, and two hundred years before that it is likely that tablets for *bona fides* acts did not exist at all, since 'chirograph' implies importation from the Greek tradition and *bona fides* acts themselves were recognized by the praetor only in the late second century BC.[18]

The trajectory of development in physical form and content visible even in what survives therefore suggests that both diptychs and formal acts – and formal acts on diptychs – were older; that the use of a wooden tablet was sufficiently characteristic and weighty as a 'Roman legal document' that a newer type of act would adopt it; that sealers brought social weight to both types of act but had different primary functions in sealing; and that 'good-faith' acts and their physical format initially emphasized (and protected) the *fides* of author and sealers to a greater extent. It would seem, therefore, that an understanding of the role such a wooden document played is rooted in a time earlier than that of the surviving documents, and in the formal acts with their performative rituals and their attesting witnesses. The complexities of form and sealing suggest, too, that the original role of wooden tablets in formal acts was more than that of mere proof. So it should be no surprise that when, in the only apparently generalizing statement about written documents from the classical jurists,[19] Gaius said that 'the purpose of writing [was] to prove the transaction more easily',[20] he also specifically limited the scope of his observation to two of the 'consensual' informal acts – mortgage (*hypotheca*, an informal good-faith contract) and marriage – two of the later acts that migrated on to tablets to share in their value. Indeed, 'writing' in legal acts was never denigrated as such by the classical jurists, who (this quotation aside) paid no generalized attention to it at all.[21]

Even if not intended to be *only* proof, wooden documents were also very useful *as* proof, and their exceptional contribution to a court case was especially acknowledged by orators. For Cicero and Quintilian, tablet-documents were a wonderful kind of super-proof: they were happy to wield them when such tablets supported the case they were arguing and recognized the need for feats of special rhetorical agility when they did not. *Tabulae* had the special and potent quality of *auctoritas* ('authority'), said Cicero,[22] and were 'difficult' to get around;[23] for Quintilian, arguing against them required 'the greatest power of eloquence'.[24] Witnesses were very important in court too, but witness-testimony written on wooden *tabulae* seems to have combined an excellent type of proof and the best form of proof into one, transforming testimony into a contribution that, like a legal document on a *tabula*, could be challenged only with great difficulty.[25] To a Cicero or a Quintilian, there was some special quality about wooden tablets, some authority, that was unmistakable and virtually unassailable, and this special quality must also have helped to perpetuate their use as *the* form to be used for legal documents through the imperial centuries. Doubling the text protected the writing and sealers added their own weight, but it was writing on wood that fixed the act or the testimony and made it authoritative. It may, indeed, have been the very existence of a tablet-document that was most important, since even when adduced in court there is no one clear example of their actually being opened: they could do their work without their strings being cut.[26]

This appreciation of the wooden tablet's power by orators who wielded or faced them in court is reinforced and in part explained by the wider cultural understanding of such forms. Authoritative finality was also thought to characterize, for example, wooden account-*tabulae*, tablets announcing repaid vows, tablets of the census, the *tabulae* of the priests recording religiously significant events of the year, the tablets of the praetor's edict, and tablets used for prayers read out by magistrates.[27] The special rhythmic and formulaic language of legal tablets finds parallels in the language of these other *tabulae*, again pointing backwards to formulations perhaps as old as the fourth- or third-century Republic, after which the use of such tablets, often as part of a larger ritual, contributed to the creation of social and political order and an appropriate relationship between Romans and their gods.[28] The quality of being embedded in larger acts that had to be performed correctly is one of the sources of this authoritative finality: a tablet was a crucial element of such an act – for example, the taking of the census[29] – that was not complete until all the writing was done and all the rituals had been performed. Wooden legal tablets were similarly embedded in the old formal acts of Roman law, as Gaius's description in the second century AD of the ceremony of bringing a mancipatory will into existence makes clear.[30]

Specific words had to be spoken in a certain order, in front of witnesses; gestures (striking a scale with a piece of bronze, and handing over the bronze) had to be made; the tablets had to be held in the hand of the testator, who then had to speak a specific formula. The Roman-citizen witnesses (*testes*) were there to judge the correctness of this ritual performance, crucial to its legal validity, and this performance included the tablets themselves, to which they affixed their seals.[31] Wooden tablets of such acts were generated as part of the act itself, were necessary for its efficacy, and authoritatively embodied and completed it.

These wooden documents, with their acknowledged intrinsic powers buttressed by the social weight of the men who sealed them, were recognized as peculiarly and characteristically Roman by the peoples whom they ruled. Roman citizens travelled with their own wooden documents or drew them up in the far-flung places where they found themselves: hence deposits not just from Campania, but also from the provinces, and especially (although not exclusively) from army camps. Terms were also transliterated, like τάβλα for *tabulae* (in, for example, a new inscription preserving testamentary dispositions from Cappadocia[32]). In Dacia, many of the surviving wooden tablets may have been employed by non-Roman citizens (the status of the participants in these legal acts is disputed and there are anomalies in the execution of the acts).[33] In the eastern Empire, the format of these documents was imitated by non-Romans, producing the (so-called) papyrus double-document. In this, the text of the act was written across the grain of the papyrus at the top of the document, with a second copy written beneath it; the top version was rolled over and sewn shut; and the names of the witnesses were written on the back of the papyrus, next to the knots from the sewing. Provincials who were not Roman citizens could not technically use formal-act legal forms, but could imitate what they thought the Romans valued in the execution of a document: inner copy, outer copy, protection, attestation, and witnessing. Such double-documents are not all that common and seem to be used especially for sales of property, such as slaves, that might be moving from one province to another, or for documents aimed at circumstances in which one could (one imagined) meet up with a Roman official. Such, for example, seems to have been the point of a papyrus double-document of honourable discharge for sailors-turned-legionaries heading for Egypt,[34] as well as the guiding assumption behind much of the dossier of documents taken by a Jewish woman named Babatha into the Judaean Desert at the time of the Bar-Kochba Rebellion: she had not only 23 double-documents, but also three copies of an outline of a Roman *formula* of the *actio tutelae*, such as a magistrate would issue to a Roman judge to specify the issues to be determined. Babatha was in litigation with the guardians of her son after the death of his father, but was also in some sort of family tangle with the clearly Roman Julia Crispina, and was preparing herself (it would seem) to come off well in an arena where Roman expectations might well reign supreme.[35] Roman documentary habits were a Roman pattern that had an impact on the understandings and expectations of provincials, and thus also on legal life in the provinces of the Empire.

In many Roman provinces, especially those in the East, the substantive law that had existed before the Romans remained in place, and so too did the associated documentary habits, especially well-attested in Egypt, but attested also in the epigraphy of Greece and Asia Minor and the papyrus and parchment finds from Mesopotamia. Such papyrus documents were valuable and useful for their protagonists, and accepted in local courts, but with no sense of the special value and weight that Romans attached to wooden tablets in their own courts. Papyrus legal documents, coming as they did from a non-Roman tradition and hardly influenced by Roman substantive law before AD 212,[36] seem to have carried little weight in Roman courts, but over time other documents on papyrus, like personal letters, gained in value – depending on who had written them. Cicero was fairly contemptuous about *litterae* ('letters' – so ephemeral!) unless they clearly supported his case, but Quintilian was rather more circumspect: holograph letters came to be seen as reflecting the *fides* (good or bad) of the author, and everyone was carefully appreciative and admiring where letters of the emperors (and eventually imperial officials) were concerned.[37] This changing attitude towards personal documents on papyrus was not a negative comment on the authoritative value of wooden documents but an argument made in addition to it, and it represented a potential expansion of the arsenal of courtroom weaponry. As the deployment of evidence in Apuleius's defence of himself on a charge of magic before the provincial governor in the second century shows, letters and such, depending on their source, could be valuable, but only as a supplement to the – already acknowledged – preponderant weight of tablets, which he used to make his final and most important points.[38]

Long before late antiquity, then, and before Roman jurists started to interest themselves seriously in matters of documentation, proof, and whether writing was a crucial component of a legal act or not, writing on a wooden tablet had established itself as being of superlative value and importance. It was a significant and necessary component of a formal legal act, had *auctoritas*, could record first-person legal acts as well as personal testimony and turn them into established facts, and was recognized as a supreme form of proof in a courtroom setting. Over time, the physical form of the wooden tablet could (literally) expand to incorporate and also convey the *fides* of those who sealed it; and in its perfected form in the second century AD it was, as Apuleius's case shows, nearly invincible in demonstrating what had happened, what was true, and which people should not be offended by impertinent challenges to what they had attested and sealed shut. Other types of writing – at least those on papyrus – offered mild competition to writing on wood but only because they too could demonstrate the *fides* and standing of the document's author: great, in the case of the emperor; lesser in the case of everyone else. So writing was important, and increasingly so over time, but it was writing of a certain sort, in documents constructed in a certain way and of a certain shape, that was for centuries most important, for reasons that went far back into Rome's religious and legal past.

Wooden tablets were also used in Roman legal procedure. Their deployment initially parallels that of the tablets used as templates for prayers, the tablet fixing a set text for proper reading aloud when extreme verbal correctness was crucial (a necessary obsession of late-Republican jurisconsults, who were mocked for it by Cicero[39]). Under the formulary procedural system (the second of the three classical systems),[40] most likely the *formula* (given by the praetor to guide the judge) – in carefully accurate language – and the accusation (*nomen deferre*), in a criminal case, were written on tablets, as were the later *inscriptio* and *libellus* (of accusation).[41] The Campanian finds reveal many more types of procedural tablets, including *vadimonia* (promises to appear), attestations that one had appeared (*tabulae sistendi*), the setting of days for a hearing, the formal passing to the giving of the judgment (*intertium*), and the judgment itself; there also survive interrogations, declarations, and the performing of oaths, all of which, like witness-testimony, seized and finalized, in an authoritative way, otherwise transitory experiences.[42] Many of these documents came as a surprise to scholars, since most other information about legal procedure had stressed its oral qualities before the late-antique period.[43] These wooden documents are not a way of making a record of an entire trial but instead fix important but individual contributions *to* the procedure of a trial and mark successive stages *of* a trial as they were completed. But the concept of the *tabula* for a perspective of the entire trial is important too, for Roman magistrates kept some records of their actions in office, records called *publicae tabulae*, and when these actions included hearing court cases (as city-magistrates or governors), information about the trial (plaintiff and defendant, advocates for and against, verdict) was entered into them, and their quality thought to reflect on the magistrate's character and probity. This initially tight focus on the magistrate's activities gradually expanded, after AD 284, to include more and more information about the trial, and more and more verbatim information from such trials came to be used in subsequent trials. The 'tablet' here was fixing and adding authority to the record of an event, and – as a metaphor for the magistrate's entire archive, when papyrus rather than wood was later used – became another locus through which individual legal acts could achieve finality and validity. 'Reading into the *publicae tabulae*' or 'entering into the *acta*' (as this process was also known) made written legal acts presumptively and authoritatively true.

Only in the later second century AD and after did legal writers like Gaius – jurists and the trained staffs of the emperors – start to construct rules for a clear system of proof, and in handling questions and problems try to assess the role of writing, especially in the formal legal acts in which writing had for centuries been embedded. The way they tackled problems, which often arose because some formal ceremonial element had been omitted from the performance of these acts, shows that they recognized writing as one of the formalities of an act, along with gestures and formulaic language: they explored where the essence of a multi-component formal act might lie, sometimes alighting on an abstract quality (such as *obligatio verbis*, 'obligation in words' or *voluntas*, 'intent'); they made compensatory arguments when one element had been mistakenly omitted or was flawed in execution, thus acknowledging that elements like writing and speech were complementary rather than primary and secondary (so Ulpian could say 'more was announced and less written' when there was a problem with a will); or, in (especially) the fifth and sixth centuries, they (finally) deemed formal elements – physical materials, special words in a set order, gestures – unnecessary, and identified writing as the all-encompassing ceremonial quality that made an act valid.[44] Justinian was notably thorough in his own legislation in imposing common requirements on written documents of all sorts, while also systematizing and granting particular strength to the 'public document' drawn up with the assistance of a public notary.[45] Changes of this sort reflect the gathering strength of the emperor as both the actual and the symbolic font of the Roman law of the Empire,[46] but also reflect the long traditions and beliefs about the embedded quality of writing that inspired respect and interest in petitioners, jurists, and the emperor's legal advisors and writers.

Because jurists and emperors weighed in on these issues so late, their opinions are where this story ends rather than where it begins. What the written wooden documents of Roman law meant to those who used them, and then to the orators who confirmed but also grappled with their weight and importance in court, was established long before the law's intellectuals turned their razor-sharp gaze on them. Because of their close association with the emperor, Severan and late-antique jurists could write in his name and with his powers and gradually adjust what the role of writing was to be; even so, traces of what writing once meant are clearly perceptible in the answers they give and the opinions they propose. Physical form, embedded writing, proper ceremonial vouched for by witnesses, and sealing by the same imparted an antique strength to wooden documents that was appreciated for centuries.

Notes

1. See, e.g., M. Kaser, *Das römische Privatrecht*, 2nd edn. (Munich, 1971), vol. 1, 231.
2. For more extensive treatment of most of the arguments in this chapter, see E. A. Meyer, *Legitimacy and Law in the Roman World.* Tabulae *in Roman Belief and Practice* (Cambridge, 2004).
3. Cic. *Part.* 130; *Top.* 96; *Caec.* 51; *Att.* 12.17 and 16.11.7; *Q. Rosc.* 37; and (the anonymous) *Rhetorica ad Herennium* 2.13.
4. The contents of the four largest collections (Dacia, and the three from Campania) are described in detail in the chapter by Wolf, 65–78.
5. North African tablets, C. Courtois, L. Leschi, C. Perrat, and C. Saumagne, *Les tablettes Albertini: actes privés de l'époque vandale* (Paris, 1952). For removal of requirements for formality, see n. 44 below.
6. *CIL* IV 3340 no. 1 (AD 15).
7. *AE* 2007.370.
8. The only surviving examples of a second exterior copy in a triptych are from Herculaneum: G. Camodeca, 'Dittici e trittici nella documentazione campana (8 a.C.-79 d.C.)', in *Eburnea diptycha. I dittici d'avorio tra Antichità e Medioevo*, ed. M. David (Bari, 2007), 81–107, at 99 n. 58.
9. For a development in two phases rather than (as here) possibly four, see G. Camodeca, 'L'evoluzione della forma dei documenti giuridici romani alla luce della prassi campana', in Fides humanitas ius. *Studi in onore di Luigi Labruna*, ed. C. Cascione (Naples, 2007), vol. 1, 617–637; and Camodeca (n. 8).
10. Suet. *Ner.* 17.
11. *PS* 5.25.6.
12. W. Jongmann, *The Economy and Society of Pompeii* (Amsterdam, 1991), 226–273.
13. Plin. *Ep.* 1.9.2–3.
14. Meyer (n. 2), 115–118 and 253–265, a controversial point.
15. These distinctions in form are questioned by Camodeca (nn. 8–9), relying on unpublished material from Herculaneum and the recategorization of doubled diptychs with *sulcus* as triptychs (not followed by Wolf, cf. n. 4 above) and omitting the *CIL* material (many triptychs but mostly from one decade) from his statistical table. Two early triptychs with *bona fides* acts, TPN 43 and 86 (from AD 37), nine more triptychs from the fifties (*CIL* IV 3340.17, 40, 46, 141–143, 145–147), and two

undated triptychs (*TPN* 92 and *CIL* IV 3340.97) also stretched the names of the sealers across the entire outside face of the second tablet, but the earliest of this style of sealing now known is the Frisian chirograph from AD 29, a second (not third) *tabula* of a triptych, republished by A. K. Bowman, R. S. O. Tomlin, and K. A. Worp, '*Emptio Bovis Frisica*: the "Frisian Ox Sale" Reconsidered', *JRS* 99 (2009): 156–170.

16. *CIL* IV 3340.155 (AD 79).
17. E.g. *CIL* IV 3340.7 (AD 54).
18. Cic. *Off.* 3.70.
19. And adduced as such by M. Kaser and K. Hackl, *Das römische Zivilprozessrecht*, 2nd edn. (Munich, 1996), 369 n. 66.
20. D. 20.1.4 = D. 22.4.4.
21. Kaser and Hackl (n. 19): 361–362, nn. 1–2 and 8 (indeed, no generalized theory of proof).
22. Cic. *Top.* 24.
23. Cic. *de Orat.* 1.250.
24. Quint. *Inst.* 5.1.2.
25. Witness-statements on *tabulae*: Cic. *Quinct.* 66–67; *2 Verr.* 1.128, 1.156, 4.148, 5.102–3; *Flacc.* 21; *Clu.* 168 (read out with the man himself present), 184; Quint. *Inst.* 5.7.1 (although easier to impugn motive of witness whose statement was on a *tabula*, since he was not there to defend himself); Tac. *Dial.* 36.7.
26. See Apul. *Apol.* 89, with E. Weiss, '*Recitatio* und *responsum* im römischen Provinzialprozeß: ein Beitrag zum Gerichtsgebrauch', *ZSS* 33 (1912): 230.
27. See Meyer (n. 2), 30–36; the census and *publica monumenta* were singled out as weightier than witnesses in court, Marcel. D. 22.3.10.
28. F. Wieacker, *Römische Rechtsgeschichte* (Munich, 1988), vol. 1, 326–327, 558–559.
29. Cic. *de Orat.* 1.183 and Ps.-Dositheus 17 (*CGL* 3.55.48–56.24, 3.107.27–46), with M. Torelli, *Typology and Structure of Roman Historical Reliefs* (Ann Arbor, 1982), 5–16.
30. Gaius 2.104.
31. A. Watson, *International Law in Archaic Rome: War and Religion* (Baltimore, 1993), 10–19.
32. *SEG* LII 1464 *ter.*
33. E. Weiss, 'Peregrinische Manzipationsakte', *ZSS* 37 (1916): 136–176, with Meyer (n. 2), 181–182.
34. *CPL* 117.
35. The documents are published in P. Yadin, with H. Cotton, 'The Guardianship of Jesus son of Babatha: Roman and Local Law in the Province of Arabia', *JRS* 83 (1993): 94–108, and cf. E. A. Meyer, 'Diplomatics, Law and Romanisation in the Documents from the Judaean Desert', in *Beyond Dogmatics: Law and Society in the Roman World*, ed. J. W. Cairns and P. du Plessis (Edinburgh, 2007), 53–82.
36. Most recently, B. Kelly, *Petitions, Litigation, and Social Control in Roman Egypt* (Oxford, 2011), 29–31, with further references.
37. See Meyer (n. 2), 225–232.
38. Apul. *Apol.* 69, 78–83, 84, 87, 95–96 (all letters); 89, 91–92, 96–97, 99–101, 102 (*tabulae*).
39. Cic. *Mur.* 25; *de Orat.* 1.236.
40. See the chapter by Metzger, 283–7.
41. *Formula*: TPN 29, with W. W. Buckland and P. Stein, *A Textbook of Roman Law from Augustus to Justinian*, 3rd edn. (Cambridge, 1963), 627; *nomen deferre*: *Roman Statutes*,

no. 1, lines 26–27; *inscriptio* and *libellus*: e.g. Apul. *Apol.* 102; Ulp. D. 2.13.1.1; Paul D. 48.2.3.

42. *Vadimonia*: TPN 1–15, TH 6, 13–15; *tabulae sistendi*: TPN 16–21, also Cic. *Quinct.* 25; giving days: TPN 34–38; *intertium*: TPN 30 31; judgment: TH 79, 81, 85 (and others listed by E. Metzger, 'Roman Judges, Case Law, and Principles of Procedure', *Law and History Review* 22 (2004): 10 n. 33); interrogations: TPN 24–26; *testationes*: e.g., TPN 78, 90–91 and TH 87, 16–20, 23–24; oaths: TPN 22–23. For late antiquity, see Kaser and Hackl (n. 19), 556–557.
43. See, e.g., Kaser and Hackl (n. 19), 10–11; 556.
44. Essence: Gaius 3.92–115 (stipulation as *obligatio verbis*), 2.104–229 (mancipatory will as nuncupation – or as institution of the heir?); *voluntas*: Mod. D. 28.1.1 and Ulp. D. 29.3.2.2. Compensatory: Ulp. D. 45.1.30 and D. 45.1.134.2; Paul. D. 44.7.38 on speech and writing in stipulation, with J. Andreau, 'Registers, Account-Books, and Written Documents in the *de Frumento*', in Sicilia nutrix plebis Romanae. *Rhetoric, Law, and Taxation in Cicero's Verrines*, ed. J. R. W. Prag (London, 2007), 91–92; Ulp. D. 28.5.1.5 (quotation), Ulp. D. 28.5.9.2, C. 6.23.7 (AD 290), on nuncupation and written will. Removal of formal elements: Ulp. D. 37.11.1 pr, C. 6.23.4 (AD 239), C. 6.23.15 + 6.37.21 + 6.9.9 (AD 320/326), C. 8.37(38).10 (AD 472), C. 8.53(54).37 (AD 531). Writing as *sollemnitas*, e.g. Ulp. D. 45.1.30, Inst. 3.19.12.
45. Meyer (n. 2), 288–289, with further references.
46. M. Peachin, Iudex vice Caesaris. *Deputy Emperors and the Administration of Justice During the Principate* (Stuttgart, 1996), 14–33.

7 Patristic Sources

Caroline Humfress

1. Introduction

Since at least the legal humanists in the sixteenth century, lawyers and historians have attempted to reconstruct Roman legal texts and principles using Patristic literature from the first six centuries AD. Patristic or 'patrological' literature forms a disparate body of material, grouped together by the idea that it was written by 'the Fathers' of the Christian Church: those ancient Christian authors later acknowledged as authorities in the historical development of Christian doctrine.[1] Patristic texts stretch across a vast range of different traditions, cultural contexts, and languages (Greek, Latin, Syriac, Ethiopian, Armenian, Coptic, etc.) and include polemical works, orations, sermons, letters, and poems, as well as systematic treatises on Christian doctrine and works of Biblical exegesis and scriptural commentary. Patristic scholars, like Roman lawyers and legal historians, have their own conventional schemes of periodization and classification: for example the traditional Patristic framework of ante-Nicene/Nicene/post-Nicene divides 'the Fathers' according to whether they wrote before or after the Council of Nicaea, the first ecumenical council of the church held in AD 325 at the command of Constantine, the first Roman emperor to be baptized a Christian. In terms of the conventional periodization of Roman law, Patristic sources span virtually the entire classical period (when taken together with the Judaeo-Christian writings of the first century AD and those of the 'Apostolic fathers'), as well as the 'epiclassical' (c. AD 235–c.300), 'postclassical' (fourth–sixth centuries AD), and Justinianic (AD 527–565) periods. The 'Golden Age of Patristics' is traditionally understood to be the fourth and fifth centuries AD, and it is the Greek and Latin patristic texts from these centuries that have been quarried most heavily as potential sources of information on late Roman imperial law, administration and forensic practice. For the postclassical and Justinianic periods, the recognition that (some) Patristic texts can be used as valuable extra-legal sources tends to merge with much broader debates concerning the extent to which Roman law and society were 'Christianized' under the later Empire.[2]

If approached as literary works, Patristic texts share many characteristics with other extra-legal, literary sources for Roman law – not least in the sense that, as the Roman legal scholar J.-P. Coriat warns, searching for law (*droit*) in *any* non-legal texts raises difficulties inherent in the nature of those texts themselves.[3] We shall return to the specific challenges posed by Christian 'Patristic' texts below. The rich potential of early Christian writings as sources of information about Roman law is clearly revealed in the 'Indice dei richiami al diritto nei testi extragiuridici latini dei secoli IV-VII', compiled as a working list by the Italian Romanist Giovanni Rotondi and published posthumously in 1922, with revisions by Vincenzo Arangio-Ruiz, Pietro de Francisci, and Mario Lauria. Running to 87 pages in its printed edition, the *Index* lists a myriad of references to Roman legal texts, principles, and technical terms in Patristic and other Christian writings, alongside far fewer references identified by Rotondi in non-Christian Latin grammatical, rhetorical, and historical writings. The first heading of the *Index* covers 'Law in general, the efficacy and enforcement of the laws' and includes entries such as: '*ius* e *iustitia*: Aug.[ustine] *Enarr. In Psalm* 145.15 ... *lex naturae*: Ambr[ose] *Hexaem.* 5.21.68 ... *ius Quiritium*: Hier[onymus = Jerome] *praef. ad. Paulin* ... *ius publicum* e *ius privatum*: Aug[ustine] *c. Faust. Man* 30.4 ... '. The *Index* then goes on to cite references in Patristic sources to Roman family law and legal status; to 'diritti reali' (including the distinctions between *res humani iuris/res divini iuris* and *res corporales/res incorporales*, as well as entries relating to property and its acquisition, possession and alienation, etc.); to obligations, contract, delict, and inheritance law, as well as to civil process and criminal law and procedure. The final thirty or so pages turn to the 'Storia delle fonti' and include references identified in Latin Patristic writings to archaic, Republican and imperial *leges* (including the XII Tables), *senatusconsulta*, edicts, and imperial constitutions and letters; to jurisprudential authors and texts; to late Roman and Byzantine legal compilations and *Codes*; and to legal culture, education, and other more general topics. Rotondi's general insight that late Latin Patristic sources can be read alongside other extra-legal literary sources for information about Roman law has been developed further by scholars collectively associated with the Accademia Romanistica Costantiniana (founded in 1973 and based at the University of Perugia).[4] The Accademia aims to produce a collection of all the material necessary for a reconstruction of law in late antiquity, and more specifically to provide sources for a *palingenesia* of late Roman imperial constitutions (see Section 2 below). To date, its published 'materiali per una palingenesi delle constituzioni tardo-imperiali' comprise numerous monographs, legal sourcebooks, and edited volumes, as well as a scholarly apparatus (updated in 2000), listing authors, titles, and editions of relevant Greek and Latin extra-legal literary sources from the fourth to the sixth centuries AD, divided into 'profane' and 'Christian' writers.[5]

As we shall see in Section 2, there are a number of Patristic writings that provide practitioners of Roman legal *Quellenforschung* with direct evidence for the reconstruction of primary Roman law texts. One of the major challenges, however, in reconstructing more general Roman legal concepts and principles from extra-legal literary writings lies in determining which references should count: do we include only those passages where technical (Latin) legal terms and concepts are cited in accordance with 'standard' Roman legal conventions, or do we include more allusive and/or imprecise passages that seem relevant to Roman law because of their general context?[6] Language, place and culture are important: 'In a multilingual society one language may have a particular association with a domain or activity or profession, and the choice of that language may be seen (for example) as a claim by the user to be working in the relevant activity: it marks his professional identity.'[7] For the Romans, Latin functioned as the highest technical language of lawyers and imperial administrative officials, as it still does to a certain extent today; as one late-eighteenth-century Polish commissioner for education put it, 'Latin, even if incorrect, is needed for juridical matters and by men of law.'[8] Yet the written language of Roman Christian *literature* up to the early third century AD is uniformly Greek. In studying the Greek *koine* of the 'New Testament' (as it had come to be known by the fourth century AD), in addition to the writings of first-century Apostolic Fathers and second-century Christian Apologists, historians and theologians have identified various uses and adaptations of different legal linguistic registers – including echoes of Greek as a language of local Roman administration in the East.[9] It is perhaps no coincidence, however, that the first Patristic author whose works survive in Latin is Tertullian (AD 155–220). Tertullian self-consciously deploys classical Roman legal terms and juristic concepts, alongside techniques developed from forensic rhetoric, in order to argue that Christians – despite persecution by the Roman authorities – are not opposed to Roman law and society.[10] Nonetheless, the identification of Tertullian, the Patristic Father of the church, with Tertullian, the Latin jurist whose works are excerpted in Justinian's *Digest*, is still a subject of debate.[11]

Individual early Christian writers, of course, make use of Roman law and legal argument in different ways. One way of attempting to account for these differences is to try to pinpoint the legal expertise and/or forensic rhetorical skill of a given author, using a combination of biographical information and prosopographical techniques (whilst accounting for possible narrative patterning in the late-antique genre of saints' lives).[12] Late Roman ecclesiastics came from a wide variety of social contexts, including uneducated and humble backgrounds: coal-burners, farmers, soldiers, labourers, fullers, shepherds, linen weavers, and so forth. Not all were literate, let alone literary. Those early Christian writers who did have some kind of education in grammar and rhetoric could pick up legal terminology, stories and traditions about Roman law from antiquarian writers such as Varro and Festus, as well as from 'school texts' and other philosophical and literary writings, from plays and comedies, and from Greco-Roman romance novels. Other early Christian ecclesiastics, however, had a more specific formation, having trained and/or practised as advocates and Roman lawyers (*iurisconsulti*, *assessores*, etc.). According to his hagiographer, the *scholastikos* Zacharius, Severus, the future bishop of Antioch (512–518), was an exemplary student at the law school of Beirut – mastering the civil law from Monday through to Saturday morning, then studying Sacred Scripture and the Church Fathers on a Saturday afternoon, before spending Sunday at church services.[13] In the hagiography of the early sixth-century East, 'lawyers' read Scripture and Saints read law.

In the mid-third century, the Church Father 'Gregory the 'wonderworker' – later known as 'Gregory Thaumaturgus'– studied rhetoric and Roman law with a private teacher in his hometown of Neo-Caesarea (the capital of Pontus, Asia Minor), before setting out with his brother and others for the law school at Beirut; they got as far as Caesarea in Palestine, where they continued their education with Origen, the early Christian philosopher and teacher. Gregory was subsequently consecrated bishop of Neo-Caesarea, but it is perhaps worth noting that he had originally returned home with the intention of practising law.[14] Other Christian ecclesiastics and writers who probably had some education in forensic rhetoric and/or Roman law include, for the Eastern Empire: Asterius of Cappadocia (early fourth century), Basil of Caesarea (c.330–377/9), Gregory of Nyssa (335–394), Gregory of Nazianzus (c.326–c.390), Amphilochius of Iconium (bishop in 373), John Chrysostom (347–407), Asterius of Amasea (late fourth–early fifth centuries), Jerome (c.345–419/20), Eusebius of Dorylaeum (early fifth century), Sozomen (c.400–c.447/8), and Severus of Antioch (Patriarch from 512–518), and for the Western Empire: Tertullian, Minucius Felix (third century), Arnobius (late third–early fourth centuries), Lactantius (c.250–c.325), Chromatius of Aquileia (335/40–407), Marius Victorinus (mid-fourth century), Ambrose of Milan

(339–397), 'Ambrosiaster' (late fourth century), Augustine of Hippo (354–430), Alypius of Thagaste (contemporary of Augustine), Sulpicius Severus (c.360–420), Victor of Thabbora (bishop in 411), Emeritus of Caesarea, North Africa (bishop in 411), Petilianus of Constantine, North Africa (late fourth–early fifth centuries), Paulinus of Nola (c.352–431), Prudentius (348–after 405), Germanus of Auxerre (d.448), Eucherius of Lyon (c.380–c.450), Peter Chysologus (c.380–450), Sidonius Apollinaris (c.430–c.485), Claudianus Mamertus (mid–late fifth century), and Gregory 'the Great' (c.540–604).

The extent to which legal and forensic training and practice reveals itself in Patristic and other early Christian writings depends on a number of factors, including the genre of the individual text itself and the intended audience(s). References to Roman law in an expositional homily spoken before a local congregation, for example, are likely to be analogous rather than direct: they might illustrate a point of scriptural exegesis or theological doctrine using concepts familiar to the audience from everyday life (guardianship, adoption, ownership, debt); or they might develop more involved and technical metaphors borrowed from Roman law. Gaudemet refers to these more technical uses as 'la construction juridique au service de la théologie'.[15] We also find sermons in which vivid and terrifying descriptions of the Last Judgment are constructed according to the conventions of Roman criminal trials; as Brent Shaw states: 'there is no doubt that bishops appropriated the judicial experience and preached it'.[16] Ecclesiastics, however, also used techniques of forensic argument in direct and practical contexts, such as pleading for imperial privileges and legal exemptions, as well as adapting them for use in doctrinal controversies and in disputes over ecclesiastical authority and jurisdiction.[17]

Some Patristic writings – ante-Nicene, Nicene and post-Nicene – challenge the traditions and teaching of Roman law, sometimes as part of a broader anti-Roman polemic and sometimes in the context of more circumscribed arguments, including comparisons between Mosaic law (the *lex Dei*), specific (Judaeo-) Christian precepts, and Roman law.[18] Clement of Alexandria (c.150–215), for example, claimed that the laws of Greek city-states – in particular Crete, Sparta, and Athens – had not been received from the gods of Mount Olympus (as some Hellenistic traditions claimed) but rather from the Christian God, via the lawgiver Moses.[19] For Origen, writing in third-century Palestine, the Christian God 'legislating through Jesus Christ for all men in all parts of the world' was a better lawgiver than Solon, Lycurgus, Zaleucas 'or any other legislator'.[20] In the early fifth century Augustine archly notes that the Romans had to borrow their laws from the Athenians – a reference to the (legendary) Roman deputation to Athens that preceded the drafting of the XII Tables – because their gods had given them no laws of their own.[21] As the late-fourth-century compiler of the text known as the *lex Dei* (also referred to as the *Collatio Legum Mosaicarum et Romanarum*) succinctly put it: 'you should learn, [Roman] *iurisconsulti*, that Moses established this first'.[22]

Explicit rejections of Roman legal concepts can be seen most clearly in early Christian writings concerning marriage and divorce.[23] For example, in a eulogizing letter written in Palestine in AD 399, Jerome attempted to defend a recently deceased, elite Christian woman, Fabiola, from the 'scandal' of having been divorced and remarried, stating that: 'The laws of the Caesars are one thing, Christ's are another; Papinian instructs one thing, our Paul another'.[24] In chapter three of his treatise *On Virginity*, Gregory of Nyssa went a step further and actually advised his audience to 'go to the law courts and read through the laws there', so that they might learn all the 'shameful secrets of marriage' from 'the strange variety' of relevant crimes listed in the legal texts.[25] Such contrasts between Christian and Roman morality have led some scholars to identify a new 'Christianized' jurisprudence in Patristic literature – a jurisprudence based solely on Christian ethics, reasoned out primarily from evangelical teaching and the Pauline epistles, with each Father of the church slowly constructing the new edifice from the materials provided by his predecessors.[26] For example, we find a contrast similar to the one that Jerome draws between the Roman jurist Papinian and the Christian apostle Paul in Augustine's *Sermon 52*, preached at Hippo, c. AD 410–412. In this sermon Augustine presents himself as an advocate defending the case that the Trinity is inseparably three-in-one, for his client, God, before his judges, the congregation gathered to hear the sermon. Augustine refers his 'judges': 'first to Paul [the Apostle] as a suitable *iurisperitus* in divine law' and then explains that: 'Lawyers today also have a Paul who declares the laws for litigants, not for Christians. I refer you, I repeat, to the Paul who declares the laws of peace, not of litigation.'[27] Augustine, like Jerome, thus rejects the writings of the Roman jurists in favour of the teachings of Christian Scripture, yet both Patristic authors are thereby able to showcase their own elite familiarity with Roman legal culture. Similarly, when Augustine records his suspicion that a rival 'Donatist' bishop of Hippo fears debating him because of his forensic skills in oratory, and offers to send an 'unlettered' bishop in his place, he is effectively asserting his dominance in traditional elite Roman terms.

Patristic literature offers a rich and diverse source of information about Roman law and legal culture(s), especially for the postclassical period. Patristic sources, however, need careful handling, not least as the fields of 'Patristics' and 'patrology' have their own disciplinary contours and boundaries. The present-day shape of Patristic theology, like the dogmatic study of Roman law itself, owes much to nineteenth-century conventions and scholarship. It constitutes a patriarchal and hierarchical discourse in which one of the 'most trenchant biases' is 'the privileging of retrospectively "orthodox" writings'.[28] Sections 2 and 3 thus follow the lead of more recent historical and theological scholarship in shifting our emphasis from 'Patristics' to 'Early Christian Studies'.[29] In Section 2 our source base will include early Christian writings that are not 'Patristic' but which nonetheless can help us to reconstruct Roman law texts: imperial constitutions and *codices* ('lawcodes'); juristic writings; and documentary evidence, including petitions, contracts and wills. In Section 3, 'Christian Ecclesiastics as Roman Legal Actors', I will attempt to move beyond text-based reconstructions in order to analyse Christian ecclesiastics as legal actors in their own right, thus in turn revealing what early Christian writings can tell us about Roman law as a set of social practices, rooted in specific places, times and contexts.

2. Early Christian Writings as Sources for Reconstructing Roman Law

> But let us read what the Emperor Antoninus [Caracalla] has established concerning this question: he was certainly not a Christian ... The following are the words of the Emperor mentioned above, as they appear in the *Codex Gregorianus* ...
>
> (Augustine, *On Adulterous Marriages* 2.8.7)

This section briefly surveys early Christian writings as extra-legal sources for Roman legal texts, for jurisprudential writings and substantive legal principles, and for legal documents. It also discusses the extent to which early Christian writings can help us to reconstruct Roman law principles and administrative/legal procedures, particularly with respect to the later Roman (postclassical) period. As noted above, Rotondi's 1922 'Index' gives an extensive list of promising references to Roman law in 'extra-legal' Latin sources from the fourth to seventh centuries – although not all of these references are as direct or technical as the Roman legal scholar might hope. We should also note that there is no index comparable to Rotondi's for extra-legal sources written in Greek or Syriac. My intention here is not to repeat Rotondi's list; nor is that possible, given the sheer breadth and range of early Christian texts in Greek, Latin and other languages, to provide anything that would even remotely approximate a complete overview of either the literature or the complexities involved. This section aims only to provide the reader with a general sense of the range and potential of early Christian writings as extra-legal sources for Roman law.

There are a handful of passing mentions to specific Republican *leges*, *plebiscita* and *senatusconsulta* in early Christian writings, as well as more detailed references such as Jerome's note on the *lex Falcidia* or Augustine's discussion of the *S.C. de Bacchanalibus*.[30] There are also a few allusions to the *edicta* of various magistrates, including the urban praetor at Rome.[31] Early Christian writings have played a more significant role, however, in the modern construction of *palingenesiae* of imperial constitutions, where they are used alongside legal sources and non-Christian literary texts, as well as epigraphic, papyrological and numismatic evidence, in order to reconstruct imperial texts as they appeared in the editions from which the surviving fragments were extracted.[32] As noted in Section 1, the Accademia Romanistica Constantiniana has sponsored a major and long-running initiative to produce *palingenesiae* of imperial constitutions: 'normative' rescripts, *mandata*, *edicta*, letters and other communications issued by imperial chancelleries between the ages of Constantine I and Theodosius II. Alongside 20 international conferences to date, the Accademia's series 'Materiali per una Palingenesi delle Costituzioni Tardo-Imperiali' includes volumes on Roman law in the writings of Ambrose of Milan and the letters of Pope Leo the Great, as well as *palingenesiae* of imperial constitutions for the reigns of Constantine; Constantine II, Constantius II and Constans I (337–361); and Valentinian and Valens (364–375) – all of which cite Christian sources as and when relevant.[33]

Turning now to a brief chronological overview of early Christian writings as sources for later Roman imperial constitutions, we begin with the reign of Caracalla (AD 211–217). Coriat identifies three fourth- and fifth-century Patristic texts that contain an echo of the celebrated *constitutio Antoniniana* of AD 212, though none go beyond a level of general knowledge.[34] In contrast, Augustine's treatise 'On Adulterous Marriages' (*de coniugiis adulterinis*) cites a rescript issued by Caracalla, lacking the *inscriptio* and *subscriptio* but quoted in some detail from the *Codex Gregorianus* (a semi-official collection of imperial constitutions from the reign of Hadrian up to May 291, compiled under the First Tetrarchy). Ulpian cited the same rescript in the second book of his commentary *Ad legem Iuliam de adulteriis* (D. 48.5.14.5).[35] The compiler of the late-fourth-century *lex Dei* (or *Collatio Legum Mosaicarum et Romanarum*) also apparently worked from a copy of the *Codex Gregorianus*, as well as the *Codex*

Hermogenianus. The *lex Dei* reproduces the famous Diocletianic rescript against the Manichees, probably issued in 302, in addition to an edict against close-kin marriage given at Damascus on 1 May 295.[36]

Christian sources for imperial orders relating to anti-Christian 'persecutions', on the other hand, can be notoriously tricky to evaluate as historical documents.[37] Many Christian martyr acts take the form of records of judicial proceedings, but their accuracy is much debated. It should not be assumed, however, that all imperial constitutions quoted in extra-legal Christian sources are necessarily suspect. In his *Ecclesiastical History* Eusebius of Caesarea (c. 260–339) quotes some 250 original documents in full and summarizes a further 100 or so. Two of these documents are Greek rescripts of the emperor Gallienus – it is impossible to establish whether Eusebius translated the texts himself or whether they were in fact circulating in official Greek translations, but there is no reason to doubt their genuineness.[38] In fact, books eight to ten of Eusebius' *Ecclesiastical History*, as well as his *Life of Constantine* and other writings, are crucial – albeit contested – sources for imperial pronouncements throughout the Tetrarchic and Constantinian periods – as are Lactantius' *On the Deaths of the Persecutors* and *The Divine Institutes*. The writings of both Eusebius and Lactantius are 'rich in texts and translations of original documents, since there was a strong need for authentic imperial documents to illustrate and bolster their argument or narrative'.[39] Other Christian sources that provide us with otherwise unattested early-fourth century imperial communications relate to the North African Donatist schism: in particular, Optatus of Milevis' *Appendix* to his work *Against the Donatists*, c. 370 (ten documents, of which six are imperial letters) and polemical works by Augustine of Hippo.[40]

Roman emperors addressed rescripts and letters to Christian ecclesiastics before the early fourth century, as the involvement of the emperor Aurelian (270–275) in the case of Paul of Samosata demonstrates.[41] The fourth-century establishment of the Christian Church as an institution under imperial patronage, however, meant that later Roman emperors frequently legislated on and responded directly to ecclesiastical affairs. Two volumes in the modern series *Sources Chrétiennes* conveniently collect together excerpts from imperial constitutions issued between AD 312 and 438 that relate to religious matters and were included in the Theodosian *Code*, the *Sirmondian Constitutions* and Justinian's *Code*.[42] Alongside these legal sources, there are also a number of late Roman imperial constitutions, some of which are otherwise unknown, reported in extra-legal Christian sources (see the modern *palingenesiae* noted above). The *Collectio Avellana* contains 244 communications dating from AD 367 to 533 – some written by emperors as well as addressed to them – of which over two hundred are preserved only in this collection.[43] The *Collectio Avellana* itself was probably compiled in the mid-sixth century, by a clerical notary who had access to the archives of the bishopric of Rome. The AD 411 ecclesiastical conference of Carthage, held at the command of the Emperor Honorius and under the presidency of the 'tribunus et notarius' Flavius Marcellinus, also had many legal documents read into its record, including the imperial *sanctio* for the conference itself and other imperial *mandata*, as well as a number of magisterial *edicta*.[44] In fact, the record from this council, recorded by both ecclesiastical and imperial stenographers, provides a wealth of information on later Roman forensic procedures and practices.

Conciliar Acts, proceedings and related documents from the fourth- to sixth-century regional and ecumenical councils of the church, are an important source of otherwise unattested imperial communications[45] – in particular the documents and texts transmitted as part of the Acts of the Council of Ephesus (431), the second Council of Ephesus (449, the so-called 'robber council' at which Eutyches was tried for various crimes), the Council of Chalcedon (451) and the Council of Constantinople (553).[46] When using ecumenical conciliar Acts as extra-legal sources we need to remember that the emperors themselves were part of the original intended audience and that the Acts are by no means simply disinterested records of events. As the nineteenth-century scholar Eduard Schwartz warns: 'One can, indeed one must, regard all the manuscript collections of council acts as propaganda.'[47] The later copying of imperial constitutions and other legal texts by ecclesiastical notaries and copyists should perhaps be seen from a similar perspective: the Roman imperial texts copied into the *Collectio Avellana*, for example, were assembled with mid-sixth-century (Roman) controversies in mind. Likewise 'the Sirmondian constitutions', as the text has been referred to since the seventeenth century, was copied by ecclesiastical scribes and appended to a collection of canons from Gallic church councils; the choice of these specific 16 imperial constitutions, dating from AD 333 to 425, dealing for the most part with ecclesiastical matters, undoubtedly reflects the contemporary concerns of the copyists themselves.[48]

Finally, with respect to early Christian writings as sources for later Roman imperial constitutions, we should also note the three fifth-century Greek historians of the church: Socrates, whose *Ecclesiastical History* dates to 439; Sozomen, a practising advocate in Constantinople, who completed his history around 443; and Theodoret of Cyrrhus, writing c. 449. All three wrote after AD 438 and each, like their models Eusebius and to a lesser extent Rufinus, 'included a large number of original documents, letters of bishops, synods, and emperors, especially Constantine and Constantius II. Yet they virtually ignore the almost two hundred laws included in Book 16 of the Theodosian Code.'[49] The constitutions excerpted in the Theodosian *Code* are, of course, in Latin, whereas Sozomen cites (existing) Greek translations of imperial letters, possibly sourced via his own forensic practice. From at least the mid-fifth century, then, Christian sources from the East can be used as direct witnesses to what Fergus Millar has termed 'A Greek Roman Empire'.[50]

Moving on to early Christian texts as sources for juristic writing and substantive Roman legal principles, this type of evidence can be particularly difficult to evaluate. Arnobius, Ambrose, the 'Ambrosiaster', Jerome and Augustine all refer to the postclassical Roman distinction between *leges* and *iura*, where *iura* refers specifically to juristic writings (rather than to 'law' or 'rights' in the more general sense of *droit*, *diritto*, *Recht*, etc.).[51] But direct references to particular jurists or works of jurisprudence are relatively rare. Tertullian's 'On the Crown' (*de Corona*) 4.6, for instance, is clearly related to the jurist Julian's celebrated definition of custom (D. 1.3.32) but does not name it as a source.[52] Lactantius, on the other hand, evidently had access to Ulpian's *On the Office of the Proconsul* and his *Commentary on the Edict*, as well as perhaps his *Commentary on the Provincial Edict* and treatise *On Adultery*.[53] Scholars have identified a number of other references to Roman juristic texts in early Christian literature, including allusions to Marcian in Ambrose and Ulpian in Augustine, in addition to excerpts from the writings of Gaius, Papinian, Ulpian, Paul, and Modestinus (possibly with postclassical emendation) in the *lex Dei*.[54] Modern scholars have suggested numerous references to substantive principles of Roman law – including rules concerning property, inheritance, intestacy, trusts, dowries, donations, loans, sales, pledges, and so forth – in the writings of Minucius Felix, Cyprian, Arnobius, Lactantius, the 'Ambrosiaster', Ambrose, Jerome, Augustine, Isidore of Pelusium, Asterius of Amasea, Peter Chrysologus and various monastic texts.[55] Some are more convincing than others. As Gaudemet states: 'Searching for law in extra-legal works is not without danger. If it is not absent, it may appear only incidentally, often in a veiled or imprecise way.'[56] In fact, many of the references to legal principles in later Roman Christian texts should perhaps be understood in terms of dynamic argument, rather than legal doctrine. We will return to this point in Section 3.

Some early Christian texts can be used as sources for the reconstruction of various kinds of legal documentary evidence, including *acta* from civil, 'criminal' and ecclesiastical trials as well as legal petitions. Alongside the much-debated evidence from Christian martyr acts, Optatus and Augustine reproduce legal *acta*, copied from municipal and imperial bureaucratic archives, relating to the 'Donatist' controversy.[57] In his 405/06 treatise against the works of the 'Donatist' layman and grammarian Cresconius, for instance, Augustine inserts what he claims to be a judgment of the proconsul Aelianus from almost a century earlier and then advises his audience that: 'If you wish to read all the verbal acts take yourself to the archives of the Proconsul'.[58] We also have documents associated with ecclesiastical and imperial hearings against Athanasius of Alexandria, Priscillian of Avila and Damasus of Rome, amongst others.[59] Early Christian writings also cite the texts of legal petitions addressed to emperors and magistrates, as well as those intended for use in legal processes internal to the church. Optatus, for instance, apparently cites a petition of AD 313 from a group of North African bishops to Constantine, forwarded by Anullinus, the Proconsul of Africa, and also gives an extract from the imperial rescript issued in response (I.22.2 and I.23.1). Letter 2 of the *Collectio Avellana* is a Latin petition from two priests addressed to the emperors Valentinian, Theodosius I and Arcadius (AD 383 or 384); Letter 2a is the imperial response, addressed to the PPO Cynegius.[60] Letter 17 of the *Collectio Avellana* is also a petition drafted on behalf of Christian priests, this time to the emperors Honorius and Theodosius II (AD 419); Letter 18 gives the corresponding rescript. *Collectio Avellana* Letter 232a is the copy of a petition dating to almost a century later (AD 520), addressed to the Emperor Justin I from Syrian monks, clergy and *possessores*. The texts of six petitions, some in summary form, are preserved via the Acts of the Church Council of Ephesus (431); with nine from the Acts of the Council of Chalcedon (451), three with corresponding imperial rescripts; and five from the Acts of the Council of Constantinople (553).[61] Finally, with respect to legal documents, there are a number of early Christian writings that provide evidence for the documentary forms of various kinds of (written and oral) contracts and testamentary dispositions.

Conciliar records, ecclesiastical documents and other early Christian writings also provide evidence for various Roman legal and administrative procedures and processes, at both the municipal and the provincial levels. The writings of elite Christian bishops such as Ambrose of Milan, the provincial governor of Aemilia and Liguria before his episcopal consecration as well as a former advocate and assessor (legal advisor) in the praetorian prefect's court at Sirmium, often draw sharp contrasts between the administrative functions of imperial bureaucrats and the pastoral, liturgical and ascetic functions of clerical offices. These contrasts can also include distinct attitudes towards judicial torture and penal condemnation, as well as expectations of justice.[62] Nonetheless, late Roman bishops also made use of Roman legal and administrative models to frame their episcopal activities: Gregory, bishop of Nazianzus, for instance, models his *Oration* 42 – a *logos apologêtikos* ('plea in his defence') – on the formal rendering of accounts required from imperial officials when they left military command, the government of a province or a financial office.[63] The influence of late Roman law is particularly evident, however, in the procedural rules and regulations that were developed with reference to synodal or conciliar tribunals. For example, a synodal disciplinary hearing usually opened with a personally presented *libellus* of complaint from the plaintiff, through which a demand was made that the defendant be summoned – the granting of the summons by the synod was thus to be understood as an official act, analogous to the same procedure in a late Roman civil *cognitio*.[64] Other legal procedures referred to in early Christian writings include slave manumissions conducted in Christian churches, as well as records relating to concrete cases of mediation, formal arbitration and (delegated) legal judgment undertaken by Christian clerics.[65]

In Section 2 our focus has been on early Christian writings as extra-legal sources for Roman imperial law and legal concepts, in addition to their value as sources for legal practice in the sense of providing evidence for documentary texts and concrete legal procedures. In Section 3, however, we turn more explicitly to Christian writers and ecclesiastics as concrete actors within the late Roman legal sphere.

3. Christian Ecclesiastics As Roman Legal Actors

> Most of the time, people just go along in their daily routines without reflecting on [the] law that has shaped these routines, their social relationships and attitude . . . The specific relevance or irrelevance of law usually crops up only when people have to deal with problematic situations, with disputes and in processes . . . that aim at changing routines and the law structuring them.[66]

Late Roman ecclesiastics were not only writers of texts; they were also, to varying extents, 'doers' of Roman law. Clerics owned property (including land and slaves), paid taxes, some inherited as heirs, some married and divorced, some engaged in business and trade, and so forth. One reason, then, why Roman law appears in early Christian writings is because early Christian writers used Roman law and Roman legal institutions in everyday contexts. From at least the early fourth century, however, the position of the Christian Church within Roman law and society began to change. From the emperor Gallienus onwards, Christians who had had property confiscated under the 'great' persecutions were entitled to have it restored. Moreover, emperors began to donate property to ecclesiastical officials, as well as granting other gifts, legal privileges, exemptions from personal and civic *munera*, and remissions from certain taxes to Christian clerics. In many cases these imperial grants were in response to requests from within the church hierarchy. The institutional development of the late Roman church was thus guaranteed and supported by the Roman imperial authorities (to a greater or lesser extent, depending on context and situation).[67] Two extant Constantinian laws, however, specify that all such legal privileges and exemptions are to benefit catholic clergy only: it had apparently come to the emperor's attention that 'heretics' were nominating 'catholics' for public liturgies.[68] Trying to ensure that imperial privileges and exemptions only benefited 'catholic' clergy appears as an ongoing concern in late Roman legislation and necessitated legal decisions over who was 'catholic' and who was not. Legal capacities to gather in voluntary assemblies or to hold lawful councils, along with rights to establish churches, 'by private or public undertakings' and to practise rituals and ceremonies, were all variously restricted by late Roman imperial constitutions. Behind such 'anti-heretical' laws, of course, lie innumerable pleas and petitions addressed to the imperial authorities by ecclesiastics themselves. From the early fourth century onwards, Christian clerics helped to shape new principles of Roman law relating to the church, ecclesiastical jurisdiction and Christian doctrine: 'Patristic texts transmit not only *exempla* of religious legislation promulgated by Constantine and later emperors, but also instances of ecclesiastical officials urging the enactment of specific legislative measures.'[69]

Late Roman Christian writings, then, are more than just potential extra-legal sources to be quarried for references to Roman legal texts and principles. Some were intended as direct interventions in concrete legal cases and contemporary disputes and controversies.[70] Christian clerics were involved in concrete legal cases on a number of different levels. Alongside acting as (delegated) judges and formal arbitrators – an activity referred to in modern sources under the umbrella term *episcopalis audientia* or 'bishop's hearing' – some clerics advised individual members of their congregation on concrete cases, for example property or inheritance disputes, as well as seeking advice themselves from legal experts (*iurisconsulti*/*iurisperiti*). The text of a letter written by Augustine, c. AD 422, to a practising North African *iurisconsultus* named Eustochius begins:

'Since you owe honest responses to all those who consult you, how much more do you owe such to us, the ministers of Christ'.[71] Augustine then asks Eustochius for *responsa* on a number of detailed legal points concerning slavery and the status of the children of *coloni*, and also specifies that he would like to know what has been established either in jurisprudential writings or by imperial constitutions concerning those who function as managers. These questions had been prompted by certain imperial laws that had been brought to Augustine's attention; moreover, Augustine states that he has had these imperial constitutions copied and is attaching them to his letter for Eustochius to read. That Augustine was also accustomed to looking up previous cases in the municipal and proconsular records himself, and then applying them to pressing legal matters, is also evident from Augustine's ('New') Letters 28* and 29*.

Some late Roman ecclesiastics also sought to develop creatively new socio-legal principles, as and when concrete situations demanded. For example, in his Letter 83 Augustine discusses the case of a certain Honoratus, who had been a monk at Thagaste in North Africa (Augustine's home town), before he was ordained as a priest in the neighbouring town of Thiava. Around AD 405 Honaratus had died intestate, without any family that could claim the right of legal succession to his goods. An equitable solution to the problem had been proposed by Alypius, then bishop of Thagaste: part of Honoratus' goods should be granted to the church at Thiava and the other part would be given to his former monastery. The citizens of Thiava, however, had objected to this split and Alypius appealed to Augustine to mediate. Augustine (eventually) decided against the monastery and in favour of the church: Honoratus' goods should devolve to the church in which he had been ordained, but in future cases concerning clerics or monks where legal heirs to their property did exist, the inheritance should pass to them in accordance with the rules of Roman civil law. Augustine also states that the right of a monastery's succession to the goods of one of its monks should be allowed only in the case of express testamentary stipulations to that effect. Papyrological evidence provides a number of examples of such monastic wills and testaments from Byzantine Egypt.[72]

As discussed in Section 2, the use of early Christian writings as extra-legal sources poses specific challenges and problems to the legal historian, some peculiar to individual texts and some relevant to 'Patristic'/'Early Christian' literature in general. Nonetheless, alongside papyrological evidence, this type of source material can offer a wealth of information in terms of how Roman law was (mis-)understood, ignored, invoked, adapted and manipulated in concrete historical situations and contexts.

Early Christian writings can help us to frame important questions from various 'sociology of knowledge' perspectives: How did legal texts circulate and in what form at any given time and place? Were there circles of legal book-copyists or lenders within particular regions, or did individuals look beyond provincial boundaries for particular texts? For example, Augustine asked Alypius, bishop of Thagaste and a former *assessor* (legal expert) to the court of the *comes largitionum Italicarum*, to check for a copy of an (anti-heretical) law whilst he was on a visit to Rome – Augustine wanted to circulate the imperial constitution and make it more widely known (Letter 10*.4). In addition, Augustine's writings detail numerous problems in actually getting provincial magistrates to enforce the imperial laws that were brought to their attention: 'The laws were not lacking, but slept in our hands as if they did not exist'.[73] How widespread was access to legal knowledge within specific cities and provinces? Were legal experts available for consultation by letter and in person in all towns and/or villages? What role did notaries play in urban life, and when did individuals seek them out to draft documents and give legal advice?

These are not just questions concerning (late Roman) law in practice or law in action. Early Christian writings also help us to see how law and socio-legal authority, in any given locality at any given time, is shaped from the ground up as well as from the top down. The sheer breadth of early Christian literature allows us to ask questions such as *why* given individuals might have chosen to mobilize late Roman courts or ecclesiastical legal processes when they did (there were always alternatives). This focus leads, in turn, to an exploration of choice-making and behaviour in terms of multiple socio-legal contexts. For example, the anonymous *Life of Alexander 'the Sleepless'*, probably written down in the Eastern Empire during the late fifth/early sixth centuries, narrates the life and conduct of the blessed Alexander, a wandering Christian 'holy man' who 'feared neither imperial authority, nor the threats of magistrates, nor the accusations of the populace, nor the wicked recommendations of bishops' (Alexander had apparently himself served as a clerk on a prefect's office staff before conversion).[74] Chapters 40–49 of the life narrate some of the troubles that Alexander encountered when he stayed in Antioch, including a sub-deacon named Malchus who complains that people now take their disputes to the holy man instead of him: 'my authority in the court was the one source of revenue that I had'. Malchus seeks permission from his bishop to drive Alexander out of the city, but in the meantime has the holy man beaten up. The people of the city protest to the bishop, and the bishop in turn petitions a military commander to exile Alexander to Chalcis in Syria. The military commander agrees, but later in the narrative we find Alexander being tried for heresy before an imperial magistrate. In this (hagiographical) narrative, then, legal or 'quasi-legal' authority is attributed to the holy man, the sub-deacon, the bishop, the military commander and the imperial magistrate. More importantly, the narrative highlights the strategic choice-making activity of Malchus (and to a lesser extent the people of Antioch) as they negotiated between various options on the ground. Early Christian texts like the *Life of Alexander 'the Sleepless'* can thus help us to understand legal practice as one aspect of a much broader repertoire of social and cultural behaviour.

If we approach early Christian texts according to the localities and times in which they were written, rather than as a single genre of 'early Christian literature', and then combine them with other relevant literary, documentary, numismatic and material evidence, we may be able to build up pictures of regional variation and multiple local 'Roman' cultures and traditions. These local cultures and traditions, moreover, do not just provide the background or 'unavoidable social context' for legal behaviour; they structure legal behaviour itself.[75] As the anthropologist Tim Jenkins puts it, 'laws are not, in the local instance, primary'.[76] Legal historians may be tempted to assume that 'the law is there and [that] disputants meet in a landscape naked of normative habitation'; but in fact, on the ground, we find a 'landscape populated by an uneven tangle of indigenous law. In many settings the norms and controls of indigenous ordering are palpably there, the official law is remote and its intervention is problematic and transitory.'[77] Early Christian texts, written from particular standpoints in concrete times and places, may not grant us unmediated access to Roman law(s), but they do enable us to recognize that normativity is itself an aspect of social practice.

Notes

1. On the technical distinction between patrology and patristics, see O. Bardenhewer, *Geschichte der altkirchlichen Literatur* (Freiburg, 1902–1932, reissued 2007).
2. B. Biondi, *Il Diritto Romano Cristiano*, 3 vols. (Milan, 1952–1954); E. Dovere, *Ius Principale e catholica lex (secolo V)* (Naples, 1999); L. de Giovanni, *Istituzioni scienza giuridica codici nel mondo tardo-antico. Alle radici di una nuova storia* (Rome, 2007); and K. M. Girardet, *Kaisertum, Religionspolitik und das Recht von Staat und Kirche in der Spätantike* (Bonn, 2009).
3. J.-P. Coriat, *Le Prince Législateur* (Rome, 1997), 897. See also the chapter by Winkel, 11–13.
4. See http://giurisprudenza.unipg.it/index.php/2013-03-19-10-54-24 (last accessed 7 October 2014).
5. R. Bruno Siola, S. Giglio, and S. Lazzarini, eds., *Auctores latini e graeci tardae aetatis (saec. IV–VI a. D) quorum scripta ad propositum opus utilia videntur.* (Milan, 1985; 2nd revd. edn. by G. M. Facchetti, 2000).

6. Z. B. Carusi, 'Diritto romano e patristica', in *Studi giuridici in onore di Carlo Fadda* (Naples, 1906), vol. 2, 79; also J. Gaudemet, 'L'Apport du Droit Romain à la Patristique Latine du IVe Siècle', *Miscellanea Historiae Ecclesiasticae* 6 (1983): 166.
7. J. N. Adams, *Bilingualism and the Latin Language* (Cambridge, 2003), 356.
8. Compare Gregory Thaumaturgus (c. AD 213–c.270), *Address of Thanksgiving to Origen*, 7.
9. On the Gospels and Pauline texts, see A. N. Sherwin-White, *Roman Society and Roman Law in the New Testament* (Oxford, 1963) and O. Eger, 'Rechtswörter und Rechtsbilder in den Paulinischen Briefen', *Zeitschrift für die neutestamentliche Wissenschaft* 18 (1918): 84–108. Cf. J. W. Martens, *One God. One Law. Philo of Alexandria on the Mosaic and Greco-Roman Law* (Boston, 2003) and S. Lieberman, 'Roman legal institutions in early Rabbinics and in the Acta martyrum', *Jewish Quarterly Review* 35 (1944): 1–57.
10. The secondary literature is extensive; see, esp., A. Beck, *Römisches Recht bei Tertullian und Cyprian. Eine Studie zur frühen Kirchenrechtgeschichte*, 2nd edn. (Aalen, 1967); R. D. Sider, *Ancient Rhetoric and the Art of Tertullian* (Oxford, 1971); I. Cadoppi, 'Sul lessico giuridico nell'Apologeticum di Tertulliano', *Acme* 49 (1996): 153–165.
11. The juristic fragments are collected by O. Lenel, *Palingenesia iuris civilis* (Leipzig, 1889), vol. 2, cols. 341–343. See now J. Harries, 'Tertullianus & Son?', in *A Wandering Galilean: Essays in Honour of Seán Freyne*, ed. Z. Rodgers et al. (Leiden, 2009).
12. On Christian authors in the late Latin West, see J. Gaudemet, *Le droit romain dans la littérature chrétienne occidentale du III au V siècle* (Milan, 1978); D. Liebs, *Römische Jurisprudenz in Africa, mit Studien zu den pseudopaulinischen Sentenzen* (Berlin, 2005); D. Liebs, *Römische Jurisprudenz in Gallien (2. bis 8. Jahrhundert)* (Berlin, 2002); D. Liebs, *Die Jurisprudenz im spätantiken Italien (260–640 n. Chr.)* (Berlin, 1987); and D. Liebs, 'Römische Provinzialjurisprudenz', *ANRW* II.15 (1976): 288–362.
13. Zacharius Scholasticus, *Life of Severus*, ed. M. A Kugener, *Patrologia Orientalis* 2 (1907): 46–92.
14. J. Modrzejewski, 'Grégoire le Thaumaturge et le droit romain. À propos d'une édition récente', *RHDFE* 49 (1971): 321–22.
15. Gaudemet (n. 12), 30.
16. B. D. Shaw, 'Judicial nightmares and Christian memory', *Journal of Early Christian Studies* 11 (2003): 549. See also M. Z. Kensky, *Trying Man, Trying God. The Divine Courtroom in Early Jewish and Christian Literature* (Tübingen, 2010), 293–342.
17. See C. Humfress, *Orthodoxy and the Courts* (Oxford, 2007).
18. On Roman law and Rabbinic texts, see C. Hezser, 'Roman Law and Rabbinic Legal Composition', in *The Cambridge Companion to The Talmud and Rabbinic Literature*, ed. C. E. Fonrobert and M. S. Jaffee (Cambridge, 2007), 144–163.
19. Clement of Alexandria, *Stromateis*, I.27.
20. Origen, *Against Celsus* IV.73. Compare Eusebius of Caesarea, *Proof of the Gospel*; Asterius of Amasea, *Sermon* 5.13–15; and Julian, *Against the Galileans*, 141D and 184B.
21. Augustine, *City of God* 2.16; cf. Livy 3.31.8–3.33.7.
22. *Collatio* 7.1 (*FIRA* 2.562). See now R. M. Frakes, *Compiling the Collatio Legum Mosaicarum et Romanarum in Late Antiquity* (Oxford, 2011).
23. See, in general, A. Arjava, *Women and Law in Late Antiquity* (Oxford, 1998).
24. Ep. 77.3, ed. I. Hilberg, *Corpus Scriptorum Ecclesiasticorum Latinorum*, vol. 55 (Vienna, 1912), 39.
25. Gregory of Nyssa, *De Virginitate*, ed. W. Jaeger, J. P. Carvanos and V. W. Callahan, in *Gregorii Nysseni Opera ascetica*, vol. 8, pt. 1 (Leiden, 1952), 261.

26. G. L. Falchi, 'L'influenza della patristica sulla politica legislativa *de nuptiis* degli imperatori romani dei secoli IV e V', *Augustinianum* 50.2 (2010): 351–407.
27. Augustine, *Sermon* 52.9 (translation by Edmund Hill, slightly modified).
28. A. Yoshiko Reed, ' "Jewish Christianity" as Counter-History? The Apostolic Past in Eusebius, Ecclesiastical History and the Pseudo-Clementine Homilies', in *Antiquity in Antiquity: Jewish and Christian Pasts in the Greco-Roman World*, ed. G. Gardner and K. L. Osterloh (Tübingen, 2008), 210.
29. See D. G. Hunter and S. A. Harvey, *The Oxford Handbook of Early Christian Studies* (Oxford, 2008).
30. Jerome, continuation of Eusebius' *Chronicle*, ed. R. Helm, *Eusebius Werke 7: Die Chronik des Hieronymus* (1956), 240; Augustine, *City of God* 6.9.1.
31. G. Rotondi, 'Indice dei richiami al diritto nei testi extragiuridici latini dei secoli IV–VII', in *Scritti Giuridici*, ed. V. Arangio-Ruiz and P. de Francisci, (Milan, 1922), vol. 1, 554.
32. J.-P. Coriat, 'La palingénesie des constitutions impériales. Histoire d'un projet et méthode pour le recueil de la législation du principat', *Mélanges de l'Ecole française de Rome, Antiquité* 101.2 (1989): 894.
33. P. Silli, *Testi Costantiniani nelle Fonti Letterarie* (Milan, 1987); M. Sargenti and R. Bruno Siola, *Normativa Imperiale e Diritto Romano negli Scritti di S. Ambrogio* (Milan, 1991); F. Pergami, *La Legislazione di Valentiniano e Valente (364–375)* (Milan, 1993); P. O. Cuneo, *La Legislazione di Costantino II, Costanzo II e Costante (337–361)* (Milan, 1997); and P. Stefania, *Religio e Ius Romanum nell'epistolario di Leone Magno* (Milan, 2002). Also, on Julian, E. Germino, 'La legislazione dell'imperatore Giuliano: primi appunti per una palingenesi', *Antiquité Tardive* 17 (2009): 159–174.
34. Coriat (n. 32), 903, noting Augustine *City of God* 5.17; John Chrysostom, *Homilies on the Acts of the Apostles* 48.1; Sidonius Apollinaris, *Letter* I.6.2.
35. For both texts, see J. de Churruca, 'Un rescrit de Caracalla utilisé par Ulpien et interprété par Saint Augustin', in *Collatio Iuris Romani. Études Dédieés à Hans Ankum*, ed. R. Feenstra et al. (Amsterdam, 1995), vol. 1, 71–80.
36. S. Corcoran, *The Empire of the Tetrarchs. Imperial Pronouncements and Government AD 284–324*, revd. edn. (Oxford, 2000), 33, 127.
37. See T. D. Barnes, *Early Christian Historiography and Roman History* (Tübingen, 2010).
38. Eusebius, *Ecclesiastical History* 7.13. See, in general, Silli (n. 33) and T. D. Barnes, *Constantine and Eusebius* (Cambridge, Mass. 1981).
39. Corcoran (n. 36), 19.
40. See J.-L. Maier, ed., *Le Dossier du Donatisme*, 2 vols., (Berlin, 1987–1989).
41. See F. Millar, 'Paul of Samosata, Zenobia and Aurelian: The Church, Local Culture and Political Allegiance in Third Century Syria', *JRS* 61 (1971): 1–17.
42. *Les Lois Religieuses des Empereurs Romains de Constantin à Théodose II. Volume I: Code Théodosien XVI* (Sources Chrétiennes, vol. 497), ed. J. Rougé et al. (Paris, 2005); *Les Lois Religieuses des Empereurs Romains de Constantin à Théodose II. Volume II: Code Théodosien 1–XV, Code Justinien, Constitutions Sirmondiennes* (Sources Chrétiennes, vol. 531), ed. J. Rougé et al. (Paris, 2009). See also E. Magnou-Nortier, *Le Code Théodosien, Livre XVI et sa Réception au Moyen Âge* (Paris, 2002); J.-N. Guinot and F. Richard, eds., *Empire Chrétien et Église aux IVe et Ve siècles. Intégration ou 'concordat'? Le Témoignage du Code Théodosien* (Lyon, 2008).
43. O. Guenther, ed., *Epistolae Imperatorum Pontificum Aliorum Inde ab a. CCCLXVII usque DLIII datae Avellana Quae Dicitur Collectio (Corpus Scriptorum Ecclesiasticorum Latinorum* 35). (Prague – Vienna – Leipzig, 1895).

44. S. Lancel, *Actes de la Conférence de Carthage en 411* (Sources Chrétiennes 194, 195, 224 and 373). (Paris, 1972–1991).
45. G. Barone-Adesi, *Richerche sui Corpora Normativi dell' Impero Romano* (Turin, 1998), vol. 1, 101–105.
46. See R. Price and M. Gaddis, *The Acts of the Council of Chalcedon I–III* (Liverpool, 2005); R. Price, *The Acts of the Council of Constantinople of 553 with Related Texts on the Three Chapters Controversy* (Liverpool, 2009). F. Millar, 'Un dossier d'accusation déposé auprès du praeses de Syrie seconde pour transmission à Justin Ier', *Antiquité Tardive* 18 (2010): 231–242 gives a brief overview.
47. Quoted from T. Graumann, '"Reading" the first council of Ephesus 431', in *Chalcedon in Context. Church Councils 400–700*, ed. R. Price and. M. Whitby (Liverpool, 2009), 28 n. 5.
48. M. Vessey, 'The Origins of the Collectio Sirmondiana: A New Look at the Evidence', in *The Theodosian Code: Studies in the Imperial Law of Late Antiquity*, ed. J. Harries and I. Wood, 2nd edn. (London, 2010), 178–199.
49. A. Cameron, *The Last Pagans of Rome* (Oxford, 2010), 69.
50. F. Millar, *A Greek Roman Empire. Power and Belief under Theodosius II (408–450)* (Berkeley and Los Angeles, 2006).
51. See P. Bianchi, *Iura-Leges. Un'Apparente Questione Terminologica della Tarda Antichità. Storiografia e Storia* (Milan, 2007).
52. Gaudemet (n. 12), 22.
53. Carusi (n. 6), 91; V. Marotta, *Ulpiano e l'Impero II: Studi sui libri de officio proconsulis e la loro fortuna tardoantica* (Naples, 2004), vol. 2, 81–83.
54. On possible postclassical revision(s) see H.J. Wolff, 'Ulpian XVIII ad edictum in Collatio and Digest and the Problem of Postclassical Editions of Classical Works', in *Scritti Ferrini*, ed. A. Gemelli (Milan, 1949), vol. 4, 64–90.
55. In addition to works already cited above see on Cyprian: T.G. Fogliani, *T. C. Cipriano. Contributo alla ricerca di riferimenti legali in testi extragiuridici del III sec. d.c.* (Modena, 1928); A. Hoffmann, *Kirchliche Strukturen und römisches Recht bei Cyprian von Karthago* (Paderborn, 2000); on Lactantius, Arnobius and Minucius Felix: C. Ferrini, 'Le cognizioni giuridiche di Lattanzio, Arnobio e Minucio Felice', *Memorie dell'Accademia delle Scienze di Modena*, ser. II, 10 (1894): 195–210; F. Felice, 'Su le idee giuridiche contenute nei libri V e VI delle Istituzioni di Lattanzio', *Rivista internazionale di scienze sociali e discipline ausiliarie* 5 (1894): 581–586; on 'Ambrosiaster': O. Heggelbacher, *Vom römischen zum christlichen Recht. Iuristische Elemente in den Schriften des sogenanntes Ambrosiaster* (Freiburg, 1959); on Jerome: G. Violardo, *Il pensiero giuridico di San Girolamo* (Milan, 1937); on Augustine: E. Albertario, 'Di alcuni riferimenti al matrimonio e al possesso in Sant' Agostino', *Rivista di Filosofia Neo-scolastica*, suppl. to vol. 23 (1931): 367–376; M. Roberti, 'Contributo allo studio delle relazioni fra diritto romano e patristica tratto dall'esame delle fonti Agostiniane', *Rivista di Filosofia Neo-scolastica*, suppl. to vol. 23 (1931): 305–366; D. Nonnoi, 'Sant'Agostino e il diritto romano', *Rivista Italiana per le Scienze Giuridiche* 12 (1934): 531–622; F.G. Lardone, 'Roman Law in the Works of St. Augustine', *Georgetown Law Journal* (1956): 435–456; on Isidore of Pelusium: E. Lyon, 'Le droit chez Isidore de Péluse', *Etudes d'histoire juridique offertes à Paul Girard* (Paris, 1913), vol. 2, 209–222; on Asterius of Amasea: E. Volterra, 'Considerazioni teologico-giuridiche di Asterio di Amasea', *Rivista italiana per le scienze giuridiche* n.s. 4 (1929): 3–10; on Peter Chrysologus: N.J. Ristuccia, 'Law and legal documents in the Sermons of Peter

Chrysologus', *Journal of Late Antiquity* 4.1 (2011): 124–156; on monastic works: C. Neri, 'Ci sono testimonianze giuridiche nelle fonti monastiche?', *AARC* 15 (2005): 107–117.

56. Gaudemet (n. 6), 166.
57. See K.M. Girardet, *Kaisergericht und Bischofsgericht. Studien zu den Anfängen des Donatistenstreites (313–315) und zum Prozeß des Athanasius (328–346)* (Bonn, 1975); D. Liebs, *Vor den Richtern Roms, Berühmte Prozesse der Antike* (Munich, 2007), 159–168.
58. Augustine, *Against Cresconius* 3.81.
59. See Liebs (n. 57), 169–178; and K.M. Girardet, 'Trier 385. Der Prozess gegen die Priszillianer', *Chiron* 4 (1974): 577–608 on Priscillian. Also G. Puglisi, 'Giustizia criminale e persecuzioni antieretiche (Priscilliano e Ursino, Ambrogio e Damaso)', *Siculorum Gymnasium* 43 (1990): 91–137; A. Coskun, 'Der Praefect Maximinus, der Jude Isaak und der Strafprozeß gegen Bischof Damasus von Rom', *Jahrbuch für Antike und Christentum* 46 [2003] (2005): 17–44.
60. See also Lucifer of Cagliari, *Libellus Precum* (= A. Canellis, *Supplique aux Empereurs* (Sources Chrétiennes vol. 504) (Paris, 2006), 224–226.
61. D. Feissel, 'Pétitions aux Empereurs et formes du rescrit dans les sources documentaries du IVe au Vie siècle', in *La Pétition à Byzance*, ed. D. Feissel and J. Gascou (Paris, 2004), 45–49 (nos. 15–20; 21–29; and 37–39). On conciliar *acta* and early 'canon law' see the chapter by Helmholz, 396–8.
62. See K. Uhalde, *Expectations of Justice in the Age of Augustine* (Philadelphia, 2007); B. A. Berkowitz, *Execution and Invention: Death Penalty Discourse in Early Rabbinic and Christian Cultures* (Oxford, 2006).
63. S. Elm, 'A Programmatic Life: Gregory of Nazianzus' Orations 42 and 43 and the Constantinopolitan Elites', *Arethusa* 33.3 (2000): 418–419.
64. A. Steinwenter, 'Der Einfluss des römischen Rechtes auf den antiken kanonischen Prozess', in *Congresso Internationale di Diritto Romano* (Rome, 1935), vol. 2, 228.
65. C. Humfress, 'Bishops and Law Courts in Late Antiquity. How (Not) to Make Sense of the Legal Evidence', *Journal of Early Christian Studies* 19.3 (2011): 375–400.
66. F. von Benda-Beckmann and K. von Benda-Beckmann, 'The dynamics of change and continuity in plural legal orders', *Journal of Legal Pluralism and Unofficial law* 53–54 (2006): 24.
67. See further E. Herrmann-Otto, *Ecclesia in re publica. Die Entwicklung der Kirche von pseudo-staatlicher zu staatlich inkorporierter Existenz* (Frankfurt, 1980).
68. C.Th. 16.2.1 (possibly 31 Oct. AD 313, no place or addressee recorded); see also C.Th. 16.2.6 (addressed to Ablabius PP, issued 1 June AD 329, according to Seeck).
69. Barone-Adesi (n. 45), 85.
70. Humfress (n. 17), esp. Part III.
71. Augustine, *Ep.* 24*, trans. Eno (1989).
72. L. MacCoull, 'Apa Abraham: Testament of Apa Abraham, Bishop of Hermonthis, for the Monastery of St. Phoibammon near Thebes, Egypt', in *Byzantine Monastic Foundation Documents*, ed. J.P. Thomas (Washington, D.C., 2000), 51–58; also R. Bagnall, 'Monks and property: rhetoric, law, and patronage in the Apophthegmata Patrum and the papyri', *Greek, Roman and Byzantine Studies* 42 (2001): 7–24.
73. Augustine, *Against Cresconius* 3.47.51.
74. D. Caner, *Wandering Begging Monks. Spiritual Authority and the Promotion of Monasticism in Late Antiquity* (Berkeley and Los Angeles, 2002), 251–252.

75. N. Mezey, 'Law as Culture', *Yale Journal of Law and the Humanities* 13 (2001): 35.
76. T. Jenkins, *The Life of Property* (New York, 2010), 116.
77. M. Galanter, 'Justice in Many Rooms: Courts, Private Ordering, and Indigenous Law', *Journal of Legal Pluralism and Unofficial Law* 19 (1981): 23[underline in original].

8 Justinian and the *Corpus Iuris Civilis*

Wolfgang Kaiser

1. Jurists' Law and Imperial Legislation Before Justinian

The Consolidation of Jurists' Law and the Transmission of Juristic Writings

Classical Roman legal science produced a great variety of legal literature, but the crisis of empire which began after the assassination of emperor Alexander Severus in March 235 caused this literary production to dry up.[1] It was only under Diocletian (who ruled from AD 284–305) that jurists of the time once again published legal compendia, treatises on specific issues, and collections of imperial constitutions under their own names (below, 120). But legal textbooks and more demanding works on legal problems are no longer attested in this period.[2] At the same time, authors whose names we do not know published works under the names of renowned late-classical jurists (pseudo-epigraphic works) – probably in order to enhance the reputation of their works.[3] One example is *Pauli Sententiae*, probably dating from the end of the third century. Around AD 330 the last known pseudo-epigraphic work – Pseudo-Ulpian's *Opinionum libri sex* – was produced.[4] In addition, the works of the classical jurists continued to be copied frequently. For the most part, however, only small fragments of late-antique manuscripts with legal content have survived;[5] the exception is the *Institutes* of Gaius.[6] From the time of Constantine (who reigned from AD 306–337) the available legal literature therefore consisted of the works of the classical jurists, some few new works by authors whose names are known, and those new productions which circulated under the names of classical jurists. This stock of legal literature did not expand until Justinian's age and formed the basis for his great collection of jurists' law (or 'jurisprudence'), the *Digest* (see Section 2).

The fact that the jurists' writings as sources of law were now fixed also led to legislation by the emperors. In AD 321 Constantine declared void critical notes (*notae*) by the jurists Ulpian and Paul on the works of Papinian.[7] In AD 327 (or 328) the same emperor affirmed that the *Pauli Sententiae* were just as valid as Paul's other writings.[8] One hundred years later an address to the senate (*oratio*) by Valentinian III of 7 November 426 dealt in great detail with imperial legislation and jurisprudence.[9] The part dedicated to jurisprudence regulated the citation of the jurists' writings in court (the 'Law of Citations'). Some writings were admissible without preconditions: those of Papinian, Paul, Gaius, Ulpian, and Modestinus. If a party wished to cite the work of another jurist, he had to produce at least two manuscripts of the work concerned. In cases where the views of the jurists differed, the majority was to prevail. If opinions were split equally, the judge was to follow the view of Papinian, who was held in high esteem in late antiquity. The 'Law of Citations' was included in the Theodosian *Code*, which was valid throughout the empire (below, 121), and also in the first edition of Justinian's *Code* of AD 529 (below, 123–4). Justinian explicitly freed the *Digest* commission from the constraints of this law (below, 124).

Imperial Legislation and the Collections of Imperial Constitutions

In late antiquity legislation by the emperors became the most important source of law. The classical jurists had already included imperial rescripts in their works on many occasions. In Diocletian's reign, the first actual collections of imperial constitutions were created: the Codex Gregorianus and the Codex Hermogenianus, named after their respective authors.[10] Gregorius (who is not otherwise attested) put together a collection of imperial constitutions in chronological order, from Hadrian to Diocletian.[11] He completed it in or a little after AD 291. The collection was subsequently expanded to include constitutions from the later years of Diocletian's reign. Aurelius Hermogenianus, who was praetorian prefect under Diocletian and also wrote a work containing legal rules, continued chronologically where the Codex Gregorianus left off and completed the first edition of his collection in AD 295.[12] Both collections remained in circulation until the time of Justinian and formed part of the material from which the *Codex Iustinianus* was created (below, 123).

About 150 years after these two *codices* another collection of imperial legislation was produced, the *Codex Theodosianus*.[13] This time, however, the collection was promulgated as an imperial enactment – just as Justinian's *Code* would be later. First, in March 429 the eastern Roman emperor Theodosius II (who ruled from AD 408–450) put together a commission consisting mainly of high-ranking officials, which was to collect general laws from the time of Constantine up to his own reign (C.Th. 1.1.5). The project failed, however, for unknown reasons. In December 435 (C.Th. 1.5.6) Theodosius II again appointed a commission, which completed its work after about two years. In an enactment dating from 15 February 438 Theodosius II conferred on this collection – the *Codex Theodosianus* – the force of law in the eastern part of the empire, effective from 1 January 439.[14] A little later the Theodosian *Code* was also published in the west.[15] It contains laws dating from 306 to 437 and is a genuine codification – that is to say, all original imperial laws from the period covered by the Theodosian *Code* lost their legal validity. The Theodosian *Code* is made up of 16 books,[16] which are divided into titles according to subject matter. Within each title, the constitutions appear in chronological order. At the beginning of each constitution there is a note stating the names of the emperors who enacted it and the persons to whom it is addressed (inscription), and at the end the place and date of the enactment are given (subscription). The constitutions are, however, no longer complete. The commission was to leave out all superfluous parts – for example, the introduction and the ending. It had explicit permission to modify the text of the constitutions and was under no obligation to indicate when it had changed the text. If necessary, the commission could allocate different parts of a single constitution to different titles. The same principles were also applied later in the production of Justinian's *Code* (below, 123–4). The extent to which a text in the Theodosian *Code* has been modified can, however, only be known when the constitution concerned has also been transmitted elsewhere: this is not often the case. One example is the *constitutiones Sirmondianae*,[17] a compilation of 16 late-antique imperial constitutions from the years AD 333 to 425 concerning ecclesiastical law. Ten of these constitutions are also transmitted in the Theodosian *Code*.

Originally the commission of 429 – after completing its work on imperial legislation – was to collect the jurists' law. This, however, did not happen. It was not until 100 years later that Justinian could realize a project of this magnitude. In the east the Theodosian *Code* remained law until Justinian's *Code* came into force on 16 April 529. In the west the Theodosian *Code* continued to be influential until the high middle ages, especially in the form of an extensive extract which was included in the Visigothic *Lex Romana Visigothorum* of AD 506 and was widespread in Gaul even after the collapse of the Visigothic kingdom.[18]

Legal Education

In order to understand fully the conditions under which Justinian could put his plans of codification into practice, it is necessary to consider late-antique legal education in the eastern part of the empire. In Berytus (Beirut) organized legal education[19] is attested as early as the beginning of the third century.[20] In Constantinople Theodosius II established a law school run by the state in AD 425 (C.Th. 14.9.3). By the end of the fifth century legal education also took place in Antioch and Alexandria. We can gain more detailed insights into the course of legal education from a law of Justinian dating from 16 December 533 (*const. Omnem*: below, 126). This law introduces reform of the programme of legal studies and for this purpose gives an account of the old curriculum which Justinian had found to be inadequate. Before Justinian's reform legal education was based on a five-year plan of study which encompassed the reading of selected legal works as well as the imperial constitutions.[21] Our evidence for the methods which law professors used to explain the jurists' texts in class also dates from the period between the middle of the fifth century and Justinian's reform.[22] The sources of law and legal terminology were in Latin, but the classes were taught in Greek. Justinian made use of the law professors' expertise for the first edition of the *Code*, and even more so for his codification of jurisprudence and for the second edition of the *Code* (below, 124).[23]

Thematic Collections

Even before Justinian's time there were works which collected excerpts from various jurists' writings and ordered them thematically. Remains of a collection which must originally have been rather extensive and which was probably produced in Rome around AD 320 are still extant in a Vatican manuscript (*Fragmenta Vaticana*). Neither the author nor the original title of the collection is known. The work was divided into titles according to subject matter (e.g., *Ex empto et vendito, De usu fructu*, and so on); each title contained relevant excerpts from the writings of classical jurists and from imperial constitutions.[24] Excerpts from juristic writings are preceded by the name of the jurist, the title of the work, and the number of the book from which the excerpt is taken (e.g., FV 119: *Ulpianus libro II de officio proconsulis* . . ., 120: *Ulpianus libro XXXIII ad edictum* . . ., and so on). Some significantly shorter works with excerpts from jurists' writings and imperial constitutions have also survived – for example, the *Consultatio veteris cuiusdam iurisconsulti*, which was created in the reign of Theodosius II and Valentinian III in southern France,[25] and the *Lex Dei* (*Collatio legum Mosaicarum et Romanarum*), a juxtaposition of Mosaic and Roman Law which was produced in Italy (probably in Rome) between AD 392 and 438.[26] The authors of these works are not known either. At the beginning each excerpt names the jurist, the work, and the number of the book, and in most cases the title (or chapter) heading too (e.g., Cons. 6.8: *Libro II sententiarum Pauli titulo ex empto et vendito*; Coll. 2.3.1: *Papinianus libro definitionum secundo sub titulo de iudicatis*). Justinian's *Digest* also gives for each excerpt the name of the jurist, the work, and the number of the book; the title heading, however, is not mentioned.

2. THE REIGN OF JUSTINIAN

The Legislation of Justinian

On 1 August 527 Justinian,[27] who was already co-regent with his uncle Justin I, acceded to the imperial throne in Constantinople. He died on 14 November 565 after reigning for 38 years. Within the first years of his reign (528–534) he realized three great legislative projects – the *Digest*, the *Institutes*, and the *Code* – collectively known as Justinian's compilation. Furthermore, in the 30 years after that he enacted a great number of laws – the *Novels* – which were to apply either throughout the empire or only in a certain territory. In the high middle ages the Glossators referred to the whole of Justinian's legislation (compilation and *Novels*) as the *corpus iuris*.[28] *Corpus iuris civilis*, the name that is common today, is first found as the title of a print edition in 1583.[29]

Six months after his accession Justinian arranged for the creation of a new collection of imperial constitutions (*const. Haec*, 13 February 528) which was to bear his name: *Codex Iustinianus*.[30] This process was necessary, Justinian argued, in order to reduce the great number of imperial constitutions and thus also the number of court proceedings (*const. Haec pr.*). The new *Code* was to encompass and replace the earlier collections (the codes of Gregorius, Hermogenian, and Theodosius) and the laws enacted subsequently. The commission appointed for this task mainly consisted of high-ranking imperial officials, including already Tribonian (on whom, see below, 124). The other members were Theophilus, a professor of law in Constantinople, and two advocates of the court of the praetorian prefect of the east.[31] The collection was to be arranged in titles according to subject matter (*const. Haec* § 2). Within each title – as in the earlier collections – the laws were to be ordered chronologically. The commissioners were explicitly authorized to leave out or change text; in particular, they were to delete what was obsolete or contradictory (*const. Haec* § 2). The work was completed quickly and, after little more than a year, on 7 April 529 Justinian could by means of *const. Summa* enact the *Codex Iustinianus*, conferring on it the force of law in the whole empire as from 16 April 529. From this date all earlier constitutions and the Theodosian *Code* were no longer in force (*const. Summa* § 3). Justinian ordered the *Code* to be sent to all provinces (*const. Summa* § 5). As little as five years later, however, a second edition of the *Code* followed. For this reason the only parts of the first edition to have survived are the two constitutions *Haec* and *Summa*, which also appear at the beginning of the second edition of the *Code*, and some small fragments of the text.[32] The first edition still contained the Law of Citations of Valentinian III (see Section 1). Some conclusions about the further contents of the first edition can be drawn from a few isolated remarks found in works by law professors.[33]

A little more than a year after the enactment of the first edition of the *Code* Justinian directed his attention to jurisprudence. Between July 530 and about September 531 he authoritatively decided a number of controversies among the classical jurists (*quinquaginta decisiones* – the Fifty Decisions).[34] Six months after beginning this revision of the jurists' law Justinian directed constitution *Deo auctore* of 15 December 530 to Tribonian, who in the meantime had risen to the post of *quaestor sacri palatii* (a kind of minister of justice). The constitution appointed a commission which was to survey the traditional jurists' law, shorten it, bring it up to date, and compile it in a new, contemporary codification: the '*Digest* or Pandects' (*Digesta vel Pandectae*: *const. Deo auct.* § 12). The commission was to base its decisions on objective considerations alone; favouring certain jurists – as in the Law of Citations (see above, 120) – was explicitly prohibited (*const. Deo auct.* § 6). The double name ('*Digest* or Pandects'), each part of which had already been used by classical jurists in the titles of their works, was chosen in order to underline the work's aspiration towards comprehensiveness. Justinian stated that the collection was necessary because the traditional jurists' law was so extensive that it had become unmanageable (*const. Deo auct.* § 1). The *Digest* commission had 17 members (the 'compilers'). It was chaired by Tribonian; the other members were one high-ranking official, four respected law professors (Theophilus and Cratinus from Constantinople, Dorotheus and Anatolius from Berytos), and 11 advocates of the court of the praetorian prefect of the east[35] (*const. Tanta/Dedoken* § 9). They were assisted by an unknown number of chancellery officials[36] and scribes. The commission read the works of those classical jurists who had possessed – at least as far as known in Justinian's time – the *ius respondendi*[37] and whose works were still available. In total, there are excerpts from 38 jurists in the *Digest*. The great bulk of the material is taken from the late-classical jurists Ulpian and Paul; about two-fifths and one-fifth of the excerpts, respectively, originate from them. The commission was able to complete its work within three years. The commissioners, especially the law professors, had long been familiar with the original writings, and this certainly made it easier for them to locate related texts and select the relevant passages from the material. The hypothesis that the *Digest* is based on extensive earlier collections of jurists' law (*predigesto*) is now out of date.

Building upon a tradition of introductory works (*institutiones*) which had already been written by the classical jurists, Justinian also made plans for an elementary textbook for first-year students (*const. Deo auctore* § 11). After work on the *Digest* had been completed, a commission with three members (Tribonian, Theophilus, Dorotheus) created – probably in the second half of 533 – the 'Institutes or Elements' (*Institutiones sive Elementa*). Justinian prefaced the work with a short introductory law (*const. Imperatoriam*) dating from 21 November 533 and addressed to the *cupida legum iuventus* ('young people yearning to study the laws'). The commission used the elementary works of classical jurists,[38] especially the *Institutes* and the *Res cottidianae* of Gaius, but also the *Institutes* of Marcianus, Florentinus, and Ulpian (*const. Imperatoriam* § 6). The *Institutes* take into account Justinian's reforming legislation, but often they also sketch the earlier state of the law (*const. Imperatoriam* § 5). Again and again the reader is referred to the *Digest* for further details on a certain subject. On 16 December 533 Justinian published the *Digest* and the *Institutes* through a constitution, of which a Greek and a Latin version have survived (*const. Tanta/Dedoken*); the two versions of the constitution are more or less identical in content. On 30 December 533 the *Digest* and the *Institutes* obtained the force of law throughout the empire (*const. Tanta/Dedoken* § 23), including North Africa, which had only recently been recaptured from the Vandals. The original juristic writings could no longer be cited in court proceedings (*const. Tanta/Dedoken* § 19). Several safeguards were put into place to protect the text of the compilation against corruption in the course of copying and re-copying of the manuscripts for distribution.[39] In the law schools the study of the original writings of the classical jurists was replaced by the *Digest* and the *Institutes* (below, 126–7).

While work on the *Digest* was ongoing Justinian continued to decide juristic controversies and to legislate on other matters. This meant that the *Code* of 529 soon became outdated. Therefore, after the work on the *Digest* had been completed, the *Code* was revised by a smaller committee made up of members of the *Digest* commission; this committee was also chaired by Tribonian. Through the *const. Cordi* of 16 November 534 Justinian brought into force the revised edition of the *Code* (*Codex repetitae praelectionis*), effective from 29 December 534. After some major military successes in the course of the reconquest of Italy – probably around 540 – Justinian had all three of these works (the *Digest*, the *Institutes*, and the revised edition of the *Code*) sent there. In 554 he re-affirmed their validity in Italy.[40] By the time the revised edition of the *Code* came into force Justinian had already made plans for a codification that would also collect his subsequent legislation. This new collection was to bear the title *novellae constitutiones* (*const. Cordi* § 4). These plans, however, were not realized (below, 138–9). The law professors of the time frequently referred to laws Justinian enacted after 29 December 534 as a 'new law', a 'new constitution' (*novella lex/constitutio*;in Greek: *νεαρὰ διάταξις*), or simply as *novella* or *νεαρά*; sometimes even Justinian himself used this description.[41] The name '*Novels*' for Justinian's laws dating from 535 or later is still used today. The first *Novel* was enacted as early as 1 January 535; the last dates from 25 March 565. In 554 Justinian ordered his legislation from 535 on to be published in Italy too.[42] Most of the extant laws date from the period between 535 and 541. Unlike the constitutions in Justinian's *Code*, these later laws have mostly survived unshortened (below, 138–9).

Legal Education Under Justinian

By means of *const. Omnem* of 16 December 533 Justinian reformed the legal curriculum[43] and limited legal education to the law schools of Berytos, Constantinople, and Rome. The teaching of law was now based on Justinian's three great works of codification. The new curriculum lasted five years. At the beginning the *Institutes* were taught, followed by the *Digest*. Not all parts of the *Digest* were treated in lectures; some were left to private study. The fifth year was reserved for the *Code*. The *Novels* were necessarily taken into account because of the changes to the law they contained. It is possible that later a sixth year of study was added, dedicated solely to the *Novels*. The teaching activities of the law professors – who referred to themselves as *antecessores* ('those who lead the way') – yielded a rich literature in Greek including introductions (*indices*), word-for-word translations (*kata poda*) as an aid to understanding the Latin text, and explanations of certain words and references to other parts of Justinian's legislation (*paragraphae, parapompae*). An introductory course in Latin to the *Novels* has survived (below, 140). The methods used by the *antecessores* are relatively well attested. Towards the end of the ninth century emperor Leo VI created a great codification (later called *Basilica*;[44]), which was based on Justinian's legislation. For this work Leo's compilers did not draw directly on the Latin text of the *Digest*, the *Institutes*, and the *Code*; instead, they used the Greek paraphrases or translations which had originated in legal education. Furthermore, scholars added glosses to the manuscripts of the *Basilica* (*scholia*[45]); these explanatory notes are based on works used in legal education which are now lost and thus significantly enhance our knowledge of the literature created by law professors in Justinian's time.

3. The *Digest*

Composition and Content

The *Digest* comprises 50 books. The arrangement of the material within it is based on the *Codex Iustinianus* and the praetorian edict (*const. Deo auct.* § 5). The books – with the exception of D. 30–32 – are divided into titles with title headings (rubrics). Each excerpt is headed by a note or 'inscription' which states the name of the jurist, the work, and the number of the book from which the excerpt was taken. This method had also been used in earlier collections of excerpts (above, 122–3). Justinian divided the *Digest* into seven *partes* which bore some relation to the organization of the legal curriculum before his reform.[46]

Within each title the excerpts are generally arranged in an order which was first discovered by Friedrich Bluhme in 1820.[47] The *Digest* commission had divided the juristic writings into three large groups or masses: the edictal mass, the Sabinian mass, and the Papinian mass. The masses take their names from the works with which they begin. The edictal and Sabinian masses are roughly similar in extent (about 575 books or *libri* each); the Papinian mass comprises about half as many books as each of the other two masses (292 books).[48] The division of the material into three masses implies a corresponding division of labour within the *Digest* commission.[49] Generally, each of these masses appears within each individual title, although their order varies. On occasion the compilers removed an excerpt from its place in one mass and inserted it into another when this seemed more appropriate.[50]

The first book of the *Digest* contains titles on law and justice, legal history, the sources of law (D. 1.1–4), the law of status (D. 1.5–7), the division of things (D. 1.8), the law on senators (D. 1.9), and on the jurisdiction of officials of the state (D. 1.10–21). The great majority of the 50 books of the *Digest* is concerned with private law (D. 2–47); D. 48 contains public criminal law; D. 49 deals with appeals procedure (D. 49.1–13) and with the law of the imperial treasury, the fisc (D. 49.14). D. 50 has titles on the law concerning municipalities (D. 50.1–12) and on various specialized areas of law (D. 50.13–15). An extensive title at the end provides information on the legal meaning of certain expressions (D. 50.16). The last title (D. 50.17) contains a great number of juristic rules.

Changes to the Original Texts: Interpolations

It is very important for our knowledge of classical Roman law to gain an understanding of how and to what extent Justinian's compilers – in accordance with their mandate – altered the text of the excerpts they included in the *Digest* (interpolations).[51] Occasionally constitutions of Justinian explicitly tell us about changes to the law.[52] Furthermore, we know that in all instances where certain obsolete institutions occurred in the classical texts, the compilers replaced them with the institutions used in Justinian's time. Examples can be found in the law of property (where the compilers inserted *traditio* for *mancipatio*), in family law (*actio dotis* for *actio rei uxoriae*), in the law of obligations (*fideiussio* for *sponsio*), and in inheritance law (*legatum per damnationem* for *legatum per vindicationem*). Incongruities in language or in substance within a passage may imply alterations to the text (especially omissions) by the compilers, but to suspect interpolations based purely on the use of certain expressions or on the assumption that the compilers held certain preconceptions of the law is no longer accepted.

Clarity about the alterations and omissions made by the compilers can be achieved only in those cases in which the same text has not only survived in the *Digest* but is also attested elsewhere – for example, in one of the collections of juristic writings produced before Justinian's time (above, 122–3). The following example is included in the *Digest* as well as in the *Lex Dei* (or *Collatio*). It is taken from Ulpian's comment on the third chapter of the *lex Aquilia*, which deals with damage to property through *urere, frangere, rumpere* (burning, breaking, smashing). The case at hand is concerned with burning. Corresponding text is shown in italics; additionally, where the wording is identical the text is underlined.

D. 9.2.27 (excerpts)	Coll. 12.7 (excerpts)
Ulpianus libro octavo decimo ad edictum.	*Ulpianus libro XVIII ad edictum*, sub titulo "si fatebitur iniuria occisum esse, in simplum" et[53] cum diceret:

7. *Item si arbustum meum vel villam meam incenderis, Aquiliae actionem habebo.*	1. *Item* si insulam meam adusseris vel *incenderis, Aquiliae actionem habebo,* idemque est, et *si arbustum meum vel villam meam.*
8. *Si quis insulam voluerit* meam *exurere et ignis etiam ad vicini insulam pervenerit, Aquilia tenebitur etiam vicino*: *non minus* etiam *inquilinis* tenebitur *ob res eorum exustas.*	3. Item *si quis insulam voluerit exurere et ignis etiam ad vicini insulam pervenerit, Aquilia tenebitur* lege *vicino etiam, non minus inquilinis ob res eorum exustas,* et ita Labeo libro XV responsorum refert.
...	...
12. *Si, cum apes meae ad tuas advolassent, tu eas exusseris,* *legis Aquiliae actionem competere* *Celsus ait.*	10. Item Celsus libro XXVII digestorum scribit: *si, cum apes meae ad tuas advolassent, tu eas exusseris,* quosdam negare *conpetere legis Aquiliae actionem,* inter quos et Proculum, quasi apes domini mei non fuerint. Sed id falsum esse *Celsus ait,* cum apes revenire soleant et fructui mihi sint. Sed Proculus eo movetur, quod nec mansuetae nec ita clausae fuerint. Ipse autem Celsus ait nihil inter has et columbas interesse, quae, si manum refugiunt, domi tamen fugiunt.
Ulpian in the 18th book on the edict	*Ulpian in the 18th book on the edict* under the title 'If it is admitted that someone was killed unlawfully. To the simple amount' and when he said:
7.	1. Likewise, if you burn down or *set fire to* my tenement-house, *I will have the action under the Aquilia,*
If you *set fire to my plantation of trees or my country house, I will have the action under the Aquilia.*	and the same is true if you burn down or set fire to *my plantation of trees or my country house.*
8. *If someone wanted to burn down* my *tenement-house and the fire also reached the neighbour's tenement-house, he will be liable under the Aquilia also to the neighbour*: *no less* will he also be liable *to the tenants because of their burned property.*	3. Likewise, *if someone wanted to burn down* a *tenement-house and the fire also reached the neighbour's tenement-house, he will be liable under the* Lex *Aquilia to the neighbour also, no less to the tenants because of their burned property,* and this is what Labeo relates in the 15th book of his Responses.

12. *If, when my bees had flown to yours, you burned them, the action under the lex Aquilia is available,*	10. Likewise, Celsus in the 27th book of his *Digest* writes that, *if, when my bees had flown to yours, you burned them,* some deny that *the action under the lex Aquilia is available*, among them Proculus, as if the bees had not been my property.
Celsus says.	But this is wrong, *Celsus says*, because bees usually return and the benefits are due to me. But Proculus was moved by the fact that they are neither tame nor locked in in such a way. Celsus for his part, however, says that there is no difference between them and pigeons, which, if they flee from the hand, nevertheless flee back home.

At the beginning of the example the compilers combined two cases into one (Item si *insulam – meam* was contracted to *Item – habebo*). They left out Ulpian's references to other jurists (*et ita Labeo – refert* and *Item Celsus – scribit*). Furthermore, they settled differences of opinion among the jurists and omitted Ulpian's account of the differing views (*legis Aquiliae actionem competere Celsus ait* instead of *quosdam negare – tamen fugiunt*). In this example no clauses or whole sentences were added by the compilers; it is, however, attested on some occasions that the compilers did this, too.

Editions, Transmission, and Textual Criticism

Today the authoritative edition of the *Digest* is that of Theodor Mommsen.[54] It was published in the years 1868 to 1870 (*editio maior*).[55] Only a few years later a simplified version of this edition, with a much shorter critical apparatus, was produced: the *editio minor*. It was first published in 1872 and was frequently reprinted. Starting with the eleventh reprint (1908) the *editio minor* was revised by Paul Krüger. Krüger on occasion made improvements to the text, expanded the critical apparatus, and included the results of Otto Lenel's palingenetic research. The result is that the *editio maior* and the *editio minor* no longer match exactly.

The transmission of the *Digest*, which can be only sketched here, is marked by the survival of one almost complete manuscript from late antiquity, the *Codex Florentinus Digestorum*.[56] The large manuscript comprises about 900 sheets (1800 pages), which today are divided into two volumes. It was probably produced in a scriptorium in the east, perhaps in Constantinople. Apart from the loss of some individual sheets and the fact that one double-sheet was already missing in the exemplar from which the *Codex Florentinus* was copied,[57] the *Codex Florentinus* is complete; in particular, it includes the passages of text written in Greek. Apart from the *Codex Florentinus*, only fragments and relics of *Digest* manuscripts from late antiquity have survived.[58]

One fascicle of a manuscript that was created in Burgundy at the beginning of the ninth century is extant. It contains the end of the *Institutes* and the beginning of the *Digest*.[59] The remainder of the manuscript is lost. The fascicle has only survived because it was accidentally bound into a manuscript of the *Epitome Iuliani* (below, 140). It seems that the *Institutes* and the *Digest* were copied directly from a late-antique manuscript.

So far as is known today, the medieval textual tradition of the *Digest* – the *Digest* vulgate – began around the middle of the eleventh century.[60] The two oldest manuscripts known today are the ms. Vat. lat. 1406 (dating from the second half of the eleventh century) and ms. Paris BN lat. 4450 (from the end of the eleventh century). The medieval manuscripts divide the text of the *Digest* into three parts (*Digestum vetus, Infortiatum, Digestum novum*), the exact delineation of which seems to have varied over time.[61] In the medieval manuscripts the passages in Greek are either missing completely or are severely mutilated. All medieval manuscripts of the *Digest* go back to one mother manuscript, which cannot be further dated and is now lost.[62] This mother manuscript is, in turn, dependent on the *Codex Florentinus*. This can be seen from the fact that many errors in the *Codex Florentinus* also appear in the medieval manuscripts. Occasionally, however, the vulgate manuscripts' readings are superior to those in the *Codex Florentinus*, and they feature text which is missing in the Florentine manuscript. Yet the improvements to the text are by no means comprehensive; the medieval manuscripts correct far from all the known gaps and errors in the *Codex Florentinus*. The origin of these manuscripts' superior readings is a question which has yet to be satisfactorily answered. The traditional model assumes that the copy of the *Codex Florentinus* (or the copy of the copy, etc.) which served as the mother manuscript for the medieval textual tradition was corrected by comparing it to a different manuscript of the *Digest*, which is lost today.[63]

In addition to the Latin textual tradition we have the indirect Greek tradition, which goes back to the works used in legal education in Justinian's time (above, 126). Depending on how faithful to the original texts the works of the *antecessores* were, they make it possible to draw conclusions about the original Latin text and expand the basis for textual criticism.[64] In those instances where the Greek tradition confirmed the readings of the medieval manuscripts Mommsen used them to emend the text of the *Codex Florentinus*.

One example in which the text of the *Codex Florentinus* can be improved with the help of the other branches of tradition is the following. At the end of D. 8.4.1 the *Codex Florentinus* (vol. 1, f. 140va/1–5) reads:

> *Ideo autem hae servitutes praediorum appellantur, quoniam sine praediis constitui non possunt: nemo enim potest servitutem adquirere vel urbani vel rustici praedii nisi qui habet praedium.*
>
> 'This is why these servitudes are called praedial because they cannot be created without there being estates [= *praedia*]. In fact, no one can acquire a servitude over either an urban or a rustic estate unless he has an estate.'

In the medieval manuscripts the text continues (see, e.g., the ms. Paris BN lat. 4450 f. 87r/34–39):

> *Ideo autem hae servitutes praediorum appellantur, quoniam sine praediis constitui non possunt: nemo enim potest servitutem adquirere vel urbani vel rustici praedii nisi qui habet praedium nec quisquam debere nisi qui habet praedium.*
>
> ' . . . unless he has an estate and no one can be bound [by a servitude] unless he has an estate.'

The indirect Greek tradition shows that the addition is, indeed, part of the original text of the *Digest*, as Basilica 58. 4.1 shows:

> *Οὐδεὶς δουλείαν ἔχειν ἢ χρεωστεῖν δύναται εἰ μὴ ὁ ἔχων ἀκίνητον.*
>
> 'No one can hold or be bound by a servitude unless he has an estate.'

Whereas Mommsen in his *editio maior* still considered the text of the *Codex Florentinus* to be accurate (*editio maior*, vol. 1, 264, 6–10), Krüger in the *editio minor* correctly features the expanded text which is attested by the medieval manuscripts and confirmed by the Greek tradition. The reason why the passage is missing in the *Codex Florentinus* is that the scribe – misled by the fact that the words *nisi qui habet praedium* occur twice – inadvertently skipped a line.

4. THE *INSTITUTES*

Composition and Content

The *Institutes*[65] are made up of four books; the books are divided into titles, the titles into paragraphs. Within the titles the text is continuous; the juristic writings from which the text is taken are not named. The *Institutes* start with law and justice and the sources of law (Inst. 1.1–2). After that the material is arranged according to the scheme of *personae – res – actiones* (persons – property – actions), which had already been used in earlier works: the law of persons (Inst. 1.3–26); the law of property (Inst. 2.1–9), inheritance law (Inst. 2.10–3.12), and the law of obligations (Inst. 3.13–4.9); and civil procedure (Inst. 4.11–17). At the end there is one title summarizing criminal law (Inst. 4.18).

Editions and Transmission

The authoritative critical edition of the *Institutes* was produced by Paul Krüger.[66] This edition – without any changes – is printed in the *editio minor* before the *Digest*.

No manuscripts of the *Institutes*[67] from Justinian's time are known. The oldest fragments we have date from the end of the sixth or the beginning of the seventh century (ms. Verona Bibl. Cap. XXXVIII (36)). Fragments from the ninth century and excerpts in a collection intended for ecclesiastical use have been found in Italy.[68] In France the *Institutes* have so far been attested only fragmentarily – together with the *Digest* – in Burgundy at the beginning of the ninth century (ms. Berlin Staatsbibl. lat. fol. 269, above, 131). Around the middle of the ninth century a copy of the *Institutes* was available in Fulda (or Mainz).[69] From the end of the tenth or the beginning of the eleventh century complete manuscripts from Italy have survived. An extensive introductory course on the *Institutes* in Greek (*index*) which was taught by the *antecessor* Theophilus (see above, 123–5) at the end of 533 or in 534 has been preserved almost completely and is an important aid to the textual criticism of the *Institutes*.

5. The Codex *Iustinianus* Repetitae Praelectionis

Composition and Content

The *Codex Iustinianus*[70] comprises 12 books. Unlike the Theodosian *Code*, Justinian's *Code* deals in the first place with ecclesiastical law (C. 1.1–13),[71] followed by the sources of law, the position of the emperor in the legal system (C. 1.14–25), and the administration of the empire (C. 1.26–57). Books 2 to 8 deal with private law, book 9 with criminal law, and books 10 to 12 are predominantly concerned with the law of the fisc, municipal administration, the colonate, and subordinate offices. The books are divided into titles. Within the titles the imperial constitutions are arranged in chronological order. At the beginning of each constitution the emperor who enacted it and the addressee are named (see above in connection with the Theodosian *Code*); at the end the date of the enactment is given (subscription).

Interpolations

The concrete changes which the compilers of the *Code* made to the originals can again only be seen in those instances where the same text has been transmitted twice, in particular when a constitution is also included in the Theodosian *Code*.[72] Parallel transmission of material taken from the *Codex Gregorianus* or the *Codex Hermogenianus* is very much rarer.

A law enacted by the emperors Gratian, Valentinian II, and Theodosius I in AD 383 will serve as an example for alterations in the text. The constitution deals with the rights of the seller of an estate if the price paid by the buyer is lower than the actual value of the estate. The law is included in the Theodosian *Code* as well as in Justinian's *Code*.

C. Th. 3.1.4	C. 4.44.15
Quisquis maior aetate	*Quisquis maior aetate*
atque administrandis familiarum suarum curis idoneus comprobatus	
praedia, etiam procul posita, distraxerit,	*praedia etiam procul posita distraxerit,*
etiamsi praedii forte totius quolibet casu minime facta distractio est,	
repetitionis in reliquum, *pretii nomine vilioris,*	paulo *vilioris pretii nomine repetitionis* rei venditae
copiam minime consequatur.	*copiam minime consequatur.*

Neque inanibus immorari sinatur obiectis, ut vires sibimet locorum causetur incognitas, qui familiaris rei scire vires vel merita atque emolumenta debuerit.	*Neque inanibus immorari sinatur obiectis, ut vires sibimet locorum causetur incognitas, qui familiaris rei scire vires vel merita atque emolumenta debuerat.*
Whosoever of legal age	*Whosoever of legal age*
and of proven capability to administer the affairs of his own property	
sold estates, even if they are situated far away,	*sold estates, even if they are situated far away,*
and even if, perhaps, in some case not the whole estate was sold,	
shall not have the possibility to claim the **rest** *on the ground that the price was too low.*	*shall not have the possibility to claim* the **sold estate** *on the ground that the price was* a little *too low.*
And he shall not be allowed to cause delays through unfounded objections of the kind that he alleges that the value of the estates had not been known to him, he who had to know the value or worth and the yield of his own property.	*And he shall not be allowed to cause delays through unfounded objections of the kind that he alleges that the value of the estates had not been known to him, he who had to know the worth and yield of his own property.*

The version in the Theodosian *Code* requires that the seller be of legal age and capable of managing his affairs. Justinian's *Code* speaks only of the necessity of the seller being of legal age; the second requirement is completely left out. Justinian's *Code* also omits the passage which explains that the sale of part of the estate suffices; probably this passage was simply seen as unnecessary. The next alteration to the text, however, signifies an actual substantive change in the law: in the version in the Theodosian *Code* the seller demands that the buyer now also pay the 'rest' – that is, the difference between the price originally agreed and the actual value of the estate – and the emperor refuses this demand. In Justinian's *Code*, by contrast, the seller demands the return of the sold estate, and the law in this version states that this is not possible if the price is only a little below the actual value of the estate. Here the compilers of Justinian's *Code* altered the text of the original constitution in order to include a change in the law which had taken place since the enactment of the original: under Justinianic law the seller of an estate could rescind the sale if the price was lower than one-half of the actual value of the estate. The buyer could avoid this by paying, in addition, the amount by which the price fell short of the full value.[73] If, however, the difference between the price and the actual value of the estate was only small, the seller had no right to rescind the sale – so says the law in the version in Justinian's *Code*. The last part of the law, which states that ignorance of the value of one's own property cannot serve as a pretext for rescinding contracts, was left unchanged. So the types of interpolations seen in the example are the complete omission of passages (*atque – comprobatus*, *etiamsi – distractio est*) and changes to the wording (*repetitionis in reliquum*, *pretii nomine vilioris – paulo vilioris pretii nomine repetitionis rei venditae*).[74] Elsewhere in Justinian's *Code* the addition of passages is also attested.[75]

Editions, Transmission, and Textual Criticism

The authoritative edition of the *Codex Iustinianus* was produced by Paul Krüger and published in 1877.[76] There was also an *editio minor* with an abbreviated critical apparatus. It was first published in 1877 and reprinted a number of times. Starting with the ninth reprint (1915), in the course of revising the *editio minor* of the *Digest* (see Section 3) Paul Krüger also expanded the *editio minor* of the *Codex Iustinianus*.

The manuscript transmission of Justinian's *Code* is inferior to that of the *Digest*. A late-antique manuscript which in appearance and age is similar to the *Codex Florentinus* has survived only fragmentarily, in the form of a palimpsest.[77] We also have smaller fragments of manuscripts from late antiquity.[78] Excerpts in collections and the remnants of complete manuscripts have survived from the early middle ages.[79] The great majority of the manuscripts which are extant date from the high middle ages.[80] Some of the early manuscripts no longer contain the original number of constitutions, which is due to an intentional thinning out. Occasionally, missing constitutions have been added in the margins. Most of the early manuscripts, however, feature complete inscriptions and subscriptions, which are often omitted in the later transmission because they are of no practical legal value. The *Summa Perusina*,[81] which is a commentary on a complete manuscript of Justinian's *Code* probably dating from the seventh century, does not preserve the original text of the *Code* but does at least preserve the inscriptions.[82] Here too reconstruction of the text is aided by instructional works in Greek, especially by the *Kata poda* of the *Code* written by the *antecessor* Thalelaius (above, 126); it takes the place of the *Code* in the *Basilica*.

The medieval Latin transmission – except for the Veronese palimpsest – no longer contains the Greek constitutions of the *Code*. These constitutions must be added from collections of east Roman church law (for example, the *Collectio tripartita*,[83] the *Collectio XXV Capitulorum*,[84] the *Collectio LXXXVII Capitulorum*,[85] and so forth)[86] or from the *Basilica* and their *Scholia*. There, however, the constitutions have not always survived in their original form but only in paraphrases.

6. The Novels

Form and Subject Matter

Like the laws enacted by his predecessors, the *Novels* of Justinian[87] might be applicable in a certain province, a certain region (comprising several provinces), or in the whole of the empire. The great majority of Justinian's *Novels* survive in Greek. In late antiquity, laws were not published by a central authority. There was no Official Journal; instead, they were sent directly to a functionary of the state or of the church. The addressee was named in the inscription. Different addressees could receive differing versions of the same law. The addressees of laws which were to be valid throughout the empire were usually the praetorian prefects, who were in charge of the great territorial subdivisions of the empire – the praetorian prefectures.[88] At the time of Justinian's accession there were two praetorian prefectures: Oriens – that is the east – with Constantinople as its capital; and Illyricum, with its capital of Thessaloniki.[89] At the end of 533, after some military successes Justinian again established a praetorian prefecture for Northern Africa (Carthage). From 537 the praetorian prefect for Italy (Ravenna) was again also appointed by eastern Rome.

Occasionally official notes have survived in the transmission of the *Novels* which record that other functionaries (and not only the addressee named in the inscription) were also to receive copies of a certain *Novel*. According to a note on Justinian's *Novel* on marriage law of 18 March 536, copies of the law were sent not only to the praetorian prefects, but also to the prefect of the city of Constantinople, the *magister officiorum*, the *comes sacrarum largitionum*, the *quaestor sacri palatii*, three generals, and the *comes rerum privatarum*.[90] If a law was concerned with ecclesiastical matters, the highest dignitaries of the church – the patriarchs – also received copies.[91] Of Justinian's *Novel* of 16 March 535 on the ordination of bishops and clerics, for example, copies are attested not only for the patriarch of Constantinople, but also for the patriarchs of Alexandria, Antioch, and Jerusalem, and for the praetorian prefects of the east and of Illyricum.[92] It is likely that if a law was to apply throughout the empire, copies were sent to all state and church officials whose area of responsibility was affected. The copies could differ depending on to whom they were addressed, taking into account, for example, the differing legal competencies of the individual addressees.[93] There is no one single 'original' of empire-wide *Novels*.

Usually, the recipients had to make the law known to their subordinate officials in the capital and especially in the provinces. Laws which were to apply throughout the empire could be published by putting them up for public display. Here, too, a publication 'pyramid' came into being, on which the epilogues of the *Novels* contain detailed instructions.[94] The laws were displayed in the cities and towns of the provinces. The actual locations of the displays, however, are rarely known. *Novels* touching on ecclesiastical matters were also put on display in churches. It seems that the *Novels* did not come into force at the time of their enactment by the emperor but only when they were published locally; the time at which they became law could, therefore, vary from region to region.[95]

As to their subject matter, the *Novels* cover all areas of the law,[96] among them administrative law (for example, public offices and the organization of the provinces), tax law, private law, criminal law, and frequently also ecclesiastical law (monasticism, preconditions for ordination, church property).[97] Only a short time after the second edition of the *Code* had come into force the *Novels* already revised it in several important fields: *Novel* 1 of 1 January 535 changed the law on heirs' compulsory shares according to the *lex Falcidia*; *Novel* 22 of 18 March 536 reformed marriage law and was in turn amended by *Novel* 117 of 18 December 542.

Editions, Transmission, and Textual Criticism

The authoritative edition of the *Novels* was begun by Rudolf Schöll and completed after his death by Wilhelm Kroll. It was first published in 1895; the last reprint dates from 1912.[98] The edition is based on the most comprehensive collection of predominantly Greek *Novels* which has survived, the Collection of 168 *Novels*, but it also takes into account the indirect Latin transmission in the *Authenticum* (for both, see below, 139). In the Schöll/Kroll edition the *Novels* regularly are arranged synoptically in two columns: the Greek text in the left column, the Latin translation of the *Authenticum* (if extant) in the right. Latin *Novels* and those in Greek for which there is no counterpart in the *Authenticum* are set in one column. The edition also includes a collection of 13 *Novels* of Justinian – the 'Thirteen Edicts' – and an appendix comprising additional *Novels* which were transmitted outside the collections. The edition does not include the epigraphic evidence.[99] The earliest edition featuring the Greek text of the *Novels* was created by Gregor Haloander and was published in Nuremberg in 1531.[100]

The *Novels* have survived in a number of (private) collections of varying extent. The plans for an official collection never came to fruition. In spite of the complexities of the transmission and the ensuing difficulties for reconstruction of the text, this also has one advantage: the individual

Novels are mostly transmitted in their entirety.[101] This means that in the case of the *Novels* those parts of a law which were of no practical legal value – and which were, therefore, omitted by the compilers of the Theodosian *Code* and Justinian's *Code* from the laws they included in their respective collections – have been preserved. The introduction in particular can provide important insights into what led to a certain piece of legislation, the motives behind it, and the ways in which the emperors portrayed themselves in their role as legislators.

Only a small fragment of a Latin *Novel* of Justinian written on papyrus (PSI 1346)[102] and a larger fragment of a *Novel* concerning Egypt (P. Oxy. 4400) have survived from late antiquity. The collections of *Novels* are therefore decisive for their transmission. The most comprehensive collection comprises 168 items (*Collectio CLXVIII Novellarum*).[103] It was created under Justinian and then extended up to the reign of Tiberius II. The collection includes 158 *Novels* of Justinian (or rather 156, as 2 Latin *Novels* occur twice); 4 *Novels* of Justin II (who reigned from 566–572); 3 *Novels* of Tiberius II (who reigned from 574–575); and, at the end, 3 edicts of praetorian prefects. Up to *Novel* 120 the *Novels* are arranged chronologically. Originally, the collection was bilingual, so included Greek as well as Latin *Novels*. The most important textual witness is the ms. Venezia Bibl. Marc. 179, which dates from the end of the twelfth or the beginning of the thirteenth century and originates from southern Italy.[104] It contains most of the Greek *Novels* but not the (originally 16) Latin ones. The *Collectio CLXVIII Novellarum* is also transmitted by the ms. Firenze Bibl. Med. Laur. plut. 80. 4ff. 1r–194v + Leiden UB Periz. F 35ff. 1r–2v (second half of the thirteenth century; probably from southern Italy),[105] but here too the Latin *Novels* are missing and the Greek text has been shortened and altered. The collection is also attested indirectly via the Breviary of Theodore of Hermoupolis (between 575 and 602).[106]

The *Authenticum* is based on a collection of (at least) 134 *Novels* of Justinian.[107] The collection mostly comprised Greek *Novels* and only a few (14) Latin ones. The Latin *Novels* have survived in the original; but, instead of the Greek *Novels*, the *Authenticum* features word-for-word translations of the Greek originals into Latin (*Kata poda*). These translations originated in the law schools of Justinian's time.[108] It seems that the *Kata poda* were originally written above the Greek text. The transmission of the *Authenticum* did not begin until the high middle ages.[109] The manuscripts vary in the number of *Novels* they contain.

Both the *Collectio CLXVIII Novellarum* and the collection on which the *Authenticum* is based were probably created in Constantinople.[110] These two main branches of transmission[111] are supplemented by a number of secondary transmissions – for example, the collection of the Thirteen Edicts (containing 13 *Novels* of Justinian), the *Collectio Ambrosiana* (14 *Novels* of Justinian in revised versions),[112] the *Collectio LXXXVII Capitulorum*, and the *Collectio XXV Capitulorum* (containing four *Novels*, three of them in their entirety).[113]

Only paraphrases of *Novels* are included in the *index* of the law professor Iulianus who taught in Constantinople (124 *Novels* of Justinian)[114] and in the *Syntagma novellarum* of Athanasius of Emesa[115] (153 *Novels* of Justinian, 3 *Novels* of Justin II).[116] Iulianus' *index*, the *Epitome Iuliani*, is an introductory course on the *Novels* in Latin, probably intended for students coming from the Latin-speaking west. The manuscripts of the *Epitome Iuliani*, which mostly date from the early middle ages, transmit a number of additional Latin *Novels* which are not attested elsewhere.[117] *Novels* also appear in scattered transmission[118] and in epigraphic testimonies (rescripts).

The Language of the Novels

When Justinian acceded to the throne the eastern Roman empire was already bilingual. In the territory administered by the praetorian prefect of the east, Greek was spoken almost exclusively. The prefecture of Illyricum, by contrast, was bilingual: in the northern part (the Danubian provinces) Latin was spoken, in the southern part the population spoke Greek. In Northern Africa, which became part of the empire at the end of 533, only Latin was spoken. As to Italy, at least from 537 the praetorian prefect of Italy was appointed by eastern Rome.

Novels in Latin are predominantly concerned with those parts of the empire where Latin was spoken (Northern Africa, Italy) or with internal matters of administration. Three *Novels* in Latin are attested which were to apply throughout the empire.[119] For Illyricum we know of *Novels* in Latin as well as in Greek. Accordingly, *Novels* whose scope of application was limited to Greek-speaking areas (for example, the eastern provinces or Egypt) were in Greek only. There is no certain evidence of empire-wide *Novels* in Greek.[120] Today only one *Novel* is extant in a Greek and a Latin version. It dates from 15 June 535 and deals with usurious money-lending to peasants (*Novels* 32 and 34).[121] The *Novel* applied in the diocese of Thracia, in the prefecture of the east. The Greek version addressed to the governor of the province of Haemimontus and the Latin version addressed to the governor of the province of Moesia secunda have survived.

As far as empire-wide *Novels* are concerned, an indication in a *Novel* dating from 1 May 538 (*Novel* 66) attests that there were two versions of an earlier *Novel* concerning inheritance law: a Greek version addressed to the praetorian prefect of the east (and probably also to the praetorian prefect of Illyricum), and a Latin version addressed to the praetorian prefect of Africa. The latter has not survived. It seems preferable to assume that those *Novels* which were intended to apply in the whole of the empire generally were bilingual and so existed in both a Latin and a Greek version.[122] In Italy, however, the Latin versions appear not to have been widely available: Pope Gregory the Great, in a letter to the *defensor* John dating from August 603, cites two *Novels* of Justinian only in a Latin *Kata poda*.[123]

Notes

1. D. Liebs, 'Jurisprudenz', in *Die Literatur des Umbruchs. Von der römischen zur christlichen Literatur 117 n. Chr. bis 284 n. Chr.*, ed. K. Sallmann (Munich, 1997), 83–217; B. H. Stolte, 'A Crisis of Jurisprudence? The End of Legal Writing in the Classical Tradition', in *Crises and Roman Empire. Proceedings of the Seventh Workshop of the International Network Impact of Empire (Nijmegen, June 20–24, 2006)*, ed. O. Hekster et al. (Leiden, 2007), 355–366.
2. D. Liebs, 'Recht und Rechtsliteratur', in *Restauration und Erneuerung. Die lateinische Literatur von 284 bis 374 n. Chr.*, ed. H. Herzog (Munich, 1989), 55–73.
3. Liebs (n. 2), 65–69, 71.
4. Liebs (n. 2), 68; D. Liebs, 'Ulpiani Opinionum libri VI', *TR* 41 (1973): 279–310.
5. They can be found in R. Seider, *Paläographie der lateinischen Papyri vol. 2.2: Juristische und christliche Texte* (Stuttgart, 1981); E. A. Lowe, *Codices Latini Antiquiores*, vols. 1–11 and suppl. (Oxford, 1934–1971; 2nd edn. of vol. 2.2, 1972). On P. Haun III. 45, see D. Nörr, 'P. Haun III 45 und der verlorene Traktat Modestins zum Vermächtnisrecht', *ZSS* 127 (2009): 53–114; F. Nasti, *Papyrus Hauniensis de legatis et fideicommissis. Pars prior (P Haun. III 45 recto + CPL 73 A e B recto)* (Naples, 2010). On the Fragmenta Londiniensia anteiustiniana, see S. Corcoran and B. Salway, 'A Lost Law-Code Rediscovered? The Fragmenta Londinensia anteiustiniana', ZSS 127 (2009): 677–678.
6. On the Veronese palimpsest of the *Institutes* of Gaius and on the fragments from Antinoe, see H. L. W. Nelson, *Überlieferung, Aufbau und Stil von Gai Institutiones* (Leiden, 1981).
7. See the excerpts in C.Th. 1.4.1 and in C.Th. 9.43.1. It is a matter of controversy whether there are two laws or two fragments of the same law.
8. C.Th. 1.4.2; on the date see O. Seeck, *Regesten der Kaiser und Päpste für die Jahre 311 bis 476 n. Chr.* (Stuttgart, 1919), 178.
9. See C. Wetzler, Rechtsstaat und Absolutismus. *Überlegungen zur Verfassung des spätantiken Kaiserreichs anhand von CJ 1.14.8* (Berlin, 1997), who also provides further information on the other parts of the *oratio*.
10. See Liebs (n. 2), 60–62, 62–64; S. Corcoran, *The Empire and the Tetrarchs. Imperial Pronouncements and Government*, 2nd edn. (Oxford, 2000), 25–42; S. Corcoran, 'The Publication of Laws in the Era of the Tetrachs', in *Diokletian und die Tetrarchie*, ed. A. Demandt et al. (Berlin, 2004), 56–73; S. Corcoran, 'The Tetrachy. Policy and Image as Reflected in Imperial Pronouncements', in *Die Tetrarchie. Ein neues*

Regierungssystem und seine mediale Präsentation, ed. D. Boschung and W. Eck (Wiesbaden, 2006), 31–61; M.U. Sperandio, *Codex Gregorianus. Origini e vicende* (Naples, 2005); S. Connolly, *Lives behind the Laws. The World of the Codex Hermogenianus* (Bloomington, 2010), reviewed by D. Liebs, *ZSS* 129 (2012): 711–724. Older literature can be found in L. Wenger, *Die Quellen des römischen Rechts* (Vienna, 1953), 534–536. On newly discovered fragments which belong most probably to a manuscript of the Codex Gregorianus, see S. Corcoran and B. Salway, 'Fragmenta Londiniensia Anteiustiniana: Preliminary Observations', *Roman Legal Tradition* 8 (2012): 63–83.

11. On the outward appearance of the imperial constitutions in the *Codex Gregorianus* and the *Codex Hermogenianus*, see Corcoran (n. 10, 2000), 42–48. On Gregorius as the name of the author, see D. Liebs, *Hofjuristen der römischen Kaiser bis Justinian* (Munich, 2010), 81–83. See further Liebs (n. 2), 61; Corcoran (n. 10, 2000), 33; Sperandio (n. 10), 291–299.
12. Liebs (n. 2), 63; Corcoran (n. 10, 2000), 37.
13. Edition: *Theodosiani libri XVI cum constitutionibus Sirmondianis*, ed. T. Mommsen (Berlin, 1905). *Codex Theodosianus*, ed. P. Krüger, vol. 1: books 1–6 (Berlin, 1923); vol. 2: books 7–8 (Berlin, 1926). For a translation, C. Pharr, *The Theodosian Code and Novels and the Sirmondian Constitutions. A Translation with Commentary, Glossary and Bibliography* (Princeton, 1952).
14. From the very extensive literature, see P. Krüger, *Geschichte der Quellen und Litteratur des römischen Rechts*, 2nd edn. (Munich – Leipzig, 1912), 324–331; Wenger (n. 10), 536–542; H. Siems, 'Codex Theodosianus', in *Reallexikon der germanischen Altertumskunde*, (Berlin – New York, 1984), vol. 5, cols. 47–52; J. Matthews, *Laying down the Law: a Study of the Theodosian Code* (New Haven, 2000); J. Harries and I. Wood, eds., *The Theodosian Code. Studies in the Imperial Law of Late Antiquity*, 2nd edn. (Bristol, 2010).
15. On this: L. Atzeri, *Gesta senatus Romani de Theodosiano publicando. Il Codice Teodosiano e la sua diffusione ufficiale in Occidente* (Berlin, 2008).
16. On the arrangement of the material, see Siems (n. 14), 49.
17. Edition: Mommsen (n. 13), 907–921.
18. On the continuing influence of the Theodosian *Code*, see M. Conrat, *Geschichte der Quellen und Literatur des römischen Rechts im früheren Mittelalter* (Leipzig, 1891; repr. Aalen, 1963).
19. On legal education in late antiquity, see B. Kübler, 'Rechtsunterricht', in *RE* IA.1 cols. 400–404; P. Collinet, *Histoire de l'école de droit de Beyrouth* (Paris, 1925), 207–259; D. Liebs, 'Juristenausbildung in der Spätantike', in *Juristenausbildung in Europa zwischen Tradition und Reform*, ed. C. Baldus et al. (Tübingen, 2008), 31–45.
20. On Berytos in particular, see Collinet (n. 19), 13–115; J. H. W. G. Liebeschuetz, 'Berytos', in *Reallexikon für Antike und Christentum*, suppl. 1 (Stuttgart, 2001), cols. 1038–1041; L. Jones Hall, *Roman Berytos. Beirut in Late Antiquity* (London – New York, 2004), 195–220.
21. For details, see Liebs (n. 19), 34–36.
22. D. Simon, 'Aus dem Codexunterricht des Thalelaios. B. Die Heroen', *ZSS* 87 (1970): 315–394; D. Liebs, 'Esoterische römische Rechtsliteratur vor Justinian', in *Akten des 36. Deutschen Rechtshistorikertages, Halle an der Saale, 10.–14. September 2006*, ed. R. Lieberwirt and H. Lück (Baden-Baden, 2008), 72–74 (with further lit.); Liebs (n. 19), 41–43.

23. On legal education in the West, see D. Liebs, *Die Jurisprudenz im spätantiken Italien* (Berlin, 1987); D. Liebs, *Römische Jurisprudenz in Gallien (2. bis 8. Jahrhundert)* (Berlin, 2002); and D. Liebs, *Römische Jurisprudenz in Africa mit Studien zu den pseudopaulinischen Sentenzen*, 2nd ed. (Berlin, 2005).
24. Liebs (n. 23, 1987), 150–162.
25. Liebs (n. 23, 2002), 138–141 (with information on the two authors); Krüger (n. 14), 346–348; G. Zanon, *Indicazioni di metodo giuridico dalla Consultatio veteris cuiusdam iurisconsulti*, 2nd edn. (Naples, 2009).
26. Liebs (n. 23, 1987), 162–174; W. Kaiser, *Die Epitome Iuliani. Beiträge zum römischen Recht im frühen Mittelalter und zum byzantinischen Rechtsunterricht* (Frankfurt, 2004), 993; U. Manthe, 'Wurde die Collatio vom Ambrosiaster Isaak geschrieben?', in *Festschrift für Rolf Knütel zum 70. Geburtstag*, ed. H. Altmeppen et al. (Heidelberg, 2010), 737–754; R. Frakes, *Compiling the Collatio Legum Mosaicarum et Romanarum in Late Antiquity* (Oxford, 2011).
27. From the extensive literature, see J. A. Evans, *The Emperor Justinian and the Byzantine Empire* (Westport, Conn., 2005); M. Maas, *The Cambridge Companion to the Age of Justinian* (Cambridge, 2005); A. Demandt, *Die Spätantike. Römische Geschichte von Diocletian bis Justinian, 284–565 n. Chr.*, 2nd edn. (Munich, 2008), 231–249; M. Meier, *Das andere Zeitalter Justinians. Kontingenzerfahrung und Kontingenzbewältigung im 6. Jahrhundert n. Chr.* (Göttingen, 2003); M. Meier, ed., *Justinian* (Darmstadt, 2011).
28. Accursius, gl. *veniunt* on Inst. 3.18.2: *Item iudiciales vagae sunt per totum corpus iuris* ('judicial stipulations are scattered throughout the whole of the Corpus iuris').
29. *Corpus juris civilis* in *IIII. partes distinctum . . . Authore Dionysio Gothofredo J. C.* (Geneva, 1583).
30. Justinian frequently used his name as an attribute, e.g. for new public offices he created (such as the *Praetor Iustinianus Pisidiae*) or for towns (e.g., Prima Iustiniana for his town of birth).
31. See 137.
32. On the fragments (particularly P. Oxy. 1814), see S. Corcoran, 'Justinian and his two Codes. Revisiting P. Oxy. 1814', *JJP* 38 (2008): 73–111; S. Corcoran, 'New Subscripts for Old Rescripts: The Vallicelliana Fragments of Justinian Code Book VII', *ZSS* 126 (2009): 401–422; S. Corcoran, 'The novus codex and the codex repetitae praelectionis: Justinian and his codex', in *Figures d'empire, fragments de mémoire: pouvoirs et identités dans le monde romain impérial (IIe s. av. n. è.–VIe s. de n. è.)*, ed. S. Benoist et al. (Villeneuve d'Ascq, 2011), 425–444.
33. D. Simon, 'Aus dem Codexunterricht des Thalelaios. C. Interpolationsberichte', *RIDA* 16 (1969): 283–308. On legal education in Justinian's day, see 126.
34. Most recently M. Varvaro, 'Contributo allo studio delle quinquaginta decisiones', *Annali del seminario giuridico della università di Palermo* 46 (2000): 359–519; C. Russo Ruggeri, *Studi sulle quinquaginta decisiones* (Milan, 1999); Wenger (n. 10), 572–576.
35. On the praetorian prefect of the East, see 137.
36. The names of some of them have been preserved in a law of Justinian dating from 23 May 535 (*Coll. CLXVIII Novv.* 35).
37. Justinian assumed that such an imperial privilege for certain jurists had existed. This is occasionally doubted in modern literature: for details, see K. Tuori, *Ancient Roman Lawyers and Modern Legal Ideals. Studies on the Impact of Contemporary Concerns in the Interpretation of Ancient Roman Legal History* (Frankfurt, 2007).

38. A. Zocco-Rosa, *Imp. Iustiniani institutionum palingenesia*, 2 vols., (Catania, 1908, 1911).
39. *Const. Tanta/Dedoken* §§ 21–22 state that no abbreviations may be used, that numbers must be written in full, and that comments may not be written into the body of the text. On the last point, see H. J. Scheltema, 'Das Kommentarverbot Justinians', *TR* 45 (1977): 307–331.
40. See the *Novel* of 13 August 554, ch. 11 (in Schöll-Kroll edn. (n. 98 below), 800, lines 38–39): *Iura insuper vel leges codicibus nostris insertas, quas iam sub edictali programmate in Italiam dudum misimus, obtinere sancimus* ('Furthermore, we ordain that the jurists' law [= *iura*] and the imperial legislation [= *leges*] which are included in our compilations and which we sent to Italy some time ago prefaced by an edict shall be valid'). A number of earlier *Novels* had, however, claimed validity in Italy even before that: see, most recently, W. Kaiser, 'Zum Zeitpunkt des Inkrafttretens von Kaisergesetzen unter Justinian', *ZSS* 127 (2010): 193–200.
41. It was, however, in use earlier, also by Justinian: see W. Kaiser, 'Zur äußeren Gestalt der Novellen Justinians', in *Introduzione al diritto bizantino. Da Giustiniano ai Basilici*, ed. J. H. A. Lokin and B. H. Stolte (Pavia, 2011), 169–173.
42. See the *Novel* of 13 August 554, ch. 11 (in Schöll-Kroll edn. (n. 98 below), 800 lines 40–42): *Sed et eas, quas postea promulgavimus constitutiones, iubemus sub edictali propositione vulgari, <et> ex eo tempore, quo sub edictali programmate vulgatae fuerint, etiam per partes Italiae obtinere* ('But we also command that those laws which we promulgated subsequently shall be made known to the public prefaced by an edict and that, from the time when they were made known to the public prefaced by an edict, they shall also be valid for the territories of Italy').
43. Kübler (n. 19), 400–404; Collinet (n. 19), 207–259; P. Pieler, 'Byzantinische Rechtsliteratur', in *Die hochsprachliche profane Literatur der Byzantiner*, ed. H. Hunger (Munich, 1978), vol. 2, 400–428; Liebs (n. 19), 32–36. On legal education in Justinian's time, see also the essays in H.J. Scheltema, *Opera minora ad historiam iuris pertinentia* (Groningen, 2004).
44. Edition: *Basilicorum libri LX, Series A (Textus)*, ed. H.J. Scheltema et al., 8 vols. (Groningen, 1955–1988).
45. Edition: *Basilicorum libri LX, Series B (Scholia)*, ed. H.J. Scheltema et al., 13 vols. (Groningen, 1953–1985).
46. *Prota*: D. 1–4, *Pars de iudiciis*: D. 5–11, *Pars de rebus*: D. 12–19, *Quarta pars*: D. 20–27, *Quinta pars*: D. 28–36, *Sexta pars*: D. 37–44, *Septima pars*: D. 45–50.
47. F. Bluhme, 'Die Ordnung der Fragmente in den Pandektentiteln', *Zeitschrift für geschichtliche Rechtswissenschaft* 4 (1820): 257–472.
48. D. Mantovani, *Digesto e masse Bluhmiane* (Milan, 1987); D. Mantovani, 'Le *masse* bluhmiane sono tre', *Seminarios Complutenses de derecho romano* 4 (1993): 87–119; W. Kaiser, 'Digestenentstehung und Digestenüberlieferung', *ZSS* 108 (1991): 330–350. A revised table showing which works belong to which masses can be found in T. Honoré, *Justinian's Digest. Character and Compilation* (Oxford, 2010), 151–161.
49. On the way the *Digest* commission worked see T. Honoré, *Tribonian* (London, 1978) and Honoré (n. 48), reviewed by T. Wallinga, *Edinburgh Law Review* 16 (2012): 119–122.
50. A table can be found in Honoré (n. 48), 162–209.
51. On this: Wenger (n. 10), 854–865; in detail F. Wieacker, *Römische Rechtsgeschichte* (Munich, 1988), vol. 1, 154–182.

52. Some examples from the law of status: C. 7.17.1 (AD 528): abolition of the *adsertor* in the action for freedom; C. 6.7.1 (AD 531): abolition of Latin citizenship; from inheritance law: *Const. Tanta/Dedoken* § 6a: abolition of the *SC Trebellianum*, § 6b: abolition of *caduca*.
53. The words *et cum diceret* can be explained either as a continuation of the rubric which has been corrupted in transmission (O. Lenel, *Palingenesia iuris civilis* (Leipzig, 1889), vol. 2, col. 526 n. 2) or as an addition by the author of the *Collatio*.
54. An overview of earlier editions of the *Digest* can be found in E. Spangenberg, *Einleitung in das roemisch-justinianeische Rechtsbuch oder Corpus iuris civilis Romani* (Hannover, 1817; repr. Aalen, 1970), 645–950. For details on the work on the *Digest* done by the Humanists, see H. E. Troje, *Crisis digestorum. Studien zur historia pandectarum* (Frankfurt, 2011).
55. *Digesta Iustiniani Augusti*, 2 vols. (Berlin, 1868–1870).
56. On the manuscript, its scribes and correctors, see W. Kaiser, 'Schreiber und Korrektoren des Codex Florentinus', *ZSS* 118 (2001): 133–219. It takes its name from the city of Florence where it is now kept in the Biblioteca Medicea Laurenziana.
57. On this, see, Kaiser (n. 56), 138 n. 17, 139 n. 19, 192.
58. See W. Kaiser, 'Digesten (Überlieferung)', in *Der Neue Pauly*, ed. H. Cancik et al. (Stuttgart – Weimar 1999), vol. 13, col. 846. On the Neapolitan fragments of the *Digest*, see most recently, B. Stolte, 'Some Thoughts on the Early History of the Digest Text. Appendix: Ms. Naples IV. A. 8 foll. 36–39 rescr.', *Subseciva Groningana* 6 (1999): 103–119; on the Pommersfelden fragments, see A. J. B. Sirks et al., *Ein frühbyzantinisches Szenario für die Amtswechslung in der Sitonie: Die griechischen Papyri aus Pommersfelden (PPG) mit einem Anhang über die Pommersfeldener Digestenfragmente und die Überlieferungsgeschichte der Digesten* (Munich, 1996), 137–142; on the transmission of D. 10.2 in agrimensorial manuscripts, see B. Stolte, 'Finium regundorum and the Agrimensores', *Subseciva Groningana* 5 (1992): 61–76, and most recently W. Kaiser, 'Spätantike Rechtstexte in agrimensorischen Sammlungen', *ZSS* 130 (2013): 273.
59. Ms. Berlin Staatsbibl. lat. fol. 269ff. 183–190, on which see, most recently, Kaiser (n. 26), 387–415.
60. On this, C. Radding and A. Ciaralli, *The Corpus iuris in the Middle Ages. Manuscripts and Transmission from the Sixth Century to the Juristic Revival* (Leiden – Boston, 2007).
61. The later canonical division was: *Digestum vetus*: D. 1–24.2; *Infortatium*: D. 24.3–38; *Digestum novum*: D. 39–50.
62. On the transmission, see W. Kaiser, 'Zur Textkritik von D. 19, 1, 30, 1 (Africanus, 8 quaest.)', in *Africani quaestiones: Studien zur Geschichte und Dogmatik des Privatrechts*, ed. J. Harke (Berlin – Heidelberg, 2011), 57–59; W. Kaiser, 'Besserlesungen in den Vulgathandschriften gegenüber Codex Florentinus und Basiliken? Zur Genuinität der erneuten Inskription vor D. 3, 5, 30, 3 (Pap. 2 resp.) in den Handschriften des Digestum vetus', *Römische Jurisprudenz. Dogmatik, Überlieferung, Rezeption. Festschrift für Detlef Liebs zum 75. Geburtstag*, ed. K. Muscheler (Berlin, 2011), 302–303.
63. Recently it has been suggested as an alternative that, conversely, an incomplete copy of the *Digest* was completed using a copy of the *Codex Florentinus* (similar to the process that can be seen in the manuscripts of the *Codex Iustinianus*).
64. See B. H. Stolte, 'The Value of the Byzantine Tradition for Textual Criticism of the Corpus Iuris Civilis. "Graeca leguntur"', in Lokin and Stolte (n. 42), 667–680. On the relevance of two newly discovered palimpsest manuscripts of the *Basilica* for textual

criticism, see B. Stolte, 'Zwei neue Basilikenhandschriften in der Wiener Nationalbibliothek II: Rechtshistorische Analyse. Mit 30 Tafeln', in *Quellen zur byzantinischen Rechtspraxis. Aspekte der Textüberlieferung, Paläographie und Diplomatik. Akten des internationalen Symposiums, Wien, 5.–7.11.2007*, ed. C. Gastgeber (Vienna, 2010), 139–151.

65. On this, see Wenger (n. 10), 600–610; Nelson (n. 6), 267–291; E. Metzger, *A Companion to Justinian's Institutes* (Ithaca, 1998); G. Luchetti, *Nuove ricerche sulle Istituzioni di Giustiniano* (Milan, 2004).
66. *Institutiones Iustiniani*, ed. P. Krüger (1st edn., Berlin, 1867; 4th edn., Berlin, 1921).
67. On this: Kaiser (n. 26), 693–695; Radding and Ciaralli (n. 60); Macino (2008).
68. On the *Capitula legis Romanae* (*Lex Romana canonice compta*), see Kaiser (n. 26), 493–522, 579–588.
69. W. Kaiser, 'Ein unbekanntes Zitat von Institutiones Iustiniani 3, 6 pr.–8 in einer Abhandlung des Hrabanus Maurus zum Ehehindernis der Verwandtschaft', in *Festschrift für Rolf Knütel zum 70. Geburtstag*, ed. H. Altmeppen et al. (Heidelberg, 2010), 513–557.
70. A. Giomaro, *Il Codex repetitae praelectionis. Contributi allo studio dello schema delle raccolte normative da Teodosio a Giustiniano* (Mursia, 2001); Wenger (n. 10), 569–572, 638–651; P. Jörs, 'Codex Iustinianus', in *RE* IV.1 (Stuttgart, 1900) cols. 167–170.
71. The *Code* begins with the law of the emperors Gratian, Valentinian II, and Theodosius I of 380 which declares Christianity to be the state religion.
72. On parallel transmissions, Wenger (n. 10), 643–648. The textual differences between the *Codex Iustinianus* and the *Codex Theodosianus* are pointed out by Mommsen in his edition of the *Codex Theodosianus* (above, n. 13).
73. C. 4.44.2 (Diocl., AD 285; interpolated).
74. The difference in the form of the verb at the end (*debuerat* instead *debuerit*) may come from the copy of the *Codex Theodosianus* used by the compilers of the *Codex Iustinianus* or it may have occurred in the course of the manuscript transmission of the *Codex Theodosianus* or the *Codex Iustinianus*.
75. See, e.g., C. 4.38.14, which is an exact reproduction of C.Th. 3.1.6 (Grat., Valent., Theod.; AD 391), but limits the applicability of the constitution by adding a clause at the end: *nisi lex specialiter quasdam personas hoc facere prohibuerit* ('unless a law specifically prohibits certain persons from doing this').
76. *Codex Iustinianus*, ed. P. Krüger (Berlin, 1877).
77. Ms. Verona Bibl. Cap. LXII (60); Lowe (n. 5), vol. 4, 511; an apographum can be found in P. Krüger, *Codicis Iustiniani fragmenta Veronensia* (Berlin, 1874).
78. Radding and Ciaralli (n. 60), 37.
79. Kaiser (n. 26), 703–704; Radding and Ciaralli (n. 60).
80. On the manuscript transmission, see G. Dolezalek, *Repertorium manuscriptorum veterum Codicis Iustiniani*, 2 vols. (Frankfurt, 1985); C. Tort-Martorell, *Tradición textual del Codex Iustinianus. Un estudio del libro 2* (Frankfurt, 1989); on new finds, see S. Corcoran (n. 32, 2009), 401–422; S. Corcoran, 'After Krüger: Observations on Some Additional or Revised Justinian Code Headings and Subscripts', *ZSS* 126 (2009): 423–439.
81. Edition: *Adnotationes codicum domini Justiniani (Summa Perusina)*, ed. F. Patetta, *BIDR* 12 (1900). On the facsimile edition of the manuscript ms. Perugia, Bibl. Capitolare 32, see Kaiser (n. 40), 626–629.

82. On this: Liebs (n. 23, 1987), 276–282; Kaiser (n. 26), 335–346.
83. Edition: *Collectio tripartita. Justinian on Religious and Ecclesiastical Affairs*, ed. N. van der Wal and B. H. Stolte (Groningen, 1994), XIII–XXXV.
84. Edition: *Collectio XXV capitulorum*, ed. G. E. Heimbach, in *Anekdota* vol. 2 (Leipzig, 1840), XXVII–XL, 145–201.
85. Edition: *Collectio LXXXVII capitulorum*, ed. G. E. Heimbach, in *Anekdota* vol. 2 (Leipzig, 1840), XLI–LXVI, 202–237.
86. For details Krüger (n. 76), X–XI.
87. For details, see F. Biener, *Geschichte der Novellen Justinians* (Berlin, 1824, repr. 1970); Wenger (n. 10), 652–679.
88. Demandt (n. 27), 292–294; A. H. M. Jones, *The Later Roman Empire 284–602. A Social, Economic and Administrative Survey*, 3 vols. (Oxford, 1964).
89. On the plans for moving the seat of the prefecture to *Iustiniana prima* (Caričin Grad), see W. Kaiser, 'Die Zweisprachigkeit reichsweiter Novellen unter Justinian. Studien zu den Novellen Justinians (I)', *ZSS* 129 (2012): 393–394.
90. *Coll. CLXVIII Novv.* 22 (in Schöll-Kroll edn. (n. 98 below), 186 line 33–187 line 21). On the officials, see Demandt (n. 27) and Jones (n. 88).
91. W. Kaiser, 'Zur Ausfertigung justinianischer Novellen an staatliche und kirchliche Würdenträger', in *Novellae constitutiones. L'ultima legislazione di giustiniano tra oriente e occidente, da Triboniano a Savigny. Atti del Convegno Internazionale Teramo, 30–31 ottobre 2009*, ed. L. LoSchiavo et al. (Naples, 2011), 25–30.
92. *Coll. CLXVIII Novv.* 6 (in Schöll-Kroll edn. (n. 98 below), 47, lines 29–35); Kaiser (n. 91), 30–36.
93. Kaiser (n. 91), 54–57.
94. Insights into the publication within the church hierarchy can be gained from the epilogue of the *Novel* of 16 March 535 (in Schöll-Kroll edn. (n. 98 below), 47, lines 14–28).
95. On this (and on the opposing view), see Kaiser (n. 40), 172–201. On Justinian's legislation being sent to Italy, see 126.
96. A systematic overview can be found in N. van der Wal, *Manuale Novellarum Justiniani. Aperçu systématique du contenu des novelles de Justinian*, 2nd edn. (Groningen – Amsterdam, 1998); a chronological one in T. C. Lounghis et al., *Regesten der Kaiserurkunden des oströmischen Reiches von 476 bis 565* (Nicosia, 2005).
97. For further references see Kaiser (n. 91), 25 n. 3.
98. *Corpus iuris civilis* vol. 3: Novellae, ed. R. Schöll and G. Kroll; 4th edn., Berlin, 1912.
99. See M. Amelotti, *Le costituzioni giustinianee nei papiri e nelle epigrafi*, 2nd edn. (Milan, 1985) and the overview in D. Feissel, 'Les actes de l'État impérial dans l'epigraphie tardive (324–610): Prolégomènes à un inventaire', in *Selbstdarstellung und Kommunikation. Die Veröffentlichung staatlicher Urkunden auf Stein und Bronze in der römischen Welt*, ed. R. Haensch (Munich, 2009), 97–128.
100. On the reconstruction of the text of the *Novels* in the age of Humanism, see H. E. Troje, *Graeca leguntur: die Aneignung des byzantinischen Rechts und der Entstehung eines humanistischen Corpus iuris civilis in der Jurisprudenz des 16. Jahrhunderts* (Cologne – Vienna, 1971); H. E. Troje, *Humanistische Jurisprudenz. Studien zur europäischen Rechtswissenschaft unter dem Einfluß des Humanismus* (Goldbach, 1993); and most recently Troje (n. 54).
101. On the composition of a late antique imperial constitution, see F. Dölger and J. Karayannopoulos, *Byzantinische Urkundenlehre* (Munich, 1968), 77.

102. S. Corcoran, 'Two Tales, Two Cities: Antinoopolis and Nottingham', in *Wolf Liebeschuetz Reflected: Essays Presented by Colleagues, Friends, and Pupils*, ed. J. Drinkwater and B. Salway (London, 2007), 194–200.
103. P. Noailles, *Les collections de novelles de l'empereur Justinian. Vol. 2: La collection grecque des 168 novelles* (Paris, 1914), with detailed information on the manuscripts; W. Kaiser, 'Die Zweisprachigkeit reichsweiter Novellen unter Justinian. Studien zu den Novellen Justinians (I)', *ZSS* 129 (2012): 397–402.
104. L. Burgmann et al., *Repertorium der Handschriften des byzantinischen Rechts. Teil 1: Die Handschriften des weltlichen Rechts (Nr. 1–327)* (Frankfurt, 1995), 339 n. 296.
105. Burgmann (n. 104), 85–86 n. 67, 119 n. 95.
106. *Theodori scholastici Breviarium Novellarum*, ed. K. E. Zachariae von Lingenthal in *Anekdota* (Leipzig, 1843), 1–165.
107. Edition: *Authenticum. Novellarum constitutionum Iustiniani versio vulgata*, ed. G. E. Heimbach (Leipzig, 1846–1851, repr. 1974); *Corpus iuris civilis* vol. 3 (above, n. 98); literature can be found in Kaiser (n. 89), 404 n. 65; L. LoSchiavo, 'Il codex graecus e le origini del Liber authenticorum. Due contributi alla storia dell'Authenticum', *ZSS* 127 (2010): 115–171.
108. H. J. Scheltema, 'Subseciva XI. Das Authenticum', *TR* 31 (1963): 275–279.
109. See now L. LoSchiavo, 'La riscoperta dell'Authenticum e la prima esegesi die Glossatori', in *Novellae constitutiones. L'ultima legislazione di giustiniano tra oriente e occidente, da Triboniano a Savigny. Atti del Convegno Internazionale Teramo, 30–31 ottobre 2009*, ed. L. LoSchiavo et al. (Naples, 2011).
110. Kaiser (n. 103), 427–428.
111. On the vocabulary of the Greek *Novels*, see A. M. Bartoletti Colombo, *Novellae, pars Graeca*, 7 vols. (Milan, 1984–1989); on the Latin *Novels* and the *Kata poda* in the *Authenticum*, A. M. Bartoletti Colombo, *Novellae, pars Latina*, 10 vols. (Milan, 1977–1979).
112. The readings are included in the apparatus of the Schöll-Kroll edn. On the collection, see S. Troianos, 'Die Collectio Ambrosiana', in D. Simon, *Fontes minores II* (Frankfurt, 1977), 30–48.
113. On the edition of the two collections, see above nn. 84, 85.
114. Edition: *Iuliani epitome Latina Novellarum Iustiniani*, ed. G. Hänel (Leipzig, 1873). For details on the *Epitome Iuliani*, see Kaiser (n. 26) and LoSchiavo (n. 107).
115. Edition: *Das Novellensyntagma des Athanasios von Emesa*, ed. D. Simon and S. Troianos (Frankfurt, 1989).
116. D. Simon, 'Das Novellenexemplar des Athanasios', in D. Simon, *Fontes minores VII* (Frankfurt, 1986), 117–140, 129, 134–139.
117. On the appendices of the manuscripts of the *Epitome Iuliani*, see Kaiser (n. 26), 347–374.
118. See the index in Burgmann (n. 104).
119. Kaiser (n. 103), 432.
120. Kaiser (n. 103), 453.
121. W. Kaiser, 'Unterschiede zwischen griechischen und lateinischen Ausfertigungen von Novellen am Beispiel des Gesetzes vom 1. Juni 535 über Darlehen an Bauern. Studien zu den Novellen Justinians (II)', *ZSS* 129 (2012): 475–500.
122. Kaiser (n. 103), 472.
123. W. Kaiser, 'Nachvergleichungen von Novellen- und Codexzitaten in einer frühmittelalterlichen Sammlung mit Exzerpten aus dem Register Gregors d. Gr. (Reg. 13, 49 [50])', *ZSS* 125 (2008): 603–613.

Part IV

PRIVATE LAW IN ROMAN SOCIETY

9 Slavery, Family, and Status

Andrew Lewis

1. Introduction

This chapter considers the key legal institutions that governed the lives of Roman citizens and others who were affected by Roman law. The background is the central question of how a person became a legitimate Roman citizen; interlinked with this is the unique Roman institution of paternal power. These key themes are reflected throughout the law on adoption, marriage and divorce, and on tutors and guardians. The chapter considers these questions not just as a matter of legal doctrine but also, so far as possible, in their social context. It also deals with the place occupied by slaves and freedmen alongside the elaborate legal institutions applicable to freeborn Roman citizens.[1]

Subordination was a permanent feature of Roman social and legal life. Only a few, exclusively male, Roman citizens possessed full legal rights in both private and public life. The majority of free male citizens and nearly all free female citizens were subordinate within their families and as such were denied full status in private law. Male citizens over the age of puberty, later settled at 14 years of age, were in principle able to participate as citizens in public life, but in private law they remained subordinated to their fathers and other male ascendants. A very large proportion of the population was not free at all: as slaves they lacked all personal rights in either private or public law.

In the course of the first century AD the little Spanish town of Irni was granted an urban charter. This has recently come to light in the form of several bronze tablets designed to be displayed in the forum of the town and recovered from their resting place by means of metal detectors. Amongst the provisions of the charter, which was of a standard type promulgated throughout the western part of the Roman Empire but only very partially preserved elsewhere, was a section on family law headed: 'That those who become Roman citizens remain in the same *manus*, *mancipium* and *potestas*'.[2]

The clause dealt with the situation which arose when, by whatever means, citizens of the town of Irni obtained Roman citizenship, a process we will glance at later in this chapter. The three key terms *manus*, *mancipium*, and *potestas* are used to describe different sorts of subordinate status. Those in *manus* are wives bound to their husbands by the old formal modes of marriage. *Mancipium* in the usage of the jurists is a term for a peculiar temporary status created in the process of emancipation, but it seems to have been the original Roman term for slavery: *mancipi* is a term for slaves. *Potestas* is a term used classically to describe both the father's power over his children and the master's power over his slaves. The two situations share enough in common juristically for the anomaly to be borne, but socially speaking it must always have been a curiosity. Because it is by far the most common term for subordination, we start with *potestas*.

2. POTESTAS

Potestas means power, and in this context it refers to the absolute control the one with *potestas* wields over the subordinate. As already noted, in classical law it is used in what appear to us – and must indeed in most contexts have appeared to the Romans – to be two very different social situations: slaves are said to be in the *potestas* of their master, and children in the *potestas* of their *paterfamilias* (their father or older male ascendant).

Slaves[3]

Slaves in Roman law were regarded as the property of their masters. They lacked all personal rights and responsibilities. They could be dealt with as animals, bought and sold and mistreated at will. Some imperial legislation limited the powers of masters to inflict serious harm or to kill their slaves, but their very enactment demonstrates the lack of a general restriction.

The earliest slaves were those enemies captured in war.[4] The Romans acknowledged as a general principle that prisoners of war lost their previous status, making provision for the case where a Roman was captured by the enemy. Such a prisoner lost his Roman citizenship until such time as he was able to regain it on returning to Roman territory, a process known as *postliminium*. Slaves captured by the Romans in war were the property of their captors. Those born to slave mothers in Rome were also slaves. As no personal relationships were recognized within slavery it did not matter who the child's father was. Additionally, by legislation under Claudius, the *SC Claudianum* of AD 53, the offspring of a freewoman who was living with a slave without the slave owner's permission were born slaves, and the woman herself reduced into slavery. By agreement with the slave's owner the woman might remain free whilst only her issue became slaves. Gaius tells us that this latter provision was abolished under Hadrian (AD 117–138).[5]

In the early Republic it was possible for a Roman citizen to be reduced to slavery as a punishment for manifest theft, although it also appears that they were sold to foreigners out of Rome, across the Tiber (*trans Tiberim*). Later, those condemned to death or to work in the mines became slaves from the moment of condemnation, their property forfeited to the state. These were not the property of individual masters but rather of the state, and are sometimes referred to as public slaves.

In some cases apparent free persons could be reduced to slavery. Those who gained their freedom from their masters, as a result of processes to be discussed shortly, might in certain circumstances have this freedom revoked for ingratitude. During the Republic this might occur by the simple will of the master, but the formalizing of hitherto informal manumission meant that in the Empire it required an imperial decree, although efforts were made to create a formal process of recall.[6] A free person who arranged to have himself sold into slavery fraudulently, hoping subsequently to recover his freedom and to share in the profits, was held to have become a slave: Hadrian held that if the purchase price were returned he might recover his freedom without express manumission. Where free children were sold into slavery the general principle was that this could not change their status, but it was later ruled that in the case of the newborn the purchaser was entitled to have the child redeemed for whatever he was worth as a slave. In effect this made the child a slave, though on redemption he was recognized as freeborn rather than a freedman.

The effects of slavery were, to the modern eye, considerable. No personal relationships were recognized between slaves so there was no marriage and no familial responsibilities. Because they lacked legal personality slaves could not enter into contracts on their own account or own property. Nor were they directly publicly liable for any wrongdoing for which they were morally responsible: rather, the master was liable, though he had the right to surrender the slave in discharge of his liability – the so-called noxal surrender. Lacking their own capacity, however, slaves were able to act on behalf of their master, managing his property and creating commercial obligations on his behalf. This was the more valuable as Roman law, perhaps for this very reason, was slow to permit one free person to act as another's agent.

Manumission A slave could be released from slavery by his master. It must always have been open to a master to treat his slave more generously and give him a measure of independence, but until the praetor intervened towards the end of the Republic to restrict masters' profligacy the slave who was informally released at his master's will was always liable to be reduced once again to slavery. From an early date, however, devices existed whereby a slave might acquire independence: a striking characteristic of these legal devices is that the slave thereby acquired full Roman citizenship. In later times this almost miraculous transition from the least of beings to the most important of citizens was curious; when Rome was but one small city-state amongst other Latin city-states it was perhaps not so surprising. Even during the Republic, however, a freedperson (someone who had acquired citizenship on release from slavery) was distinguishable from a free person, born into that status.

The earliest method for releasing a slave seems to have been incorporation in the census list. This list (or, rather, lists), created every five years or so, determined those entitled as Roman citizens to exercise their vote in one of the various voting categories of the Republican assemblies. By directing his slave to present himself before the censors, the enrolling magistrates, the master offered the slave his freedom, which was confirmed by the magistrates' action of enrolment. There must always have been an element of fiction in this device as one must suppose that the magistrates were normally concerned only to enrol those already entitled to vote. A less public but still formal mechanism existed in the form of manumission *vindicta*. This takes the form of a compromised lawsuit, bearing its fictive character on its face. The master wishing to release his slave procures a friend to litigate the question of the slave's status with him. Such a procedure might fairly be used in a case, say, where the slave's status – perhaps a child sold into slavery – was genuinely in doubt. The litigants appeared before the praetor as if for the preliminary stage of the lawsuit, the claimant (*adsertor libertatis*) made his claim, the defendant master remained silent, and, consequently, the praetor declared the slave to be free. Again, as with manumission *censu*, we can observe the combination of the master's will and the magistrate's authority combining to create a new, free citizen. But a genuine case would result in a freeborn citizen (*ingenuus*) hitherto improperly held in slavery, whereas manumission produces a citizen who is a freedperson (*libertinus*) who obtains a subservient status. Not eligible for public office, he continues to owe duties to his former master. A third means existed for formally freeing slaves. A master might, in his will, grant his slaves their freedom as a legacy. Such slaves could be expected to show their gratitude by appropriate displays of grief at the funeral, but the master's generosity was exercised at the expense of the heir and, in the case of large estates, the public good. Legislation at the turn of the eras restricted both the number of slaves who could be released in this way, proportional to the size of the estate, and the status into which they would come on release. Those who were under the age of 30 acquired their freedom only as Latins, not as Roman citizens.[7]

Latin status conferred rights somewhat greater than those exercised by foreigners. It had its origin in the shared culture of the Latin city-states of which Rome was originally one. By the end of the Republic the former Latin city-states had all acquired rights of Roman citizenship, but there continued a number of Latin colonies, founded elsewhere in the Mediterranean, whose citizens continued to enjoy only Latin status. It was open to Latins to acquire Roman citizenship in various ways. The *lex Aelia Sentia* of AD 4 borrowed the notion in order to create a class of freedpersons for whom Roman citizenship was a goal to be achieved. This they could do by serving in the fire service or performing other public duties, or, alternatively, by marrying another Latin and producing a child, at which point all three persons, parents and child, could apply for citizenship.[8]

Those slaves whose masters did not arrange to free them formally by census, will, or *vindicta* could nevertheless, as we have seen, be allowed an informal measure of freedom. Such liberty was initially enjoyed only until the master chose to revoke it, the slave having no legal standing to object. Towards the end of the Republic, and possibly only in the early Empire, the praetor began to offer legal protection to former slaves who could show that they had been granted freedom before the master's friends or in a similar public manner. Such slaves were said to be free under the protection of the praetor (*in libertate tuitione praetoris*). By granting or refusing actions the praetor could ensure that they retained their independence. The status was, however, fragile, and a *lex Junia* of unknown date formalized their status as Latins: they were known as Junian Latins to distinguish them from others.[9]

EFFECTS OF SLAVERY The slave was regarded as lacking all capacity, even to form personal relationships. Slave unions were, of course, known, but there was no legal restriction on the master's right to separate partners and their children. It was, however, easy to be misled, and the jurist Paul has to point out that the mere use of standard terms like *uxor*, *pater*, and *filius* in relation to slaves creates no rights,[10] and, as he says elsewhere, it is not easy to tell a freeman from a slave.[11]

Slaves were used to manage property and goods belonging to their masters – for example, being put in charge of a shop or a ship. For this and other purposes it was usual for masters to grant slaves rights over part of their property, called the slave's *peculium*. Strictly speaking, this was a private arrangement between master and slave which could be reviewed at any time without legal restriction. But in practice it gave rights to third parties in dealings with the slave and to this extent the master was bound. The praetor permitted actions to be brought in effect against a slave-manager either on the basis of the *peculium* or on the master's express or implied authority. In either case it was the master's economic interests which were at stake, although in the former case there was a form of limited liability, the limit being the size of the slave's *peculium*.

If a slave committed an act which in a citizen would have amounted to a wrong inviting legal redress, theft, or damage to property, then the master was in principle liable. However, in some circumstances he was able to escape by the expedient of handing the offender over to the victim in expiation – the so-called noxal surrender.

Freedmen *(Lībertīnī)*[12]

Those citizens who had been freed from slavery did not enjoy full equality with the freeborn Roman. Most of the restrictions were matters of public or constitutional law, limiting their voting rights and preventing their standing for office. But they also continued to owe duties to their former master, now their patron. During life this involved showing respect (*obsequium*), which limited their rights to sue the patron and obliged them to perform certain agreed services. The former master could punish them with impunity as the praetor would decline to allow a complaint 'from one who was but yesterday a slave and is now free'.[13] There was a mutual obligation to provide for each other in time of need. On death the patron was a freedman's intestate heir if there were no children. If the freedman made a will then the patron took shares with all but children under the praetorian scheme of succession.

Those freed as Junian Latins were in a similar situation during their life, but on death their property reverted to their former master. This was not succession, and any family of the deceased was wholly excluded, a situation which troubled Justinian who abolished the status ('in their last breath they lost both life and liberty').[14] Slaves who had been seriously punished by their masters were on manumission placed in a special class of *dediticii*, assimilated to conquered peoples not granted a constitution by reason of their treachery. Unlike Latins they were debarred from ever becoming citizens and were required to live at least 100 miles from Rome.

Children

A peculiarity of Roman law, recognized as such by the Romans,[15] was that the subordination of members of the family to the *paterfamilias*, or eldest male progenitor, was life-long, being in principle ended only by the death of the *paterfamilias*. All those who were born of a valid Roman marriage were in *patria potestas* (paternal power), and indeed the jurists discuss the institution of marriage principally from this perspective. Although most were in the *potestas* of their natural relatives, it was possible to create such subordination artificially by process of adoption. Conversely, those who were freed from *potestas* (typically through the death of their *paterfamilias*) before they came to maturity were free from subordination but required the assistance of tutors in order to manage their property.

The subordination of paternal power (*patria potestas*) applied only in private law and did not restrict capacities in public office. The Romans enjoyed stories which pointed up the potential conflicts this could create, as when a consul meeting his father on horseback in the street ordered him to dismount in deference to his status as chief magistrate.[16]

(I) SONS Although many of the features of subordination affected both males and females equally, the social restrictions imposed upon women in Rome ensured that most are discussed only in the case of sons. Additional legal restrictions upon daughters are dealt with separately below.

Although a *paterfamilias* exercised extensive powers of control over his subordinates, he was expected to exercise power in the context of a family council and not arbitrarily. In classical times the *paterfamilias* was not able to punish disobedience with death. Ulpian says that a father should not kill his son unheard, but rather accuse him before the governor; Hadrian deported a father who killed his son, observing that paternal power should be expressed in mutual respect not violence:[17] the somewhat restrained manner in which this limitation on paternal power was expressed reveals the extent of its residual force on the Roman mind.

LEGAL CAPACITY Subordinate members of the Roman family, even though freeborn, lacked basic legal capacity in private law. In this they were little different from slaves. Correspondingly, any capacity attributed to them belonged to their *paterfamilias*: any property they acquired was acquired for him and any benefits under contract accrued to him. Like slaves, they could be accorded a *peculium* with which to deal. From the time of Augustus this came more and more to be regarded as the property of the son. In particular, Augustus permitted property acquired whilst serving with the legions to be kept separate from paternal property (the *peculium castrense*): it could be disposed of by military will.[18] Under Constantine these rights were extended to property acquired in any public service, *quasi castrense* and to property acquired from the mother (*bona materna*).[19] These differences from the *peculium* of slaves reflect the free status of sons and the expectation that they will eventually acquire full legal status.

Like slaves, sons-in-power were formally incapable of being sued in the case of wrongdoing for lack of legal capacity. The *paterfamilias* could and was made liable, however, and at least in theory retained the liberty of surrendering the offender in discharge of his responsibility. Justinian, in stressing how unlikely it seems to him that one could surrender a son let alone a daughter in such circumstances, merely serves to indicate the potency of the idea.[20]

The *paterfamilias*' consent was required for a child's valid marriage, and until the end of the second century AD he could compel a divorce without reason: imperial legislation merely imposed a requirement that it be not exercised capriciously, and even under Justinian it remained available for substantial cause.[21]

EMANCIPATION Whilst under *patria potestas* a child of whatever age remained subordinate to the *pater* until he died. At that point his children would acquire independence, becoming (in the untranslatable legal phrase) *sui iuris*. It was possible in some circumstances for a father to free his son or daughter from his power during his own lifetime. A consequence was that the child so emancipated left its birth family, losing any inheritance rights or likelihood of support. To bring this about the jurists of the mid-Republic utilized a rule of the Twelve Tables: 'If a father sell his son three times the son is to be free from the father.'[22] It is plausibly suggested that the rule was originally intended to restrain, or at least minimize, the capacity of the father to abuse his power by selling his son's labour by *mancipatio*, the formal sale and conveyance required for *res mancipi* which included slaves. We may suppose that in an agricultural society such labour might be in demand at harvest time but at other times the son's buyer might not wish to carry the extra expense of his keep and so return him to his father. Whilst in the hands of the purchaser, the son was in effect in a state of slavery (*in mancipio*), and a formal manumission *vindicta* would be needed to release and return him to his father's power. Under the Twelve Tables rule repeated sales would result in a situation where, if so released by the purchaser, the son became independent, although as a formally released slave he would owe his former master a duty of *obsequium*. The jurists' scheme simply consisted in having the father sell his son to a friend who would release him, returning him to the power of his father, and having this repeated three times. A twist was provided at the end, however, to avoid the father losing his rights completely: after the third sale, the son being *in mancipio* to the purchaser, the latter would convey him formally back to his father, to whom he was now said to be in a position of subordination as a slave, *in mancipio* but not, owing to the rule of the Twelve Tables, *in potestate*. Now, when the father manumitted his son *vindicta* the latter acquired his independence but continued to owe respect to his (former) *paterfamilias*.

Legitimation Other than by birth within a Roman marriage, to be discussed below (165), children could enter paternal power by being legitimated or through adoption. We only hear of legitimation by the subsequent marriage of the parents in the late Empire. Constantine permitted it for existing situations, prohibiting it for the future; only under Justinian was it made generally available in cases where the parents might have been married at the time of conception, thereby excluding cases of adultery.[23]

Adoption and Adrogation Adoption was a common event in Roman families of high status. It was often utilized as an inheritance strategy by those who lacked natural descendants who could inherit as a matter of civil law. At civil law those who were adopted left their family of origin and became fully and exclusively members of their adopted family. Roman religion was in origin a series of family cults; responsibility for maintaining the family's worship and memorialization of its ancestors fell on the *paterfamilias* as head of the family. Each independent Roman citizen, a person *sui iuris*, was in principle the head of his own family; in consequence, his adoption into another family raised a religious question, balancing the termination of his existing family against the possible prolongation of the cult of the family into which he was to be adopted. Adoption in these circumstances – strictly speaking, adrogation – required both religious and legislative scrutiny.

In the Republic adrogation was effected by means of private legislation in one of the popular assemblies, the *comitia curiata*. This consisted of the members of the *comitia centuriata* presided over by the chief priest, the *pontifex maximus*. Both parties, the adopter and the adoptee, had to be present in the assembly, so it was not possible to adrogate persons below the age of puberty or women, who could not attend. The religious investigation, to establish the propriety of the adoption, once perhaps rigorous, became a formality as the importance of the ancestral religion diminished. The proposal – the formal question or *rogatio* – was put to the assembly, and on its passing the adoptee became a member of his new family.[24]

Having been independent (*sui iuris*) before his adoption, on being adrogated the adoptee fell under the *patria potestas* of his adoptive father. All of his property became the property of his new father and henceforward, until he should regain his independence on his father's death, he ceased to have a separate legal personality in private law. Cicero's enemy Clodius, born into the patrician family of the Claudii, arranged his own adrogation (and subsequent emancipation) by a plebeian, so as to be qualified to stand for election as a tribune of the plebs.[25]

In the case of those who were still under *patria potestas* in their family of birth, the formal barriers to adoption were different. It was considered necessary to first break the power of the birth father before creating a new *potestas* link in the new family. To this end the jurists implemented a strategy which made use of the legal device already utilized to permit emancipation. The *patria potestas* of the birth father was broken by means of three sales to a friend, after the third of which the son was *in mancipio* to the friend. At this point it was open to the adoptive father to claim him as his son but Gaius, our main source for this procedure, says that it was more convenient (*commodius*) for the birth father to receive him *in mancipio* as in the case of emancipation and for the adoptive father to make his claim from him.[26] This is done by commencing a formal legal action before the praetor claiming that he is his son. There is a plausible basis for such a claim in a case where someone's son is being improperly and mistakenly held as another's slave: in such a case the matter might need to go before a judge for determination. In this fictive version of the lawsuit the claim before the praetor goes undefended, with the result that the praetor awards the suit to the claimant and with the effect that the adoptee becomes his son. The formal legal result is the re-establishment of a paternal bond but all are aware that this is a new, rather than a recovered, status. It became the practice of such adopted sons to add to their new name a *cognomen* indicative of their origin. The emperor Augustus was born Gaius Octavius Thurinus: on adoption by Julius Caesar he became Gaius Julius Caesar Octavianus.

Because the adoptee by *adoptio* as opposed to *adrogatio* was already under another's power, the legal effects of the adoption process were less marked. But the adopted person still changed families, lost all rights of inheritance in the birth family, and became legally unrelated to members of the previous family. These effects were moderated in the later Empire as family relationships were recognized as surviving these legal moves.

Tutelage In the case of sons, tutelage applied to those under puberty who lacked a *paterfamilias*, normally because of the death of their father following the grandfather's death.

At civil law, by a rule attributed to the Twelve Tables, in the absence of a *paterfamilias* a son fell under the tutelage of his nearest male agnate, typically an uncle. Agnates are those related by descent through males only. The original explanation of this institution, known as *tutela legitima*, was to protect the family inheritance. On the death of the son below the age of puberty, before he could procreate legitimate offspring and before the age at which he was allowed to make a will, the property would pass to the nearest agnate. In the meantime, therefore, the agnate was permitted to ensure that his pupil did not dissipate the estate.

When a *paterfamilias* contemplated the possibility of his dying leaving a son under the age of puberty, he was permitted to make provision in his will for a tutor to the son. Such a tutor took precedence over the *tutor legitimus*, whose rights on intestacy were in any case compromised by the provisions of the will.

If a person below puberty had no identifiable agnates and no testamentary tutor had been appointed, the *lex Atilia* (of unknown date before 186 BC, when it is mentioned in Livy) authorized the praetor to make an appointment.[27] Originally the praetor acted in concert with the tribunes of the plebs, but under the Empire the *praetor tutelaris* acted alone following an examination (*cognitio*).

Conditions and Duties As a general rule, a tutor had to act when appointed: this reflects the earlier notion that he was in effect acting in his own interest. An agnatic tutor was required to give security that he would protect the pupil's property: one that would not was in effect excluded from acting. A person appointed by the praetor had the right to nominate another more suitable. Soldiers were exempt, as were – by imperial legislation – teachers, orators, and doctors. Otherwise, testamentary and Atilian tutors could advance various excuses for not serving: poverty, illiteracy, public office, or holding three existing tutorships.[28] In addition, a testamentary tutor could escape if he could show that he had only been appointed out of dislike! Only men could be tutors before the postclassical period: thereafter a mother could be appointed if there were no testamentary or agnatic tutor and she undertook not to remarry.[29]

Justinian forbade those under 25 to be tutors: apparently, though we only know this from this passage, it had earlier been a reason to be excused.[30]

The tutor had two basic functions: to administer the pupil's property where he was incapable of doing so, and to provide authority for certain transactions undertaken by the pupil.

The administration required of the tutor was of the pupil's property, not of his person. There was no obligation to educate the pupil. A tutor administering the pupil's property acted on his own account and not as agent for the pupil, but he could be held liable subsequently for acting fraudulently or for not showing the diligence of a good *paterfamilias*. In later law, restrictions were placed upon his ability to alienate property: an *oratio* of Severus in AD 195 forbade alienation of property in the country, extended to all property after Constantine.[31] As soon as a pupil became capable of making decisions, then the administration of his property became his own responsibility. But there remained some actions which required the authorization of his tutor.

The tutor was required to provide authorization for all civil law transactions performed by the pupil. It is likely, but uncertain, that the pupil was required to be present at such transaction, at whatever age, so that it was the joint participation of both tutor and pupil which created a valid act. If able to speak (not an *infans*) the pupil performed the spoken words. A failure to provide authorization by the tutor might in some circumstances lead to his being liable for fraud or negligence in his management.

If a pupil acted without authority then his actions could benefit but not harm his interests. So if he received a payment of a debt without authority this did not discharge the debtor, but if he bought goods he could sue for delivery of the goods though he was not liable to pay the price. However, a pupil was not permitted to take advantage of his position, and an attempt to reclaim the loan or actually obtain the goods without payment could be defeated by an appeal to good faith.[32]

Ending of Tutelage, Curatorship, and Liability of Tutor Tutelage of boys ended on their entering puberty. This was in origin a matter of fact, although the Proculian school of jurists advanced the notion that this was presumed to occur at the age of 14. Thereafter the youth acquired full capacity to deal with his own property without scrutiny or assistance; however, the praetor could be asked to intervene in a case where a person aged under 25 had been taken advantage of, requiring the other party to restore the youth's position to the *status quo ante*. As a consequence, those under 25 found it difficult to enter into commercial transactions with others without some independent scrutiny. This was provided by a *curator*, who would be appointed by the praetor at the youth's request in order to validate his transactions.[33] Although in principle voluntary, the institution became regularized. Meanwhile, as noted, the tutor could be called to account for his stewardship of the tutelage. Earlier remedies were absorbed in the classical period by the praetorian *actio tutelae* which held the tutor liable for fraudulent and negligent acts, being later extended to cover cases of inaction – for example, failure to provide authorization, to the pupil's loss.[34]

(II) DAUGHTERS The position of daughters within the household was similar to that of sons, save for two matters in which she was in a worse position.[35] We are told that she was incapable of acquiring anything, even for the benefit of her *paterfamilias*.[36] This limitation on her ability to act as an agent for her father did not add to the restrictions imposed in practice (although not in law) upon her social engagement outside the family and is probably to be regarded as a reflection of it.

More significantly, a daughter who lacked a *paterfamilias* fell under perpetual tutelage. This was originally designed to protect the interests of those who would inherit from her. As she was incapable, as a woman, of making a will, and was unrelated at civil law to her own children, her property could be lost only through her marriage *in manu* or prodigality. Both were controlled by placing her under the tutelage of her nearest male agnate, her natural heir. The agnate's rights were abolished under Claudius (except in the case of patrons of freedwomen).[37] Thereafter a woman might have a tutor appointed in her *pater*'s will (though she might be offered the right to choose one), failing which she had one appointed by the praetor. In either case the woman might apply to the praetor for a replacement, in effect giving her control.[38]

Tutors of women in perpetual tutelage were not expected to administer, but only to provide the *auctoritas interpositio* which was necessary to enable her to dispose of landed property or make a will once this became possible under Hadrian.[39] In the pre-classical period *auctoritas* would also have been required for marriage in *manu* (at least by *confarreatio* and *coemptio*, but arguably also for *usus*).

The jurists of the classical age invent spurious explanations for the phenomenon of perpetual tutelage, the basis of which they little understood: hence Gaius's 'weakness of mind' and Ulpian's 'ignorance of legal matters'.[40] Gaius has the grace to add that 'this seems more specious than true'.[41]

It is perhaps worth emphasizing that, although women were socially disadvantaged in Rome, as in nearly all pre-modern societies, the major limitations upon their legal capacity stemmed from the common subordination of all children to their *paterfamilias*. Although, unlike their male siblings, they remained subject to perpetual tutelage on their father's death, this was limited to the requirement for *auctoritatis interpositio*, a restriction which was of minimal importance with the diminution in importance of formal conveyance by *mancipatio* and the availability of mechanisms for selecting a complacent tutor. This apart, single women in Rome in theory possessed the full range of capacities to deal with their own property, and the disappearance of *manus* from the late Republic meant that marriage imposed no additional legal restraints.

3. MANCIPIUM

Although presented in our sources as part of a series of formal legal manoeuvres in connexion with emancipation and adoption, there is evidence that the status of *mancipium* was a substantial reality until the end of the Republic. This impression is reinforced by the appearance of the term together with *manus* and *potestas* in the *lex Irnitana* of the early Empire, quoted above (151). Although we cannot be certain what status distinctions existed in the peregrine communities to which the clause applied, it is clear that the Romans expected them to deploy a range which encompassed all three types of status. As we have seen, *potestas* elides two quite different types of subordination within the family: that of slaves and that of children. *Manus* applies only to women subordinated within marriage. *Mancipium* seems to be a term to describe the temporary subordination of a freeborn person to a stranger, a status akin to slavery but without the permanent loss of free status that this involved. In particular, one manumitted from *mancipium* recovers his freeborn citizen status and is in no way affected by the inconveniences of freed (*libertinus*) status. However, as most of our information comes from a period when the status has become largely formalized as part of legal procedures it is difficult to be certain. Gaius reports an opinion of the jurist Labeo, a contemporary of Augustus, regarding the status of a child born to one *in mancipio* pending his release after a third mancipatory sale in the course of an emancipation. The child is said to be subordinated *in mancipio* like his father. Gaius reports that in his own day this was no longer true and the child's status was in suspense.[42] If the one *in mancipio* is eventually manumitted, then the child falls under his *patria potestas*; but were he to die *in mancipio*, the child would become independent without any apparent need for an act of manumission: *mancipium* has become merely a fictive stage in the emancipation process. But Labeo's decision belongs in a world in which *mancipium* has real effects, and a child born to one *in mancipio* seems to require release from it.

4. *MANUS* AND MARRIAGE[43]

The Roman jurists pay little regard to marriage except as a means by which a *pater* obtains *potestas* over his children born in a legitimate Roman marriage. Early Roman marriage involved the subordination of a wife to her husband: she was said to be *in manu*, in the hand of her husband. Where, as often, he was himself under *patria potestas*, she was additionally subordinate to his *paterfamilias*. Free marriage without *manus* developed later and rapidly became the norm in late Republican and imperial Rome. It is convenient to discuss it first.

Marriage *Sine Manu*

To effect a valid marriage there must be capacity (*conubium*) between the parties.[44] A freeborn Roman citizen could freely marry another freeborn Roman citizen by the middle of the Republic, although before the *lex Canuleia* of 445 BC there had been a bar to marriage between patrician and plebeian, as laid down in the Twelve Tables. Until the Empire there was a limitation on marriage between the freeborn and the freed, descendants of manumitted slaves, though the exact details are uncertain. In the later Empire a formal limitation was again imposed upon marriage between the senatorial class and the freed: the wife of the emperor Justin, Justinian's adoptive father, was declared to be freeborn so that he could marry her. That there were further limitations in practice is illustrated by the legislation of Justin permitting marriage with reformed actresses, which paved the way for his nephew Justinian's marriage to Theodora.[45]

Certain relatives could not intermarry. These included ascendants and descendants, including adoptive relationships even if terminated, and siblings (but here a former adoptive relationship was not a bar). Uncles and aunts could not marry their nieces and nephews, except that legislation was passed under Claudius to permit marrying a brother's daughter, in his case Agrippina. This was reversed by Justinian. Even where there was *conubium* a marriage might be barred where there was a risk of undue influence: tutors were unable to marry their female pupils owing to a *senatusconsultum* of Marcus Aurelius *circa* AD 175. Provincial governors could not generally marry in their province.[46]

The parties to a marriage needed to be capable of consummating it: for females this was early fixed at 12 years of age. In the classical period the Sabinian and Proculian schools of jurists disagreed on whether it was fixed at 14 for boys (the Proculian view) or still had to be a matter of fact requiring inspection, as the Sabinians and the older view maintained.[47]

Although the position was possibly different in early law, by the late Republic the consent of both parties to a marriage was required. Those incapable of such consent – the mad – were unable to marry for this reason. But the consent might be only nominal: Celsus holds that, although consent cannot be compelled, an allegation that the consent given was constrained will not of itself invalidate a marriage.[48]

Where a partner to a marriage was in someone's *potestas*, that person had also to agree for the marriage to be valid. This is still stated to be the law by the jurist Paul, writing in the early third century AD,[49] despite the fact that entering into a free marriage did not alter the married person's personal status. Anyone subordinate to a *paterfamilias* before marriage remained so afterwards. That the concern was not entirely about legal rights is reflected in the fact that, if the *paterfamilias* were a grandfather, the father, in the intervening generation, had also to agree.

In strict law there was no need for any formal element to supplement the consent of the parties (and their *patresfamiliarum*). As Ulpian says, marriage is made in the mind not in bed.[50] But proof of marriage would frequently require some evidence of form. The forms of *manus*-marriage were unambiguous, but as free marriage grew up as a substitute for these no standardization was achievable. Moreover, as noted before, the jurists were not interested in marriage as such, for it transformed few if any legal relations, but only as a means for the creation of *patria potestas*. The most common sign of marriage was the leading of the woman into the marriage home. The juristic texts which speak of it being possible for a man to be married in his absence, but not for a woman to be, mean that in the husband's absence a woman may be led to the matrimonial home by another. It is likely that with both parties present no further action than consent was necessary for a marriage to be created. We learn of other peripheral acts involving the use of fire and water and words such as 'Wherever you are Gaius, I am Gaia'.[51] But none of these was essential. Nor was it necessary that the marriage be consummated.

Marriage *Cum Manu*

Very different were the older forms of marriage leading to the wife's subordination *in manu*. There were three ways in which such a marriage might be established.[52] *Confarreatio* was a religious rite, possibly originally restricted to patricians. The ritual involved sacrifice and the offering of cakes of wild wheat or spelt (*far*) and the use of solemn words in the presence of ten witnesses. In the Republic the priests of the State religion had to be both married themselves in this form and be themselves the offspring of a *manus*-marriage. Both the complexity of the ceremony and the consequences for the woman of subordination in marriage led to its disuse, according to Tacitus, and legislation was passed under Tiberius to enable priests to marry using the forms but without the legal consequence to enable the needs of religion to be met.[53] *Coemptio*, a form of fictitious bride-purchase, was the standard form for ordinary Romans wishing to enter into such a marriage. The woman would be mancipated to her husband, in the presence of a scale-holder and witnesses. Gaius tells us that special words were used to indicate that the purpose of the formal sale was marriage and not servitude, but in view of the result – the subordination of the woman within her husband's family – this may be a later rationalization.[54] It seems likely that this form of marriage died out at the beginning of the Empire. These forms did not exhaust the possibilities of creation of *manus*-marriage. Gaius tells us that, if a man and a woman lived together for a year as husband and wife, then at the end of the year the woman entered her husband's *manus* by *usus* (use). The similarity to the mode of acquiring another's property by a year's *usucapio* is striking. Gaius, writing at a time when free marriage was the norm, assumes that the parties were already married, but it is probable that originally this was a mode by which those who were unmarried formally became married in the standard form in which the wife was subordinated. We are told of various devices developed to prevent the presumption of *manus* arising – such as the wife's absenting herself from her husband for three consecutive nights, applying a rule of the Twelve Tables.[55] By Gaius' time such subterfuge was no longer necessary and there may have been legislation to this effect in the late Republic which has not come down to us.[56]

A woman *in manu* had left her family of birth and joined her husband's family. She was said to be in the *manus* of her husband and in the *potestas* of his *paterfamilias*, if any. She is sometimes said to be *in filiae loco* to her husband, in the position of a daughter, but this is more a comment on her acquiring rights of inheritance similar to a daughter than on her social position.

Divorce

Manus-marriage could be dissolved by appropriate actions. A ceremony of *diffarreatio* served in case of marriage by *confarreatio*; for those married by *coemptio* or *usus* a process of *remancipatio* to the former *paterfamilias*, or *emancipatio* if there were none such, served to terminate both the marriage and the wife's subordination to her husband.

In the case of free marriage, formed by the consent of both parties, dissent – a settled will not to remain married on one side – was sufficient to terminate the union. The Augustan *lex Julia de adulteriis*, which imposed penalties on those who formed sexual relations whilst married to another, forced the introduction of a witnessed transaction with seven witnesses (borrowed from the participants in an *emancipatio*) to free those who intended to remarry from the risk of accusation of adultery.[57] Divorce, like marriage, remained a matter of will or lack of it until the end of the Roman period. When after the conversion of Constantine Christian emperors sought to restrain unjustified divorce in accordance with Christian doctrine, this had to be effected by means of criminal sanctions on those who continued to exercise their legal powers.[58]

Dotal Property

Although a matter of property and not strictly connected with status, it is convenient to state here the basic features of the law relating to *dos* (dowry). The existence of a dowry was one of the principal overt markers of the existence of a free marriage. It was not, however, a necessary feature of the institution and had to be specifically created. To create a *dos* on marriage, property was transferred, actually or potentially, from the wife or her family to the husband or his family. The conditions under which the dotal property could be enjoyed depended upon the details of the arrangement. Fundamentally it belonged to the husband (or his *paterfamilias*) during the marriage, but he was bound to exercise care in its management and not to dissipate it. Further conditions might be attached to it by agreement between the parties.

On the termination of the marriage, by death or divorce, the fate of the dotal property depended both upon its manner of creation and the actual circumstances of the termination. The jurists distinguish a number of types of *dos*. *Profectitia* was *dos* provided by the bride's father or ancestor (or by another on his behalf). Where a marriage ended by the wife's death, *dos profectitia* returned to the donor if he were alive but, if not, it was retained by the husband. If there were children from the marriage, then the husband could retain one-fifth of the whole for each child against the donor. Where the husband died, the wife took the dotal property: it was her means of support and in effect a share in her own family property. If the marriage ended in divorce, then in principle the wife took the *dos*, but if she or her father caused the breakdown without sufficient justification, the husband was entitled to retain one-sixth for every child from the marriage up to three (i.e., up to half of the dowry). He could also claim a retention if the wife's adultery occasioned the breakdown. When the wife herself provided the *dos* it was termed *adventitia*. This the husband kept on his wife's death, whilst it returned to her, on general principle, on his. *Dos* provided by anyone else was *receptitia*. This was always regulated by agreement about how it was to be returned. The dotal property became the husband's on marriage and it did not automatically transfer at the end of the marriage. The above rules are in effect the conditions under which actions could be brought to require him to re-convey.[59]

The Roman system of dotal property was modified in the later Empire under the influence of Greek law practice, within which there was a preference for mutual gifts. *Donatio ante nuptias* was a gift made before marriage by the husband to the wife, though the property itself continued to be managed by the husband. Legislation provided that the *donatio* was to go to the survivor of the marriage or to the one divorced, but the rules were frequently changed in the later period.[60]

Gifts Between Husband and Wife

In the old form of *manus*-marriage a married woman owned no separate property and both partners were members of the same family as regards inheritance rights. But in the Empire those marrying freely remained separate persons in separate families. On death, wills apart, members of their respective families became entitled to inherit, but spouses ranked quite low down on the praetorian scheme of intestate succession. In these circumstances the possibility that marriage partners might transfer significant elements of their wealth to each other during the marriage came under scrutiny at the moment of inheritance and a rule, of uncertain date and origin, arose that no gift between husband and wife was valid. Exceptions included small gifts as presents and gifts subsequently validated by being confirmed in a will (which had the effect of trumping the rights of intestate heirs).

5. CITIZENS, LATINS, AND *PEREGRINI*

To be a Roman citizen in the Roman world was a privilege. As the apostle Paul of Tarsus discovered, his Roman citizenship, unexpected in the person of an itinerant Jewish preacher, could protect him from the casual brutalities of Roman governance.[61] As far as Roman private law was concerned, although the fullest status was only available to citizens, it was only a smaller number within this group, those who were not in someone else's *potestas*, who enjoyed the greatest of rights. The Roman law of persons is largely a study of those whose rights are limited in some way or other, whether by lack of freedom or its consequences, by subordination, by gender, or simply by being foreign.

In early Rome there was a distinction between patricians and plebeians. This may have originated in a racial distinction, perhaps between a ruling caste of Etruscan origin and local indigenes. After 445 BC intermarriage between the two groups was permitted, but a sense of patrician social superiority persisted until the end of the Republic and indeed into modern use. There were two privileged orders of citizens in the imperial period. Senators became an order under Augustus, reflecting an existing sense of superiority of those descended from members elected to the Senate, whether of patrician or plebeian family. Equestrians (knights) were in origin from families wealthy enough to serve in the early citizen army on horseback. This military aspect ceased to be of importance in the late Republic when all Roman soldiers served in the infantry legions, cavalry being provided by auxiliaries. Membership of the order was for life only and not inheritable, and it conferred distinction in judicial, financial, and military life.

In the later Empire a class of *coloni* emerged, a precursor of the serfs of the post-Roman period. Though not formally unfree, the *coloni* were in effect tied to the land they worked. The position was hereditary and those who sought to escape it could be compulsorily returned to their land.

As we have seen, one surprising way of attaining Roman citizenship was to be freed from Roman slavery, albeit not all so freed acquired citizenship immediately in the early imperial period. For those free persons who lacked it, Roman citizenship could be gained by performing a variety of public services – for example, by building and operating ships to carry grain to Rome, or mills to grind grain for Rome. It could be purchased, as by the Roman tribune who was amazed to discover that his prisoner, a Jew from Tarsus named Paul, was himself freeborn.[62]

Citizenship might also be conferred on individuals or communities by the emperor as a boon. Claudius was criticized for doing this too freely. Pliny records a typically convoluted case involving his personal physician, Harpocras, for whom he requested a grant of Roman citizenship. The emperor Trajan initially responded favourably. It then emerged that as Harpocras was an Egyptian by origin he should first have acquired citizenship of Alexandria before becoming a Roman. Trajan somewhat reluctantly granted this too.[63]

A Roman who was captured in war (as opposed, say, to being captured by pirates, as Julius Caesar once was) lost his citizenship. For the period of his captivity he was incapable of exercising his rights as an owner of property, his marriage was dissolved, and any *potestas* over his former subordinates was in suspense.[64] On recovering his freedom his rights revived as soon as he entered Roman territory, *postliminium*. But he needed to repossess all his previous property and to remarry his wife, if she were still available and willing. If he died a captive, he was fictitiously presumed to have died at the moment of capture, so any will made previously took effect on that basis.

The Romans recognized the application of local customary laws of their foreign subjects in both local and Roman courts. Those (the majority) who did not possess Roman citizenship were classed as *peregrini* (foreigners) and had only such rights as the Romans were willing to grant them. In private law terms this meant that, whilst they could have dealings with Romans, some essential features of the Roman legal system, particularly those relating to commercial and property matters, were denied to them.

Latins

A hybrid status was occupied by the peoples of historic Latium, noted above in connexion with slavery (155). As Latins, citizens of nearby cities, the Romans had accorded them limited rights of intermarriage and commerce, probably on a reciprocal basis, as early as the fifth century BC. Following the Social War of 91–88 BC, Roman citizenship was granted to all Latin communities in Italy. However, there were a number of colonies established elsewhere in the Mediterranean which had been granted a limited form of Latin right (not including the right of intermarriage) and these survived – and were indeed added to – in the period up until the grant of citizenship to all under Caracalla around AD 212.

Dediticii

Communities defeated by the Romans in war would typically be permitted to retain their existing legal and social customs, although they were regarded as foreigners in Roman law. But where no agreement was reached with such defeated peoples they were regarded as being in a lower category, called *dediticii*, with whom few or no dealings were expected.[65] The status virtually disappeared in imperial times, although it was artificially retained for a certain class of manumitted slave, as noted above (156).

Constitutio Antoniniana

Around the year AD 212 the emperor Caracalla (formally Marcus Aurelius Severus Antoninus, who reigned from AD 198–217) granted Roman citizenship to all free persons in the Roman world. It was apparently a single grant (our direct knowledge of the provision is limited) transforming the status of all existing Latins and peregrines without altering the laws by which such statuses could continue to be created in the future. Justinian's discussion of Latinity implies that it remained a status for certain manumitted slaves until his own act which abolished it.[66] Among the more important persistent effects of the constitution was to absorb into the Roman citizen body people with distinctive legal traditions, particularly those of the Greek East. This transformed certain aspects of Roman law, including marital property as noted above (169).

Notes

1. See J. A. Crook, *Law and Life of Rome* (London, 1967; repr. Ithaca NY, 1984), chs. 2 and 4; J. F. Gardner, *Family and* Familia *in Roman Law and Life* (Oxford, 1998); for the later period, J. Evans Grubb, *Law and Family in Late Antiquity* (Oxford, 1995). See also the articles collected in *The Family in Ancient Rome: New Perspectives*, ed. B. Rawson (London, 1986, repr. Ithaca NY, 1993); *Marriage, Divorce and Children in Ancient Rome*, ed. B. Rawson (Oxford, 1991); *The Roman Family in Italy: Status, Sentiment and Space*, ed. B. Rawson and P. Weaver (Oxford, 1997). Useful collections of materials in translation are J. F. Gardner and T. Wiedemann, *The Roman Household: A Sourcebook* (London, 1991); B. W. Frier and T. A. J. McGinn, *A Casebook on Roman Family Law* (New York, 2003); J. Evans Grubb, *Women and the Law in the Roman Empire: A Sourcebook on Marriage, Divorce and Widowhood* (London, 2002).
2. *Lex Irn.* ch. *22: Ut qui civitatem Romanam consequentur maneant in eorumdem manu mancupio potestate.*
3. Detailed accounts of the law of slavery are to be found in W. W. Buckland, *The Roman Law of Slavery* (Cambridge, 1908), and A. Watson, *Roman Slave Law* (Baltimore, 1987).
4. Inst. 1.2.20.
5. Gaius 1.84.
6. Tac. *Ann.* 13.26.
7. Cf. Gaius 1.44.
8. Gaius 1.28ff.
9. Gaius 1.22.
10. D. 38.10.10.5.
11. D. 18.1.5.

12. The position of those freed from slavery is covered in S. Treggiari, *Roman Freedmen during the late Republic* (Oxford, 1969), and A. M. Duff, *Freedmen in the Early Roman Empire* (Cambridge, 1958).
13. D. 47.10.7.2.
14. Inst. 3.7; C. 7.6.1.
15. Gaius 1.55.
16. J. A. Crook, '*Patria potestas*', *CQ* 17 (1967): 113–122.
17. D. 48.8.2; D. 48.9.5.
18. Inst. 2.12 pr.
19. C. 12.30.1; C. 6.60.1.
20. Inst. 4.8.7.
21. C. 5.17.5.
22. *Si pater filium ter venum duit filius a patre liber esto*, quoted in Gaius 1.132.
23. C. 5.27.5.
24. Gaius 1.99ff.
25. Cic. *Dom.* 34ff.
26. Gaius 1.134.
27. Gaius 1.185; Livy 39.9.
28. D. 27.1 deals with excuses from tutelage.
29. C. 5.35.2, 3.
30. Inst. 1.25.13
31. D. 27.9.1; C. 5.37.22 pr.
32. D. 18.5.7.1.
33. D. 4.4.1.
34. Inst. 1.20.3.
35. The particular position of women is considered in J. F. Gardner, *Women in Roman Law and Society* (London, 1986); for the wider context, see A. Arjava, *Women and Law in Late Antiquity* (Oxford, 1996).
36. Gaius 3.104.
37. Gaius 1.157.
38. Gaius 1.173.
39. Cf. Gaius 2.112.
40. Gaius 1.144; UE *de tut.* 11.
41. Gaius 1.190.
42. Gaius 1.135.
43. Specific studies of marriage in Rome include P. E. Corbett, *The Roman Law of Marriage* (Oxford, 1930, repr. 1969); S. Treggiari, *Roman Marriage:* iusti coniuges *from the Time of Cicero to the Time of Ulpian* (Oxford, 1991).
44. Cf. Gaius 1.76.
45. C. 5.4.23; generalized by Justinian: Nov. 117.6.
46. D. 23.2.59–60; D. 23.2.57.
47. Cf. Gaius 1.196.
48. D. 23.2.21–22.
49. D. 23.2.2.
50. D. 50.17.30.
51. Plutarch, *Quaest. Rom.* 30.
52. Gaius 1.110ff.
53. Tac. *Ann.* 4.16; Gaius 1.136.

54. Gaius 1.123.
55. Aulus Gellius, *NA* 3.2.13.
56. Gaius 1.111.
57. D. 24.2.9.
58. C.Th. 3.16.1.
59. For a good short survey of various forms of dotal property, see Gardner (n. 1), 85ff.
60. W. W. Buckland, *A Textbook of Roman Law*, 3rd edn. by P. Stein (Cambridge, 1963), 111.
61. *Acts of the Apostles*, 22:25.
62. *Acts of the Apostles*, 22:28.
63. Pliny, *Ep.* 10.6–9.
64. Gaius 1.129.
65. Gaius 1.14.
66. Inst. 1.5.3.

10 Property

Paul du Plessis

1. Introduction

In most textbooks on Roman law, the treatment of the law of property is divided into four topics, namely (i) the types of 'things'; (ii) the different modes of acquisition and alienation of ownership of property; (iii) ownership and possession; and finally (iv) limited real rights in property.[1] That this division is based on a certain elegant logic cannot be denied. After all, it is only really possible to understand a branch of private law if one understands the scope of that branch of law, the ways in which it functions in relation to the larger legal order, and the rights operating within it. With that said, although this treatment of the Roman law of property is largely based on the original Roman legal sources, it presents a more ordered and settled picture than is visible in those sources. As modern scholarship increasingly begins to acknowledge that Roman legal thought (with specific reference to their logic and understanding of categories) was not necessarily the same as nineteenth-century German legal thought, these basic structures need to be reassessed.[2] As a starting point, two of the most famous teaching manuals on Roman law, the *Institutes* of Gaius and those of Justinian, will be re-examined. Although these manuals were produced under different circumstances and for different audiences, it is well known that the compilers of Justinian's *Institutes* in the sixth century AD used the second-century manual of Gaius as their blueprint. Since both of these works were designed to be introductory teaching manuals setting out the basics of the law, an examination of their content should provide a clearer understanding of the structure of this branch of private law.

What little is known about Gaius and his work indicates that the *Institutes* was written as a textbook for use in teaching Roman law to his pupils.[3] It is impossible to tell whether Gaius' manual was used as a textbook in a formal setting or whether it was used unofficially to teach his followers privately.[4] Nothing is known about the rest of the curriculum, but it is worth mentioning that Gaius' textbook, written towards the end of the second century AD, only really deals with the *ius civile* as it applies to Roman citizens. As it was written a few decades before the wholesale granting of citizenship to most free inhabitants living within the boundaries of the Roman Empire in AD 212, the textbook has a specific focus and should be read as such.

Because of the existence of a number of introductory imperial decrees in which Justinian set out his vision for a manageable compilation of Roman law accessible to all, more information is known about the *Institutes* of Justinian compiled in the first half of the sixth century AD.[5] According to these sources, the *Institutes* of Justinian was compiled after the *Digest* project had been finished, as Justinian had by then realized that this anthology of juristic writing from the classical period would be too overwhelming and detailed for beginner law students. He therefore instructed a three-man commission to compile an introductory work in which the basic tenets of the law were explained (drawing on the model of Gaius), updated to reflect Roman law of the sixth century AD. This textbook was designed to be the teaching material for the first year of a degree in law, the rest of which consisted of a study of the *Digest* and finally the *Code*. As Justinian gave all the parts of this compilation the force of law, it replaced all earlier law books as authoritative sources.

For the purposes of this chapter, the nineteenth-century table of contents drawn up by Eduard Böcking to accompany the *Institutes* of Gaius will be used to structure the discussion.[6] While it is of course a product of nineteenth-century German legal thought, it represents the topics covered by Gaius accurately and allows for comparison with the corresponding sections of the *Institutes* of Justinian. Böcking divided Gaius' treatment of the law of property, located in book two, into three broad topics, namely (i) the types of 'things'; (ii) the acquisition and alienation of individual objects; and (iii) the acquisition and alienation of patrimony in its entirety. This threefold division accurately represents Gaius' discussion, although contemporary Romanists would classify (iii) as the law of succession, a separate sub-branch of law with great affinity to the law of property and indeed classified by Gaius as a 'mode of acquisition'. Owing to page constraints, this branch of law will not be included in this chapter, but it is worth noting that in the Roman legal mind the connection between the law of property and that of inheritance was an intimate one.[7]

II. THE LAW RELATING TO THINGS

A. Things are either in the category of private wealth or not (Inst.Gai. 2.1)
  1) the main division of things: those under divine law, and those under human law
    a) under divine law (in the estate of no one) (Inst.Gai. 2.2)
      i) sacred and religious things (Inst.Gai. 2.3–7)
      ii) sanctified things are also in a certain sense under divine law (Inst.Gai. 2.8)
    b) under human law (generally someone's property) (Inst.Gai. 2.9)
      i) public things (no one's property) (Inst.Gai. 2.9)
      ii) private things (belonging to individuals) (Inst.Gai. 2.10–11)
  2) Corporeal and incorporeal things (Inst.Gai. 2.12–14)
  3) Capable of mancipation or not (Inst.Gai. 2.14a–18)

FIGURE 10.1: Böcking's Rendition of Gaius' Treatment of the Different Types of Things

The Types of 'Things'

Figure 10.1 sets out Böcking's rendition of Gaius' treatment of the first of the three broad topics, namely the different types of 'things'.[8]

Gaius' decision to place this topic first suggests that he was attempting to define the scope of this branch of law with reference to its content. Providing his audience with a survey of the types of 'things' which formed the subject of the law of property enabled the reader to form a clearer understanding of the scope of this branch of private law. Böcking's rendition of the structure of Gaius' discussion of the different types of 'things' identifies three sub-topics, namely things subject to human or divine law; things which are corporeal or incorporeal; and finally things which are capable of *mancipatio* or not. In the mind of Gaius, therefore, these three topics formed the parameters within which the law of property operated. The first sub-topic (things subject to human or divine law) appears to have a delimiting function, since 'things subject to divine law' generally fell outside the scope of the law of property, but the remaining two sub-topics seem to fulfil a different role as they describe the characteristics of certain 'things', all of which are subject to private ownership.[9] This suggests that Böcking's rendition of the sub-topics as being of the same *genus* perhaps simplifies Gaius' original intention with these three sub-topics.

If these three sub-topics were chosen by Gaius to provide both limiting and explanatory functions, is it possible to draw any conclusions from the way in which they were structured? It seems safe to assume that the classification of some objects as being capable of *mancipatio* and others not is the oldest, yet Gaius places it at the end of his discussion on the types of 'things'. It is preceded by a discussion of corporeal and incorporeal things which, judging from the examples of limited real rights cited, must be taken to be a more recent category.[10] It therefore seems that Gaius structured the three sub-topics comprising his discussion of the different types of 'things' in the following manner: first he introduced the branch of private law using a delimiting category of human and divine law;[11] thereafter he introduced two further explanatory sub-topics in order of importance and relevance at the time – first corporeal and incorporeal things, followed by the older classification of things capable of *mancipatio* or not.[12]

The content of these three sub-topics allows further insights into Gaius' structuring of the discussion. Gaius' overarching introduction is that some things fall into the category of private wealth while others do not. This is followed by the *summa divisio*, whereby some things fall under divine and others under human law. Things subject to divine law belong to no one and examples of these are sacred, religious, and sanctified things. This category is set against those things which are subject to human law and generally (but not always) belong to an individual, such as public and private things. While Böcking's rendition is accurate, there are some perplexing questions in the detail, which suggest that the Roman understanding of these categories (if they are categories at all) was rather different. First, Gaius does not link his introductory statement – that some things fall into the category of private wealth while others do not – with the next sentence in which he sets out the *summa divisio*. It is left to the reader to make the logical connection that things falling into the category of private wealth are subject to human law whereas things falling outside are subject to divine law. Böcking correctly interpreted it in this sense, but it is only in paragraph 9 that Gaius links things subject to human/divine law to the concept of private property. No justification for this tangent is provided. Second, if sacred, religious, and sanctified objects are taken to be examples of things subject to divine law (is this a *numerus clausus*?), this provides further insights into Gaius' conception of this latter term. The statement in Gaius 2.4 that sacred things are consecrated to the gods above and sanctified things to the gods below at first suggests a religious connotation (in the wider sense), but subsequent passages show that these terms had a mainly public/civic meaning. This is hardly surprising given the connection between the state and religion in Roman society.[13] Sacred things are those consecrated by public authority of the Roman people (with a specific dispensation for land in the provinces), while religious things become such through a private act (the burial of a body), provided the owner of the land did the burying. A similar allowance is made for land in the provinces which cannot be held in private ownership. Finally, Gaius relates that sanctified things are also subject to divine law 'in a certain sense' (*sanctae quoque res, velut muri et portae, quodam modo divini iuris sunt*). It is not known why this qualification was required, but it suggests that sanctified things did not sit well with the established division.

Having established the scope of the law of things, Gaius proceeded to discuss two common classifications found in this branch of law, namely corporeal/incorporeal and those capable of *mancipatio* or not. The discussion of these two sub-topics in Gaius is straightforward and does not contain anything novel. After a rudimentary definition of corporeal property as things which can be touched, Gaius lists a number of examples. From these it would seem that Gaius wished to stress that 'real rights' (*quae in iure consistunt*), whether full or limited, should be seen as incorporeal things. The final topic of discussion – things which are capable of *mancipatio* and those which are not – contains the controversial *numerus clausus* of things classified in that way, together with a tangential discussion about whether beasts of burden are deemed to be such at birth or only once broken in and whether wild animals can ever be said to be beasts of burden. This discussion clearly shows Gaius as having Sabinian sympathies.

When Gaius' discussion of the different kinds of 'things' is compared to that of the compilers of Justinian's *Institutes*, differences appear. Before embarking on a comparison of this kind, it is important to stress that the structure of the *Institutes* of Justinian as depicted in the table of contents produced by Paul Krueger (Figure 10.2), does not contain the same level of detail as that of Böcking.[14] Gaius had structured his introduction around three broad topics (things subject to human/divine law, corporeal/incorporeal things, and things capable of *mancipatio* or not). Such a division into three broad topics does not appear in the *Institutes* of

BOOK TWO

1) The Classification of Things
2) Incorporeal Things
3) Servitudes
4) Usufruct
5) Use and Habitation
6) Usucapion and Long-Term Possession
7) Gifts
8) The Power to Alienate
9) Acquisition through Other People

FIGURE 10.2: Krueger's Table of Contents for the *Institutes* of Justinian

Justinian. Instead, the compilers of Justinian grouped matters together in a number of comprehensive paragraphs (beginning with Inst. 2.1 on the classification of things). These paragraphs show the extent to which Justinian's compilers altered the classical Roman law of property. First, the discussion concerning things capable of *mancipatio* or not has been eliminated completely from the introductory discussion in Inst. 2.1 to reflect the abolition of this legal institution in Justinianic law. Second, the discussion of corporeal/incorporeal property has been separated from the introductory paragraph on the classification of things to form a separate paragraph in Inst. 2.2. The discussion of things subject to human/divine law, while remaining in Inst. 2.1, has been altered to reflect the law of Justinian.

To appreciate the nature of this transformation, more detail is required. At the start of book 2 of Justinian's *Institutes*, the reader is informed that all things either form part of private wealth or they do not. This is followed by a statement that things can either be property common to all men by virtue of the law of nature or property belonging to the state, to the corporation, or to nobody. No indication is given as to whether this latter classification applies only to things which form part of private wealth, but this seems unlikely given the broader context. In this respect, the compilers of Justinian's *Institutes* followed the same line of reasoning as Gaius. The compilers of Justinian's *Institutes* provide a number of examples of the first two categories – things which belong to everyone by virtue of the law of nature and those which belong to the state. The discussion also mentions that the law of all peoples (the *ius gentium*) permits the public certain rights in property which belongs to everyone. As far as corporate property is concerned, a full list is not provided but merely a few examples, alongside the notion that anything whose ownership vests in the citizen body is treated as corporate property. This is a new category, which did not appear in the *Institutes* of Gaius. The final category – things belonging to nobody – contains a discussion of things which are sacred, religious, and sanctified. As such, it is a contraction of two of Gaius' ideas, namely that some things are subject to divine law and that this category of things is not subject to private ownership. When the content of these three concepts (sacred, religious, and sanctified things) is investigated, certain changes become visible. First, the distinction between sacred and religious things found in Gaius (one consecrated to the gods above, the other to the gods below) has disappeared completely. Second, the act of transforming property into sacred property no longer resides with the public authority of the Roman people but is instead left to the church and its officials. By contrast, the act of making property religious remained unchanged as a private act, but with more detail about the position of co-owners and others with an interest in the land. Finally, the description of sanctified things remained largely unchanged, except for the inclusion of a reference to penalties for those who interfere with such property.

Acquisition (and Alienation) of Individual Things

Böcking's rendition of Gaius' treatment of the second broad topic in Figure 10.3, the acquisition of individual things, demonstrates the importance of the Roman concept of legal status. It comes as little surprise that Gaius used the position of a free Roman citizen as his starting point, given that his work focused on the *ius civile*. This sub-category was separated

B. Acquisition (and alienation) of individual things

1) by the person who acquires (or alienates)
   a) acquisition or alienation by state law
      i) by those with normal power of alienation
         aa) corporeal things: actual delivery of a thing not capable of mancipation; mancipation; assignment in court (Inst.Gai. 2.19–27)
         bb) incorporeal things: incorporeal things are incapable of delivery; but some can be dealt with only by assignment in court, such as urban praedial servitudes, a usufruct and an inheritance; others can also be mancipated, such as rustic praedial servitudes. None of this applies to obligations which are transferred by novation (Inst.Gai. 2.28–39)
         cc) usucapion of movables and immovables whether capable of mancipation or not; division of ownership so that one person can be owner by quiritary right and another has the thing in his estate until he has usucapted; usucapion of things delivered to us by a non-owner; sometimes the usucapion will not work to the advantage of the possessor in good faith of another's thing; usucapion by someone who knows he possesses another's thing (Inst.Gai. 2.40–61)
      ii) sometimes an owner does not have the power to alienate and a non-owner does (Inst.Gai. 2.62–64)
   b) acquisition by natural law
      i) delivery, first taking, capture from an enemy (Inst.Gai 2.66–69)
      ii) force of a river, alluvial accretion, an island formed in a river (Inst.Gai. 2.70–72)
      iii) a superstructure becomes part of the land, a plant put into our land, corn sown in our land; what someone writes on my paper becomes mine, but not what he paints on my board (Inst.Gai 2.73–78)
      iv) making a new kind of thing from another's material (Inst.Gai 2.79)
2) acquisition and alienation by people under guardianship (Inst.Gai 2.80–85)
3) acquisition through those in power, in marital subordination or in bondage (Inst.Gai 2.86–96)

FIGURE 10.3: Böcking's Rendition of Gaius' Treatment of the Acquisition of Individual Things

from two further ones which were devoted to those persons who, while free, were subject to certain restrictions in the acquisition of ownership on account of guardianship. The rationale for separating categories one and two appears to be that those in the latter category could still acquire ownership of things, but they required permission for such an acquisition. The final category seems to have been created to distinguish those who could acquire personally from those through whom we could acquire ownership of things because of their relationship to us, such as on account of *potestas*.

Of the three sub-categories mapped out here, the first (acquisition by the person who acquires or alienates) is by far the most comprehensive. Within this category, an internal division exists between modes of acquisition according to state law and those according to natural law. As is evident from an examination of the 'state-law' modes, these are all legal creations peculiar to Roman citizens. Acquisition by state law is further divided into two sub-categories, namely instances of the normal power of alienation and instances where the person's right of alienation has been curtailed. The first category deals with the stock 'state-law' modes of acquisition. Again, the emphasis placed on the distinction between corporeal and incorporeal property suggests that it was a more recent category. The treatment of usucapion as a mode of acquisition of property according to state law is particularly informative as it introduces the concepts of peregrine and bonitary ownership. The second sub-category, detailing examples where a person's right of alienation has been curtailed, refers to issues of state law such as rights in the wife's dowry. Acquisition through natural law as a category contains stock examples and need not be discussed in detail. The two remaining categories – those people under guardianship and those subject to marital subordination – contain some interesting insights. First, in relation to guardianship, the focus of Gaius' discussion is on the position of women and wards (of either gender). Second, in relation to marital subordination, he mentions that ownership can be acquired either via free persons or slaves.

When Gaius' treatment of the acquisition of ownership is compared to the corresponding passages in Justinian's *Institutes* (see Figure 10.2), it is clear that the compilers of the latter had a different structure in mind. First, the threefold categorization of Gaius based on legal status has been abandoned in favour of longer paragraphs with little evidence of an underlying structure. This is to be expected since the distinction between citizen and non-citizen had long since ceased to be relevant, although it must also reflect changes in the rules on guardianship and marital power. In the second place, the category of acquisition by state law appears much transformed on account of the abolition of *mancipatio*. Possibly as a result of this complication, the compilers of Justinian chose to commence the discussion about the acquisition of ownership (Inst. 2.1.11) with reference to the natural-law modes. The discussion of the natural modes of acquisition has been expanded considerably and continues until the end of Inst. 2.1.35, where it is followed by a brief excursus on the acquisition of fruits and on delivery as a mode of acquisition. As Figure 10.2 illustrates, Inst. 2.2–7 represent a series of loosely connected topics which range from incorporeal things to gifts as a mode of acquisition of ownership, but a closer reading reveals a more complex relationship. As Inst. 2.2.3 shows, the leading discussion is that of incorporeal things (the subject of Inst. 2.2) from which, as the final paragraph shows, Inst. 2.3, 4, and 5 should follow. When viewed in this manner, it becomes clear that the compilers of Justinian's *Institutes* wished to highlight three main topics, namely incorporeal things, usucapion and its development (already visible in its most basic form in Gaius), and gifts as a mode of acquisition. In the two final paragraphs, the power to alienate (Inst. 2.8) has been altered to take account of the abolition of the guardianship of women, while in Inst. 2.9 the number of examples in which someone is able to acquire ownership through others has increased considerably.

From this survey of the structure of Gaius and of Justinian in relation to the law of property, it should be evident that their discussions lack one central element. Most modern textbooks on Roman law emphasize the type of right which is found in the law of property. The right at the basis of the law of things was the real right (*ius in rem*), 'real' being from the Latin noun *res* ('a thing'). For all the apparent importance of these concepts in modern discussions of the Roman law of property, they do not feature prominently in the discussions in Gaius' or Justinian's *Institutes*, designed though they were to introduce the law of property to beginner law students.

A final question that requires exploration is whether any conclusions may be drawn from the structuring of the law of property in other parts of the Justinianic compilation of Roman law. Since the arrangement of the *Digest* was apparently based on the order of the codified praetorian Edict produced by the jurist Julian during the reign of the Emperor Hadrian, it provides little in the way of information regarding the structure of the law of property. While property is an important topic in the *Digest*, juristic discussion of the law of property only really features in a handful of titles. The earliest mention is in book 6, which deals with *vindicatio* and the *actio Publiciana*. Books 7 and 8 deal with usufruct and servitudes generally. The only other book in which the law of property is comprehensively discussed is book 41, which deals with topics as diverse as ownership, possession, and usucapion. From this it would seem that the arrangement of the books and titles that deal with the law of property does not provide much insight into its structure, apart perhaps from reinforcing the obvious point that this branch of law cannot be understood fully without taking the legal process into account.

The following survey of the Roman law of property will not provide an account of the development of each rule of law or legal concept: these matters are thoroughly explored in systematic surveys found in most textbooks on Roman law. Instead, this survey will highlight certain themes which have emerged in those surveys, with a view to providing a new narrative for the Roman law of property.

2. *Ab Urbe Condita* to the Enactment of the XII Tables

The likely origins of the Roman concept of property and its original nature are much debated.[15] It is, for example, unclear whether the early Roman concept of property was 'home-grown' or not. Various property regimes existed in the ancient Mediterranean before the establishment of the Roman state, and the Romans may have used these as inspiration for the creation of their own.[16] But source material for this period is so sparse that it is impossible to determine the nature of this concept in early Roman law. It seems plausible that it would have started out as a factual (customary) rather than legal concept, since a fledgling city-state with a small territory hardly requires much more. It also seems plausible that the early notion of 'ownership' was perhaps first limited to chattels only.[17] The traditional narrative, found in most earlier works on Roman property law, is of an 'evolution' from communal to individual ownership of land (which is thought to have come into existence by the time of the enactment of the XII Tables in the mid-fifth century BC) via first the *gens* and then the *familia*.[18] The recognition of individual ownership of chattels and land seems to have gone hand in hand with early attempts at classifying certain types of property.[19] The primary distinction drawn in the XII Tables was between *res mancipi* and *res nec mancipi*.[20] The origins and motivation for this distinction most likely lay in the utility of the former for agricultural production. Given their special significance, the transfer of 'ownership' of *res mancipi* in early Roman law required the performance of a ritual known as *mancipatio*.[21] The legal consequence of *mancipatio* was to give the transferee *mancipium* over the object.[22] This term is thought to be the historical ancestor of the concept of ownership (*dominium*) of classical Roman law.[23] The legal consequences of a *mancipatio* are particularly visible where this ritual was performed on account of a 'sale'. Here it also generated *auctoritas*, a type of guarantee of title to the extent that the transferor was called upon to help prove 'ownership' where the transferee's entitlement to the object was challenged.[24] The fact that sale was singled out for special attention suggests that it may have been an important reason for *mancipatio* in early Roman law. Acquiring 'ownership' of anything else (*res nec mancipi*) did not require a *mancipatio* to be performed, but how ownership was transferred remains unclear. It has been suggested that it could be done using a formal legal procedure known as *cessio in iure*, where the parties had to appear before a magistrate who then assigned 'ownership' of the property to one party.[25] This is an important point. For both categories of property, formality was required when transferring 'ownership'. This tells us something about the Roman approach to 'ownership' of property in the earliest period. Any transfer of 'ownership' of property outside the *familia* required legal formality. It also suggests that the *familia* and the larger *gens* may have been largely self-sufficient entities in terms of the production of commodities. Mainly for these reasons, since formality increases the potential for error, a third method whereby 'ownership' of property could be acquired seems to have arisen in early Roman law, namely through prescription, the continued use of the property of another for a period of time (*usus auctoritas*).[26] According to the XII Tables the period of prescription for chattels was one year and for land two years. The short time periods reflect the size of Roman territory and may also be connected in some way to agricultural production. It has been suggested that there were no formal legal requirements for prescription.[27] This seems true, but since such a large part of Roman property law during this period must have been based on custom, it cannot be said definitively. Related to the rise of individual ownership of chattels and land in early Roman law is the concept of possession. Much like the classical concept of ownership (*dominium*), the concept of possession in classical Roman law (as a legal concept and as the counterpoint to ownership) seemingly did not yet exist in early Roman law.[28] On a practical level, however, possession in the sense of physical control must already have had some legal significance in early Roman law, given the existence of an early form of acquisition of 'ownership' by continued 'possession' for a certain period of time.

The XII Tables also mentioned certain 'limited real rights' that individuals could hold over another's property.[29] They are all related in some way to agricultural production. These 'limited real rights' included those created by the contract of pledge (*pignus*) and its historical antecedent, which are known to have agricultural roots. Others included the right to a path or a water source or to drive one's cattle over the property of another (collectively called 'rustic servitudes' in classical Roman law). The relationship between these and the early Roman concept of ownership remains disputed.[30]

The extent to which the early Roman-law concept of property and property rights is rooted in custom can be seen from the nature of the legal remedies used to enforce these rights.[31] One of the archaic forms of civil procedure, the action at law known as the *legis actio sacramento* (*in rem*) ('by oath'), seems to have been mainly used for this purpose.[32] Gaius' *Institutes*, our main source for this early form of procedure, states that it could be used in all cases where a specific statute did not exist to deal with the issue.[33] It therefore would have been the prime legal remedy for property disputes. This procedure had a number of peculiarities.[34] Both parties had to appear before a magistrate and assert their claim over the object. These claims had to be supported by a fixed sum of money – the amount depending on the value of the property in question – that was provided as a wager of the truth of the assertion. After hearing both arguments, the magistrate assigned 'interim possession' of the object in dispute to one party until the end of the proceedings. The party who lost the suit forfeited his wager to the state treasury as penalty. Another of the archaic forms of civil procedure, the *legis actio per iudicis arbitrive postulationem* (by petition for a judge or arbitrator), might also have been used in the law of property, especially in the division of property held in common.[35]

Before we move on to the republic, one final observation about the XII Tables is required. If, as is now generally accepted, the XII Tables was nothing more than a redaction in writing of some of the most controversial areas of Roman customary law,[36] then the fact that many areas of property law are contained in it suggests that the customary law on property was starting to become a source of discontent in the context of the 'struggle of the orders' and could no longer be regulated purely by custom. It is also important to view the early Roman law of property in the context of the knowledge of the law and the 'pontifical monopoly' over legal interpretation.

The growth of the Roman republic from the late years of the sixth century BC to its fall at the start of the first century BC is dominated by a number of political events which are inextricably linked to land and land ownership. Traditionally, the conclusion of the Second Punic War in 201 BC is taken as a watershed moment in the legal development of the republic, although in reality the Roman concept of property was most probably shaped by a number of different events.[37] In the period between the enactment of the XII Tables and the Second Punic War, Rome expanded her influence progressively across the Italian mainland through conquest and treaty, as is evidenced by the circumstances surrounding the Latin War of 340–338 BC. Once (most of) the Italian mainland had been subjected to the authority of Rome, a series of wars (collectively known as the Punic Wars) with the Carthaginians, mainly on account of access to trade routes, gave the Romans overseas territories. These territories had to be governed and issues surrounding land (specifically the legal status of such lands and the entitlements of local inhabitants to such land) had to be resolved.[38] This period also marks the start of the Roman obsession with the mapping out and classifying of the status of different types of land.[39] The final event, which had a significant impact on the formation of the Roman law of property, was the Gracchan land reforms (133–111 BC). This attempt to give land to war veterans at the expense of the patrician-dominated senate demonstrates the politically sensitive nature of land and land ownership in the Roman republic and set the tone for the events of the next century. These political events also need to be viewed within the context of certain major legal innovations which occurred during the course of the republic, namely the introduction of the office of the praetor as well as the rise of the profession of the jurist.[40]

The exact route whereby the early Roman concept of *mancipium* became the concept of *dominium* of classical Roman law is unclear, but it is commonly accepted that this development occurred during the republic.[41] In all likelihood, both the acquisition of new territories, first in Italy and later abroad, as well as the effect of the Gracchan land reforms contributed to the formation of the Roman legal concept of *dominium*, which is thought to have come into existence by the start of the first century BC.[42] Linked to this, and as a precursor to the development of *dominium*, possession as a legal concept developed in republican law.[43] The concept in its various forms was, according to Kaser, already widely known in Roman law by the third century BC.[44] Possession must have been particularly useful as a legal concept in defining the nature of the entitlement of those individuals who held land in the provinces.[45]

During the republic, a less formal mode of acquisition of ownership arose alongside *mancipatio* and *cessio in iure* to deal with the transfer of ownership of *res nec mancipi*. The rise of this mode, called *traditio* (delivery), suggests a growth of the category of *res nec mancipi*. It arose sometime between the third and second centuries BC and was therefore most likely linked to the increased economic importance of *res nec mancipi* as well as the influx of foreigners after the conclusion of the Second Punic War.[46]

The third method of acquiring ownership of property, prescription, underwent substantial changes in republican law. The early Roman law concept, *usus auctoritas*, was transformed into *usucapio* (possibly during the second century BC), and various legal requirements for its operation were introduced.[47] This development in particular suggests the growth of a more sophisticated legal concept of property in Roman law.

The number of 'limited real rights' which individuals could hold over the property of another increased during the republic. A category of *servitus* (servitudes) appears which contains both the original rustic servitudes of early Roman law and a number of urban servitudes, the latter no doubt a product of the increased urbanization of the Roman population.[48] The exact legal nature of these 'limited real rights' during the republic remains unclear, which is to be expected given the developmental state of ownership and possession during this period.[49] The increasing complexity and sophistication of Roman property law during this period can be seen, for example, in the rise of two further types of entitlement to the land of another: the lease of state land (later known as *emphyteusis*), and the right to lease a building (*superficies*).[50]

The rise of the formulary procedure and the impact of praetorian innovation upon the *ius civile* had an important effect on the remedies of early Roman law. A new proprietary remedy arose in the context of the formulary procedure.[51] This new remedy, the *formula petitoria* (ownership *formula*), differed from its predecessor (it has been suggested by Buckland that there may have been an intermediate remedy, *agere per sponsionem*).[52] The main advantages of the new remedy were that it dispensed with the wager, while at the same time strengthening the legal significance of 'interim possession' by placing the proof of ownership on the party who had not been granted possession.

The praetor also developed another important proprietary remedy during the republic, to deal with uncertainties surrounding ownership under Roman civil law. Sometime in the first century BC the *actio Publiciana* was created to assist individuals who, through no fault of their own, had failed to acquire ownership for good cause (*causa*) and who had lost possession before prescription (*usucapio*) could run its course.[53] The action contained a legal fiction that the time period for prescription had already passed. The significance of this action and the protection which it afforded are a matter of some debate.[54]

Possession in the Roman law of the republic came to be protected by interdicts, a summary procedure that occurred in front of the praetor. Information about the origins of interdicts is scarce.[55] The main advantage of possessory interdicts as a remedy was that they did not enquire about the legality of the possession but merely preserved the status quo. An interdict thus often served as a precursor for a more comprehensive legal process in which the true state of affairs was ascertained. The praetor then commanded the offending party to abstain from any attempt to interfere with the possession. Failure to do so resulted in a fine. While the possessory interdicts were useful in protecting property rights, the fact that they were required in the first place suggests a fairly unsettled property regime which would be in keeping with the political and societal turmoil of the late republic. It is also clear from celebrated court cases like Cicero's defence of Aulus Caecina that the legal interpretation of newly introduced possessory interdicts could be problematic.

2. THE EMPIRE

The main legal themes of the early Empire (the principate) are consolidation (the praetorian Edict was formally 'closed' in AD 130 during the reign of the emperor Hadrian and enacted as statute) and refinement (through juristic writing). The role of the praetor as the main agent of legal reform was slowly replaced by the emperor and his imperial bureaucracy. A new form of civil procedure, the *cognitio extra ordinem*, which coincided with the increased bureaucratization of the imperial administration, was also introduced during this period and would gradually overtake the formulary procedure.[56]

The intellectual refinement of Roman law characteristic of the early Empire found expression in attempts to classify and structure areas of private law. Thus, as mentioned above, according to Gaius, there were two kinds of property in Roman law: property capable of private ownership, and property incapable of private ownership (along with further sub-classifications).[57] Although Gaius' attempt at classification is of course not the earliest, it is comprehensive and demonstrates the mindset of the jurists of this period. The extent to which the Roman concept of 'ownership' had matured is evident from the various categories mentioned in the sources.[58] The standard and most important form was Roman ownership in accordance with the *ius civile*, described as *dominium* or Quiritary ownership.[59] It was restricted to Roman citizens or those foreigners who had been granted a special dispensation by the Roman state (*ius commercii* – right of commerce).[60] Ownership of land seems to have been a particularly complex issue, especially prior to AD 212 when most free inhabitants of the Empire acquired Roman citizenship.[61] All 'provincial land' belonged to the state (senatorial and imperial provinces) and thus could not be privately owned in the sense that *dominium* could be acquired over it. Since the majority of the Roman Empire's inhabitants lived in the provinces, however, Roman law had to grant them some rights similar to ownership over such property. The rights that individuals could acquire over provincial land are sometimes referred to as provincial 'ownership', but little is known about this institution. Possession as a legal concept must have been particularly important in this context.[62]

As for the modes of acquisition of ownership, certain changes are visible. *Mancipatio* and *cessio*, while still in existence, continued to decline in importance.[63] Physical delivery of the object combined with the intention to transfer ownership (*traditio*) became the dominant mode of acquisition of corporeal property.[64] The third method of acquiring ownership (*usucapio*) was substantially transformed. These changes are undoubtedly linked to the intellectual refinement of the Roman concept of ownership and the complex legal status of land in the provinces.[65] This probably also accounts for the introduction of a variant form of prescription to deal with 'ownership' of provincial land (*longi temporis praescriptio*).

Another consequence of the attempts at classification in classical Roman law is the identification of 'natural-law' modes of acquisition of ownership.[66] These were distinguished from the 'civil-law' modes mentioned above in that they were common to all people and not limited to Roman citizens. They must be of some antiquity, especially the 'seizing' of ownerless property (*occupatio*). These methods of acquiring ownership had probably existed in some form since early Roman law.[67] Legal remedies available for the protection of ownership and possession became sophisticated in classical Roman law.[68] The earlier *sponsio* and the *formula petitoria* were now unified and classified as variant forms of the *rei vindicatio*, the main proprietary remedy available to the *dominus*.[69] This remedy was available under Roman civil law solely to an owner (*dominus*) who had lost possession of his property and wished to recover it from anyone currently in possession of it.[70] Alongside the *vindicatio*, a number of legal remedies arose in classical Roman law to protect ownership. Possessory interdicts increased in number and were classified according to their function (acquisition, retention, and recovery)[71].

In keeping with the attempt at classification in classical Roman law, 'limited real rights' over property belonging to another were expanded and classified. Thus, the legal measures in the XII Tables on infringements by neighbours were developed further and placed in a single category.[72] Similarly, a distinction was drawn between rural praedial servitudes (the oldest category already extant in the XII Tables) and urban praedial servitudes.[73] Other real rights over property belonging to a third party, such as those created by pledge and hypothec, continued to develop.

The main theme of the late Empire is one of 'crisis and recovery'.[74] The 'crisis of the third century' – that is, the period of chaos following the death of Alexander Severus – had a profound impact upon the organization and governance of the later Roman Empire. The gradual separation of the Roman Empire into the East and the West, begun most notably during the reign of Diocletian and his successors in the fourth century AD, had a profound impact upon the Roman law of property. The end of Roman rule in the West in AD 476 gave rise to a smaller Roman Empire. In the West, Roman law was replaced by a mixture of Roman and indigenous Germanic customary law (or perhaps this merely signalled a *de iure* recognition of a legal pluralism which had in fact existed for some time), while in the East, classical Roman law continued to exist in some form.[75]

Owing to the fact that the source material (mostly the Theodosian *Code*) for this period deals mainly with public (imperial) law rather than private law, much remains unclear about the survival of classical Roman property law in the so-called 'post-classical' period of AD 284–476.[76] Nothing is known about the fate of Gaius' scheme of classification during this period. Given the broad outline of the decline of Roman law in the West after AD 476, and given the absence of any reference to classification in the Romano-Germanic law codes of the period, it must be assumed to have disappeared. By this time, elements central to his classification had been undermined. Diocletian, for example, had effectively abolished the distinction between Italic and provincial land by imposing upon Italic land taxes similar to those levied on provincial land.[77] In the East, on the other hand, knowledge of this scheme was preserved and remained sufficiently available to be used by the compilers of Justinian's *Institutes* in the sixth century AD.

Modern scholars have identified a number of features of the law of this period. First, legal sources of the late Empire indicate a general confusion in terminology.[78] Second, a general decline in legal sophistication and an abandonment of the distinction between contract and conveyance led to a transformation of the modes of acquisition of ownership.[79] Acquisition of ownership by prescription (*usucapio*) and its variant form *longi temporis praescriptio* were replaced by a vulgarized form of prescription which had very few legal requirements apart from continuous possession for either thirty or forty years depending upon the circumstances.[80] There is no direct evidence about the fate of the natural-law modes of acquisition of ownership.

Legal remedies to protect ownership and possession adapted to the circumstances of the period.[81] The late Empire saw the decline and eventual abolition of the formulary system in favour of the *cognitio* system.[82] Since the latter was not predicated upon the existence of stock *formulae* in the praetorian Edict, the notion of the action and its *formula* went into decline. Not much is known about the fate of the possessory interdicts; they probably did not survive in the West, though some may have endured in the East in a vulgarized form (*actio momentaria*).[83] Given the broad themes identified by modern scholars, it seems unlikely that much of the sophistication of real rights over the property of another in classical Roman law would have remained. As an example, one might mention the notion of hereditary lease (*emphyteusis*) generating a real right over imperial property. It developed in the third century AD.

3. Justinianic 'Recovery and Restoration'

The 'restoration' of classical Roman law in the Justinianic project is well documented and need not be examined in detail. Rather, the main changes introduced by the Justinianic compilers will be highlighted here. It is important to establish why these were necessary and what they sought to achieve.[84]

In relation to the classification of the law of property, certain changes were introduced as set out above. Justinianic law abolished the distinction between *res mancipi* and *res nec mancipi* (possibly reflecting the postclassical position under Diocletian, whereby Italic land came to be taxed as well).[85] Although the distinction was in all likelihood by this time merely a historical relic, its abolition nonetheless triggered a number of other changes, especially in relation to the modes of acquisition of ownership.

The distinction between ownership and possession found in the classical Roman law of property was revived.[86] *Dominium* – that is, Quiritary ownership under Roman civil law – was reintroduced. The other forms of ownership, such as peregrine and provincial ownership, were abolished, although many of these must at this stage have been merely archaic legal concepts preserved in the writings of the classical jurists contained in the *Digest*, and their abolition must have been an attempt to adapt the law of the *Digest* to the circumstances of the period.[87] The other forms of ownership (peregrine and provincial) only really made sense in an empire where the personality principle in law prevailed. Since

AD 212, when most free inhabitants of the Roman Empire were given citizenship, the principle of personality had been replaced by territoriality and these were no long relevant. It also stands to reason that the reintroduction of the distinction between ownership and possession would have an effect on the concept of possession.[88] As with ownership, a terminological adjustment was required. The different terms used in classical Roman law were abolished and replaced by a single term, *possessio*, which described legal possession with the intention of being the owner. All other forms of possession were described as natural or corporeal possession (*possessio naturalis/corporalis*).[89] Although classical Roman law had required both a physical and a mental component for possession to continue, Justinianic law held that possession could be retained through a mental intention alone.[90]

The modes of acquisition of ownership also reflected changes which had been introduced elsewhere. The most important change in this area of the law was the abolition of *mancipatio* as a mode of conveyance.[91] The compilers of the *Corpus iuris civilis* erased it (sometimes rather clumsily) from the legal texts of the classical period, although traces of it remained. *Cessio in iure* suffered a similar fate. Although it was never officially abolished in Justinianic law, it had already fallen into disuse in the classical period.[92] *Traditio* was instated as the standard mode of acquisition of ownership. It seems that it had to be based on some just cause (sale, donation, etc.), but the texts are unclear.[93]

The acquisition of ownership through the passing of time (*usucapio*) was comprehensively reformed in Justinianic law.[94] These changes are well documented and need not be discussed in detail. Suffice it to say that they must have been necessitated by the changes introduced in relation to ownership and possession in classical Roman law.

The 'natural-law' modes of acquisition of ownership, discussed in the *Institutes* of Gaius, were also taken up in Justinian's *Institutes*, as mentioned above (190). Certain changes were introduced where the law had changed since the classical period.[95]

Limited real rights over the property of another were reconstituted in their classical form, again with certain changes to reflect the law of Justinian's period.[96] Furthermore, the law of neighbours was developed and refined under Justinianic law.[97]

The *vindicatio* again, with slight variations, became the standard remedy available to the owner to recover property from a third party.[98] The classical scheme of possessory interdicts was restored, although some simplification of procedure occurred on account of the changes in civil procedure during this period.

4. Conclusions

This chapter of two halves is designed to make two larger points about the Roman law of property. The first is to argue that more attention needs to be paid to the structure of this branch of law as presented in the *Institutes* of Gaius and of Justinian. When surveying the 'evolving' structure of the Roman law of property as presented by these two teaching manuals, more attention needs to be paid to the legal thought (logic, understanding of concepts and categories) which underpinned these structures. Roman legal thought is not modern legal thought, and the Romans had a unique way of looking at law which was informed by their own world view. The second point which this chapter seeks to make is that any account of the 'development' of Roman property law from the founding of Rome (*ab urbe condita*) to the publication of the *Digest* cannot be wholly internally focused. While until now much has been done to demonstrate how concepts evolved with time, such an internal narrative has become dis-associated from the larger narrative surrounding the Roman Empire.[99] This needs to be addressed. Property – specifically land – does not just have a legal dimension; it is rooted in the social, economic, and political narratives of the Romans and should be viewed from these perspectives as well.[100]

Notes

1. See, e.g., J. A. C. Thomas, *Textbook of Roman Law* (Amsterdam, 1976), part III, chs. 10–15.
2. See T. Leesen, *Gaius Meets Cicero: Law and Rhetoric in the School Controversies* (Leiden, 2010) and D. Lehoux, *What Did the Romans Know? An Inquiry into Science and Worldmaking* (Chicago, 2012).
3. See the excellent yet much underrated work by O. Stanojević, *Gaius Noster – Plaidoyer pour Gaius* (Amsterdam, 1989), chs. 3–5. On the person of Gaius, see also T. Honoré, *Gaius* (Oxford, 1962). On the text of Gaius see the recent work by F. Briguglio, *Il Codice Veronese in trasparenza. Genesi e formazione del testo delle Istituzioni di Gaio* (Bologna, 2012).
4. Stanojević (n. 3), ch. 8. Gaius' teaching should be seen within the context of Roman legal education of the second century AD.
5. See the *Prooemium* to the *Institutes* (*const. Imperatoriam Maiestatem*).
6. E. Böcking, *Gai Institutionum Commentarii Quattuor* (Leipzig, 1855) [as augmented by Seckel and Kuebler].
7. See, e.g., the interesting work by R. Saller, *Patriarchy, Property and Death in the Roman Family* (Cambridge, 1994).
8. The English translation is from W. M. Gordon and O. Robinson, *The Institutes of Gaius* (Ithaca, 1988).

9. See M. Kaser, *Römisches Privatrecht*, 17th edn. by R. Knütel (Munich, 2003), § 18.I.2a. More generally, M. Crawford, 'Aut sacrom aut poublicom', in *New Perspectives on the Roman law of Property*, ed. P. Birks (Oxford, 1989), 93–98.
10. For an interesting discussion of the relationship between the Roman understanding of *res incorporales* and that of nineteenth-century German legal scholars, see G. Turelli, ' "*Res incorporales*" e beni immateriali: categorie affini, ma non congruenti', *Teoria e Storia del Diritto Privato* (online journal: http://www.teoriaestoriadeldiritto privato.com) 2012 (5): 1–17.
11. On the *summa divisio*, see U. Vincenti, *Categorie del Diritto Romano*, 2nd edn. (Naples, 2008), 96–99.
12. On this secondary division, see Vincenti (n. 11), 99–112.
13. See C. Ando, *The Matter of the Gods: Religion and the Roman Empire* (Berkeley, 2008), 59–92.
14. See vol. 1. of the *Corpus iuris civilis* (Berlin, 1954).
15. M. Kaser, *Eigentum und Besitz im älteren römischen Recht*, 2nd edn. (Cologne, 1956) remains one of the most influential books on this topic.
16. Compare G. G. Archi, 'Il concetto della proprietà nei diritti del mondo antico', *RIDA* 6 (1959): 229–249. See, most recently, the thought-provoking book by P. Garnsey, *Thinking about Property: From Antiquity to the Age of Revolution* (Cambridge, 2007), esp. chs. 1 and 2.
17. For an anthropological comparison, see, e.g., M. Gluckman, *Politics, Law and Ritual in Tribal Society* (Oxford, 1965), 36–38.
18. G. Diósdi, *Ownership in Ancient and Preclassical Roman Law* (Budapest, 1970), 37 and generally ch. 3; M. Kaser, 'Über "relatives Eigentum" im altrömischen Recht', *ZSS* 102 (1985): 1–39; L. Capogrossi Colognesi, 'La proprietà in Roma dalla fine del sistema patriarcale alla fioritura dell'ordinamento schiavistico', in *La Terra in Roma antica: Forme di Proprietà e Rapporti Produttivi*, ed. L. Capogrossi Colognesi (Rome, 1981), vol. 1, 135–169; Kaser (n. 9), § 22.II.1; L. Capogrossi Colognesi, 'Per la storia della proprietà romana', *Labeo* 18 (1972): 373–398.
19. Diósdi (n. 18), 21–26; Kaser (n. 9), § 18.I.3a.
20. H. F. Jolowicz and B. Nicholas, *Historical Introduction to the Study of Roman Law*, 3rd edn. (Cambridge, 1972), pp. 137–140.
21. Jolowicz and Nicholas (n. 20), 143–149.
22. M. Varvaro, '*Manu(m) conserere* e *omnibus verbis vindicare* (Gellius 20.10.7)', in *Le Dodici Tavole: dai Decemviri agli Umanisti*, ed. M. Humbert (Pavia, 2005), 267–309.
23. Diósdi (n. 18), 57, Vincenti (n. 11), 112–122.
24. Diósdi (n. 18), 75–81.
25. Jolowicz and Nicholas (n. 20), 149–151.
26. Jolowicz and Nicholas (n. 20), 151–152; Kaser (n. 9), § 25.I.1–2.
27. Diósdi (n. 18), 90.
28. Diósdi (n. 18), 124. For a discussion of the different historical roots of possession in Roman law, see Kaser (n. 9), § 19.II.1.
29. Kaser (n. 9), § 28.I.1.
30. Diósdi (n. 18), 108; see also, more generally, R. Feenstra, '*Dominium* and *ius in re aliena*: The Origins of a Civil law Distinction', in Birks (n. 9), 111–122.
31. Cf. the chapter by Metzger, 281–3.
32. Diósdi (n. 18), 105–106; Kaser (n. 9), § 27.I.
33. Gaius 4.13.

34. See, extensively, C. A. Cannata, '*Qui prior vindicaverat*: la posizione delle parti nella *legis actio sacramento in rem*', in *Mélanges Felix Wubbe*, ed. J. A. Ankum et al. (Fribourg, 1993), 83–96.
35. Gaius 4.17a; Kaser (n. 9), § 81.II.2.
36. Cf. the chapter by Ibbetson, 26–7.
37. On Italy in the Republic, see K. Lomas, 'Italy during the Roman Republic: 338–331 BC', in *The Cambridge Companion to the Roman Republic*, ed. H. Flower (Cambridge, 2004), 199–224.
38. For an interesting example of how this was done, see J. S. Richardson, 'The *Tabula Contrebiensis*: Roman Law in Spain in the Early First Century B.C.', *JRS* 73 (1983): 33–41, and P. Birks, A. Rodger, and J. S. Richardson, 'Further Aspects of the *Tabula Contrebiensis*', *JRS* 74 (1984): 45–73.
39. See, generally, O. Dilke, *The Roman Land Surveyors: An Introduction to the Agrimensores* (Newton Abbot, 1971).
40. Cf. the chapter by Ibbetson, 28–9.
41. Kaser (n. 9), § 22.II.
42. Kaser (n. 9), § 22.II.2 has suggested that this development may be linked to the increased sophistication of the law (e.g., the development of other areas of law) as well as to changes in Roman legal procedure.
43. Kaser (n. 9), § 19.II.1–2. See also, generally, G. Wesener, '*Ius possessionis*', in *Festschrift für Max Kaser zum 70. Geburtstag*, ed. D. Medicus et al. (Munich, 1976), 159–178.
44. Kaser (n. 9), § 19.II.
45. Kaser (n. 9), § 19.II.2.
46. Diósdi (n. 18), 73; Kaser (n. 9), § 24.IV.1.
47. Diósdi (n. 18), 145–146; Kaser (n. 9), § 25.II.
48. Jolowicz and Nicholas (n. 20), 268; Kaser (n. 9), § 28.I–III.
49. M. Kaser, 'Altrömisches Eigentum und *usucapio*', *ZSS* 105 (1988): 122–164.
50. Some debate remains over the precise origins of these two institutions. Jolowicz and Nicholas (n. 20), 269–270, relying on the views of Mitteis, suggest that they may have existed, albeit de facto rather than in law in the republic. Others suggest a later date for their introduction: see W. W. Buckland, *A Textbook of Roman Law from Augustus to Justinian* 3rd edn. by P. Stein (Cambridge, 1963), 275–276.
51. Diósdi (n. 18), 149–154.
52. Buckland (n. 50), 675. See, most recently, L. Capogrossi Colognesi, *Proprietà e Diritti Reali* (Rome, 1999), ch. 4.
53. J. A. Ankum and E. Pool, '*Rem in bonis meis esse* and *rem in bonis meam esse*: Traces of the Development of Roman Double Ownership', in Birks (n. 9), 5–42; L. Vacca, 'Il c[osí]. d[etto]. *Duplex dominium* e l'*actio publiciana*', in *La Proprietà e le Proprietà*, ed. E. Cortese, (Milan, 1988), 39–74. See also Capogrossi Colognesi (n. 52), ch. 5.
54. Diósdi (n. 18), ch. 4.
55. Jolowicz and Nicholas (n. 20), 261–263; Kaser (n. 9), § 21.1; L. Capogrossi Colognesi, '*Dominium* e *possessio* nell'Italia Romana', in Cortese (n. 53), 141–82. See also G. Giliberti, '*Dominium caesaris*', *Index* 24 (1996): 199–228.
56. Kaser (n. 9), §§ 87, 88.
57. Gaius 2.1.
58. F. Schulz, *Classical Roman Law* (Oxford, 1954), 338–343.
59. Diósdi (n. 18), 131, 135–136; Kaser (n. 9), § 22.II.2. See also G. G. Archi, 'L'aspetto funzionale del '*dominium*' romano', *BIDR* 61 (1958): 61–79.

60. Kaser (n. 9), § 22.II.2. See also F. Piccinelli, *Studi e ricerche intorno alla definizione 'dominium est ius utendi et abutendi re sua quatenus iuris ratio patitur'* (Naples, 1980), an important recent work on this topic.
61. See, e.g., Siculus Flaccus, *De Condicionibus Agrorum*, specifically on Italic land; the date of the work is unknown but thought to be of the second century AD: B. Campbell, *The Writings of the Roman Land Surveyors: Introduction, Text, Translation and Commentary* (London, 2000), xxxvii.
62. For an interesting account of the history of the Roman concept of possession in the civilian tradition, see Capogrossi Colognesi (n. 52), ch. 6.
63. Schulz (n. 58), 344–348.
64. Schulz (n. 58), 349–353; Diósdi (n. 18), 139, 143.
65. Kaser (n. 9), § 22.II.2.
66. Schulz (n. 58), 361–366; Kaser (n. 9), § 26.I–III.
67. Diósdi (n. 18), 121.
68. Schulz (n. 58), 368, 378.
69. Kaser (n. 9), § 27.I.3.
70. Kaser (n. 9), § 27.I.3. See also B. Kupisch, *In integrum restitutio und vindicatio utilis bei Eigentumsübertragungen im klassischen römischen Recht* (Berlin, 1974) for a more extensive account.
71. Kaser (n. 9), § 21.I.2.
72. Kaser (n. 9), § 28.I. On these, see, generally, A. Rodger, *Owners and Neighbours in Roman Law* (Oxford, 1972), and most recently Capogrossi Colognesi (n. 52), ch. 2.
73. Schulz (n. 58), 381–399.
74. Compare P. Garnsey and C. Humfress, *The Evolution of the Late Antique World* (Cambridge, 2001), 52–82.
75. For an example of this, see I. Wood, 'Administration, Law and Culture in Merovingian Gaul', in *From Roman Provinces to Medieval Kingdoms*, ed. T. Noble (London, 2006), 358–375.
76. A systematic comparison of the law with the treatise by Agennius Urbicus, *De Controversiis Agrorum* (if, as cautiously suggested by Campbell (n. 61), xxxii, it dates from the late fourth/early fifth century AD, it may provide new insights into this period).
77. Thomas (n. 1), 136.
78. E. Levy, *West Roman Vulgar Law* (Philadelphia, 1951), 19–71, 84–99; Kaser (n. 9), §§ 19.III.1, 22.II.3.
79. Levy (n. 78), 127–148, 156–176; Kaser (n. 9), § 24.V.1.
80. Kaser (n. 9), § 26.IV.1.
81. Levy (n. 78), 202–276.
82. Kaser (n. 9), § 88.
83. Kaser (n. 9), § 21.III.
84. See C. Humfress, 'Law and Legal Practice in the Age of Justinian', in *The Cambridge Companion to the Age of Justinian*, ed. M. Maas (Cambridge, 2005), 161–184.
85. Kaser (n. 9), § 18.I.3a.
86. Kaser (n. 9), § 22.II.4.
87. Kaser (n. 9), §§ 22.II.4, 21.III.1.
88. Kaser (n. 9), § 19.VI.2.
89. Kaser (n. 9), § 19.VI.2.
90. Kaser (n. 9), § 21.II.2.
91. Kaser (n. 9), § 24.V.1–2.

92. Kaser (n. 9), § 24.III, V.
93. Kaser (n. 9), § 24.V.1a. Compare R. Evans-Jones and G. MacCormack, '*Iusta causa traditionis*', in Birks (n. 9), 99–109.
94. Kaser (n. 9), § 25.IV.2a–b.
95. Kaser (n. 9), § 26.I–III.
96. Kaser (n. 9), § 29.I.7.
97. Kaser (n. 9), § 23.III.
98. Kaser (n. 9), § 27.I.
99. See J. Pölönen, 'The Case for a Sociology of Roman Law', in *Law and Sociology*, ed. M. Freeman (Oxford, 2005), 398–408.
100. See, e.g., the work of B. W. Frier and D. Kehoe, 'Law and Economic Institutions', in *The Cambridge Economic History of the Greco-Roman World*, ed. W. Scheidel et al. (Cambridge, 2013), 113–143.

11 Succession

David Johnston

1. Introduction

Adam Smith observed that 'there is no point more difficult to account for than the right we conceive men to have to dispose of their goods after death'.[1] Roman law, however, was remarkably precocious in arriving at the view that a person was entitled to dispose of his property by means of a will. This principle once accepted, the Roman jurists lovingly elaborated the formal requirements for making a valid will and the various dispositions that it could contain, such as legacies or other bequests, manumission of slaves, and appointment of tutors. In doing so they constructed a massively complex edifice. Even the surviving fragments of the jurists' commentaries and discussions occupy 11 out of the 50 books of Justinian's *Digest*. Among other things they consider in minute detail the appointment of heirs and substitutes in the event that the first-appointed heir predeceased the testator, and they examine the precise linguistic requirements for making a legacy of a particular type and the legal consequences that flow from the use of one type of legacy rather than another.

This chapter could attempt to give a short account of these detailed technical rules,[2] but there is a risk that that might not be very interesting. Instead, the aim here will be to provide a survey on a more general level. This is because it is crucial to view the law of succession in the broader context of Roman social history. Clearly, a fundamental issue for the functioning of Roman society is how the Romans chose to transfer property between generations.[3] There is an issue of economic history here too. And also, at the upper end of the social scale, there are ramifications for political history.

2. Succession on Intestacy

Heirs on Intestacy

By the time of the XII Tables of about 450 BC, Roman law already regulated both testate and intestate succession. In other words, there were rules on how to make a valid will. There were also rules about devolution of the estate if the deceased person had made no will or the will was invalid, for example because it failed to comply with formal requirements.

Distribution of the estate on intestacy depended on a classification of types of heir. Children who were released from paternal power (*patria potestas*) on the death of the deceased had the first claim on his estate, in equal shares. They were known as the *sui heredes*. It is a difficult term to translate literally – more or less 'own heirs'. In the mid-second century AD the jurist Gaius explained that they are called this because they are household heirs and even during their father's lifetime are regarded in a way as owners of the family property (Gaius 2.157). A testator might have no *sui heredes*; women never did, since they did not enjoy paternal power. In that case the next best claim was that of the nearest agnate or agnates, if there was more than one equally closely related. Agnates were relatives of the deceased who traced their relationship to him through the male line only. Again, a deceased might not have any agnates (freedmen, for instance, by definition did not, and if they left no children then their patron succeeded to their estate). In the absence of a nearest agnate, members of the *gens* or extended family were entitled to claim the inheritance. This, however, appears to have applied only in early law. Apart from this, there is virtually no trace in Roman law of a notion that the wider community ought to be a (or the) beneficiary in the event of the death of one of its members.

The law of succession is an area of Roman law which demonstrates particularly clearly what may be called the dualism of the Roman legal system. On the one hand there was the *ius civile* (civil law), made up of the XII Tables, statutes passed by the legislative assemblies, and their authoritative interpretation. On the other there was *ius honorarium* (the law of the magistrate, in this context the praetor).[4] By imaginative approaches to the situations in which he would grant an established remedy or when he might refuse it, the praetor was able to bring about remarkable changes in the shape of the civil law. The praetor came to admit claims that he regarded as equitable although they were not recognized under *ius civile*, and to reject claims that he viewed as unjust although they were legitimate at civil law. In doing this he presided over the formation of a new body of law in which some quite radical departures from tradition were made.

In the law of succession on intestacy the praetor innovated on the scheme established in *ius civile* by elaborating the circumstances in which he was willing to grant an order for possession of the estate (*bonorum possessio*). A rather complicated hierarchy of claimants was introduced. Under this system those with the best claim were the children, including not just *sui heredes* but also those who had been emancipated by the deceased and so in the strict sense were no longer within the family; next came agnates; then cognates (that is, those related to the deceased but not necessarily through the male line, according to their degree of proximity); finally, the praetor recognized the claim of the surviving spouse on the estate of his or her deceased spouse. It is not so much the details that interest us here as two broader points: first, that the praetorian innovations aligned the law of succession much more closely with family relationships, notably by recognizing that it was not just those who could trace their relationship through the male line who should have a claim; second, the praetor recognized the entitlement of the surviving spouse – but since that ranked below all claims based on relationship it confirmed that the abiding principle was that marriage did not involve community of property.

Justinian's law swept away the distinctions made in the classical law. There was now no sign of *sui heredes* or any distinctions based on agnatic or cognatic relationship (or between male and female in general). Instead, in two laws Justinian set out an order of succession on intestacy by reference to three classes; in each class the person nearer to the deceased would exclude the claim of the more remote. The first claim was that of descendants; next, ascendants and brothers and sisters; and last, other collaterals (*Novels* 118 (AD 543) and 127 (AD 548)). The result is that the categories of the classical law have no continuing significance for the systems that borrowed from and built upon Roman law.

Testation and Intestacy

The question arises whether, at least among the propertied classes of Rome, it was common to make a will. The evidence on this is not unequivocal. Some literary sources at least imply that testation was regarded as a duty or *officium*: in particular, Cato is said to have regretted having lived a single day intestate.[5] Sir Henry Maine regarded testation as being so much the norm that he wrote of the Roman 'horror of intestacy'.[6] Although that appears to be overstated, on balance it does appear that the propertied Roman was very likely to make a will, especially if he was male.[7] The evidence of such wills as survive suggests that the Roman testator was most likely to appoint his children – particularly his sons – as the heirs under his will.[8] They of course are precisely the people who would have had the first claim if the deceased had died without leaving a valid will. But that perhaps tells us something: by contrast with other societies, it is notable that Roman law neither gave any preference to male children over female children nor precedence to the oldest child over younger ones. It is clear that a system of unregulated partible inheritance such as this has a strong tendency to fragment property. The effects of fragmentation are likely to be all the more significant and marked in a society such as that of classical Rome, in which membership of a particular social class depended on the amount of property that a person owned. Although the evidence does not allow any clear or firm conclusion on the point, it is at least tempting to speculate that the desire to avoid fragmentation of the estate may have encouraged Roman testators to make wills, precisely because by doing so they could leave their property to their children in unequal shares.

3. Testate Succession

Making a Will

The earliest wills could be made only at a twice-yearly assembly (*comitia calata*) or when war was imminent (*in procinctu*). In due course a form of will for everyday use was developed. This was the will made by bronze and scales (*testamentum per aes et libram*). By the end of the republic it had suppressed the other forms of will. Bronze and scales were a standard feature of formal acts in early Roman law, and making a will in that manner followed the same pattern as (for instance) conveying certain kinds of property by the formal conveyance of *mancipatio*. In the presence of a scale-bearer (*libripens*) and five witnesses the testator made a formal conveyance of his estate (*mancipatio*) to a trustee (*familiae emptor*) and declared his intentions regarding his estate. On grounds of confidentiality the declaration soon came to be made in writing; by this means the will came into being, and the conveyance itself became no more than a formality. There were developments in the requirements for execution of a valid will. From an early date the praetor was willing to accept a will that did not comply with the requirements set out above, or where there had been no formal ceremony of *mancipatio*, provided it was sealed by seven witnesses. This was adapted in postclassical law to require that the testator and the seven witnesses should subscribe the will.

It was open to any Roman citizen who was of age to make a will. A woman could make a will with the authority of her tutor. The formal requirements for validity were strict. The essential feature of a Roman will was the appointment of an heir or heirs. The jurist Gaius described this as the source and foundation (*caput et fundamentum*) of the will (Gaius 2.229). The testator could name one or more heirs and could also provide for substitute heirs, in the event that those appointed predeceased him or did not accept appointment as heir. Some surviving examples contain elaborate series of substitutions in more than one degree.

The first provision in the will had to be the appointment of the heir in set words. There were also formal requirements for disinheriting certain people. The *ius civile* protected the expectations of a testator's children by requiring that certain formalities be observed. Male children, if not appointed heirs, had to be disinherited by name. Female children could be disinherited by a general clause of disherison, without being specifically named. The praetor extended the rule to require that even an emancipated son ought to be appointed or disinherited expressly.

Position of the Heir

The heir or *heres* was regarded for most purposes as stepping into the shoes of the deceased. Although certain rights did not survive the death of the deceased (for example, usufruct) and certain obligations were extinguished by his death (such as mandate, partnership, marriage, delictual obligations except to the extent the heir had benefited from the proceeds), the general principle was that the heir enjoyed the same rights and obligations as had the deceased.

The whole estate of the deceased devolved on the heir. That included debts, and the heir's liability was unlimited. For this reason appointment as an heir to a particular estate might be extremely undesirable. Apart from the financial burden, there was the prospective ignominy of being the subject of bankruptcy proceedings. For these purposes the *sui heredes* were in a different position from others. Under the *ius civile* they had no power to refuse appointment as heir: for that reason their full title was *sui et necessarii heredes* (see Gaius 2.56–8). This had the unfortunate consequence that if the estate was insolvent, bankruptcy proceedings would take place in the name of the *sui heredes* themselves. In order to mitigate this consequence, the praetor recognized that *sui heredes* who had not involved themselves with the estate could abstain from being recognized as heirs. The result was that any bankruptcy proceedings would be in the name of the deceased, and creditors would be unable to enforce their claims against the *sui heredes*.

There was one further kind of heir who could not refuse appointment (*heres necessarius*), and this was a slave who was freed by the testator in his will and at the same time appointed heir. Although there was in his case no means of avoiding being implicated in any bankruptcy proceedings, even here the praetor provided some protection by allowing the slave to keep his own property separate from that of the estate (Gaius 2.155).

Other heirs appointed in the will were free to accept or reject appointment and were formally recognized as heirs only once they had accepted or otherwise dealt with property of the estate in such a way as to be regarded as accepting. There is some evidence that, in order to spare their children the burdens and responsibilities of being heirs, some testators preferred to disinherit them and appoint someone else as an heir. That person might then be requested by *fideicommissum* (see below, 206–9) to transfer the property to the children.[9] In Justinian's law a new institution, the privilege of inventory or *beneficium inventarii*, provided that an heir must, within 30 days of knowing of his right to the estate, begin to make an inventory of it. If he did so, his personal liability would not extend beyond the assets set out in the inventory.

Taking Possession of the Estate

The *ius civile* provided an action by means of which the heir could claim possession of the estate: *hereditatis petitio*. It is not necessary to examine the details here.[10] It is, however, worth noting that, alongside this traditional civil-law claim, there grew up a new praetorian institution, *bonorum possessio*, an order for possession of the estate. This has already been mentioned in relation to succession on intestacy. Such orders were also available even where there was a will. They may be divided into two: possession in accordance with the will (*secundum tabulas*), and contrary to the will (*contra tabulas*). *Bonorum possessio* was in effect an entire system of inheritance which ran in parallel to that of the *ius civile*. In strict law, the person to whom the praetor awarded *bonorum possessio* was not heir (Gaius 3.32). He would, however, obtain possession of the estate, although there might be competition between a number of claimants to obtain possession. It is not unfair to characterize the rules as excessively detailed and complex, and in the circumstances it is not surprising that there was a gradual move towards simplification of the system, culminating in the fusion of the praetorian system of *bonorum possessio* and the civil-law system of appointment as *heres*.[11]

The Content of a Will

The only essential content of a will was the appointment of an heir, but in it a testator might also appoint tutors to his children, manumit slaves, and charge his heir to pay legacies. The appointment of tutors by will had been recognized as early as the XII Tables. In the early empire statutory restrictions were placed on the number of slaves who could be manumitted by will, apparently because of concerns about the number of freedmen created in this way. The limits depended on how many slaves the deceased had, but regardless of that an absolute maximum of 100 was imposed (*lex Fufia Caninia* of 2 BC; Gaius 1.42–3).

Legacies

Legacies are worth somewhat closer consideration.[12] Roman society was one in which the wide dispersion of property by legacy on death appears to have been common. This was a means of recognizing social obligations which had been incurred by means of the complex demands of friendship and patronage.[13] The corollary, however, is that there was a real risk that legacies charged on an estate might be so numerous and extensive that there was no incentive for an heir to accept appointment. And without an heir, the provisions of the will would be ineffective. The legislator therefore stepped in to regulate the position. The most important and enduring of statutes directed at this issue was the *lex Falcidia* (40 BC), the finer points of which were still under discussion by jurists centuries later.[14] It provided that, if legacies exceeded three-quarters of an estate, then they were cut back *pro rata*. This had the effect that the heir was guaranteed that the entire estate would not be consumed by the legacies, leaving him empty-handed. To the modern eye perhaps the most striking point is that anybody should think of leaving more than three-quarters of his estate to persons other than his heirs.

In Justinian's *Digest* the various types of legacy are discussed at length. The main (but not the only) forms were the legacy *per vindicationem*, which made the legatee owner of the object of the legacy and entitled him to claim it by *vindicatio*; and the legacy *per damnationem*, which imposed an obligation on the heir to make payment. It is, however, less the legal form than the wide range of content of legacies which is interesting as a matter of social history. It is not possible here to discuss this exhaustively, and the following is no more than a selection of the more interesting points. Books 33 and 34 of the *Digest* devote attention to such curiosities as legacies of dowry, wine, farm equipment, *peculium* (a fund given to a slave or dependent child to administer), and *penus* (furniture). *Digest* 33.1 is concerned with legacies of annuities, mostly to old retainers. These were payments of annual sums for the remainder of the lifetime of the payee. The jurists interpreted these as a series of annual payments, each of which was conditional on the legatee still being alive when the date for the particular instalment came round.[15] *Digest* 33.2 deals with legacies of a life interest in property or usufruct. It appears to have been common practice for a testator to leave ownership of property to his children, subject to a usufruct in favour of his widow. That entitled her to enjoy the use and profits of the property during her lifetime or for whatever period the testator stipulated. There are also quite numerous instances both in the *Digest* and in surviving epigraphic evidence of legacies left for public or philanthropic purposes, often to towns. In the jurists' terminology, these were legacies *sub modo*. For example: 'Lucius Titius left a legacy in his will of 100 to his home town, Sebaste, so that from the interest on it games should be celebrated in his name every other year'.[16] Legacies for constructing buildings, paving roads, and heating public baths are also not uncommon. The obvious attraction of choosing a non-natural person such as a town as the legatee was its durability: it came under a continuing obligation to carry out the purpose for which the legacy had been given. Although there are evident difficulties in such arrangements as time goes by, not least since their endurance depends on there being someone interested in securing compliance with the terms of the legacy, the evidence suggests that the popularity of this kind of legacy was enduring.

Fideicommissa The *fideicommissum* or trust was an important alternative to the legacy.[17] It evolved as a legal institution from the beginning of the empire. Prior to that, the *fideicommissum* had been regarded as generating no more than a moral obligation. The emperor Augustus changed this by charging the consuls with the responsibility for enforcing certain *fideicommissa*. This jurisdiction was replaced by that of two standing praetors for *fideicommissa* under Claudius; they were later reduced to one. The procedure before these magistrates was the new extraordinary procedure (*cognitio extra ordinem*).[18] The *fideicommissum* was a request made by a testator to a person who benefited from his estate. Typically it was a request to transfer part or all of it to another person. A simple *fideicommissum* such as a request to make a payment to a beneficiary would look much the same as a legacy, the difference being that the only person who could be charged with the payment of legacies was the heir, whereas anyone who benefited from the estate could be charged with a *fideicommissum*.

One of the initial attractions of *fideicommissa* was that they could benefit people who were unable to become heirs or legatees under *ius civile*. This would in principle apply to proscribed persons and to foreigners. It might also apply to those who fell foul of the Augustan marriage legislation (*lex Iulia de maritandis ordinibus* of 18 BC and *lex Papia Poppaea* of AD 9), by virtue of which (subject to a number of exceptions depending on the closeness of their relation to the deceased) unmarried adults were debarred from receiving inheritances or legacies, and married but childless adults were permitted to receive only half of what they had been left. A logical problem resides, however, in trying to understand how far magistrates can really have enforced *fideicommissa* in favour of those who had been subjected to restrictions by the *ius civile* or by statute. There is at any rate no doubt that so far as *fideicommissa* created loopholes in the law, these were progressively restricted: for example, the *SC Pegasianum* of AD 73 debarred the unmarried and childless from benefiting by way of *fideicommissum*.[19]

THE USES OF *FIDEICOMMISSA* The simplest kind of *fideicommissum* was one which, like a legacy, was directed at having a particular item conveyed to a particular beneficiary. But the flexibility of the institution was such that it was possible to do a number of more elaborate things. One was to ask a person to free a slave.[20] More adventurously, a testator's heir could be asked to make over the entire estate to some other person (*fideicommissum hereditatis*) either immediately, after an interval, or on his own death. As Gaius explains, 'When we have written "Let Lucius Titus be heir", we can add "I ask and request of you, Lucius Titius, that as soon as you are able to accept the inheritance you make it over to Gaius Seius".' (Gaius 2.250) Here Lucius Titius was to transfer the estate immediately; in other cases the heir was asked to transfer it only after an interval; commonly this was on his own death.[21] Functionally, this is equivalent to the legacy of a usufruct (see above, 205–6): in effect, the enjoyment of a life interest and the ultimate title are split. As with usufruct, it appears that this method was sometimes used to divide rights in property between the testator's widow and his children. Equally, there appear to be cases where it was used to protect the interests of children against their stepmothers.[22]

Since a *fideicommissum* could be charged on a person other than the heir, it was possible to use it so as to affect later generations. Scaevola provides numerous examples, of which the following is one: 'A father prohibited his son and heir from alienating or mortgaging lands and entrusted to his faith that they would be preserved for his legitimate children and other relatives.'[23] Here, on his father's death, the son became owner of the land, but it was not his to dispose of, since the father's will already determined who was to receive it. This kind of arrangement could have operated over several generations, although it seems to have been valid in classical law only if the beneficiaries could be identified. The most remote beneficiaries who were regarded as identifiable were the immediate issue of those living at the date of death of the person who set up the *fideicommissum*.[24] This kind of device might in principle have been employed in order to generate family settlements of property lasting for a number of generations, as occurred in Europe in early modern times. For Rome, however, there is some but not much evidence that this was done. While Justinian did legislate to set a maximum four-generation limit on such arrangements, there is little to suggest that this was a response to widespread use or abuse of *fideicommissa* of this kind.[25]

Fideicommissa could be imposed not simply on the heir under a will, but on anybody who received a benefit from the deceased on succession. This applied not just to legatees (or for that matter the beneficiaries of *fideicommissa*) but also to those who succeeded as heirs on intestacy. As Paul observed, '*Fideicommissa* can be charged on heirs on intestacy, since the paterfamilias is regarded as intentionally leaving them his estate on intestacy.'[26] Here, paradoxically, the *fideicommissum* made it possible to die without leaving a will and yet still determine where some or all of the estate was to go. Since it was possible to charge a *fideicommissum* on the prospective heir on intestacy, there was in fact no need to make a will at all. Nonetheless, in classical times (up to the mid-third century AD or so) there is no indication that making wills declined in favour of creating *fideicommissa* on intestacy. What is notable, however, is that in post-classical writings the term *fideicommissum* is often used in contrast to testamentary succession. This may suggest an increased role for intestacies which fell to be regulated by *fideicommissum*, as opposed to 'pure' intestacies governed by the default rules of the civil law.

While a will required set words for appointing an heir and charging legacies, no formal constraints affected *fideicommissa*. This led to the development of a practice of asking that a will, if it turned out to be formally invalid, should be upheld in fideicommissary form. That stratagem could work, as long as it was possible to identify that the testator was indeed attempting to create a *fideicommissum*. An example appears in an opinion of Scaevola recorded in Justinian's *Digest*: '"I, Lucius Titius, have made this will without any legal expert, observing the reason of my own mind rather than excessive and miserable pedantry; if I have done anything without legality and skill, let the wishes of a sane man be treated as valid in law." He then appointed his heirs. A question arose when the property was claimed on intestacy.'[27] Here, in spite of the testator's plea, the will was void, but the jurists were willing to allow the shares set out in the will to be claimed on the grounds that they could be regarded as *fideicommissa*.

It appears that the lasting attraction of *fideicommissa* lay in part with the flexible procedural advantages of *cognitio extra ordinem* and principally in their lack of legal formality. Under Justinian the two institutions of legacy and *fideicommissum* were fused. The unitary system which resulted was much closer to the *fideicommissum* than to the legacy. Justinian regarded the *fideicommissum* as the more 'humane' of the two institutions, so the informal nature of the *fideicommissum* was extended to legacies. Where the rules of the two institutions conflicted, Justinian determined that those of the *fideicommissum* should apply. The result was an institution of great flexibility, apt both for straightforward bequests and for more elaborate strategies of succession over one generation or more.

4. FREEDOM OF TESTATION AND STRATEGIES OF SUCCESSION

Freedom of Testation

Certain formal requirements for making a valid will and other testamentary dispositions have already been mentioned. These, however, in no sense restricted freedom of testation; all they did was require that set forms be followed. From the XII Tables onwards Roman law allowed the testator a great degree of freedom. Provided he complied with the formal requirements, he could validly dispose of his property as he saw fit.

Towards the end of the republic, however, it came to be recognized that certain relatives of the testator should share in his estate. They could challenge the will by raising court proceedings in the form of the complaint of the undutiful will (*querela inofficiosi testamenti*). A challenge could be mounted by any descendant or ascendant who could show that he or she had received less than a quarter of the share of the estate to which he or she would have been entitled had the testator died intestate, and that the testator had had no good reason for cutting him or her out. Relatives who challenged successfully would receive their whole intestate share. The claim appears to have rested on a fiction that the will was so 'undutiful' that the testator cannot at the time of making it have been in his right mind. The logical consequence of that would be that the whole will should be avoided, but in fact the practice was to set it aside only so far as necessary to cover the successful claimant's share. Although there were perfectly good and accepted reasons for disinheriting relatives, the jurists do not discuss them, and they are left to the attention of the rhetorical treatises. Only in late classical law is there imperial legislation referring to certain classes of people who could validly be disinherited without further inquiry into their conduct: examples are those leading immoral lives, and gladiators.[28] In AD 542 Justinian brought this legislative development to its natural conclusion by promulgating a lengthy list of accepted grounds for disinheriting relatives.[29]

It is nonetheless appropriate to stress the limitations of this inroad on freedom of testation. For a testator with three children, each child would have a prospective share of one-third of the estate on intestacy. In order to bar the *querela*, each would have to be left not less than a quarter of that – namely one-twelfth. The testator would remain free to do as he wished with the remaining three-quarters of the estate. These figures were adjusted somewhat by Justinian in his later legislation[30] so that, in relation to claims brought by descendants only, the testator was entitled freely to dispose of two-thirds of his estate (if he had up to three children) or half (if he had more than that). The figures remained the same so far as other claimants were concerned. The *querela* therefore amounted to a modest first step in protecting the expectations of relatives. But by recognizing that there was such a thing as a fixed expectation it marked a sea change in the Roman approach to testate succession. One remarkable feature of the *querela* is that, unlike almost all other innovations in the law of succession, it owed nothing to the work of the praetor. Indeed, litigation took place not in the praetor's jurisdiction but before the *centumviri*, a large lay 'jury' much frequented by aspiring and established orators.[31]

Strategies of Succession

The Roman had at his or her disposal a remarkable range of legal institutions in order to regulate the devolution of his or her estate on death. The evidence in the *Digest* does not, of course, allow us to draw direct conclusions about what happened in practice. But it is surely legitimate to draw from the evidence preserved there some conclusions about how or how well the law facilitated various strategies of succession and what strategies the Roman testator, armed with these legal institutions, chose to pursue.[32]

In general, the overwhelming impression is that the concern of the Roman testator was primarily with arranging the destination of his or her property within the circle of his or her living kin and freedmen; it was not with devising grand schemes for posterity. So, for example, most of the *fideicommissa hereditatis* now attested, while they could have been employed for more elaborate purposes, appear to have been drafted with reference to the current generation and with an eye to directing benefits to those who were actually living in the testator's household. Two further, general points may be made. First, it is quite striking how many of the wills quoted in the *Digest* are concerned with directing benefits to the testator's freedmen, who would of course bear his surname (*nomen*). This secured for him a degree of commemoration in posterity. Second, given the harsh incidence of mortality, testators had good reason to be preoccupied with ensuring that provision was made for their immediate descendants, with anticipating the possibility (or likelihood) that some of their children might predecease them, as well as with considering what arrangements to make for the event that one of the parents died before their children grew up to adulthood.

Earlier it was suggested that the desire to avoid fragmentation of the estate may have encouraged Roman testators to make wills, precisely because by doing so they could leave their property to their children in unequal shares. Nonetheless, the surviving evidence does not suggest that this freedom was typically allowed to produce great inequality. So, for example, Modestinus cites a will in which the paterfamilias is at pains to ask his daughter not to be angry that in his will he has left more property to her brother and to remind her of the various burdens that her brother will have to bear.[33] Clearly, from one text one cannot draw any conclusions of wide-ranging validity, but this is at least consistent with the view that emerges from other evidence that a typical will might be expected to leave substantial property to each of a testator's children, even if it did not leave them precisely the same amount.

NOTES

1. A. Smith, *Lectures on Jurisprudence*, ed. R. Meek, D. Raphael, and P. Stein (Oxford, 1978), 63.
2. The leading modern account is by P. Voci, *Diritto ereditario romano*, 2 vols. (Florence, 1963, 1967).
3. On this theme in general, see, esp., F. von Woess, *Das römische Erbrecht und die Erbanwärter* (Berlin, 1911); E. Champlin, *Final Judgments* (Princeton, 1991); cf. also K. Hopkins, *Death and Renewal* (Cambridge, 1983), ch. 4.
4. See, the chapter by, Ibbetson, 34.
5. Plut. *Cato* 9.6.
6. H. Maine, *Ancient Law*, 8th edn. (London, 1880), 223. Cf. also D. Daube, 'The Preponderance of Intestacy at Rome', *Tulane Law Review* 39 (1965): 253–62; J. Crook, 'Intestacy in Roman Society', *Proceedings of the Cambridge Philological Society* 19 (1973): 38–44.
7. Champlin (n. 3), 46–9.
8. Champlin (n. 3), 107–20. For a valuable discussion of surviving documentary evidence of Roman wills, see M. Amelotti. *Il testamento romano* (Florence, 1966).
9. D. 28.2.18 and 38.2.12.2.
10. Instead, see, most recently, M. Müller-Ehlen, *Hereditatis petitio* (Cologne – Weimar – Vienna, 1998).
11. For details, W. W. Buckland, *A Textbook of Roman Law*, 3rd edn. by P. Stein (Cambridge, 1963), 381–98.
12. See, in general, G. Grosso, *I legati nel diritto romano* (Turin, 1966).
13. L. Boyer, 'La fonction sociale des legs d'après la jurisprudence classique', *RHD* 43 (1965): 333–408; R. Saller, *Personal Patronage under the Early Empire* (Cambridge, 1982).

14. See D. 35.2.
15. D. 33.1.4.
16. D. 33.1.21.3.
17. See, in general, D. Johnston, *The Roman Law of Trusts* (Oxford, 1988); V. Giodice Sabbatelli, *La tutela giuridica dei fedecommessi fra Augusto e Vespasiano* (Bari, 1993); V. Giodice Sabbatelli, *Fideicommissorum persecutio: contributo allo studio delle cognizioni straordinarie* (Bari, 2001).
18. For this, see the chapter by Metzger, 287–9.
19. For the details, U. Manthe, *Das senatus consultum Pegasianum* (Berlin, 1989).
20. G. Impallomeni, *Le manomissioni mortis causa: studi sulle fonti autoritative romane* (Padua, 1963).
21. D. 35.1.102; D. 36.1.56; D. 36.1.60.8. Cf. L. Desanti, Restitutionis post mortem onus. *I fedecommessi di restituirsi dopo la morte dell'onerato* (Milan, 2003).
22. For differing views on this point, see M. Humbert, *Le remariage à Rome: Étude d'histoire juridique et sociale* (Milan, 1972), 207–40, and S. Treggiari, *Roman Marriage* (Oxford, 1991), 392.
23. D. 32.38 pr.
24. D. 31.32.6.
25. Nov. 159 (AD 565).
26. D. 29.7.8.1.
27. D. 31.88.17.
28. C. 3.28.11 (AD 224); C. 3.28.19 (AD 293).
29. Nov. 115.
30. Nov. 18 (AD 536).
31. Plin. *Ep.* 1.18.3, 4.24.1, 6.12.2; cf. Buckland (n. 11), 615.
32. On this theme and what follows, see, above all, R. Saller, *Patriarchy, Property and Death in the Roman Family* (Cambridge, 1994), ch. 7.
33. D. 31.34.6.

12 Commerce

Jean-Jacques Aubert

Historians of the Roman economy appear to agree that during the period 200 BC–AD 200 the Gross Domestic Product of the overall empire grew, however moderately. They explain this phenomenon partly as the result of a reduction in transportation costs and in 'transaction costs' – that is, the sum of the costs of looking for opportunities for exchanging goods and services, reaching agreements between parties through contracts, and enforcing transactions.[1] This reduction is said to be due, among other causes, to the development of a common legal system, 'especially in the field of commercial law'.[2] This statement raises the following questions: What is 'Roman commercial law'? Where does it come from? How did it develop? And how does it fit in the wider field of Roman law? This chapter will attempt to provide some answers.

1. Law of Commerce, Commercial Law, Business Law

A standard handbook of Roman law states unambiguously at the outset: 'Ein besonderes Handelsrecht haben die Römer daneben nicht ausgebildet.'[3] However, there is no dearth of books and articles entitled or explicitly dealing with *Diritto commerciale romano* or *L'histoire du droit commercial romain*.[4] Behind this apparent contradiction lurk both a question of definition and a recurrent and continuing scholarly debate about the way to approach the Roman legal institutions that governed trade and other economic activities.[5] We can evaluate the usefulness, sophistication, and shortcomings of the Roman law of commerce against the standard of commercial law and business law.[6]

According to a strict definition, 'commercial law' is a set of legal rules originating with merchants, designed for merchants, and enforced – partly, at least – by merchants. Scholars looking for Roman 'commercial law' focus on sources of law, legal interpretation, practical application, and jurisdiction. The former two are quite accessible through extant sources, the latter two mostly blurred through lack of evidence.

Historically, the definition proposed above applies to the law developed in western Europe, mostly Italy and France, during the middle ages. Thus 'commercial law' (*ius mercatorum*, *lex mercatura*: law merchant) was meant to be more pragmatic and flexible, less bookish, and less dominated by scholars than Roman and Canon laws. Its purpose was to satisfy the needs of commerce, facilitating transactions, expediting proceedings through separate jurisdictions and procedures, and transcending the limits of national legal systems as an early form of international law. Its provisions inevitably reflect the concerns and interests of an identifiable socio-economic class of people, namely traders. 'Commercial law' was a part of private law and its status with regard to civil law has fluctuated through history. Distinct at first, it tended to merge and become absorbed by the latter, as in Swiss or Italian law, and eventually become a subfield of the law of obligations. Or else, 'commercial law' opened up to other fields of law and became more inclusive in terms both of the people it governed and the types of issues and transactions it dealt with, thus evolving into 'business law'.[7]

In the middle ages, cases of 'commercial law' were heard in special courts. As litigation frequently involved people of different national and social origins, judges based their decisions on a mixture of mercantile codes and usages, while paying particular attention to good faith. The formalism of legal procedure was somewhat relaxed, and judicial decisions were rendered on the basis of considering facts rather than legal technicalities.[8]

Originally, 'commercial law' was mostly maritime law, with an emphasis on contracts related to sales, transportation, and money-lending. With time, the nature of trade became more diverse and more complex. 'Commercial law' also applied to land-based trade (in the context of fairs and markets), including production, storage, and distribution, and to people involved in any economic activity. A final development even took consumption and consumer protection into consideration. A standard modern treatise of (British) commercial law deals with property, contract (mostly sales and partnerships), agency, payment instruments and systems, financing, insolvency (in connection with company law), and the resolution of commercial disputes through litigation or arbitration.[9]

While 'commercial law' was exclusively concerned with identifiable (registered) businesses and exclusively applied to business transactions performed by well-defined groups of people, traders, and professional businessmen, such restrictions came to be seen as counterproductive and called for adjustment. So the modern trend is for 'commercial law' to evolve into 'business law', disregarding the specific status of both structures and people, and combining elements of both private and public law. Legal practitioners thus deal with all kinds of issues relating to the multifarious aspects of commercial life.[10]

Because 'business law' is more inclusive than 'commercial law', and because of the reciprocal 'civilizing' of commercial law and 'commercializing' of civil law which resulted in the development of 'business law', it seems appropriate to look at Roman legal institutions, both private and public, in their historical development from the earliest time until the period of classical law. The purpose is to evaluate their commercial relevance, usefulness, and adequacy in comparison with both later 'commercial law' and 'business law'. The following survey will show that while the appellation of Roman 'commercial law' is unsustainable, the Roman law of commerce shares many features with modern 'business law', features which extend far beyond the scope and limits of the Roman law of obligations.

2. Towards a History of Roman Business Law: From Barter to Sale

'Buying and selling originate with exchange or barter.' These are the opening words of the title on sale in Justinian's *Digest*, excerpted from Paul's commentary on the praetorian edict (D. 18.1.1 pr.). Trade certainly existed before the extant sources reveal how Roman law dealt with it. In a pre-monetized society, the exchange of goods and services was presumably based on barter or exchange (*amoibè* or *permutatio*).[11] In spite of the symmetrical feature of barter that both parties were equally uncertain about the quality of goods to be obtained,[12] classical jurists viewed barter as an impediment to trade because of the difficulty of matching demand to supply. To be sure, some commodities (such as cattle, metals, slaves, staples) were deemed universally desirable and used as monetary instruments at a very early date. The consensus on a constant medium of exchange eventually took the form of coinage. While relying on bronze bullion (*aes rude/grave*), the Romans started using Greek coinage by the fifth or fourth century BC and coined their own by the early third. Barter undoubtedly gave rise to disputes in early Rome, but there is no trace of any litigation connected with it. It is possible that it was not legally recognized before a much later period and that social control was sufficient to settle such disputes. Besides, non-monetary commercial exchanges must have existed throughout Roman history, especially wherever and whenever currency was a scarce commodity and monetization an unfamiliar abstraction. Even though the geographer Strabo, active in the Augustan period, associates barter with backwardness and the uncivilized way of life typical of marginal, unassimilated tribes,[13] it must have been a Roman reality all along.

Classical Roman jurists knew of the practice of barter and dealt with it rather marginally. In the first century AD Sabinus and Cassius thought of it as equivalent to sale, while Nerva and Proculus disagreed with them.[14] The mid-second-century jurist Gaius,[15] following Sabinus, underlines its antiquity by citing Homer[16] and reports earlier disputes concerning its contractual status. Around the time of Trajan, Sextus Pedius and Aristo, both cited and followed by Paul a century later,[17] address issues by analogy with the consensual contract of sale (*emptio venditio*). Paul – the only classical jurist whose works are excerpted in the title of the *Digest* dealing with barter (D. 19.4, *De rerum permutatione*) – wonders about the nature of the obligation arising from such a transaction, buyer (*emptor*) and seller (*venditor*), price (*pretium*) and goods (*merx*) being indistinguishable from one another, causing difficulty in the event of non-delivery or eviction.[18] It is only in the late classical period that barter was promoted from the status of 'unenforceable *pactum*' to that of so-called 'innominate real contract'. Justinian's *Code* preserves several imperial constitutions from the mid- and late third century AD on the subject.[19] This suggests that payments in kind may have increased when the Roman monetary system was in disarray, and the need to regulate this type of commercial exchange may have become more urgent.

The history of barter in Roman law serves as a reminder that not all economic transactions were necessarily sanctioned by law.[20] For commerce in general the first (that is, both the earliest and most prominent) problem to be dealt with is legal recognition and therefore jurisdiction.

3. *Ius Commercii* and International Law

Among the first policies enacted by the republican state after the revolution of 509 BC, an important step was to establish and define commercial contacts with neighbours, both immediate (Latins and other Italic people in the region) and further afield (Etruscans, Greeks, and Carthaginians, to name only the most important ones). Polybius records the content of a series of treaties between the Romans and Carthaginians.[21] In the first treaty (c. 509–507 BC), it was agreed that trade carried on by the Romans in Sardinia, Sicily, and Africa – all Carthaginian territories at the time – should be strictly controlled and guaranteed by the state. Transactions were to be concluded through an auctioneer (*kèrux*) and a scribe (*grammateus*), both of whom engaged the Carthaginian state's good faith (*pistis*) towards sellers. There is no mention of reciprocity. This sounds like protection against piracy, ransom, or extortion, as the distinction between such practices and trade is sometimes blurred. The second treaty (c. 348 BC)[22] explicitly forbade piracy and opened up trade in Sicily and Africa for the Romans and at Rome for the Carthaginians: traders of each nation had the same rights as the natives.[23] This meant that the exchange of goods between Romans and Carthaginians had the same legal validity in either place as between fellow countrymen. A third (or fourth?)[24] treaty of c. 278 BC reasserted these provisions. Subsequent treaties, while redefining areas of respective power and influence, did not question the basic trade agreement, the text of which, interestingly, was engraved on bronze tablets and preserved in the aediles' office.[25]

Whereas Polybius does not enter into detail on the legal aspects of arrangements for international trade, Dionysius of Halicarnassus[26] reports in the context of the so-called *foedus Cassianum* (a treaty concluded in about 493 BC with neighbouring Latin communities) that contracts between Romans and Latins would be enforced in court within ten days, wherever they had been concluded. This provision implies that in any court of law Romans and Latins would enjoy identical legal standing, with equal protection by the law recognized and enforced by the respective courts. This would have excluded the potential conflicts arising from competing legal systems and inaugurated a form of international (or supranational) law (*ius gentium*).[27] In addition, plaintiffs are guaranteed a speedy trial, facilitated by the fact that discrepancies between legal systems should be irrelevant. This arrangement would be known subsequently to the Romans as *commercium/ius commercii*,[28] namely the right to make formal contracts, to acquire property, and to resort to courts according to Roman law and procedure.[29] It was, or became, part of a larger package (*isopoliteia*) including the right to intermarry (*conubium*) and to participate in civic life (*suffragium*). This interpretation is based on the terms of the settlement of 338 BC, by which Latins were deprived of various rights they had previously enjoyed.[30] It is quite possible that *commercium* allowing Latins to benefit from the protection of Roman law went beyond the rights secured through the Romano-Carthaginian treaties.[31] It is also likely that the scope of *commercium* was limited in comparison with Roman citizenship and did not come close to extending to these privileged foreigners (*peregrini*) a legal protection equal to that enjoyed by Roman citizens.[32]

4. Commerce in Early Legislation

The issue of legal recognition of commercial transactions concluded with foreigners was taken up in the first Roman 'codification' of law known as the XII Tables, traditionally dated to about 451–450 BC. Foreigners (*hostes*),[33] presumably with *commercium*, can have their day in court (table 2.2), possibly with some degree of priority over other cases with respect to international treaties.[34] Foreigners could only acquire ownership through formal conveyance, such as *mancipatio*.[35] The seller or transferor would have to protect the buyer or transferee against eviction by a third party for an unlimited period of time, because the one- or two-year period of prescription (*usucapio*) which applied to Roman citizens did not apply to foreigners but was everlasting (tables 6.3, 6.4).[36]

The XII Tables contained some dispositions offering potential for innovation. Take, for example, the law of contracts (6.1): 'When someone shall perform a *nexum* or a *mancipatio*, rights (*ius*) will be defined by what the tongue has pronounced.' *Nexum* is an early form of loan performed like *mancipatio*, 'by means of bronze and scales' (*per aes et libram*) and guaranteed by the pledge of the very person of the debtor.[37] Regarded as unduly risky and anti-social in its consequences, it was abolished in the late fourth century by a *lex Poetelia Papiria* (326 or 313 BC).

Mancipatio proved a more durable institution. The provision in the XII Tables introduces a verbal dimension to the formal act, allowing the parties to specify the terms of the contract to be concluded. Originally the solemn utterance before witnesses or *nuncupatio* may have been more or less fixed, prescribed words being imposed on the parties. The fact that the same ritual *per aes et libram* was performed in widely different contexts – such as the making of a will or a donation, the conveyance of property, the constitution of a dowry or servitude, the emancipation of a dependant, or the contracting of a loan – would point to a wider range of prescribed statements. In pre-classical Roman law, contractual obligations were overwhelmingly oral, the *stipulatio* (oral contract) being flexible – and liable to become increasingly so – enough to address adequately most social and economic needs. *Nuncupatio* and *stipulatio* share the faculty of clarifying intentions in any legal situation. In both cases only one party's intention is clarified.

It is remarkable that the XII Tables, for all the provisions (between 88 and 109) that are preserved or reconstructed, have little to say about commerce.[38] Table 3.5 and 3.6 allude incidentally to periodic market-days (*nundinae*). Some other clauses are pregnant with important features of later legal developments in the law of commerce, such as the civil liability of masters for the (wrong)doings of their dependants (table 8.2 and 12.2, *noxa*), deceit (table 8.10, *fraus*), and malice aforethought (table 8.9, *dolus malus*). Much of the law, however, is concerned with criminal law, police regulation, and civil procedure. This latter field, with its reliance on the role of magistrates, would despite its formalism prove instrumental in the development of much of the Roman law of commerce over the next three centuries or so (mid-fifth to late-second century BC).

5. The Pros and Cons of Civil Procedure

In the archaic and mid-republican periods, civil litigation fell within the scope of one of five actions of the law (*legis actiones*) or general remedies granted by a magistrate endowed with jurisdiction based on *imperium*. These remedies ranged from the taking of a pledge (*pignoris capio*) or personal execution (*manus iniectio*) to the initiating of judicial procedure in front of the magistrate (*iudicis arbitrive postulatio*), on the basis of a specific claim (*condictio*) which was at times stated under oath (*sacramentum*). Plaintiffs had to resort to one of these remedies (*actiones*) according to the nature of the claim. If none of the remedies fitted the case, there was no claim. Some remedies were more flexible than others. However, because of its excessive formalism, this archaic system of civil procedure underwent a natural evolution while keeping some of its key features: the two-step procedure, first in front of the magistrate (*in iure*), then before a judge (*apud iudicem*); and the turning point of the joinder of issue (*litis contestatio*), whereby the parties agreed on the legal framework, sanctioned by the magistrate, within which the appointed judge(s) would have to evaluate the facts. This legal framework was eventually described in a written formula instructing the judge(s) about the path to follow and leading to two opposite outcomes of the forthcoming trial ('if it appears that . . ., then condemn; if not, then absolve'). Whatever happened thereafter, the joinder of issue extinguished the plaintiff's claim.[39]

Commercial transactions could often – but not always – be enforced through the existing set of original remedies. Some situations, however, called for new solutions. Additional remedies came to be created over the next centuries by statutes, such as the *lex Marcia* against usury in 104 BC,[40] or by magistrates' edicts. Remedies came to be divided into those of the civil law (*actiones civiles*) and those introduced by magistrates (*actiones honorariae*), whether the praetor or the aedile. Since magistrates were free to deliver – or not – a legal remedy upon one party's request, the available remedies tended to mushroom. Since the magistrate's edict was valid for the duration of his tenure of office, a recognized *actio* could technically be refused (*denegatio actionis*), although social pressure may have played a part in the quest for consistency. Adventurous magistrates might be expected to create new *actiones* if and when they considered that the situation or their sense of equity allowed them to do so. Creativity could take various forms. When a remedy existed but did not exactly fit the situation, the magistrate could grant an *actio utilis* that extended the scope of the original remedy. If the existing but unsatisfactory remedy was based on a statute, the magistrate could introduce a fiction in order to meet the situation, such as the fiction that a party was a Roman citizen even though he was an alien (*peregrinus*). If Roman law provided no remedy to address the issue even remotely, the magistrate could create one based on his perception of the situation (*actio in factum*). Faced with an actual legal problem, the magistrate was allowed – and expected – to devise a legal solution, leaving it to the judge to decide whether the facts that had led to the solution were correct. As will be seen later on, this instrument proved to be most efficient in dealing with issues related to commercial life.[41]

It is obvious that this system, introduced between the fourth and second centuries BC and called the *ordo* or formulary system, gave great power to magistrates in charge of granting *actiones*. To alleviate the suspicion of arbitrariness and to give a sense of coherence to the administration of justice, magistrates who had jurisdiction were required to announce ahead of time when and in what circumstances they would grant a remedy (*actio*). They did so through their (yearly) edict. We know next to nothing about the circumstances in which they devised their edicts, but we can imagine that outside inspiration or pressure may not have been totally foreign to their decisions. Pressure from whom remains debatable, but jurists and professionals involved in all kinds of business transactions unavoidably come to mind.[42] Edictal law should be regarded as the ad hoc answer to legal problems and situations, whether foreseen or encountered. In this sense, it can be said that at least in its private law elements the Roman law of commerce was essentially a law originating with traders and adapted to the requirements of traders, although not exclusively traders. The *ius honorarium* introduced by magistrates in order to aid, supplement, or correct the existing civil law was geared towards protecting and promoting the interests of the community.[43] Economic interests must have ranked high on the list. Unfortunately, the details mostly escape us.

During the fifth and early fourth centuries BC, justice was administered by the consuls. Admittedly, plebeian aediles, two in number, may have had some jurisdiction, the extent of which is unclear. In 367 BC, if not before, new magistracies reserved to patricians were created: both the praetorship and the curule aedileship were devised to compensate for the loss of power resulting from sharing the consulship with plebeians. The new magistracies diluted some of the consuls' powers, thus allowing patricians to retain control over them. These new magistrates held *potestas*, including the right to issue edicts and to enforce their authority, and they held *imperium*, the basis of their judicial power (*iurisdictio*).[44] With the addition of further praetors in and after 241 BC who dealt with foreigners (*peregrini*) and later held provincial governorships, these magistrates (praetors and aediles) were responsible for legal matters and the supervision of markets. Their part in the development and implementation of the Roman law of commerce is attested by what remains of the edicts they promulgated over several centuries. Roman business law is first and foremost edictal law. However, individual edicts were necessarily phrased as briefly as possible and therefore left much room for interpretation. This is where the jurists stepped in, and edictal law must be approached through the juristic writings of the classical period, often the very source from which edictal law can be reconstructed. In the next sections, both sources of law will be examined in order to assess the making and refining of Roman business law. One should remember, however, that several centuries may have elapsed from the time a remedy was created until the time the legal texts commenting on it were written, before later finding their way into the *Digest*.

6. The Edict of the Curule Aediles

In their capacity as magistrates of the city, the curule aediles were in charge of supervising the markets. What remains of their edicts[45] goes back at least to the first half of the second century BC and is known through citations preserved in the *Digest* (D. 21.1, *De aedilicio edicto et redhibitione et quanti minoris*) and the work of the second-century AD antiquarian Aulus Gellius.[46] These cover two topics: the sale of slaves (*mancipia*), and the sale of animals (*iumenta, ferae*). The edict stipulates (i) that buyers of defective slaves will be granted a remedy for rescission (*actio redhibitoria*) if the seller has concealed a specific defect, whether or not he was aware of it; and (ii) that a remedy for diminution of the price (*actio aestimatoria* or *quanti minoris*) will be available to buyers cheated of what was owed to them, including qualities advertised that turn out to be lacking. The former kind of claim was available for 60 days or 6 months; the latter for a year.[47]

The aedilician edict was traditional: aediles were in office for one year only and usually they did not have the legal training necessary to be innovative. Like their better-known senior colleagues, the praetors, aediles tended to borrow most or all of their edicts from their predecessors. In time this resulted in a rather static document, eventually codified by Salvius Iulianus in the age of Hadrian, perhaps as an appendix to the praetorian edict (*edictum perpetuum*). We do not know when the aedilician edict ceased to be modified, but some first-century AD documentary evidence suggests that it was still viewed as dynamic under Nero, if not later.[48]

The content of the aedilician edict is mostly lost, perhaps due to its eventual merging with the praetorian edict. However, the reconstructed text gives several examples of how a slave may be defective. The aediles are said to have done everything possible to avoid ambiguity,[49] but there was ample room for elaboration. For all its flexibility and pragmatism, edictal law would be inadequate without interpretation by the jurists. Faced with provisions phrased briefly and of general scope, over several centuries the jurists took on the task of adjusting these provisions to the requirements of social and economic life within a logical framework. Title 21.1 of the *Digest* includes 62 excerpts from classical juristic writings on the subject. The earliest authority quoted in them is Cato (presumably the Elder),[50] followed by several republican jurists. It provides valuable evidence about ancient slavery and the slave trade. The late republican jurist C. Trebatius Testa, for instance, downplayed bad breath as the result of poor oral hygiene, a condition that Apuleius could have treated adequately two centuries later.[51] The Flavian jurist Sextus Pedius discusses the case of the bed-wetter and distinguishes between slaves suffering from a bladder condition and those who are too drunk or too lazy to get up at night.[52] Mental defects are taken seriously: slaves hooked on games or art works are considered defective by the late second-century AD jurist Venuleius Saturninus.[53] At stake were the smooth running of the slave trade, consumer protection, and the expected productivity of slave labour.

The animal trade presented similar problems but seemingly triggered less discussion on the part of the jurists[54] or less interest on the part of the compilers: dangerous animals, including dogs, should be kept away or chained, so that they do not attack people, thus causing damage calling for monetary penalties. Animals should be sold with the trappings (*ornamenta*) they wore at the time of sale, lest the sale be rescinded or a diminution of the price be granted. Interestingly, the aediles consider sales (and returns) in bulk, for instance for a pair of mules. This applies to slaves as well, be it a company of actors or simply siblings.[55]

Diminution of the price could be obtained through the *actio quanti minoris/aestimatoria*, which the aediles mentioned only in connection with animals,[56] but which the jurists showed to apply to slaves as well.[57] This is typical of the work of classical jurists. We know of provisions dealing with partnerships of slave dealers (*societates venaliciariorum*),[58] the castration of young slaves,[59] and the definition of trappings (*ornamenta*).[60] Consumer protection, however, was not limited to the sale of slaves or animals, at least by Diocletian's time.[61] Besides, Ulpian points out that the aedilician edict applies to sales only and not to other categories of contract such as hire and lease (*locatio conductio*), because such contracts were never under aedilician jurisdiction or – and the introduction of an alternative explanation would be telling if the whole passage were not interpolated – because the contracts are different.[62]

Although the aediles were in charge of supervising local markets and their edicts were recognized not only in Rome but also in the rest of Italy and apparently across the empire by the second century AD,[63] the scope of aedilician law was dwarfed by praetorian law. This is confirmed by the fact that few classical jurists are known to have commented on the aedilician edict: Ofilius and possibly Labeo in the late republican and Augustan periods, Caelius Sabinus and Sextus Pedius in the first century AD, Pomponius and Gaius in the second, Paul and Ulpian in the early third. It is likely that the aedilician edict eventually became an appendix to the praetorian edict, since the curule aediles' competences were progressively absorbed by other magistrates and imperial officials.[64]

7. The Praetor's Edict

Both the urban and peregrine praetors issued edicts, which were valid and possibly binding during their one-year term in office, at the end of which individual edicts could either be dropped or renewed by transfer into the successor's edict.[65] Dio Cassius reports that in 67 BC a plebeian tribune named C. Cornelius introduced a plebiscite (*lex Cornelia de edictis/ de iurisdictione praetoris*) compelling all praetors – and possibly governors as well – to abide by their own edicts; their edicts contained the basic principles (*dikaia*) according to which they would administer justice but not all remedies (*dikaiomata*) which were required in order to enforce contracts. This piece of legislation was part of a larger package aimed at curbing corruption on the part of the senatorial class and ensuring legal consistency. It may have re-enacted an earlier custom or law that had been neglected or breached during the 80s and 70s BC.[66]

The making of praetorian edicts during the republic and early empire is something of a mystery.[67] Of all the edicts preserved or reconstructed, none can be dated precisely and a few only roughly. Vague *termini ante quos* are provided by quotation, mention, or allusion in the commentaries on the edict by republican and Augustan jurists such as Servius Sulpicius Rufus, Ofilius, or Labeo. The sum of those edicts that had been retained over the years was codified in about AD 130 to form the *Edictum Perpetuum*. What remains of the edict of the urban praetor was reconstructed by Otto Lenel in the nineteenth century on the basis of the structure of Justinian's *Code* and *Digest* and the numerous quotations preserved in the *Digest*, especially from the commentaries on the edict by Paul (80 books) and Ulpian (81 books).[68] What survives amounts to 292 entries (*rubricae*) distributed into 45 titles in 5 parts. For many of the 292 entries, nothing but the title is preserved or can be reconstructed. The order does not necessarily correspond to the chronology of their introduction into the edict; there are reasons to believe that the arrangement was revisited even shortly before – if not at the time of – its final codification. On the basis of a comparison of the space devoted to various parts of the edict in Paul's and Ulpian's commentaries as opposed to Sextus Pedius' commentary on the first-century-AD edict, it appears that some dispositions that affect business may have been shifted to a different section. At some point in the late first or early second century AD (possibly at the time of the codification of the edict), the law of indirect agency seems to have been severed from its original context (the special liability of seamen, innkeepers, and stable-keepers for what was entrusted to them in the course of business) and linked with banking and financing on the one hand and consensual (good faith) contracts on the other.[69]

The urban praetor's edict contributes a great deal to our knowledge of Roman business law, since 9 titles out of 45, and more than 40 rubrics out of 292, deal with legal issues concerning commerce.[70] Unsurprisingly, this means maritime law; banking; agency; contracts between private individuals, and between private individuals or companies and the Roman government; securities; and procedure. The question is whether any of the edicts concern traders to the exclusion of other actors participating in legal transactions. The answer is unambiguously positive, although such cases are rather limited.

Title XIX of the edict (§§ 106–112) introduced the good-faith remedies (*De bonae fidei iudiciis*) that are central to economic activities. The real contract of deposit (D. 16.3), *fiducia* as a form of real security,[71] and the consensual contracts of mandate (D. 17.1), partnership (D. 17.2), sale (D. 19.1), and hire (D. 19.2) were all devised during the mid-republican period. They usefully supplemented the older, flexible but formal oral contract of *stipulatio* in that they considered questions of will, permission, and awareness (or the lack of it) in relation to the parties to a contract. By enabling transactions to be carried out without the presence of one or both parties, they opened the door to a major innovation: the law of indirect agency (see below, 228).

8. Sale

The consensual contract of sale (*emptio venditio*) was introduced by the second century BC. At the minimum, buyer and seller had to reach a specific agreement on both the object of sale and its price. The usual terms of the contract could be modified or specified through *stipulatio* or *pactum*. In practice, the parties' agreement was often made explicit – and strengthened – by the written record (*chirographum*) of what sounds like a *stipulatio*. The seller had to warrant his title to the object of sale and its quality (that is, lack of defects). The buyer, who originally bore all the risks of the transaction ('caveat emptor'), came to enjoy the protection of the law enforced by the aediles, praetors, and, later on, prefects, in accordance with established standards of good faith.[72] The Roman law of sale, for all its sophistication and prominent importance in commercial life, was not specific to the business community.[73] Other areas of law, such as transportation or agency, are more likely to have been the preserve of merchants.

9. Transportation

The law of carriage, for both land- or sea-transport of people and goods, combines several areas of law, including the consensual contract of hire (*locatio conductio*, D. 19.2; C. 4.65), whose object could be either the means of transportation (*res* in the form of pack or draft animals, mounts, porters, wagons, ships, storage rooms), the task (*opus*), or the services provided by professionals (*operae*). Specific modes of financing were developed (maritime loans or *faenus nauticum*, D. 22.2; C. 4.33), as well as early forms of insurance against the enormous risks connected with navigation (*lex Rhodia de iactu*, D. 14.2), and rules about safekeeping (*custodia*) in storage (*horrea*) or in transit (*naves, cauponae, stabula*, D. 4.9 and 47.5).

Provisions in the edict call for a higher standard of liability on the part of shippers and inn- or stable-keepers for goods entrusted to their care in the course of their business. The operators (*exercitores*) of the ship, inn, or stable are responsible for wrongdoing (including theft) by their employees, whether slaves or free, because they chose their staff and had a chance to vet them. By analogy, innkeepers were also responsible for the wrongdoing of their guests, at least those who lived there on a permanent basis, as opposed to passing travellers and passengers on a ship.[74] The owner of the stolen property could sue either the thief under civil law or the operator under praetorian law.[75] If the operator had guaranteed the safekeeping of the goods, he could sue the thief himself.[76] The duty of safekeeping was conditioned by the operators' free choice (*arbitrium*) in accepting the goods to be watched. In that sense, Ulpian considers the praetor's edict 'most useful'.[77] The drafting of the edict is most economical, and the terminology is elucidated by the jurists: 'seaman' (*nauta*) designates the operator of a ship (*exercitor*) or his agent (*magister navis*), not the crew. Along the same lines, the 'inn-' or 'stable-keeper' (*caupo* or *stabularius*) is the person in charge of the facilities, either as operator (*exercitor*) or as manager (*institor*);[78] 'ship' is understood as including river-boats and rafts;[79] 'goods' (*res, merces*) mean not only merchandise but also personal belongings transported as luggage or clothing.[80] The praetor provides the general rule, the jurists determine its scope, and the judge sees to its application.

The remedy brought against the operator or manager was based on the initial contract of hire or deposit that bound him to the plaintiff. It called for different standards of liability: fault (*culpa*) in the former case, fraud (*dolus*) in the latter.[81] Cases not covered by the edict – for instance, for lack of fault or fraud on the part of the operator or because no price was paid for the service – gave rise to an *actio in factum*.[82] If the damage was caused by one of the sailors' slaves who was not a sailor himself, the operator would nevertheless be liable to an *actio utilis*.[83] Conversely, operators could avail themselves of a defence (*exceptio*) in the event of an act of God (*vis maior*), such as shipwreck or attack by pirates or bandits.[84] Thus the law took into account the reality of commercial life by striking a balance between the interests of customers and those of business people.[85]

10. Banking

The praetorian edict contains two dispositions concerning professional bankers (*argentarii, argentariae mensae exercitores*). The so-called *receptum argentarii* was an informal promise or guarantee to pay a client's debt on an agreed day.[86] Surprisingly, this arrangement bound the banker and creditor and left out the debtor. In addition, the nature and very existence of the debt were irrelevant. Despite its obvious usefulness for banking, the *receptum argentarii* is little attested in the legal sources because it was merged in late antiquity with the wider ranging, more general *constitutum debiti*.[87]

The money that the banker agreed to pay probably came from the customer's account. The praetor rightly compelled bankers to produce accounts upon request from judicial authorities (*EP* § 9a, b, *De edendo*). Ulpian regards the rationale for this edict as most equitable.[88] The praetor arranged for reciprocity, the banker being entitled to ask for production of accounts by an opponent, unless the banker had the means of achieving the same result through documents readily accessible to him because of his occupation.[89] Gaius explains that bankers (*argentarii*) have a special obligation to produce their accounts because their trade has a *publica causa*, which means that the Roman people had a vested interest in regulating the profession.[90] For that reason, according to the third-century jurist Callistratus, women were banned from it.[91]

11. Money-lending

The edict deals with loans for consumption (*mutuum*, D. 12.1; C. 4.1–2), loans for use (*commodatum*, D. 13.6; C. 4.23), pledge (*pignus*, D. 13.7; C. 4.24), and set-off (*compensatio*, D. 16.2; C. 4.31). These legal institutions were needed in commercial life, in terms of credit, security, and payment, but were by no means restricted to the activities of professional traders. It is tempting, however, to explain the sophistication and sometimes paradoxical and adventurous nature of some arrangements as dictated by the requirement of specialized trading.[92] The edict on deposit (*EP* § 106) originally followed the edict on *compensationes* (*EP* § 100), before the shift of the title dealing with agency presumably occurred (*EP* §§ 101–5).[93]

12. AGENCY

Agency is undoubtedly one of the most significant areas of progress in the field of Roman business law.[94] As a matter of principle Roman law was averse to the idea that one person's action could engage another's liability, although there was no problem in benefiting from it. Slaves' wrongdoing did, however, give rise to noxal liability on the part of their master.[95] This somewhat contradictory position precluded the concept of agency, so important in economic life – even more so given the negative attitude of the Roman elite towards trade and commerce.[96] The patriarchal nature of Roman society offered a way to overcome this obstacle: persons in power (*in potestate, alieni iuris*), such as sons, daughters, other descendants, and especially slaves, had no legal capacity of their own. The praetor, aware of this asymmetrical state of affairs, had only to extend the liability of the principal to contracts made by his agent.[97] To that effect a set of six remedies was created over the course of time, presumably between the late third and early first centuries BC: the title in the edict 'On the dealings of the ship's captain, business manager, and person in power' contains one of the boldest and most ingenious creations of praetorian law,[98] the early history of which is unfortunately blurred, but can be reconstructed on the basis of a few classical – and therefore much later – legal texts.

Ulpian records that the praetor attended first to remedies given for the full amount (*in solidum*) on the basis of contracts concluded with persons in power.[99] Remedies giving rise to a liability limited to the amount of the *peculium* or the extent of enrichment (*dumtaxat de peculio aut de in rem verso*) and those based on the contracts of non-dependent persons should therefore be regarded as later additions or extensions. Gaius expressly says that the praetor started with the grant of a remedy in relation to authorized transactions carried out by a dependant (the *actio quod iussu*) and added by analogy two further remedies for transactions concluded by dependent ship's captains (*actio exercitoria*) or business managers (*actio institoria*).[100] The liability of the father or master was based on his willingness to allow contracts to be made with his dependant. This willingness was expressed through the appointment (*praepositio*) of the ship's captain (*magister navis*) to a ship or the business manager (*institor*) to a business. It is possible (although not certain) that originally the *actio institoria* was available only in the context of the management of a shop (*taberna*).[101] Alternatively, a rural context, such as the Catonian villa, may have provided the original *Sitz im Leben* of the *actio institoria*, since non-legal sources refer to *institores* under the titles of *vilici* and *actores* in this context.[102] The extension to other types of business – such as workshops, credit institutions, and so forth – would only be natural.

Whether ships should be regarded as a later extension is a controversial question. Gaius' *Digest* and Justinian's *Code* each present the *actio exercitoria* before the *actio institoria*.[103] This suggests that by the time of the composition of the *Edictum Perpetuum* the order reflected the prominence – not necessarily the priority – of the *actio exercitoria* over the *actio institoria*. On the other hand, both Gaius and Ulpian stress the particularity of the conditions in which a ship's captain works in comparison with a business manager:[104] the distance separating agent and principal from one another in the context of trade by sea makes it more difficult for third parties to check the agent's legal status and scope of authority. Sub-appointments are more readily acceptable in the case of a ship's captain than a business manager 'for practical reasons'.[105] It also seems that, by contrast with business managers, ship's captains are presented as not being dependants. I believe this to be the result of a later development: third parties could elect whether to sue the ship's operator (*exercitor*) or the ship's captain. The operator had no remedy against third parties contracting with his captain, supposedly because he did not need one since he could sue the captain on the contract of employment or mandate which defined the relationship between principal and agent. Ulpian notes, however, that in practice the prefects in charge of the corn supply (*annona*) and provincial governors assisted informally.[106] The peculiarities of agency in the context of trade by sea explain why two distinct but related remedies were necessary and may suggest that the *actio exercitoria* developed from a more general *actio institoria* into a ground-breaking legal instrument, both remedies eventually applying to the contracts of independent agents.[107]

The main legal issue discussed by the jurists in connection with both remedies is the scope of the appointment (*praepositio*). In order to give rise to the principal's full liability, the contract concluded by the agent must pertain to the business of which he or she (women and children could be appointed[108]) is in charge. Republican and Augustan jurists such as Servius and Labeo and their successors list various types of activity in connection with which specific transactions may give rise to an *actio institoria* or *exercitoria*, thus contributing to the definition of business and enterprise in the Roman world.[109] The scope of the appointment was implicitly conditioned by the nature of the business and could be expressly spelled out in a charter (*lex praepositionis*) used as a job description.[110] Any extension (*iussum*) or limitation (*proscriptio*) had to be publicly posted and advertised. Appointments combining two (or more) types of activities under the responsibility of the same manager are attested.[111]

Ulpian also discusses cases of sub-appointment, joint managers working for a single operator, and joint operators appointing a single manager either within a partnership (*societas*) or as joint owners.[112] The last configuration has been identified as the possible ancestor of company law, so prominent in modern commercial law.[113] The Roman law of indirect agency also applied to collectivities, both private and public, such as companies of publicans, professional and religious associations (*collegia*), and towns (*municipia* and *coloniae*).[114]

The second part of the praetorian edict on indirect agency deals with those remedies that strictly apply to transactions carried out by dependants. The *edictum triplex*[115] includes the *actio quod iussu* (D. 15.4), mentioned above as the likely original remedy for full liability of the principal, and two further remedies, eventually intertwined as the *actio de peculio aut de in rem verso* (D. 15.1–3), which imposed limited liability on the part of the principal on account of contracts concluded with his dependant.[116] Connected with the *actio de peculio* was a sixth remedy (*actio tributoria*, D. 14.4), whereby the principal was treated like any ordinary creditor when the agent's insolvency gave rise to an action on his *peculium*.[117] The order in which the various remedies appear in the *Digest* and presumably in the edict (§§ 101–5) cannot reflect the chronology of their respective creation. The transfer of the *actio quod iussu* to the very end of the series (D. 15.4) suggests that the order reflects the relative importance of each remedy in comparison with the others, the *actio quod iussu* being at best subsidiary in the classical period. It is therefore telling that the *actiones exercitoria* and *institoria* applying to contracts concluded by both dependent and independent appointees had taken precedence over all the others by the time of redaction of the *Edictum Perpetuum* in the second century AD. Accessorily, the reconstructed relative chronology of the creation of the so-called *actiones adiecticiae qualitatis* (with the addition of the *actio tributoria*) and their respective order in the edict indicate that the praetor favoured the interests of third parties who contracted with dependent agents rather than those of the principals whose liability was engaged.

Gaius reports that provincial governors (*proconsules*) ensured that those who contracted with persons in power obtained their due: if the *actio exercitoria, institoria,* or *tributoria* did not apply, the governor would grant the *actio quod iussu* for full liability provided authorization for the transaction existed; or the *actio de in rem verso* for the enrichment obtained from the transaction; or, in the last resort, the action based on the *peculium*.[118] The order of preference is altogether clear, and reflects the sense of equity (*ex bono et aequo*) of the political or judicial authority in relation to the third party. In one case, the owner of a runaway slave who had been appointed to lend money and to accept security (*pignus*) fought off a suit from barley traders who had been promised payment on behalf of customers. Interestingly, the prefect of the corn supply stepped in on behalf of the traders and decided to hold the master liable in full, pointing out that the slave was notoriously in the habit of being involved in various businesses, such as renting warehouses (*horrea*). The early third-century jurist Paul, who reports the advice he gave in the emperor's *consilium*, argued for considering the slave's payment as a type of guarantee (*fideiussio*), presumably as opposed to a *receptum argentarii*. On appeal, the prefect's decision was upheld by the emperor.[119]

13. THE PROVINCIAL EDICT

Ancient legal commentaries leave no doubt that the bulk of edictal law pertaining to commercial life was established through the praetorian edict and then developed by the jurists. As the case discussed in the last paragraph shows, provincial governors and prefects also used their *ius edicendi* to intervene when needed. Gaius' lone commentary on the provincial edict (in 30 books, as compared with only 10 for his commentary on the praetorian edict)[120] suggests that a general provincial edict, distinct from individual edicts applying to distinct provinces, existed by the second century, but that it was not so different from the praetorian edict as to justify separate treatment by any other classical jurist. Like the edict of the curule aediles, it may have been absorbed in the *Edictum Perpetuum* at some point.

The situation may have been different in the republican period. We happen to know something of Cicero's own edict as governor of Cilicia in 51/50 BC through his letters to his friend Atticus. In the winter of 50, Cicero was approached both by the Salaminians of Cyprus and by M. Scaptius and P. Matinius, agents of M. Iunius Brutus, for the recovery of a debt owed by the Salaminians to Brutus. The disagreement bore on the interest to be paid. Cicero stated that he had promised in his edict that he would not allow more than 12 per cent annually compounded interest whereas Scaptius was asking for 48 per cent simple interest.[121] Scaptius relied in opposition to Cicero's edict on a senatorial decree passed a few years before (56 BC) compelling the governor of Cilicia to honour a bond which was in blatant contravention with the *lex Gabinia* of 68/67 BC forbidding Romans to lend money to provincial communities. The details of the story and its outcome need not concern us here. Cicero obviously felt constrained by the terms of his own edict (described in a later letter),[122] although not by those of his predecessor in the position of governor of Cilicia. Cicero's provincial edict, kept intentionally short, was derived from the Asiatic edict of Q. Mucius Scaevola (consul in 86 BC) and divided into two parts: one was considered exclusively provincial and dealt with civic accounts (*rationes civitatum*), debt, rates of interest, contracts, and regulations applying to publicans; the other part contained the usual edictal material and dealt with such things as inheritance, possession, and sale of goods. Some rules remained unwritten, but Cicero boasts that he would let provincials use their own laws in their own courts, thus maintaining the fiction of restored autonomy. In disputes between publicans and provincials, the governor's protection of the provincials amounted to no more than a temporary measure, advertised as such in order to put pressure on the Greeks to settle as quickly as possible: after a fixed deadline the provision of the provincial edict regarding the rate of interest would give way to the terms of their agreement. Provincial governors, like aediles and praetors, used their *ius edicendi* both before and during their term of office, enabling them to react to unexpected circumstances and problems while at the same time exposing them to undue pressure on the part of groups and individuals and to the risk of self-contradiction.[123] In addition, local customs (*mos regionis*) and laws could be taken into account.[124]

The combined creativity of curule aediles, urban and peregrine praetors, and provincial governors provided ample material for the jurists to adjust the law to the needs of the business community in a growing and increasingly interconnected Mediterranean world. The flexibility of law-making through temporary or permanent edicts combined with a constant, recurring, and diverse exposure to neighbouring legal systems, especially in the Greek east, and blended new ingredients into the old Roman legal system. Cicero's Salaminian issue brought him into contact with the Greek institution of *syngrapha*, which (like the better attested *chirographum*) eventually shifted into Roman law as a form of written contract in addition to real, oral, and consensual contracts.[125]

Unsurprisingly, the Greeks were mostly influential in the field of maritime law. In spite of what the Romano-Carthaginian treaties of the early republican period (cf. above, 216–17) may suggest, the Romans were late – in relation to the Greeks and Carthaginians – in developing trade by sea and their own sea power. The Mediterranean world, especially in the east, was already bursting with commercial activities in the classical and Hellenistic periods. Navigation was regarded as being – and to some extent was – a dangerous activity, and the Greeks had devised some legal institutions aimed at minimizing the financial risks attached to it: the bottomry loan (*foenus nauticum*) and compensation for jettison of property (*iactus*) are two forms of maritime insurance in which the Roman jurists elaborated apparently pre-existing arrangements familiar to the trading community. How these arrangements passed into Roman law – provided they were actually borrowed and not simply reinvented as the logical solution to a universal problem – is a mystery, but it is fairly clear that the edict was not the way.[126]

14. Maritime Loans

Maritime loans are attested in the Roman world as early as the second century BC.[127] The loan (*pecunia traiecticia*) was made by private investors or professional bankers – acting as middlemen – to a shipper or group of shippers in a partnership and had to be repaid only if and when ship and cargo reached the agreed destination. Ship and cargo were considered securities for the loan, whose duration was limited in time (for example, 200 days in the case of one Callimachus, for a trip from Beirut to Brindisi).[128] In case of shipwreck, attack by pirates, or acts of God, the creditor would bear the loss. On the other hand, if the voyage was successful, the creditor was entitled to collect interest at a much higher rate than the 12 per cent annually which the law permitted for regular loans. Many points remain problematic, and unfortunately neither the nine excerpts in the *Digest* (D. 22.2, from Servius Sulpicius Rufus to Ulpian) nor the four Diocletianic constitutions from the *Code* (C. 4.33) provide more than hints. It is not clear, for instance, on what ground the legal limit on the rate of interest could be exceeded. We know of no statute, senatorial decree, plebiscite, or edict abrogating it, although no fewer than four laws on usury were proposed or passed between 217 and 192 BC.[129] The jurists and the drafters of imperial constitutions insist on the notion of *periculum creditoris* (moneylender's risk), an allocation of risk that possibly reveals a favourable bias towards shippers, who had to show only good faith.[130] Maritime loans sound like a necessary evil akin to both speculation and insurance against disasters.

15. The Rhodian Law on Jettison

Disasters did strike, although unevenly. Greek and Roman literature, including Paul's report in the Acts of the Apostle,[131] betray both fascination for and familiarity with standard procedure during storms at sea. To rescue the ship, part or all of the cargo sometimes had to be jettisoned. Those whose goods had been saved thanks to the others' – sometimes unwilling – sacrifice were called to contribute to the loss. The Roman jurists acknowledge the routine resort to foreign usage,[132] the so-called *lex Rhodia de iactu*, the Rhodian origin of which is little more than hypothetical. From what can be reconstructed on the basis of D. 14.2 and Pseudo-Paul's *Sententiae*,[133] it seems that a contribution was expected not only in the case of jettison but also for ransom paid to pirates, according to late republican and Augustan jurists like Servius, Ofilius, and Labeo.[134] They and later classical jurists devised a very sophisticated system of estimating the respective market value of goods lost, damaged, or saved. Although the *lex Rhodia* was not included in any edict and should be regarded as a mere appendix to the law of hire and lease (*locatio conductio*), the title dedicated to it was placed between the *actio exercitoria* (D. 14.1) and the *actio institoria* (D. 14.3) by the compilers of the *Digest*, because the owners of the jettisoned goods had a remedy against the ship's captain, and because the *lex Rhodia* was akin to a *lex contractus* or *lex praepositionis*, in that it expounded the terms of the contract of hire between shipper and merchants.[135]

The legal status of the usage is uncertain but is somewhat illuminated by a very controversial text by the late-second-century jurist Volusius Maecianus, the alleged author of a monograph on the *lex Rhodia*.[136] A petitioner writes to the emperor to complain about being robbed by islanders after a shipwreck. The emperor's answer, based on an earlier ruling by Augustus, specifies that the *lex Rhodia* applies whenever it is not in conflict with Roman law. Taken at face value, the text indicates that a legal vacuum could – or had to – be filled by existing usage, whatever it is and whatever its origin; foreign customs are better than nothing, and Roman lawmakers could not be expected to cover all situations. Maritime law was obviously permeable to external input.

16. PUBLIC LAW: REGULATION AND EXPLOITATION

The combination of edictal law and jurisprudence, and the occasional adoption of international or local norms (laws and customs) certainly facilitated the development of commerce by providing the business community with adequate legal instruments and protection. However, there is another side to the coin, reflecting social and political concerns and fiscal necessities. This is where public law steps in.

Starting in the early republican period, a series of *leges fenebres* tended to limit the rate of interest before banning interest altogether, although unsuccessfully. Other public laws bearing on commercial activities regulated the food supply (*leges annonariae/frumentariae*), luxury consumption (*leges sumptuariae*), the occupation of agricultural land (*leges agrariae*), and taxation.[137] The point was to preserve the social order and the political power of the elite. One such law, the *plebiscitum Claudianum* of 219/218 BC, reiterated in slightly different form by the *lex Iulia repetundarum* of 59 BC, barred senators and their sons from owning – although not from operating – ships of large capacity (over 300 amphoras), so excluding them from lucrative public contracts connected with the food supply and hampering the marketing of the produce of ever-growing agricultural estates.[138] The ban may have been instrumental in developing the *actio exercitoria* and its extension to non-dependent captains of ships. The activities of shippers (*navicularii*) drew the attention of imperial government officials and gave rise to an abundant legislation into late antiquity. At stake was the reliability of the food supply of Rome and, from the fourth century, that of Constantinople. Organized in associations (*collegia, corpora*), at first the shippers enjoyed privileges such as exemption from compulsory public services; they ended up fulfilling a public service even against their will.[139]

State control over economic activities was not limited to shipping and became a general phenomenon in the fourth and fifth centuries. Unsurprisingly, it affected trades connected with the food industry (bakers, meat sellers, and so on), but it also extended to other commercial activities.[140] It was mostly exercised through taxation: in the republican and early imperial periods, trade was subject to all kinds of taxes, above all tolls and custom duties (*portoria*) at both municipal and imperial levels.[141] It is difficult to estimate the impact of taxation on the volume of trade, but it is clear that the burden increased with time: from the reign of Constantine until AD 498, a special tax in gold and silver called *collatio lustralis* or *chrysarguron* was collected on behalf of the imperial treasury from merchants, who therefore had to be registered.[142] By then, the time of laisser-faire and promotion of commercial activities on the part of public authorities was long gone.

Traders were not just considered a fiscal golden hen by a needy government. The attitude of lawmakers towards them had changed. The preamble of Diocletian's Price Edict (AD 301) accuses them in no uncertain terms of greed and selfishness and of being the cause of uncontrollable inflation, threatening them and their agents (*institores*) with capital punishment unless they desist from speculating and abide by the law setting maximum prices, possibly unrelated to market prices. A few years later, Lactantius claimed that the ill-advised imperial policy resulted in both slaughter and scarcity of goods.[143] In spite of its failure and eventual repeal the measure shows that it was soldiers rather than traders who had the emperor's ear.

17. Conclusion

To the question 'was Roman business law *designed for* traders?' we can propose a qualified answer: looking at the time of its development during the republic and principate, there is no doubt that edictal law and jurisprudence jointly produced legal institutions of unprecedented efficiency, offering pragmatic solutions to practical problems, occasionally borrowed from subject communities. This is true of private law. As for public law, it was concerned with social stability and fiscal necessity, not economic growth, and should be viewed as a permanent hindrance.

To the question 'was Roman business law *inspired by* traders?' the answer is less clear-cut. Roman magistrates and jurists invariably belonged to the elite. The dominant ideology would have liked us to think of it as a landed aristocracy, but the evidence suggests that senatorial, equestrian, and curial families were heavily – for senators, perhaps indirectly – involved in commercial activities, in spite of legal prohibitions and social pressures. The pragmatic nature of edictal law and the flexibility in its application attested in juristic writings make it difficult to rule out close and recurring contacts between the business community and lawmakers (and this is suggested by Cicero's occasional indiscretion). The sheer volume of legal opinions preserved in the *Digest* cannot be allowed to blur the fact that Roman business law is mostly edictal law, explained and extended by the jurists.

To the question 'was Roman business law *enforced by* traders or, at least, in special courts reserved for traders?' the answer can only be a negative one: there is not much evidence for a Roman equivalent to the Greek *emporikai dikai*.[144] Roman courts were composed either of *recuperatores* or a single judge or arbiter, who were selected from a list of respected people, some of whom could have been businessmen (*negotiatores*).[145] In the imperial period, jurisdiction passed to civil servants (*praefecti*, *praesides*, *iudices*) whose interests scarcely coincided with those of traders, and whose technical competence rested less on their personal legal expertise and practical experience than on the services of their staff. The evident worsening of the condition of traders in late antiquity does not point towards their receiving judicial privileges.

Notes

1. As suggested by the New Institutional Economics school of thought: see D. North and R. P. Thomas, *The Rise of the Western World: A New Economic History* (Cambridge, 1973); D. North, *Structure and Change in Economic History* (New York – London, 1981); D. North, *Institutions, Institutional Change and Economic Performance* (Cambridge, 1991); and P. Malanima, 'Progresso o stabilità? Il mercato nelle economie preindustriali', *Studi storici* 50 (2009): 7–8.
2. E. Lo Cascio, 'The early Roman empire: the state and the economy', in *The Cambridge Economic History of the Greco-Roman World*, ed. W. Scheidel, I. Morris, and R. Saller (Cambridge, 2007), 619 and 626 (quotation); W. V. Harris, 'Roman governments and commerce, 300 BC–AD 300', in *Mercanti e politica nel mondo antico*, ed. C. Zaccagnini (Rome, 2003), 282, 285; M. Silver, 'Roman economic growth and living standards: perceptions versus evidence', *Ancient Society* 37 (2007): 192 (quoting A. Wacke and H. W. Pleket), 210–11, 217–20; T. Terpstra, 'Roman law, transaction costs and the Roman economy: evidence from the Sulpicii archive', in Pistoi dia tèn technèn. *Bankers, Loans and Archives in the Ancient World. Studies in Honour of Raymond Bogaert*, ed. K. Verboven, K. Vandorpe, and V. Chankowski (Leuven, 2008), 345–69.
3. M. Kaser, *Das römische Privatrecht*, 2nd edn. (Munich, 1971), 474 ('The Romans did not develop a specific, autonomous commercial law.')
4. See, most recently, P. Cerami and A. Petrucci, *Diritto commerciale romano. Profilo storico*, 3rd edn. (Turin, 2010). Cf. also A. di Porto, 'Il diritto commerciale romano. Una "zona d'ombra" nella storiografia romanistica e nelle riflessioni storico-comparative dei commercialisti', *Nozione, formazione e interpretazione del diritto dall'età romana alle esperienze moderne. Ricerche dedicate al Prof. Filippo Gallo*, ed. M. Marrone (Naples, 1997), vol. 3, 413–52, citing G. Carnazza, *Il diritto commerciale dei Romani* (Catania, 1891); M. Bianchini, 'Diritto commerciale nel diritto romano', in *Digesto delle Discipline privatistiche. Sezione commerciale IV* (Turin, 1989), 320–33; M. Bianchini, 'Attività commerciali fra privato e pubblico in età imperiale', in *Fides, Humanitas, Ius. Studi in onore di Luigi Labruna*, ed. C. Cascione and C. Masi Doria (Naples, 2007), 423–38 (with some reservations). L. Labruna, 'Il diritto mercantile dei Romani e l'espansionismo', in *Le strade del potere*, ed. A. Corbino (Catania, 1994), 115–37, coins the term 'diritto mercantile'. Others speak only of 'istituti commerciali del/nel diritto romano': cf. C. Fadda, *Istituti commerciali del diritto romano. Lezioni dettate nella R. Università di Napoli nell'anno scolastico 1902–1903* (Naples, 1903; repr. with note by L. Bove, 1987); P. Cogliolo, *Gli istituti commerciali nel diritto romano. Corso compilato dall'Avv. E. Finzi e dallo studente G.G. Traverso, Anno accademico 1921–1922* (Genova, 1922); and A. Földi, 'Eine alternative Annäherungsweise: Gedanken zum Problem des Handelsrechts in der römischen Welt', *RIDA* 48 (2001): 85.
5. The debate started anew in Italy in the late 1980s: cf. Bianchini (n. 4) and di Porto (n. 4). It was subsequently carried on at various conferences: see, e.g., J.-F. Gerkens, reporting on the SIHDA conference of 2001 in *RIDA* 50 (2003): 489–516; Circolo Toscano 'Ugo Coli' at the Certosa di Pontignano (12–14 Jan. 2006); and the Fourth OxREP conference, 1–4 October 2009, including A. J. B. Sirks, 'Law, commerce and finance in the Roman empire', in *Trade, Commerce and the State in the Roman World*, ed. A. I. Wilson and A. K. Bowman (Oxford, forthcoming).

6. For surveys in English, cf. J. A. Crook, *Law and Life of Rome, 90 B.C.–A.D. 212* (Ithaca NY, 1967), ch. 7, 206–49; D. Johnston, *Roman Law in Context* (Cambridge, 1999), ch. 5, 77–111.
7. J. H. Merryman, *The Civil Law Tradition. An Introduction to the Legal Systems of Western Europe and Latin America*, 2nd edn. (Stanford, 1985), 12–13, 98–100, 146–7.
8. R. Goode, *Commercial Law*, 3rd edn. (London, 2004), 3–6.
9. Goode (n. 8).
10. C. Champaud, *Le droit des affaires*, 5th edn. (Paris, 1994); D. Legeais, *Droit commercial et des affaires*, 15th edn. (Paris, 2003); F.-X. Lucas, *Le droit des affaires* (Paris, 2005); D. Kelly, A. Holmes, and R. Hayward, *Business Law*, 5th edn. (Abingdon – New York, 2005). For the combination of private and public laws, cf. Goode (n. 8), 10; and Lucas, 8.
11. P. Meylan '*Permutatio rerum*', in Ius et lex. *Festgabe zum 70. Geburtstag von M. Gutzwiller* (Basel, 1959), 45–64. F. Kudlien, '*Mutator* und *permutatio* als finanz- und handelstechnische Termini', *MBAH* 20 (2001): 48–54 rightly points out that the word *permutatio* has various meanings.
12. N. Morley, *Trade in Classical Antiquity* (Cambridge, 2007), 59: contrast sale, where the seller has the advantage of knowing the quality of the goods on sale.
13. Strabo 3.3.7 (on Lusitanian mountain-dwellers, trading through exchange/*amoibè* or bullion); 7.5.5 (on Dalmatians). Cf. J. de Churruca, 'Le commerce comme élément de civilisation dans la *Géographie* de Strabon', *RIDA* 48 (2001): 41–56.
14. Paul D. 18.1.1.1.
15. Gaius 3.141.
16. *Iliad* 7.472–75.
17. D. 19.4.1.3 and D. 19.4.2.
18. D. 19.4.1–2; cf. D. 18.1.1 pr.-1; and Ulp. D. 21.1.19.5, possibly interpolated. Cf. R. Zimmermann, *The Law of Obligations. Roman Foundations of the Civilian Tradition* (Oxford, 1990), 250–2; 532–7; Johnston (n. 6), 78–9.
19. C. 4.64.1–8.
20. Cf. J.-J. Aubert 'L'économie romaine et le droit de la représentation indirecte sous la République romaine', in Cascione and Masi Doria (n. 4), 215–30 on the situation in fourth-century Athens.
21. Polyb. 3.22–27.
22. cf. Livy 7.27.
23. Polyb. 3.24.
24. Livy 9.43.
25. Polyb. 3.26; E. Ferenczy, 'Die römisch-punischen Verträge und die Protohistorie des *commercium*', *RIDA* 16 (1969): 259–82; B. Scardigli, *I trattati Romano-Cartaginesi* (Pisa, 1991); D. Nörr, 'Osservazioni in tema di terminologia giuridica predecemvirale e di ius mercatorum mediterraneo: il primo trattato cartaginese-romano', in *Le Dodici Tavole. Dai Decemviri agli Umanisti*, ed. M. Humbert (Pavia, 2005), 147–89, esp. 171–7, who sees in Polyb. 3.22.8 a reference to two common forms of sales (auction and written contract) and suggests a possible interpretation for the term *telos* (*auctoritas*) as the effect of the contract.
26. 6.95.
27. Nörr (n. 25), 183–4, with reference to H.-J. Wolff, *Das Problem der Konkurrenz von Rechtsordnungen in der Antike* (Heidelberg, 1979).
28. *UE* 19.5.

29. T. Mayer-Maly, '*Commercium*', *TR* 71 (2003): 1–6; Nörr (n. 25); and G. Minaud, *Les gens de commerce et le droit à Rome* (Aix-en-Provence, 2011), ch. 1 (§§ 19–70, esp. 35–36).
30. Livy 8.14.10.
31. L. Capogrossi Colognesi, 'Ius commercii, conubium, civitas sine suffragio. Le origini del diritto internazionale privato e la romanizzazione delle comunità latino-campane', in Corbino (n. 4), 3–64; D. Kremer, 'Trattato internazionale e legge delle Dodici Tavole', in Humbert (n. 25), 191–207.
32. M. Kaser, 'Vom Begriff des *commercium*', in *Studi in onore di V. Arangio-Ruiz* (Naples, 1953), vol. 2, 131–67, suggesting that *mancipatio* rather than in *iure cessio* was made available to foreigners as a formal means of conveying property.
33. cf. Cic. *Off.* 1.37.
34. Kremer (n. 31), 197–203.
35. *UE* 19.4.
36. Pace Kremer (n. 31), 203–6; and M. Humbert, 'Il valore semantico e giuridico di vsvs nelle Dodici Tavole', in Humbert (n. 25), 393–7. References to the XII Tables are given according to the numbering in *Roman Statutes.*
37. Varro *LL* 7.105.
38. J.-J. Aubert, 'The Republican economy and Roman law: regulation, promotion, or reflection?' in *The Cambridge Companion to the Roman Republic*, ed. H. I. Flower (Cambridge, 2004), 164–5. As W.V. Harris suggested to me, the archaic rules may have been superseded by the time the law found its way into the extant literary sources.
39. For details, see the chapter by Metzger, 283–4; Gaius 4.11–30; A. Borkowski and P. du Plessis, *Textbook on Roman law*, 3rd edn. (Oxford, 2005), 63–83.
40. Gaius 4.23.
41. For details, see the chapter by Metzger, 284; Gaius 4.30–47; J. Gaudemet, *Institutions de l'Antiquité*, 2nd edn. (Paris, 1982), 615–20.
42. E.g. Cic. *2 Verr.* 1.119. The evidence is more telling for a later period: cf. Nov. 136 (AD 535); Nov. 106 (540); Nov. 110 (541); Ed. Just. 7 (542) and 9 (date unknown) for the influence of moneylenders on imperial legislation. Cf. A. H. M. Jones, *The Later Roman Empire, 284–602. A Social, Economic, and Administrative Survey* (London, 1964), 350, 1139 n. 63.
43. Pap. D. 1.1.7 and Marci. D. 1.1.8.
44. The question of the *imperium* of the curule aediles is debated: see G. Impallomeni, *L'editto degli edili curuli* (Padua, 1955), 109–21; F. Reduzzi Merola, 'Ventes d'esclaves sur les marchés de Campanie', in *Routes et marchés d'esclaves. 26e colloque du GIREA*, ed. M. Garrido-Hory (Besançon, 2001), 325 n. 18.
45. See FIRA I 66.
46. *NA* 4.2.1. See Impallomeni (n. 44), 90–136; D. Pugsley, 'The Aedilician edict', in *Daube Noster. Essays in Legal History for David Daube*, ed. A. Watson (Edinburgh – London, 1974), 253–64.
47. Gai. D. 21.1.28; Ulp. D. 21.1.19.6 and D. 21.1.38 pr. (about *iumenta*). Cf. J.-J. Aubert, 'Vitia animi: tares mentales, psychologiques, caractérielles et intellectuelles des esclaves en droit romain', in *I diritti degli altri in Grecia e a Roma*, ed. A. Maffi and L. Gagliardi (Sankt Augustin, 2011), 236–48.
48. Reduzzi-Merola (n. 44), based on TPSulp 43 (21 Aug. 38) (possibly also TPSulp 42 and 44); TH 59–62 (between AD 47 and 63); and Petr. *Sat.* 53.9–10. Cf. J. de la Hoz Montoya, 'Neron y el impuesto sobre la venta de esclavos', *SDHI* 74 (2008): 376–80.

49. Ulpian D. 21.1.1.7.
50. Ulpian D. 21.1.10.1.
51. D. 21.1.12.4; Apuleius *Apol.* 6.
52. D. 21.1.14.4, cited with approval by Ulpian.
53. D. 21.1.65 pr.
54. D. 21.1.38, 40, and 41.
55. Ulp. D. 21.1.38.1, 14; Paul D. 21.1.39.
56. D. 21.1.38 pr. and 13.
57. Gai. (1 *ad ed. aed. cur.*) D. 21.1.18 (false advertisement); Ulp. D. 21.1.19.6 (deadlines: six months for *actio redhibitoria*; one year for *actio quanti minoris*); D. 21.1.31.5, 31.10 (joint purchase), 31.16 (successive claims by buyer); Pomp. D. 21.1.36 (bulk price); Paul D. 21.1.43.6 (complementary remedies); Paul D. 21.1.47 pr. (extinction of buyer's claim after slave's manumission); Ulp. D. 21.1.61 (undeclared servitude).
58. Paul D. 21.1.44.1.
59. Ulp. D. 9.2.27.28.
60. Paul D. 50.16.74.
61. C. 4.58.4.
62. D. 21.1.63.
63. Cf. FIRA 3.87–88 (AD 139 and 142, Dacia); FIRA 3.133 (AD 151, Side in Pamphilia) and 132 (Seleucia in Pieria, AD 166).
64. Dio 53.2.2 and 54.2.3. Cf. C. Giachi, *Studi su Sesto Pedio. La tradizione, l'editto* (Milan, 2005), 65–70, esp. 67 n. 147.
65. T. C. Brennan, *The Praetorship in the Roman Republic* (Oxford, 2000). On the peregrine praetor, cf. D. Daube, 'The peregrine praetor', *JRS* 41 (1951): 66–70; F. Serrao, *La* 'iurisdictio' *del pretore peregrino* (Milano, 1954).
66. Dio 36.40.1–2; Asc. *Corn.* 59.8–9 (Clark) = 48 (Stangl); and Cic. *2 Verr.* 1.46.119 on Verres deciding contrary to his own edict. Cf. G. Rotondi, *Leges publicae populi romani* (Milan, 1912), 371; M. Griffin, 'The tribune C. Cornelius', *JRS* 63 (1973): 209; P. Pinna Parpaglia, *Per una interpretazione della 'lex Cornelia de edictis praetorum' del 67 A.C* (Sassari, 1987), and P. Pinna Parpaglia, '*Lex Cornelia de edictis*, mutui feneratizi, certezza del diritto', *Labeo* 38 (1992): 372–8; and N. Palazzolo, 'Sulla *lex Cornelia de edictis*', *Labeo* 37 (1991): 242–5.
67. See the chapter by Ibbetson, 34. A. Guarino, 'La formazione dell'editto perpetuo', *ANRW* II.13 (1980), 62–102, esp. 68–76 for the distinction between *edictum perpetuum* (promulgated at the beginning to the year of office) and *edictum repentinum* (promulgated during the year of office), as opposed to *denegatio actionis* (denial of a remedy); D. Mantovani 'L'édit comme code', in *La codification des lois dans l'Antiquité. Actes du colloque de Strasbourg, 27–29 novembre 1997*, ed. E. Lévy (Paris, 2000), 257–72.
68. FIRA I 65.
69. C. Giachi, 'Storia dell'editto e struttura del processo in età pre-adrianea. Un'ipotesi di lavoro', in *Rivista di diritto romano*, http://www.ledonline.it/rivistadirittoromano/attipontignano.html, 14 n. 23 on the transfer of *EP* §§ 101–5 (*Quod cum magistro navis, institore eove qui in aliena potestate est, negotium gestum erit*) from their theoretical original place just after § 78 (*De his quae cuiusque in bonis sunt – In factum adversus nautas caupones stabularios*) to a place between §§ 95–100 (*De rebus creditis*) and *EP* §§ 106–12 (*De bonae fidei iudiciis*).

70. *EP* § 9 (*De edendo – argentariae mensae exercitores*); *EP* §§ 49–50 (*De receptis*); *EP* § 78 (*De his quae cuiusque in bonis sunt – In factum adversus nautas caupones stabularios*); *EP* §§ 95–100 (*De rebus creditis*); *EP* §§ 101–5 (*Quod cum magistro navis, institore eove qui in aliena potestate est, negotium gestum erit*); *EP* §§ 106–12 (*De bonae fidei iudiciis*); *EP* §§ 183–5 (*De publicanis*); *EP* §§ 218–23 (*Quemadmodum a bonorum emptore vel contra eum agatur*); *EP* §§ 269–79 (*De exceptionibus*).
71. Gaius 2.60.
72. See TPSulp 42 (Puteoli, AD 26), 43 (Puteoli, AD 38), 44 (Volturnum, first century AD); FIRA III 132–42 (all documents of early and late imperial date). On sale, cf. Gaius 3.139–41; D. 18.1–19.1; Crook (n. 6), 215–21; Johnston (n. 6), 79–84; Zimmermann (n. 18), 230–337.
73. With the possible exception of the sale of wine, cf. B. W. Frier, 'Roman law and the wine trade: the problem of "vinegar" sold as wine', *ZSS* 100 (1983): 257–95, 292.
74. Ulp. D. 47.5.1.6.
75. D. 47.5.1.3.
76. D. 47.5.1.4. See *EP* § 49 (*De receptis*) and § 78 (*In factum adversus nautas caupones stabularios*) A. Petrucci kindly points out that Gaius D. 4.9.2 includes the innkeeper's liability for theft committed by travellers (*viatores*) in case of *receptum*. Ulpian follows suit for passengers in a similar position D. 4.9.1.8. On *locatio conductio*, see now P. du Plessis, *Letting and Hiring in Roman Legal Thought: 27 BCE–284 CE* (Leiden, 2012).
77. D. 4.9.1.1.
78. D. 4.9.1.2–3, 5.
79. Labeo D. 4.9.1.4.
80. Vivianus, Pomp. D. 4.9.1.6–8.
81. Ulp. D. 4.9.3.1.
82. Ulp. D. 4.9.3.1, Paul D. 4.9.6.
83. Ulp. D. 4.9.7.3.
84. Labeo cited by Ulp. D. 4.9.3.1.
85. P. Huvelin, *Etudes d'histoire du droit commercial romain (Histoire externe – Droit maritime)* (Paris, 1929), 115–59; Zimmermann (n. 18), 514–26 (*receptum nautarum cauponum stabulariorum*); P. Gröschler, Actiones in factum. *Eine Untersuchung zur Klage-Neuschöpfung im nichtvertraglichen Bereich* (Berlin, 2002), 70–9.
86. Lenel *EP* § 50.
87. D. 13.5 and C. 4.18 (*De pecunia constituta*). Cf. Crook (n. 6), 232–3, 243; Zimmermann (n. 18), 511–14; J. Andreau, *La vie financière dans le monde romain. Les métiers de manieurs d'argent (IVᵉ siècle av. J.-C.–IIIᵉ siècle ap. J.-C.)* (Rome, 1987), 597–602; J. Andreau, *Banking and Business in the Roman World* (Cambridge, 1999), 43–4, 58 with reference to TP 151 (= FIRA 3.131e, AD 62) as a possible example from practice; A. Petrucci, Mensam exercere. *Studi sull'impresa finanziaria romana (II secolo a.C.–metà del III secolo d.C.)* (Naples, 1991), 378–83; A. Petrucci, *Profili giuridici delle attività e dell'organizzazione delle banche romane* (Turin, 2002), 57–65; A. Petrucci, in Cerami and Petrucci (n. 4), 143–9.
88. D. 2.13.4 pr.-1.
89. D. 2.13.6.8–9. See *EP* § 9 (*De edendo – argentariae mensae exercitores*); cf. Andreau (n. 87, 1987), 551; Andreau (n. 87, 1999), 30–49, esp. 46; Petrucci (n. 87, 1991), 141–71; Petrucci (n. 87, 2002), 23–27, 140–53; Petrucci in Cerami and Petrucci (n. 4), 191–203.

90. D. 2.13.10.1. See Petrucci (n. 87, 2002), 18 and 123, n. 30. On *causa* as a ground for legal action, cf. Borkowski and du Plessis (n. 39), 258–9, with reference to Ulp. D. 2.14.7.4.
91. *Opera virilis*: Call. D. 2.13.12. Cf. Andreau (n. 87, 1987), 497. The nature of the *edictum monitorium* is uncertain.
92. Sirks (n. 5), with reference to Ulp. D. 12.1.9.8; Celsus D. 12.1.32; and Ulp. D. 16.3.7.2 (insolvency of *nummularii*).
93. Cf. above, with Giachi (n. 69).
94. F. Serrao, *Impresa e responsabilità a Roma nell'età commerciale: forme giuridiche di un'economia-mondo* (Ospedaletto, 1989); Zimmermann (n. 18), 34–67, esp. 45–58; J.-J. Aubert, *Business Managers in Ancient Rome. A Social and Economic Study of* Institores, *200 BC–AD 250* (Leiden – New York – Cologne, 1994); Cerami, in Cerami and Petrucci (n. 4), 36–67.
95. Cf. above, XII Tables 8.2 and 12.2 (as per order in *Roman Statutes*); Ulp. D. 4.9.3.3; D. 4.9.7.4.
96. Cic. *Off.* 1.150–51.
97. Ulp. D. 14.3.1. The blurring of criminal and civil liability is touched upon in Ulp. D. 21.1.23.4–5.
98. *EP* §§ 100–5 (*Quod cum magistro navis institore eove qui in aliena potestate est negotium gestum erit*). The latest work on this part of the edict (*formulae*) is M. Miceli, *Sulla struttura formulare delle* actiones adiecticiae qualitatis (Turin, 2001), esp. 185–228; and M. Miceli, *Studi sulla 'rappresentanza' nel diritto romano* (Milan, 2008).
99. D. 15.1.1 pr.
100. Gaius 4.70–71.
101. Földi (n. 4), 78–84.
102. Aubert (n. 94), 117–200.
103. Gaius 4.71; D. 14.1, 14.3; C. 4.25.
104. D. 14.1.1 pr.
105. D. 14.1.1.5.
106. Ulp. D. 14.1.1.17–18 (*extra ordinem*) to be compared with Ulp. D. 14.3.1, citing the late second-century jurist Marcellus; and Gai. D. 14.3.2. Cf. B. Sirks, 'Sailing in the off-season with reduced financial risk', in Speculum iuris. *Roman Law as a Reflection of Social and Economic Life in Antiquity*, ed. J.-J. Aubert and B. Sirks (Ann Arbor, 2002), 139.
107. J.-J. Aubert, 'Les *institores* et le commerce maritime dans l'empire romain', *Topoi* 9 (1999): 145–64. On the *actio exercitoria*, cf. D. Gaurier, *Le droit maritime romain* (Rennes, 2004), 79–95, and M. Zimmermann, 'Die Haftung des Reeders mit der actio exercitoria: Ein Beitrag zur ökonomischen Analyse des römischen Rechts', *ZSS* 129 (2012): 554–70.
108. Ulp. D. 14.1.1.21 and 14.3.7.1; Gai. D. 14.3.8. Cf. Aubert (n. 94), 43, 56, 140–1, 193, 372, 224–6, 292–3, 419–20. The impact of the *SC Velleianum* (c. AD 46) (*EP* § 105; D. 16.1; C. 4.29) on the ability of women to act as agents is unclear.
109. Ulp. D. 14.3.5.1–15 and 14.3.13 pr.; Paul D. 14.3.16 and D. 14.3.17 pr.
110. For *lex praepositionis* as a kind of *lex contractus*, cf. J.-J. Aubert, 'En guise d'introduction: contrats publics et cahiers des charges', in *Tâches publiques et entreprise privée*, ed. J.-J. Aubert (Neuchâtel – Geneva, 2003), 1–25; J.-J. Aubert, 'Corpse disposal in the Roman colony of Puteoli: public concern and private enterprise', in Noctes Campanae. *Studi di storia antica ed archeologia dell'Italia preromana e romana in memoria*

di Martin W. Frederiksen*, ed. W. V. Harris and E. Lo Cascio (Naples, 2005), 141–57; J.-J. Aubert, 'L'estampillage des briques et des tuiles: une explication juridique fondée sur une approche globale', in *Interpretare i bolli laterizi di Roma e della Valle del Tevere: Produzione, storia economica e topografia*, ed. C. Bruun (Rome, 2005), 53–9; J.-J. Aubert, 'Dealing with the abyss: the nature and purpose of the Rhodian sea-law on jettison (*Lex Rhodia de iactu*, D. 14.2) and the making of Justinian's *Digest*', in *Beyond Dogmatics. Law and Society in the Roman World*, ed. J. W. Cairns and P. du Plessis (Edinburgh, 2007), 157–72; J.-J. Aubert and G. Raepsaet, 'Un mandat inscrit sur une sigillée argonnaise à Liberchies-Geminiacum', in L'*Antiquité classique* 80 (2011): 139–56.

111. Ulp. D. 14.1.1.12 (*certa lex*); D. 14.3.11.2–6 (*proscriptio*); D. 14.3.13 pr. (double appointment); Gai. D. 14.5.1 (*iussum*). Cf. J.-J. Aubert, 'Workshop managers', in *The Inscribed Economy. Production and Distribution in the Roman Empire in the Light of* instrumentum domesticum., ed. W. V. Harris (Ann Arbor, 1993), 171–89; Aubert (n. 94), 6–14, 50–2, 335; Aubert (n. 110, 2003, 2005, 2005, 2007); E. Jakab, 'Vertragspraxis und Bankgeschäfte im antiken Puteoli: *TPSulp* 48 neu interpretiert', in Verboven et al. (n. 2), 321–44; Aubert and Raepsaet (n. 110), (mandate).

112. D. 14.1.1.5; D. 14.1.1.13–14 and 14.3.11.5; D. 14.3.13.2.

113. A. di Porto, *Impresa collettiva e schiavo 'manager' in Roma antica (II sec. a.C. – II sec. d.C.)* (Milan, 1984), 169–204; Aubert (n. 94), 54–7 and 62–3, with references; see also Paul D. 14.3.14. For Roman company law, cf. Crook (n. 6), 229–36.

114. Aubert (n. 94), 325–47; J.-J. Aubert, 'La gestion des collegia: aspects juridiques, économiques et sociaux', *CCG* 10 (1999): 49–69. On publicans, cf. *EP* §§ 183–5; D. 39.4, with Gaius' commentary *ad edictum praetoris titulo de publicanis*; and L. Maganzani, *Pubblicani e debitori d'imposta. Ricerche sul titolo edittale* de publicanis (Turin, 2002).

115. Ulp. D. 15.1.1.1.

116. *Actio quod iussu*: A. M. M. Schleppinghoff, Actio quod iussu. *Die Geheissklage (und ihre Bedeutung für die Entwicklung des Stellvertretungsgedanken im 19. Jahrhundert* (Diss, Cologne University, 1996); G. Coppola Bisazza, *Lo* iussum domini *e la sostituzione negoziale nell'esperienza romana* (Milan, 2003). *Actio de peculio*: J.-J. Aubert, 'Productive investment in agriculture: *instrumentum fundi* and *peculium* in the later Roman Republic', in *Agricoltura e scambi nell'Italia tardo-repubblicana*, ed. J. Carlsen and E. Lo Cascio (Bari, 2010), 167–85; J.-J. Aubert, '*Dumtaxat de peculio*: What's in a *peculium* or the extent of the principal's liability', in *New Frontiers: Law and Society in the Roman World*, ed. P. du Plessis (Edinburgh, 2013), 192–206 with earlier bibliography. *Actio de in rem verso*: T. Chiusi, *Die* actio de in rem verso *im römischen Recht* (Munich, 2001).

117. *Actio tributoria*: T. Chiusi, *Contributo allo studio dell'editto* 'de tributoria actione' (Rome, 1993).

118. D. 14.5.1.

119. Paul D. 14.5.8.

120. R. Martini, *Ricerche in tema di editto provinciale* (Milan, 1969), 103–28; B. Santalucia, *L'opera di Gaio* 'ad edictum praetoris urbani' (Milan, 1975).

121. Cic. *Att.* 5.21.10.

122. Cic. *Att.* 6.1.15–16.

123. Cic. *Att.* 5.21.10–13 (13 Feb. 50); 6.1.15–16 (22 Feb. 50); 6.2.7–10 (early May 50). Rotondi (n. 66), 373–4 (*lex Gabinia*). Cf. G. Pugliese, 'Riflessioni sull'editto di Cicerone in Cilicia', in *Synteleia V. Arangio-Ruiz*, ed. A. Guarino and L. Labruna

(Naples, 1964), vol. 2, 972–96; Martini (n. 120), 11–102; L. Peppe, 'Note sull'editto di Cicerone in Cilicia', *Labeo* 37 (1991): 14–93; and L. Maganzani, 'L'editto provinciale alla luce delle *Verrine*: profili strutturali, criteri applicativi', in *La Sicile de Cicéron. Lectures des* Verrines, ed. J. Dubouloz and S. Pittia (Besançon, 2007), 127–46.

124. Ulp. D. 25.4.1.15, admittedly in a different context.

125. Gaius 3.134; E. A. Meyer, *Legitimacy and Law in the Roman World. Tabulae in Roman Belief and Practice* (Cambridge, 2004), 12–19, 125–68.

126. Crook (n. 6), 223–5. Cf. in general Huvelin (n. 85), 184–218; J. Rougé, *Recherches sur l'organisation du commerce maritime en Méditerranée sous l'empire romain* (Paris, 1966); Gaurier (n. 107), 97–133. On the Greek *daneion nautikon*, cf. S. Schuster, *Das Seedarlehen in den Gerichtsreden des Demosthenes: mit einem Ausblick auf die weitere historische Entwicklung des Rechtsinstitutes: dáneion nautikón, fenus nauticum und Bodmerei* (Berlin, 2005).

127. Plut. *Cato Maior* 21.6. Cf. D. 22.2 and C. 4.33, with W. Litewski, 'Römisches Seedarlehen', *Iura* 24 (1973): 112–83; A. Biscardi, Actio pecuniae traiecticiae. *Contributo alla dottrina delle clausole penali*, 2nd ed. (Turin, 1974); L. Casson 'New light on maritime loans: P. Vindob. G. 19792 (= *SB* VI 9571)', in *Studies in Roman Law in Memory of A. Arthur Schiller*, ed. R. S. Bagnall and W. V. Harris (Leiden – New York, 1986), 11–17; L. Casson, 'New light on maritime loans: P. Vindob. G 40822', *ZPE* 84 (1990): 195–206; Zimmermann (n. 18), 181–6; H. Ankum, 'Some aspects of maritime loans in old-Greek and in Roman law', in *Mélanges I. Triantaphyllopoulos*, ed. I. Velissaropoulou-Karakosta et al. (Komotini, 2000), 293–306). This type of loan occasionally appears in the papyri, e.g. *SB* III 7169 (with *Berichtigungsliste* = *BL*, second cent. BC) for a trip to the Somali coast (with Roman names: ll. 12, 19, 21); *SB* III 7170 (id.); *SB* XIV 11850 (*BL*, Theadelphia? Feb. 13, AD 149); and *SB* XVIII 13167 (*BL*, so-called Muziris papyrus, mid-second cent. AD) for a trip from Alexandria to India and back.

128. Scaev. D. 45.1.122.1; Johnston (n. 6), 95–6; and Sirks (n. 106), 142–9.

129. Rotondi (n. 66), 99.

130. Moneylenders had influence on legislation in a later period, cf. *Nov.* 106 (540) and 110 (541); cf. Jones (n. 42), 350.

131. Acts 27:14–20.

132. In the 7th century Isid. *Etym.* 5.17 speaks of Rhodian laws of maritime commerce as 'antiquitus mercatorum usus'.

133. *PS* 2.7.

134. Paul D. 14.2.2.3.

135. Zimmermann (n. 18), 406–12; E. Chevreau, 'La lex Rhodia de iactu: un exemple de la réception d'une institution étrangère dans le droit romain', *TR* 73 (2005): 67–80; Aubert (n. 110, 2007); and N. Badoud, *La lex Rhodia de iactu* (forthcoming).

136. D. 14.2.9.

137. Rotondi (n. 66), 92–100.

138. Livy 21.63; Cic. *2 Verr.* 5.17.44–18.45; and *PS* (Leiden fragment published in 1956) 3 (p. 5), ll. 7–11; Aubert (n. 38), 166–8 and 178, n. 17; A. Tchernia, 'Le *plebiscitum Claudianum*', in *Vocabulaire et expression de l'économie dans le monde antique*, ed. J. Andreau and V. Chankowski (Bordeaux, 2007), 253–78, with a telling calculation of the capacity of the ship.

139. Cf. the chapter by Sirks, 340–1; B. Sirks, *Food for Rome* (Amsterdam, 1991); L. de Salvo, *I* corpora naviculariorum*: economia privata e pubblici servizi nell'impero romano* (Messina, 1992).

140. *Pistores, suarii, pecuarii, boarii, vinarii*, etc. Cf. the chapter by Sirks, 341–2; C. book 11; C.Th. books 10 and 14; Sirks (n. 139, 1991), 307–413; Földi (n. 4), 85–7.
141. J. France, Quadragesima Galliarum. *L'organisation douanière des provinces alpestres, gauloises et germaniques de l'empire romain* (Rome, 2001) for Gaul; M. Cottier et al., *The Customs Law of Asia* (Oxford, 2008) for Asia Minor; and R. Delmaire, *Largesses sacrées et* res privata. *L'*aerarium *impérial et son administration du IVe au VIe siècle* (Rome, 1989), 275–312 for late antiquity.
142. C.Th. 13.1; C. 11.1 (abolition in the East); Jones (n. 42), 351, 431–2; Delmaire (n. 80), 254–74, esp. 367 n. 41, with reference (for registration) to C.Th. 16.2.15.1 (359 or 360); and P. Oxy. L 3577 (28 Jan. 342). Cf. also Minaud (n. 29), § 298. Other taxes on trade are attested: *siliquaticum, canon telonei* and *transmarinorum*, on which see Jones (n. 42).
143. *Edictum Diocletiani et collegarum de pretiis rerum venalium*, ed. M. Giacchero (Genoa, 1974), 1: 134–7, esp. ll. 64–136; Lact. *Mort.* 7.6–7. Cf. S. Corcoran, *The Empire of the Tetrarchs: Imperial Pronouncements and Government, AD 284–324*, revd. edn. (Oxford, 2000), 205–33.
144. E. E. Cohen, *Ancient Athenian Maritime Courts* (Princeton, 1973); E. E. Cohen, 'Commercial law', in *The Cambridge Companion to Ancient Greek Law*, ed. M. Gagarin and D. Cohen (Cambridge, 2005), 300–2; and A. Lanni, *Law and Justice in the Courts of Classical Athens* (Cambridge, 2006), ch. 6 ('Maritime Cases'), 149–74. The Roman evidence collected by Minaud (n. 18), § 365 (Cic. *2 Verr.* 2.13.34; *CIL* XIV 2630; SHA, *Alexander Severus* 33.2; C.Th. 14.7.1 (397); C. 3.13.7 pr. (502); Isid. *Etym.* 5.17) is inconclusive, with the possible exception of the passage from the *Historia Augusta*.
145. Cic. II *Verr.* 2.13.32–34.

13 Delicts

A. J. B. Sirks

1. General[1]

A delict in Roman law was reprehensible behaviour which the law punished by imposing an obligation on the perpetrator towards the victim. The imposition of the obligation was a punishment and so could be directed only at the perpetrator, but the obligation itself could consist of a fine, compensation for the loss, or a combination of the two.[2] In contrast to public crimes, for which anybody could sue, only the victim of a delict (or on his death his heir) could sue the perpetrator. Delictual actions were penal actions in the sense too that, just as with public crimes, once the perpetrator had died, no action was possible against his heir. However, in some cases where compensation was the sanction, the delinquent's heirs could be sued to the extent to which through succession they had been enriched by the delict.

The penal nature of delicts can also be seen in the fact that they were cumulative. They could be cumulative against one person, who could be sued and condemned for more than one delict committed in a single act (such as wounding a slave and in doing so at the same time insulting his owner), or they could be cumulative against several people, so that if two people jointly stole something both could be sued and condemned, each for the full amount.[3] Delicts are mentioned as early as the regal laws (between 753 and 509 BC) and the XII Tables (c. 455 BC, the Decemviral period). The regal laws imposed the sanction *sacer esto* for, for example, the intentional killing of a free man (Numa Pompilius 12)[4] and for a child who flogged his parents (Servius Tullius 1).[5] *Sacer esto* most likely meant that the perpetrator was outlawed and might be killed by the relatives of the killed person without their being liable to revenge. The implication may be that the relatives could ask for whatever compensation they wanted; whereas for the negligent killing of a man the perpetrator was liable to surrender a ram to the agnates of the deceased (Numa Pompilius 13).[6] Yet the distinction with (public) crimes remains unclear, by contrast to the situation under the XII Tables. Under the XII Tables singing a shaming song was a delict (table 8.1), as was casting a spell on another's crops (table 8.8); cutting another's crops by night was punishable by death or, in the case of a perpetrator who was under age (*impubes*), by flogging and a double indemnity (table 8.9); burning down a granary was punished by flogging and death on the stake if intentional, or, if done negligently, by paying an indemnity or being castigated (table 8.10). Accidental killing incurred liability for payment of a ram (table 8.24a, a reprise of the regal law). The XII Tables also contained several other rules on wrongful loss, injury, and *furtum* (see 248, 254, 258). These and other crimes and delicts remained in force so far as not set aside wholly or partly by later legislation.

For the early Principate there are around 30 delicts known to Roman law (they cannot all be dealt with here). About five have a sanction in the form of compensation for loss caused by damage. The remainder have one in the form of a fine. Some delicts were considered more important or complicated than others. Wrongful loss, injury, and *furtum* (theft in a wide sense) were apparently considered the most important. In late antiquity and in Justinian's times (AD 527–565), owing to the shift from the formula to the *cognitio* procedure, the private delicts lost much of their private character.[7]

2. *Furtum* (Theft in a Wide Sense)

Furtum was a delict of a much wider scope than theft is nowadays. It included theft but also unauthorized intentional use of another's thing, attempted theft, and help and assistance with *furtum*. The victim did not have to be the owner, but could also be a usufructuary, a pledgee, or other person, as long as he had an interest in the thing not being stolen: 'If a thing given in pledge be taken from the creditor, we grant him the action for theft although the pledge is not one of his assets; indeed, we grant him the action not only against a third person but even against the owner of the thing.'[8] He could claim a fine of twice, three times, or four times the value of the thing stolen. Condemnation entailed infamy. The thing which was the object of *furtum* became a *res furtiva* (a 'stolen object') and, as long as it had not returned to the possession of its owner, could not be acquired by usucapion.

The origins of *furtum* are obscure. The Romans gave an etymological explanation of the word, as derived from *(au)ferre* ('to carry away'); but modern linguistics conclude that this is impossible. However, it does tell us what was typical of *furtum* for Romans of about AD 300.

Asportation (carrying away) was certainly a criterion later on, but so was *contrectatio* ('handling', 'meddling'). So the ambit of *furtum* through the ages is a point of debate.

This delict already appears in the XII Tables. At this time several punishments are mentioned. According to Gaius, the XII Tables stated that in the case of the *fur manifestus* (a culprit caught red-handed), the magistrate would scourge him if he was a free man and assign him to the person against whom he had committed *furtum*; if he was a slave, he would be put to death. As the slave Sceparnio says in Plautus' play,

> I'll just put this urn down in the middle of the road. But what if someone were to steal this sacred urn of Venus? I'd get into trouble. I fear that woman framed me up to get me caught with the sacred urns of Venus. The magistrate would rightly kill me with a noose if he saw me with it, because it is inscribed: it shouts out whose it is.[9]

Gellius says that a thief who was under age (*impubes*) would, at the discretion of the praetor, be scourged; then the damage caused had to be made good. So the jurists of the Republic discussed whether the free adult was assigned as a slave or assigned in debt slavery to pay off the debt. But the XII Tables (tables 8.12, 8.13) also said that, if *furtum* was committed at night, the thief might be killed; he could be killed if he was caught during the day only if he resisted arrest.[10] The punishment of scourging and full loss of status or life (*poena capitalis*) is strongly reminiscent both of expiation (XII Tables 8.9, 8.10) and treason. Perhaps *furtum manifestum* originally meant breaking into a house in order to steal.[11] If so, it was soon secularized and extended. In the second century AD and later the victim might only kill the thief, at night or day, if it was impossible to hand him over to the authorities. The victim could also press for a public prosecution,[12] but this did not preclude him from privately suing the thief. As Birks observed, for *furtum manifestum* (when the culprit was caught red-handed), there need not be asportation: merely touching sufficed.[13] Later praetorian edicts were issued which imposed for this delict a fine of four times the value of the thing stolen. The XII Tables (table 8.15) had also provided a fine of double for *furtum non manifestum* (non-manifest theft), and a triple fine for *furtum conceptum* and *furtum oblatum* (see below, 249). These were also included in later praetorian edicts.

Apart from this, the victim, who remained owner, could vindicate his property. Or, if the thief no longer had the stolen object, he could use the *condictio furtiva* in order to claim its value as compensation.[14] If one spouse had stolen from the other, instead of the action on *furtum* there was the *actio rerum amotarum* (the action for things removed), which was available after divorce.

Commentaries from the first centuries AD discuss what manifest *furtum* is. The general opinion was that if the thief was caught on the spot, or as long as he was seen with the stolen thing on his way to his lair, it was manifest. After that it became non-manifest *furtum*, for which the fine was double the value. If the stolen thing was found at somebody's house after a formal search, a threefold fine was imposed on the owner of the house (*furtum conceptum*). If the thing had been deposited with him, he in his turn could sue and claim the threefold fine from the depositor (*furtum oblatum*). There was also a threefold fine for refusal to let one's house be searched (*furtum prohibitum*).

The rules may seem straightforward, but the practice was more complicated. The act of *furtum* had to be done against the will of the owner. If the thief honestly thought that the owner had consented, there was no *furtum*. Conversely, if the owner did not mind, the thief was not guilty, even if he had acted in the belief that the owner did not consent. Moreover, if the thief believed he was taking his own property, although it was in fact another's, this was not *furtum*: the intention (*dolus, animus furandi*) to steal was necessary: 'If a person deposited a purse containing twenty coins and received another purse, which he knew contained thirty, the giver being in error, it is settled that he is liable in theft only for ten, if he thought that his twenty were included in the purse.'[15]

The value of the object could also present problems. The true value was taken, not what the thief thought it was. But the true value did not have to be the value of the object as such:

> One who takes away wax tablets or *cautiones* is liable in theft not only for their intrinsic value but for what they represent, which means the amount of the sum contained in the document, if, that is, their interest is that great; thus if a chirograph records a sum of ten gold pieces, we say that that is the sum to be doubled'.[16]

What if the value had increased or decreased after the theft? Could the estimate of value given at joinder of issue, the moment in litigation at which the parameters of the legal case were set, be adjusted? 'Again, if the thing had deteriorated, assessment was to be directed to the time of the actual theft. But if it had become more valuable, it is twofold the subsequent higher value which should be the basis of assessment, because the better view is that the theft still continues.'[17] If the decoration of a platter made the platter more valuable, that value was to be taken, not the value of the material of the platter: 'A person who scrapes [the decoration] off a platter, steals the whole of it and is liable in the action for theft for the owner's full interest.'[18]

A further problem arose if a thief had taken part of a whole – for example, a bushel from a heap of grain. Was the estimate to be of the bushel or of the heap?

> It is a common question whether a person who takes a pint from a heap of corn steals the whole heap or only what he removes. Ofilius thinks that he steals the whole heap; similarly, Trebatius says that one who touches the ear of a person touches the whole person. And in the same way, one who opens a wine jar and abstracts a small quantity of wine therefrom is deemed a thief not only of what he takes but of the whole contents. But the truth is that these people are liable in the action for theft only for what they took.[19]

Ofilius and Trebatius were jurists of the 1st century BC and for them *contrectatio* (the touching or handling of something that belonged to another) alone sufficed for *furtum*: hence one merely had to decide what was touched, and that was the heap or the full jar. Contrary to that was Ulpian's solution, which applied the idea of asportation: *furtum* was for him primarily a taking away (which necessarily included a touching). That view was dominant in the later second century AD, and consequently the fine was based on the value of what was taken away.

Furtum was a broad concept. A creditor-pledgee who did not return the pledge after the debt was paid committed *furtum* if this was done intentionally;[20] knowingly to accept an undue payment was *furtum*;[21] so too was retention of lost property for the purpose of gain (*lucri faciendi causa*).[22] Along the same lines is the unauthorized use of another's property: 'A man who takes draught animals which he has borrowed further than he should or who uses another's property without the owner's consent is guilty of theft.'[23] There is no asportation here: it is a case of what we now call *furtum usus*. In these cases the *contrectatio* criterion is clearly applied and means unauthorized handling. What we now call *furtum possessionis* is similar: 'An owner who takes away the thing in which another has a usufruct will be liable for theft to the usufructuary.'[24] A usufructuary had a right to possess the property for the time of the usufruct, while the owner retained a property right. Theoretically he could not steal his own goods, but what he did here was to take away their possession. Yet if he had lent something, he could take it back without committing *furtum*, unless the borrower had an interest in it – for example, for compensation for his expenses. In short, there had to be a right to possess, as for the creditor-pledgee or the tenant.[25]

But it could be more complicated:

> If, again, a person opens or breaks into something which is too heavy to be removed, an action for theft will lie against him not for the whole contents but only for what he removes, because he could not remove the whole thing. In the same way, suppose the man opened a closet that he could not remove in order to handle [*contrectet*], and he did handle [*contrectavit*] some of the contents; although he could remove individual items within it, if he could not remove the whole closet, he would be a thief of the things that he did take away but not of the rest. But if he could take the whole receptacle, we say that he is thief of all, even though he opened it to take away one or some items; and so says Sabinus.[26]

We see how *contrectatio* comes to be more specifically defined, with asportation as the crucial element of *furtum*. But was it still sufficient for attempted theft? If it was done with theft in mind, was it *furtum*? Attempt as such was not punished: 'A person who enters an enclosure for the purpose of theft is not yet a thief even though he entered for the purpose of stealing. What then? By what action will he be liable? It could be the action for injury [*iniuria*] or he could be (criminally) charged with violence, if he made a forcible entry'.[27] On the other hand, the requirement of asportation was widened to what *could* have been taken away (*contrectatio* remaining a condition). In this way it could, as here, include a form of attempt. Handling or touching combined with the possibility of taking away the whole sufficed for a man to be guilty of *furtum*, and so the fine was based on the whole.

Help and assistance with *furtum* (*ope consiliove*) were treated as *furtum non manifestum*.[28] But what was help? There is the case of advising a slave to flee. A slave who fled was considered to have stolen himself, which made him a *res furtiva* and thus incapable of being usucapted. When did advice amount to help?

> One who persuades a slave to run away is not a thief. For one who gives another evil counsel of this sort is no more liable for

> theft than one who advises another to throw himself from a height or to kill himself; such conduct does not give rise to the action for theft. But if one person persuades the slave to run away, so that he may be taken by a third person, the persuader will be liable for theft, because the theft was done with his help and advice [*ope consilio*].[29]

But the next case could be tricky:

> If two slaves incite one other and run away together, neither is thief of the other. But what if they hide one another? Can it be that they are thieves then, one of the other? It can be said that each steals the other just as, if third persons took them individually, they would be liable as if each had abetted the other.[30]

Because of the noxal liability of owners for their slaves (see below, 265–7), each owner here might sue the other.

And then there are cases which remain for us enigmatic, like: 'Someone lent you heavier weights when you were buying by weight; Mela writes that he will be liable to the vendor for theft as also will you if you are aware of the facts; for you do not acquire the goods with the owner's consent when he is in error over the weight.'[31] That the buyer was guilty of *furtum* if he knew is no surprise and the lender would be guilty of assistance, but is Mela's view that it is *furtum* merely to provide false weights? Mela lived at the very beginning of the first century AD, when both *contrectatio* and asportation were used as criteria. The lender lent – knowingly, we assume – his own weights, which the innocent seller used. The seller suffered a loss, but the lender was not enriched. Is this not rather a case of fraud?

Another case is this: 'If, when my tame peacock escaped from my house, you chased it so that it disappeared, I could have the action for theft against you if someone else should take it.'[32] How can this have been *furtum*? The view of J. A. C. Thomas might provide the explanation here. He suggested considering *furtum* from the point of view of the victim and defining it as causing deprivation to him in a wide sense.[33] That would bring all cases neatly under one denominator. One may go a step further and refine this deprivation as a loss of control – that is, a loss of *potestas* or *dominium*. The peacock has gone away and apparently will not return, having lost its will to return. By that means its master has lost control. That suggestion also fits with *furtum* of children and of a wife held in power (*in manu*): *furtum* would be a challenge to this power.[34]

Some authors (such as Watson,[35] Thomas, Nicholas,[36] Albanese,[37] and Zimmermann) see in cases such as that of the peacock the indication that *furtum*, from originally involving mere asportation, had expanded to a very wide delict in the last century of the Republic, namely any patrimonial loss caused by the wrongful intent (*dolus*) of another and which was not covered by the *lex Aquilia*. A reaction grew up against the width of *furtum*, and in various ways its scope was reduced – for example, by Sabinus' criterion that it must be done in order to gain. It was in this context that *contrectatio* was devised, in order to cover attempt. This view is understandable if one reads (wrongly, according to Birks[38]) *ferre* (taking) in *furtum*. But it still does not explain the penalty in the XII Tables for *furtum manifestum* by night where nothing needed to be asported. Thomas suggested that *contrectatio* included every way in which an owner was deprived of his property (parallel to the introduction of the *lex Aquilia* which covered loss through damage);[39] Watson suggested that there had to be a physical handling.[40] On the other hand, Birks and Jolowicz maintained that *contrectatio* was the basic criterion.[41] Theophilus, a law professor teaching in AD 533–534, explained *contrectatio* as 'to behave like an owner in respect of a thing and to do to it things which are appropriate to an owner'. This is the inverse of taking away or opposing the power of the owner; and only this view explains why the thief is not culpable if he thinks he acts with the approval of the owner, or if the owner does not object; hence, *contrectatio* has to be the original element. Theophilus' definition also fits Thomas's view as rephrased. The peacock was lost: this implied a loss for its owner. He was indeed deprived of it, but it was also no longer under control of its owner (as expressed in its now lost will to return). The chaser behaved as if he had the right to strip the peacock from its intention to return (*animus revertendi*).

In the Decemviral period, theft of use may have been more frequent than theft by asportation. As noted, the word *furtum* cannot be connected with asportation; we cannot assume that this was its original meaning. *Contrectatio* will have been the original element: interference with the power of the *paterfamilias*, and it would have included asportation. There is the story of an embassy which was invited on several nights to dine with a Roman family and every time saw the same silver plates. It appeared that only one family in Rome owned silver plates. If true, and it is certain that in early times even the leading families were living modestly, this situation had certainly been transformed by the first century BC, when Rome had conquered the world and riches had been amassed. Theft by asportation will have been the common form of *furtum* from then on, reducing mere *contrectatio* in that new context to the form of *furtum usus* and a form of attempt. A parallel shift in the learned discussion of *furtum* will have occurred. We can see this in the famous definition of Paul: 'Theft is a fraudulent interference [*contrectatio*] with a thing with a view to gain, whether of the thing itself or of the use or possession of it. This natural law proscribes.'[42] This also explains the increased interest in defining attempt, and help and advice. A further trend is that of letting the authorities deal with theft: the victim was supposed to hand over a thief, caught in the act, and let the authorities investigate and punish him. However, already by the middle of the second century AD handing over a thief to the authorities implied that one preferred public handling of the case and would be satisfied with its simple value as compensation.[43]

3. Injury (*Iniuria*)

Ulpian explains neatly in his commentary on the edicts on *iniuriae* what *iniuria* (injury) was: 'specifically, "wrong" [*iniuria*] is the designation for contumely [*contumelia*]. . . . contumely, scathingly insulting, derives from scathing or deriding [*contemnere*]'.[44] Injury had a wide meaning or application. Already the XII Tables had a fine of 25 asses for *iniuria* (table 8.4: 'If he do injury (to another?), 25 (asses) are to be the penalty.'). Whether this was already restricted to insult or also covered injuries not covered by other sections of the XII Tables, we do not know. After all, we have very little of this legislation. Generally it is thought that around 200 BC *iniuria* covered wounding and insult. Later on the praetorian edict had a general action and four special actions for specific cases of injury, while injury as wounding may by that time have been covered by the *lex Aquilia*.[45] The sanction was undoubtedly a fine. The edicts found a competitor in the *lex Cornelia de iniuriis* of 81 BC. This statute specifically covered the beating or thrashing of a person, forceful entry into his house, and all injuries physically caused; but it also included publishing writings meant to bring a person into disrepute (a decree of the senate extended this to anonymous writings). These statutory crimes were subsequently included in the praetorian edicts under the general delict of injury. The actions could not be brought against the heirs of the culprit, or by the heirs of the injured person.

First the general edict. Injury could be committed by a physical act, such as slapping a person's face, or by words, such as scolding. It had to bear upon what we would call one's personality rights: 'Every contumely is inflicted on the person or relates to one's dignity or involves disgrace: it is to the person when someone is struck; it pertains to dignity when a lady's companion is led astray; and to disgrace when an attempt is made upon a person's chastity.'[46] This itself shows that the ancient personality was a much wider concept. The status of the injured person mattered; an insult to one's children might be considered an insult to the father, likewise an insult to one's wife or fiancée might be an insult to her husband or fiancé (but not conversely: engaged or married women were subordinated in this respect to their men). Even harm done to a slave might be an injury to his owner: it depended on the nature and way it was done. But an injury had always to be done with the intention to injure: 'Thus, someone can suffer an injury, even though unaware, but no one can perpetrate one without knowing that he commits an injury, even though he does not know to whom he is doing it. Hence, if someone strikes another in jest or during a contest, he will not be liable to the action for injury.'[47]

It is not surprising that some things were considered injury which we would not regard in that way (and vice versa, of course). Thus if a teacher chastised a pupil, it was not an insult, since he merely wanted to correct him (yet, if excessive, it would constitute fault[48]). Further, social level played a great role. Freedmen had to be respectful to their patrons and could only sue for injury if it constituted aggravated injury – for example, being treated as if they were slaves; the same applied to children who were not in paternal power, while those still in it could never raise an action. What 'aggravated' meant is specified in several texts. It depended on the social position of the person, the place, the time it happened, and whether it was accompanied by physical force – in short, it depended on the circumstances. One such a case is: 'If a man claims as his slave someone whom he knows to be free, . . . he is liable to the action for injury.'[49] Suggesting that a free person was a slave was a grave injury. Hindering somebody from using public property was an injury too:

> If someone prevent me from fishing in the sea or from lowering my net. . .., can I have the action for injury against him? There are those who think that I can. And Pomponius and the majority are of opinion that the complainant's case is similar to that of one who is not allowed to use the public baths or to sit in a theatre seat or to conduct business, sit or converse in some other such place, or to use his own property; for in these cases too, an action for injury is apposite.[50]

In antiquity 'public' meant that something was indeed common to all citizens. Hindering somebody in using this was an injury to his citizenship;

it implied that he did not participate fully. Injury could also apply where we would find nuisance:

> If the owner of lower premises, with the intention of smoking [something] out, causes smoke in the premises of his neighbour above, or if the owner of the upper premises throws or pours anything into those below, Labeo says that the action for injury does not lie. I think this is wrong, if it is done with the intention of injury.[51]

The injured person had to specify in detail the injury he claimed to have suffered, and he had to estimate his injury, but the judge would set the fine. Condemnation brought infamy, which in its turn barred the condemned person from public functions. In the fourth century AD the punishments were scourging for slaves, beating with cudgels for freemen of the lower orders, and relegation or exile for the higher orders.

Special edicts existed for shouting abuse in a group (*convicium*), bringing young boys, girls, or married women into disrepute (*de pudicitia adtemptata*), and shaming somebody (*ne quid infamandi causa*). Theoretically these delicts could have been addressed by the general edict, as Labeo himself says about the last of them.[52] It is indeed an unresolved question whether the general edict was issued after the special edicts in order to comprise all cases not covered, or whether the special edicts were issued after the general edict in order to give more attention to these specific forms of injury.

Convicium was mob shouting, and the shouting had to be against good morals. Plutarch gives an example:

> Finally, when Pompey came to attend a court case, Clodius stood in a prominent position and put a series of riddles to the gangs of louts he led, who had no respect for anyone or anything: 'What do you call a lewd military commander?' 'What do you call a man in search of another man?' 'What do you call a man who scratches his head with one finger?' And like a chorus which has been well trained in its responses, cued by Clodius, giving his toga a shake, they shouted in answer to each question 'Pompey!'.[53]

All of these questions suggested that Pompey was effeminate and a catamite, surely behaviour against good morals; it was aggravating too, considering the place where it happened. Pompey, however, did not sue Clodius.

Reputation was perhaps not everything, yet for many it meant much. Girls and married women had to think of theirs and, as this edict implies, they could not readily go out without an escort; the same may apply to boys. *Pudicitia* (chastity) was a great virtue for both girls and boys: 'In the first place, as a boy and as a youth, despite his attractive looks he escaped all malicious gossip', wrote the younger Pliny in praise of his protegé Ummidius Quadratus.[54] Being followed closely by somebody quickly suggested an illicit affair: 'It is one thing to accost, another to follow. A person accosts who verbally solicits chastity; he follows who silently walks close behind; an assiduous proximity more or less suggests something disreputable.'[55] But the following had to be contrary to good morals. The edict punished those who accosted, followed, or succeeded in luring the escort away.

Shaming (*infamari*) was punishable too. The edict was in fact very wide in purport, almost as wide as the general edict. But in practice it was directed at more specific conduct:

> And so whatever one does or says to bring another into disrepute gives rise to the action for injury. Here are instances of conduct to another's disrepute: to lower another's reputation, one wears mourning or filthy garments or lets one's beard grow or lets one's hair down or writes a lampoon or issues or sings something detrimental to another's honour.[56]

The first instances suggested that the victim was in some way connected with death, or that he was accused of something reprehensible (only close relatives of an accused could wear filthy garments[57]). The edict referred to a 'song', but a lampoon was also covered. There were other ways to bring disrepute to a person: for example, spreading doubts about his financial solvency: 'Similarly, if someone announces that he is selling a pledge to denigrate me, as though he had received it from me, Servius says that I can bring the action for injury.'[58]

Another edict (*si ei qui in alterius potestate erit*) covered injury done to somebody in another's power, sons and daughters, grandsons and granddaughters in paternal power. Further, the edict *qui servum alienum adversos bonos mores verberavisse* sanctioned the thrashing or torturing of somebody's slave against good morals and without the owner's consent. It was of course always permitted to correct or reform a slave physically,[59] or to torture him to investigate something. But if it was outrageous, it would be against good morals or could be considered an affront to his master and the master could sue; or the magistrate would sue. A final edict (*si quid aliud factum esse*) was a kind of general clause: if anything else was alleged which implied injury, the praetor could take the measures he considered appropriate.

4. Wrongful Loss (*Damnum Iniuria*)

In comparison with other ancient laws, the attention paid to wrongful loss, the delict dealt with by the *lex Aquilia*, is remarkable. There had been regal laws on killing, and there had been special rules in the XII Tables on killing and damaging (see above, 247), but the origins of the *lex Aquilia* have always been sought in a few specific XII Tables wrongs (such as table 8.2: 'If he has maimed a part (of a body), unless he settles with him, there is to be talion'; table 8.3: 'If he has broken a bone of a free man, 300, if of a slave, 150 (asses) are to be the penalty'). The *lex* itself, probably a comprehensive compilation of several individual rules,[60] was on the other hand surprisingly wide, and it would widen further in the course of time. Its aim was to cover loss as suffered by the victim.

The statute was enacted by a plebiscite and, since it was always called a *lex*, it is assumed that it was enacted after the *lex Hortensia* of 287 BC, which made plebiscites equivalent to statutes. It is likely that it was enacted before 217 BC. Some think it is of a later date but accept in any case that it dates from before the first century BC. The delict it regulates is *damnum iniuria*, which is to be translated as 'loss in the context of/caused by a wrong', albeit essentially the loss had to be caused by physical injury.[61] As Ulpian relates, it (partially?) took the place of several older rules, by which he may have meant the XII Tables and subsequent rules. The statute had three chapters. Chapter 1 provided, for the killing (*occidere*) of a slave or four-footed animal of the category of livestock, compensation of the highest value the killed slave or animal had had in the year prior to the killing. Cardascia argues that this was a rough method in order to avoid loss by price fluctuations.[62] Chapter 2 condemned an adstipulator (that is, a co-promisee) who had fraudulently released the common debtor to pay compensation. Chapter 3 ruled that, where somebody had burned, broken, or smashed (*urere frangere rumpere*) another's property, he had to pay compensation for what it was worth in the nearest 30 days. Later Sabinus in the first century AD interpreted this as the highest value in that period. It is unclear whether the period was the 30 days before or after the damaging. Perhaps this was intentional. The costs of wounding could only be established afterwards, but the loss caused by destruction of an object could be assessed from the previous period. The statute provided for compensation of the loss suffered. The delict was, notwithstanding its compensatory goal, penal in the sense that it could not be raised against the heirs of the delinquent (except for enrichment); but it could be raised by the heirs of the victim.

The definition of Chapter 1 was strictly maintained: it had to be a direct violent act of killing like clubbing. That of Chapter 3 was extended, first by fiction ('as if he had broken'), and later by grammatical extension to all kinds of deterioration (*corrumpere*).

The ambit of the statute was further extended in several ways to cover cases which did not fall directly under its wording and therefore could not be granted an *actio directa*. Reconstructions of the *actio directa* have been put forward. The most recent suggestion is that of Nörr,[63] namely that the formula contained an *intentio* (a description of the event in terms of the statute) and then as sequel 'whatever it appears that the defendant should give the plaintiff under the *lex Aquilia*, the judge must condemn him to give to him; or else exonerate him'. In other cases – for example, where a usufructuary had suffered a loss, or loss had been caused indirectly – an adapted action was granted, either an *actio utilis* or an action on the case (*actio in factum*). In the latter case the situation was described in the *demonstratio* of the action, and, if the description proved to be right, the judge was directed to apply the *lex Aquilia*. Such a simple reference to the statute would explain, as already suggested by Rodger, the extensive attention which is given to the statute itself in the commentaries.[64] As for requiring damage to property, in the end even pure patrimonial loss could be claimed by an *actio in factum*.[65] Further, by an *actio utilis* a free person could claim medical expenses,[66] while a *paterfamilias* could claim medical expenses and loss of income for wounding and mutilation of a son in power.[67] These situations are reminiscent of the XII Tables (table 8.3).

Causation

The real extension of the statute was achieved by introducing or developing legal concepts. The wording of the law dealt with some specific cases, chiefly defined by a verb. *Occidere* (to slay to death) is direct and presumes killing by one's own hand, most likely with a club or other blunt instrument. What if the killing is by poisoning? By starving? The Romans solved this by distinguishing a philosophical concept underlying this: causation. *Occidere* was a case of directly causing death, whereas poisoning and starving were doing this by providing an (indirect) cause of death (*mortis causa*). For these cases, actions *in factum* were used. So if somebody gave someone poison by his own hand, it would be a direct action, but if he let the victim drink it himself, it would be an action *in factum* because a cause of death was provided.[68] If somebody was thrown from a bridge and drowned because he could not swim, in the second half of the first century AD Celsus considered this direct killing, presumably because the victim did not bring about his own death but simply succumbed passively.

But by moving away from the immediate and direct killing, the Romans got into more complicated questions of causality. What if a slave was wounded, but died a week later? The question became whether his owner could sue for the wounding alone under chapter 3 or for killing under chapter 1, or even for both? Was it possible to see death as a consequence of the wounding? If not, death could not be attributed to the defendant. Celsus said it could not, but in the middle of the second century AD Julian – and apparently all jurists by some 50 years later – assumed that it could, taking the moment of wounding as the moment of killing. The reason may be – by application of Stoic theories of causation – that if a wound was mortal (the outcome would prove this), the body would at that moment already be mortally wounded and equivalent to being dead.[69]

Here is another school example: a mortally wounded slave takes refuge in a house, which collapses over him: is the assailant liable for killing? Ulpian (around AD 200) thought that he was only liable for wounding. Stoic theories give an explanation for this. The wound is an antecedent cause which makes the body mortally wounded. The quality of being mortally wounded is only a statement of truth if death follows from it. The collapse prevented verification of this, and therefore the only true statement was that he was wounded: 'the collapse of the house did not allow it to emerge whether or not he was killed'.[70] The same reasoning was applied if a slave was mortally wounded but somebody else killed him.[71] Starving a slave to death was a cause of death, not killing, and so an action *in factum* was applicable.[72] If two people together killed a slave – one holding him, the other killing him – then both were liable, the first by an action *in factum*: this was a case of joint causes.[73] But what was a mortal wound? 'But if someone gives a light blow to a sickly slave and he dies from it, Labeo rightly says that he is liable under the *lex Aquilia*; for different things are lethal for different people.'[74] Thus early in the first century AD the adage 'you take your victim as you find him' already applied. Justinian schematized all of this: the *actio directa* applied in case of damage caused *corpore corpori*, 'by a body to a body'; the *actio utilis* where it was caused by a body but not to a body (*corpore* but not *corpori*); and the *actio in factum* if caused neither *corpore* nor *corpori*.[75]

A true school example brings several questions together:

> Further, Mela writes, when some people were playing with a ball, and one of them hit it hard and it knocked the hands of a barber with the result that the throat of a slave whom the barber was shaving was cut by the jerking of the razor, that the person in whom the fault [*culpa*] lies is liable under the *lex Aquilia*. Proculus says the fault [*culpa*] is the barber's, and surely, if he was carrying on shaving in a place where people customarily played games or where there was much going to and fro, it will be imputed to him; but it is a fair point that if someone entrusts himself to a barber who has his chair in a dangerous place he has only himself to blame.[76]

Mela, early in the first century AD, speaks of *culpa*, but the case is about both causality and fault. The causality is multiple: the person who hits the ball causes the ball to hit the arm of the barber, the arm of the barber involuntarily (we assume) cuts the throat of the slave. Hence the barber did kill, but involuntarily and rather as an instrument. From that point of view the hitter of the ball indirectly caused death (*actio in factum*). The barber killed, but in principle did not act unlawfully – he was pushed – so the statute does not apply, as Proculus said of a similar case in the first half of the first century AD.[77] At that point the question turns to *iniuria*: there was *iniuria*, which is now understood more broadly as negligence (see below, 262). If the barber worked at a dangerous place, says Proculus, he will have acted unlawfully because he was negligent in choosing the place to work. And Ulpian adds that the slave may have been the cause himself. As with the slave who walked through a field where people were practising throwing javelins and was hit,[78] he placed himself in a dangerous place and was the cause of his own death. From that perspective only one cause can bring liability and indeed, in Roman law a contributory cause set aside any other liability.

Iniuria

As appears from this example, the element of *iniuria* was refined. The statute itself contained the word, and its probable meaning was 'a wrong', causing a wrongful loss intentionally (with *dolus*). It is assumed that originally 'wrong' meant an act done *non iure*, 'without right' or 'against the law'. The law allowed you to kill a thief in case of *furtum manifestum* at night, so that was done *iure* (lawfully). Similarly, a slave caught in adultery could be killed by the husband.[79] Self-defence also meant that what was done was not done *non iure*,[80] although in the Principate this applied only if the assailant could not be arrested; otherwise one was guilty of murder.[81] Theoretically the statute imposed liability for killing negligently or accidentally. Perhaps the verb *occidere* implied only a deliberate act. However, since the XII Tables (table 8.24) considered negligent killing reprehensible, we may assume that this too, being clearly *non iure*, fell directly under the *lex Aquilia*. In this respect this delict differed from other delicts where intention (*dolus*) was always required. It would be in line with this that the concept of *culpa* began to fill out the element of *iniuria*. 'Wrong' could now mean negligence, fault, recklessness, carelessness, all in an objectivised sense. Where the perpetrator was a craftsman, *culpa* could also mean lack of skill (*imperitia*). And, as we saw before, it was linked with causality. This is because the act which was the cause was either voluntary (*dolus*) or it was involuntary (*casus*) – 'Throwing a weapon is an act of the will, to wound somebody you do not want to is an accident'[82] – or else it was still an act of the will but could have been avoided (negligence): 'Agitations of the mind fall also into the category of unwittingness and imprudence. Though they are voluntary (they can be restrained by reproach and admonishment), still they have so much impulse of their own, that they are considered to be sometimes compelled or certainly unwitting (acts).'[83]

This is all neatly summarized in a famous text of Paul, from around AD 200:

> If a pruner threw down a branch from a tree and killed a slave passing underneath (the same applies to a man working on a scaffold), he is liable only if it falls down in a public place and he failed to shout a warning so that the accident could be avoided. But Mucius says that even if the accident occurred in a private place, an action can be brought on account of his fault [*culpa*]; and he thinks there is fault [*culpa*] when what could have been foreseen by a diligent man was not foreseen or when a warning was shouted too late for the danger to be avoided. Following the same reasoning, it does not matter much whether the deceased was making his way through a public or a private place, as the general public often make their way through private places. But if there is no path, the defendant should be liable only for intentional wrongdoing [*dolus*].[84]

Since Mucius Scaevola (around 100 BC) introduced foreseeability as an element of negligence, *culpa* was standard from quite an early date. It included even the slightest degree of fault.[85] The earlier view was more restricted: throwing down branches on private land did not make you liable at all, since it was *iure* to do what you wanted on your land, and consequently the cause was imputed to the victim himself. Causality and *iniuria* were connected. Hence Proculus could say that a man who was pushed and killed did not act with *iniuria*: he did not do it intentionally or negligently, although he was the direct cause.

Negligence could also indirectly lead to causing and so to liability:

> In the action which arises under this title, both intentional wrongdoing [*dolus*] and fault [*culpa*] are punished; and so, if a man sets fire to stubble or thorns in order to burn them up and the fire escapes further afield and spreads and burns another's crops or vineyard, we shall ask whether this occurred through his inexperience [*imperitia*] or negligence [*neglegentia*]. If he did it on a windy day, he is guilty of a fault [*culpa*] (for even he who provides the opportunity [*occasionem praestare*] is deemed to have caused the loss); and he who did not see to it that the fire did not spread stands in the same position. But if he saw to everything that he should have done or it was a sudden squall of wind that extended the fire, he is free of fault [*culpa*].[86]

In this case somebody does what is allowed (*iure*), but if he is to do it, he must be experienced or, if he is inexperienced, be careful. If this is the case, we may expect the fire to be contained. An external cause like a squall of wind is then considered *vis maior* (force majeure). However, if he is careless or inexperienced, he creates an opportunity for external causes which otherwise would not have effect. Burning on a windy day is not diligent. Although he did not intend this and everything happened involuntarily, he did intend at the outset to do something which was able to set this chain of causation in motion.

The role of negligence may be explained by a Stoic refinement of the antecedent cause. A cause did not under all circumstances unavoidably lead to its consequences but could be conditional. 'If a slave is wounded, but not mortally, and he dies of neglect, the action will be for wounding, not for killing.'[87] The antecedent cause was conditional: the wound was not mortal if proper care was provided, so the absence of this additional cause, owing to negligence, prevented its fulfilment.[88] Likewise shaving on the street is not dangerous as long as one takes care not to do it in a busy place (or, if it is being done there, the customer should avoid this barber).

A loss could be caused by more than one person, in which case all were liable; and payment by one did not release the others: it was after all a penal action.[89]

Compensation

Another issue was compensation. The word *plurimi* ('the highest') could be interpreted in more than one way and so respond to complicated situations. It could refer to the object itself and would then refer to its highest market value in the preceding year (in the case of chapter 1) or in the nearest 30 days (for chapter 3). Sentimental values were not taken into account: 'If you kill my slave, I think that personal feelings should not be taken into account (as where someone kills your natural son whom you would be prepared to buy for a great price), but only what he would be worth to the world at large.'[90]

But *plurimi* could also be interpreted differently. It could cover what we now call consequential losses. Where a child in paternal power was wounded, his *pater* had a claim for the medical costs, but also for what he lost in income by his son's services.[91] 'For under the *lex Aquilia*, we sue for the amount of the loss suffered, and we are said to have lost either whatever we could have gained or what we are obliged to pay out.'[92] In short, lost gains and incurred costs were indemnifiable.

Another case: What if your slave had been instituted heir but was killed before you as his owner could accept the inheritance? This was not so difficult: the value of the slave was increased by the inheritance, he could be sold for that price, and that was the value of the compensation.[93] What if your horse was one of a four-in-hand and killed? It takes a great deal of time to train horses to do this. Here the value of the horse was its value as such, but the loss in value of the four-in-hand was added to this. In this example probably another criterion for loss was applied, which Ulpian formulated: 'But are we assessing only his body, how much it was worth when he was killed, or rather how much it was worth to us that he should not be killed? We use this rule, that the assessment should be what he was worth to the plaintiff.'[94] This different method, 'the worth of not being killed', which we also see applied for injury (see above, 258–9), was accepted alongside the old one, and the plaintiff was free to choose. It provided a solution to the question raised by the example of the four-in-hand. Further, destroying a will, or a chirograph which proved a claim for money, involved liability for the amount the plaintiff could claim.[95]

So far as procedure is concerned, the statute originally allowed only the owner to raise a claim, but this was extended to those with an interest similar to the owner, such as the usufructuary.[96] The plaintiff raised a claim with the magistrate, who would then ask the defendant whether he denied it or not. If he denied it, the *lex Aquilia* doubled the estimate of the compensation claimed ('litiscrescence': it did not apply to the praetorian actions *utilis* and *in factum*). Denial (*infitiatio*) related to the facts of the case. Suppose somebody acknowledges the wounding or killing of a slave and later discovers that the slave was not wounded or killed or had died a natural death: then the procedure comes to an end.[97] Perhaps it also extended to denying that the statute applied; we do not know. It might be that the parties agreed on all the facts but not about the amount of compensation; in that case the judge merely decided that point.[98]

5. NOXAL LIABILITY

Persons of full legal standing (*sui iuris*) were liable for the delicts they committed. With slaves and children in paternal power (*alieni iuris*) who committed delicts the situation was complicated. In their case a slightly complex way of suing was adapted, known as noxal action after the word *noxa* for wrong or loss caused by persons *alieni iuris*. Celsus explains in the context of the *lex Aquilia* how this came about: the XII Tables contained a provision 'if a slave commits theft or commits harm [*noxa*] or injures'. Following Celsus, we must assume that it went on to say that the slave was punishable. We know that with theft a slave was scourged and turned over to the victim of the theft. Perhaps something like that originally happened in cases of wrongful damage.

Under the *lex Aquilia*, however, it was the owner who was liable for his slave's delicts and not the slave. Presumably this was because the statute aimed at compensation for the loss caused. It would be of no help to hold a slave liable, since a slave had no property. But the different approach of the XII Tables was not abolished, and the *lex Aquilia* apparently supplemented it (or was understood to supplement it). The two systems were fused. If a slave committed a delict (wrongful loss, *furtum*, injury), his owner was cited before the magistrate on account of the slave and asked whether he wanted to defend him. If the owner refused, the slave was at once assigned by the magistrate in ownership to the plaintiff. If the owner took the defence upon him, the action was allowed as a noxal action, using the phrase from the XII Tables. The owner had a second opportunity to repudiate his defence of the slave, since in the condemnation the owner was given the choice either of accepting liability to pay the compensation or surrendering his slave on account of *noxa* (noxal surrender, *noxae deditio*). The same procedure applied to children in paternal power but, if their *pater* refused to defend them, they were allowed to defend themselves. Justinian abolished this. He further provided that slaves had to work off the debt, after which they were to be returned.

Noxal liability only applied where the owner (or *pater*) did not have knowledge of the delict. That was understood in this way: '"knowledge" should be taken to mean knowledge on the part of someone who has the power to prevent'.[99] In all other cases the owner was directly liable in his own person.

The rule became complicated in relation to ownership. What if a slave was meanwhile sold or inherited or enfranchised or owned by more than one person? Or a child was adopted or emancipated? Who was to be cited as master? The general rule was that whoever was the owner of the slave at the moment litigation started was cited and liable, not the person who was owner at the moment of the delict. This rule is comprised in the adage *noxa caput sequitur* ('the wrong follows the head'). Usually head is understood to mean the head (*caput*) of the slave, but it might also refer to the owner, who had legal standing (*caput*), which legally a slave did not have. Perhaps the phrase even refers to the change from the XII Tables to the *lex Aquilia*.[100] Under the *actio de pauperie* (see below, 267) the same rule applied. In practice it does not make a difference. Mutatis mutandis, the same applied to children in paternal power. Manumission or emancipation after the delict made the slave or child in person liable and released their former owner or *pater*.

In the case of *iniuria*, in later times the punishment for slaves was a thrashing (see above, 257). But in the second century that was not unusual, as this text shows:

> When a slave effects an injury, he obviously commits a delict; and just as in the case of other delicts, so also a noxal action for injury will issue; but it is in the master's discretion whether he will submit the slave to a thrashing to mollify the victim of the injury; the master will not be obliged to present him for a thrashing, but he will have the option of allowing him to be thrashed or, if that would not satisfy the affronted person, of giving him in surrender on account of *noxa* or of accepting an assessment in legal proceedings.[101]

Here, if the owner did not want to defend his slave, the magistrate had the opportunity to have him thrashed but not to surrender him. We can also see that primarily the owner was supposed to exercise his power to discipline his slave.

6. ANIMALS, *PAUPERIES* (LOSS, CAUSED BY AN ANIMAL)

Animals were wild or, if they were tame, could still exhibit wild behaviour. If a wild animal or a tame one acting wildly caused harm, its owner and not the animal was liable: 'Servius writes, this action lies when a four-footed animal does harm because its wild nature has been excited.'[102] Noxality was also applied to damage and losses caused by animals on their own. If they were under control, their owners or masters would be liable under the *lex Aquilia*: 'Julian says the *lex Aquilia* only applies to this extent: it applies to a person who had a dog on a lead and caused it to bite someone; but if he was not holding it, an *actio in factum* must be brought.'[103] The victim could sue the owner with the *actio de pauperie*, the action on loss caused by an animal. The action was penal, so if the animal died before joinder of issue the action failed.[104] The owner had the choice either to pay the sum to which he was condemned or to surrender the animal.[105] This delict was already included in the XII Tables.[106] If the loss was large, it would be profitable to turn the animal over. If after joinder of issue such an animal was killed, under the *lex Aquilia* its owner could claim not the value of the animal as such but his interest in surrendering it: 'the assessment must not be according to the beast's physical value, but to the amount of liability in the case involving the *pauperies* action' which obliges him 'to pay the amount that it would have profited the owner to make a surrender on account of *noxa* rather than pay the assessment of the issue'.[107] Alongside this action the aedilician edict provided a non-noxal remedy.[108]

The harm could be done to slaves and animals, but the wounding of free people (*sui* and *alieni iuris*) was most likely the primary concern of the delict. They could sue for the 'expenses of medical treatment and the loss of employment [*operae amissae*] and of the opportunity of taking a job caused by the party being disabled', but 'that is not to say that disfigurement can be taken into account, because the body of a free person is not susceptible of assessment (in court).'[109] It is evident that the Romans were well aware of how the consequences of wounding could affect somebody's earning power and that it mattered to them.

7. Other Delicts

There were other delicts, such as cutting and stealing trees (*actio arborum furtim caesarum*, D. 47.7) or desecrating graves (*actio de sepulchro violato*, D. 47.12). Of these, *rapina* or *actio vi bonorum raptorum* (robbery) was the most important. It was the combination of *furtum* with force and was punished with a fourfold fine if sued within a year (after that, for the simple value). One-quarter of the fine was meant to compensate the victim.

Alongside the delicts where intention (or negligence) was required, there were delicts where intention was not necessary. If something was thrown or poured out of a building, regardless of who did it the occupier had to pay double damages, including medical costs for free people, or 50 *aurei* if a free man was killed (*actio de deiectis vel effusis*).[110] If something was placed on an eave or projecting roof in a place where people usually passed by, an action on the case was given for 10 *solidi* against the person who placed it, if it could injure people if it fell (*actio de positis vel suspensis*).[111] If an employee of an inn-keeper, livery man, or shipmaster had stolen or damaged goods belonging to a customer, his master was liable,[112] according to Ulpian and Justinian, because he had been negligent in choosing such bad employees. There are several theories on the grounds for liability in these cases: negligence, risk liability, vicarious liability, or liability on account of public policy. The Byzantines classified them as quasi-delicts and added the liability of a judge for his errors (*iudex qui litem suam fecit*).

Notes

1. The bibliography on delicts and particularly the *lex Aquilia* is immense. For surveys and literature the reader is referred to Kaser, *Das römische Privatrecht*, vol. 1, 146–165, 609–634; vol. 2, 425–440; Kaser and Knütel, *Römisches Privatrecht*, §§ 50–51; Zimmermann, *Obligations*, 902–1130.
2. Authors such as Kaser consider the sum claimed in penal actions to be a fine, intended to placate the injustice done. Because under the *lex Aquilia* the sum claimed was the same as the loss suffered, Kaser is led to describe the action under the *lex Aquilia* as an action for a fine with a compensatory function. Compensation indeed redresses an injustice done, but the modern fine, of which Kaser is thinking, is not compensatory.
3. A. J. B. Sirks, 'The delictual origin, penal nature and reipersecutory object of the *actio damni iniuriae legis Aquiliae*', *TR* 77 (2009): 303–353.
4. FIRA I, 13 no. 16.
5. FIRA I, 17 no. 6.
6. FIRA I, 13 no. 17.
7. See the chapter by Metzger, 287–9.
8. D. 47.2.12.1; but if the owner had no such interest, he could not sue: Inst. 4.1.13(15).

9. Plautus, *Rudens* 473–478.
10. Gaius 3.189–190.
11. A. J. B. Sirks, 'Furtum and manus / potestas', *TR* 81 (2013): 465–506.
12. D. 47.17.1.
13. P. Birks, 'A Note on the Development of Furtum', *Irish Jurist* 8 (1973): 349–355.
14. D. 13.1.20.
15. D. 47.2.21.1.
16. D. 47.2.47 pr.
17. D. 47.2.50 pr.
18. D. 47.2.22.2.
19. D. 47.2.21 pr.
20. D. 47.2.52.7.
21. D. 13.1.18, D. 47.2.43 pr.
22. D. 47.2.43.4.
23. D. 47.2.40.
24. D.47.2.15.1.
25. D. 19.2.6; D. 47.2.14.2 and 12.
26. D. 47.2.21.8.
27. D. 47.2.21.7; the reference to the criminal charge relates to the *lex Julia de vi privata*.
28. D. 47.2.34.
29. D. 47.2.36 pr.; it still constituted wrongful loss: Inst. 4.3.16.
30. D. 47.2.36.3.
31. D. 47.2.52.22.
32. D. 47.2.37; it is generally assumed that the part 'if someone . . . it' is a later addition, because it does not make the chasing person a thief.
33. J. A. C. Thomas, 'Contrectatio, Complicity and Furtum', *Iura* 13 (1962): 69–88.
34. Gaius 3.199: 'Sometimes theft may be committed of free persons, as, for example, if a person has carried off one of our children in our power, or our wife under marital power, or my adjudicated debtor'.
35. W. A. J. Watson, 'Contrectatio as an Essential of Furtum', *Law Quarterly Review* 77 (1961): 526–532.
36. B. Nicholas, 'Theophilus and Contrectatio', in *Studies in Justinian's Institutes*, ed. P. Stein and A. D. E. Lewis (London, 1983), 118–124.
37. B. Albanese, 'La nozione del 'furtum' nell'elaborazione dei giuristi romani,' *Jus* 5 (1958): 315–326 (also in Albanese, *Scritti Giuridici* (Palermo, 1991), vol. 1, 99–110).
38. Birks (n. 13).
39. Thomas (n. 33).
40. Watson (n. 35).
41. Birks (n. 13); H. F. Jolowicz, *Digest XLVII, 2, De Furtis* (Cambridge, 1940).
42. D. 47.2.1.3.
43. D. 47.2.57(56).1.
44. D. 47.10.1 pr.
45. D. 9.2.13 pr.
46. D. 47.10.1.2.
47. D. 47.10.3.2–3.
48. D. 9.2.5.3–4.
49. D. 47.10.12.
50. D. 47.10.13.7.

51. D. 47.10.44.
52. D. 47.10.15.26.
53. Plut. *Pomp.* 48.
54. Plin. *Ep.* 7.24
55. D. 47.10.15.22.
56. D. 47.10.15.27.
57. D. 47.10.39.
58. D. 47.10.15.32.
59. D. 47.10.15.38.
60. F. Pringsheim, The Origin of the 'lex Aquilia', in *Mélanges Lévy-Bruhl*, Paris 1959, 233–244 (= *Gesammelte Abhandlungen* (Heidelberg, 1961), vol. 2, 410–420).
61. *Iniuria*, a noun, has here an adjectival role, defining the nature of the loss. *Damnum* means 'loss', not damage. See D. Daube, 'On the Use of the Term Damnum', in *Studi Solazzi*, (Napoli 1948), 93–156.
62. G. Cardascia, 'La portée primitive de la loi Aquilia', in *Daube Noster: Essays in Legal History for David Daube*, ed. A. Watson (Edinburgh, 1974), 53–75.
63. D. Nörr, 'Zur Formel der *actio legis Aquiliae*', in *Festschrift für Rolf Knütel zum 70. Geburtstag*, ed. H. Altmeppen et al. (Heidelberg, 2009), 833–48.
64. A. F. Rodger, 'The Palingenesia of the Commentaries Relating to the Lex Aquilia', *ZSS* 124 (2007): 145–197.
65. D. 9.2.33.1; Inst. 4.3.16.
66. D. 9.2.13pr. The text has *liber homo*, which is interpreted by Kunkel as *liber homo bona fide serviens*, while others consider this a Byzantine interpolation (see Zimmermann (n. 1), 1016–1017). Yet neither argument makes sense given that a free man could sue for compensation for wounding in the case of *pauperies* and the delict *de deiectis vel effusis*, and D. 9.2.11.8 makes sense only if a free man could already sue *utiliter* for being wounded.
67. D. 9.2.7 pr.
68. D. 9.2.7.6.
69. D. 9.2.21.1.
70. D. 9.2.15.1.
71. D. 9.2.11.3. See A. J. B. Sirks, 'The Slave Who Was Slain Twice: Causality and the lex Aquilia (Iul. 38 dig. D. 9, 2, 51)', *TR* 79 (2011): 313–351.
72. D. 9.2.9.2.
73. D. 9.2.11.1.
74. D. 9.2.7.5.
75. Inst. 4.3.16.
76. D. 9.2.11 pr.
77. D. 9.2.7.3.
78. D. 9.2.9.4.
79. D. 9.2.30 pr.
80. D. 9.2.4 pr.
81. D. 9.2.5 pr.
82. Cic. *Top.* 64.
83. Cic. *Top.* 64; see 263.
84. D. 9.2.31.
85. D. 9.2.44 pr.
86. D. 9.2.30.3.

87. D. 9.2.30.4.
88. Without this condition, determinism would be the outcome: it would not matter whether one took care of a wound or not. Now it depended on free will.
89. D. 9.2.11.2; 9.2.19.
90. D. 9.2.33 pr.
91. D. 9.2.7 pr.
92. D. 9.2.33 pr.
93. D. 9.2.23 pr.
94. D. 9.2.21.2.
95. D. 9.2.41.1, 40; as in the case of *furtum*, see 249, D. 47.2.47 pr.
96. D. 9.2.17–19.
97. D. 9.2.23.11–24, 25.
98. D. 9.2.25.2.
99. D. 9.4.4 pr.
100. A. J. B. Sirks, 'Noxa caput sequitur', *TR* 81 (2013) 81–108.
101. D. 47.10.17.4.
102. D. 9.1.1.4.
103. D. 9.2.11.5.
104. D. 9.1.1.13.
105. D. 9.1.1 pr.
106. D. 9.1.1 pr.
107. D. 9.2.37.1.
108. D. 21.1.40–42.
109. D. 9.1.3. Cf. the *actio de deiectis vel effusis* (Section 7, 268).
110. D. 9.3.1.
111. D. 9.3.5.6–13.
112. D. 4.9, D. 47.5.

14 Litigation

Ernest Metzger

The Romans resolved civil disputes by recourse to litigation based on law. Litigation was guided by formal procedures which underwent reform by statute, praetorian innovation, and imperial enactment. The earlier procedures depended to a high degree on the initiative of the plaintiff and the cooperation of the defendant. The later procedures depended to a greater degree on the power of the courts to compel obedience.[1]

1. Surviving Evidence of Civil Procedure

Our understanding of Roman procedure relies on diverse sources, none of which is satisfactory on its own, and even taken together are only adequate.[2] Physical evidence has been lost with time, but the problem is deeper. The Romans did not reflect on their procedural law in the way they reflected on their private law.[3] They did not linger over modes of pleading or representation. If a rule of procedure was unfair or inappropriate, it was mended without a view to the system of litigation as a whole. This prevented the Romans from appreciating that their procedural law had a tradition and an evolution, and that there was something to be learned from studying older law. The result is that the Romans treated old rules as if they were old newspapers. Justinian's compilation and the Theodosian *Code* are sources for the procedure of late antiquity, but scarcely for the earlier forms. Justinian was particularly ruthless: rules that had fallen out of use were either discarded by the compilers or altered to be fit for re-promulgation. Occasionally the compilers performed these tasks clumsily and the shadow of some earlier law makes itself known through an artless interpolation. But what we miss in Justinian, in strong contrast to his treatment of private law, is even a cursory discussion of old and new law side by side.

The discovery of Gaius' *Institutes* in the early nineteenth century partly answered this need. Gaius wrote in the middle second century AD, and the surviving portions of book 4 give us an overview of the *legis actio* and formulary procedures.[4] His treatment is brief but preserves many details. We are especially indebted to him for his discussion of the *legis actio* procedure, in which his interest was almost wholly historical, and which leaves only the barest traces in other sources. Even the formulary procedure was falling out of use when he wrote, so that what he gives us of that procedure is something like a 'potted account' of the main features, rather than the description of an observer or the 'how-to' manual of a practioner.[5]

Among literary authors Cicero (106–43 BC) is the principal source. In certain speeches procedure is front and centre (*pro Caecina*, *pro Quinctio*), while in others, details of procedure can be extrapolated from single passages or even passing remarks.[6] Other important authors are Aulus Gellius (AD 125/8–ca. 180), who saw service as a judge and recorded thoughts and observations on the law, Horace (65–8 BC), Pliny the Younger (AD c. 61–c. 112), and Macrobius (fifth century AD). Plautus (third–second century BC)[7] is rich but requires special care, because the procedure he describes is not always Roman, and because he often uses a rule of procedure for humorous effect, requiring the reader to divine the law and the joke at the same time.

Quintilian needs special mention as a source, because he was long underappreciated. Proceeding from the part truth, part conceit that Justinian's *Corpus iuris* is 'legislation', the natural lawyers and their equally enthusiastic systematizers in the nineteenth century gave special place to the legal sources that were, after all, the raw material for their systems. Literary sources were sidelined, and Quintilian's *Institutio oratoria* (and, for that matter, Cicero's rhetorical works) were seen to belong to another discipline altogether. We now appreciate far better that Quintilian is a valuable source for procedure; much of what took place in litigation was unwritten in the law and shaped by the work of advocates.[8]

Statutes and records of private affairs survive in inscriptions: their value to the study of procedure is enormous.[9] Even imperfectly preserved, they come to us free from abbreviation, interpolation, and so forth. They convey rules and customs that were uninteresting to subsequent generations, and events that were ephemeral even to contemporaries. As such they can give us a direct view of daily life in the courts and, substance aside, their drafting gives us clues to juristic practice.

Many new and valuable inscriptions were discovered only in the last century. We now possess, for example, several Roman formulae and can compare them to Gaius' description.[10] Among the most valuable of the new discoveries are the collections of first-century waxed tablets from Herculaneum and Puteoli, both of which include documents prepared for litigation.[11] Another valuable new source is the *lex Irnitana*, a copy of a model 'town charter' prepared for *municipia* in Spain. The *lex Irnitana* contains detailed rules on conducting lawsuits, and many of the rules directly reflect the practice in Rome.[12]

2. The Scope of the Law

Litigation was governed by law but the law was not comprehensive: litigants supplemented the law with practices that acknowledged but were not determined by the law, and advocates conducted trials based on rules and practices developed outside the operation of the law altogether. The present day owes its comprehensive laws of procedure to its enthusiasm for testing its systems against wider principles such as 'hear both sides' and 'due process', and reforming the law to suit. Roman procedure was not deaf to these principles nor resistant to improvement, but there were no means to challenge the validity of questionable law in a way that might have led to wider reflection and a more comprehensive body of rules. This is why it is somewhat jarring to see modern scholars do what the Romans never did: assess Roman procedure for its fidelity to certain 'principles of procedure'.[13] We know, for example, that the Romans favoured publicity in their proceedings, and that at times they avoided taking decisions in a defendant's absence, but to treat these features as conscious aspirations wrongly suggests that the Romans were somehow anticipating a better and more complete system.[14]

In fact the law of procedure, until very late, concerned itself with a limited number of issues, the principal ones being summons, joinder of issue or establishing the claims, and the instigation of trial. Execution of judgments was rudimentary until the creation of appropriate devices under the imperial *cognitio* procedure. The limited scope of procedural law reflected the limited authority of the magistrates[15] who enforced it. From at least the time of the Twelve Tables, and through the principate, much of the ordinary civil litigation took place in two distinct stages, and the magistrate presided over the first stage only. This was the so-called *in iure* stage. Generally speaking, this stage was devoted to isolating the issues for trial. In some cases this could be a complex task to perform, requiring special findings of fact, interim remedies, or sanctions for disobedience. At bottom, however, this stage had a modest goal – to produce the trial agenda – and the law of procedure developed to assist the magistrate in that goal. The law extended hardly at all into the second stage of the lawsuit, the trial before the judge (*apud iudicem*). This was the stage at which witnesses and evidence were presented and a judgment given. There were no laws to assist the judge comparable to those that assisted the magistrate.

Thus, the Roman practice of dividing the lawsuit into two stages left the trial stage relatively unregulated. There were important exceptions: the judge was answerable for certain mistakes and misbehaviour (usually reflected in the form or timing of the judgment), and in some circumstances a litigant could return to the magistrate to have the lawsuit restored to an earlier, pre-trial state of affairs (*restitutio in integrum*, discussed below, 277). But for the most part the trial was conducted according to other rules: the rhetorical conventions cultivated by the orators who spoke on behalf of the litigants. In the republic these were the *patroni*, men of wealth and standing, later named *advocati* as they came to be drawn from less elevated ranks and became more professionalized. They imported Greek rhetoric and nurtured it into a peculiarly Roman discipline.[16]

3. The Two Stages

The two-stage proceeding is striking and, not surprisingly, has invited scholars to consider and describe its general character.[17] An enduring description (or at least an enduring point of departure) is Moriz Wlassak's from the nineteenth century: a voluntary submission to state-sanctioned arbitration. His description drew of course on the largely unregulated second stage, but also on the relatively 'light touch' exercised by the magistrate in the first stage, and on the seemingly contractual nature of the event (*litis contestatio*) by which the second stage was set in motion. But, if litigation was at the outset a species of arbitration, then it could not have been unitary in origin, with a single figure (king, then magistrate) exercising full judicial powers. Thus, writers after Wlassak, such as Leopold Wenger, sought to disprove Wlassak by showing that the Roman kings did indeed possess full judicial powers, a proposition for which there are a few (though suspect) sources. Others, such as Kaser, have criticised Wlassak's view directly on the argument that even in the earliest period of litigation, that of the *legis actio*, state compulsion was present and the parties were undeniably at odds.

At bottom the answer turns on the (conjectural) origins of the *judge*: where did the impetus come from to create a separate decision-maker?

The arbitration theory makes him the creation of the parties; the unitary-in-origin theory makes him a 'state concession' to, for example, democratic pressures or the magistrate's burdens of office. A further state-concession explanation, put forward by Kaser, was influential for many years. This was the explanation that all judicial duties may originally have been concentrated in a king, but this would only be the case so long as lawsuits were decided by, for example, magic and ritual. When lawsuits came to be decided by *law*, this effected a division of responsibility: the magistrate (or king) performed acts of will, such as orders to act or refrain from acting, and these are distinct in character from decision-making, which relies on knowledge of the rights that obtain in a particular case. Thus, the divided procedure would reflect a new-found desire of two contesting parties to find an impartial decision-maker with knowledge of the relevant rights.[18]

Yet newer studies, and new evidence, have perhaps revived the arbitration model somewhat. The judicial selection procedures, now visible in great detail in the *lex Irnitana*, reveal themselves to be strikingly consensual (Birks). A study of *editio*, a form of pre-trial notice (Bürge), though revealing *litis contestatio* to be less 'contractual' than Wlassak believed, ironically shows it to be more consensual. And a comparison of the procedures of the Twelve Tables with other primitive modes of litigation suggests that early Roman litigation may have been more concerned with keeping the peace among members of a close community than with parsing every grievance into legal claims (MacCormack). The consensual features now appear so prominent that we are perhaps justified in giving the arbitration theory a second look. Jolowicz's view – that early Roman litigation was arbitral even in the face of a hostile party and a measure of state compulsion – now seems quite plausible.[19]

4. Challenges, Reviews, Appeals

Until the principate and the arrival of the *cognitio* procedure, a disappointed litigant had limited means for challenging a judgment or the decision of a magistrate; none of the available means could be described as 'appeal'.[20] Before *cognitio*, a lawsuit proceeded in a (to us) back-to-front manner, with the higher authority (the magistrate) making certain final decisions before the matter was passed to the lower authority (the judge). In theory, this ought to clear the stage of appealable issues before trial. In practice, it might be necessary not to 'appeal the case' to a higher authority, but to revisit a matter that the magistrate had earlier decided. A litigant might, for example, seek the *auxilium* of a tribune or the veto of another magistrate.[21] This must have been rare, however. The more usual method for revisiting a magistrate's decision, and the method addressed at length in the praetor's edict,[22] was to seek *restitutio in integrum* ('restoration to an earlier state of affairs'). This was a special praetorian remedy, often invoked to relieve a litigant from the legal effects of a transaction deemed to be unfair in that instance. The remedy resembled an appeal, however, when a litigant had lost his right to bring an action and equity demanded that that right be restored. This might occur, for example, if a litigant had innocently sued a person who lacked the capacity to be sued, or if a litigant's action had expired because a magistrate's own negligence had allowed it to do so. A further means to challenge the legal sufficiency of a judgment, somewhat analogous to *restitutio*, was for a losing defendant to mount a challenge when the prevailing party brought an enforcement action (*actio iudicati*). The need to furnish security, and the risk of a double condemnation in the event that the challenge failed, made this a perilous course.

Quite a separate avenue for challenging a judgment was to bring a personal action against the judge.[23] Aside from some possible pre-edictal roots, this type of proceeding belonged to the formulary procedure, and specifically to lawsuits that were brought before the lay *unus iudex*. The grounds on which these actions were granted is not perfectly clear: the evidence is patchy, and it is difficult to distinguish the grounds set down in the praetor's edict from the grounds set down later in a *lex Iulia de iudiciis privatis* (17 BC, discussed below, 282). Properly speaking these actions were not a species of appeal or even a substitute for appeal, but a tool of administration: the state machinery lacked the means to manage the trial, and opted to 'manage the judge' instead. He was given a single commission and charged with performing it properly at the risk of personal liability. Aside from certain errors of calculation, easily avoided, he was bound (1) to give judgment within the proper time, and (2) not to give judgment in the face of certain unexpected events, for example a party's illness. It is unlikely that a judge who crossed these lines would face certain condemnation, at least after the passage of the *lex Iulia*; many of the errors for which a judge was responsible could be easily corrected (although after execution of a defective judgment, perhaps not.)

From the principate onwards, an increasing number of cases were brought under the *cognitio* procedure, and because the authority to adjudicate these cases derived ultimately from the emperor's *imperium*, appeals could now be taken to the emperor himself or to persons or institutions to whom he delegated this authority.[24] The appellate authority, moreover, could reform the judgment, where *restitutio* had only allowed earlier proceedings to be annulled. For the principate the sources are more spare, but it appears that civil appeals were variously permitted to the urban praetor (from Roman litigants), to the senate (from provincial litigants), and in the late principate to the *praefectus praetorio*. We would expect, however, that in the usual case appeals would be taken from the delegated judge to the delegating magistrate or, where relevant, a provincial governor. In the later empire the judicature was much altered, with cases being heard at first instance in local courts and provincial governors' courts, and more rarely before the now multiple *praefecti praetorio* and in the courts of regional *vicarii* (deputies of the *praefecti*). Second or even third appeals might be heard from these courts upwards, though the governors' courts were usually the last resort for local matters.

5. Principal Models and Special Proceedings

From the monarchy to the dominate, civil procedure evolved through three periods:

> *Legis actiones*. A procedure nominally, if not in fact, determined by statute (*lex*), guided by strict pleading, and marked by certain archaisms. It is older than the Twelve Tables, and had largely disappeared by the second century BC.
>
> *Ordo iudiciorum*, or formulary procedure. A procedure guided by a brief written statement, assembled from model clauses ultimately founded on the law. The statement constituted the question to be adjudicated. The procedure's origins may lie in the peregrine praetorship (242 BC), and its use declined through the principate.
>
> *Cognitio*.[25] A procedure marked by an official's undertaking to investigate and adjudicate a claim according to the law. Its origins are in the power of the emperor, and it became the usual form of procedure from some undetermined time in the principate.

This account is accurate, though incomplete. The three periods describe the different frameworks within which a civil lawsuit passed from summons to execution. Within each of these frameworks, however, narrow and limited proceedings could take place. Such proceedings had a short duration and followed a unique procedure; each was used to resolve one or more type of controversy. For example, a specific proceeding might be necessary to determine the ownership of a slave or its servile status, a litigant's disobedience, or the genuineness of a debt. Such proceedings met certain needs that the main forms of action could not adequately meet. The most important of these was the need to enforce the magistrate's authority. For whatever reason, the power to enforce obedience to magistral orders came slowly to civil litigation, reaching a measure of efficiency only with the contempt procedure of the later principate and dominate. Before that time, magistrates relied on certain special proceedings.

An important example is *missio in possessionem*: a magistrate with *imperium* gives the possession of another's goods and allows their sale.[26] Among other uses, it was a procedural instrument used to enforce judgment debts and also, significantly, used against those who resisted the magistrate's authority by concealing themselves or otherwise leaving themselves undefended. A current of opinion holds that *missio* was available even against a person who resisted private summons (*in ius vocatio*, discussed below, 282), but there are reasons to doubt that this was the case.[27]

A second example is the praetorian stipulation.[28] This belonged to the formulary procedure, though it followed a sequence of events at least partly familiar to the *legis actio* procedure. The praetor, instead of ordering a party to perform at the risk of penalty, would order a party to make a conditional promise to his opponent. The transaction was therefore a compulsory stipulation, creating a conditional debt. Diverse matters were handled in this way, including *operis novi nuntiatio* (a stipulation for assurance from a neighbour who is contemplating hazardous work), *cautio damni infecti* (a stipulation against impending damage), and *vadimonium* (a stipulation to return after proceedings *in iure* have been interrupted). There are interesting examples of the latter in the finds from Herculaneum and Puteoli. Local magistrates sometimes lacked the jurisdiction to hear a case locally, and were charged with deciding whether the case ought to be heard in Rome or by a provincial governor. But this required a special evidentiary proceeding to determine whether the subject matter of the case, or the amount in controversy, did indeed make a local trial impossible. If the case could not be heard locally, the proceeding would conclude with a praetorian stipulation. One party (or perhaps both?) promised the other to appear at the remote tribunal, and to pay a sum if he did not appear.[29]

Interdict

The most important of these special proceedings, however, was the interdictal proceeding.[30] Interdicts are attested from the second century BC and were perhaps the earliest form of praetorian intervention. An interdict was a command that issued from a magistrate with *imperium* and was aimed either at bringing order to a disorderly (and perhaps unpeaceful) state of affairs, or at forestalling some undesirable event. The magistrate, on application, ordered a person to do something or to refrain from doing something. An inquiry of the facts was not needed for an order to issue, and there were even instances where it issued *ex parte*. This seems remarkable until we appreciate that the order was not directed against a person *per se*, but against a person who was, in fact, as he was alleged to be. What this means in practice is that a magistrate, considering an interdict, need not decide whether the plaintiff had a valid claim in law, but only whether the plaintiff was in a deserving position relative to the *alleged* position of the defendant. If, for example, a person had allowed another the use of his property for some indefinite period (a so-called *precarium*), and the grantee refused to return it on demand, it was enough for the magistrate to appreciate that the greater possessory right would lie with the grantor if the grantor's story were true. The magistrate would then order the grantee to restore, not 'the property', but 'that which he holds *precario*'.[31] In inserting the proviso, the magistrate is hedging: the grantor may in fact have no such right. A second example: if a person believed that another had done something injurious on his land, such as erecting a structure, and had done so 'by force or stealth' (*vi aut clam*), the magistrate would not simply order restoration, as he did not have the facts before him; he would instead order the restoration of 'that which was performed *vi aut clam*'.[32] Again, the magistrate is hedging.

Speed was the principal advantage in the interdictal procedure: small and uncontested affairs could be disposed of without trial; possession could be quickly secured when ownership was disputed; a 'new possession' could be obtained, for the sake of equity, when time was of the essence.[33] But the advantage of speed was at the defendant's expense. The unusual construction of the interdict did not allow the free incorporation of defences, and in any event the interdictal proceeding did not allow a defendant to prove his defence as he would at trial. A defendant who believed his side had merit was therefore put in the position of making a later challenge, not to the interdict itself (which was final), but to the assumption on which the interdict issued. This required a trial on the merits, which would proceed under a *legis actio* or, later, under a formula. The groundwork for the trial was usually set by mutual promises, expressed as stipulations: the interdicted person promised to pay a sum if, for example, he had disobeyed the interdict to restore that which was performed *vi aut clam*. This required him to prove at trial that he had not acted *vi aut clam*, or possibly that some other factor made his conduct lawful. The other party made a corresponding promise to pay a sum if his opponent had not disobeyed the interdict. Under the formulary procedure, a more careful defendant, unsure whether he could show he had acted properly, could instead elect, at the time that the interdict issued, to go to trial on a formula permitting him (in the event judgment went against him) to obey the interdict in lieu of condemnation.

6. Legis Actio

The *legis actio* procedure was a strict and formal method for identifying claims that deserved further prosecution.[34] By later Roman standards the claims were highly 'unparticularized'. The specific grievance was unacknowledged, the litigant receiving instead an off-the-peg statement that he had been aggrieved in one of the limited permissible ways, along with the state's approval to seek redress, whether by trial or execution. The state expressed its approval in one of five general forms. Certain forms (*legis actio per sacramentum*; *per condictionem*; *per iudicis postulationem*) allowed the plaintiff to seek redress before a judge or judges at trial, while other forms (*per manus iniectionem*; *per pignoris capionem*) allowed the plaintiff to seek direct redress against, respectively, a debtor or the debtor's property. The differences among the forms lay partly in the underlying substantive claim (e.g., a personal claim would usually be brought under *per sacramentum in personam* or *per condictionem*), but mostly in the procedure. The *per condictionem* interposed a delay before trial; the *per iudicis postulationem* required a similar delay, but was used only when a specific statute authorized it; the *per sacramentum* was preceded by an elaborate wager; the *per manus iniectionem* and *per pignoris capionem* were highly prescribed modes of execution.

Litigation by *legis actiones* had several obvious shortcomings. The off-the-peg claims required the most careful pleading (Gaius 4.11, 30) and it was not possible to include affirmative defences. A representative could not appear in a litigant's place. Non-citizens did not participate: the entire process was, at bottom, a means to bring the authority of the civil law to Roman citizens. This last shortcoming is a serious one, and it is widely accepted that alternative methods of expressing claims must have existed when the peregrine praetorship was created in 242 BC. The origins of the formulary procedure (or some close predecessor) are usually dated to about this time. Quite apart from the problem of peregrine litigants, the availability of claims based on either the urban or peregrine praetor's own authority (*ius honorarium*) will have required the use of formulae.

Yet litigation by *legis actiones* continued alongside the use of formulae, and in the second century BC a *lex Aebutia*[35] appears to have adjusted the use of the two forms of procedure in some way. The traditional view, set out by Moriz Wlassak, is that before the *lex Aebutia*, the only way to enforce a claim under the civil law was via the *legis actiones*. The formulary procedure, even if used in the court of the urban praetor, would adjudicate only praetorian, not civil, law. On this explanation the *lex Aebutia* first permitted formulae for civil law actions between Roman citizens. There are, however, other views.[36] The *legis actiones* were dealt a more serious blow by a *lex Iulia de iudiciis privatis* (17 BC),[37] which seems to have abolished their use in most cases. They remained as an alternative form of proceeding in cases of *damnum infectum* (to forestall damage to one's property by a neighbouring property), and in cases before the centumviral court (see below, 283).

Course of Proceedings

Though the forms of action eventually gave way to formulae, the underlying procedures proved to be more lasting.[38] This is remarkable, given that these procedures are founded on a few terse provisions of the Twelve Tables.[39] A person who wished to bring a lawsuit was himself responsible for bringing the defendant physically to the magistrate. This summons (*in ius vocatio*) was purely private and, moreover, inadequately supported by state enforcement.[40] Until the later development of praetorian measures against reluctant litigants, the law simply gave 'cover' to a plaintiff who used force against a refusing defendant. The defendant himself had a single alternative: if he did not wish to come at that moment, he could give a person in his place. The role of this person, the *vindex*, is not perfectly known, but it appears that he undertook to produce the defendant at a later time.[41]

Proceedings *in iure* were oral, and the main tasks were to obtain a claim in one of the permissible forms, and to receive a judge or judges. It might not be possible to achieve this on a single occasion and, in any event, certain *legis actiones* interposed a period of delay before the judge was selected. This created the problem of how to induce a defendant to return. The earlier law relied on sureties (*vades*).[42] How the defendant gathered these *vades* on the spot, and how he satisfied the plaintiff that the *vades* were acceptably solvent, were two recurring problems which perhaps led to the later practice of using personal bonds (*vadimonia*).

The final event *in iure* was *litis contestatio* ('joinder of issue').[43] At this juncture the parties made declarations (apparently before witnesses), the effect of which was to erase any claims that arose from the matter being litigated, and replace them with the triable issue or issues described in the *legis actio*. It was not possible to relitigate those claims after *litis contestatio*, even if the matter did not reach judgment.

Iudex, Arbiter, Centumviri

Most lawsuits requiring a trial would pass to a *iudex* or *arbiter*. By the end of the republic the distinction between the two was all but lost, but originally, it appears, an *arbiter* was selected when a matter was essentially uncontested but something remained for decision, possibly requiring a wide power of discretion: for example, the division of an inheritance or the assessment of a sum owing.[44] The selection of a lay *iudex*, with full power to resolve and decide contested matters, was the more usual practice. A far smaller number of suits under the *legis actiones* passed to the centumviral court, comprising 105 members (often but not always sitting in panels) and led by magistrates, but drawn from elected representatives from each Roman *tribus*. This court, possibly of great antiquity, had a limited subject-matter jurisdiction whose boundaries are not wholly clear from the sources. Certain matters of inheritance certainly belonged to it, and perhaps also questions of status.[45]

7. FORMULARY PROCEDURE

The formulary procedure was marked by an improved system of pleading and the introduction of new, largely praetorian rules of enforcement.[46]

Pleading

Litigants were no longer required to plead the words of the civil law. They were now allowed to plead the event which triggered the assistance of the law, and the law could be either civil or praetorian in origin. This new freedom was possible because the praetor, in his yearly edict, now announced in advance which events would win the right to bring an action. Thus, litigants knew that if they described to the praetor how, for example, they had created a contract, they would win the right to bring an action on the contract. The praetor simplified the task by setting out his intentions in plain language, and by providing model clauses – the actions and defences – from which the agenda for trial would eventually emerge.

The agenda was expressed as a 'formula', a brief statement of perhaps a few dozen words, addressed to the judge or judges, and written down. It was assembled from model clauses (for example: a charging clause, a defence clause, a condemnation clause). It expressed a conditional injunction, informing the judge under what circumstance he should give judgment for the plaintiff or defendant. As such it served simultaneously as a set of instructions, a judicial commission, and a summation of the pleadings. It was also a very concise expression of a legal remedy, and formulae therefore became the objects of juristic study.

A formula awarded only monetary damages. This was not because the law lacked the imagination to do otherwise; more exotic remedies were available from magistrates in other proceedings. The preference for monetary damages might conceivably reflect something deep in Roman legal thinking: that injuries created debts, and that legal process should locate and assess those debts.[47] On the other hand, remedies such as performance would have been difficult to enforce in any event.[48] The judge's commission ended when he gave judgment, and enforcement was left to a second, wholly separate, proceeding. Roman magistrates had, over time, become expert in bringing pressure to bear on reluctant debtors, and a plaintiff seeking enforcement in a second proceeding could hardly do better than have in hand a judgment debt. In short, litigation at this period was particularly suited to the debt model.

Praetorian Lawmaking

The praetor now had considerable powers to fashion remedies, and he used these powers to create new rules of procedure. He was in a unique position both to see and to cure procedural abuses, and used a range of 'devices' to enforce appropriate behaviour: actions, defences, oaths, and obligations. For example, he discouraged vexatious litigation over simple debts by allowing the creditor to demand an extra penalty if a stubborn debtor insisted on going to trial but then lost.[49] He developed the old system of oaths (*iusiurandum in iure*), by which two parties could put any fact or legal conclusion out of contention; a system of actions and defences prevented parties from reopening these matters.[50] He developed a range of praetorian stipulations by which defendants could be compelled to return after an interruption *in iure*.[51] He created a punitive action against a defendant who, when summoned, neither came nor gave a *vindex*.[52]

Course of Proceedings

Aside from the use of formulae and the new procedural rules, the course of proceedings remained much as it was under the *legis actio* procedure. As before, a plaintiff could use summons (*in ius vocatio*) to begin proceedings; he could also now use *editio*, a term which described one of several methods for informing a defendant about the nature of the impending lawsuit.[53] Summons remained a private affair (now supported by the punitive action just mentioned). Ideally the two litigants would advance quickly to the selection of a formula and judge, and from there to *litis contestatio*, but when a magistrate concluded his business for the day there might well be litigants remaining to be heard. To ensure the return of the several defendants, the magistrate would order the pending matters to resume on the day after the next; this allowed a plaintiff, with the magistrate's backing, to demand a promise (*vadimonium*) from his opponent that he would return on that day.[54] The litigants' ultimate goal was to secure a formula from the magistrate, and in many cases this will have been an uncontroversial event: the plaintiff selected an action, the defendant selected any defences, and if the magistrate were satisfied, for example, that the action would not be barred by *res judicata*, he would proceed to assemble the formula.

Litigants could now appear through representatives; these representatives were often simply friends of the litigant: making appearances for your friends was among the duties of friendship.[55] It was not, however, possible for the acts or statements of the representative to bind the principal.[56] The representative 'stood in for' rather than 'stood for' the principal. This was particularly true of the more formal class of representative, the *cognitor*, who for the sake of his principal might allow his own name to be inserted in the condemnation clause of the formula. The gravity of the *cognitor*'s undertaking makes sense when we consider that the case might have to be prosecuted at a remote tribunal, where the principal cannot easily make a personal appearance at *litis contestatio*.[57] The other class of representative, the *procurator*, was more generally a mouthpiece and negotiator for his principal, and because his actions alone (unlike the *cognitor*'s) could not give any assurance to his principal's opponent that the matter was being disposed of once and for all, he was obliged to furnish security.

Joinder of issue (*litis contestatio*) was, as before, the final event *in iure*, and as before it served to consume the parties' claims while substituting new claims. The formula was now the expression of those new claims. It is a significant step to exchange irrevocably one's present position for a new position with an uncertain outcome, and thus a defendant's participation at *litis contestatio* continued to be voluntary.[58] This is perhaps why the judicial selection procedures were so solicitous of the defendant.[59] The names of prospective judges were displayed on an annual list (*album iudicum*), divided into a number of rosters (*decuriae*). By a process of alternating rejection (*reiectio*), the plaintiff and defendant would in turn strike out entire *decuriae*, the defendant making the final strike. From the *decuria* remaining, they would strike out the names of their less desired candidates, the defendant again making the final strike. If the parties so agreed, they might forgo *reiectio* and choose a candidate outright, whether from the list or not. The plaintiff would have the unilateral choice of candidate only if the defendant refused to participate in *reiectio*. The consensual nature of these selection procedures has many explanations: that it encourages settlement, that it lends decency to the office of the judge, that it helps to assure impartiality. The more cynical view is that with less consensual selection procedures, the defendant would not participate in *litis contestatio*.

Some formulae in civil trials appointed a small panel of judges (usually three or five) called *recuperatores*.[60] Their names were drawn from the same *album iudicum*, but the litigants had less freedom to choose. A pool of potential judges was chosen from the *album* either by lot (if they so agreed) or by *reiectio* (and again, a non-participating party would have to accede to his opponent's selection). The panel was then selected from the pool by lot. Unlisted persons could not be selected by agreement, as in ordinary cases. As Nörr points out, the magistrate had comparatively greater power over selection, and this fact (among others Nörr enumerates) perhaps made recuperatorial trials particularly suited to provincial practice. Another inference is that selection was less consensual because a defendant, for some unknown reason, required less persuasion to participate in a recuperatorial trial. This last inference ought to give some clue to the grounds on which recuperatorial trials were granted, but of all questions surrounding *recuperatores*, this is the most difficult. The trials may have their origin in disputes between nations, and may have been granted in private matters where a strong public interest underlay the suit. Judgments appear to have been speedier, but whether this was true of all recuperatorial trials, or whether speed was attendant on the type of case being heard, is unclear. The *lex Irnitana*, while giving many new details on the selection of *recuperatores*, gives up relatively little on their jurisdiction; we now know that at Rome there was a monetary threshold for granting these trials.

The nature of the trial itself was discussed above (285–6). It remains to add that trials were very much a public affair, held out-of-doors or in basilicas; private homes might themselves have contained the open space to accommodate trials and attendant crowds.[61] It was not necessary for both parties to be present at trial, though a judge risked liability if he gave judgment in the absence of a party who had a permissible reason for being absent.[62] The form in which judgment was given is unknown, but it seems unavoidable that it should be written down.[63] A plaintiff who prevails would (it seems) need a written judgment if he intended to bring an enforcement action, and a defendant who prevails would be equally eager to defend against any effort to reopen the matter.

8. COGNITIO

The *cognitio* procedure has no single and identifiable origin.[64] It is strongly identified with the authority of the *princeps*, though the power of republican magistrates to investigate and adjudge controversies was longstanding. The praetor exercised *cognitio*-like powers when, for example, he conducted *interrogatio* or granted interdicts – arguably whenever he paused from the assembly-line granting of routine actions to consider a subsidiary matter with closer attention.[65] But certain features of *cognitio* were genuinely different, the most profound difference being its (at least nominally) undivided nature: trials were not conducted by a lay judge chosen by the parties, but directly by the holder of *imperium* or his deputy. Accordingly, in the absence of any founding legislation, one looks for the origins of *cognitio* in instances of 'direct adjudication'. For example: Augustus committed to the consuls the enforcement of testamentary trusts (*fideicommissa*), leading eventually to a dedicated court; municipalities were permitted special proceedings to enforce public gifts (*pollicitationes*); special proceedings were created for the disposition of property that would otherwise pass to unmarried or childless persons but, under Augustus' *lex Papia Poppaea*, passed to the *aerarium* or *fiscus*.

It is unclear how quickly *cognitio* became the usual procedure in civil cases. The formulary procedure is evident in first-century epigraphic sources from Italy and the provinces, and apparently thriving, and yet there is evidence from Suetonius (on Augustus) and Tacitus (on Nero) describing the management of appeals from the decisions of *iudices* in Italy and the provinces.[66] It is disputed whether these are *cognitiones* or formulary. Even in Rome itself the picture is cloudy. Frier has pointed to a passage in Tacitus' *Dialogus* (39.1) where Maternus, describing the state of

Flavian oratory, states that *fere plurimae causae* are decided in conditions which, to us, strongly suggest *cognitio*.[67] The statement is surprising, given that the *lex Iulia* that reformed the formulary procedure was relatively new and very much in force. It is conceivable the *lex Iulia* made the use of lay judges in some way undesirable and thus drove litigants, where possible, to use professional judges, but this is only a guess.

Course of Proceedings

Summons under the formulary procedure had been a private act. Under the *cognitio* procedure both the execution and enforcement of summons was supported by the administrative machinery.[68] The forms of summons evolved; of the earlier forms, *litis denuntiatio* was the most usual. The plaintiff (so it appears) prepared and delivered to the defendant a notice to appear which in some way evidenced the authority of the court. A stronger form of written summons (*litterae*[69]) was prepared by the tribunal and delivered by the plaintiff to a defendant who resided at a distance. Defendants who were otherwise unreachable could be 'summoned' by public notice (*edictum*). All of these methods of summons were enforced by means of a contempt procedure (*contumacia*).

The contempt procedure is a hallmark of *cognitio* and needs special mention because it marks an abrupt change from the formulary procedure.[70] Under the formulary procedure, as already noted, the defendant's participation was voluntary. A magistrate had used his edict to bring pressure to bear where he could, but its effect was limited, and the edictal manner of expression, offering remedies against opponents who acted in such-and-such a way, required the aggrieved party to take the first steps. The contempt procedure was more plainly a means to punish disobedience to the command of a magistrate or judge. Its role in the summons of the defendant is the most striking. A defendant could be summoned, and fail to appear, three times without consequence, but at that point a 'peremptory summons' was issued, and if this were ignored the matter could proceed to disposition in the defendant's absence. If the plaintiff presented proof in support of his claim, he could receive judgment in his favour, and the defendant was closely restricted in his ability to appeal against the judgment.

The proceedings under *cognitio* were much changed.[71] Litigants did not frame their claims as specific actions and exceptions as in the formulae, but set them out as rights supported by the law. *Litis contestatio* still existed but its principal effects were gone: it was no longer a 'novated obligation', and the event itself did not consume the right to claim. Aspects of a trial that were handled somewhat clumsily under the formulary procedure, such as the summoning of witnesses, adjournments, and examination by *interrogatio*, were handled efficiently by direct order, usually supported by the power of the contempt procedure. Judgments were no longer restricted to monetary damages.

The procedure developed further in the dominate under aggressive legislation.[72] From the middle of the fifth century, a lawsuit was begun with a so-called *libellus conventionis*, a written complaint prepared by the plaintiff and delivered to the judge, setting out the facts on which the plaintiff based his claim, along with a request for the defendant to be summoned. The 'libellary process' gave the judge an opportunity to scrutinize the claim before issuing the summons. This period also saw changes to the rules of evidence (some rather retrograde), and the closer control of judges to prevent abuses of their office. This period as a whole shows a less thoughtful system of procedure and an imperial bureaucracy more jealous of its power.

9. Legacy

Legis Actiones

The principal legacy of the *legis actiones* is the modern law of unjust enrichment.[73] Claims of debt were apparently too cumbersome to prosecute under the earliest *legis actiones*, and in the late third century BC two *leges* simplified these claims considerably by introducing the *legis actio per condictionem* – a simple claim that something was owing. When this kind of claim was later prosecuted by formula (the *condictio*), it retained its simple character: the formula alleged the existence of a debt without explaining how the debt was alleged to have come about (*causa debendi*). The bare assertion of a debt, without *causa debendi*, proved to be a convenient vehicle for many different claims that happened not to fit under the heads of property, contract, or delict.

Formulary Procedure

The principal legacy of the formulary procedure is the institutional scheme as reflected in the modern civil law. The formulary procedure required the differentiation of actions, and each action, in turn, was triggered by a certain event: winning the right to bring a particular action required a litigant to allege the occurrence of the corresponding event.[74] To the extent that the institutional scheme differentiates among persons, delicts, contracts, and property, it is built upon these separate events.

Cognitio

The principal legacy of the *cognitio* procedure is the romano-canonical procedure and the modern systems that derive from it.[75] Roman procedure was studied, systematized, and written upon from the twelfth century onwards as part of the broader revival of interest in Roman law. The procedure that developed in the church courts was to a large degree an original creation, but drew heavily on Roman sources. The Romano-canonical procedure spread into the lay courts of Europe, where its systematization was a great attraction.

Notes

1. The **leading reference work** on civil procedure is M. Kaser, *Das römische Zivilprozessrecht*, 2nd edn. by K. Hackl (Munich, 1996). **Other general reference works**: J. L. Murga, *Derecho romano clasico. 2. El proceso* (Zaragoza, 1980); G. Pugliese, *Il processo civile romano [1. Le legis actiones. 2. Il processo formulare]* (Milan, 1962/63). **Reference works on narrower topics**: B. Albanese, *Il processo privato romano delle 'legis actiones'* (Palermo, 1987); F. Bertoldi, *La* lex Iulia iudiciorum privatorum (Turin, 2003); G. Cervenca, *Il processo privato romano: le fonti* (Bologna, 1983); A. H. J. Greenidge, *The Legal Procedure of Cicero's Time* (Oxford, 1901); K. Hackl, 'Der Zivilprozeß des frühen Prinzipats in den Provinzen', *ZSS* 114 (1997): 141–59; K. Hackl, 'Il processo civile nelle province', in *Gli ordinamenti giudiziari di Roma imperiale. Princeps e procedura dalle leggi Giulie ad Adriano*, ed. F. Milazzo (Naples, 1999), 299–318; M. Indra, *Status Quaestio. Studien zum Freiheitsprozess im klassischen römischen Recht* (Berlin, 2011); W. Litewski, *Der römisch-kanonische Zivilprozess nach den älteren ordines iudiciarii* (Krakow, 1999); D. Mantovani, *Le formule del processo privato romano. Per la didattica delle istituzioni di diritto romano*, 2nd edn. (Padua, 1999); K. W. Nörr, *Romanisch-kanonisches Prozessrecht: Erkenntnisverfahren erster Instanz in civilibus* (Heidelberg, 2012); N. Palazzolo, *Processo civile e politica giudiziaria nel principato*, 2nd edn. (Turin, 1991); G. Provera, *Lezioni sul processo civile Giustinianeo* (Turin, 1989); D. Simon, *Untersuchungen zum justinianischen Zivilprozess* (Munich, 1969); W. Simshäuser, *Iuridici und Munizipalgerichtsbarkeit in Italien* (Munich, 1973); M. Talamanca, 'Il riordinamento Augusteo del processo privato', in *Gli ordinamenti giudiziari di Roma imperiale. Princeps e procedura dalle leggi Giulie ad Adriano*, ed. F. Milazzo (Naples, 1999), 63–260; U. Zilletti, *Studi sul processo civile Giustinianeo* (Milan, 1965). **Shorter or introductory works**: V. Arangio-Ruiz, *Corso di diritto romano. Il processo privato* (Rome, 1951); V. Arangio-Ruiz, *Cours de droit romain: les actions* [*Antiqua*, 2], ed. L. Labruna (Naples, 1980); A. Biscardi, *Lezioni sul processo romano antico e classico* (Turin, 1968); W. W. Buckland, *A Text-Book of Roman Law*, 3rd edn. revd. by P. Stein (Cambridge, 1963), 604–744; C. A. Cannata, *Profilo istituzionale del processo privato romano* (Turin, 1982/89); J. A. Crook, *Law and Life of Rome, 90 BC–AD 212* (Ithaca, 1967), ch. 3; J. A. Crook, 'The Development of Roman Private

Law', in *CAH* vol. 9, 2nd edn. by J. A. Crook et al. (Cambridge, 1994), 544–46 ('The law of actions'); D. Johnston, *Roman Law in Context* (Cambridge, 1999), ch. 6; H. F. Jolowicz and B. Nicholas, *Historical Introduction to the Study of Roman Law*, 3rd edn. (Cambridge, 1972), 175–232, 395–401, 439–50; M. Kaser, 'The Changing Face of Roman Jurisdiction', *Irish Jurist* (n.s.) 2 (1967): 129–43; G. I. Luzzatto, *Procedura civile romana* (Bologna, 1945/48); G. Nicosia, *Il processo privato romano: corso di diritto romano* (Turin, 1986/2012); E. Seidl, *Römische Rechtsgeschichte und römisches Zivilprozessrecht* (Cologne, 1962), 157–84; A. A. Schiller, *Roman Law: Mechanisms of Development* (The Hague, 1978), 188–218, 433–41; M. Talamanca, 'Processo civile (diritto romano)', in *Enciclopedia del diritto* 36 (1987): 1–79; M. Talamanca, *Istituzioni di diritto romano* (Milan, 1990), 273–378; O. Tellegen-Couperus, *A Short History of Roman Law* (London, 1993), 21–24, 53–59, 89–93, 128–30; J. A. C. Thomas, *Textbook of Roman Law* (Amsterdam, 1976), chs. 5–9.

2. Schiller (n. 1), 188–218, 433–41, discusses and translates into English a handful of sources on procedure. More thorough, though (like Schiller) somewhat out of date, is Cervenca (n. 1).
3. 'Rules of procedure could be found in many parts of the Corpus iuris but the Romans had never gathered them systematically or studied procedure as an autonomous subject.' R. Feenstra, 'Law', in *The Legacy of Rome: A New Appraisal*, ed. R. Jenkyns (Oxford, 1992), 410.
4. Additional portions of book 4 were uncovered in the last century, the first ('Oxford fragments') among the Oxyrhynchus papyri, published in 1927, and the second ('Florentine [or Antinoite] fragments') on parchment fragments discovered in Cairo and first published in 1935. The earlier known portions of the *Institutes*, preserved in the *Digest* and in the *Epitome* of Gaius, do not contain any of book 4. A full account of the sources for the *Institutes* is given in H. L. W. Nelson, *Überlieferung, Aufbau und Stil von Gai Institutiones* (Leiden, 1981), and a full account of the Veronese palimpsest – the main source – is given in F. Briguglio, *Il Codice Veronese in trasparenza. Genesi e formazione del testo delle Istituzioni di Gaio* (Bologna, 2012), who reports also on new efforts to read the manuscript (new photographs are in F. Briguglio, *Gai codex rescriptus in Bibliotheca Capitulari Ecclesiae Cathedralis Veronensis* (Florence, 2012)). The principal editions in English are W. M. Gordon and O. F. Robinson, eds., *The Institutes of Gaius* (London, 1988), and F. de Zulueta, ed., *The Institutes of Gaius*, 2 vols. (Oxford, 1946–53). A new critical edition, published by Duncker and Humblot, is in preparation; recent volumes are edited by H. L. W. Nelson and U. Manthe. A volume treating book 4 has not yet appeared. How this new critical text might be affected by the work of Briguglio, cited above, is unclear.
5. Two authors with practical information on procedure are: Marcus Valerius Probus (latter 1st century AD), who lists abbreviations used in statutes, edicts, and other sources affecting procedure and their meanings (*De notis iuris fragmenta* in *FIRA* 2.451–60), and Sextus Pompeius Festus (latter 2nd century AD), whose abridgment of Marcus Verrius Flaccus' *De verborum significatu* preserves many terms used in litigation (*Sexti Pompei Festi de verborum significatu*, ed. W. M. Lindsay (Leipzig, 1913)).
6. For the procedure in Cicero, Greenidge (n. 1) is old but still valuable. See also A. Lintott, 'Legal Procedure in Cicero's Time', in *Cicero the Advocate*, ed. J. Powell et al. (Oxford, 2004), 61–78; B. Frier, *The Rise of the Roman Jurists: Studies in Cicero's Pro Caecina* (Princeton, 1985); J. Platschek, *Studien zu Ciceros Rede für P. Quinctius* (Munich, 2005); J. Harries, *Cicero and the Jurists: From Citizens' Law to the Lawful State*

(London, 2006), ch. 7; E. Metzger, *Litigation in Roman Law* (Oxford, 2005), 19–44, 163–66 (*pro Quinctio*); J. G. Wolf, '*Vadimonium* in Ciceros Rede pro Quinctio', *SDHI* 74 (2008): 79–97.

7. See, e.g., A. Scafuro, *The Forensic Stage: Settling Disputes in Graeco-Roman New Comedy* (Cambridge, 1997); L. Pellecchi, *Per una lettura giuridica della 'Rudens' di Plauto* (Faenza, 2012).

8. On the use of Quintilian, see O. Tellegen-Couperus, 'Introduction', in *Quintilian and the Law: The Art of Persuasion and Politics*, ed. O. Tellegen-Couperus (Leuven, 2003), 12–17. On the role of advocacy and its relation to law, see J. A. Crook, *Legal Advocacy in the Roman World* (Ithaca, 1995), ch. 1; B. Frier, 'Finding a Place for Law in the High Empire: Tacitus, Dialogus 39.1–4', in *Spaces of Justice in the Roman World*, ed. W. Harris and F. de Angelis (Leiden, 2010), 67–87. For a study of Roman advocacy using Quintilian generously, see L. Bablitz, *Actors and Audience in the Roman Courtroom* (New York, 2007), 141–204.

9. The standard reference for statutes is M. H. Crawford, ed., *Roman Statutes*, 2 vols. (London, 1996). Many records of private affairs are collected in *FIRA* 3 ('Negotia'), though this does not include the great majority of records discovered in the twentieth century, on which see below (274).

10. This group of sources divides into 'model formulae' (essentially templates that litigants would complete) and 'completed formulae' prepared for specific litigation.

Of the former type: **(1)** the *lex de Gallia Cisalpina* (1st century BC), ch. 22, a statute prescribing laws for Cisalpine Gaul, and containing two model formulae to be used for trial when a person fails to make the required performance in a proceeding for *damnum infectum*: see *Roman Statutes* (n. 9), no. 28; F. J. Bruna, *Lex Rubria: Caesars Regelung für die Richterlichen Kompentenzen der Munizipalmagistrate in Gallia Cisalpina* (Leiden, 1972), 28–30, 107–19; **(2)** the *Tabula Contrebiensis* (87 BC) from Botorrita in Spain, preserving on bronze the judgment in a border dispute: see CIL I^2 2951a; B. Díaz Ariño, *Epigrafía Latina Republicana de España* (Barcelona, 2008), 95–98; J. S. Richardson, 'The *Tabula Contrebiensis*: Roman Law in Spain in the Early First Century BC', *JRS* 73 (1983): 33–41; P. Birks, A. Rodger, and J. S. Richardson, 'Further Aspects of the Tabula Contrebiensis', *JRS* 74 (1984): 45–73; **(3)** *Lex rivi Hiberiensis* (AD 117–38), an inscription containing a decree governing an irrigation community on the Ebro in Hispania Citerior, and including a formula for a trial on the imposition of a penalty: see M. H. Crawford and F. Beltrán Lloris, 'The Lex rivi Hiberiensis', *JRS* 103 (2013): 233; F. Beltrán Lloris, 'An Irrigation Decree from Roman Spain: *The Lex Rivi Hiberiensis*', *JRS* 96 (2006): 147–97; D. Nörr, 'Prozessuales (und mehr) in der Lex Rivi Hiberiensis', *ZSS* 125 (2008): 108–88; **(4)** a legal fragment from Egypt, PSI VII 743 *recto* fr. e (ca. AD 100), part of an instructional work used for teaching Greek, containing the *condemnatio* for a formula seeking an *incertum*, the formula translated into Greek and then presented in the Roman alphabet: see S. Ciriello and A. Stramaglia, '*PSI* VII 743 *recto* (Pack^2 2100): *Dialogo di Alessandro* con i ginnosofisti e testo giuridico Romano non identificato', *Archiv für Papyrusforschung* 44 (1998): 219–27; D. Nörr, 'PSI VII 743r fr. e: Fragment einer römischen Prozeßformel? Bemerkungen zum vorhadrianischen Edikt und zu den Hermeneumata Pseudodositheana', *ZSS* 117 (2000): 179–215.

Of the latter type: **(5)** A formula in an action on a debt from Puteoli (1st century AD), preserved on a waxed tablet: TPSulp 31, in Camodeca, *Tabulae pompeianae Sulpiciorum* (n. 11); **(6)** three formulae in papyri (P. Yadin. 28, 29, 30) from the province of Arabia (ca. AD 124), partly prepared in anticipation of a suit on guardianship to be tried before a panel of judges in Judaea: N. Lewis, ed., *The Documents from the Bar Kokhba Period in the Cave of Letters: Greek Papyri* (Jerusalem, 1989), 118–20; H. Cotton, 'The Guardianship of Jesus Son of Babatha: Roman and Local Law in the Province of Arabia', *JRS* 83 (1993): 94–108; D. Nörr, 'The *Xenokritai* in Babatha's Archive (Pap. Yadin 28–30)', *Israel Law Review* 29 (1995): 83–94; D. Nörr, 'Prozessuales aus dem Babatha-Archiv', in *Mélanges de droit romain et d'histoire ancienne. Hommage à la mémoire de André Magdelain* (Paris, 1998), 317–41.

11. The Herculaneum tablets were discovered in the 1930s and texts were published in succeeding decades by G. Pugliese Carratelli and V. Arangio-Ruiz. See further the chapter by Wolf, 61–84. In the last two decades G. Camodeca has re-edited many of these texts, and a new edition is forthcoming. The Puteoli tablets were discovered in 1959 near Pompeii. Many of them relate to a family, the Sulpicii, that engaged in banking activities. The critical edition is Giuseppe Camodeca, ed., *Tabulae Pompeianae Sulpiciorum (TPSulp). Edizione critica dell'archivio puteolano dei Sulpicii* (Rome, 1999). The two collections are introduced and discussed in P. Gröschler, *Die* tabellae-*Urkunden aus den pompejanischen und herkulanensischen Urkundenfunden* (Berlin, 1997). The Puteoli tablets are discussed in their economic context in J. Andreau, *Banking and Business in the Roman World*, trans. by J. Lloyd (Cambridge, 1999), 71–79, and there is a popular account in D. Jones, *The Bankers of Puteoli: Finance, Trade, and Industry in the Roman World* (Stroud, 2006). For a fascinating and provocative treatment of Roman tablets generally, see E. A. Meyer, *Legitimacy and Law in the Roman World: Tabulae in Roman Belief and Practice* (Cambridge, 2004).
12. The critical texts are: Julián González, 'The Lex Irnitana: A New Copy of the Flavian Municipal Law', *JRS* 76 (1986): 147–243 (with English translation); F. Lamberti, *Tabulae Irnitanae: municipalità e 'ius Romanorum'* (Naples, 1993) (with Italian translation). Some new readings and supplements are given in M. H. Crawford, 'The Text of the Lex Irnitana', *JRS* 98 (2008): 182. A brief description is given in E. Metzger, 'Agree to Disagree: Local Jurisdiction in the *lex Irnitana*', in *Judge and Jurist: Essays in Memory of Lord Rodger of Earlsferry*, ed. A. Burrows, et al. (Oxford, 2013), 213–15.
13. See Kaser and Hackl (n. 1), 8–11; Seidl (n. 1), 162–67.
14. For more on this subject, and literature, see E. Metzger, 'Roman Judges, Case Law, and Principles of Procedure', *Law and History Review* 22 (2004): 243–75.
15. For the sake of exposition this chapter uses 'magistrate' as a shorthand for the various office holders with authority to administer justice. This includes, e.g., consuls, praetors, aediles, local *duumviri* or *praefecti iure dicundo*, governors, *praefecti praetorio*, *vicarii*, and, of course, the emperor.
16. See K. Tuori, 'A Place for Jurists in the Spaces of Justice?' in *Spaces of Justice in the Roman World* (n. 8), 45–48; J. Powell and J. Paterson, 'Introduction', in *Cicero the Advocate* (n. 6), 10–18; Crook (n. 8); J.-M. David, *Le patronat judiciaire au dernier siècle de la république romaine* (Rome, 1992); A. A. Schiller, *Roman Law: Mechanisms of Development* (The Hague, 1978), 569–77.
17. For what is given below (275–6), see A. Bürge, 'Zum Edikt *De edendo*', *ZSS* 112 (1995): 1–50; Kaser and Hackl (n. 1), 29–30, 79; M. Kaser, 'Nuovi studi sul processo civile Romano', *Labeo* 15 (1969): 190–98; M. Kaser, 'Prätor und Judex im römischen Zivilprozess', *TR* 32 (1964): 329–62 (modifying the views expressed in 'Zum Ursprung des geteilten römischen Zivilprozessverfahrens', in *Ausgewählten Schriften*

(Naples, 1976), vol. 2, 385–409); M. Kaser, 'Römische Gerichtsbarkeit im Wechsel der Zeiten', in *Ausgewählten Schriften* (Naples, 1976), vol. 2, 419–49 (= 'The Changing Face of Roman Jurisdiction' (n. 1)); H. R. Hoetink, 'The Origin of the Dual Mode in Roman Procedure', *Seminar* 5 (1947): 16–30; Jolowicz and Nicholas (n. 1), 176–78; G. MacCormack, 'Roman and African Litigation', *TR* 39 (1971): 221–55; J. M. Kelly, *Roman Litigation* (Oxford, 1966), ch. 1; J. M. Kelly, *Studies in the Civil Judicature of the Roman Republic* (Oxford, 1976), 125–29; H. F. Jolowicz, 'The judex and the arbitral principle', *RIDA* 2 (1949): 477–92.

18. This is the view set out in Kaser, 'Prätor und Iudex' (n. 17) and 'Römische Gerichtsbarkeit' (n. 17). It was promptly criticized by Jolowicz and Nicholas (n. 1), 177 n. 2, as 'too rational'.
19. See, esp., Jolowicz (n. 17), 488–91. His views are reflected in his *Historical Introduction* (with Barry Nicholas, cited in n. 1), at 176–78. Cf. Kaser and Hackl (n. 1), 30: 'Das in dieser Unterwerfung, die notfalls vom Staat erzwungen wird, liegende Element der Gemeinsamkeit im Verhalten der Parteien reicht für die Annahme eines Schiedsvertrages nicht aus.'
20. For what is given below (276–8), see A. H. M. Jones, 'Imperial and Senatorial Jurisdiction in the Early Principate', in *Studies in Roman Government and Law* (Oxford, 1968), 67–98; Jolowicz and Nicholas (n. 1), 216, 229–30, 400; Thomas (n. 1), 109, 113–14; P. Stein, '"Equitable" Remedies for the Protection of Property', in *New Perspectives in the Roman Law of Property: Essays for Barry Nicholas*, ed. P. Birks (Oxford, 1989), 191–92; Metzger (n. 6), 117–20.
21. See Cic. *Quinct.* 65, 69.
22. O. Lenel, *Das Edictum Perpetuum*, 3rd edn. (Leipzig, 1927), 109–30.
23. The literature on this subject is enormous. The newer literature should be favoured, because the *lex Irnitana* discovered in 1981 has added a great deal to our understanding. See, most recently, E. Metzger, 'Remedy of Prohibition against Roman Judges in Civil Trials', in *Judges and Judging in the History of the Common Law and Civil Law from Antiquity to Modern Times*, ed. P. Brand and J. Getzler (Cambridge, 2012), 177–91; E. Metzger, 'Absent Parties and Bloody-Minded Judges', in *Mapping the Law: Essays in Memory of Peter Birks*, ed. A. Burrows and A. Rodger (Oxford, 2006), 455–73; A. Gómez-Iglesias, 'Lex Irnitana *cap. 91*: lis iudici damni sit', *SDHI* 72 (2006): 465–505; R. Scevola, *La responsibilità del iudex privatus* (Milan, 2004); D. Mantovani, 'La "diei diffissio" nella "lex Irnitana"', in *Iuris Vincula: Studi in onore di Mario Talamanca* (Naples, 2001), vol. 5, 13–72. O. F. Robinson has written a series of articles on the uses of judges' liability in Justinian: 'Justinian's Institutional Classification and the Class of Quasi-Delict', *Journal of Legal History* 19 (1998): 245–50; 'The "iudex qui litem suam fecerit" explained', *ZSS* 116 (1999): 195–99; 'Justinian and the Compilers' View of the *iudex qui litem suam fecerit*', in *Status Familiae*, ed. H.-G. Knothe and J. Kohler (Munich, 2001), 389–96; 'Gaius and the Class of Quasi-Delict', in *Iuris Vincula: Studi in onore di Mario Talamanca* (Naples, 2001), vol. 7, 120–28.
24. See S. Randazzo, 'Doppio grado di giurisdizione e potere politico nel primo secolo dell'impero', in *Roman Law as Formative of Modern Legal Systems. Studies in Honour of Wiesław Litewski*, ed. J. Sondel et al. (Krakow, 2003), vol. 2, 75–94; Kaser and Hackl (n. 1), 501–10; D. Liebs, 'Roman Law', in *CAH* vol. 14, 2nd edn. by A. Cameron et al. (2000), 240–41; I. Buti, 'La "cognitio extra ordinem": da Augusto a Diocleziano', *ANRW* II.14, 54–58; L. Fanizza, *L'amministrazione della giustizia nel principato* (Rome, 1999), 11–60.

25. Textbooks commonly refer to *cognitio* in various forms: *cognitio extra ordinem, cognitio extraordinaria, iudicia extraordinaria*. From at least the middle empire one could refer to this new, now common, mode of procedure as *extraordinaria* or *extra ordinem* (Paul 1 *sent.* D. 3.5.46.1; Inst. 4.15.8). It is widely accepted that the term was coined to distinguish this form of procedure from the *ordo iudiciorum* (or *iudiciaria*) – that is, the formulary procedure. See Randazzo (n. 24), 79 and n. 15. Compare W. Turpin, 'Formula, *cognitio*, and Proceedings *extra ordinem*', *RIDA* (3rd ser.) 46 (1999): 544–62.
26. For what is given below, see Platschek (n. 6); Kaser and Hackl (n. 1), 222–23, 427–29; Thomas (n. 1), 112–13; Jolowicz and Nicholas (n. 1), 217, 228–29.
27. Kaser and Hackl (n. 1), 222, outline the common opinion (with literature). It rests substantially on events recounted in Cicero, *pro Quinctio*, where Cicero's client has been subjected to *missio* and where, according to a widely held view, the client's absence took place before proceedings had been initiated. To the contrary, new evidence from Puteoli and Herculaneum (above, n. 11) suggests that Cicero's client was ignoring the praetor's compulsory order to reappear. See Metzger (n. 6), 30–38, 163–66.
28. Metzger (n. 6), 37–38, 161–63; E. Metzger, 'Lawsuits in Context', in *Beyond Dogmatics: Law and Society in the Roman World*, ed. J. Cairns and P. du Plessis (Edinburgh, 2007), 204–5; É. Jakab, *Praedicere und cavere beim Marktkauf* (Munich, 1997), 223–29; Kaser and Hackl (n. 1), 429–32; A. M. Giomaro, 'Ulpiano e le stipulationes praetoriae', in *Studi in onore di Arnaldo Biscardi* (Milan, 1983), vol. 4, 413–40; A. M. *Giomaro, Cautiones iudiciales e officium iudicis* (Milan, 1982).
29. See TH 14 (n. 11) with Indra (n. 1), 106–9; TPSulp 27 (n. 11).
30. For what is given below (279–81), see Gaius 4.138–70; Kaser and Hackl (n. 1), 408–21; Buckland (n. 1), 729–44; Frier (n. 6); A. Watson, *The Law of Property in the Later Roman Republic* (Oxford, 1968), 86–89; A. Watson, *Law Making in the Later Roman Republic* (Oxford, 1974), 41–42; Jolowicz and Nicholas (n. 1), 230–32, 259–63; Stein (n. 20), 188–89.
31. The form of the interdict is given in D. 43.26.2 pr.: *Quod precario ab illo habes aut dolo malo fecisti ut desineres habere, qua de re agitur, id illi restituas.*
32. The form of the interdict, as reconstructed, is: *Quod vi aut clam factum est qua de re agitur id, si non plus quam annus est cum experiundi potestas est, restituas*. See D. 43.24.1 pr.; Mantovani (n. 1), 88.
33. Obtaining a 'new possession' is a more aggressive use of possessory interdicts; examples are interdicts to assist *bonorum possessio* and possession of a tenant's property by a landlord under the *interdictum Salvianum* (see M. Kaser, *Das römische Privatrecht*, 2nd edn. (Munich, 1971), vol. 1, 472–73).
34. For what is given below (281–2), see Gaius 4.10–31; Jolowicz and Nicholas (n. 1), 175–90; Tellegen-Couperus (n. 1), 21–24; de Zulueta (n. 4), vol. 2, 230–50; Crook (n. 1, *CAH*), 544–46; Kaser and Hackl (n. 1), 25–148, esp. 44–60, 64–81; Greenidge (n. 1), 49–75.
35. Gaius 4.30; Gell. *NA* 16.10.8.
36. The newest view, and among the most engaging, is that of Talamanca, who follows Wlassak to some degree. Talamanca looks back to the time before the *lex Aebutia* but after the creation of the peregrine praetorship, suggesting the urban praetor founded on his own *imperium* the authority to grant civil actions, as well as developing his own 'honorary actions' for use by Roman citizens: these would exist side-by-side with the

legis actiones. The *lex Aebutia* would then have 'legalized' the formulary procedure for civil actions, giving those actions the civil effects they would have lacked when based only on the praetor's *imperium*. Talamanca (n. 1, 'Il riordinamento Augusteo'), esp. 74–76, 199–203. For other views see M. Kaser, 'Die lex Aebutia', in *Studi in memoria di Emilio Albertario* (Milan, 1953), 25–59 (the statute permitted formulae for actions formerly brought by *legis actio per condictionem*); P. Birks, 'From *Legis Actio* to *Formula*', *Irish Jurist* (n.s.) 4 (1969): 356–67 (the statute limited whatever tactical advantages a plaintiff enjoyed in selecting between the two forms of procedure); Crook (n. 1, *CAH*), 146 (similar to Talamanca: the statute ensured that actions sued by formulae could not be sued upon again).

37. Gaius 4.30; *lex Irn.* ch. 91 (n. 12, this chapter); Kaser and Hackl (n. 1), 153–57.
38. For what is given below (282–3), see Kaser and Hackl (n. 1), 64–69; Pugliese (n. 1, *Le legis actiones*), 253–63; Kelly (n. 17, *Roman Litigation*), ch. 1; MacCormack (n. 17); Buckland (n. 1), 609–30.
39. XII Tables 1.1–4, 6–10; see also Paul 1 *ed.* D. 50.17.103.
40. Kelly (n. 17, *Roman Litigation*), ch. 1; cf. Kaser and Hackl (n. 1), 222. The use of *missio* in this context is doubtful, as noted above (n. 27). Paul says that a fine (*multa*) will be imposed against those who do not come when summoned before a municipal magistrate, but that rustics will be spared, and that for others some sort of prejudice must be shown: Paul 1 *ed.* D. 2.5.2.1.
41. See Kaser and Hackl (n. 1), 66, 224 and the literature cited in R. Domingo, *Estudios sobre el primer título del edicto pretorio* (Santiago de Compostela, 1993), 56 n. 140. The awkward text is Gaius 1 *leg. duo. tab* D. 2.4.22.1, which suggests that the *vindex* undertook to defend his principal.
42. Varr. *LL.* 6.74; Gell. *NA* 16.10.8; Livy 3.13.8; Kaser and Hackl (n. 1), 68–69. Gellius speaks of *subvades*; Livy speaks of multiple *vades*, each liable to a specific sum. One hypothesis is that a defendant 'cumulated' *vades* until he reached a satisfactory level of assurance.
43. Kaser and Hackl (n. 1), 75–77, 79–81. Cf. A. Watson, *International Law in Archaic Rome: War and Religion* (Baltimore, 1993), 10–19 (on 'testes estote').
44. Kelly (n. 17, *Studies*), 117–19; Talamanca (n. 1, *Istituzioni*), 289–90.
45. On the composition and jurisdiction of the centumviral court, see Kaser and Hackl (n. 1), 52–56; Kelly (n. 17, *Studies*), ch. 1. On the physical space it may have occupied, see Bablitz (n. 8), 61–70.
46. Our main source for the details of the formulary procedure is Gaius 4.30–187. See Kaser and Hackl (n. 1), 220–382; Johnston (n. 1), 112–18; E. Metzger, 'Formula', in *Oxford International Encyclopedia of Legal History*, ed. S. N. Katz (New York, 2009); E. Metzger, *A New Outline of the Roman Civil Trial* (Oxford, 1997), ch. 5; Jolowicz and Nicholas (n. 1), 199–225; Crook (n. 1, *Law and Life of Rome*), 73–87; Talamanca (n. 1, *Istituzioni*), 298–360.
47. See, e.g., Gaius 3.180: *Nam tunc obligatio quidem principalis dissolvitur, incipit autem teneri reus litis contestatione: sed, si condemnatus sit, sublata litis contestatione, incipit ex causa iudicati teneri.*
48. Stein (n. 20), 187. In certain cases, performance could be *encouraged* by including a special clause in the formula (*clausula arbitraria*) threatening condemnation if a performance was not tendered.
49. Gaius 4.171. On its praetorian origins, see D. Liebs, 'The History of the Roman *Condictio* up to Justinian', in *The Legal Mind: Essays for Tony Honoré*, ed. N. MacCormick and P. Birks (Oxford, 1986), 165 n. 9 (with literature).

50. Kaser and Hackl (n. 1), 266–69; E. Metzger, 'Having an Audience with the Magistrate', in *Spaces of Justice in the Roman World* (n. 8), 37–41.
51. Described briefly in Gaius 4.184–187. See Metzger (n. 6), 8–10, 65–94.
52. Gaius 4.46. The remedy is criticized for giving the plaintiff a second action with, perhaps, no greater promise of victory than the first: I. Buti, *Il 'praetor' e le formalità introduttive del processo formulare* (Naples, 1984), 296–98. However, the remedy very effectively thwarts a defendant who makes himself scarce until the plaintiff's right of action expires; the clock begins to run anew under the penal action.
53. Bürge (n. 17). A *vadimonium* was not used at this stage of proceedings. See Metzger (n. 28, 'Lawsuits in Context'); cf. Kaser and Hackl (n. 1), 231.
54. The postponements to the day-after-the-next are described with the words *intertium dare* in the *lex Irnitana*, our main source for this institution. See Metzger (n. 28, 'Lawsuits in Context') and in more detail, Metzger (n. 6), chs. 5, 6, and 7. The details are contested; full discussion of all views is given in Metzger (n. 6), 123–32. The contrary view is set out most thoroughly in J. G. Wolf, 'Intertium – und kein Ende?' *BIDR* 39 (2001): 1–36.
55. See, e.g., Ulpian 6 *ed.* D. 3.1.1.2.
56. Kaser and Hackl (n. 1), 209–17.
57. As evidenced in a recently uncovered inscription, TPSulp 27 (n. 11). The evidence is discussed in Metzger (n. 28, 'Lawsuits in Context'), 190–92, 204–5. Gaius describes the two permissible formulae for appointing a *cognitor*: Gaius 4.83. The second formula omits any mention of the action being brought, which seems curious until we recall that this is precisely the right formula to use when two *cognitores* are being sent to prosecute the case away from home, as in TPSulp 27, and the ultimate form of the action is therefore unknown to the litigants.
58. Kaser and Hackl (n. 1), 289–90.
59. Our knowledge of the judicial selection procedures relies a good deal on the *lex Irn.* chs. 86, 87, 88. There may be subtle discrepancies from the practice at Rome, but the two obvious ones are (1) the number of *decuriae* (three in Irni; five in Rome after Caligula) and (2) the qualifications for selection for the *album* (the property threshold was modest in Irni). For what is given below, see P. Birks, 'New Light on the Roman Legal System: The Appointment of Judges', *Cambridge Law Journal*, 47 (1988): 36–60; Kelly (n. 17, *Studies*), 125–29; Bablitz (n. 8), 93–103; Kaser and Hackl (n. 1), 192–96; Metzger (n. 46, *New Outline*), ch. 5.
60. For what is given below, see *lex Irn.* (n. 12) chs. 88, 89; P. Yadin (n. 10) 28, 29, 30; Birks (n. 59); Frier (n. 6), ch. 5; Kaser and Hackl (n. 1), 197–201. The most thorough recent research on *recuperatores* is by Nörr: see, above all, D. Nörr, 'Zu den Xenokriten (Rekuperatoren) in der römischen Provinzialgerichtsbarkeit', in *Lokale Autonomie und römische Ordnungsmacht in den kaiserzeitlichen Provinzen vom 1. bis 3. Jahrhundert*, ed. W. Eck (Munich, 1999), 257–301. Cf. Nörr (n. 10, 'The Xenokritai in Babatha's Archive'), 83–94. If, as Nörr argues, the 'xenokritai' named in (among other sources) the formulae in the Babatha archive (early 2nd cent. AD) denote *recuperatores*, this may suggest that the panel was drawn from an *album* at least partly comprising peregrines.
61. See Frier (n. 6), 204–5; Bablitz (n. 8), 51–70. Cf. Kelly (n. 17, *Studies*), 121–24.
62. Metzger (n. 23, 'Absent Parties'), 459–68.
63. Frier (n. 6), 227.

64. See, most recently, Randazzo (n. 24); J. M. Rainer, 'Zum Ursprung der extraordinaria cognitio', in *Roman Law as Formative of Modern Legal Systems* (n. 24), vol. 1, 69–74; Buti (n. 24), 34–9.
65. Talamanca (n. 1, *Istituzioni*), 361.
66. Suet. *Aug.* 33.3; Tac. *Ann.* 14.28.
67. Frier (n. 8).
68. For what follows, see Buti (n. 24), 44–6.
69. Also referred to as summons by *evocatio*, a term which encompasses the tribunal's broad power to summon.
70. For what is given below (288–9), see A. Steinwenter, *Studien zum römischen Versäumnisverfahren* (Munich, 1914); T. Kipp '*contumacia*' in *RE* vol. 4 (1901), col. 1165; Kaser and Hackl (n. 1), 477–81.
71. See Buti (n. 24), 47–54; Kaser and Hackl (n. 1), 485–501.
72. Kaser and Hackl (n. 1), 570–607; Simon (n. 1), esp. 37–63.
73. Gaius 4.17b–20; Liebs (n. 49); R. Zimmermann, *The Roman Law of Obligations* (Oxford, 1996), 835–6.
74. See P. Birks, 'Definition and Division: A Meditation on Institutes 3.13', in *The Classification of Obligations*, ed. P. Birks (Oxford, 1997), 17–18.
75. See R.C. van Caenegem, *History of European Civil Procedure* [International Encyclopedia of Comparative Law, vol. 16.2] (Tübingen, 1987), 11–23, 32–43, 45–53; J. A. Brundage, *The Medieval Origins of the Legal Profession* (Chicago, 2008), ch. 5.

Part V

CRIMINAL AND PUBLIC LAW

15 Crime and Punishment

Andrew Lintott

1. Introduction

For the modern reader there is an immediate problem of definition about Roman criminal law. In current systems civil and criminal law are distinguished by procedure, by the source of the suit or prosecution, and by the nature of the judgment. Criminal cases are characterized by the fact that a public authority prepares the charge, a particular form of trial is used, and judgment is given in favour of the state rather than those who were in fact wronged. At Rome too, while civil procedure was marked out by the distinctive two-part process discussed elsewhere in this volume, criminal cases had characteristic forms to be examined here. However, ancient Rome had no public prosecutor or prosecution service. That function was performed either (i) by certain magistrates, under the Republic tribunes or aediles; (ii) by wronged parties or their relatives; or (iii) by individual citizens for a variety of motives, under statutes which permitted any Roman citizen to bring an action on behalf of another citizen or the Roman people. As for judgments, a successful prosecution in a trial for 'recovery' in the *quaestio de repetundis* (regularly described in modern works in English as the 'extortion court') might involve both a penalty to the state and compensation, sometimes penal, to wronged individuals. Furthermore, the boundary between civil and criminal prosecutions was not that found nowadays under English and similar legal systems. Under the Republic and early Principate theft was a matter for prosecution by a civil action as a private wrong. Assault, battery, and personal affront were similarly private wrongs until Sulla's statute on injuries (*de iniuriis*) which, although it changed the mode of trial, still seems to have provided for the penalty to be paid to the injured party. Similarly, violent expulsion from property first became a matter for specialized civil actions in the late Republic but was then subjected to criminal action under Augustus' statute about violence.[1] There is also the interesting borderline territory of administrative law, where transgression of public statutes or corruption or negligence in their execution might be prosecuted either in the form of a civil or criminal action.[2]

In legal discussion criminal law is and was the poor relation of civil law. In the Augustan period Ateius Capito wrote *On Public Trials* (*De iudiciis publicis*). He was followed in the 'classical period', two centuries later, by Marcianus, Macer, and Paul. There were also works on penalties (*De poenis*) by Venuleius Saturninus, Modestinus, and Paul, while Callistratus wrote on criminal inquiries (*De cognitionibus*). Such works made an important contribution to Books 47–9 of Justinian's *Digest*. However, they seem to have been largely concerned with assembling relevant material rather than with general principles or critical analysis of the working of the criminal law. One reason for this may have been the very nature of the material. There never was a systematic criminal code. The Twelve Tables of the fifth century BC dealt for the most part with civil actions and, while provisions about crimes are to be found, they seem to be answers to particular problems rather than an attempt to mark out the area of criminal law. Augustus passed a statute about public trials (*de iudiciis publicis*), but this was an adjunct to a number of statutes on particular offences, some of them his own, others the work of Julius Caesar or legislators of the late Republic. This last period was indeed a very creative one in the history of the criminal law, as we shall see, but by the same token unstable owing to legal experimentation and the effect of powerful political conflicts.

If we look for the principles that lay behind the original development of the criminal law, a central one is *vindicatio*, related to the modern Italian *vendetta*. Cicero regarded this as part of natural law, an instinct by which we repel from ourselves and those dear to us violence and insult through self-defence and revenge.[3] Other natural principles are respect for the divine and for fatherland and parents – *religio* and *pietas*. While such principles are active from the earliest phases of the criminal law, as the Republic develops we see something which the great Greek historian of Rome, Polybius, saw as a critical function of the popular element in the Roman constitution during the second century BC – that is, the reward of virtue and the punishment of vice. This, in his view, and in that of the Athenian lawgiver Solon, was an essential requirement if any community was to be coherent.[4] Control of behaviour was even more necessary for a community that aspired to rule the whole Mediterranean. In spite of much criminal legislation, social coherence lapsed, thus contributing to the civil strife of the late Republic. It was, therefore, natural that Augustus, when he sought to legally buttress the monarchy that he had acquired by force, should reform and extend the criminal law as part of his commission from the senate to supervise the morality of the people.

Before we examine the origins of the criminal law, it is worthwhile to consider briefly its topographical location. Talk of 'courts' may immediately mislead, as it gives the impression of confined indoor spaces. Jurisdiction in a civil lawsuit was exercised by the praetor originally in the open Comitium, then in a Forum, although the hearing might take place in a private house.[5] Under the Republic, on the other hand, a *iudicium publicum* of a criminal case was by definition a trial in public as well as a public trial. A magistrate prosecuted from the *rostra* in the Forum Romanum, before holding a vote there or in another place of assembly. The jury-courts that were introduced in the last two centuries of the Republic met in the open air in the neighbourhood of one of the tribunals in the Forum – the latter were little more than elevated platforms large enough to accommodate the chair of the presiding magistrate and space for a few essential aides. The seats of the jurors were also elevated,[6] while the parties to the case sat or stood below on the Forum pavement. The jurors, if bored, might walk about, chat with each other or in groups, or send a slave to find out the time.[7] By then the earliest basilicas were enclosing the Forum and it was even possible to watch what was going on from their upper stories.[8] The Forum had indeed become an open-air theatre with several competing stages. When in 45 BC Julius Caesar tried king Deiotarus of Galatia *in camera*, Cicero as defending counsel complained about the unusual procedure, but it was a portent for the future.[9] Under the Principate regular lawsuits were held inside the new, larger basilicas built in the reign of Augustus; other trials took place inside the senate-house or in an imperial residence. Proceedings thus came to resemble more closely those of a modern court, and this affected the atmosphere of trials and the techniques used by advocates.

2. THE ORIGINS OF CRIMINAL JUSTICE

As elsewhere, the criminal law in Rome seems to have begun with the regulation of private retaliation and with measures to define and manage religious pollution. It assumes a society built up of nuclear families under the authority of a *paterfamilias*, which are themselves part of wider agnatic groups. In laws ascribed to various kings we find the deliberate murderer of a free man defined as *paricidas* (best interpreted as kin-murderer) and thus liable to the same sort of reprisals as murder within the kinship group; involuntary homicide is expiated by the public sacrifice of a ram for the agnates of the deceased. Assaults by sons or daughters-in-law on parents, which are severe enough to cause a cry for help, lead to the consecration of the assailant to the gods of the parents.[10] Whether it led to death or not, this placed the perpetrator outside the community of the kinship group or the people as a whole.

Legal regulation was extended in the Twelve Tables, the law-code created – allegedly after popular pressure – in the first century of Republican government. However, this was still a society characterized by self-help and *justice populaire* in the pursuit of security and the repression of crime. In both civil and criminal suits it was for the injured party, if alive, and/or his family and friends to bring the accused before a magistrate. A thief, if he came by night or by day with a weapon, could be killed on the spot, but only after an outcry (*plorare*) was raised to summon friends and neighbours to assist and witness the justice of any such execution. For other forms of theft, where guilt was established after due legal procedure, a range of penalties was laid down, including subjection as a bondsman to the person robbed (*addictio*).[11] For personal injury exact retaliation (*talio*, 'an eye for an eye') was prescribed for the maiming of a limb, unless an agreement for compensation was made, and appropriate financial penalties for lesser injuries (the parallel with the Old Testament is obvious, but we know also of a similar provision being inserted into a law-code for the Greek city of Thurii in southern Italy in the same period).[12] All of these penalties assume actions brought by the injured parties similar to those '*legis actiones*' used, for example, to claim property or sue for the repayment of a debt.

As for murder and other capital offences, there survive three allusions from the Tables to specific forms of execution – in cases of false testimony, arson, and the transportation of crops by magic – but nothing about procedure.[13] It is the view of a number of scholars now, since the work of Wolfgang Kunkel, that capital crimes against individual citizens were also prosecuted by private actions, though not in a two-part action but solely before a magistrate, perhaps the consul (then called *praetor*) or the 'investigator of homicide' (*quaestor parricidii*). The traditional view, by contrast, has been that such capital prosecutions took place in an elaborate procedure before a popular assembly, such as was also used to try crimes against the community as a whole.[14]

This issue can only be understood in the light of an interpretation of early Roman politics, but first it is important to register a feature of Roman society which is related to the *justice populaire* discussed earlier. A citizen was expected to cry for help to his neighbours (*plorare*) when confronted with a malefactor; he might similarly cry for help to his fellow citizens (*provocare*) when being (in his view) unjustly treated by someone in authority. Cicero claims that this custom went back to the regal period and this is certainly possible but, according to the accounts of the annalists many centuries later, it became important in the conflict between patricians and plebeians which developed after the establishment of the Republic. *Provocatio* is also associated with appeal to the tribunes of the plebs who were created for the first time in this period as spokesmen for the common people.[15]

Statutes entrenching *provocatio* as a legal right are ascribed by our sources to the first year of the Republic (509 BC) and the immediate aftermath of the deposition of the ten-man commission which created the Twelve Tables (449 BC). However, since a statute of 300 BC declaring execution in defiance of *provocatio* to be illegal was not backed by any specific sanction, modern scholarship has tended to be sceptical about the real existence of the two earlier statutes. Equally, Theodor Mommsen's view that *provocatio* was an integrated part of any assembly trial is not borne out by the evidence for such trials. This does not mean, on the other hand, that before 300 BC *provocatio* did not exist and so restrain de facto a magistrate from using capital punishment in the face of popular disapproval. In the late Republic *provocatio* was regarded as a cornerstone of the liberty of the individual Roman citizen. More specifically, it is likely that it influenced the nature of capital criminal trials in the early Republic. However, it would not necessarily have entailed that all such trials had to take place in a popular assembly, since a manifestly guilty criminal would not have found support among the people if he appealed for their help.[16]

Cicero, when arguing that his enemy Clodius had not used due legal process to drive him into exile, describes what he claimed was the traditional form of process for capital trials before the assembly. A magistrate held three public investigations of the accused – where witnesses could be called and the accused had a right to reply – followed after a due interval by a final accusation and vote by a formal assembly on the same day. A municipal law from Bantia in southern Italy, apparently modelled on Roman practice, incorporates a similar process but with four, not three, preliminary investigations. A text in Livy suggests that in certain circumstances a single accusation and vote was sufficient.[17] In the light of this evidence of variation in procedure, we cannot be sure what the earliest form of assembly trial was: perhaps that which was completed on a single day. Cicero also cites a clause in the Twelve Tables which forbade, first, the proposal of laws directed against individuals and, second, voting on the life (*caput*) of a citizen except in the 'greatest' or 'very great assembly'. He took this to mean the military assembly (*comitia centuriata*) – which was where the final vote in a capital trial before an assembly took place in his day – one distributed into centuries of military origin and so organized that it privileged wealth and age. However, it might simply mean a well-attended (and so quorate) assembly.[18] Moreover, there is evidence in Republican history for capital decisions in other assemblies, where the citizens were simply organized in voting divisions (*tribus*).[19] It is therefore probable that, when Cicero claimed that this clause of the Twelve Tables prescribed the only form of capital assembly trial in the past, this was a misinterpretation based on current practice.

It may seem paradoxical that capital prosecutions before an assembly were conducted under the mature Republic by tribunes of the plebs, who were associated with defending the rights of the individual. The tribunes were, according to Roman tradition, created originally as spokesmen by the plebs during their revolutionary 'secession' from the patricians in 494 BC. To ensure the tribunes' security, the plebs took an oath that their persons should be sacrosanct – that is, immune from physical violation: anyone who assaulted a tribune was liable to the vengeance of the plebs. From this immunity sprang the tribunes' capacity to protect ordinary citizens (*auxilium*) and to block the actions of other magistrates (*intercessio*). However, there is also a tradition in the annals that they used this status to prosecute enemies of the plebs before assemblies of the plebs.[20] It has been suggested that the clause that Cicero cited from the Twelve Tables was deliberately designed to nullify this practice and ensure that such prosecutions could not be made purely in the plebeian interest.[21] This depends on the questionable assumption that Cicero understood the clause correctly. However, it is likely that, while trials before assemblies for offences against the community as a whole were a feature of Roman criminal justice from the early Republic, if not the regal period, the activities of tribunes contributed to the development of such trials and hence in due course it became customary for them, rather than other magistrates, to prosecute in capital cases. Who the prosecuting magistrates were before this task fell to the tribunes remains uncertain. An antique formula was known in the late Republic, in which the prosecutors for treason (*perduellio*) were a two-man commission (*duumviri*), but we do not know whether this was a special measure or the regular procedure of the early Republic.[22]

Amid so many uncertainties, at best some probable suggestions may be made about the procedure that had developed by the middle Republic. First, it is likely that prosecutions of capital crimes, such as murder and arson, against private individuals were normally prosecuted by private initiative before a magistrate. If these led to *provocatio* (an appeal against the magistrate) then there might be recourse to an assembly either by the magistrate judging the case or a tribune who gave support to an appeal, but not otherwise. In public matters prosecutions before the assembly were mounted by tribunes and, in non-capital cases, by aediles. These might involve three or more investigative hearings before the final accusation and vote, if the nature of the offence needed to be established, but, if offence and penalty were clear-cut, could be completed in a day. There is also evidence for justice being exercised by the *triumviri capitales*, the board of three men in charge of the prison and executions. They had absorbed the function of an earlier board of three, the *triumviri nocturni* – which maintained the night watch against fires, thieves, runaway slaves, and other malefactors. They exercised against such people a form of summary justice or coercion – for runaway slaves, flogging and return to their masters. The *triumviri* are also attested as receiving denunciations for murder and carrying an offensive weapon. It is not clear how far they could proceed with these beyond accepting or rejecting the charge. They could perhaps incarcerate those who appeared guilty of murder, and even execute slaves or free men of inferior status.[23]

Special circumstances required special measures. Mass lawbreaking against the public interest, such as treason by a group of people in war, could not be handled in a regular assembly trial. Here investigation of the crime and sentence were left to a magistrate, the senate, or a special commission, although it was usual for the assembly to give its fiat to the procedure either before or afterwards, thus avoiding any offence against the *provocatio* laws. *Ad hoc* tribunals of investigation, normally called *quaestiones*, to deal with capital or non-capital public cases became common in the second century. These were established either by statute or decree of the senate and took the form of an inquiry by a magistrate or magistrates assisted by a panel of assessors (*consilium*), whom they themselves chose. Information might be laid before the tribunal, but formal prosecution was not necessary, as we see in accounts of the inquiries into the Bacchanals in 186 BC and the murders in the Silva Sila in 138 BC.[24] Defendants, however, could speak themselves or be represented by advocates. The magistrates were empowered to reach a verdict, in which they might be influenced but not bound by their assessors' views, and to pass sentence. This procedure, better suited to the unravelling of complex cases, is very similar to that which eventually came to prevail under the Principate and was then termed *cognitio*: indeed, Cicero uses this term for the investigation of the murders by the staff of the contractors in the Silva Sila.[25] However, law does not necessarily develop in the simplest way. In fact, these *ad hoc* tribunals led in the late Republic to perhaps the most remarkable creation in Roman criminal law, the permanent tribunal of investigation (*quaestio perpetua*).

3. Permanent Tribunals: The Criminal Courts of the Late Republic and Early Principate

Our knowledge of these courts derives in part from sections of their statutes that survive in the *Digest* and other juristic sources, but, more importantly, from two kinds of contemporary source. We have an incomplete but nevertheless lengthy text of a statute establishing a permanent tribunal (*quaestio perpetua*) to investigate money which should be recovered (*de repetundis*) because it had been improperly extorted by Romans in authority. This is inscribed on fragments of a bronze tablet, which were once in the library of the dukes of Urbino but then passed to Cardinal Bembo about AD 1500.[26] We also have other smaller bronze fragments with parts of the texts of other statutes of this sort.[27] The second source is the texts of Cicero: written versions of the speeches he gave in these courts and rhetorical treatises that *inter alia* discussed the best methods to be used in criminal pleading. Thanks to the survival of the bronze fragments we know most about the *quaestio de repetundis* and to some extent have to extrapolate conclusions about the other tribunals from its procedure. However, caution is required, especially as it is clear that through successive laws court procedure, jury selection, and even the definition of the offences to be tried by the various tribunals altered over time.

We have already discussed the *ad hoc* tribunals which were established from the middle Republic onwards. In the second century some of these were augmented or replaced by permanent tribunals: for example, by 142 BC a permanent tribunal concerning assassins (*quaestio de sicariis*) had come to exist in place of those that had from time to time been established earlier. This is one factor in the background to the law passed by Lucius Calpurnius Piso in 149 BC, establishing the first *quaestio de repetundis*. Another is the private procedure that had been set up originally for the recovery of money by non-Romans, where the hearing took place not before a single judge but a jury of *recuperatores* (recoverers) – a procedure characterized by strict time-limits and a continuing supervision by the magistrate of the jury's hearing of the case and the execution of the verdict. A special version of this procedure had been set up by the senate in 171 BC for the benefit of Spanish plaintiffs against former Roman magistrates.[28] It was supervised by the praetor then appointed to govern Spain, with five *recuperatores* appointed for each defendant. One of the accused was acquitted and two deserted their bail and went into exile before a verdict could be reached, thus frustrating any substantial recovery of extorted money and demonstrating the inadequacy of purely civil procedure in such cases.

The first form of suit provided for the *quaestio de repetundis* by Piso's law was a traditional form of Roman civil action, the *legis actio sacramento*, which could only be performed by Roman citizens or perhaps their Latin allies. Thus, if other allies or foreigners wished to use this law, as most scholars believe, they could only do so through a Roman patron. Conviction led to simple restitution. The jurors seem to have been of senatorial rank; the panel was probably not very large.[29] This procedure underwent a revolutionary change through the statute we possess on the bronze fragments from Urbino, which, we can infer with some certainty, was passed in the second tribunate of Gaius Gracchus (122 BC). The statute was directed against the improper acquisition of property above a certain minimum sum through force, menaces, fraud, or the solicitation of favours, by Roman magistrates, senators, or senators' sons. At this time official brutality was not covered, except in so far as it produced financial loss; nor was the unsolicited receipt of gifts or bribes.[30]

Prosecution was described both as *petitio* (suit), a term appropriate to a civil action, and *nominis delatio* (denunciation), a term appropriate to the laying of information about a criminal to a tribunal of inquiry. The right to prosecute was granted first to the victims themselves and their relatives, second to men acting for an allied king, an allied community, or a fellow-citizen in such a community (the use of *cognitores* (legal representatives) was already accepted in Roman civil law). After the denunciation had been accepted, the court might grant a prosecutor the help of a Roman *patronus*, but the principle was that a wronged foreigner could have direct access to a Roman criminal court.[31]

The procedure for assembling a jury was elaborate. The relevant praetor was required every year to select and register on an *album* (a white board) a panel of 450 jurors between the ages of 30 and 60, domiciled within a certain range of the city of Rome (the specific distance is not preserved). The positive qualifications for this panel are unclear, but it is likely that they were members of the order of knights (*equites*) and/or possessed appropriate property. Those excluded were senators and their relatives, those who had held a minor magistracy, and former senators who had been stripped of their rank because of their disgraceful conduct. The aim was clearly to eliminate those who were generally likely to have connections or sympathy with the accused. This was reinforced in the selection of the trial jury, where the defendant was required to disclose to the prosecutor anyone on the panel connected to him by kinship, as close as a cousin, as well as stepfathers, stepsons, and relatives by marriage, and members of the same guild or association (*collegium* or *sodalitas*). The prosecutor then offered the defendant 100 jurors, who were similarly in no way connected with himself: if they had been disclosed as connected with the defendant, that was the prosecutor's affair. The defendant in turn selected 50 of these, or, if he failed to do so, the praetor acted for him. Throughout this procedure there was concern for publicity: the names of both the panel and the trial jury were made available for copying, and the praetor and the parties concerned took oaths in public that they were acting according to the law.[32]

The praetor was required to use his authority to assist in the collection of evidence and witnesses from Italy: up to 48 could be formally summonsed by the prosecutor and the production of public documents could be demanded. A prosecutor from abroad would have had to bring foreign witnesses with him. Because of the damage to the bronze, we have little detail of the trial procedure (but see below, 313–14). It is clear that the presiding praetor could ask questions, but the verdict was a matter for the jury alone. It was the praetor's task to ask if enough of the jury had made up their minds to enable a vote to be taken: if more than a third said *non liquet* ('the matter is not clear'), the hearing was prolonged until two-thirds were prepared to vote, but jurors who refused to vote on more than two occasions were to be fined 10,000 sesterces – a considerable sum even for a wealthy man. Voting was by ballot with tablets marked with *A(bsolvo)* on one side and *C(ondemno)* on the other: the voter was required to delete one of these, or both if he wished to register no vote. The voter had to conceal the vote on his ballot as he placed it in the box, but to keep his arm bare so as to make plain that he was not stuffing the box with illegal ballots. A man was condemned if there was a greater number of 'C's than the number of 'A's, provided that it also exceeded the number of 'no vote' ballots.[33]

As soon as a man was condemned, he either had to give guarantors to the praetor for the sum he was liable to pay or submit to the seizure of his property. In the estimation of damages (*litis aestimatio*) that followed, it was the jury's task to determine the precise amount of damages to be awarded to each injured party. The damages were penal, double the loss sustained by each victim, except for offences committed before the passage of the law. Furthermore, successful prosecutors were offered rewards: non-Romans could receive full Roman citizenship if they wanted or alternatively the right of *provocatio* and freedom from military service and public duties in their own communities. Rewards, probably of this second kind, were also offered to Roman citizens. The statute excluded any kind of intervention from outside, so no appeal or *provocatio* would have been valid against the court's decision. There was also an entrenchment clause (*sanctio*), not preserved but mentioned elsewhere in the text, which, to judge from examples preserved on other inscriptions, would have threatened with penalties anyone who sought to frustrate the working of the law.[34]

In the next 50 years subsequent statutes changed and changed again the selection and composition of the jury until a compromise was reached in 70 BC, whereby the panels were composed one-third of senators and two-thirds of non-senators, selected from the album by lot and then alternate rejection by prosecution and defence. Around 100 BC the procedure for bringing charges was altered so that, after the original prosecution was made, further prosecutors might come forward; a jury was required to select the most appropriate one in a process called *divinatio*. The selected prosecutor was then allowed time to investigate the charges abroad (*inquisitio*). This led in practice to most cases being undertaken by Roman citizens who were practising advocacy. The provision for up to two extensions of the hearing without penalty was replaced by a compulsory two-part trial (*comperendinatio*). Moreover, a new procedure was devised to pursue money which the condemned man had passed on to others (*quo ea pecunia pervenerit*). These measures arguably led to more efficient and comprehensive prosecutions, but the part that might be played by non-Roman plaintiffs was reduced. The centrality of compensation for the injured party was diminished when the remit of the court was extended to the receipt of freely given bribes, including those directed at judicial corruption. Furthermore, in the late Republic various breaches of the rules laid down for the behaviour of Roman magistrates in the provinces were made liable to prosecution in this court, although they involved no financial loss to the allies. Certain forms of misconduct were even treated as capital offences – for example, the receipt of money in return for an unjust capital condemnation.[35]

Because the *quaestio de repetundis* was one of the easier means to procure the downfall of a high-ranking Roman, it was the subject of political controversy on the grounds that its procedures were themselves an avenue of corruption. It became, nevertheless, the model for other permanent criminal courts. It seems to have been imitated by Lucius Saturninus, when he introduced (in 103 or 100 BC) a tribunal to deal with the 'diminution of the majesty of the Roman people' (*de maiestate populi Romani minuta*), an all-embracing concept of political misconduct which was understood to cover unconstitutional behaviour, military incompetence, and treason. In Sulla's legislation (82–1 BC) existing tribunals concerning assassins (*de sicariis*), poisoners (*de veneficis*), electoral bribery (*de ambitu*), and embezzlement (*de peculatu*) were reformed on this model, if they had not been before. New tribunals were established to deal with forgery (*de falsis*) and assault or insulting behaviour (*de iniuriis*), and shortly afterwards another for political violence (*de vi*). The court dealing with assassins was also made responsible for trials of *parricidium* (the term now meant the murder of either parent). *Parricidium* was characterized by the peculiar and dreadful sack penalty – precipitation into water in a sack together with a cock, a viper, and a monkey. A law of Pompey (of 55 or 52 BC) extended this crime to cover the murder of any close relative or patron, but reserved the sack penalty for those who confessed or had been caught in the act. Sulla seems to have wanted the permanent tribunals to take over the exercise of criminal justice both over Rome and, where the crime was capital, over the communities of Italy too, especially in view of his restriction on the powers of tribunes, who were deprived of the right to legislate or prosecute before an assembly. In 70 BC the tribunes' powers were restored, but we hear of only one prosecution carried out by a tribune and one by an aedile in the last 20 years of the Republic.[36]

The rich, largely Ciceronian evidence for the late Republic allows us to fill out the picture of the operation of criminal tribunals. The presidency of the tribunals was allotted partly to praetors in their year of office, and partly to 'judges of the inquiry' (*iudices quaestionis*), senators just below the rank of praetor, who had formerly been aediles. After 70 BC there were three divisions of jurors: senators, knights (*equites*), and so-called tribunes of the treasury (*tribuni aerarii*) – wealthy men who did not possess equestrian status. Each album had perhaps 300 members. Equal numbers from these three albums were allotted to a case and were in turn reduced through alternate rejection by prosecution and defence, leaving a trial jury that varied from about 50 to about 75 (the 3 final panels were not required to be exactly equal). One law about a form of electoral corruption introduced a variation on this, based on the voting districts for the assembly.

In courts other than the *quaestio de repetundis* there was no selection of a prosecutor, and the trial was expected to follow on the tenth day after the acceptance of the original accusation as legitimate, with the allotment of the jurors complete. Prosecution in political cases, such as those *de repetundis* or *de maiestate*, was undertaken usually by cadet members of the elite or by members of the equestrian order who specialized in advocacy (Cicero's prosecution of Verres, when already a senator, was an exception). The prosecutor was frequently either connected to those injured through friendship or patronage or an enemy of the defendant for personal reasons. Prosecution for murder tended to be carried out by professional advocates, usually on behalf of the kin of the victim. By the late Republic informing had become a profession, and prosecutors could also expect to receive evidence from members of the accused's household, including slaves. Defence counsel were the best advocates and the most eminent senators that the defendant could summon to his aid.[37]

The speeches of those prosecuting and those defending took place before the examination of witnesses. However, summaries of their testimonies had to be deposited with the court beforehand and sealed with the seals of the jury. Witnesses were examined and cross-examined, and this was followed by a debate (*altercatio*) between the parties about the reliability of the evidence and its implications. Some defence testimonies were merely praise of the defendant's character. In general, a witness statement was not a disinterested statement of fact. It was expected to come to a conclusion about the guilt or innocence of the accused and so to contribute directly to the prosecution or defence.[38] Equally, the advocates were not purely servants of the court. Prosecutors stood in a relation of patronage to their clients and frequently had a personal interest in the case, while defence counsel put at their client's disposal not only their ability as advocates but the authority deriving from their status, which was granted to the client in friendship. A defence counsel was in effect at the same time a witness to character.

Defendants, their families, and friends wore mourning during the trial. This was not merely a visual aid for the conclusions of defence speeches but could also be deployed in last minute personal appeals to the jury as they voted. The vote of the jury was final in this period. Appeal to the assembly in cases of treason and violence was only introduced by Mark Antony after Caesar's death in a measure that was rescinded but probably revived.[39] Similarly, a person could not normally be accused again on the same charge, unless it could be shown that the prosecution had been collusive, and therefore deliberately ineffective (*praevaricatio*).[40]

In a trial for recovery (*de repetundis*) a considerable time might elapse between prosecution and verdict, owing to the period that might be allocated to the prosecutor for investigation abroad and the two-part trial. Other procedures were swifter. Trials in *quaestiones* were normally confined to the ten hours between the first hour and the eleventh hour each day, to judge from Julius Caesar's later regulations for his colony at Urso. There were limitations on the length of speeches in trials *de repetundis* from at least Sulla's legislation onwards.[41] However, the hearing of witnesses might be exceedingly time-consuming. In 52 BC, when Pompey set up special courts to deal with violence and bribery, he deliberately compressed the timetable. The first three days of each trial were devoted to the hearing of witnesses, and only at the end of this were the written versions of their testimonies sealed. Then on the fourth day the speeches were held – the prosecution being allotted two hours, the defence three – and the vote was held on the same day.[42]

In the early Republic, as we have seen, the consequence of condemnation after a private prosecution was either execution in a prescribed fashion, subjection to the injured party as a bondsman, or a financial penalty. Public criminal prosecutions before an assembly were either capital or for a fine proposed by the prosecutor. However, it became the practice for the defendant to be allowed to escape into exile at the last moment before the decision of the critical voting division was announced. In consequence, the exile of the condemned man was formally recognized, but he was forbidden 'fire and water' – that is, if he were to return to Roman soil, he would be an outlaw and could be killed on sight. In the late Republic statutes regulating criminal tribunals prescribed exile through the ban on fire and water as the regular form of capital penalty.[43] Before the unification of Italy under direct Roman rule, which followed the Social War (90–87 BC), exile could be less than a day's journey from Rome in the allied towns of Tibur (Tivoli) and Praeneste (Palestrina), although such enclaves surrounded by Roman territory were highly restrictive. In the late Republic exile meant, at least in theory, banishment from peninsular Italy and could be extended to a specific distance from Rome, as it was for Cicero (400 or 500 miles); Cicero, moreover, was excluded from Sicily and Malta.[44]

Even at the end of the Republic many offences now regarded as crimes remained matters for prosecution by injured parties through civil actions. The scope of the criminal law had been extended, however, and the new permanent criminal tribunals were a convenient way to pursue both offences against the community and certain offences against individuals. The adversarial procedure in these courts gave defendants maximum scope to escape the charge. Moreover, although the prosecutors were often skilled advocates and were given important privileges in collecting evidence, they lacked the support available to those of the present day. Nevertheless, an examination of known outcomes in the court for recovery (*quaestio de repetundis*) suggests a conviction rate of about 50 per cent.[45]

4. The Augustan Reforms

Julius Caesar is said to have planned a codification of the law, but he achieved no more than a few piecemeal reforms. His statute about recovery (*repetundae*), an immensely complex one incorporating specific rules for the behaviour of provincial governors and perhaps introducing the concept of a capital offence in this court, was passed in his first consulship (59 BC).[46] In his dictatorship he confined service as a juror or judge to senators and knights; he also reformed the tribunals on treason (*maiestas*) and violence. The penalty was exile, combined with loss of property at home.[47] We find him exercising criminal jurisdiction in the Forum as dictator over an accusation of treason in the case of Quintus Ligarius; he also tried king Deiotarus on a similar charge in his own house. In this respect his actions were a precedent for what was to happen under the Principate. After Caesar's death Mark Antony legislated in 44 BC for an additional division of jurors who did not possess equestrian status but had apparently a wealth qualification. This was rescinded in 43 BC, but a third division was probably restored by the triumvirs.[48]

Augustus claims in his *Res Gestae* that in both 19 and 11 BC he was offered by senate and people the position of 'curator of laws and morals with supreme power and without colleague' but did not accept any magistracy without precedent. Instead he carried out the measures required by the senate through his tribunician power[49] – that is, by using it to legislate through the plebeian assembly. His judicial measures seem to have formed part of the ensuing reforms, enacted before the emperor departed for Gaul in 16 BC.[50] His general statutes about procedure in public and private trials (the *lex Iulia de iudiciis publicis* and the *de iudiciis privatis*) are only known to us through a scattering of references and allusions. We have more substantial evidence for his reforms to the system of permanent criminal tribunals in both the legal sources and other literature. It seems that in these reforms he was essentially building on late-Republican foundations. However, there were also developments that in the longer term brought about a revolution in court procedure. Augustus followed Caesarian precedent in using his *imperium* to preside over certain trials at Rome himself. Moreover, through a facet of the tribunician power granted to him in 30 BC, he judged cases on appeal.[51] A further alternative to Republican procedure was created, when towards the end of the reign the senate was granted jurisdiction in cases involving the majesty of the Roman people, this being understood to embrace that of the senate and the imperial house.

Under Augustus there were originally three divisions (*decuriae*) of judges and jury-members, from which it seems that two albums were drawn each year: one for private and one for public cases. Senators were not excluded and the remainder had equestrian status.[52] A fourth division was then added from those of an inferior property qualification to judge private cases for less significant sums of money. A fifth was to be added by the emperor Gaius, but Galba is said to have refused to add a sixth.[53] The emperor may originally have selected the members of the divisions, but by the end of Augustus' reign the task of drawing up the equestrian list, like that of reviewing membership of the senate, had been delegated to a commission of senators.[54] The minimum age for jurors was reduced to 25 years. Members of the albums were expected to be available for the whole period designated for judicial business – the so-called *rerum actus*. Augustus made available for judicial business 30 days among those allocated to recently created festivals – although not including those relating to the imperial family – and created a judicial vacation in November and December.[55]

A uniform process for accusation was created that no longer required an initial summons before the president of the court but was effected by a written denunciation (*libellus* or *subscriptio*). If this was accepted, the accuser was allowed a period to collect evidence (*inquisitio*) and then had to notify the defendant of the date fixed for the trial.[56] The emperor Claudius was later to complain that accusers, once the charge had been accepted for trial, were lax in actually bringing it to court.[57] We hear of various other rules ascribed to Augustus' law. For example, witnesses could not be compelled to testify against relatives by blood (as far as the grade of cousin) or marriage;[58] neither party was permitted to enter the house of a juryman during a trial.[59] These rules may have existed in earlier statutes regulating individual criminal courts. However, the increase to 12 in the number of defence counsel permitted is ascribed specifically to Augustus.[60]

New laws were passed for existing crimes – electoral bribery (*ambitus*), embezzlement (*peculatus*), and violence (*vis*). The law about bribery actually mitigated the existing penalty, perhaps because the direct and indirect influence of the emperor on elections made extreme sanctions unnecessary. Otherwise, the changes seem to have been mainly a matter of identifying particular forms of illegal behaviour. *Peculatus* was extended by a *lex Iulia de residuis* to cover specifically the retention for private use of money received for a public purpose or in the course of a public transaction.[61] The law or laws about violence distinguished between public – that is, against public authority – and private violence. The most interesting new inclusion in public violence was improper official brutality, the coercion of Roman citizens through bonds or flogging or their execution in defiance of *provocatio* (exceptions were made for the coercion of confessed or condemned criminals, of actors because of their degraded profession, and of those subject to military discipline).[62] The explanation of the incorporation of such matter in a law about violence may be that behaviour of this kind might provoke a riot. *Provocatio* seems originally to have been understood as appeal to the public, but was soon reinterpreted as appeal to the emperor (see below, 318). Augustus also created tribunals for new crimes. One (*de annona*) dealt specifically with fraud in connection with the corn-supply, interference with it, or conspiracy to raise prices.[63] Another was of much greater significance as it introduced the criminal law into matters that earlier had largely been left to self-help and family justice.

Under the Republic certain flagrant sexual offences had been prosecuted by aediles before an assembly,[64] but our admittedly inadequate sources suggest that requital for the majority of offences had been left to fathers and husbands, who, preferably after a family council, were allowed to chastise women of the family and their lovers physically and even execute them.[65] There is some evidence for Republican laws which limited this sort of self-help.[66] Augustus' *lex Iulia de adulteriis* on the one hand had elaborate regulations restricting self-help, and on the other required such offences to be prosecuted by the father of the woman or her husband – the latter on pain of being prosecuted himself as a pimp if the offending pair were not accused. It should be noted that *adulterium* covered not only adultery but any kind of illicit sexual act (*stuprum*). Under the new regime a father could still kill his daughter and her lover, provided that he caught the pair in the act, that he killed both at once, that the act took place either in his own house or that of his son-in-law, and that the woman was legally either in his power (*potestas*) or that of her husband.[67] A husband, however, was forbidden to kill his wife, and could only kill his wife's lover if they were caught in the house and the lover fell into one of the categories of degraded persons (*infames*), including slaves, freedmen of the family, actors, dancers, and prostitutes.[68] Complaisant husbands were not permitted, as a famous letter of the younger Pliny shows.[69] In such processes slaves were permitted to give evidence against their masters and mistresses and many accusations arose through information laid by members of the household.[70] In this period many offences against individuals and their households were still not subject to prosecution in a criminal court, and Augustus' innovation here can only be understood in the context of his other measures about marriage: it was a determined effort to reinforce the sanctity of the institution and the family home.

5. Trials Before the Emperor and the Senate

It is a moot point how far one should seek to find a strict legal justification for the justice administered by the emperor himself. The element most easily grounded is his power to hear appeals. According to the historian Dio,[71] in 30 BC Caesar Octavianus (as Augustus then was) was granted for life the power of the tribunes, defined as 'defending those appealing to him inside the *pomerium* [the formal city boundary] and outside up to a mile, . . . judging cases on appeal, and casting the vote as it were of Athena in all criminal courts'. The foundation of this power was the *auxilium* all Republican tribunes possessed individually. However, it was supplemented in the first place by a power to hear appeals, which Republican tribunes had in certain cases exercised as a college, although not individually nor against the decisions of criminal tribunals: indeed, it was on the popular assemblies that Mark Antony had wished to confer this right to hear appeals against condemnations for violence and treason.[72] Secondly, there was 'the vote as it were of Athena', a reference to that cast by the goddess in favour of Orestes in Aeschylus' *Eumenides*, which tied the votes of the Athenian jurors and produced acquittal. Many scholars have wished to press the parallel to the utmost and understand this as a privilege to acquit a defendant if he or she was being condemned in a criminal tribunal by the margin of a single vote, but it would have been an insult to grant to the victor in the civil wars a privilege that could have been exercised rarely, if ever. It is better to see this as a kind of royal prerogative to grant pardon, even if the person was guilty.[73] The nearest Republican precedent for this would have been the acquittal by the assembly of a person condemned by a magistrate in one of the earlier forms of criminal inquiry (*quaestio*), such as the tribunes sought in the case of Q. Pleminius.[74]

Augustus' exercise of primary jurisdiction in the city was, according to Suetonius,[75] frequent. It can only have occurred in the period when he was regularly at Rome exercising consular or proconsular power – that is, at the time of his criminal legislation in 18–17 BC and then again after his return from Gaul in 13 BC. His trials of persons from the empire outside Italy, such as Aulus Stlaccius Maximus from Cyrene in 7–6 BC,[76] were justified by his *proconsulare imperium maius*, the power that allowed him to override provincial governors throughout the Roman empire. On the other hand, jurisdiction in the city had not been a matter for Republican consuls in the middle and late Republic. No doubt an antiquarian justification could have been found for it, if necessary, but by this time little disguise remained for the dynastic monarchy that Augustus was founding, for which *auctoritas*[77] was the euphemistic term employed by Augustus himself and generally used in modern scholarship. In any case, the trials could have been interpreted as part of Augustus' supervision of laws and morals. His practice was not imitated by Tiberius, who was criticized by Tacitus for merely sitting as an assistant to praetors on the wing of their tribunals;[78] Claudius did follow Augustus' precedent and consequently was lampooned and denounced after his death for his litigiousness and the holding of trials in his own houses.[79] Nero made promises to avoid Claudius' practice on his accession, but these eventually went for nothing when he was threatened by the Pisonian conspiracy,[80] and we do not find objections to the principle of imperial jurisdiction subsequently. In Tacitus' portrayal of oratory under Vespasian, however, the cases pleaded before the emperor are only those concerning the emperor's freedmen and procurators.[81]

The senate was always dependent on the magistrate who convened it for its agenda and the translation of its decrees into action. Under the Principate this meant that its decisions were largely subordinated to the legal powers and informal authority (*auctoritas*) of the emperor. However, its close relationship to the emperor came to increase its power in more than one respect. One was that its decrees were given the force of laws. Hence, we find a series of *senatus consulta* which reinterpreted the existing criminal statutes, extended their remit, or changed the procedure of the courts.[82]

Under the Republic the senate was not a court. It did, it is true, investigate the evidence against the leading Catilinarian conspirators at Rome in 63 BC, apparently extracting confessions from them.[83] In the subsequent debate, however, that led to their being sentenced to death, the accused were neither present themselves and able to speak nor even represented, which could hardly be described as judicial procedure even by the standards of the time. Trials in the senate for offences that could be construed as damaging Rome's *maiestas* seem on our evidence first to have occurred late in Augustus' reign. After Ovid had been 'relegated' – that is, banished through consular authority – in AD 8, he complained that he had not been condemned either by a criminal tribunal or a decree of the senate.[84] At this time Augustus probably used the senate to condemn his granddaughter, Ovid's alleged lover, as he had previously (2 BC) his daughter Julia.[85] However, the first certain example of this sort of trial is that of a man whose primary offence was against the *maiestas* of the senate itself, the orator and pamphleteer Cassius Severus, who had defamed distinguished men and women in his writings.[86] Furthermore, about AD 11–12 a former proconsul of Asia, Volesus Messala, accused under the law about recovery (*de repetundis*), was brought before the senate on account of the brutality that had accompanied his extortion, a matter about which the emperor had written a commentary and submitted it to the senate: this in effect redefined the *repetundae* charge as *maiestas*.[87]

Even before this Augustus had devised a new swift form of process for *repetundae* cases where there was no capital charge, which in effect resembled a civil process for compensation before *recuperatores* (the sort of process provided in 171 BC). We possess a full text of this in Greek – an account of legal procedure second only in its detail to that provided by the *lex repetundarum* – because it was incorporated by the emperor in one of his Cyrene edicts.[88] The measure was expressed in a decree of the senate proposed by the consuls of 4 BC, Calvisius Sabinus and Passienus Rufus, on the basis of a memorandum drawn up in the emperor's council (*consilium*). The plaintiffs were first to approach the senate, which was empowered to allot a group of nine senators of differing ranks, excluding relatives and enemies of the defendant, who were to be reduced by alternate rejection to five. There was a limit on prosecution witnesses being summoned from outside Italy; judgment was to be given within 30 days, and the judges were to deliver their opinion openly. This sort of procedure was used against Granius Marcellus, after a *maiestas* charge against him was rejected by the senate in AD 15 and, as an interim measure, against Marius Priscus, when he was prosecuted by Tacitus and the younger Pliny in the senate in AD 100.[89]

The law of *maiestas*, on the most plausible view,[90] was that passed by Julius Caesar as dictator, but both the crime itself and the penalty became subject to development and re-interpretation under the emperors. It is now abundantly clear from the text of the decree of AD 20 relating to the condemnation of Gnaeus Piso the previous year that *maiestas* now included the majesty of the imperial household.[91] Moreover, the senate imposed penalties exceeding those prescribed by the *lex Iulia*.[92] In Pliny's time, it was argued in the senate both that it was limited by the law and, alternatively, that it was free to improvise penalties to suit the magnitude of crimes or mitigate the severity of the law.[93] As for procedure in the senate, this owed something to the example provided by the criminal tribunal (*quaestio perpetua*), but was changed by the very nature of the senate itself, a massive jury, whose members all possessed the right to deliver an opinion when asked for their verdict, including making proposals about the penalty. Other features in which early senatorial trials differed from the *quaestio perpetua* are the prosecution of men while they still held office, the presence of magistrates among the accusers, and, above all, the frequent participation of the emperor himself.[94]

The senate decree about the trial of Gnaeus Piso for *maiestas* refers successively to the speeches by Piso's accusers and by the man himself, the reading of letters and the memoranda Germanicus sent to Piso, and the hearing of witnesses from every rank.[95] If this is a temporal sequence, then procedure in this case came close in outline to that of a regular criminal tribunal. From Tacitus we learn that the four speakers for the prosecution were allocated a total of two days and the three speakers for the defence three days:[96] these periods seem to have included the reading of documents and hearing of witnesses. In the trial of Marius Priscus and Flavius Marcianus under Trajan – in which the accusation *de repetundis* was extended to cover not only Priscus' receipt of money in exchange for a condemnation but Marcianus' bribery of Priscus – the first prosecutor, the younger Pliny, spoke and the defence replied, then Tacitus spoke for the prosecution, and the defence replied; the presentation of evidence (*probationes*) followed.[97] The shape of the trial thus resembled the two-part structure prescribed for the *quaestio* by Republican legislation, except that no evidence was given in the first part. However, the trial of Caecilius Classicus and his accomplices in the same period had three parts, which the prosecution divided between different defendants.[98]

During the century that separated Ovid's exile from Pliny's advocacy in the senate, a procedure devised originally for what were thought especially heinous offences against the regime seems to have been extended to regular crimes covered by the laws of the criminal tribunals, provided that the chief defendants were senators or at least important members of the equestrian order. Senatorial procedure had to be adapted to conduct trials, but the basic principle of complete consultation of the membership present could not be avoided. Senators kept one eye on the Republican and Augustan statutes but, as befitted a body which since Augustus had itself the power to alter the criminal law, asserted, when judging cases, the senate's right to decide what in its view was just, even if up to that point it had not been legal practice. Indeed, a number of the innovative *senatus consulta* arose from the trial of particular cases: for example, a decree making provincial governors responsible for the conduct of their wives arose from the trial of Gaius Silius in AD 24.[99]

6. *Cognitio* – Investigation by Magistrates or Officials

Cognitio was the term used for a criminal investigation by a magistrate or magistrates assisted by a *consilium* of advisers. This procedure, as has been seen earlier, existed before the creation of permanent criminal tribunals, and it was still employed at Rome from time to time during the late Republic to deal with special offences, such as the *quaestio Mamilia* about the receipt of bribes from King Iugurtha in 110 BC.[100] It was also the regular form taken by a criminal trial before a provincial governor in person, assuming that he did not refer the matter to one of the courts in the province. When the Roman emperor, by virtue of his *proconsulare imperium maius* in the Roman empire, became the ultimate source of justice for Rome's allies and subjects, *cognitio* was the form taken by cases referred to him directly or on appeal. Augustus also, as we have seen, exercised this form of justice at first instance over certain cases from Rome and Italy, although the practice was to arouse disquiet among the elite when later followed by Claudius. In the longer run, to an increasing extent *cognitio* came to replace the operations of the permanent criminal tribunals in respect of cases arising at Rome or in Italy.[101] However, this was not, and could not have been, achieved simply by multiplying trials before the emperor in person, but required the delegation of judicial powers to magistrates or other appointees. As under the Republic, *cognitio* was a convenient way of proceeding against mass offences and also permitted the investigation of behaviour, believed criminal, which did not fall neatly within the categories of offence listed in the statutes governing the permanent criminal tribunals.[102] Moreover, the denouncing of an offender to a magistrate for judicial investigation required less action and commitment than the procedure for accusation before a permanent tribunal and would have been less likely to deter those of inferior status who lacked suitable patrons.

It is hard to establish how soon *cognitio* by subordinates of the emperor developed at Rome and how quickly and completely it supplanted the *quaestiones perpetuae*. The *praefectus urbi* was originally devised by Augustus as a kind of minister of public security, hence his command of the urban cohorts.[103] This was the situation in Tiberius' reign, but by AD 61 under Nero the prefect's jurisdiction in certain criminal cases was so well established that a man was condemned to exile by the senate for bringing accusations before a *quaestio perpetua* in order to avoid their being heard by the prefect of the city, his plan being to mishandle the prosecution in the *quaestio* and so prevent the defendant being tried again – in Roman terms a form of *praevaricatio*.[104] The poet Statius' praise of Rutilius Gallicus, prefect under Domitian in about AD 90, suggests that the latter's jurisdiction was then especially exercised over common criminals who violently disturbed the peace, whether at Rome or elsewhere in Italy – men who might be imprisoned or flogged.[105] However, under Trajan, Pliny sat as assessor to the prefect in a case where two promising young orators were speaking on either side, which suggests a defendant of some status and importance, perhaps accused of murder or violence[106] By the time Ulpian wrote his work *On the Duties of the Prefect of the City* in the early third century, the prefect had become a universal criminal magistrate for cases up to 100 miles from the city of Rome with powers of punishment appropriate for persons of high rank.[107]

Limited jurisdictions inferior to that of the city prefect were acquired by the prefect of the watch (*praefectus vigilum*) in matters relating to fires and theft,[108] and perhaps by the prefect of the corn-supply (*praefectus annonae*),[109] in order that the latter could determine whether a fine for corn-hoarding was appropriate. More important in the long term were the judicial powers granted to the prefects of the guard (*praefecti praetorio*).[110] The first securely attested to have acted as a judge at Rome is Q. Marcius Turbo under Hadrian.[111] Later, in the reign of Marcus Aurelius we find on a well-known inscription from Saepinum the prefects Bassaeus Rufus and Macrinius Vindex threatening the local magistrates with an inquiry and punishment because of their interference with flocks belonging to the imperial treasury.[112] Unfortunately we have no idea of the scope of the praetorian prefects' judicial activity before the late empire, when it was wide-ranging.

It is generally assumed that *cognitio* (investigation by magistrates) had supplanted the operations of the criminal tribunals at Rome by the epoch of the great classical jurists at the beginning of the third century AD. However, due to the scarcity of evidence it may be better to leave the question open. The younger Pliny certainly knew of a praetor in charge of a *quaestio perpetua*.[113] In the third century AD Paul's prescription of the written form to be used for accusations for adultery had just two alternative addressees – a praetor (who in this era can only have been the man in charge of the criminal tribunal) or a proconsul (the authority in a province).[114] Hence, we should assume that the *quaestio de adulteriis* was still functioning. As for the alleged 3,000 accusations for adultery arising from Septimius Severus' legislation that the historian Dio Cassius claims to have seen inscribed on the album when consul in about AD 205,[115] it seems as likely that these were originally addressed to the appropriate praetor as to one of the prefects or the emperor himself (whether Dio was considering them for possible hearing in the senate or not).

7. Other Developments in the Principate

The crimes prosecuted under the statutes of the late Republic and Augustus were extended and redefined by decisions of the emperor or senate. For example, an unidentifiable decree of the senate embraced offences committed in the municipalities in the law against electoral bribery (*ambitus*); by then, according to Modestinus, the elections in Rome were totally controlled by the emperor.[116] The 'extortion' or recovery law (*de repetundis*) was applied to the activities of those who were neither Roman magistrates nor senators.[117] New categories of violence were specified as actionable under the statute; in two rescripts of Hadrian the homicide law (*de sicariis et veneficis*) was interpreted to cover wounding with the intention to kill and killing through culpable negligence;[118] Sulla's law about forgery was refined in AD 16 by a decree of the senate in relation to wills and later by other measures,[119] as were the provisions against false and collusive accusation (*calumnia* and *praevaricatio*) through a senatorial decree of AD 61.[120] A number of forms of insulting or outrageous behaviour, the majority of them probably already actionable under Sulla's *lex de iniuriis* or other statutes, were singled out for investigation by *cognitio* and in some cases (e.g., the rape or seduction of boys or girls) for capital punishment.[121]

More interesting, however, is the extension of the criminal law into matters previously left to civil actions or not subject to legal action at all. By the early third century AD the *cognitio* procedure was being used to investigate not only offences that were actionable by prosecution before one of the criminal tribunals but also those outside that field. It is not clear whether there were any major steps in this direction or simply a piecemeal development through a series of imperial edicts or rescripts.[122] Convicted hoarders of goods, including foodstuffs, who were termed *dardanarii*, could be 'relegated' or forced to do public works.[123] We find the term *stellionatus* used to describe various refined types of fraud, including corrupt practice in the sale of goods and granting of security.[124] The violation of graves became a crime.[125] Certain kinds of theft were distinguished for criminal action, including theft by night or with a weapon (capital offences under the Twelve Tables), cattle-rustling, looting, housebreaking, and theft from the baths.[126]

8. PENALTIES UNDER THE PRINCIPATE

By the time of Julius Caesar's death the capital penalty in the statutes governing the criminal tribunals seems generally to have become banishment in the shape of interdiction of fire and water. However, a full capital penalty was exacted for certain treasonable actions both under the triumvirate and during Augustus' reign.[127] Under Tiberius it is clear that those condemned in the senate on a capital charge might face execution, and from then onwards one of the yardsticks by which the senatorial order judged emperors was whether they approved of executing members of the elite or not. In practice, this was mitigated by the possibility of avoiding humiliation through being allowed to commit suicide. Moreover, suicide before condemnation might induce the emperor to be generous in conceding the property of such persons to their family. The Augustan laws, like those of the late Republic, provided rewards for accusers, both in the form of preferment in the pursuit of public office and financial compensation, the latter to come from the estates of the condemned.[128] The Republican concept of exile, moreover, had now become somewhat outdated. Exiled men had been able to pass the time in an agreeable Greek city. We find Augustus by contrast selecting islands for the banished, which were intended to be penally restrictive if not necessarily uncomfortable. His daughter Julia went to a villa on Pandateria off the coast of Latium, her lover Sempronius Gracchus to Cercina off Tunisia; Cassius Severus was sent first to Crete and then, when he would not give up writing lampoons, to the small rocky island of Seriphos in the Aegean.[129]

By the time of the classical jurists the range of non-financial penalties had been extended and their nature refined through decisions by emperors or the senate. Moreover, they were varied according to not only the nature of the crime but also the status of the criminal. It seems to have been mainly the elite who could profit from the concession of exile under the Republic; common criminals were likely to be killed or rendered virtual slaves. Under the Principate a distinction developed between 'the more honourable' (*honestiores*) and 'the more humble' (*humiliores*).[130] Signs of this can be seen in second century AD rescripts about local senators,[131] but the full elaboration of the distinction probably came only in the Severan period. For the more honourable the supreme penalty was now execution by the sword, not by the traditional axe or rope. The ban on fire and water was no more, replaced by deportation to an island with confiscation of property. The more humble, including slaves, might be crucified, hanged, burnt alive, or exposed to the beasts; less drastic penalties, but likely to bring a slow death, were condemnation to the mines or to public work – that is, hard labour.[132] *Relegatio* had now become a criminal penalty, milder than deportation in that it was temporary not permanent. Penalties might be aggravated by beatings with sticks or whips, dependent on the victim's status. Prison was still in theory a measure for detention before trial or execution, but in practice it was frequently used as a punishment.[133] When Christianity came to dominate the empire, the cruelty of penalties generally was not reduced but, if anything, intensified.[134]

9. Conclusion

About AD 200 the main lines for the development of criminal law had already been set. Our discussion has been of the law of Rome and Italy, but the evolution of the Roman empire meant that this law became relatively less important than the law exercised in the provinces: it is in this context that we should view the decline of both the criminal tribunals and the judicial function of the senate and the corresponding growth of *cognitio* by magistrates. In the later empire Rome and Italy were to become provinces and the system of provincial justice – based on the governor, the judges he appointed, and appeal to the emperor or deputies he appointed – became the general model for procedure. In the new system local justice was dispensed by a *defensor civitatis* subject to the governor; legal advisers were appointed to provincial governors; appeal from most of the governors was directed to the praetorian prefects or their deputies (*vicarii*) in each diocese: in effect, justice became one element in an hierarchically organized administration.[135] Accusation became little more than the laying of information, though threatened with dire penalties if it were proved to be calumny. The substantive law essentially grew through an accretion of imperial decisions in response to particular situations, which led to a mass of incoherent material. Only occasionally were there attempts to set this in order, above all the Theodosian *Code* of AD 438.[136]

It may be argued that in the course of Roman history criminal law became increasingly determined by lawyers. However, the forces that created it were for the most part political: it was a response to the needs of the community, as its leaders perceived them, and what they believed to be popular sentiment. As such the creation and reform of criminal justice were essentially reactive, like most political measures, rather than the articulation of basic concepts. However, in spite of the lack of theory in the work of the lawyers of the Principate in the criminal field, consideration of the statutes and decrees by which the law was created suggests that those behind them did in fact deliberate about principle. For example, it was a decision of principle by those who introduced the permanent criminal tribunals in the late Republic to assign judgment to a large jury, as impartial as could be assured, as a half-way house between a popular assembly and the circle of assessors that a criminal investigator had previously gathered around him. It was equally a matter of principle to reward accusers beyond compensation. The legislators doubtless had examples from the laws of the Greeks before them,[137] but to transpose these into a Roman context required more than simple imitation. The codification of law that Cicero advocated and Julius Caesar promised was a mirage. Nevertheless, Augustus' criminal legislation, in spite of the special pressures that determined elements in it, suggests that he aimed to create a system for the long term. It is a tribute to what he and his Republican predecessors created that the subsequent substantive law was for the most part a series of glosses on their work.

NOTES

1. A. Lintott, *The Constitution of the Roman Republic* (Oxford, 1999), 109, 125–9.
2. See, e.g., *Roman Statutes*, no. 7 lines 7–13.
3. Cic. *Inv.* 2.66.
4. Polyb. 6.14.4–5; Cic. *ad Brut.* 23.3.
5. Vitr. 6.5.2; A. Lintott, 'Legal Procedure in Cicero's time', in *Cicero the Advocate*, ed. J. Powell and J. Paterson (Oxford, 2004), 62–4; F. Coarelli, 'I luoghi del processo', in *La repressione criminale nella Roma repubblicana fra norma e persuasione*, ed. B. Santalucia (Pavia, 2009), 3–13.
6. Cic. *Rosc. Am.* 12.
7. Cic. *Brut.* 200.
8. Val. Max. 9.12.7.
9. Cic. *Deiot.* 5–7.
10. FIRA I pp. 9, 13–4, 17; W. Kunkel, *Untersuchungen zur Entwicklung des römischen Kriminalverfahrens in vorsullanischer Zeit* (Munich, 1962), 39ff.; J. D. Cloud, '*Parricidium* from the *lex Numae* to the *lex Pompeia de parricidiis*', *ZSS* 88 (1971): 1–66.
11. *Roman Statutes*, no. 40 I.17–21; Lintott (n. 1), 13, 24, 33 n. 2.
12. *Roman Statutes*, no. 40 I.13–15; *Exodus* 21.23; Diod. 12.17.4; Lintott (n. 1), 25–6.
13. *Roman Statutes*, no. 40 VIII.5–6, 12.
14. Kunkel (n. 10), 97ff.; A. Lintott, *Violence in Republican Rome*, 2nd edn. (Oxford, 1999) 150.
15. Lintott (n. 1) 11–16, 24; A. Lintott, '*Provocatio* from the Struggle of the Orders to the Principate', *ANRW* vol. I.2, 226–67.
16. Lintott (n. 15), 226–8, 235–8; Lintott (n. 14), 150–4.
17. Cic. *Dom.* 45; *Roman Statutes*, no. 13 lines 13–17; Livy 25.3.12–18, 4.7–11; A. Lintott, '*Provocatio* e *iudicium populi* dopo Kunkel', in *La repressione criminale nella Roma repubblicana fra norma e persuasione*, ed. B. Santalucia (Pavia, 2009), 15–24.
18. *Roman Statutes*, no. 40 IX.1–2; Lintott (n. 1), 150–1.
19. Polyb. 6.14.7–8; Livy 25.3–4; R. Pesaresi, *Studi sul processo penale in età repubblicana* (Naples, 2005), 123–59.
20. Lintott (n. 1), 32–4.
21. J. Bleicken, 'Ursprung und Bedeutung des Provokationsrechtes', *ZSS* 76 (1959): 352ff; Lintott (n. 1), 151.
22. B. Santalucia, *Diritto e processo penale nell'antica Roma*, 2nd edn. (Milan, 1998), 22–3, 54–5.
23. Lintott (n. 1), 102–5; W. Nippel, *Public Order in Ancient Rome* (Cambridge, 1995), 22–6; Kunkel (n. 10), 97ff.; C. Cascione, *Tresviri capitales. Storia di una magistratura minore* (Naples, 1999).

24. Cic. *Brut.* 85ff.; Kunkel (n. 10) 45ff.; Lintott (n. 1) 157–8; A. Lintott, *Judicial Reform and Land Reform in the Roman Republic* (Cambridge, 1992), 11–12.
25. Cic. *Brut.* 87.
26. Lintott (n. 24), 66–70; *Roman Statutes*, no. 1.
27. *Roman Statutes*, nos. 5–9, 11, 27.
28. Livy 43.2; Lintott (n. 24), 12–14; A. Lintott, 'The *Leges de Repetundis* and Associate Measures under the Republic', *ZSS* 98 (1981): 164–76; C. Venturini, 'La repressione degli abusi dei magistrati romani ai danni delle popolazioni soggette fino alla *lex Calpurnia* del 149 a.c.", *BIDR* 72 (1969): 19–87.
29. Lintott (n. 24), 14–16.
30. *Roman Statutes*, no. 1; Lintott (n. 24), 88ff.
31. Lines 1–12.
32. Lines 12–28.
33. Lines 30–56.
34. Lines 57–88.
35. Lintott (n. 24), 27–9; Lintott (n. 28), 186–205.
36. D. 47.10.5; D. 48.8–10, 14; Lintott (n. 14), 109–24; J. D. Cloud, 'The Constitution and Criminal Law', in *CAH* IX (1994), 514–30.
37. Lintott (n. 5), 74–7; A. Lintott, '*Delator* and *Index*: Informers and Accusers at Rome from the Republic to the early Principate', *Accordia Research Papers* 9 (2001–3): 109–14.
38. Asc. *Corn.* 60–1 (Clark); Quint. *Inst.* 6.4.1ff.; A. Lintott, *Cicero as Evidence: A Historian's Companion* (Oxford, 2008), 20–1.
39. Cic. *Phil.*1.21; J. T. Ramsey, 'Mark Antony's Judicial Reform and its Revival under the triumvirs', *JRS* 95 (2005): 20–37.
40. Lintott (n. 24), 137–9 on *lex rep.* 56.
41. *Roman Statutes*, no. 25, ch. 102; Cicero, *Verr.* 1.32; 2 *Verr.* 1.25; *Flacc.* 82.
42. Asc. *Mil.* 39, ll. 20–4 (Clark).
43. Cic. *Rab. perd.* 16; *Clu.* 170; *Sull.* 89; *Sest.* 146. *Contra* G. P. Kelly, *A History of Exile under the Roman Republic* (Cambridge, 2006), 39ff.
44. Cic. *Att.* 3.4; Plut. Cic. 32.1; Dio 38.17.7.
45. Lintott (n. 28), 209–12.
46. Lintott (n. 28), 198–205.
47. Suet. *Iul.* 41.2; 42.3; 44.1; Cic. *Phil.*1.23.
48. Ramsey (n. 39).
49. *Res Gestae* 6.1–2.
50. Cf. Dio 54.18.2–3.
51. Dio 51.19.6.
52. *Roman Statutes*, nos. 37–8, *Tab. Heb.* 8, 11, 17, 31; *SC de aquaeductibus*, Fronto, *de aq.*101 (= FIRA 1 no. 41).
53. Suet. *Aug.* 32.3; *Calig.*16.2; *Galb.* 14.3.
54. Suet. *Aug.* 37; Tac. *Ann.* 3.30; V. Ehrenberg and A. H. M. Jones, *Documents Illustrating the Reigns of Augustus and Tiberius*, 2nd edn. (Oxford, 1976), no. 209.
55. Suetonius, *Aug.* 32.2–3; O. Behrends, *Die römische Geschworenenverfassung* (Göttingen, 1970).
56. Santalucia (n. 22), 190–1.
57. FIRA I no. 44, col. III.
58. D. 22.5.4, cf. FIRA I no. 68, V, 116–8.

59. D. 48.14.1.4.
60. Asc. *Scaur.* 20, ll. 14–16 (Clark).
61. D. 48.13.5. pr.–1.
62. D. 46.6.7; *PS* 5.26.1–2; Lintott (n. 15), 265–6.
63. D. 48.13; cf. Dio 54.17.1 for changes in the appointment of *curatores*.
64. E.g. Livy 8.22.2–3; 10.31.9; 25.2.9.
65. S. Treggiari, *Roman Marriage: Iusti Coniuges from the time of Cicero to the time of Ulpian* (Oxford, 1991), 264ff., with doubts about the last point.
66. Sall. *Hist.* 1.61M = Plut. *Sull.*41.3; *Collatio* 4.2.2.
67. D. 48.5.23, 24.
68. D. 48.5.25.
69. Plin. *Ep.* 6.31.4–6.
70. Tac. *Ann.* 3.25.
71. 51.19.6.
72. See n. 39, this chapter.
73. J. M. Kelly, Princeps Iudex. *Eine Untersuchung zu der Begrundung der kaiserlichen Gerichtsbarkeit* (Weimar, 1957), 17ff.; *contra*, e.g., J. Bleicken *Senatsgericht und Kaisergericht* (Göttingen, 1962), 71.
74. Lintott (n. 15), 241–3, 263–4.
75. Suet. *Aug.* 33.
76. FIRA I no. 68, II.
77. Santalucia (n. 22), 216f.
78. Tac. *Ann.* 1.75.
79. Sen. *Apocol.* passim; Suet. *Claud.*14–15.
80. Tac. *Ann.* 13.4; 15.55ff.
81. Tac. *Dial.* 7.1.
82. FIRA I no. 68, V; Santalucia (n. 22), 206–13.
83. Cic. *Cat.* 3.8–15; *Sull.* 36–42; Sall. *Cat.* 46.6–47.4.
84. Ov. *Trist.* 2.131–2.
85. Tac. *Ann.* 1.53; 3.24.
86. Tac. *Ann.* 1.72; 4.21; *Dial.*19.1; 26.4.
87. Tac. *Ann.* 3.68, cf. 67; Sen. *Ira* 2.5.5.
88. FIRA I no. 68, V; R. Sherk, *Roman Documents from the Greek East* (Baltimore, 1969), no. 31.
89. Tac. *Ann.* 1.74; Plin. *Ep.* 2.11.5.
90. J. E. Allison and J. D. Cloud, 'The *lex Iulia Maietatis*', *Latomus* 21: (1962) 711–31; Santalucia (n. 22), 195–6, 256–7.
91. W. Eck, A. Caballos, and F. Fernandez, *Das senatus consultum de Cn. Pisone patre* (Munich, 1996), 40, lines 32–3.
92. Tac. *Ann.* 3.50–1; 4.20.
93. Plin. *Ep.* 2.11.4; 4.9.17, cf. 5.20.7.
94. Y. Rivière, *Les délateurs sous l'empire romain* (Rome, 2002), 161ff.
95. Eck et al. (n. 91), 40, lines 23–5.
96. Tac. *Ann.* 3.10–11, 13.
97. Plin. *Ep.* 2.11.14–18; 4.9.3–15.
98. Plin. *Ep.* 3.9.
99. Tac. *Ann.* 4.19–20; cf. D. 1.16.4.2.
100. Sall. *Jug.* 40.

101. T. Mommsen, *Römisches Strafrecht* (Leipzig, 1899), 346ff.
102. Santalucia (n. 22), 213.
103. Tac. *Ann.* 6.10–11; *Hist.* 3.64.
104. Tac. *Ann.* 14.41.
105. Stat. *Silv.* 1.4.9–16, 39–48.
106. Plin. *Ep.* 6.11.
107. D. 1.12.1 *pr.*, 4, 13; Santalucia (n. 22), 221–4; D. Mantovani, 'Sulla competenza penale del *praefectus urbi* attraverso il *liber singularis* di Ulpiano', in *Idee vecchie e nuove sul diritto criminale romano*, ed. A. Burdese (Padua, 1988), 171–223.
108. D. 1.15.3.1, 5; D. 47.2.57.1.
109. D. 48.2.13; D. 48.12.3.1.
110. D.1.11.
111. Dio 69.18.3–4.
112. FIRA I no. 61.
113. *Ep.* 5.9.3.
114. D. 48.2.3. But see P. Garnsey, 'Adultery Trials and the Survival of the *Quaestiones* in the Severan Age', *JRS* 57 (1967): 56–60.
115. Dio 77(76).16.4. See F. Millar, *A Study of Cassius Dio* (Oxford, 1964), 204–7 for the date.
116. D. 48.14.1.
117. D. 48.19.38.10; Santalucia (n. 22), 258f.
118. Santalucia (n. 22) 260ff.
119. D. 48.10; Santalucia (n. 22), 263f.
120. D. 48.16; Santalucia (n. 22), 264f.
121. D. 47.10.35; D. 47.11.1.1–2.
122. Santalucia (n. 22), 266–8.
123. D. 47.11.6.
124. D. 47.20; L. Garofalo, *La persecuzione dello stellionato in diritto romano* (Padua, 1992).
125. D. 47.12.
126. D. 47.17, 18.
127. Tac. *Ann.* 1.10.
128. S. H. Rutledge, *Imperial Inquisitions: Prosecutors and Informants from Tiberius to Domitian* (London & New York, 2001); Rivière (n. 94); Lintott (n. 37).
129. Tac. *Ann.* 1.53; 4.2; X. Lafon, 'Les îles de la mer Tyrrhénienne: entre palais et prisons sous les Julio-Claudiens', in *Carcer. Prison et Privation de Liberté dans l'antiquité classique: Actes du colloque de Strasbourg (5 et 6 décembre 1997)*, ed. C. Bertrand-Dagenbach (Paris, 1999), 149–61; Y. Rivière, 'L'Italie, les îles et le continent; recherches sur l'exil et l'administration du territoire impérial (Ier–IIIe siècles)', *Entretiens Fondation Hardt* 54 (2008): 261–310.
130. P. Garnsey *Social Status and Legal Privilege in the Roman Empire* (Oxford, 1970); R. Rilinger *Humiliores – Honestiores* (Munich, 1988).
131. D. 49.19.15; D. 48.22.6.2.
132. See, esp., D. 48.19.8, 19, 28.1, and 28.11ff.; Santalucia (n. 22), 249ff.
133. D. 48.19.8.9; Y. Rivière, 'Détention préventive, mise à l'épreuve et démonstration de la preuve (Ier–IIIe siècles ap. J.-C)', in Bertrand-Dagenbach (n. 129), 57–73; J.-U. Krause, *Gefängnisse im Römischen Reich* (Stuttgart, 1996); J.-U. Krause, 'Prisons et crimes dans l'Empire romain', in Bertrand-Dagenbach (n. 129), 118–28; A. Lovato, *Il carcere nel diritto penale romano (dai Severi a Giustiniano)* (Bari, 1994).

134. Krause (n. 133); J. Harries, *Law and Empire in Late Antiquity* (Cambridge, 1999), 135f.
135. Santalucia (n. 22), 269–80; A. H. M. Jones, *The Later Roman Empire* (Oxford, 1964, repr. 1973), vol. 1, 470–522; vol. 2, 1202–20.
136. Harries (n. 134).
137. Lintott (n. 24), 31–2.

16 Public Law

A. J. B. Sirks

1. Introduction

Public law is, as Ulpian put it, the law *quod ad statum rei Romanae spectat*, 'which regards the state of the Roman commonwealth'. It therefore covers everything that does not concern the affairs of individual citizens: what we now call constitutional, criminal, and administrative law. This chapter does not cover the substance of criminal law.[1] It is concerned with 'public' law, meaning constitutional as well as administrative law, both at the level of the empire and at the local level. It considers the formal elements of public law in the pre-imperial period, and the formal and substantive elements of public law during the imperial period, as well as further changes made under Diocletian and up to the end of the fifth century AD.

2. The Constitution of the Empire

For a better understanding of the whole public law of the Roman empire, it is useful to recall the situation in the Mediterranean in the republican period. The Mediterranean world at that time was a tapestry of independent city-states, each with its own written – or often unwritten – constitution, exercising its own foreign policy, having its own legislation, jurisdiction and administration, and imposing its own taxes on its citizens and residents. The major exception to this was Egypt, where the pharaoh was sole ruler, commander of the army, lawgiver, and judge. Rome was, originally, just another city-state with its own institutions. They were the senate, with advisory power (originally consisting of the heads of the patrician families, with the addition of former magistrates); the elected magistrates, with legislative and executive power (consuls, praetors, aediles, censors, dictator); and the people's assemblies, with legislative power (the *populus Romanus* and the *plebs*). When larger entities began to be created, such as the Macedonian kingdom and its successor states, and the successor to all of these, the Roman empire, the existing constitutional structures were maintained. For Rome that meant that institutions designed for a city and its surrounding region now had to work for an ever-increasing and ultimately enormous area. By the first century BC it became clear that this was not possible. We do not know precisely what designs Julius Caesar had in mind. Perhaps it was indeed (as his detractors claimed) a monarchy modelled on the Hellenistic kings; that would have been better suited to a large territorial state than the republican constitution. But his murder made clear that that was very threatening to a large part of the Roman elite who wanted to keep the old system.

Once Antony and Cleopatra had been defeated and the civil war had come to an end, Rome's empire stretched all around the Mediterranean Sea, roughly bounded in the North by the Rhine and Danube, in the East by the Euphrates and Tigris, and in the South by the Sahara. All territories had formally been subjected to the Roman people (meaning Rome, Italy, and certain colonies) as provinces. Only a few towns such as Marseilles were, as *civitates liberae et foederatae*, formally on a par with Rome. The provinces were governed by former magistrates of Rome, appointed by the Roman senate. The situation now became complicated. Formally, the republican institutions persisted, but they had been crafted for a city-state and were not fit for an empire such as this.

Reform was necessary. But Caesar's adoptive son Octavian (later Augustus) was very conscious of the resistance to Caesar's aspirations and, after he had removed all opposition by 27 BC, thought it wise to retain the republican constitution. He did so by modifying it to the extent that alongside the unwritten customary constitution was an unwritten addendum, which effectively transferred most legislative and judicial power and the command of the army to him and his designated successors (who would also adopt the name of Caesar). Certain formal decisions provided the basis for the constitutional position of the emperor. On 13 January 27 BC, in a session of the senate, Octavian laid down all his powers as triumvir. He was then awarded the title 'Augustus', and the provinces were divided between him and the senate. He was to govern seven provinces with legions; the other twelve were to be governed by senatorial appointees. Augustus also received proconsular power (*imperium proconsulare*) and the command of the army. In 23 BC the power of a tribune (*tribunicia potestas*) was awarded to him as well. Both titles implied the right to issue edicts. After 12 BC he became *pontifex maximus* too. These three attributes remained constant for every emperor that followed. In addition, in the early years of the empire, at the accession of each new emperor a statute was passed in which these powers were awarded to him.[2] They included the power to do everything which was in the interest of the state (*ex usu rei publicae*), such as concluding treaties. One of these, the *lex de imperio Vespasiani*, is preserved. Until AD 383 imperial titles still continued to mention *tribunicia potestas* and *imperium proconsulare*.

At the beginning of the principate the emperor was still just one of several constitutional organs, alongside the assemblies of the Roman people (the *comitia* and the *concilium plebis*) and the senate, albeit his position was now one of overwhelming authority and power. This changed: in the first century both the *comitia* and *concilium plebis* disappeared, and by the end of the second century the senate was reduced to a formality. It remained so. In AD 330 Constantinople was made the second capital, with its own senate and functionaries, but that did not change the situation. Its members were co-opted from sons of senators; high functionaries also became members; and the emperors could always appoint senators. Emperors were by this time appointed by the army, and the senate formally confirmed the candidate who had proved himself superior to the others. All the provinces were now governed by governors, appointed by the emperor alone.

Diocletian (who ruled from AD 284–305) changed the constitution. The empire would now have two emperors, called Augusti, who would each govern half of the empire. Each would appoint a future successor, called Caesar, who would administer a part of his half and succeed him after a certain period. The empire was divided into a number of praetorian prefectures, each prefecture into dioceses, each diocese comprising a number of provinces. Diocletian more than doubled the number of provinces, to over a hundred. He further separated the military administration from the civil administration. Governors were now pure civil servants. Military commanders ultimately reported to *magistri militum* and *magistri equitum*, who in their turn reported to the emperor. The administration was subject to checks: one could appeal against decisions.

Diocletian's creation of two Augusti and two Caesars did not last long. As soon as AD 324 Constantine seized sole power. The other innovations, however, did remain. Prospective emperors still needed the support of an army, but we can also see that being related to a former emperor was a point in a candidate's favour. We see the same pattern here as is found with the senate and town councillors: birth and family ties became strong factors. But by now the army offered opportunities for social climbing: Valentinian and Valens began as soldiers; still later, barbarian generals exercised great influence and occupied high office. By that time (mid-fourth century) the powers of the emperor had fused into a customary amalgam of legislative, judicial, and administrative power, and after AD 383 the references to *tribunicia potestas* and proconsular *imperium* were dropped. The transfer of power, now complete, became the core of the unwritten constitution, the emperor being sole lawgiver, supreme judge, supreme administrator, and army commander. The republican institutions survived in a merely formal sense, although in the west the senate remained, politically and economically, a formidable power block. When Theodosius died in AD 395, his two young sons were without difficulty accepted as emperors. From that time the dynastic principle was a constitutional and almost conclusive factor in succession to the empire. It can be seen in the marriage policy of the emperors and usurpers: Pulcheria, the sister of Theodosius II, married the general Marcian to legitimize him as the successor to her brother; the usurper Petronius Probus forced a daughter of Valentinian III to marry his son.

3. Legislation in the Empire

The constitutional development also had an impact upon the way legislation was made. The republic knew of statutes (*leges rogatae*), plebiscites (*plebiscita*), resolutions of the senate (*senatusconsulta*), and edicts (*edicta*). Statutes were still enacted in the first century. However, we do not find any trace of the popular assemblies (*comitia*) in the second century; and, significantly, after the second century the reference to a person's voting tribe, which used to be added in names just before the cognomen, is no longer mentioned in inscriptions. Resolutions of the senate are still found in the second century (although certainly needing imperial approval), but with the Severan emperors the emperor's speech in the senate (*oratio in senatu habita*) itself appears as a source of law. That implies that a *senatusconsultum* was superfluous now. Later on it was enough that a letter from the emperor was read in the senate by his representative. Thus, by the beginning of the third century these sources of law were at an end; the plebiscite had already suffered the same fate even under Augustus.

Although the emperor had since the beginning of the second century been de facto the sole lawgiver, supreme judge, and administrator of the empire, that certainly did not imply that he had absolute power. It is repeatedly stated that a good emperor subordinates himself to the rule of law,[3] and the emperor himself said so: 'our authority depends on the authority of the law' (*de auctoritate iuris nostra pendet auctoritas*).[4] This was not mere propaganda and ideology. Practice and legislation were a development of the existing structures rather than brusque innovation, and mostly a response to litigation or problems which had arisen at the lower levels of government.[5] Private individuals could also appeal against decisions of officials.

New sources of law now made their appearance. The instructions given to governors (*mandata*) gained force of law. New law also derived from the emperor's jurisdiction and his interpretation of existing law. This made customary law into written law. As supreme judge the emperor could interpret existing rules in his judgments or replies to individual petitions and, if it was of general purport, a new interpretation would be effective. All imperial rulings were now conveniently categorized as 'constitutions'. According to a constitution of AD 426 (the so-called Law of Citations),[6] confirming existing practice, imperial letters sent to officials were to be accepted as general rules if they were general in purport and contained a reference to an edict, for example when they contained an order that they should be published everywhere by edict (this must already have been the case at the beginning of the fourth century) or if they were said to constitute a general rule, a *lex generalis*. They then acquired the force of an edict (*lex edictalis*). Thus, we see in the late empire three main sources of formal imperial legislation: the *oratio*, the *lex edictalis*, and of course the edict proper (*edictum*). Although in practice there was no difference between these, the formal differences were still observed. All of them were published: for *senatusconsulta* it was sufficient to deposit them in the archives; for the others the text was put on display. It is not clear whether imperial legislation became effective immediately upon the speech or imperial approval, on the signing of the letter or edict, or upon publication. The last would lead to the law coming into force at different times in the provinces.

In the republic and early principate a governor could issue an edict for his province and by that means create substantive provincial law. Pliny's letters to Trajan show the measure of Roman involvement in provincial and local affairs.[7] Edicts of prefects and governors were still issued and had force in their areas, yet they now could not prevail against general rules issued by the emperor. References in private law to regional custom or law (*mos* or *lex regionis*) exist but not much is known about this: the best documented is a specific rule on manumission for the province of Macedonia before and after the *constitutio Antoniniana* (AD 212).[8] In administrative law there certainly were specific provincial or regional arrangements. Criminal law was based on two pillars: (i) customary law together with a number of statutes on particular crimes; and (ii) the power of the authorities to maintain public order, with considerable discretion in the application of sanctions. There was also some military law.

But the main body of law – that is, private law – was customary, largely laid down in the succinct and discrete formulae (actions) of the praetorian edict. It was commentary by the jurists on the edict after its canonization in AD 138 and their attempts to systematize the law in their various writings which made this law into a written law, which also included legislation such as constitutions and mandates to governors. As 'ancient law' (*ius vetus*) all of these had in any case by the beginning of the fourth century acquired legal force: 'we confirm all the writings of Papinian, Paul, Gaius, Ulpian and Modestinus'.[9] Their authenticity had for that reason become a matter of imperial interest.[10] Modifications were made by later legislation.

4. Jurisdiction in the Empire

Originally the Mediterranean city-states had their own jurisdictions; their incorporation into the empire did not change this as such, except for criminal and administrative law where the Roman authorities, in the form of the provincial governor, exercised jurisdiction. If the town was not a Roman one, the governor would also handle civil cases between Romans; after the *constitutio Antoniniana* of AD 212, which granted Roman citizenship to almost all non-Romans, this applied to everybody. But it did not have to end there. The function of emperor also included a judicial aspect, namely that of judge. He might, like any other respectable citizen, act as a judge in private matters, but in addition we see that Tiberius admonished judges, while Claudius liked to sit as a judge himself.[11] Later on appeals were also lodged with the emperor. The appeal as an institution most likely developed from the fact that one could appeal from an agent or delegate to his principal. In the first century AD *procuratores fisci* were introduced, representing the emperor, and in general the emperors appointed the governors as their representatives. Thus, it will have been natural to appeal from them to their principal, the emperor. Further, in criminal law there existed the *provocatio ad populum* in capital cases: if a magistrate had condemned a citizen to death, the condemned could appeal to the *plebs* or *populus*. Since the emperor exercised the *tribunicia potestas*, it is easy to understand how this became *provocatio ad principem*. The result of all of this was that in the second century the emperor was the supreme and ultimate judge in almost all legal cases. This was primarily exercised by him in person, in his council (*consilium*).[12] The exceptions were small cases at the local level, and cases of extortion and treason, in which the senate acted as a separate court. The procedure followed on appeal was that of extraordinary *cognitio*. In other words, the formulary procedure did not apply.[13] The *cognitio* was rather formless and characterized by the fact that the entire procedure (examination of the plea, acceptance, examination of the case, and judgment) took place before one and the same magistrate; by contrast, the two stages of the formulary procedure were divided between magistrate and judge. *Cognitio* was used for private, criminal, and administrative processes alike, which were distinguished only by special rules and the substantive law applicable. Military commanders judged military cases at first instance. In criminal and civil cases one could appeal the judgment from a local council or court or magistrate to the provincial governor; similarly in military cases. From him one could appeal again to the emperor or to his representative. If the latter had been given delegated power to judge (*vice sacra iudicans*), no final appeal to the emperor was possible (as with the *comes sacrarum largitionum*: see Section 9). Citizens could also file a petition. Both litigants in a case and officials could submit a petition to the emperor for advice on interpretation and would receive an answer (*rescriptum*) which again, if of general purport, would be valid in other cases. Private collections were made (such as the Apokrimata, during Septimius Severus' visit to Egypt in 200).[14] The Gregorian and Hermogenian *Codes* were collections of rescripts most likely made from imperial records which gained universal acceptance.[15] A work of the fourth century, the Fragmenta Vaticana, combines extracts from legal authors with rescripts and other constitutions, arranged under headings according to subject matter.[16]

5. The Imperial Bureaucracy

Trajan transformed the imperial administration from a domestic staff (for instance, Claudius had often used his own freedmen) into a civil service, with a career to be followed through various levels, as well as remuneration. The emperor himself was assisted by prefects, a council, secretaries, other officials, and offices (*scrinia*). This administration was accompanied by the development of an administrative law, which followed the same procedure and route of appeal as did private and criminal law. Broadly speaking, the tasks of the central administration were safeguarding public order and taxation (later, this became largely an imperial task itself: see Section 9); providing justice; defending the realm; providing and maintaining the main roads and state communications (the postal system); and safeguarding the provision of public distributions in Rome (later on in Constantinople, and also in Alexandria and Carthage). At a provincial level these tasks fell to the governors of the provinces, who if there were troops stationed there were at the same time military commanders (in the principate not all provinces had legions stationed in them). They reported straight to the emperor. The praetorian prefects were in charge of the provincial administration including taxation. In the fourth century we also find among others the *comes sacrarum largitionum* for the state treasury and the *comes privatarum rerum* for the management of the imperial domains, while the *quaestor sacri palatii* was responsible for drafting legislation (previously this had been done by the praetorian prefects). The provision of the public distributions in Rome was under the supervision of the prefect for the *annona*. Rome itself was governed by the urban prefect, as later was Constantinople. These prefects were, like the governors, formally lieutenants for the emperor. Elaborate rules regulated the organization and competences of these offices.

This does not mean that there was no corruption or bribery in the Roman empire or abuse of power: on the contrary, already in the republic a statute had been passed against corruption; later came the *lex Iulia de repetundis*; and the emperors repeatedly issued measures against corrupt practices, such as in AD 414: 'With remedies well planned Our Clemency provides against the dissimulation and the petty corruption (*corruptela*) of the offices of the prefect of the city and of the prefect of the annona.' In this case the context was covering up (naturally for payment of money) that a shipmaster had delivered less public grain in Ostia than he should have. The guilty officer was to be sent to Africa. If the prefect of the annona allowed the shipmaster to delay his case (in the hope, of course, of permanently delaying it), he and his office were to be fined five pounds of gold.[17] Sometimes the emperor admitted his own helplessness: 'But since very often in some cases we are so constrained by the shameless greed of petitioners for such [confiscated] property that we even grant requests which should not be allowed.'[18] A corps of officials, the *agentes in rebus*, was set up in the fourth century to inspect the functioning of the administration and to spy; unfortunately they often abused their position. So corruption was repudiated, one could try to seek redress against administrative abuse, and redress was given – but how often we do not know. Lower down the scale, recourse to a more powerful person could always help against a local potentate, as long as the latter was not too well connected higher up in the system. The rise of bishops as arbiters may indicate that they offered better prospects at the lower levels of the system. But in the end the large number of rescripts in Justinian's *Code* which are reproduced from the Gregorian and Hermogenian *Codes* (dating from about AD 293 and after AD 294 respectively) testify that at least in the first three centuries the system of appeal and petition must have provided redress to the people at large. In the fourth century the emperors relied more on internal checks, as the legislation on this point shows.

6. Imperial Administrative Tasks

Defence, public order, and taxation were of course the primary public tasks of the emperor. For the first there was the army; the second was maintained through the provincial governors and the army; and the third was farmed out to tax farming companies but from the third century was included in the imperial administration (see Section 9). But there was more. Augustus had assumed responsibility for the public distributions in Rome and in general for its provisioning in times of shortage, the *cura annonae*. For this he appointed a prefect for the *annona*, who had a small staff and who contracted out the transport of grain for the distributions. The grain itself was levied as an additional tax in Egypt and Africa. But in the course of the second century AD public bodies appear which comprised investors, ship owners, and transporters (*navicularii*). They received immunity from guardianship as long as they invested half of their assets in companies engaged in providing grain or olive oil for the Roman market or in transporting these to Rome, or themselves provided transport to Rome. In the third century in the provinces of Africa and Egypt a similar public body – a *corpus naviculariorum* – was instituted, consisting of landowners who had to invest in the building and maintenance of ships which, with the ships of other landowners, were organized into a fleet. This fleet, managed by the *corpus*, would transport grain for the public distributions from Africa to Ostia, where it was unloaded. For the unloading and subsequent transportation to Rome similar public bodies (*corpora*) existed. Those participating in these *corpora* received immunities from other public duties. The landowners were, for example, freed from the decurionate (i.e., serving as local councillors). In order to keep its accumulated capital intact, membership of the *corpus* became compulsory in the third century; it was considered an *origo*: being heir to a member made one liable to membership. Theoretically this created a self-sustaining body, but there were factors which threatened to reduce it, like the marriage of a decurion's son to the daughter of a *navicularius* (which might make her property subject to the decurionate), and rules were issued to amend these flaws in the system. In addition members tried to enjoy the privileges without investing too much, or they abused the rules: for instance, after receiving a cargo one had two years to return the receipt, given in Ostia, to the authority that sent the cargo. Some abused this by selling the cargo at a high price elsewhere and buying other grain at a low price. The complications of the system led to a body of rules and exceptions, with procedural safeguards.[19]

After Constantinople had been founded as a second capital, public distributions were established there as well. Egypt became its sole supplier, with its *corpus*. In the winter of AD 408/409 a crisis in transportation was overcome by using transporters outside the *corpus*, paying them a good reward. This led to a change in the set-up: by AD 534 the *corpus* consisted of landowners who had to contribute to a common chest, out of which these transporters were paid. As a result rules on transportation were reduced to supervision of transport and emergency requisition of ships.

A public body was also set up in Rome for the milling and baking of the grain which was distributed publicly. This *corpus pistorum* consisted of a number of *pistores* (miller/bakers) who were bound to this both personally and in respect of their assets. Membership was probably voluntary in the second century, but in the early third century it became compulsory. Here also membership was considered an *origo*. If a *pistor* had only daughters, the son-in-law had to manage the enterprise. A *pistor* could also leave his enterprise to the *corpus*, which would appoint a manager. In this case he formally became owner but, in order to avoid alienation of the property, it was treated as if it were property comprised in a dowry (*dotis nomine*) and by that means made inalienable. Later on even assets acquired subsequently were treated as if held *dotis nomine*.[20] As with the *navicularii*, a body of administrative law governed this system.

Further public bodies with membership as a public duty were those of the *saccarii*, the people who filled the sacks with grain and loaded and unloaded the ships in Ostia and Rome. In the middle of the third century, for five months of the year the public distribution of grain was supplemented in Rome with one of meat. For that a public body of pig merchants, the *corpus suariorum*, was set up. Landowners in Lucania and Britti (nowadays Basilicata and Calabria) had to deliver a number of pigs (*canon suariorum*) or to pay the equivalent in money: the pig merchants had to drive these pigs to Rome, to make up any shortfall with money, and to deliver all of this to the prefecture. Similarly, the maintenance of roads and the public postal system came to be a charge, this time imposed on adjoining landowners. As with other charges, an appeal was possible.

Lastly, certain services considered to be in the public interest were also regulated by public law. The workers in the mints and in the state factories for such things as arms and textiles for the imperial house, and the purple dye fishers, were likewise collected into corporations, subjected to rules of membership based on *origo*, and supervised. All these public bodies disappeared in the west with the falling away of imperial power.

7. The Constitution of Cities

When Rome expanded, its territory came to include existing towns and their surrounding territories. Some were included in Roman territory as *civitates liberae et foederatae* (such as Marseilles); others were subjugated. Under Roman rule they naturally lost their power to act as internationally independent actors and to have an army and, once incorporated into the imperial administration, they had (with some exceptions) to pay taxes to Rome. Rome sought to befriend the ruling classes by granting them citizenship, since this cemented its control. Thus the cities could continue to handle their own law and affairs and usually kept their existing constitution (*lex loci*) and administrative structure. The constitutional differences between towns slowly disappeared. The grant of Roman citizenship in AD 212 reduced their independence still further. It seems that by the end of the third century, if not before, all towns were treated equally by the imperial administration. Some privileges or special rules remained, such as the admissibility to the decurionate of sons of a marriage between a decurion's daughter and a non-curial in Antioch[21] or immunity from guardianship over children not from Troy.[22] Some towns enjoyed the *ius Italicum*,[23] which probably implied freedom from the obligation to pay land tax (tribute). What remained of citizenship of a town was the liability for public duties and functions and domicile (the *origo*: see below, 343–4). Local administration remained the domain of the cities, albeit once again under the control of the governor. He restricted himself to keeping order in towns. But even this modest aim might involve considerable influence on local constitutions, such as fixing the number of decurions or supervising elections.[24]

Roman towns were usually ruled by local elites, represented in local councils (*curiae*) whose members were called *decuriones* (the remainder of the citizens being classified as *plebs*). We find these designations in legal texts for all towns. Perhaps the Romans imposed their model and terminology on peregrine towns, but it is also possible that it was a widespread Mediterranean model and that the Roman terms are used generically. Election to the council may originally have been the rule (although it certainly was not universal), but from the second century AD co-option was standard. As a rule the town councillors chose their sons (*curiales*) as candidates. The decurions also had to meet a minimum wealth requirement. In this way they formed a local elite. Theoretically they were kept in check by the governors, but the introduction in the middle of the fourth century of *defensores civitatis* ('defenders of the town') appointed by the emperors shows that more control was needed.[25] These officials had to guard against mismanagement and to safeguard proper justice. Other offices appear after the beginning of the fourth century, such as the *curator civitatis* and *pater civitatis*. All being appointed by the imperial administration, they slowly encroached upon the traditional role of the councils and magistrates. By the end of the fifth century the role of the *curia* was considerably diminished.[26]

We see in the east under Anastasius (AD 491–518) how decisions previously taken by the council were now formally delegated to a group of the most important locals, including the bishop and the largest landowners. This development is probably due to the increasing presence of wealthy imperial officials in towns, who were not subject to the decurionate. Some of these officials may have been the sons of those decurions. In the east the council continued to exist alongside these new oligarchies, but probably only as a body of persons subject to public duties. In the west the *curiae* enjoyed a longer life, probably owing to their function regarding *gesta municipalia*, which were (also) used as public records for private matters.[27] But in both cases we see a decline in public building, maintenance of streets, and public services. In both parts of the empire the rise of the bishop in administration is remarkable. According to Liebeschuetz, this shift was more than simply the continuation of local oligarchies under a different name or setting: the bishop stood next to the council and was part of the larger organization of the Church. But his rise was also due to the weakening of the local administrative system.[28] Everyone in a town will have been equally subject to criminal law, provincial law, and administrative law, whether by virtue of existing Roman law or law established by the emperor or the governor. But particular rules of a town on summoning people to carry out functions, or other rules of this kind, could continue to apply. Likewise, we see regional differences in administration. Since from the third century all towns were equally subject to the imperial government (and since Diocletian Italy had been treated in the same way as any other province), a person's home-town now had purely administrative significance: as *origo* it determined who was eligible – or could be summoned – for the honorific functions (*honores*) and public duties (*munera*) of a town; as such it had a role throughout administrative law. As a criterion, the *origo* became widely used (for example, for the corporations for imperial tasks: see Section 6). But it was not a criterion based on heredity; and public obligations or professions did not become hereditary. The attribution of *origo* followed the rules for citizenship. Citizenship was automatically accorded based on the criterion of descent: a person born of a legitimate marriage became a citizen of his paternal home-town; one born of an illegitimate marriage or a 'natural' child became a citizen of the maternal home-town. And even those obligations which were imposed on heirs of members of a public body in the course of the third century (such as the *navicularii*: see Section 6) or on a landowner (as with *munera patrimoniorum*) were imposed on a person on taking possession of the assets which were registered as liable with the *corpus* or land according to the fiscal registration – and not merely because of being heir. Similarly the *origo* was decisive in the fourth and fifth century in the case of the colonate, a situation in which somebody was subjected to the owner of a particular estate, although here the *origo* was changed from the home-town to the fiscal registration of the particular land. In view of its importance, much administrative law dealt with questions of *origo* and conflicts of liability regarding public obligations. To the *origo* further criteria might be added, like a requirement of sufficient capital. These were the basis for nomination, after which a formal imposition determined the selection. Elaborate rules were issued on these matters.

8. Administration of Cities

Local administration was done by the citizens themselves, by way of an honorific function (*honor, honores*) or a public duty (*munus, munera*). Contemporary texts classify duties into those burdening the patrimony, those requiring personal exertion, and those demanding both. The first had to be done by all; the others could only be executed by men. A citizen was domiciled in his home-town and could be summoned for public duties there. Those who were merely resident (*incolae*), such as immigrant German barbarians, other foreigners, and citizens of other towns could be called for duties in the town of their residence as well as in their home-town. The major posts were reserved for the decurions. Being a *duovir* (mayor), *quaestor*, or *quinquennalis* was an honour, while other tasks were considered duties without status, such as being *curator operis faciendi*, in charge of a public work, or guardianship. Sometimes there was a small municipal staff to assist, usually of scribes. Some duties were considered 'dirty' (*sordidus*) and probably only executed by the *plebs*. The same applied to all other duties, of which there were many. Local organization depended on citizens executing all kinds of tasks, done nowadays by specialized local services or contracted out by the community. For example, local landowners had to maintain the roads (*munus sternendae viae*). There were menial duties like cleaning irrigation channels or acting as night watchman (*nuktophylax*). By the beginning of the fourth century the levying of taxation had been added to the local administrative tasks. But honour or not, it had to be done and if there were not enough volunteers, it was imposed. This explains why as early as the second century we find rules on the imposition of these duties by the council or (presumably indirectly) by the governor.[29]

Charges were assigned according to a finely tuned system of rules. A citizen could offer himself voluntarily for a charge; often the retiring official nominated a candidate who could raise objections, such as not being rich enough to sustain the burden or the potential deficits or claims it involved, or propose a more suitable candidate. In the end the council would elect him (in which case he could appeal to the governor) or acknowledge his objection. The elected official would then either accept his duty or appeal to the provincial governor. Usually personal surety was required as well. At the end of his term there was a year within which claims against him on account of mismanagement could be raised. Completion of the duty brought a period of immunity from new charges. The lower duties were imposed in a similar procedure.

In the late third century in Oxyrhynchus a certain Ptolemaeus, son of a chief priest, was proposed for a second office, that of public banker. Previously another person, Pasion, had been nominated, but he was not rich enough. Ptolemaeus opposed his own nomination, saying: 'I entreat you, I cannot serve. I am a man of moderate means. I live in my father's house.' And he said that two offices at the same time were too much. But the councillors said: 'Upright, faithful Ptolemaeus'; and the result was that the exegetes said: 'You elected him on account of his good faith.'[30] But was a son of a chief priest really of modest means? Was Ptolemaeus really pressed? Or did he merely feign modesty? Was it part of a ritual? And was there really no one else who could do the job? That could indeed have been the case, but if so it might have been coincidental and does not prove that it became difficult to fill posts.

Nevertheless, we do see a shift in the third and fourth centuries AD towards more pressure to perform duties. The cause is not clear. It is often assumed that enthusiasm for local public administration dwindled in these centuries. The reality may have been more complicated. First, the situation will have differed from place to place. The welfare of one town may have declined, causing problems in its administration, while that of another increased. The towns of Africa, for instance, seem to have prospered well into the third century. In the second century AD, however, we already find imperial admonitions to replenish the councils with plebeians and illegitimate sons. That may indicate a shortage in candidates; but it may also indicate that councils tended to become oligarchies, like the senate, raising the standards for admission. So we find elaborate rules on such things as whether a son born to a decurion after his banishment counts as a decurion's son: he is, if conceived before that; but if conceived afterwards, he is not.[31] Other rules concern immunities, liability for other duties, and so on. The possibility of joining the imperial service, the army or (from the fourth century) the Church, with their immunity from civic charges, threatened the administration of towns. Rules were issued to counter the negative effects of this.

Much legislation, particularly in the late empire and transmitted in the *Codes* of Theodosius and Justinian, is about imposition of duties. Councillorship itself was now a duty that could be imposed. But this still does not exclude the possibility that there was a continuing public spirit: legislation of this kind would still be necessary if a minimal number of towns had used up their reserves. We may assume that normally the number of councillors would have been sufficient to ensure that the duties continued to be performed, with a reserve. Problems arise when the reserve is insufficient, although that still means that a proportion of public obligations is performed without difficulty. But we do not have numbers. As early as the second century a system of exemptions (*excusationes*), vacancies (*vacationes*), and immunities (*immunitates*) applied. A person who was called for a personal public office or duty could raise an exemption such as age or number of children and would be exempt for the period for which this exemption was applicable. Performance of a duty itself gave rise to a 'vacancy', so that one was free of this and other personal duties for a certain period. Some were fortunate enough to avoid all such claims by virtue of an immunity granted as a privilege. (In practice, the distinction between these terms is not always strict.) So, for instance, Diocletian and Maximian granted students an exemption until their twenty-fifth birthday:

> To Severinus and other law students from Arabia. Since you state that you are occupied in studying the liberal arts and especially law, while you are staying in the city of Berytus in the province of Phoenicia, we direct, taking into consideration the public good as well as your hopes, that none of you shall be called away from your studies until the age of twenty-five.[32]

Understandably, immunities were sought after.

Mixed obligations, such as the decurionate, required both personal performance and capital. In this case lack of capital could provide an exemption. Women were by virtue of their sex unfit for public offices, with the exception of certain priesthoods. For public obligations which encumbered only patrimonies, on the other hand, there was no escape, whether for men or women, young or old: they had always to be performed,[33] unless another patrimonial duty excluded this, as in the case of those who had to run ships for the transportation of public goods, who did not have to be decurions.

Many tried to evade nominations, either because they were too burdensome or out of self-interest. All kinds of tricks were used. Thus registering as a *colonus* (that is, a subjected person) would – so it was hoped – make one unfit for the decurionate, which had to be exercised by unsubjected persons. But the emperors did not accept this and ordered the recall of the registration ('every frustrative action based on privilege or birth status . . . shall be barred').[34] A curious way to escape was to cohabit with a slave woman: 'Therefore, if . . . any man shall be found to have alienated his patrimony and have consigned it to the master of the slave woman, the municipal senate shall be permitted to make a diligent investigation.'[35] The precise scheme is unknown, but the decurion made himself financially ineligible by transferring his assets in trust to another (this will have involved sham sales and transfers) and his eventual future offspring ineligible owing to their birth status (assuming that the arrangement involved ultimately transferring his children to him, after which he could free them). The fact that the decurion transferred his assets to the slave's master strongly suggests that it was not just a scheme for love affairs.

Another cause of shortage was the immunity provided by the Christian church. Some might want to become bishops, clerics, or lead a secluded life as monks. Joining the Church was of course not reprehensible, but some may simply have viewed it as an alternative but more agreeable career. The emperors tried to remedy this drain by providing that a decurion or curial who became a cleric had to surrender a quarter of his assets to the town council. The council could then make this property over to a curial who was otherwise too poor to become a decurion and to carry out duties. Still, the number of available people must have dwindled, and this in turn will have raised the burden for the others. Yet there will still have been people eager to fulfil these offices spontaneously, since they gave their incumbents the status of decurions and so provided a social ladder.

We find the same tendency with other public bodies which were set up during the second and early third centuries to ensure a steady supply of public distributions in the capitals (see Section 6). As with the town administrations, these bodies were supposed to run themselves with a great measure of independence. As with the public charges mentioned already, most of the rules were concerned with keeping up the numbers of the public bodies and with conflicts with other public duties assigned to their members. But as membership of one body gave immunity from other duties, since the imperial service in both its civil and military branches likewise gave immunity, and since the decurions formed a reservoir of educated and moneyed people, it is possible that the drain on a common fund of human and financial capital grew too big, reserves became too thin, and that these problems were in the end generated by the system itself. The real challenge was the public duties system. One has therefore to read the texts in the *Codes* with care: they deal with problematic situations; the unproblematic ones are rarely mentioned, if at all.

Other charges such as cleaning channels or keeping watch at night, which were executed by the city *plebs*, were not coveted and a drain occurred here too. In the fourth century we find the formation of groups (*collegia*) of plebeians responsible for such 'dirty' tasks. These groups were replenished by the children of members (*collegiati*) according to the *origo* principle. Membership of such a group was a *munus* and it was enforced.

9. Empire and Cities: Taxation

Taxation is nowadays a prime public task, and an important body of public law on taxation exists. In the republic and early empire, taxes were farmed out by the Roman state to collecting companies (*societates publicanorum*). The conditions of these contracts were a private matter. Only after many complaints by provincials about the oppressive behaviour of the companies did Nero publish the conditions of the contracts. At some point, however (the end of the second century according to some authors, but more likely later), levying the land tax (*tributum*) and its accompanying surcharges as well as the poll tax (*tributum capitis*) was entrusted to local decurions and put under the supervision of the praetorian prefectures and other offices, such as the *comes sacrarum largitionum*. Collection of customs dues remained farmed out. This was certainly the position by the beginning of the fourth century. The freedom from taxes which Italy had enjoyed was removed. The Theodosian *Code* includes a body of law on taxation which was needed to direct the provincial and local authorities and to ensure the equitable imposition and levy of taxes. It also contains procedural rules. The basis of the land tax at that time, and probably already by the end of the second century, was an evaluation of the productivity of land according to different categories. In the assessment a landowner had to declare 'land: how many *jugera* have been sown in the last ten years; vineyards: how many vines they have; olive-groves: how many *jugera* and how many trees they have; meadows: which have been mowed in the last ten years and how many *jugera*; pastures: how many *jugera* are estimated; the same for coppices'.[36] On the basis of these statistics, the taxpaying capacity of every town was calculated, and at the higher levels that of every province, diocese, and prefecture. On the other side of the account, anticipated expenditures were added up. Using a proportional scheme, these were then redistributed by reference to prefectures, dioceses, provinces, towns, and finally landowners through *indictiones*. In this redistribution surcharges were included.[37] If later on more income was required in order to meet expenditure, a *superindictio* would be imposed. The poll tax was apparently a fixed sum. Legal challenges to the imposition of tax and charges were possible, and appeal was possible too, which led to some case law. The *comes sacrarum largitionum* was in fiscal litigation the highest judge.

10. Public Law: Writings and Doctrine

The Romans did not theorize on their constitution, and there is no such thing as a developed constitutional law, let alone doctrine about it. So far as administration is concerned, in due course a body of substantive law on public law came into being, and jurists at the end of the second century wrote treatises about it. Papirius Iustus collected imperial rulings in his *De constitutionibus*; Callistratus wrote his *De iure fisci* ('On fiscal law'); Paul collected imperial decisions in his *Sententiae*; while Ulpian wrote *De officio proconsulis* ('On the office of a proconsul'), Hermogenian an *Epitome*, a compendium of public law, and Arcadius Charisius *De muneribus civilibus* ('On public obligations'). On criminal law there were specialized works such as Papinian's *De adulteriis*, Marcian's *De publicis iudiciis*, and Modestinus' *De poenis*. There is even Macer's *De re militari*. The great commentaries of Ulpian and Paul on the edict also dealt with public law. As for the law of procedure, *cognitio extraordinaria* – the mode of procedure which gradually came to dominate – was basically the same for private, public, and criminal law. Some treatises were written about it too, such as Callistratus' *De cognitionibus* ('On litigation'), or Ulpian's *De appellationibus* ('On appeals'). These treatises mainly describe the law and cite imperial decisions which had a general purport, but they also discuss doctrinal questions and systematize the law. Much legislation on administrative law, extending to criminal law, imperial administration, taxation, and local administration, was collected in the three earlier *Codes* (Gregorian, Hermogenian, and Theodosian) and later in Justinian's *Code*. Extracts from the kinds of treatises just mentioned were included in the *Digest*. This legislation was certainly founded on a system, but from the piecemeal references that remain it is often not easy to discern it.

II. Summary

The constitution of the Roman empire was in effect relatively simple. The supreme administrator was the emperor. All imperial administrative officers, such as provincial governors and army commanders, were essentially his assistants and delegates. From the time of Diocletian the governor was responsible for civil matters, while the military commander was responsible for defence and public order. Independent bodies in the provinces of Africa and Egypt took care of the transportation of grain for the public distributions in Rome and Constantinople. The provincial governors too were supervised by the prefect, and from Diocletian onwards by *vicarii* (lieutenants, appointed over dioceses) and then by prefects. Rome and Constantinople were governed independently by urban prefects with *vicarii*. All prefects were responsible to the emperor. This administrative structure was essentially the structure through which complaints about taxes and charges proceeded and through which appeals were made. Litigants would submit their cases to a magistrate – in the provinces the governor and in Rome and Constantinople the urban prefect or his *vicarius*. This was also the judicial structure, since separation of powers was unknown. General administrators such as those just mentioned issued rules, judged cases, and administered.

Although it was not as extensive as private law, this public (administrative) law, together with a reasonably effective system of procedure, must have provided citizens with an adequate level of protection against abuse by state officials and others. There are many references in the Theodosian *Code* to bribes and abuse by officials, but its constitutions also show an abiding imperial concern to ensure the fair application of law.

Notes

1. See instead the chapter by Lintott, 301–31.
2. Gaius 1.8; Ulp. 1 inst. D. 1.4.1 pr.

3. E.g. Plin. *Pan.* 65.1.
4. C. 1.14.4 (AD 429), still in force in AD 534.
5. C. 1.14.2–3.
6. C. 1.14.3, fragments of which are preserved in C.Th. 1.4.3, C. 1.14.2 and 3, C. 1.19.7, and C. 1.22.5.
7. E.g. Plin. *Ep.* 10.16 sets out how he examined the finances of the city of Prusa, which he found to be in a dismal state of administration.
8. See M. S. Youni, 'Transforming Greek practice into Roman law: manumissions in Roman Macedonia', *TR* 78 (2010): 311–40.
9. C.Th. 1.4.3.
10. Cf. C.Th. 1.4.1–3.
11. Suet. *Claud.* 23; *Tib.* 33.
12. See, e.g., D. 28.4.3 pr.; D. 32.97.
13. See the chapter by Metzger, 287–9.
14. W. L. Westermann and A. A. Schiller, *Apokrimata: Decisions of Septimius Severus on Legal Matters* (New York, 1954).
15. D. Liebs, 'Recht und Rechtsliteratur,' in *Restauration und Erneuerung. Die lateinische Literatur von 284 bis 374 n. Chr. (Handbuch der lateinischen Literatur)*, ed. R. Herzog (Munich, 1989), 64–65.
16. Liebs (n. 15), 60–64.
17. C.Th. 13.5.38.
18. C.Th. 10.10.15 (AD 380).
19. Mainly found in the Theodosian *Code.* See, in general, on these public bodies, A. J. B. Sirks, *Food for Rome* (Amsterdam, 1991). On *origo*, see A. J. B. Sirks, 'The Colonate in Justinian's Reign', *JRS* 98 (2008): 126–28.
20. See A. J. B. Sirks, 'Late Roman Law: The Case of *dotis nomen* and the *praedia pistoria*,' *ZSS* 108 (1991): 178–212.
21. C.Th. 12.1.51; a concession to the Greek custom of the *epiklerate*?
22. D. 27.1.17.1.
23. D. 50.15.1.
24. E.g. Plin. *Ep.* 10.39.
25. See R. Frakes, *Contra Potentium Iniurias: The Defensor Civitatis and Late Roman Justice* (Munich, 2001).
26. See A. Laniado, *Recherches sur les notables municipaux dans l'empire protobyzantin* (Paris, 2002).
27. See F. M. Ausbüttel, *Die Verwaltung der Städte und Provinzen im spätantiken Italien* (Frankfurt – Bern – New York – Paris, 1988).
28. J. H. W. G. Liebeschuetz, *Barbarians and Bishops: Army, Church, and State in the Age of Arcadius and Chrysostom* (Oxford, 1990), 228–35, for the example of Synesius in Cyrenaica.
29. See, e.g., D. 48.4.1.3, D. 50.4.14.
30. P. Oxy. XII.1415.
31. D. 50.2.2–8; see further A. J. B. Sirks, 'Die Nomination für die städtischen Ämter im römischen Reich', in *Stadt – Gemeinde – Genossenschaft. Festschrift für Gerhard Dilcher zum 70. Geburtstag*, ed. A. Cordes, J. Rückert, and R. Schulze (Berlin, 2003), 13–22 (also deals with entry requirements for the sons of senators).
32. C. 10.50.1.

33. C.10.42.6.
34. C.Th. 12.1.33.
35. C.Th. 12.1.6 (AD 319).
36. Ulp. D.50.15.4.
37. See J.-M. Carrié, 'Diocletien et la fiscalité', *Antiquité Tardive* 2 (1994): 33–64.

Part VI

BYZANTIUM AND BEYOND

17 THE LAW OF NEW ROME: BYZANTINE LAW

Bernard H. Stolte

1. INTRODUCTION

The afterlife of Roman law took various shapes, as will transpire from other chapters in this section. Underlying most of them is the assumption that Roman law lived on in a Latin-speaking environment. After all, the Roman jurists had written in Latin, and Justinian had codified juristic writings and imperial legislation in that language, even though the majority of his subjects were Greek-speaking. The miraculous rebirth of Roman law in northern Italy in the eleventh century would never have occurred if Justinian had not adhered to the Latin language. The influence of Roman law on canon law and political theory would have been different and perhaps even lacking altogether, and the same holds good for the career of Roman law in the modern world.[1] So what of the law in New Rome?

In theory the law of New Rome began with the foundation of Constantinople in AD 330. Important as that event may have been, it is almost irrelevant to the history of Roman law. To be sure, it was a milestone on the way towards a more permanent division of the Empire, which, however, did not come about until much later. Even the division between Arcadius and Honorius in AD 395, a suitable starting-point for the period we now understand by 'late antiquity', did not mark the inception of Byzantine law. Much could be said about the development of the law in late antiquity, but it should not be under the heading 'Byzantine law'. 'Byzantine' is an invention of western historiography to indicate a geographical and cultural environment which, however, understood itself as Roman. In few areas is this as obvious as in the law. What, then, is Byzantine law? When did the development of Roman law in the eastern half of the Roman world branch off in a direction which was truly different from what happened in the west?

Given the lack of continuity in the west, the question is actually misconceived. It was the west which went its own different way. In the east, after Justinian's codification, development ran a predictable course: the new authoritative text was taught, commented upon, and summarized, and, where necessary, the legislator intervened with additional legislation, the *novellae constitutiones*. Famous schools were those of Constantinople and Beirut, legislation of course being restricted to the capital; insofar as teaching took place in other cities such as Rome, it has left few traces and may fairly soon have ceased altogether. The development of Roman law in the west seems to have come to a standstill, to be resumed in the different world of northern Italy almost five centuries later.

In spite of the initial successes of Justinian's generals in the reconquest of former territories in the western half of the Mediterranean world, it soon became clear that the future of the Roman empire lay in the east. In other words, from the end of the sixth century onwards, geographically the empire in actual fact covered predominantly Greek-speaking territory, Latin being just one of many minority languages. Inevitably, the language of the law then changed from Latin to Greek. The clearest sign of this development is the fact that Justinian himself started to legislate in Greek: the *novellae constitutiones* were issued in Greek, with some exceptions which are readily explained by their intended audience.[2] It is not the law that branches off in a different direction; it is the language of the law – and even that only partially, since technical terminology remained Latin. Moreover, in legal teaching and practice, Greek had already long been in use.

If we must have a precise starting-point for Byzantine law, I propose 534, when the codification had been completed, the first Greek *Novels* were issued, and – more significantly – the new legislation was taught and applied in Constantinople and elsewhere. It is from this point that a development began which was unique to the eastern Mediterranean world and never really became part of a common legal tradition shared with the west. Since this development was separate from the western tradition that we denote as Roman, it makes sense to give it a different name: let us by all means stick to historiographical convention and call it 'Byzantine'.

In his chapter on Justinian and the *Corpus iuris civilis*, Kaiser has given an outline of legal teaching in the age of Justinian.[3] In the present context it is worth emphasizing that we actually possess extensive remains of this teaching, consisting of translations, lecture notes, summaries of, and commentaries on, the various parts of Justinian's legislation.[4] Together they afford a unique insight into how Justinian's contemporaries understood and explained the legislation. But there is still more to these writings, which had been written in many cases by the very jurists who sat on the committees responsible for drafting the codification.

First and foremost, they are the closest we can get to the inception of Byzantine law. Elsewhere I have suggested that two transformations of Roman law took place in the first decade or so of Justinian's reign.[5] The first was the codification itself: at this point the old juristic writings ceased legally and materially to exist. The second was the 'appropriation' of the Latin codification in the form of Greek writings by translators, exegetes, and commentators. It is true that theoretically the Latin text of the codification had sole authority, but to all intents and purposes the Greek versions served *in loco parentis*. They were to be the basis of subsequent development: not only are they quoted in later juristic writing, but many passages are repeated, often literally, in later legislation. In short, they are the first generation of Byzantine law – unthinkable, of course, without the Justinianic codification.

Moreover, owing to their origin, they are witnesses to the sixth-century text of the Justinianic legislation. For that very reason these *Graeci interpretes*, as they were then called, were to join the western Roman legal tradition through the efforts of the Humanists, of whom more below (369). Modern editors of the various parts of the legislation have followed in the footsteps of the humanists.

This chapter sets out to deal with Byzantine law in the context of Roman law. Byzantine law began as Roman law, and the way in which it developed is one of many strands in the history of Roman law. Byzantine law went its own course, in a language and a cultural environment different from those we habitually imagine when confronted with Roman law. In spite of all the differences, Byzantine law never lost sight of its origin and never hesitated to proclaim it. Playing down this aspect would be distorting its history. Indeed, these pages will bring out continuity rather than change. Byzantinists may consider this statement a contribution to perpetuating a one-sided, traditionalist picture of Byzantium as the decline and fall of ancient Rome. I can only say that I hope it will help Romanists to look occasionally over the ever-higher fence that seems to separate the students of east and west.

2. THE EARLY CENTURIES: THE COMMON HISTORY

Although there are good grounds for making the history of Byzantine law begin with the completion of the Justinianic codification, it is impossible to leave out the preceding centuries. Indeed, precisely since the

Justinianic codification is at one and the same time the final restatement of the Roman law of antiquity and the point of departure for Byzantine law, a treatment of Byzantine law which does not incorporate the Roman antecedents is unthinkable.

In the Justinianic codification, Roman and Byzantine law are bound up inextricably. The difference between the Romanist and the Byzantinist lies merely in the direction of their view: the Romanist is inclined to see the Justinianic legislation as the storehouse of materials from which to construe the classical past – and is therefore usually less interested in the *Novels* – whereas the Byzantinist will look at what happened after the promulgation of the codifcation – that is, the *Novels* and much else.

Since Kaiser's chapter (119–48) deals with Justinian and the *Corpus iuris civilis*, it may suffice here to refer the reader to his words (indeed to much of this book) as the indispensable prologue to what followed. In one respect, however, yet another prologue is required. The Byzantine state was a Christian state. Just as it is impossible to write its political and cultural history without taking into account the role of the Church, it is equally unthinkable to restrict a survey of Byzantine law to secular law. Byzantine law was founded not only on the Justinianic heritage, but also on the legislative work of the first four ecumenical (and various local) councils. In the present context, however, this will be left to one side insofar as it is not connected with Roman law.

3. The *Antecessores*: Teaching the First Generation of Byzantine Lawyers

Understanding and applying the new codification must have been a linguistic challenge, at least for aspiring law students, the vast majority of them Greek-speaking. Illyricum, Africa, and Italy were Latin-speaking, and students from those parts must have experienced similar difficulties with Greek texts. As it happens, we are well-informed about the way this problem was confronted. The details, with numerous examples, are found in a very concise but seminal book by H. J. Scheltema.[6]

Teaching took the form of two courses: in the first, by way of introducing the law, professors (*antecessores*) gave a paraphrasing Greek translation or adaptation of the Latin text; in the second, on the basis of the original Latin text, they gave a legal explanation of that text, again in Greek. The first course was called *index*, the second one *paragraphai*;[7] the original Latin text was called *to rhèton*.

Teaching of the imperial constitutions codified in the *Code* and subsequently augmented by the *Novels* employed a special aid in addition to the two already mentioned. Given language rather more complicated than one finds in the *Institutes* and *Digest*, recourse was had to word-for-word (*kata poda(s)*, 'on the heels') translations, which were written above the words of the original. This produced a series of words rather than a syntactically coherent text; and when these 'translations' were detached from their source and perhaps rewritten, their syntax continued to betray their origin. A large number of examples in Greek can be found in the scholia on the Basilica (see Section 4), but to Romanists another example is more familiar: the *Authenticum*. It started life as a Latin *kata-poda* translation of the Greek *Novels* for Latin-speaking students and circulated in the Latin west independently of the (literally) underlying text. Before its origin was recognized, its 'bad' Latin led to hypotheses which were wide of the mark. Another Latin collection of *Novels* circulating in the west, the *Epitome Juliani*, also originated in teaching the Greek *Novels* to a Latin-speaking audience: it was originally a course of *paragraphai*.[8]

It is this process of appropriation and especially teaching that generated the humus from which Byzantine law grew. Justinian's legislation was being translated, summarized, and interpreted in a language that precluded circulation of the results in the Latin-speaking west, just as the *Authenticum* and the *Epitome Iuliani*, though Byzantine by origin, were a basis for developments in which the Byzantine east did not take part. In Byzantium, the Greek representations *in loco parentis* took the place of their Justinianic originals and were understood and applied in an environment entirely different from eleventh-century northern Italy. It is hardly surprising that the result was different too, but it was definitely Roman law. Indeed, it is more surprising that it remained so 'Roman'. The explanation for the latter phenomenon is partly to be found in the history of the normative sources.

This is not the place to go into detail about the succession of the various longer and shorter compilations of Byzantine law, of which there are several historical accounts; all of them begin in late antiquity and include the Justinianic era. The fullest are by van der Wal and Lokin in French and, most recently, by Troianos in Greek.[9] Both incorporate canon law. The present author has contributed a summary of 'legal literature', secular as well as ecclesiastical,[10] and Pieler has written an extensive treatment of secular Byzantine legal writing considered as literature.[11] The addition of the word 'literature' indicates the nature of these last two works, but also applies to the first two: they all deal with normative sources and 'learned' legal writing but do not pay systematic attention to documentary sources stemming from legal practice. 'Sources' is understood largely to refer to normative sources, a perfectly legitimate choice, the more so since for most of Byzantium's history documentary sources are relatively scarce.

It is the history of the normative sources, then, that raises the question of continuity and change of Roman law in Byzantium.

4. Byzantine Law: Continuity or Change?

Scheltema compared the Greek representations of the Justinianic originals with *tesserae* from which subsequent generations composed their mosaics.[12] The simile is most apposite: the resulting compilations were different each time yet the same, and thus suggest change yet continuity. This is not to say that Justinian's successors did not legislate, but it is strange to note that only rarely were these post-Justinianic *Novels* incorporated into later compilations, expressly or tacitly. This seems to raise a question over the principle that a later statute derogates from an earlier one (*lex posterior derogat legi priori*) so familiar from Roman law. We should not be over-hasty with that conclusion. The very name of the *Novels* – *nearai meta ton Kodika diataxeis*, 'new constitutions after the *Code*' – suggests that the emperors were conscious of making amendments to the *Code*, and references to the maxim of *lex posterior* are not infrequent. But it is clear that the Byzantine understanding of that model was not the same as the Roman.

Two inferences may be drawn from this. First, the recurrence of the Justinianic legislation in later compilations kept the Byzantine legal system very 'Roman'. The introductory textbook par excellence always remained Justinian's *Institutes* in the paraphrase by Theophilus.[13] A return to the sixth century[14] is particularly striking in the most extensive compilation of Byzantine law, the *Basilica* (short for *ta basilika nomima*, 'the imperial laws') of about 900,[15] essentially an imperially sanctioned Greek rendering of the Justinianic legislation in which the titles of *Digest* and *Code* were amalgamated and (parts of) Justinianic *Novels* were added. The relevant (Justinianic) legislation on a given subject was now at last to be found within one title, but the purpose of the collection seems to have been to assist consultation of the original legislation rather than to replace it with a new codification. This impression is reinforced by the addition of commentaries; these consisted once again in fragments of antecessorial texts written in the sixth century in order to elucidate the *Digest*, *Code*, and

Novels (the so-called 'old scholia': see below, 369–70). Shorter compilations such as the *Ecloga*, *Procheiron*, and the *Eisagoge* order the material differently, but the texts are mostly recognizably Justinianic. To investigate the nature and purpose of these 'law books', we should look at their preambles and at what has been included and omitted. All in all, the overwhelming impression is one of continuity. Needless to say, this is why the Byzantine material is useful for textual criticism of the *Corpus iuris civilis*, an aspect on which interest in Byzantine law on the part of Romanists has traditionally focussed (see also Section 9).

Second, the history of Byzantine law should not be confused with the history only of the normative sources. Change there was, but it was not necessarily reflected in these sources. In order to trace the development of Byzantine law, one has to cast one's net wider. It is in the *Novels*, of Justinian as well as of his successors, that individual emperors address contemporary problems. Similar indications may be found in non-legal literature. Given the apparent continuity that emerges from the successive normative compilations, it would be useful to check this picture against series of court cases. Unfortunately these are not readily available. The examples that survive show, on the one hand, adherence to the Roman legal system and terminology but, on the other, occasional divergences from the Roman norm, sometimes explicitly, sometimes tacitly. In short, it is from evidence of 'law in action' that we may trace the development of Roman–Byzantine law.

5. Byzantine Legal Language: Latin, Greek, and Greek

For several centuries, Byzantine legal language remained recognizably Roman. To be sure, the language was Greek, but its technical vocabulary was Latin. Latin adages had been taken over unchanged, although their fate in the manuscripts shows that the scribes did not really understand the Latin they were copying. Linguistically more interesting are nouns, adjectives, and verbs: they were from Latin roots but given Greek endings, so that the words could be declined and conjugated as if they were Greek.[16] Originally they were written with Latin letters, including their Greek endings. Traces of Latin script are found in carefully written legal manuscripts as late as the twelfth century and even beyond, although the scribes were understandably seduced by Greek endings to write these more or less frequently with Greek characters. In the latest modern edition of Theophilus' *Paraphrasis Institutionum* the editors attempted to reconstruct the oldest attainable version: they interpreted the presence of 'at least one Latin character in at least one manuscript at that specific place' as grounds for printing an entire word or name in Latin script according to a 'normalized' orthography.[17] Literally every page of the edition contains such words, which stand out immediately in this Greek environment through their small Latin capitals.

The Latin vocabulary was eventually replaced by *exellenismoi*: translations into Greek. Two examples may suffice. The Latin *emptio* (purchase) is found in early Byzantine legal texts as EMPTION, with the Greek feminine article and treated as a noun of the third declension according to the pattern of roots ending with *-n*. In later texts, and sometimes in 'exhellenized' versions of older ones, EMPTION becomes *agorasia*. This should not be considered indicative of substantive change in the contract of sale. More interesting is the Latin *translatio (legatorum)*, which figures as TRANSLATION. The Latin verb is *transferre*, but in Byzantine legal language the verb has been formed from the root TRANSLAT- and becomes TRANSLATEUEIN. The later Greek translation of the noun, which replaces TRANSLATION, is *metathesis*.

The average Byzantine citizen will have been bewildered by this highly technical vocabulary. In Justinian's *Novels* it is found only rarely, but their Greek is far from simple. If we leave the question of literacy on one side, the real problem for the average citizen must have been that of 'diglossia': on the one hand there was everyday spoken Greek, of which the Greek of the New Testament gives an impression but which of course developed over the centuries, and on the other hand the purist, atticizing, literary Greek of higher written expression. The two were increasingly divergent and must have already differed considerably by the sixth century, not to mention later times.[18]

So far as the Greek used in legal matters was concerned, there were at least three different forms. For legislation an ornate, sometimes very complicated language was preferred, which corresponded to the rhetorical conventions of literary Byzantine Greek. The written language the jurists employed in their translations, summaries, and commentaries made use of the technical vocabulary described above and also of a much simpler, clearer syntax. This is the language of Theophilus and other *antecessores*. These writings are the ones that are probably of the greatest interest to the Romanist. Contact between a lawyer and his client and between a judge and the parties would be in an entirely different spoken Greek, the contemporary everyday language. It would not be an exaggeration to imagine a difference similar to that between formal Latin and the emerging vernaculars of the early Middle Ages.

6. Legal Practice: The Evidence

Evidence from legal practice is very unevenly distributed over space and time. Several of Justinian's *Novels* are imperial reactions to practical problems that had been brought to the emperor's attention. For the same period we have one other rich source. In the sixth century, Egypt was still firmly under Byzantine domination. The papyri are a vast body of evidence of what this meant in practice.[19] Although they are much less abundant for provinces such as Palestine, Arabia, and Syria, it is now widely believed that there is no reason to regard these parts of the Near East as differing greatly from Egypt, so that we may extrapolate the evidence of the Egyptian papyri to other provinces of the empire. This evidence suggests that legislation issued in the capital reached the provinces, although there is less agreement on the measure of its penetration into daily life. Various questions arise, but this much is clear: these papyri are evidence of how Byzantine law was applied in a province of the empire. Greek was the dominant language, but we should not forget papyri in other languages such as Coptic.[20]

After the loss of Egypt in the seventh century we have to rely in principle on other sources. The new masters did not force their subjects to abandon their traditional way of life, but their 'tolerance' of course applied more in the sphere of private law than in public law. In any case, legislation from Constantinople no longer influenced what went on in these territories. For the legal historian of Byzantium, the loss of Egypt means the loss of a rich source of documentary evidence. For the next couple of centuries we are forced to base ourselves mainly on indirect evidence such as saints' lives. To make matters worse, for the seventh and eighth centuries few imperial *Novels* have been preserved. The promulgation of the *Basilica* in about 900, while of inestimable value for our knowledge of Justinian's legislation, is of little use to the historian of Byzantine legal practice.

From the eleventh century dates the *Peira* ('Experience'), mainly a collection of excerpts stemming from the practice of Eustathios Rhomaios, a judge in the High Court of Constantinople. Unfortunately the actual cases are often unclear, which is explained in part by the fact that the anonymous author was not so much reporting them as trying to write a textbook. But the collection does convey an idea of the sort of cases the court had to deal with and the way in which a judge applied legislation in actual cases.[21]

Evidence is available not only from the secular sphere but also from an ecclesiastical context. Actual cases are reported in the twelfth-century commentary on the *Nomocanon of Fourteen Titles* and the *Corpus canonum* by Theodore Balsamon.[22] Another source is the register of the patriarchate of Constantinople of the fourteenth century, which contains a considerable number of judicial decisions.[23] The archives of the monasteries of the Holy Mountain document, among other things, transactions concerning property; these range from the tenth century to the present.[24] When secular structures were on the verge of collapse, a bishop's court was often still available and dealt with non-ecclesiastical cases too. A late example is documentation from the activity of Chomatenos in Epirus in the late twelfth and early thirteenth centuries.[25]

In all these sources, whether secular or ecclesiastical, one finds evidence of the application of Roman law in Byzantine form. But which part of Roman law was actually in use? And to what extent was Roman law changing in Byzantine hands? To the first question a tentative answer may be found in short selections such as the *Ecloga* of the Isaurian emperors Leo III and Constantine V of 741.[26] To judge from the number of surviving manuscripts, the *Ecloga* was very successful. It contains predominantly Justinianic provisions and gives an indication of which parts of Roman law had a role to play in legal practice. In the same manuscripts one often finds other short texts. Among them are the three so-called *leges speciales* (the Farmers' Law, the Seamen's Law, and the Soldiers' Law).[27] Their nature and purpose have been much discussed and no consensus has been reached. They have been variously dated from the late sixth to the eighth centuries and are, in varying degrees, less dependent on Justinian's legislation. Not all of them are laws in the formal sense. Here too it seems reasonable to see them as a mirror of the law actually in use. Their names indicate the special spheres in which their provisions would apply. Similar indications of less ambitious sets of rules that had some real influence on daily life may be seen in other texts often found in the same manuscripts as the *Ecloga*: the *Mosaic Law*[28] and the so-called *Appendix Eclogae*.[29]

7. A History of Byzantine Law?

To what extent was Roman law changing in Byzantine hands? What is 'Byzantine law in context'? The best available answers are still to be found in Zachariä's *Geschichte des griechisch-römischen Rechts*, now more than 100 years old.[30] It has still not been superseded – not for want of new material, but by virtue of the quality of the original and the immensity of the work involved in its revision. The late Alexander Kazhdan pleaded strongly for a revision with the rhetorical question 'Do we need a new history of Byzantine law?' He was answered by Ludwig Burgmann as well as by myself, along different lines but to the same effect: yes, but it is not going to be written in the foreseeable future and even then probably not in a manner that would have been to Kazhdan's taste.[31] In essence, this is all a case of mistaken identity: Kazhdan reproached legal historians for believing that formal sources represented reality and therefore for neglecting data from other sources such as saints' lives. But no legal historian holds such a view; or, rather, Kazhdan's understanding of 'reality' is not the same as what most legal historians set out to describe.

A history of Byzantine law should ideally take on board both the legal 'reality' of the structure of the formal legal sources and information about what these texts were supposed to do: how, in the course of the centuries, they contributed to ordering society, settling disputes and so forth. The former is mainly Roman law in Greek dress. The latter, which is of both legal and non-legal origin, shows that Byzantine society often developed independently of its Roman heritage; in any case, Byzantines dealt with this heritage in a decidedly different way from their ancestors. The ultimate result would be a history showing, on the one hand, a strong continuity in the formal sources, and on the other hand, change – as postulated by Kazhdan and never denied by others.

A history of Byzantine law would show a society in which legislation and 'law-in-action' interacted in a way different from Rome in antiquity. For one thing, the role of legislation was different.[32] For the student of Roman law the Byzantines' adherence to the Justinianic legislation is a bonus, since this has preserved information that would otherwise have been lost. These texts, however, do not provide direct access to the way this version of Roman law was applied in Byzantium. There is an obvious parallel with the position of the *Corpus iuris civilis* in the western legal tradition. Its survival and distribution do not directly inform us about medieval or early modern legal practice. Without the work of the Glossators and, building on that, the Commentators, the *Corpus iuris civilis* would have been an interesting historical phenomenon but surely of little use to the practising lawyer. Of course, the tradition of the *ius commune* embraces far more than just repetition of Justinian's words, and in that respect the case of Byzantine law is the same. In Byzantium, Roman law was at the forefront to the very end, but it did not play the same role as it did in the *ius commune* in (re)creating and maintaining a legal system fit for use in the contemporary world.

It is no small achievement that Zachariä's history of Byzantine law already went some way towards an ideal history. Let us briefly look at two areas, matrimonial property and real property, in order to put this into perspective.

Zachariä believed that the Byzantines had parted company with the Romans in legislating for a new system of matrimonial property based on joint ownership; that it was the Isaurian *Ecloga* of 741 that effected this; and that the wider context of this change was the union of Roman law with Christian doctrine in the hands of the Byzantines, as is sometimes (over-enthusiastically) alleged of Byzantine law in general. This assertion has not been able to withstand closer scrutiny. In the regime of matrimonial property, the *Ecloga* shows a great deal of continuity with Justinianic Roman law.[33] Equally, it is not easy to describe Byzantine matrimonial property as a system, as Dieter Simon has shown for a later period.[34]

As to real property, it suffices to read the concluding pages (§ 64) of Zachariä's treatment of 'Das Grundeigenthum insbesondere' to realize that in Byzantium we gradually leave familiar Roman ground. After a comparison of eastern and western law, Zachariä's conclusions were (i) 'that for the various kinds of real property ("Grundbesitzes") the Byzantines knew no different law of succession from the one applicable to personal property', and (ii) 'that a proper feudal bond remained foreign to the Byzantines'.[35] A new history might wish to rewrite these pages, since it would be able to take into account many documents not accessible to Zachariä. First of all, of course, consensus would be needed on what exactly is understood by feudalism.[36] And we should not forget that legal relations concerning real property and their description also presented – and still do present – problems to western medieval lawyers and their historians.

For the time being, everyone will continue to make grateful use of Zachariä's *Geschichte*.

8. Afterlife and Reception of Byzantine Law

The life of a legal system is bound up first of all with the society, and often the state, in which it developed. The Byzantine empire, the legitimate successor of the Roman empire, lived on until the fall of Constantinople in 1453. But as is well known, the end of a state need not be the end of its legal system. Byzantine law, considered here as part of the afterlife of Roman law, is a case in point. The key to understanding its success lies in the defining characteristics of Byzantium: the Greek language and the Orthodox faith. Where an historical awareness of these characteristics, coinciding with the right political conditions, survived the collapse of the state, Byzantine law often lived on. This is true of Greece in particular, where after 1453 the population under Turkish domination was allowed to follow 'Roman' (that is, Byzantine) law under the responsibility of the Patriarch of Constantinople. When, on independence in the early 1820s, the nascent Greek state adopted a constitution, it immediately confirmed 'the remaining laws of the Christian emperors of Constantinople'.[37]

Generally speaking, the canon law of the Orthodox Church preserved a certain amount of Byzantine law of secular origin. In that sense one aspect of the survival of Byzantine law is the spread and survival of Orthodoxy. It is certainly responsible for the following two interesting cases, in which the presence of Byzantine law cannot readily be explained by the historical existence of the Byzantine empire. These are cases not of the 'normal' development of Byzantine law but of its 'reception' or 'transplant': the adoption of a legal system in an area where it had not been at home as the law of the land. With the greatest hesitation a possible third case may be mentioned, though it is subject to much debate.

The first case concerns the reception of Byzantine law in eastern Europe, for which Christianization by Byzantine missionaries was crucial.[38] Byzantine ecclesiastical law, already containing imperial law, was adopted in the new churches, and several secular collections followed in its wake. Obolensky points out four reasons for interest in Byzantine laws in that part of the world. In addition to a practical reason, a political reason, and the connection with canon law, he puts forward as a cultural reason 'the immense prestige which the empire's legal tradition enjoyed in the eyes of its neighbours'.[39] The result varied from country to country, but the *Ecloga* and *Procheiron* seem to have been the most successful. Several translations are preserved.[40]

Another case is the Ethiopic *Fetha Nagast*, the 'Law of the Kings' in Ge'ez, the 'learned' language of the Ethiopian people.[41] It retained a prominent position in Ethiopia until the promulgation of a Penal Code in 1930 and again in 1957 and a Civil Code in 1960.[42] On all three occasions the *Fetha Nagast* was mentioned as the point of departure – or at least the inspiration – for the new law codes. It is a collection translated and adapted in the seventeenth century from an Arabic *nomocanon* in two parts written in 1238 by a Coptic jurist called Ibn al 'Assal. The first part deals with religious matters and need not concern us here. The second, secular part goes back to a collection in four books called 'The Canons of the Kings'. The first three of these books have been identified as versions of the *Procheiron*, the *Syro-Roman Law Book*, and the *Ecloga* respectively; the fourth draws on the Pentateuch.[43] The first and third part are cases of truly 'Byzantine' reception: the dates of their originals – 741 and the early

880s (or even 907), when Egypt had long ceased to be Byzantine (something that Ethiopia had never been) – show that we are dealing with a pure transplant. Transplants have a reason: here, once more, it is the Christian faith, but with a twist. The Copts had never accepted the creed of Chalcedon: they were monophysites. In theory, therefore, the *Procheiron* and *Ecloga* had been issued by heretic emperors. Among the 'Kings' in question was Constantine V of the *Ecloga*, who could conveniently be identified with Constantine the Great, most probably not by mistake but in a deliberate attempt to give the texts a respectable origin. Likewise, the attribution of the collection to the '318 Fathers of [the Council of] Nicaea [of 325]' fitted with the ascription to Constantine the Great. The story shows a transmission of Roman rules from Latin via Justinian to Greek to Arabic to Ge'ez. The Coptic language does not seem to have been involved, but the Copts – who were by then Arab-speaking – definitely were.

The case of the law of Ethiopia and its Coptic antecedents leads naturally to a possible third case of an entirely different nature. It concerns the hotly debated influence of Byzantine law on Islamic law. Ibn al 'Assal's work has been shown to have undergone Islamic influence,[44] which is hardly surprising when one considers for how long Egypt had been part of the Muslim world by the thirteenth century. But had Islamic law itself been influenced by Byzantine law? Lack of relevant knowledge means that the present writer can do no more than refer to Leopold Wenger's warning[45] and point to work by others. Recently, flying in the face of what seems to be traditional wisdom, Benjamin Jokisch has strongly defended a positive answer. Among other things, he construes a link between the *Digest* and Islamic law through the intermediary of the Greek Digest Summa of the so-called Anonymus.[46]

Another way of looking to the phenomenon of an afterlife of Byzantine law is to focus on the reception of one text only. The *Ecloga* of the iconoclast emperors Constantine V and Leo III has already been mentioned several times. It had at least a Slavonic, an Armenian, and an Arabic reception,[47] and its history in southern Italy should perhaps come under the same heading.[48] But the great success of the *Ecloga* should not make us impervious to the fact that there never was a wholesale reception of Roman–Byzantine law in the east on the scale and in the form of the reception of the *Corpus iuris civilis* in the west. The honour of the longest unbroken tradition, however, arguably has to go to the present Greek state, where the *Tourkokratia* did not end the application of Byzantine law, and where Byzantine law was once more confirmed on independence, finally to be replaced only in 1946 by a BGB-inspired Greek Civil Code.[49]

9. RECEPTION OF BYZANTINE LAW IN THE WEST? GLOSSATORS AND HUMANISTS

Until the time of legal humanism Byzantine law led an existence quite separate from Roman law in the west. Yet the almost contemporaneous foundation of a law school in Constantinople in 1045 and the first beginnings in Bologna just a few decades or so later offer tantalizing food for thought. So far no direct or indirect influence has been proven. The Glossators do not seem to have been the pupils of their Constantinopolitan colleagues. Medieval manuscripts of the *Corpus iuris civilis* are almost devoid of Greek.

A western presence of Greek legal texts and their use by scholars are not attested until the fifteenth century.[50] Even then, we should not think of a 'reception' of Byzantine law. What was new was rather an awareness of the opportunity of checking the received text and interpretation of the *Corpus iuris civilis* of the late Middle Ages against an authentic, earlier tradition of the *Corpus* in a different political and cultural environment. To be sure, lack of knowledge of all relevant manuscripts and restricted access to those that were known contributed to exploitation of the possibilities that was only gradual and piecemeal. An edition of the most important source, the *Basilica cum scholiis*, was produced only in 1647;[51] its replacement in the nineteenth century by Heimbach[52] was still a far cry from a satisfactory critical edition, which did not appear until the twentieth century.[53] Already in 1534 Viglius of Aytta had prepared the *editio princeps* of the *Paraphrasis Institutionum* of Theophilus; unfortunately, his source was a Venetian manuscript which was not representative of its textual tradition. An edition with full critical apparatus appeared only in 2010.[54] But although the means at their disposal were defective, the humanists were on the right track towards fully understanding the textual transmission of the Justinianic texts.

To understand this we have to return to the beginnings of Byzantine law, to the process of appropriation of the Latin texts in a Greek-speaking environment – in short, to the classroom of the first decades after the completion of Justinian's codification. The *antecessores* had to begin with and explain a Latin text. Sometimes they quoted a Latin word or passage; in rare cases they even explicitly pointed out variant readings. A *kata poda* translation into Greek was an almost direct representation of the Latin sentence over which it had been written. Even a summarizing translation can be a good indirect witness of its source. All these genres have been preserved to a greater or lesser extent in the Byzantine tradition, especially in the *scholia* on the Basilica. To take full advantage of these sources one needs, of course, to understand their nature and cultural context.

The humanists were not 'receiving' Byzantine law. On the contrary, they searched for sources containing what was in their view 'authentic' Roman law – that is, 'what Justinian had written'. They thought they found that in ancient manuscripts, especially the Florentine codex of the *Digest* and in certain Byzantine texts. Byzantine sources, then, were considered useful insofar as they enabled the scholar to come closer to Justinian, bridging a time gap of around 1,000 years. Their possibilities still have not been exploited to the full.

10. Epilogue

Language excepted, it would seem difficult to distinguish Roman from Byzantine law. In the fourteenth century a Byzantine student would still learn his secular law from Theophilus' *Paraphrasis* and consult Harmenopoulos' *Hexabiblos.* The former translates and explains Justinian's *Institutes*; the latter is a compilation drawn from various Byzantine compilations, the great majority of them ultimately going back to Justinian's legislation. There can be no doubt that Byzantine law was Roman law – and was to remain Roman even after the fall of Constantinople.

But Byzantine law is, of course, not just Roman law. As the present writer is all too painfully aware, to sketch Byzantine law as a species of Roman law is grossly unfair to legal historians of Byzantium who study Byzantine law for its own sake and not from the perspective of a Romanist.[55] For modern students of Roman law the distance in time between them and Justinian has now stretched to almost 1500 years. Modern Romanists may not be much interested in Byzantine legal practice, but they will still find it worth their while to pursue a humanist agenda.[56] In doing so they are studying not Byzantine law, but Roman law through exploiting Byzantine sources.

Our knowledge of Byzantine law has increased immensely since the humanists and is still increasing. Well-known texts have received modern critical editions, and hitherto unknown texts their *editio princeps.*[57] Nowadays editions are accompanied by a translation into an 'accessible' language. For a fairly recent development we have to thank our colleagues in the sciences: through modern multispectral photography and enhancement of digital images it has become possible to read the lower layer of palimpsest manuscripts with greater success than in the past. It is not an exaggeration to say that legal historians especially are profiting from these possibilities. Few texts become as definitively obsolete as legal texts when new legislation is issued. All Romanists are familiar with the example of Gaius' *Institutes*, of which only a palimpsest has reached us. That text was of course superseded by Justinian's *Institutes* and therefore no longer copied. Byzantine legal texts are no exception. They too are frequently found buried in the cancelled layers of manuscripts, reused for texts that were apparently considered more interesting. Occasionally the legal historian will now be able to make a journey back in time. More than once the destination will turn out to be Justinian.[58]

NOTES

1. See the chapters by Mayali, 374–95; Helmholz, 396–422; and Zimmermann, 452–80.
2. Cf. the chapter by Kaiser, 119–48; and Section 5, this chapter.
3. Kaiser, Section 2; and Section 3, this chapter.
4. See, esp., Section 3, this chapter.
5. B. H. Stolte, 'Is Byzantine Law Roman Law?', *Acta Byzantina Fennica* 2 (n.s.) (2003–4): 111–16; B. H. Stolte, 'The Byzantine Law of Obligations', in *Obligations in Roman Law. Past, Present and Future*, ed. by T. A. J. McGinn (Ann Arbor, 2012), 320–33.
6. H. J. Scheltema, *L'enseignement de droit des antécesseurs* (Leiden, 1970), repr. in his *Opera minora ad iuris historiam pertinentia*, ed. N. van der Wal et al. (Groningen, 2004), 58–110.
7. It is worth remembering that the original meaning of this word is 'what is written beside [the text]': many of these explanations were first given literally 'beside' – that is, in the margin – of the text.
8. See also W. Kaiser, *Die Epitome Iuliani. Beiträge zum römischen Recht im frühen Mittelater und zum byzantinischen Rechtsunterricht* (Frankfurt, 2004): note the significant subtitle.
9. N. van der Wal and J. H. A. Lokin, *Delineatio iuris graeci-romani. Les sources du droit byzantin de 300 à 1453* (Groningen, 1985); S. N. Troianos, *Oi peges tou buzantinou dikaiou*, 3rd augmented ed. (Athens – Komotini, 2011).
10. B. H. Stolte, 'Justice: Legal Literature', in *The Oxford Handbook of Byzantine Studies*, ed. E. Jeffreys et al. (Oxford, 2008), 691–8.
11. P. E. Pieler, 'Byzantinische Rechtsliteratur', in *Die hochsprachliche profane Literatur der Byzantiner*, vol. 2, ed. H. Hunger (Munich, 1978), 341–480.
12. Scheltema (n. 6), 1: 'Presque tous ces ouvrages . . . sont des mosaïques formées par ces textes arrangés sans cesse dans de nouvelles combinaisons.'
13. *Theophili Antecessoris Paraphrasis Institutionum*, ed. J. H. A. Lokin et al., with translation by A. F. Murison (Groningen, 2010).
14. This re-orientation in relation to the Justinianic period is connected with a cultural revival known as the 'Macedonian Renaissance': for a brief introduction from a legal perspective, P. E. Pieler, 'Anakatharsis ton palaion nomon und makedonische Renaissance', *Subseciva Groningana* 3 (1995): 61–78.
15. *Basilicorum libri LX*. Series A: Textus (8 vols.); Series B: Scholia (9 vols.), ed. H. J. Scheltema et al. (Groningen – The Hague, 1953–88). See *Subseciva Groningana* 3 (1995) for the Proceedings of the Symposium on the occasion of the Completion of a New Edition of the Basilica, Groningen, 1–4 June, 1988.

16. N. van der Wal, 'Die Schreibweise der dem Lateinischen entlehnten Fachworten in der frühbyzantinischen Juristensprache', *Scriptorium* 37 (1983): 29–53; L. Burgmann, 'Lexeis rhomaïkai. Lateinische Wörter in byzantinischen Rechtstexten', in *Lexicographica byzantina*, ed. W. Hörandner and E. Trapp (Vienna, 1991), 61–79; Theophilus (n. 13), Prolegomena, xxiii–xxvi; Indices, esp. XII: Latin words and expressions, 996–1028.
17. Theophilus (n. 13), Prolegomena, xlix.
18. For all this see R. Browning, *Medieval and Modern Greek*, 2nd edn. (Cambridge, 1983), who, however, does not deal with the phenomenon of 'legal' Greek.
19. See, e.g., P. Sarris, *Economy and Society in the Age of Justinian* (Cambridge, 2006).
20. See J. Beaucamp, 'L'histoire du droit byzantin face à la papyrologie juridique. Bilan et perspectives', *Fontes Minores* 11 (2005): 5–55.
21. D. Simon, *Rechtsfindung am byzantinischen Reichsgericht* (Frankfurt, 1973) paints a picture of the quality of the practice of the court which is in my view somewhat too negative.
22. *Syntagma ton theion kai hieron kanonon*, ed. G. A. Rhalles and M. Potles, 6 vols. (Athens, 1852–9), esp. vols. 1–4.
23. See, e.g., E. Papagianni, 'Un témoin de la réalité juridique byzantine: la jurisprudence patriarcale au XIVe siècle', *Fontes Minores* 11 (2005): 213–27.
24. *Archives de l'Athos*, ed. P. Lemerle et al., a series arranged by monastery (Paris, 1937–).
25. *Demetrii Chomateni Ponemata diaphora*, ed. G. Prinzing (Berlin – New York, 2002).
26. *Ecloga. Das Gesetzbuch Leons III. und Konstantinos' V*, ed. L. Burgmann (Frankfurt, 1983).
27. For orientation and editions, see van der Wal and Lokin (n. 9), 72–6; Troianos (n. 9), 160–79.
28. L. Burgmann and S. Troianos, 'Nomos Mosaïkos', *Fontes Minores* 3 (1979): 126–67.
29. L. Burgmann and S. Troianos, 'Appendix Eclogae', *Fontes Minores* 3 (1979): 24–125.
30. K. E. Zachariä von Lingenthal, *Geschichte des griechisch-römischen Rechts*, 3rd edn. (1892, repr. Aalen, 1955).
31. A. Kazhdan, 'Do we need a new history of Byzantine law?', *Jahrbuch der Österreichischen Byzantinistik* 39 (1989): 1–28; L. Burgmann, 'Ansinnen an byzantinische Rechtshistoriker. II: 'Do we need a new history of Byzantine law?', *Rechtshistorisches Journal* 10 (1991): 198–200; B. H. Stolte, 'Not new but novel. Notes on the historiography of Byzantine law', *Byzantine and Modern Greek Studies* 22 (1998): 264–79; cf. also B. H. Stolte, 'Balancing Byzantine Law', *Fontes Minores* 11 (2005): 74–5.
32. See also Section 4, this chapter; and esp. M. T. Fögen, 'Gesetz und Gesetzgebung in Byzanz. Versuch einer Funktionsanalyse', *Ius Commune* 14 (1987): 137–58.
33. See now L. Burgmann, 'Reformation oder Restauration? Zum Ehegüterrecht der Ecloga', in *Eherecht und Familiengut in Antike und Mittelalter*, ed. D. Simon (Munich, 1992), 29–42.
34. D. Simon, 'Das Ehegüterrecht der Pira. Ein systematischer Versuch', *Fontes Minores* 7 (1986): 193–238.
35. Zachariä (n. 30), 277.
36. See, e.g., the article on feudalism in the *Oxford Dictionary of Byzantium* (Oxford, 1991).
37. S. N. Troianos, 'Von der Hexabiblos zu den Basiliken', *Subseciva Groningana* 3 (1989): 127.
38. Here I generally follow D. Obolensky, *The Byzantine Commonwealth. Eastern Europe 500–1453* (London, 1971), ch. 10, 'Religion and Law', 377–415, esp. 404–15. Cf. also

Burgmann (n. 26), 25, pointing out that, insofar as missionaries were sent from Byzantium to the Slav countries, they understandably also adopted Byzantine ecclesiastical law. For bibliography, L. Burgmann and H. Kaufhold, *Bibliographie zur Rezeption des byzantinischen Rechts im alten Rußland sowie zur Geschichte des armenischen und georgischen Rechts* (Frankfurt, 1992).

39. Obolensky (n. 38), 405.
40. The details cannot detain us here. See, e.g., P. Angelini, 'The Code of Dušan 1349–1354', *TR* 80 (2012): 84.
41. *The Fetha Nagast. The Law of the Kings*, trans. from the Ge'ez by Abba Paulos Tzadua and ed. by P. L. Strauss, 2nd edn. (Durham, North Carolina, 2009), with an excellent introduction by Tzadua (xxxvii–xxxviii, plus bibliography), and by P. H. Sand ('Roman origins of the Ethiopian "Law of the Kings" [Fetha Nagast]', xxxix–l).
42. Tzadua in Tzadua-Strauss (n. 41), xxxviii.
43. Sand in Tzadua-Strauss (n. 41), esp. xlv–xvii, with bibliography.
44. Sand in Tzadua-Strauss (n. 41), xlvii–xviii.
45. L. Wenger, *Die Quellen des römischen Rechts* (Vienna, 1953) 318, quoted in translation by Sand in Tzadua-Strauss (n. 41), xlix.
46. B. Jokisch, *Islamic Imperial Law. Harun-Al-Rashid's Codification Project* (Berlin – New York, 2007). For a convenient summary of the main thrust of this sizeable work, see the review by R. Zimmermann, *Zeitschrift für europäisches Privatrecht* 16 (2008): 655–6.
47. Burgmann (n. 26), 24–7; *Die arabische Ecloga. Das vierte Buch der Kanones der Könige aus der Sammlung des Makarios*, ed. S. Leder (Frankfurt, 1985), with a valuable introduction; *Die slavische Ecloga*, ed. J. N. Ššapov and L. Burgmann (Frankfurt, 2011).
48. Burgmann (n. 26), 23–4.
49. Even that did not mean the end: Byzantine law can still be invoked on the Holy Mountain, Mount Athos.
50. For a full introduction, see H. E. Troje, *Graeca leguntur. Die Aneignung des byzantinischen Rechts und die Entstehung eines humanistischen Corpus iuris civilis in der Jurisprudenz des 16. Jahrhunderts* (Cologne – Vienna, 1971).
51. *Ton Basilikon biblia LX*, ed. C. A. Fabrot, 7 vols. (Paris, 1647).
52. *Basilicorum libri LX*, ed. C. G. E. Heimbach et al., 6 vols. and 2 suppls. (Leipzig, 1833–97).
53. N. 15, this chapter.
54. Theophilus (n. 13); on humanist and later editions see xxxvii–xliii.
55. For a mostly different emphasis see, e.g., the series *Fontes Minores*, 11 vols. to date (Frankfurt, 1976–).
56. B.H. Stolte, 'The Value of the Byzantine Tradition for Textual Criticism of the Corpus Iuris Civilis. 'Graeca leguntur', *Introduzione al diritto bizantino*, ed. J. H. A. Lokin and B. H. Stolte (Pavia, 2011), 667–80, with examples of the value of Theophilus' Greek *Paraphrasis Institutionum* for establishing the text of Justinian's *Institutes*. Kaiser, 128–30 gives an example for establishing the text of the *Digest*.
57. For advances made in the last decades see B. H. Stolte (n. 31), 61–5.
58. For a recent example see J. Grusková and B.H. Stolte, 'Zwei neue Basiliken-Handschriften in der Österreichischen Nationalbibliothek. I: Paläographisch-kodikologische Analyse; II: Rechtshistorische Analyse. Mit 30 Tafeln', *Quellen zur byzantinischen Rechtspraxis. Aspekte der Textüberlieferung, Paläographie und Diplomatik. Akten des internationalen Symposiums Wien, 5.–7.11. 2007*, ed. C. Gastgeber (Vienna, 2010), 107–82.

18 The Legacy of Roman Law

Laurent Mayali

Standing on one side of the entrance to the city hall of Saint Antonin, Justinian holds his book of the *Institutes* open, with the statement *Imperatoriam maiestatem non solum armis decoratam sed etiam legibus oportet esse armatam.*[1] Facing Justinian, on the other side, Adam and Eve stand next to the tree of knowledge. In the late 1130s, when the city authorities commissioned these two statues, Saint Antonin-Noble Val was a small town built around its Benedictine abbey on the pilgrims' path to Santiago de Compostella. Lying between Quercy and Rouergue in the southwestern part of the mountains that mark the southern limits of the Massif Central, it was away from the main trade roads connecting northern Italy with southern France and Spain. Yet this early reference to Justinian as legislator in a remote part of France attests to the rapid dissemination of Roman legal culture in medieval society.[2] The city hall of Saint Antonin stood as a symbol of municipal governance under the rule of its viscount. In the eyes of its citizens, these strongly symbolic sculptures represented the spiritual and temporal pillars upon which medieval society was meant to rest. Justinian's effigy further conveyed the significance of law as a model of governance that challenged the traditional practices of feudal society.[3]

By this time, on the other side of the Alps, the study of Roman law already attracted widespread interest.[4] As early as 1127, a Benedictine monk from Saint Victor of Marseille, who was on his way to Rome on his monastery's business, described in a letter to his abbot the 'crowds of students' who were 'hurrying' to Bologna for the sole purpose of studying law.[5] Seeking his abbot's consent, our monk was keen to outline the multiple advantages of this legal knowledge and its great benefits to the monastery in the endless disputes that opposed it to its quarrelsome feudal neighbours. Despite its obviously self-serving overtones, this account attested to the appeal of a legal knowledge that was equated with expertise and power.

Barely half a century earlier, the first confirmed reference to Roman law was made in a trial held at Marturi in northern Tuscany. It is generally agreed among legal historians that, with the collapse of the western empire in the fifth century, Roman law almost disappeared from the emerging European legal landscape. A handful of Germanic legislation maintained for a while a piecemeal assortment of Roman legal provisions for their newly conquered Gallo-Roman subjects. Sporadic evidence nevertheless suggests that with the collapse of the western empire most of its legal institutions eventually fell into desuetude. A few centuries later, the short-lived Carolingian episode revitalized the imperial ideal but contributed little to structuring these ideas into a coherent legal system. Under these circumstances the resurgence of Roman law in northern Italy by the end of the eleventh century remains as remarkable as it is mysterious. Such obscure beginnings for the use of Roman law in legal practice point, in the absence of public support, to the role of private initiatives on a case-by-case basis. These timid attempts did not hinder a subsequent expansion that set up the conditions for the defining influence of Roman law on emerging European legal systems.[6] By the end of the twelfth century, knowledge of Roman law was widespread among governing elites.[7] Emperors and popes, princes and bishops, lords and merchants often relied upon legal experts for advice and assistance. Medieval towns witnessed the ascension of these *legum doctores* or *iuris periti*, judges, lawyers and notaries, who enjoyed a monopoly in the exercise of the legal profession.

The appeal of Roman law was even more remarkable in a static society where innovations were considered with suspicion and long-established customs regulated conservative ways of life. Early local interest ultimately grew into substantial enthusiasm and triggered an intellectual revolution.[8] Its initial impact on daily legal practice was, however, diverse. In various parts of Europe local usages and beliefs reinforced people's sense of belonging to tightly knit communities.[9] In some areas attitudes towards the new law varied from diffidence to outright hostility, while in others the written reason was embraced as a source of much-needed legal instruments. It would thus be inaccurate to construe the resurgence of Roman law in western Europe as the triumph of a new legal system that overcame the resistance of local usages, thoroughly shaped secular legislation, redefined feudal obligations, and permanently altered the essence of ecclesiastical law. From a comparative perspective, the re-emergence of Roman law appears as a gradual process of legal transplants of varying success into communities, political circles, and nations that had little awareness of a common Roman cultural heritage and even less of a sense of Roman identity. Roman law did not mirror medieval and early modern societies, nor did it closely espouse individual or collective expectations. Within these limitations, it nevertheless shaped distinct expressions of private and public lives as it was used to convey definite conceptions of a political and social order. These paradoxes force us to reconsider in part historical accounts of this *reception* which largely depend on a legal-positivist view of the development of legal systems in European countries.

When Roman legal rules took roots on these new grounds, more than six centuries after the collapse of the western Roman empire, their rapid growth sprang from a combination of seemingly conflicting factors. On the one hand, historical reference to a long-forgotten past had a strong symbolic dimension that resonated in the classical culture of the social and political elites as a model of civism and governance. The reference to a famed past carried with it images of prestige and authority that were associated, especially after the Christianization of the empire, with public institutions and the exercise of political power. On the other hand, the adoption of new legal instruments and procedures met concrete and practical needs that could no longer be satisfied by adherence to local usage. By the end of the twelfth century, in both the private and public spheres, the increased complexity of daily transactions and a changing economic environment necessitated the implementation of new sets of rules and principles. The success of Roman law was thus conditioned by its perceived historical prestige, but also heightened by its ability to provide suitable solutions to growing legal challenges. In doing so, it also projected a conception of legality that would in turn influence the perception of existing usages and social practices, thus contributing to their conversion into a newly defined customary law.

The transformation of ancient practices into juridical rules resulted from the emergence of new concepts of law and the development of a juridical language that provided different forms of narrative and models of representation. Law was not simply the consequence of human experiences and practices. It was also the result of a cognitive process. This process perhaps reached its apex in the first decades of the thirteenth century when Accursius, the renowned author of the ordinary gloss to the *Corpus iuris civilis*, asserted that to know the law meant to know everything, since there was nothing outside the *corpus* of the law. This forceful statement did not accurately describe the reality of the contemporaneous legal order, but it does demonstrate the perceived significance of a legal system that had come to life barely a century earlier. Accursius justified his claim by quoting Ulpian's definition of jurisprudence as the knowledge of both divine and human affairs. Our doctor's enthusiasm reflected perhaps an exaggerated sense of his own importance. But despite this self-indulgence, his interpretation led to more wide-ranging conclusions which expressed the jurist's wonder at the authority of his newly-acquired knowledge. By then, in

Bologna and elsewhere in Italy and Europe, Roman legal culture surely permeated all aspects of social life. City councils adopted imperial constitutions on architecture and city planning, canonists updated the legal foundations of the Church's authority and, as Ernst Kantorowicz noted,[10] artists such as Petrarch and Dante found legitimation for their own creative powers in the civilist's interpretation of law as the 'art of good and equal'. Interpreting Roman law in such ways performed a double heuristic function: it made sense of its rules while relying on them to give meaning to new demands and ideas.

This juridical acculturation produced at least two consequences. First, as observed by André Gouron, it sanctioned the development of a normative culture firmly based on reference to the law (*ius*).[11] Second, the so-called renaissance of Roman law was less the rebirth of a long-forgotten *romanitas* than the dawn of a new legal system where the interpretation and application of Roman rules did not always follow the reasoning of former Roman jurisconsults or the pronouncements of emperors. Medieval jurists and their successors were less concerned with recovering the essence of Roman law than with making sense of diverse legal techniques and asserting their relevance for their times. In so doing, they not only focused on the meaning of obscure terms and their accurate translation but also assessed the authority of the legal reasoning that they encountered according to their own logical conclusions.

One should not assume, however, that the rediscovered Roman texts were considered a sort of ready-made handbook for finding solutions to life's legal problems. The daunting mass of written sources assembled in Justinian's compilations undoubtedly presented a significant challenge both in form and substance for people who, for the most part, enjoyed a limited command of their complex legal syntax. The challenge was further compounded at a time when the prevailing normative tradition relied almost entirely on oral transmission. In such a culture of orality, written texts yielded great authority. Roman law became known as the *ius scriptum* or the *ratio scripta* in order to indicate its unique status. The written law embodied in people's view a legal rationality that contrasted with the empirical oral tradition. With texts came words and concepts that composed a new legal terminology and became part of the language of society.

At the same time, in academic circles, the varying approaches to Roman legal sources initially stemmed from a combination of cultural shortcomings and intellectual choices. In the contemporary world of medieval scholasticism, jurists' reasoning followed the distinct patterns of *scientia* and *prudentia* that reflected the awareness of the dual function of law as abstract knowledge and a functional system of rules. But this division was not construed as an opposition between two clearly distinct methods in which the limits of legal reasoning were circumscribed by the necessities of legal practice. It was, on the contrary, the continuous interplay of *scientia* and *prudentia* that expressed the perceived plasticity of a legal system which combined – more or less harmoniously – diverse normative sources and traditions. Consequently, attempts to outline or interpret this dichotomy by drawing a distinction between theory and practice remain largely unsatisfactory in the historical assessment of the impact of Roman law on western legal culture.

The extent of Roman law's influence over time is thus measured by the emergence of new forms of legal consciousness that gradually expanded to whole communities – not just intellectual elites – in both public and private matters. In this perspective, the local resistance to Roman law rules which was emphasized by chauvinistic historiography in the first half of the twentieth century did not always imply rejection of the entire legal model. It focused instead on selective applications. For instance, it is worth noting that the affirmation of community norms versus alien Roman rules often relied on the legal technique of renunciation that was itself borrowed from Roman law, as illustrated in the widespread use of contractual provisions rejecting the application of Roman legal exceptions in contractual transactions.[12] Resistance to *ius scriptum* was thus more pragmatic than ideological. Local customs and feudal law did not constitute a monolithic and bottomless reservoir of static rules. As society changed, customs evolved and Roman legal technology quietly found its way into the reconstructed legal heritage that defined community tradition. The novelty of Roman rules was often hidden behind rhetorical reference to ancient local traditions. In the late middle ages, for every explicit denunciation of unwelcome Roman legal influence, we often count several discreet adoptions of rules that represented a significant departure from the earliest social practices. Although this process of domestic assimilation forces us to reconsider the old-fashioned history of the civil law tradition, its broader consequences for the dissemination of Roman law across Europe should nonetheless be carefully appraised.

Perhaps the main source of contention among legal scholars lies with the ambiguity surrounding the concept of *ius commune*. Historians and jurists have long referred to the period defined by the last centuries of the middle ages as the 'age of *ius commune*'. This expression conveniently fitted within the description of medieval legal pluralism. It represented an overarching system of rules that elevated Roman law to the status of a unifying model when state nationalism was still in its infancy. The interpretation of the term as a synonym for Roman law is often misleading. Its definition is at best elusive and its use subject to diverse interpretations. Although Roman law was never enforced as the common law of continental Europe, its academic status as the archetype of a legal system made it an obvious common reference. From the twelfth century onwards, multiple mentions of the *ius commune* suggest a broader meaning than the description of Roman law, since *ius commune* rules were not always viewed as having a Roman origin. Outside the writings of learned jurists (who held it as a synonym for the written law, including canon law), in legal documents from various parts of Europe the expression might equally have described local customs or legislation – the general customs of the kingdom – that defined, in people's minds, a shared legal tradition.[13] On the whole, medieval and early modern mentions of the *ius commune* instead expressed belief in the existence of a common legal language. It exemplified a form of legal reasoning that governed the understanding of the purpose of law in a given society. The romanization of European legal traditions, from the middle ages to modern times, did not rest only on the strict adoption of rules and procedures that can be traced back to a particular section of Justinian's compilations.

Ultimately, the development of this legal patchwork resulted from three main historical factors. It started as an intellectual movement that was promptly supported by political powers, both secular and ecclesiastical. It was also fuelled by pressing social demands and aided by the concomitant development of the legal profession. The cumulative effects of these underlying forces fashioned over a period of several centuries the main features of the civil law tradition.[14]

Its intellectual foundations defined the conditions for its successful adoption. The emergence of Roman law in northern Italy and its rapid expansion in continental Europe resulted in the gradual and permanent transformation of legal thinking. Its influence is perhaps nowhere more significant than in the conception of a legal system, the definition of a law-making process that clearly defines the validity and authority of legal norms and their implementation into a cohesive system of rules. From this perspective, it is not inappropriate to consider the vast legal literature of the last centuries of the middle ages and the modern period as the result of a unique European experience.

First, the success of the intellectual movement that led to the birth of medieval jurisprudence rested upon the creation of new centres of learning. These communities of masters and students (*universitas magistrorum et scholarium*) departed from the ancient model of the cathedral schools. Their open structure and larger size transformed educational standards and teaching practices. Where cathedral schools had relied upon small groups of pupils and teachers studying together a finite number of texts, the new universities grew with the expansion of groups of doctors and students who engaged in a variety of textual inquiries and topics. Legal education profited doubly from the development of these new institutions. On the one hand, they provided a stable and controlled environment for the members of the academic community. Newly founded colleges endowed by rich patrons offered free and convenient housing to numerous students from out of town. The development of copyists' workshops ensured the continuous production of copies of the texts studied. Jurists also benefited from the vicinity of adjoining disciplines that formed the curriculum of the *trivium* and *quadrivium*. Legal pedagogy initially used most of the intellectual tools acquired during the jurists' previous training in fields where scholars enjoyed longer experience in textual exegesis and in teaching its different outcomes.

The sheer mass of texts that composed Justinian's compilations, as well as their diverse origins, imposed the use of adequate heuristic methods on readers who were hardly versed in the details of Rome's legal history. The compilations' lack of a systematic arrangement added to the confusion induced by multiple repetitions and contradictory statements attributed to diverse jurisconsults or emperors. Indexing, cross-referencing, grouping, and annotating proved to be essential procedures in the gradual assimilation of this legal treasure trove. As rightly observed by Giuseppe Speciale, Accursius' ordinary gloss and the apparatus that preceded it represented the medieval equivalents of contemporary hypertexts.[15] They served identical purposes and provided their users with the necessary tools to access Justinian's data banks and retrieve basic information. Ultimately, data processing included a succession of steps that defined the content of the lectures from simple retrieval of facts to the presentation of principles and from the classification of arguments to the resolution of contradictions. Besides their obvious practical purpose, these methodological choices also reflected a distinct conception of law's function that eventually defined legal scholasticism. This particular approach to the textual tradition shaped the perception of civil law for the following centuries, up to the nineteenth-century codification movements.

The significance of the written support was further compounded by its rarity. Attempts at providing a comprehensive exegesis of Roman legal sources were constrained by the difficulty of securing reliable and complete versions of the texts. The philological challenge could not be easily solved and raised multiple unanswered questions, both theoretical and practical, about the authenticity of the texts and the authority of their provisions. A defective process of transmission of Justinian's corpus produced different consequences for the structure and content of legal education. Unreliable manuscript traditions governed access to the separate parts of the *Corpus iuris civilis*. There are reasons to believe that this breakdown caused the division of the *Digest* into three parts (*Vetus*, *Infortiatum*, and *Novum*). On the whole, this arbitrary textual distribution did not reflect any substantive preferences, nor was it motivated by a patent pedagogic strategy. The partition of the last three books of the *Code* (*Tres Libri*) seems, on the other hand, to have been the consequence of a deliberate decision to treat public law issues separately.[16] These last three books were collected separately in the *Volumen*, together with the *Institutes*, a version of the *Novels* known as the *Authenticum*, and a compilation of feudal law, the *Libri feudorum*. It is worth mentioning that this subdivision remained in use until the end of the middle ages despite the more fluent use of the various segments of this monumental work. The fact that it was still maintained in the sixteenth-century printed editions of the *Corpus iuris civilis*, notwithstanding the humanists' critical editions, is evidence of its significance in understanding the civilists' attachment to the fundamental function of the text in defining law's authority. Let us observe, however, that this textual formalism did not preclude a more systematic arrangement of legal rules. First attempts at systematization had already taken place in the last decade of the twelfth century, but this change had occurred in the neighbouring field of canon law with the composition of the first compilation of pontifical law decretals, the *Compilatio Prima* authored by Bernard of Pavia. Despite the canonists' broad reliance on Roman law in the elaboration of the laws of the Church, the new format did not influence the civilists' traditional lectures and commentaries on the *Corpus iuris*, but it certainly opened the door to more thematic expositions of distinct legal topics in numerous separate treatises of varying length.

While the tripartite arrangement of the *Digest* and the partition of the *Code* determined the structure of the lectures, the medieval fortune of the *Institutes* followed a different path. Initially written for the education of students, the four books of the *Institutes* purported to give a shorter and clearer version of the main legal issues addressed in the *Code* and the *Digest*. Its simplified structure in four books provided medieval readers with a more accessible and practical introduction to Roman law. Its availability explains its popularity among smaller academic circles outside Bologna where the scarcity of copyist's workshops made it almost impossible for students and Faculty alike to acquire samples of the necessary parts of the *Digest* or *Code*.[17] The scarcity of legal manuscripts undoubtedly explains the production of second-hand works and partial summaries that bear witness to the existence of small pockets of intellectual activity outside

Bologna. In most cases, however, the fact that they had no durable institutional support led to their disappearance, while Bologna remained for a time a unique model. While Bologna was witnessing the rise of academic dynasties and the steady growth of its student population, elsewhere in Catalonia, Languedoc, and England a handful of centres attempted to satisfy a local demand for the new *ius scriptum*. From Placentinus in Montpellier to Vacarius in Oxford,[18] former members of the Bolognese *studium* tended to the growing local interest in the law.[19] For a brief period, these short-lived schools succeeded in spreading the lessons of the Bolognese masters to a small audience of students, clerics, and public authorities who might have first encountered the new law through contact with merchants from Italian cities such as Genoa or Pisa who opened trading posts in their cities. Roman law came in these merchants' bags or in those of the clerics. Its progression followed the trading routes and the pilgrims' pathways that connected northern Italy towards the east to southern France and northern Spain and towards the north, past the Parisian schools, the fairgrounds of Champagne, and across the Channel on to religious and commercial centres. England was not immune from this intellectual epidemic. Local schools in Oxford and elsewhere served as relays for the circulation of the Bolognese teaching. At the turn of the thirteenth century, this knowledge commanded the attention of local jurists who used it as a functional reference in the consolidation of the laws of the realm.[20] Here, as elsewhere, the extent of this influence depended on the perceived usefulness of peripheral rules in the expansion of the indigenous system. From this perspective, legal transplants did not inevitably displace existing rules so much as they adjusted the scope of their application. This initial pattern of diffusion of Roman law by way of periodic interactions in academic, religious, or commercial centres remained constant for several centuries until the nation-states finally took over the legal systems of the various countries. This cultural pattern was largely responsible for the patchwork nature of romanization in western Europe, in both form and content, where practical concerns were mixed with doctrinal pursuits.

In Bologna, the situation was different. The teaching of Roman law was the cornerstone of a prosperous institution that assumed a central position in the city's affairs. Its fame was founded on the reputation of a handful of professors who asserted their command of the legal sources and advanced their authoritative opinions to enraptured audiences. Academic tradition preserved the names of these pioneers and conveyed the memory of their opinions from one generation of students to the other. Following the first lectures of Irnerius, two schools soon came into being, around 1130.

Each one expressed a distinct conception of the legal order. Disciples following the teaching of Bulgarus took pride in adopting a strict interpretation of the sources and endorsed an orthodox definition of law. Others known as the Gosiani – taking their name from the family name of their master, Martinus – chose to pay more attention to different normative sources such as equity and customs.[21] The former eventually succeeded, at least in Bologna, in imposing their academic supremacy, thus cementing the fame of their master. Its dominance reached its apex with Accursius' ordinary gloss to the entire *corpus* in the first third of the thirteenth century. Martinus' views, on the other hand, found more attentive ears in small centres where some former students or those cast out from Bologna had chosen to settle, such as Placentinus in Montpellier. From the very first lectures of Pepo and Irnerius, on to Bulgarus and Martinus and then Placentinus, Johannes Bassianus, and Azo, academic genealogies were forged from masters to disciples.[22] Knowledge of Roman law established standing in social and political circles which profited from the prominence of academia and bolstered its prestige and the authority of its members. It is sometimes difficult to distinguish scholarly dissension from institutional jockeying and academic gossip in these academic quarrels. Competition for students' attention and for the support of public authorities, secular and ecclesiastical, was no doubt heightened by a political environment which saw the two main powers, imperial and pontifical, vie for the control of Italian cities and political hegemony over various parts of Europe. Since Savigny's first history of medieval Roman law, much has been written about the rivalry of these schools. Beyond the well-publicized differences and mutual criticisms, we observe the remarkable success of a rather small intellectual community and its capacity to impose its views on society as a whole – thus reinforcing Roman law's broad authority in public affairs. For instance, Justinian's declaration on the significance of the laws as weapons in the service of imperial power in times of both war and peace was understood to confer a kind of knighthood on lawyers who were expert in the use of these arms. Likewise, Ulpian's definition of jurisprudence as the knowledge of both human and divine causes was understood as vindicating the jurists' claims to equal mastery of law and theology. The new jurisprudence was born in the vigour of these intellectual exchanges. It forged the scholarly tradition of the civil law for many centuries to come. The success of the university of Bologna and its contribution to the city's fame inspired new establishments. The thirteenth and fourteenth centuries witnessed the foundation of various law schools in Italian and European cities.

To name a few, representative of the geographical expansion, we should mention Naples, Perugia, Orleans, Montpellier, Toulouse,

Salamanca, Coimbra, and Heidelberg. The significance of legal studies grew with the foundation of each new university. It assumed a broader purpose than the mere training of lawyers and it projected a template of governance that combined *iurisdictio* with *potestas*.[23] In 1406, the victorious Florentines solemnly transferred to their city a precious war trophy seized from the defeated Pisans. In many ways, Florence's possession of the oldest known manuscript of the *Digest* – the *Littera Pisana*, afterwards known as the *Florentina* – was an assertion of the triumphant political power's claim to legal knowledge and its desire to be associated with a tradition that reinforced its historical legitimacy.

In this political environment and with the support of local elites and public authorities, each law school attempted to attract prominent scholars who added to the city's renown and often took some part in its governance. Newly anointed doctors were hired from one city to the other; some returned to the school of their hometown after years of studying and teaching in Bologna; while others alternated teaching positions with the exercise of diplomatic charges or judicial functions. In any event, academic reputation warranted the value of legal opinions and consultations that increasingly represented an important aspect of the doctors' professional responsibilities. This practical activity gave rise to a new type of legal literature that eventually influenced the teaching of law and provided a theoretical model for discussing its practical points. By then, in most of these cities, Roman legal principles were seamlessly woven into the fabric of the community's law. Manuscripts of different parts of the *Corpus iuris civilis* found their way into private libraries as legal studies were viewed as the foundation of a good education. In Paris, however, Roman law was no longer welcome. In 1219, bowing to royal pressure and out of concern for the declining study of theology, pope Honorius III forbade the teaching of Roman law. But Roman law did not disappear from the French kingdom. A few decades later, the rise of the Orleans school injected new energy into a stagnant and complacent legal scholarship.[24] Combining a refreshed methodology with a critical appraisal of Accursius' *glossa ordinaria*, Orleans masters such as Jacques de Révigny[25] and Pierre de Belleperche challenged existing doctrines and proposed new interpretations. Their opinions did not go unnoticed across the Alps. They soon found their way back to Italian schools, with the help of professors such as Cinus de Pistoia – jurist, poet, and close friend of Dante – who passed them on to their students. Standing pre-eminent among this new generation of civilists, Bartolus de Sassoferato – professor in Pisa and Perugia and Cinus' former student – epitomized the civil-law academic tradition in the first half of the fourteenth century. His authoritative commentaries on the *Corpus iuris civilis*, combined with a series of works and treatises on diverse legal matters, dominated legal doctrine until the end of the middle ages. The lasting influence of Bartolus' works, blending Roman legal doctrine with the analysis and interpretation of local laws, remains permanently associated with the fortune of the civilists' theories in the development of modern legal systems. The academic momentum stimulated by the intellectual legacy of Bartolus and his disciple Baldus de Ubaldis carried the traditional teaching of Roman law up to the end of the middle ages.

For over a period of four centuries, from Irnerius' first lectures to the doctors of the early fifteen hundreds, the teaching of Roman law had enjoyed a remarkable period of institutional stability. It rarely deviated from the original Bolognese model that was still the source of authority for the intellectual tradition of the *mos italicus*. This conservative attitude was supported by the repetitive character of commentaries which, for the most part, barely added new meaning to the opinions of preceding generations of teachers. The initial exegetic methodology favoured by the glossators had given way to the more text-independent form of the commentary. But emancipation from the confines of strict textual exegesis was limited by the time-honoured reliance on the opinions of predecessors. A narrow rigidity in the form and content of lectures was maintained, following the original structure circumscribed by the early partitions of Justinian's compilations. Apart from a few new insights authored by a handful of doctors, legal scholarship was marred by uncritical repetition of previous opinions and an absence of innovative ideas. It seemed that the initial intellectual impetus that had promoted the renewal of jurisprudence and the growth of legal knowledge had finally run its course. Institutional decline quickly followed this intellectual drought. It badly affected the universities that remained committed to the traditional treatment of the legal sources. But as student attendance and the authority of professors declined in these older centres, emerging schools explored a different path and begun to attract larger audiences. By the end of the middle ages, Europe's enduring affair with Roman law was taking a new turn.

Renaissance humanism opened up intellectual perspectives and made the study of law a challenging pursuit.[26] Philological interest in Roman and Greek authors of the classical tradition placed the emphasis on the primary value of the text. The need to produce accurate editions became a priority.[27] The humanists' scorn for the medieval jurists' poor treatment of Latin and Greek sources did not significantly challenge the substance of established civilist doctrine, but it directed the jurists' attention to the limitations of a defective manuscript tradition. This erudite approach introduced a higher level of scrutiny of legal codes while aiming to restore their original structure and essential meaning. It raised doubts about the linguistic soundness of sources that had been taken for granted and prompted a thorough re-evaluation of their textual foundations. One of the pioneering attempts at this critical evaluation came with the publication of Guillaume Budé's *Adnotationes ad Pandectas* in 1508. This work set new editorial standards and offered a methodology that changed the longstanding medieval treatment of legal sources. Budé's administrative and diplomatic responsibilities placed him at the junction of the worlds of politics and law – outside the university, but within the apparatus of the nascent early modern state. This unique position gave him the freedom to treat the *Digest* without the constraints of an ossified teaching method, thus broadening its value in a system of education that sought to instil the new values of a humanistic vision of man and nature. In Bourges, where Alciatus and Cujas introduced students to the innovative legal science, as in Freiburg with Zasius and soon in Leiden, sixteenth-century continental Europe witnessed the rise of universities which welcomed this combination of philological erudition and legal criticism. Using their academic perches in a transnational forum of ideas, legal humanists reshaped the teaching of Roman law while expanding its scope into the various corners of early modern political culture at a time when religious conflicts challenged alternative forms of normative guidance and social control. In doing so, these *legum doctores* secured the enduring success of Roman law within the mainstream expansion of national legal systems in continental Europe.[28] Away from the first medieval schools, academic law continued to enjoy lasting influence in spite of the rise of state-sponsored teaching of domestic laws.[29] This literary-juridical movement stimulated the study of Justinian's sources and restored the historical significance of his laws in the development of European culture.

From its foundation in 1575, the university of Leiden assumed a central role in the diffusion of these legal ideas.[30] For the following century, the Dutch university remained the European hub of Roman jurisprudence which, like Bologna four hundred years earlier, attracted students from all parts Europe. Following the success of their promptly published lectures, scholars such as Doneau, Noodt,[31] Vinnius, and Voet[32] personified a generation of doctors who updated the Romanist tradition in accordance with the demands of their turbulent times without stripping it of its essence. The broad availability of printing ensured the wide diffusion of their works.[33] Multiple editions placated the public demand for constant updating, thus encouraging the perception of a continuous doctrinal production.[34] The names of these legal stars were associated with the fame of the institution they served and with the conception of a systematic and practically oriented legal science. This scholarly course paved the way for the further actualization of Roman law that was eventually promoted by the seventeenth-century *Usus modernus Pandectarum*. The modernism of Justinian's compilation did not spring from an antiquarian interest in its idealized past, nor did it result from a conformist wish to reassert long lost values of imperial romanity. In this late and final stage of the European reception of the legal legacy of Rome, German jurists such as Stryck promoted the growth of a mixed legal system attentive to the requirements of domestic institutions and social order.

Reborn out of centuries of painstaking exegesis, literal interpretation, and historical criticism, Roman law was well adapted to these changing times. In the eyes of the bureaucrats who were now in charge of concocting the mixtures of the state's legal order, transplanting Roman legal principles satisfied the need for innovation without carrying the risk of uncertainty. It conferred credibility on the claim of legal stability that legitimized the power of the modern ruler. This active integration of norms from diverse legal orders represented a significant departure from the medieval model of legal pluralism that had governed the insertion of Roman rules into existing systems.[35] Now in various countries the traditional process of juxtaposition and harmonization was subsumed into a rationally structured unifying plan.

From the pioneering contributions of the glossators, through the institutional hegemony of the commentators, to the sweeping transformations introduced by the humanists, the teaching of Roman law remained for several centuries the defining component of legal education in continental Europe. Legal texts and doctrinal treatises upheld the status of Roman law both as a source of knowledge and as a normative reference for legal transplants at a time when the authority and the status of major universities transcended contested state boundaries. The subsequent introduction of lectures on national law and the creation of professorial chairs dedicated to its teaching did not result in the exclusion of Roman law from the university's stage. On the contrary, it underscored the perennial value of a legal science that combined a rigorous method of analytical reasoning and textual criticism with a systematic conception of the legal order. It also represented a reliable point of reference for fragmented domestic legal systems.

The intellectual effervescence born of the humanist impulse nurtured early modern jurisprudence. It breathed new life into the civilist tradition and placed the study of the Roman jurists' works at the core of the political process leading to the establishment of national legal systems. Balancing its status between historical representation and contemporary relevance, the renowned architects of elegant jurisprudence permanently set civil law on a doctrinal course that eventually led to the codification movement of the nineteenth century.[36] With codification, the form and the substance of the law were once again combined according to a structural model that symbolized the osmosis of the legal system with the natural order of society. Beyond the influence of natural law theory and its appeal to the significance of a rational legal order, codification promoted a model of legislation that enhanced the overall authority of law while facilitating its access and use. For this purpose, the choice of the code as a vessel for organizing and presenting successive legal provisions was more than a historical coincidence. Apart from its symbolic value, it expressed the commonly shared view that the strength of all legal rules represented more than the arithmetical sum of their diverse provisions.

Much has been written about this last phase of Europe's juridical growth. Attempts at distinguishing what was Roman from what was domestic, sorting out the imported seeds from the native plants, and eventually piecing together the asymmetrical parts of the European legal puzzle produced uneven results. Part of the fault lies with the nationalist essence of legal history which, from the second half of the nineteenth century, went through great efforts to assert its *pro domo* legitimacy and to distance itself from the history of Roman law. This enduring distinction continues to shape law-school curricula in many European countries. But the other part of the responsibility for this confusing outcome lies with eighteenth-century jurists' attempts to circumvent the side effects of legal transplants. By dissociating the transplanted organs from their functions, they focused their attention on the consequences of the imported rules. Their intellectual fine-tuning was also facilitated by the rise of a state administrative apparatus that placed the imperatives of social management above ideological contentions. The final reception of the *ius civile* in northern Europe undoubtedly benefited from previous centuries of development of an autonomous legal science, however hesitant or imperfect it may have been compared with the standards of these new times. The reception process had come full circle. The codification movement accomplished what earlier generations of jurists and scholars had not been able to achieve: the normalization of Roman law and, with the uneasy assistance of the historical school, its insertion into a legal tradition. To be sure, the integration of Roman law into national legal systems had already taken place in various European countries with various consequences. But with codification the dichotomy distinguishing Roman law from local usage was replaced by the distinction between legislation and custom.

Intellectual prowess, however remarkable, was not the sole reason for the permanence of the Romanist legal tradition through the turbulent periods of European legal history. Political considerations certainly played a great role in the effective development of national legal systems. In addition to the strategies pursued by determined popes and emperors[37] in their attempts to define the greater scope of their powers, ambitious rulers of nascent kingdoms promptly seized opportunities to assert their claims to sovereignty.[38] In doing so, they paid particular attention to the legal theories expounded by the glossators and later commentators of Roman law. Beginning with Frederic Barbarossa's *Constitutio Habita* of 1158, extending protection and forum privileges to professors and students in Bologna,[39] imperial interest in Roman legal thought reflected the ruler's dual ambitions to base his power on a combination of historical legitimacy and legal authority. In this regard, Frederic's decision to expand an earlier privilege in the form of an imperial constitution which was to be inserted as a *Novel* in Justinian's *Code*, reflected the influence of civilist doctrine on the conception of his legislative power. The four Bolognese law professors present at the Diet of Roncaglia where a belligerent Frederic met representatives of the northern Italian cities undoubtedly drew his attention to the political advantages of this legal filiation. In their solemn harangue, they compared him to the 'living law on earth', thus applying to Frederic Justinian's self-professed description of his imperial *majestas*. The use of such a formula carried profound consequences. The transition from de facto power brought by the recent success of his army to *de iure* authority changed Frederic's political status. Arriving in Roncaglia as little more than a powerful feudal warlord, Frederic left as a universal statesman.[40]

It is not difficult to understand why public authorities turned a favourable ear to the lessons of Roman legal doctrine which, when applied efficiently, could contribute to redefining the scope of their powers and justifying their claim to political supremacy. In this context the influence of Roman law proved decisive in providing the much-needed juridical template for political ambitions. Medieval jurists were skilled at using their knowledge to the benefit of their rulers and redefining the princes' power in legal terms.[41] The first glossators' interpretation of the quasi mythical *lex regia* transferring legislative power from the people to their ruler provided a most opportune explanation for the concentration of powers in the emperor's hands.[42] The people's willing relinquishment of their law-making power in favour of the emperor was deemed to be irreversible. The jurists concluded that the emperor did not act as the mere representative of the people's will but as a legislator *sui iuris*. This medieval interpretation was further supported by the reference to Ulpian's declaration that whatever pleased the prince had the force of law.[43] The combination of these two excerpts became one of the cornerstones of the juridical reinterpretation of medieval political reality. The subsequent objectification of the will of the sovereign placed law (*lex*) at the heart of the body politic. It gave new meaning to the concept of *plena potestas* that best described the prince's normative authority.

A century later, in 1231, a few years after founding the University of Naples,[44] Frederic II's promulgation of the *Liber Constitutionum* (also known as *Liber Augustalis*) completed the recent military conquest of Sicily. It also attested to the substantial influence of Justinian's precedents in legislative matters. We can observe a similar evolution in Spain, where the composition in 1265 of the *Siete Partidas* at the request of Alfonso X confirmed the significance of Romanist doctrines in the conception of royal legislation. In 1348, the adoption of the Partidas as the law of the kingdom validated the romanizing inclinations of the monarchy. In England, from the second half of the twelfth century, the influence of Roman rules was not limited to the few teaching centres, but spread to both ecclesiastical and royal administration. Its academic culture might not have been as emphatic in promoting the new law, but its spirit freely permeated public expressions of political symbols.[45] As observed by Gaines Post, the terminology of royal charters borrowed its concepts from the Roman law known to the king's advisors. They used it in defining the status of the crown.[46] Around the same time, in France the royal endorsement of the kingdom's partition into northern countries ruled by customary law and southern regions governed by the written law (that is, Roman law) acknowledged the significance of this legal tradition for a large number of the king's subjects. The presence in the king's councils of jurists trained in the school of Orleans shaped the formation of the royal administration and defined the essence of its jurisdiction.[47] We can observe, everywhere in the public sphere, the weaving of Roman legal principles[48] into the feudal thread of social solidarity and dominance that governed the relationships between vassals and suzerains and defined their respective rights and obligations.

The process of giving a juridical framework to feudal culture did not simply consist in renaming existing forms of governance. It profoundly changed the perspectives of a political philosophy that had initially relied on the ancient biblical model of kingship to outline the duties of the prince.[49] The Roman imperial ideal that was made up from the civilists' selective interpretation of Justinian's prerogatives nurtured a more pragmatic conception of the royal function and the status of the crown. On the one hand, the statement boldly asserting that the king was emperor in his kingdom captured the essence of the royal claim to sovereignty. On the other, the debate on whether the prince was bound by the laws attested first and foremost the fundamental relevance of the legal standard in evaluating the prince's powers. By the end of the middle ages, these prevailing theories were firmly established in the institutional structures that were a prelude to the emergence of the modern state and its conception of the *res publica*.[50] It would be naïve, however, to discern in these efforts the proof of early attempts at enforcing a system based on the rule of law. Juridical terminology and legalistic theories of sovereignty did not translate directly into a vision of society based on protected rights and due process of law, nor does it reflect the uniquely pluralistic character of its legal order.

A similar process took place in the Church, where Modestinus' formula defining Rome as the *communis patria* was reinterpreted for the benefit of pontifical authority.[51] By the end of the twelfth century, canon law had absorbed various Roman legal principles, thus assuring their continuous presence in the Church's legal tradition. But, contrary to what has often been incorrectly assumed, this widespread transplantation did not entirely result in the systematic romanization of the Church's law. The canonist's selective use of Roman law contributed instead to its assimilation into a broader normative domain that facilitated its reception in daily social practice. The resulting *utrumque ius* expressed the concept of a harmonious government of Christian society where pontifical supremacy was the source and the warrant of right governance. This legal process transformed the population of faithful to legal subjects. Ecclesiastical courts played a significant role in the effectiveness of this model of legal integration, thanks in large part to the reliability of the romano-canonical procedure which constituted the backbone of its judicial system.[52]

Finally, the adoption of the institutions of Roman public law was nowhere more apparent than in the growth of urban legislation which resulted from the movement towards political autonomy spearheaded by town councils. By the end of the twelfth century in southern France, members of city councils proudly bore the title of 'consul'.[53] The development of intercity commerce and the remarkable expansion of urban communities created numerous legal challenges in the regulation of collective and individual human behaviour. In this thriving environment, the lessons of the *Digest* and the *Code* introduced a much desired alternative to the rigid and ineffective feudal practices that hindered the political expectations of urban elites impatient to translate their economic power into a political status corresponding to their recent achievements. In these cities, the traditional balance of power was shifting in favour of a more entrepreneurial bourgeoisie that asserted its social ascent. From a theoretical perspective, Gaius' remarks excerpted in the *Digest* conveniently fitted their ambitions.[54] The idea that each town or community could abide by its own distinct laws resonated in the minds of the residents of towns who were seeking a change of legal status from being the lord's subjects to becoming free citizens of a self-governing community. It is in these dynamic urban environments that we find the social and economic ferment for legal change. The medieval interpretation of Gaius' statement set the legal context for the people's efforts to carve out municipal autonomy from feudal lords. The exercise of public prerogatives included the power to legislate. The enactment of statutes proclaimed each town's legal distinctiveness and supplemented its local customs with various imported additions.[55] Their learned terminology reflected the growing influence of up-and-coming legal professionals who were often counted among the towns' leadership.[56] Their legal expertise made them indispensable to the effective running of cities' public affairs as well as to the planning of more personal and familial matters. As attested by their presence as witnesses in numerous legal transactions and public documents which often followed Roman legal patterns, these lawyers exercised such diverse functions as notaries, advocates, judges, or administrators.[57] Their personal experience as former students and practising lawyers constituted an essential link between legal abstraction and social reality, thus redefining the essence of legal knowledge while contributing effectively to the diffusion of Roman legal rules in the regulation and management of community affairs.[58] In the private sphere, marriage contracts and testaments formed the new legal reality of family life, while the availability of various forms of Roman contracts introduced legal options better adapted to the needs of economic transactions. At the same time, resolution of private disputes was facilitated by the adoption of procedures and a system of proof that met people's expectations of predictability and rationality.

In conclusion, we should be careful not to overstate the influence of the legacy of Roman law in European legal culture, even in the countries where it represented the main source of the national tradition.[59] The civil law systems that govern states in continental Europe grew out of a complex and diverse set of normative sources that included customs, religious beliefs, judicial decisions, administrative regulations, and royal and local legislation.[60] Besides its symbolic value as one classical model of civilizing culture,[61] Roman law's success resided less in its technical superiority as a legal anthology than in its ability to provide a normative environment for the combination of distinct legal sources into unified national systems. In this perspective, the common European legal experience did not reside in the existence of the system of the *ius commune* but instead in the opportunity to assert distinct legal identities, using concepts and procedures outlined in the Romans' idea of *ius civile*.

Notes

1. P. Ourliac, 'Une statue de Justinien en Rouergue, vers 1140', in P. Ourliac, *Les pays de Garonne vers l'an mil. La société et le droit* (Toulouse, 1993), 167–171.
2. A. Gouron, *La science du droit dans le Midi de la France au Moyen Age* (London, 1984).
3. G. Giordanengo, *Le droit féodal dans les pays de droit écrit. L'exemple de la Provence et du Dauphiné, XIIè -début XIVè siècle* (Rome, 1988).
4. G. Dolezalek and L. Mayali, *Repertorium manuscriptorum Codicis Justiniani* (Frankfurt, 1985).
5. 'I see constantly through almost whole Italy students most of whom are from Provence, not only from my order but from many others who come in large groups to study the laws.' A. Gouron, G. Giordanengo, and J. Dufour, 'L'attrait des *leges*: note sur la lettre d'un moine victorin (vers 1124–1127)', *SDHI* 45 (1979): 504–529.
6. H. Coing, 'Das Recht als Element der europäischen Kultur', *Historische Zeitschrift* 238 (1984): 1–15; P. Grossi, *L'europa del diritto* (Rome, 2007).
7. H. Coing, *Handbuch der Quellen und Literatur der neueren europäischen Privatrechtsgeschichte. I: Mittlelalter (1100–1500)* (Munich, 1973); E. Cortese, *Il rinascimento giuridico medievale* (Rome, 1992); H. Kantorowicz and W. Buckland, *Studies in the Glossators of the Roman Law* (Cambridge, 1938; repr. with addenda and corrigenda Aalen, 1969).
8. P. Stein, *Roman Law in European History* (Cambridge, 1999), 2: 'It has indelibly impressed its character on European legal and political thought.'
9. A. Gouron, 'Un assaut en deux vagues: La diffusion du droit romain'. In *L'Europe du XIIème siècle, El Dret Comù i Catalunya*, ed. A. Iglesia Ferreiros (Barcelona, 1991), 47–63.
10. E. Kantorowicz, 'The Sovereignty of the Artist. A Note on Legal Maxims and Renaissance Theories of Art', in *De Artibus Opuscula XL. Essays in Honor of Erwin Panofsky* (New York, 1961), 267–279, reprinted in *Selected Studies* (New York, 1965), 352–365.
11. A. Gouron, 'Aux origines de l'émergence du droit: glossateurs et coutumes méridionales (XIIe-milieu du XIIIe siècle)', in Gouron (n. 2).
12. L. Mayali, 'Mythes et réalités de la renaissance juridique au douzième siècle', in *El dret comù i Catalunya III* (Barcelona, 1993), 187–202.
13. G. Giordanengo, '*Jus commune* et droit commun en France du XIIIe au XVe siècle', in *Droit romain, ius civile et droit français*, ed. Jacques Krynen (Toulouse, 1999), 219–247.
14. R. van Caenegem, *European Law in the Past and the Future: Unity and Diversity over Two Millennia* (Cambridge, 2002), esp. 73–89.
15. G. Speciale, *La memoria del diritto comune: sulle tracce d'uso del Codex di Giustiniano (secoli XII–XV)* (Rome, 1994).
16. E. Conte, *Tres libri Codicis: la ricomparsa del testo e l'esegesi scolastica prima di Accursio* (Frankfurt, 1990).
17. F. Soetermeer, *Utrumque ius in peciis: die Produktion juristischer Bücher an italienischen und französischen Universitäten des 13. und 14. Jahrhunderts*, trans. G. Hillner (Frankfurt, 2002).
18. P. Landau, 'The origins of legal science in England in the twelfth century: Lincoln, Oxford and the career of Vacarius', in *Readers, Texts and Compilers in the Earlier Middle Ages. Studies in Honour of Linda Fowler-Magerl*, ed. M. Brett and K. Cushing (Aldershot – Burlington, 2009), 165–182.
19. A. Gouron, 'La science juridique française aux XIe et XIIe siècles: Diffusion du droit de Justinien et influences canoniques jusqu'à Gratien', *Ius Romanum Medii Aevi*, part I.4.d-e (Milan, 1978).

20. P. Stein and F. de Zulueta, *The Teaching of Roman Law in England around 1200* (London, 1990), esp. xxii–xliii.
21. Kantorowicz and Buckland (n. 7).
22. G. Speciale, 'Garnerius Theutonicus' Nuove fonti su Irnerio e i quattro dottori', *Rivista internazionale di diritto comune* 2 (1991): 123–133.
23. P. Costa, *Iurisdictio. Semantica del potere politica nella pubblicistica medievale, 1100–1433*, 2nd edn. (Milan, 2002); J. Vallejo, *Ruda equidad, ley consumada: concepcion de la potestad normativa (1250–1350)* (Madrid, 1992).
24. M. Bassano, '*Dominus domini mei dixit*'. *Enseignement du droit et construction d'une identité autour des juristes et de la science juridique au studium d'Orléans (1230–1320).* (Thesis, University of Paris II, 2008), Leiden, 2013.
25. K. Bezemer, *What Jacques Saw: Thirteenth Century France through the Eyes of Jacques de Révigny Professor of Law at Orléans* (Frankfurt, 1997); K. Bezemer, *Pierre de Belleperche: Portrait of a Legal Puritan* (Frankfurt, 2005).
26. D. Maffei, *Gli inizi dell'umanesimo giuridico* (Milan, 1964).
27. H. E. Troje, *Crisis Digestorum: Studien zur historia pandectarum* (Frankfurt, 2011).
28. H. E. Troje, *Humanistische Jurisprudenz: Studien zur europaischen Rechtswissenschaft unter dem Einfluss des Humanismus* (Goldbach, 1993).
29. C. Chêne, *L'enseignement du droit français en pays de droit écrit (1679–1793)* (Geneva, 1982).
30. G. C. J. J. van den Bergh, *Die hollandische elegante Schule: ein Beitrag zur Geschichte von Humanismus und Rechtswissenschaft in den Niederlanden 1500–1800* (Frankfurt, 2002).
31. G. C. J. J. van den Bergh, *The Life and Work of Gerard Noodt, 1647–1725: Dutch Legal Scholarship between Humanism and Enlightenment* (Oxford, 1988).
32. R. Feenstra and C. J. D. Waal, *Seventeenth-Century Leyden Law Professors and their Influence on the Development of the Civil Law: a Study of Bronchorst, Vinnius and Voet* (Amsterdam, 1975).
33. M. Ahsmann, *Collegium und Kolleg: der juristische Unterricht an der Universität Leiden 1575–1630 unter besonderer Berücksichtigung der Disputationen* (Frankfurt, 2000).
34. For an appraisal of legal publications from the beginning of printing up to 1800, see the fundamental work by D. Osler, *Bibliographica iuridica*, 6 vols. (Frankfurt, 2000–2009).
35. A. Wijffels, *Qui millies allegatur: les allegations du droit savant dans les dossiers du Grand Conseil de Malines (causes septentrionales, ca. 1460–1580)* (Leiden, 1985).
36. R. Feenstra and R. Zimmermann, eds., *Das Römisch-hollandische Recht: Fortschritte des Zivilrechts im 17. und 18. Jahrhundert* (Berlin, 1992).
37. D. Maffei, *La donazione di Costantino nei giuristi medievali* (Milan, 1964).
38. G. Giordanengo, 'Le pouvoir legislatif du roi de France, (XIe–XIIIe siecles) Travaux recents et hypothèses de recherche', *Bibliothèque de l'Ecole des Chartes* 147 (1989): 283–310.
39. W. Ullmann, 'The Medieval Interpretation of Frederick I's Authentic *Habita*', in W. Ullmann, *Scholarship and Politics in the Middle Ages* (London, 1978); W. Stelzer, *Deutsches Archiv für Erforschung des Mittelalters: Monumenta Germaniae Historica*, 34 (1978): 153–162.
40. L. Mayali, '*Lex animata*. Rationalisation du pouvoir politique et science juridique (XIIè–XIVè siècles)', in *Renaissance du pouvoir législatif et genèse de l'Etat*, ed. A. Gouron and A. Rigaudière (Montpellier 1988), 155–164.
41. E. Conte and S. Menzinger, *La Summa Trium Librorum di Rolando da Lucca (1195–1234): Fisco, Politica, Scientia iuris* (Rome, 2012).
42. E. Cortese, *La Norma giuridica: spunti teorici nel diritto comune classico*, 2 vols. (Milan, 1962–1964), esp. vol. 2, 126ff.

43. D. 1. 4.1: *Quod principi placuit legis habet vigorem, utpote cum lex regia quae de imperio eius lata est populus ei et in eum omne suum imperium et potestatem conferat.*
44. M. Bellomo, 'Federico II, lo "Studium" a Napoli e il diritto comune nel "Regnum"', *Rivista internazionale di diritto comune* 2 (1991): 135–151.
45. R. Helmholz, 'Magna Carta and the ius commune', *University of Chicago Law Review* 66 (1999) 297–371.
46. G. Post, 'Status regni: Lestat du roialme in the statute of York 1322', in G. Post, *Studies in Medieval Legal Thought: Public Law and the State* (Princeton, 1964), 310–332.
47. G. Giordanengo, 'Le roi de France et la loi. 1137–1285', in *Colendo Iustitiam et Iura Condendo. Federico II legislatore del regno di Sicilia nell'Europa del Duecento*, ed. A. Romano, 345–395.
48. J.M. Cauchies, 'Selon la disposition du droit escript ... Na dispositie van het beschreve regt ... ou l'ombre naissante du droit romain dans la legislation des Pays Bas bourguignons (1488)' in *Le droit romain d'hier à aujourd'hui. Collationes et oblations. Liber amicorum en l'honneur du professeur Gilbert Hanard*, ed. Annette Ruelle and M. Berlingin (Brussels, 2009), 29–77.
49. J. Krynen, *L'empire du roi. Idées et croyances politiques en France. XIIè–XVème siècle* (Paris, 1993).
50. G. Post, 'Ratio publicae utilitatis, ratio status and 'reason of state', 100–1300', in Post (n. 46), 241–309.
51. D. 50. 1.33.
52. G. Le Bras, 'Le droit romain au service de la domination pontificale', *RHDFE* 27 (1949): 377–398.
53. A. Gouron, 'Diffusion des Consulats Méridionaux et Expansion du droit romain aux XIIe et XIIIe siècles', *Bibliothèque de l'Ecole des Chartes* (1963): 26–76.
54. D. 1.1.8, Gaius 1 inst.: *Nam quod quisque populus ipse sibi jus constituit, id ipsius proprium civitatis est: vocaturque jus civile, quasi jus proprium ipsius civitatis.*
55. M. Sbriccoli, *L'interpretazione dello statuto. Contributo allo studio della funzione dei giuristi nell'età comunale* (Milan, 1969).
56. *The Politics of Law in Late Medieval and Renaissance Italy. Essays in honor of Lauro Martines*, ed. L. Armstrong and J. Kirshner (Toronto, 2011).
57. E. Cortese, 'Legisti, canonisti e feudisti: la formazione di un ceto medievale', in *Università e Società nei secoli XII–XVI* (Pistoia, 1982), 195–281.
58. S. Stelling-Michaud, 'La diffusion du droit romain en Suisse: étudiants suisses à l'étranger et leur activité professionnelle ultérieure', *Ius Romanum Medii Aevi*, part V.12b (Milan, 1977).
59. P. Tisset, 'Mythes et réalités du droit romain', *Etudes d'histoire du droit privé offertes à P. Petot* (Paris 1959), 553–560.
60. See, e.g., P. Stein, 'Roman Law in Scotland', *Ius Romanum Medii Aevi*, part V.13b (Milan, 1968); J. Barton, 'Roman Law in England', *Ius Romanum Medii Aevi*, part V.13a (Milan, 1971); R. van Caenegem, 'Le droit romain en Belgique', *Ius Romanum Medii Aevi*, part V.5b (Milan, 1966).
61. 'Dieu a manifestement fait naître et perfectionner le droit romain afin de servir de modèle à tout ce que la prudence et la diligence humaine peut faire de mieux pour le gouvernement du monde et l'administration de la justice.' Guillaume de Maran (d. 1621), *Discours politique de l'établissement et conservation des lois et de la justice* (Toulouse, 1628), 534–535 cited by Giordanengo (n. 47), 394 n. 7.

19 Canon Law and Roman Law

R. H. Helmholz

This chapter deals with the place of Roman law in the creation and evolution of canon law, the law of the medieval church.[1] Its particular subject covers one aspect of the larger history of Roman law, assessing its influence on a different legal system, one that touched the lives of virtually all European men and women during the middle ages and into modern times. Any such assessment must embrace three separate though related aspects. First is an examination of the impact of the *Corpus iuris civilis* on the texts and substance of the medieval canon law. Second is an evaluation of the part played by the church in preserving and promoting the legal heritage of the ancient world as it was found in the Justinianic compilations. Third is a consideration of how (and how far) the two laws were blended together to form the *ius commune*, the general law common to European lands prior to the nineteenth century.

1. Introduction

Almost from its first days, and certainly from the conversion of Emperor Constantine in AD 312, the Christian church was governed by laws of its own making.[2] Called canons, these laws quickly became a recognized part of the institutional life of the church. Early ecumenical councils, like that of Nicaea (325) or Chalcedon (451), enacted canons that affected many aspects of church government, religious practice, and moral conduct – even to the point of attempting to settle a controversy over whether worshippers should kneel or stand while praying.

That said, it is equally true and significant that the world in which the Christian church grew was one governed by Roman law. When the church fathers spoke of the law, they normally meant the Roman law. This was a natural and indeed an all but inevitable way for them to speak and think, for they knew no other source of temporal government. They lived in a Roman Empire. They were subject to its law. That fact of life did not mean, of course, that they took the imperial law as possessing sovereign authority over them or the church. Jesus had said that his kingdom was not of this world; ultimate authority belonged to God. His commands were revealed in the Christian Gospel. In fact, the Roman law had played a substantial part in the persecution of the earliest Christians. For them, Roman law therefore stood under the judgement of God. Whatever its hold on human life, religious principle required a certain distance between it and governance of the church itself.

What the exact relationship between the civil law and the law of the church would be in the world was therefore uncertain. No decree fixed it. Some early steps were taken towards the creation of a separate system of ecclesiastical law, but they were hesitant steps, and it cannot be said that a true system of canon law came into existence before the twelfth century. In the first millennium of the church's existence, the promulgation of most canons was local and occasional. Their authority was unclear, their invocation in practice infrequent, and their coverage of human life incomplete. No system of regular diocesan courts, much less anything like the Roman Rota, existed to enforce the canons that did exist. Only with arrival of the movement for reform of the church led by the papacy and the revival of learning that led to the foundation of universities in the twelfth century and beyond was the Latin church's law set on a more ambitious course. The history of the canon law in the East was different in timing and substance. There are parallels, but among other differences the ties between imperial law and canon law were closer in the East.[3] Although that subject is of intrinsic interest, this volume and this chapter concentrate on the law of the West.

A signal event in the movement forwards in the Latin church was the compilation by Gratian of the *Concordia discordantium canonum* (ca. 1140), the church's first true law book. Gratian's method was to assemble a collection of apparently contradictory canons from earlier collections, finding ways to resolve the inconsistencies in them and thereby arrive at a true set of laws for the church. It was a schoolbook, but it also permitted a working out of some practical legal principles. By them, church and clergy could be governed in the world. The *Decretum*, as it was called, was followed a century later by the promulgation of the *Liber extra*, a collection of papal decretals commissioned by Pope Gregory IX and edited for clarity and consistency by St Raymond of Peñafort. This collection of Decretals built upon the *Decretum*, not diverging from it on most points, but enlarging it and filling gaps in the coverage of the earlier work. The same pattern was followed by the later collections of papal decretals that were joined together to constitute the *Corpus iuris canonici* – primarily the

Liber sextus (1298) and the Clementines (1317). When this work had been accomplished, the body of canon law was complete, and this *Corpus* remained the basic law of the Catholic church until the twentieth century. Taken all together, the texts in these books were called the *ius novum*. What came later was called the *ius novissimum*. Its importance in the history of Western law is shown not only by its longevity, but also by its ubiquity. In the course of time it exercised a strong influence on the laws received in Protestant churches.

2. The Independence of the Canon Law

Such a bald statement of the path taken by the medieval church in the creation of its own law may raise the question of whether knowledge of the canon law sheds any light on the long history of Roman law. It does. But there were always differences – some of them quite fundamental – between the canon law and the law of the empire. Understanding the relationship between the two laws requires a closer look at the nature of the canon law. It will show a continuing importance of the differences that long existed, reminding us that we must not treat the two laws as identical twins. Some of what divided them existed from the inception of the church's history. Other parts grew up gradually, dependent on historical developments that accompanied the establishment of Christianity as the established religion of European lands.

Spiritual Principles

In the developed thought of the canon lawyers, the most fundamental reason for the canon law's independence grew out of a perceived difference of purpose between the two laws. Both were part of God's plan for the world, but according to the church's jurists, the civil law's principal goal was to provide order and security in society. It regulated men's affairs to order to allow them to live together in tolerable harmony. Accepted principles of morality came into this, of course. History shows that human flourishing is impeded if the persons and property of human beings are not given at least a modicum of protection against depredation from without. The civil law aligned itself with the law of nature to enforce some basic rules of equity and to provide basic security to free men and women. But, at least in the opinion of the canonists, it did no more than that. It was an 'earth bound' system.

The canon law aimed at a higher – or at least a different – goal. The canons did encompass some quite pedestrian rules, but they too were thought to derive from laws of nature established by God. Their true purpose was to lead men and women to eternal life, to allow them to stand before God unashamed. The soul's health (*salus animarum*) of the people was therefore the canon law's paramount consideration. Other aims had to give way before it. That is, although the canon law contained many rules about human conduct on earth, they were all meant to be shaped by this transcendent goal – so the canonists repeatedly proclaimed.[4] God would eventually weigh men's sins on earth and mete out justice to them, and the church's law should appropriately serve to guide human conduct, looking forward towards that day. The task would of course require the adoption of rules – inevitably, some quite detailed – about how men and women should conduct themselves on earth, and those rules were to be fashioned to serve that ultimate purpose.

Admittedly, a firm jurisdictional divide between these two spheres of legal regulation, dependent upon a division of purpose, would have been difficult to fashion. Nor would it always have been desirable. Both of the 'two swords' were necessary. Both had been instituted by God. In the normal case, overlap existed between the two, and this was not necessarily a bad thing. In many parts of human life civil and canon law would each have a legitimate say. Adultery, for example, both upset civil society and endangered the souls of the adulterers. Roman law and the canon law alike contained many texts punishing the crime and regulating its consequences.[5] Some of the subjects that modern assumptions would place on one side of the line or the other were regarded as common to both in earlier centuries – blasphemy, for example. Insulting God, the medieval jurists held, had disastrous consequences both for human society and for the individual blasphemer. It was not, then, a 'victimless crime'. God would punish a society where it was widespread or where the governors made no effort to punish it. Of course, it was quite true that God would himself punish the blasphemer. But it was entirely consistent with canonical principles to endorse and even to adopt the provisions of Roman law that dealt with its consequences on earth.[6] A shared jurisdiction over blasphemy was allowed.

Heresy was treated in like fashion. Contrary to the modern view allowing liberty in religious matters, the canonists thought that allowing individuals free choice in religion would invite disaster in society. It would mean the loss of souls to Satan and invite disorder among the people. The canonists thus did not regard the Roman law texts dealing with blasphemy, or adultery and heresy, as 'usurping' the jurisdictional rights of the church, although they did insist that the canon law had an exclusive right to define each of these crimes. But they regarded most of the civil law's texts on these subjects as proper ways of fulfilling the Roman law's legitimate task of protecting civil society. Indeed, they took some comfort from the overlap. To them, it showed they were on the right track.

Amendments to the Law

Even where there was overlap, the difference in purpose remained, and legal consequences flowed from it. One of the most striking of these was that the canon law was considered as standing somewhere above the civil law in authority, precisely because its purpose was higher – at least, so the canonists thought. Despite the greater age and sophistication of the Roman law, they did not blush to draw this conclusion. It seemed logical. In its extreme form, it could lead to the position stated baldly by Pope Boniface VIII in *Unam sanctam* (1302): that on earth the church possessed both the spiritual and temporal swords. It had delegated the temporal sword to secular authorities, but that delegation was not irrevocable. The spiritual power, acting through the popes, could withdraw the delegation if a king or prince refused to be governed by God's commands. Priestly authority could then make good the situation that refusal created. That view never won common assent in medieval Europe, but in a less extreme form it did have legal consequences, some of which were actually greeted with general approbation by civil lawyers. Their general acceptance meant that parts of the Roman law could be 'corrected' by the canon law where receiving the civilian texts undiluted might endanger the soul's health of the people involved.

As noted, most of the 'strong' forms of this theory remained solely within the sphere of canonical theory – the canonical rule that the courts of the church could routinely intervene to correct a denial of justice in a secular court, for example. Europe's kings did not accept that they were bound to follow every dictate of the church in the administration of justice, but neither did they refuse it categorically. A good example of what it meant comes from the law of prescription. All Western legal systems, the canon law among them, have held that lapse of time can extinguish a legal right to recover property or enforce a contract. The subject occupied several titles in both the *Digest* and the *Code*.[7] The Decretals also contained a long title approving and adopting the same system.[8] Some of the prescriptive periods adopted by the canon law were in fact taken over directly from the Roman law. However, there was a difference. The Fourth Lateran Council (1215), citing biblical authority (Rom. 14:23), enacted a constitution holding that 'no prescription, whether canonical or civil, is valid without good faith'.[9] The reason behind the constitution was avowedly spiritual. If a man possesses property that rightfully belongs to another, or if he withholds payment of a legitimate debt, knowing in each case that he is acting wrongfully, he will have intended to commit a sin, a sin for which he will ultimately have to account before God. Mere passage of time will not change that. It is possible, however – indeed, in the world it happens with surprising frequency – that one of the actors involved may be quite ignorant of the rights of the other. If so, he may be in perfect good faith in retaining property that belongs to another or refusing to pay a debt he honestly believes he does not owe. Where this happened, the canon law allowed him to take advantage of prescriptive right. This was not so, however, where he had been aware of the truth all along.

The Roman law, by contrast, had allowed any kind of prescription to ripen into title, at least in certain limited circumstances. Repose promoted peace in society. Stale claims should be allowed to die. Where many years had gone by, this approach made common sense. At some point, good order in society depends on drawing a curtain on antiquated claims. The church, however, did not see things that way. The canon law looked beyond the simple passage of years, and, as the *glossa ordinaria* put it, 'the canons sought to correct the laws in this instance because of the peril to souls'.[10] Whether this 'correction' would be accepted in Europe's temporal courts remained an open question for centuries, but there is testimony from careful observers that some temporal courts did in fact adopt the canonical position.[11]

Additions to the Law

A second consequence of the differences in purpose between the canon and Roman laws made itself felt in the former's greater attention to spiritual matters. Some of that attention was directed towards simple housekeeping matters – regulating the affairs of the clergy and establishing ways of protecting church property. But it went much further too. Correct belief and correct action in matters that affected a person's salvation, the canonists thought, were the legitimate concern of the church's law. Antinomianism did not tempt them. These subjects also required more detailed regulation than could be found in the Roman law's texts. Some degree of independent regulation was needed if the church was to fulfil its true mission.

The contrast was not absolute, of course. The *Corpus iuris civilis* was the product of a Christian empire and a Christian emperor. The first title in the *Code* announced its congruence with the Holy Trinity and the Catholic faith. Later titles, including many in the *Novels*, went into more detail. They dealt with the duties and privileges of the clergy. They did not omit to regulate some matters we regard as peculiarly religious in nature – the consecration of bishops and the ordination of the clergy, for example.[12] The late antique Roman emperors even defined how marriages might be dissolved by mutual consent of the parties,[13] a ruling that would be regarded with distaste by canonists six centuries later.

During the early middle ages, the canons supplemented these imperial laws to an extent, but with the creation of the *Corpus iuris canonici* the church sought to extend its regulatory role. In consequence it came to contain many provisions not touched upon in the *Corpus iuris civilis*. An illustrative if obscure example is a title in the Decretals containing a papal letter of Innocent III. It dealt with the purification of women after childbirth, the question being how long they had to wait before entering a church. Mosaic law had contained what we could call a mandatory waiting period. Was that biblical injunction still in force? Or had the coming of Jesus impliedly abolished it? Pope Innocent III held the latter view. The old law no longer obtained. 'If after giving birth a woman wishes to enter a church in order to give thanks to God', the Pope held, 'no sin is involved, and no one should deny her entry to the church'.[14] Indeed, hers was a praiseworthy act. From it grew the English custom, not yet entirely forgotten, called 'Churching of Women'.[15] It is only a small example of the multitude of rules and principles established in the canon law that found no counterpart in the Roman law's texts. Some of them were regarded as of the greatest moment – the correct baptismal formula, for example. It was necessary for salvation. Its statement as a legal requirement, as with many others, followed from a perception that the canon law's transcendent purpose required rules not found in the temporal law.

Criminal Sanctions

A third consequence of the canon law's special nature is visible in the law of sanctions. How should men and women who violated the law be treated? In the criminal law, the church's problem was particularly acute. The whole matter could not simply have been left to the temporal power, because the church claimed a special jurisdiction over some crimes and also an exclusive power to discipline the clergy. In these areas, the question had to be faced: Should criminals be left to God, or should they be punished on earth? The former was sure to occur and sure to be accurate. It could claim biblical support (e.g., Rom. 14:10–12), and it fitted well with the church's avowedly spiritual nature. But was it enough? Without the latter, crimes might seem to observers on earth to have been left unpunished.[16] Sin might be encouraged. Without sanctions that others could see and fear, criminals might set a pernicious example. The

Bible itself produced examples where holy men acted as judges of the people (e.g., Exod. 18:1). Jesus had not altogether rejected their example.

In accepting the power to inflict punishment, however, the church purposefully diverged from the course found in the Roman law. The blood sanctions that accompanied the *ius gladii* in the civil law were refused. Afflictive corporal penalties, such as sentences that entailed compelling forced work in the mines, were forsworn. Even forcible deportation and exile played no part in the *Corpus iuris canonici*. In their place stood excommunication. It was to be the most serious sanction at the disposal of the courts of the church. It separated the contumacious sinner from receipt of the sacraments and, in its strongest form, from the communion of Christian people. It amounted to what St. Paul had described as the 'handing over to Satan' of the stubborn wrongdoer (1 Cor. 5:5).

At the same time, excommunication was meant to be medicinal in effect. It was designed to lead the wrongdoer back to the right paths. Although in the sphere of civil remedies, the canon law adopted many of the remedies found in the Roman sources – *restitutio in integrum* or *missio in possessionem*, for instance – the only penalty for disobedience to these remedial orders at the disposal of ecclesiastical courts was excommunication. Even the remedy of an interdict, by which performance of the sacraments within a territory was withdrawn or limited, amounted to a form of excommunication. A long title in the fifth book of the Decretals set out the basic rules.[17] The *Liber sextus* enlarged them.[18]

Had the medieval church been satisfied with this self-denying ordinance, the history of Western law, including the relationship between the Roman and canon laws, would have been quite different than it was. But the situation seemed less than ideal to many among the lawyers of the medieval church. Too many Christians, they thought, were reacting to sentences of excommunication with indifference or contempt. Stronger medicine was needed. A theory was at hand to meet the need: the theory that the secular power was the natural helper of the spiritual. The 'two swords' were to cooperate for the common good. This was thought to mean that if medicinal remedies failed, the church could call upon the temporal authorities to intervene with harsher penalties. The church could not act – but at the church's direction, princes could. And although Europe's kings and princes did not all fall into line behind the clerical mandates that grew from the theory, many did so in at least a limited measure. In England, it led to a system whereby any person who remained excommunicate for more than forty days could be 'certified' to the king's chancery, which would order him imprisoned until he obeyed the mandates of the church.[19] In most parts of Europe, the temporal powers readily embraced the system under which the church would surrender defendants convicted of heresy to the secular arm, so that they could be put to death by the temporal sword.[20] The canonists thus preserved the letter of its prohibition against using any but spiritual sanctions even while they ignored its spirit. In some sense, it represented a compromise with reality.

3. The Dependence of the Canon Law

Independence is thus part of the story, but it is not the whole story. The other half – in partial opposition to the first – came from the fact that the canon law was always a partial law. When the specific ways in which the canon law diverged from the Roman law were counted up, a good many things that are necessary features of any legal system remained absent. Procedural law and a law of proof were the most obvious absentees. No sophisticated system of law can exist without an orderly system for trying criminals and determining the merits of civil suits. Roman law had such a system. Its outlines were visible in the *Corpus iuris civilis*, although many parts of its procedural law were incompletely stated there and remained to be worked out in detail. The relevant question for the historian is therefore the extent to which the Roman law was taken into the canon law in this and in the other areas where the medieval church had no special reason for insisting upon enacting its own law. A related question is whether the situation changed over time.

It turns out that in virtually every aspect, the Roman law was incorporated into the church's legal system. The process has been investigated with some thoroughness, and that such incorporation occurred is widely known among legal historians. Indeed, much of it is undeniable. There has been further disagreement about the meaning of the process. Some ecclesiastical historians have minimized the canon law's debt to Roman law, ascribing many of the parallels to common 'cultural influences' rather than purposeful borrowing.[21] Others have thought it more accurate to see the process as a conscious replication or a 'canonization' of texts and principles taken from the Roman law.[22] The subject may appropriately be considered in three or four historical periods.

The Early Middle Ages

In the centuries before the formulation of the *Corpus iuris canonici*, it was natural that the clergy should have looked more immediately to the Roman law than to their own canons for most legal questions. The church had little law of its own. *Lex*, properly speaking, meant a Roman law. The early church's dependence on the civil law was pithily stated in an oft-repeated maxim, as found, for example, in the *Lex Ribuaria*: 'The church lives according to the Roman law' (*Ecclesia vivit iure Romano*).[23] That maxim has been cited often in modern studies and has been used to sum up the jurisprudence of the early middle ages. But perhaps it has been cited too often. What, exactly, did it mean in practice? That is less clear. Here we can only draw the conclusions that seem to emerge from what evidence there is. All of what there is, however, should be set against the background of a world in which formal law and law courts played a smaller part in governing human life than they later would. Custom governed the settlement of most disputes. The sophistication of many of the classical institutions had little meaning in the Barbarian West. Much was lost.[24] Indeed, the *Digest* itself seems to have disappeared from sight. Much of what was known of the Roman law was preserved in books of civilian extracts such as the *Epitome Juliani* (ca. 600), a collection of texts taken from the *Novels*, or the *Lex Romana canonice compta* (ninth century), a compilation for ecclesiastics that drew upon the *Epitome*.

Such limitations – important as they were – did not deprive the maxim of consequence. One was that it provided a clear statement of a principle: the clergy were not to be governed by the laws of the Germanic nations. They were a tribe apart. In a legal world in which the personal principle applied – that is, each person was to be judged by the law that attached to his status or nation – setting the clergy apart from the laity would have seemed (and been) a matter of importance. That 'there are two kinds of Christians' – clergy and laity – was to be a guiding principle of the canon law,[25] and this maxim can be regarded as one way of stating it. Indirectly, it would also have been one way in which the Roman law itself was perpetuated. If the clergy were to be judged by the laws of Rome, at least some of those laws had to be known. When historians have looked at whether the medieval clergy was in fact ruled exclusively by the Roman law, however, the evidence has seemed less than compelling.[26] Some of the evidence, scanty as it is when one considers how long a period was involved, suggests that the regime of customary law bore equally upon the lives of both clergy and laity.

The maxim's impact was also evident in the mass of Roman law that purported to regulate church and clergy. The Christian emperors took it as a matter of course that their duties included governance of the clergy, and that was only one part of their spiritual responsibilities. They convoked church councils and promulgated the decrees of the councils. They enacted laws that regulated the internal working of the church. The first book of Justinian's *Code*, for example, begins with titles on churches and their possessions, bishops and clerics, episcopal jurisdiction, heresy, baptism, and apostasy. The second last of these was directed principally to establishing the theological principle that the sacrament of baptism must under no circumstances be repeated.[27] In other words, even though there were undoubtedly aspects of church government beyond the reach of imperial authority, the line between the two was drawn at a different location than it would be in the twelfth century and beyond. It was balanced, of course, by recognition on the part of the emperors that imperial laws should themselves sometimes follow the canons. 'The imperial laws should not disdain to imitate the sacred canons', proclaimed the Emperor Justinian.[28] It thus worked both ways. Acceptance of the principle of cooperation on the part of the church in the West is amply demonstrated by the testimony of Christian bishops, including the Roman pontiffs. They cited the Roman law as the law in force, rightly governing the clergy and their flocks together with the canons.[29]

In a slightly different but equally compelling sense it was literally true that the medieval church lived by the Roman law. This was so because the church itself took over and incorporated large parts of it. The organizational structure of the church borrowed many of its categories from that of the empire. The division of the church into dioceses and provinces seems to have been inspired by imperial models. Clerical costume, insignia, and functions were borrowed from imperial precedents.[30] The law followed the same pattern. Legal rules taken from the Roman law determined many aspects of government within the church. It is found, as outlined above (400), in the pattern and the details of the law of prescription, though subject to the requirement of good faith as shown above (401). That meant that title to church property was subjected to loss through prescription, just as was true for secular rights and chattels. Similarly, in the church's law of marriage, support for the principle that choice of a spouse should be a matter of free will was found within the civil law's texts.[31] Marital property (generally) also followed the patterns laid out in the civil law, despite a Christian dispensation that sought to curtail freedom of divorce. Procedural rules used in the *episcopalis audientia*, the forum in which Christian bishops acted as judges with the consent of the litigants, were also apparently the same rules and procedures used in the temporal forum.

These and similar borrowings were not meant to imply that the church was being obliged to toe a Roman line. Most of them were matters of choice. This is sometimes described as 'canonizing' a civilian text.[32] That term is useful in emphasizing that the decision to follow Roman law was a voluntary act, though it should not be used to downplay the canonists' habitual dependence on the civil law. They would not have considered 'canonizing' attractive passages from the Qur'an. In the long history of the law, dependence has very often grown out of free choice; it is natural – perhaps even inevitable – where no particular reason for rejecting established and familiar law presents itself. Lawyers in the newly independent American colonies were not required to follow the English common law after they had thrown off the British yoke, for example, but they did. *Mutatis mutandis*, this was something like the position in which the church found itself after its establishment. The extent of borrowing was less, perhaps, but it was far from negligible.

The rate of canonical borrowing from the Roman law during these centuries seems to have accelerated as the new millennium approached and passed. Alongside new legislation, the rate of compilation of canonical collections increased from the tenth century onward.[33] So did their sophistication. Many of them were now organized by subject matter, rather than by date of the promulgation of the canons in them. This very fact promoted the use of Roman law, for completeness was now an aspiration of the canonists, and where the coverage of the canons was deficient, the civil law might fill the gap. And even where canons did exist, their force might be confirmed and their effect increased if Roman law texts could be added to the mix. The canonical collection of Regino of Prüm (906–915), for example, mixed Roman laws, most taken from the Theodosian *Code*, together with the decrees of synods and councils and other ecclesiastical sources.[34] The canonical collection of Anselm of Lucca (d. 1086), important in preparing the way for papal leadership of the movement for reform of the church, made unhesitating use of Roman law texts in laying out the rules guaranteeing the right of appeal to the apostolic see.[35] The *Collectio Britannica*, compiled ca. 1090 in Italy, contained excerpts from the *Institutes* and the *Digest* in several matters of importance to the clergy.[36] Similarly, the *Collectio in tres libri* (ca. 1112), product of a Roman canonist, included at least 54 texts taken from the Roman law.[37] These years are best known to historians as a time of struggle between church and state – the Investiture Contest, as it is often called. There was such a struggle. But even though the successors to the Roman emperors were on the other side, this did not cause the canonists to abandon respect for and use of the laws of the Roman emperors.

The *Corpus Iuris Canonici*

For understanding the place of the canon law in the history of Roman law, a survey of the formulation of the church's *ius novum* is of the greatest importance – far more so than piecing through the shards of evidence from the centuries before 1100. This is so for several reasons. The *Corpus iuris canonici* contained the law applied throughout Latin Christendom; it covered a much broader range of subjects than did earlier canonical collections; it was put into effect in diocesan and appellate courts throughout the church; and it attracted juristic commentary and development in a way that none of the earlier efforts did. It also lasted a very long time.

Its first component part, as noted above, was Gratian's *Decretum* (ca. 1140). This text has long presented mysteries for scholars; little is known about its author or the circumstances of its compilation. However, recent years have witnessed renewed efforts to discover the original text of the *Decretum*.[38] They may now have been crowned with the success afforded by scholarly consensus of a sort. The theory being advanced is that Gratian's original text can in fact be recovered and that it was considerably smaller than the version that quickly came to be used in the Schools and in practice. The original text was supplemented by texts added by Gratian's successors. This makes a difference for understanding the place of Roman law in the canons, because it seems that almost all the texts in the final version taken from the *Corpus iuris civilis* were added after Gratian had completed his initial version. If so, the order would show his own neglect – perhaps his distrust – of the temporal law. What happened next would also tend to show that even within the sphere of the church's jurisprudence, Roman law was regarded as a useful – perhaps an inevitable – component. Why else would Gratian's followers have rejected his own decision to exclude it?

Whatever the motivation involved, it is certain that the text of the *Decretum* used for centuries made repeated use of Roman law. Fundamental questions involving the admissible sources of law, such as the place of custom and reason, were dealt with by lifting texts from Justinian's *Code* or *Institutes*.[39] Such usage was not to the exclusion of earlier texts from the church fathers, the popes, or church councils. However, it did seem to place Roman law alongside the canons in stating the applicable law. A *dictum* of Gratian explicitly recognized that this was so.[40] Examples are many. One finds that the *Decretum* incorporated civil law texts in order to delineate the necessary qualifications of judges and lawyers.[41] It borrowed a text from the *Digest* to illustrate the effect of adoption on the prohibited degrees in the law of marriage and divorce,[42] and it adopted texts from the *Code* in the service of establishing rules for the interpretation of papal rescripts and privileges.[43] The number of such instances is far outweighed by canons that Gratian and his successors took from ecclesiastical sources. Even so, it was by no means negligible. For the future, when the *Decretum* would serve as a basic text in law faculties, it would set an enduring example.

The second part of the *Corpus iuris canonici* to be compiled was the *Liber extra*. It was the work of a Spanish canonist, Raymond of Peñafort. In 1234 it was approved as the law of the church and sent to university faculties by Pope Gregory IX. Most of it consisted of papal decretals issued in relatively recent decades, though it also included a few older authorities and some canons from church councils. It included only a tiny number of texts taken over directly from the Justinianic laws. However, some of the papal decretals it contained in fact restated and made use of Roman laws. They embraced the notion that the imperial laws were to be used by the church where the canons did not supply adequate answers to legal questions.[44] The popes were careful to qualify that usage. To be acceptable in ecclesiastical matters, imperial laws must conform to the laws of reason and they must not contradict express precepts of the church. How large that field would prove to be was never wholly clear. A decretal of Pope Honorius III stated the opinion that it would 'rarely happen' that the canons would need help from outside,[45] but the Roman pontiffs have not always been the most reliable predictors of the future. Roman laws would come to the aid of the canons in many circumstances.[46]

The extent of overlap between the two laws is particularly apparent in the titles found in the *Liber extra*. When compared to those found in the *Code*, a real pattern emerges.[47] On the one hand, some titles in the Decretals had no counterpart in Roman law. For example, titles providing detailed rules about the ordination of clerics, about the duties of archdeacons, sacrists, and wardens, and about the collection of tithes and ecclesiastical dues were new. If they were to be influenced by the Roman law, it could only be by analogy. On the other hand, there was also overlap. Titles devoted to the duties of judges, proctors, and arbiters appeared in both; they followed the same path. Titles involving court procedure – the law of presumptions, the place of the *litis contestatio*, and the regulation of appeals – also appeared in both of these law books, again alike in substance. In several matters involving the dealings of ordinary life – contracts, wills, and gifts, for example – the titles and the substance were also identical.

In arranging the *Liber extra*, Raymond of Peñafort evidently turned to the *Corpus iuris civilis*. Before that, his immediate model, the *Quinque compilationes antiquae*, had done the same. The books of the Roman law were available and he used them. Of course, they were being studied and discussed in the Schools, and perhaps it was inevitable that the compiler of an ambitious compilation like the *Liber extra* should look to what he knew as organizational principles. Lawyers are rarely great inventors.

This should not be taken to mean that Raymond followed civilian models slavishly. He did not. He omitted many of the titles and he added others to their number. For example, the Roman law's *Code* had a title on witnesses; in it was a text that dealt with the use of compulsion in requiring witnesses to give evidence.[48] Raymond inserted a title of the same name into the *Liber extra*, but he also added a new title called *De testibus cogendis vel non* – that is, a separate title to deal specifically with the question of when witnesses could, and could not, be summoned and compelled to testify.[49] In other words, he divided one title into two. We do not know for sure why he did so, but the effort seems to have been to require testimony only when it was absolutely necessary to establish the truth. Giving evidence in court required taking an oath, and an oath raised the possibility of perjury. Men and women ought not to be subjected to that danger unnecessarily. Thus Raymond included a decretal of Pope Clement III stating that unwilling witnesses were to be compelled to appear by threat of excommunication only 'if otherwise the truth of the matter cannot be otherwise elicited'.[50] In this way the Decretals both augmented and modified what was found in the Roman law. Of course, the resulting law was not greatly different in its core. The Roman system left considerable discretion on the point to judges, and so would the canon law. A difference remained, however. The canon law was both more careful and more complicated to put into practice. One sees this difference even in the titles Raymond chose to use for his compilation, and it was certainly a conscious choice.

The following books of the *Corpus iuris canonici* were compiled along much the same lines as those found in the *Liber extra*. With one exception, they require no special comment. That exception comes from the end of the *Liber sextus*, in a special title called *De regulis iuris*. It contained 88 jurisprudential principles. Some stated rules of the law of nature – no one is to be punished who is without guilt, for example (Reg. 23). Others stated starting points for sorting out competing claims to property – prior in time, prior in right, for example (Reg. 54). Others stated what we would call simple interpretative maxims – the greater includes the lesser, for example (Reg. 35). Still others stated overtly ecclesiastical rules – the fault of a person should not redound to the detriment of the church, for example (Reg. 76). Notable throughout the title is that almost all of these *Regulae* were in fact taken from the same title in the *Digest*.[51] Pope Boniface VIII, in whose name they were issued, obviously did not disdain to imitate the imperial laws in the development of workable rules for the law of the church. He did not take them all, and he did incorporate some additional maxims. All the same, his title provides a telling example of the dependence of the classical canon law upon the Roman law. It provided his starting point and most of the content that followed.

The canon law that emerged from the compilation of the *Corpus iuris canonici* was thus touched by the Roman law in three important ways. First, the sources of law and the principles by which the law was interpreted and put into practice were largely identical. The canonists took over the assumptions they found stated in the Roman law's texts. Second, although the canonists stressed the church's independence from temporal control, they accepted that the canon law would use the Roman law when the canons proved incomplete. How large that area would be may have been uncertain, but that it existed they did not doubt. And third, even in areas of the law where the canon law was stated expressly and separately, it often followed the Roman law's lead. The church's procedural law, for instance, began by restating provisions found in the civilian texts. It normally built upon them, creating a fuller body of law made necessary by the exigencies of court practice, but the starting point was the *Corpus iuris civilis*.

A telling example – one that includes a little of all three of these sources of influence – occurred with the familiar legal doctrine that ignorance of the law is no excuse. While a mistake about the facts may excuse a person who acts wrongly in accordance with his mistaken belief, the same person's ignorance of the law will not furnish a legitimate way of avoiding the consequences of violating the law. That was (and is) a basic assumption of Western jurisprudence. The canonists found it stated in an opinion of Ulpian in the *Digest*.[52] They took it into the canon law itself, using identical language,[53] and they understood it in the spirit of a still-developing civilian jurisprudence. Thus, the *glossa ordinaria* to the canonical text, the standard tool of interpretation in the canon law, cited both canonical and civilian sources, including the commentary of the greatest of medieval civilians, Bartolus of Sassoferrato, as a key to unlock its meaning.[54] The two laws stood cheek and jowl in the gloss, and that fusion came to be entirely characteristic of the common law of Europe.

The Early Ius Commune

The European common law as it came to exist in the twelfth century and beyond is called *ius commune*. The term refers to the combination of the Roman and canon laws that long served as the jurisprudential foundation for European law. Understanding its formation, its composition, and its force in contemporary jurisprudence is therefore fundamental for understanding the relationship between the canon and Roman laws.

There was, however, a complicating factor. The *ius commune* was never the only law in force in Europe. Although it was a unity and although its reach extended across many lands, in practice European law was open both to development over time and to variation from one place to another. By force of local custom and legislation, court practice accommodated rules that differed from what was found in the texts. One geographical area might adopt its own particular regime for inheritance of land – primogeniture, for example. Another might adopt a different rule – such as equal division of real property among a man's children. Such differences did not undermine the effectiveness of the *ius commune*.[55] They simply allowed for local variation within it. The *ius commune* itself made room for them by recognizing custom as a legitimate source of law. Such variations constituted the *ius proprium*. It meant the law proper to each particular location.

How, then, was the *ius commune* itself constituted? And how does one account for its impact and its longevity? Both questions can best be answered by stressing points already made. First, although the two laws were always distinct, with separate legal texts and separate faculties in the universities, they also had many areas of overlap. In most of those areas, the basic rules were the same. The procedural law used in the canon law, for example, was taken in large part from the civil law. Second, both civilians and canonists acknowledged that gaps in their own laws could legitimately be filled with the other's aid. Emperors had stated that the imperial laws should sometimes follow what the canons contained, and ecclesiastical authorities had repeatedly endorsed the civil law as a useful mine of law for church and clergy. Under a legal regime that looked automatically to the past for guidance, such endorsements encouraged a kind of fusion of the two. Third, both Roman and canon law were founded upon an assumption that law should aim for perfect justice. The teachings of natural law and Christianity were to underpin the positive law. If canon law and Roman law had different aims, as noted at the chapter's outset, they shared a conviction that law was more than the command of the legislator. So joined in assumption, the two came to be, as one modern author has put it, 'as closely connected as the two sides of a coin'.[56]

The point is best understood by examining concrete examples, and many are available. One was mentioned at the end of the previous section: the contents of the *glossa ordinaria*. From the earliest days following the revival of jurisprudence in the twelfth century, commentators wrote about the meaning of the texts. Their common conclusions appeared in glosses attached to the texts. Defining terms, suggesting interpretations, solving inconsistencies, and calling attention to other relevant texts and rules, the glosses moved the law forwards. In doing, so the commentators routinely drew upon both laws.[57] They moved easily from one to the other.

A straightforward example is provided by Roman law and tithes. Of greatest importance to the material interest of the medieval church, the canon law held that the tenth of the fruits of the earth and of men's labour was owed to God and was to be collected by God's delegates on earth, the clergy. The Roman law had no law of tithes, of course. Their source was found in the Bible (e.g., Gen. 28:22). A law to deal with the subject had to be supplied, and one was in fact supplied in a title of 35 chapters in the Gregorian Decretals.[58] The chapters in it dealt with many troublesome problems for the clergy. Tithes were not always easy to collect and they had fallen into lay hands in many parts of Europe over the course of the early middle ages. In theory the men who grew crops were required to collect them together and hand over the tenth part to the parson. But what if they sold those crops to strangers without telling them that the tithes had not been deducted? Were the innocent purchasers obliged to pay the parson a tenth part of what they had purchased, or could they escape the obligation if they were bona fide purchasers? If it was the second, the parson had a cause of action only against the seller. The question was raised in a response by Pope Innocent III to the bishop of Ely.[59] The answer, found most fully stated in the *glossa ordinaria*, was that the purchaser could indeed be sued to collect the tithe, and the justification given for this result was taken directly from the Roman law of sale. Transfer of a chattel carries with it all that belongs with that chattel unless the contrary is stated in the transfer.[60] Thus, the sale of a cow carries with it the calf conceived at the time when the calf is later born. So it was said to be with the tithe. True, the calf was a benefit whereas the tithe was a burden, but the same reasoning applied. One who takes the benefit must also take the burden. Thus, a text from Roman law served to augment the revenue of the church. It was not a great stretch, it seems. For a canonist, it was a normal process.

A slightly more complicated example of such use of Roman law comes from a decretal of Pope Urban III dealing with a contract of marriage entered into under the condition that it would be valid only if the father of the woman consented to it. Urban held that the condition would be effective, even if this placed the decision into the hands of a third party who was not present and would not himself be a party to the matrimonial bond.[61] The glossator sought to support this result, which might have been attacked as a limitation on the pure consent necessary in marriage or as insufficiently certain in outcome to be specifically enforceable. In rejecting this argument, the *glossa ordinaria* cited a title in the Roman law's *Digest* dealing with a conditional sale of a slave.[62] It held that a sale conditioned upon settlement of the slave's accounts to the satisfaction of his master was sufficiently definite, because the satisfaction being referred to was that of a reasonable man, not the simple whim of the master involved. In equal fashion, the gloss implied, the same standard could be used in assessing the father's consent. If he refused agreement arbitrarily, that would be one thing, but if he had a good reason for doing so, that would be something else. The matter could thus be judged by an objective standard, and if that standard had been met, the unfilled condition would provide a defence in an action brought to enforce the contract. The parties would then be as free to contract elsewhere as the buyer and seller of the slave had been free to make other arrangements where the accounts were not properly settled. In this case, therefore, the Roman law both furnished support for the papal decretal's ruling and served to clarify the decretal's meaning. With a clarification taken from Roman law about the nature of the condition involved, the outcome reached by Urban seemed grounded and workable. Today the conjunction of these two texts may seem incongruous. What does a contract for the sale of a slave in Roman law have to do with a Christian marriage? That question obviously did not trouble the canonist who wrote this gloss. He preferred guidance from a distinction drawn in the texts to speculation about public policy, consideration of the personal nature of marriage, or even concern for proper relations between fathers and daughters. The Roman law found in the gloss met that need.

A third example, taken from the *glossa ordinaria* to Gratian's *Decretum*, involved interpretation of a decree of the Third Lateran Council (1179). One of its canons, known from its first words as *Si quis suadente*, declared excommunication of any person who 'laid violent hands' upon a cleric.[63] The gloss posed and answered several questions about it. One was: What if the attacker was a woman? The Latin word *quis* is masculine, so it might be read so as to cover only masculine attackers. That would fit the so-called rule of lenity familiar in the criminal law. But it was not so, held the gloss. Female attackers were included. Why? The civil law's text cited in support was a rule found in the *Digest* holding that women were to be excluded from all public and civil offices.[64] That now seems a very strange choice to show that attacks by women were in fact covered by the Council's decree, and it is only when one takes account of the commentary on the *Digest* text itself that the reason for citing it becomes clear.[65] The explanation was that women were being disqualified because they were thought by nature to be unfit for public life. This was a rule subject to exceptions, some of which were found in the gloss itself, but it was based on an understanding widely accepted at the time. In this case, the lawyers read it *a contrario sensu*, meaning that if women were being excluded from an office precisely because the office was public in nature, it necessarily followed that where the office was not a public one, it should be open to women. The text could thus be read as standing for the broader proposition that unless a good reason for excluding women from the coverage of any law existed, they were to be included. It was actually a clever argument. Attacks on clerics could occur anywhere, and the resulting disparagement on the clergy would have been the same, no matter whether the attacker was male or female. No special reason for excluding women existed here, as it had in the *Digest* text. Hence, the text from the Roman law not only provided an answer to the glossator's specific question, it also supplied principles of interpretation that could be applied in other parts of the *ius commune*.

These three instances are but examples of the many uses the medieval canonists made of Roman law. It became second nature to them. In the Schools, canonists would have learned to look to the *Corpus iuris civilis* for guidance and authority. This was part of their education in law and they would have applied it to their own law. It did not, of course, preclude similar use of canonical sources. For instance, the first example given was actually an exceptional case in the Decretal title on tithes; the great majority of citations found in the *glossa ordinaria* under that head came from canonical texts. In glossing the marriage law – somewhat ironically, in light of the canon law's rejection of divorce – more use of Roman law was normal. So there was variety. However, all three examples show what became an almost reflexive response to a legal problem arising in the canon law: look to an analogous situation in the civil law and apply the reasoning or the result found in it to interpreting the church's own law.

This was one side, and the more significant side for understanding the lasting influence of the Roman law, but it should be noted that medieval civilians, commentators on the *Corpus iuris civilis*, also made reference to canonical texts.[66] They did so to a much lesser extent at the stage of the *glossa ordinaria* than the canonists had in developing their own law. Then, the Roman law was more sophisticated and complete; the canon law was less so at the time Accursius (d. 1263) put together the standard gloss on the *Corpus iuris civilis*. With the gradual move towards equal status, however, the two laws began to play a roughly equivalent role in the commentaries written on the other's texts. Much depended on the subject, of course. The canon law provided only a modicum of help with the law of last wills and testaments, for example, and the Roman law was useful only within odd parts of the canon law regulating the church's sacraments. But the blending together of the two laws, both being treated as authority useful for interpreting and augmenting the other law, had been established as normal practice for European law by the end of the thirteenth century.

The Later *Ius Commune*

What was a small lake in the twelfth and thirteenth century had become an ocean by the sixteenth century. Scholarly volumes in uncountable numbers had been written to describe, interpret, and advance the *ius commune*. No ideological divide separates the two periods, but they do look quite distinct from the outside. The enormous growth in the number and range of commentaries gives the later period a quite different appearance. There was perhaps less innovation. There was certainly more complexity, more stress on completeness, more repetition of rules, and more references made to a myriad of learned works. The enlargement responded to a real need, no doubt. By all counts, the law courts of the later middle ages and beyond dealt with more litigation than they had earlier, and much of it was complex enough to require massive and detailed treatises. Very likely, the proliferation in scholarship also responded to the growth in numbers of European universities and law faculties. Many of the *Doctores* who taught in them wished to publish the fruits of their studies. What they published provides a new vantage point from which to view the history of the relationship between the Roman and canon laws.

The first thing one observes is the existence of a class of literature which it is impossible to assign to one side or the other of the line between the two laws. Works on civil and criminal procedure are the most obvious example. The same works were used in both secular and spiritual courts. This was an amplification of an existing habit. Except for their bulk and their complexity, most later treatises on the subject were not different in essence from the procedural manuals produced in the thirteenth century. The *Ordo iudiciarius* by Tancred of Bologna (d. 1236), or the *Speculum iudiciale* by William Durantis (d. 1296) cited both laws without discriminating between them. Tancred's discussion of the office of *procuratores* and their role in litigation, for example, contained 7 citations from Gratian's *Decretum*, 17 from the Gregorian Decretals, 12 from the *Code*, 3 from the *Digest*, and 4 from Justinian's *Institutes*.[67] Here the two laws were truly fused. The same characteristic is found in juristic works of the sixteenth and seventeenth centuries, the principal difference between them and their predecessors being a multiplication of the number of citations to other commentators on the *ius commune*. Of course, much less of that literature existed at the time Tancred was writing. By 1600 it had mushroomed, and in the hands of some of the later jurists citation of the opinions of other writers on both the Roman and canon laws became something of a mania. For instance, a discussion from the elephantine treatise by Joseph Mascardus (d. 1588) of a proctor's disqualification to give evidence as a witness contains a single reference to a text in the *Digest*, 1 from the *Code* and 1 from the Gregorian Decretals, but it contains 27 separate citations from the works of other jurists.[68] In this respect, that treatise was not unusual.

A second and immediately recognizable development in the later works of the *ius commune*, one in which many of the same characteristics are evident, is the greater attention paid to courts and litigation. *Decisiones* from the courts were published in great numbers; so were *Consilia*, the opinions of jurists on questions raised in practice, used by judges to resolve actual cases or by parties to influence the judges; and also works of *Praxis* about proceedings in specific courts. The authorities in these works were the same as found in most treatises of the time, but here the *ius proprium* played a greater part. If one looks, for instance, at a collection of *Decisiones* from the Roman Rota at the end of the sixteenth century compiled by Franciscus Mantica, the same features reappear. In a decision relating to a gift between husband and wife, several texts from Gratian's *Decretum* were noted, but most of the citations to specific texts came from the Roman law.[69] Both the *Code* and the *Digest* had long titles devoted to the subject. The Decretals also contained one, but most of its chapters dealt with the effect of divorce on dowry rights, a matter not involved in the case in Mantica's collection. By contrast, a dispute about whether an archdeaconry could be created without an adequate endowment was decided largely on the basis of the canon law, including previous decisions of the Rota, although two texts from the *Digest* were also included in it.[70] Both, however, also contained references to contemporary commentaries on the *ius commune*. They show clearly that the regular intermingling of the two laws continued and intensified. This was not an academic exercise; it applied *throughout* Western Europe.[71] Even in the papal court, Roman law had an impact on the law of the church that occasionally seemed greater than that of the canon law itself.

A third feature of the later history of the *ius commune* deserving of the attention of any student concerned with the relationship between the two laws is the creation of a body of works expressly devoted to the subject. It is called the *Differentiae* literature. Although it could range more widely, most of it consisted of works called 'Of the differences between the canon law and the civil'. As its name implies, its announced purpose was to discover and describe the differences that existed between the two laws. How many were there and how significant were they? The very fact of their existence tends to show that lawyers in the sixteenth and seventeenth centuries, from which most of this literature comes,[72] regarded the subject of the relationship between the two laws as one worthy of study, and some of the literature fulfils the promise of true comparison. That by Heinrich Canisius (1548–1610), for example, begins by considering the areas where, as a matter of principle, the canon law was duty-bound to assert its independence. Where the civil law provided an occasion for sin, he noted, it should have no place in the courts of the church.[73] He then went on to give examples. In the longer part of his treatment he listed 54 instances in which either that or some other principle required a difference between the two laws. Each cited a text as authority, usually one from the canon law. Otherwise, he seemed to say, the two laws complemented each other.

This work by Canisius, it should be said, was better than most. The three examples of the class found in the *Tractatus universi iuris* (1584–86) appear almost to have been the products of a contest to see which compiler could come up with the largest number of differences. The 'winner' was Hieronymus Zanettini, whose collection listed 277 separate differences, though a few of them required stretching in order to be counted.[74] Zanettini ended by asserting that many more existed, but this was a ritual required at the end of such a list; all the jurists included something like it. When viewed objectively, the lists of differences actually confirm the mutual dependence of the two laws. A few were important, but most of the differences were predictable, small, or invented. The similarities were greater.

4. Conclusion

This chapter began by dividing the topic of the canon law's relation to Roman law into three parts: the existence of mutual influence, the preservation of Roman law, and the creation of the *ius commune*. What has the cumulation of evidence shown about each? The first was consideration of the extent to which the resources of the *Corpus iuris civilis* were used in formulating the canon law. Here, it seems clear that the connections were vital in several respects. From the earliest days, the church fathers had assumed that Roman law stated good law, although not in every area of human life. When, several centuries later, it came time to compile a systematic law for the church, its *Corpus* followed organizational patterns found in the Roman law books, incorporated parts of the individual Roman laws into its titles, and relied on Roman laws to interpret its own collections of canons and papal decretals. The church was not compelled to follow the civil law, and indeed it rejected some civil law doctrines as incompatible with the Christian religion. Overall, however, the instances of dependence were greater than those of rejection.

About the second area raised at the outset – an assessment of the canon law's role in preserving the heritage of the ancient Roman law – the picture is more clouded. That the church did help preserve the inheritance of Roman law is not open to doubt. By 'canonizing' so much of the ancient law and making repeated use of it in the centuries when the church dominated much of human life, the church did aid in the civil law's survival into the modern world. However, it is one thing to show that the church supported the ancient law. It is another to attribute Roman law's survival to the church. The revival of study of Roman law began more than a century before Gratian compiled the *Decretum*, and at first the civilians regarded the canon law with some disdain. The civil law was always more comprehensive and more sophisticated than that of the church. It could stand on its own. Would its influence have been what it was without the church? Probably yes; it would have been, in some measure. The most one can say is that without the canon law Roman law would not have been quite as pervasive a force in European history as it turned out to be.

How and why it happened that the two laws became blended together to form the *ius commune*, the third subject, is only a little less difficult to estimate accurately than the second. That it happened is a fact. That it was a reflection of the medieval belief in the interdependence of the spiritual and secular sides of life is also a live possibility. That the two were the products of the same revival of legal study in the twelfth century furnishes an additional reason for the fusion that occurred. The two were taught side by side in most European universities and many aspiring lawyers studied both. This could of course be either a cause or an effect of their interdependence. A familiar maxim of earlier centuries held that 'A legist without the canons is worth little; a canonist without the civil laws nothing at all.'[75] If we cannot quite explain the deep reasons for this fusion, we can at least be sure that this was a maxim every lawyer once knew.

Notes

1. For abbreviations used in this chapter see the table of abbreviations, and note that in this chapter while C. 1.1.1 refers (as elsewhere) to Justinian's *Code*, C. 1 q. 1 c. 1 refers to the Decretum of Gratian, Causa 1, quaestio 1, canon 1.
2. J. Witte and F. Alexander, eds., *Christianity and Law: An Introduction* (Cambridge, 2008), 1–17.
3. See A. Van Hove, *Prolegomena ad codicem iuris canonici* (Mechelen and Rome, 1945), 163–76; C. Gallagher, *Church Law and Church Order in Rome and Byzantium: A Comparative Study* (Aldershot, 2002).
4. Henricus de Segusio (Hostiensis) (d. 1271), *Summa aurea*, Proem. no. 12 (Venice, 1574), 8.
5. D. 48.5.1–45; C. 9.9.1–35; X 5.16.1–7.
6. See DD at X 5.26.2.
7. E.g. D. 44.1.1–24; C. 7.33.1–12.
8. X 2.26.1–20.
9. Lat. IV, c. 41 in *Decrees of the Ecumenical Councils*, ed. N. Tanner (1990) vol. 1, 253.
10. *Gl. ord.* ad X 2.26.20: 'et ideo canon voluit propter periculum animarum in hoc leges corrigere'.
11. E.g. Andreas Gail (d. 1587), *Observationes practicae imperialis camerae* (1595), lib. II, obs. 18, nos. 6–7: 'quia secundum canones et communem atque in camera imperiali saepius approbatam opinionem, malae fidei possessor nullo unquam tempore praescribit'.
12. Nov. 137.1–6.
13. Nov. 140.1.
14. *Gl. ord.* ad X 3 47.1: '[S]i mulieres post partum voluerint ecclesiam intrare acturae gratias Deo, nullum est peccatum, nec aditus ecclesiae illis est denegandus'.
15. M. Hill, *Ecclesiastical Law*, 2nd edn. (London, 2001) paras. 5.57, 144.
16. R. Fraher, 'The theoretical justification for the new criminal law of the high middle ages: *Rei publicae interest, ne crimina remaneant impunita*', *University of Illinois Law Review* (1984): 577–95.
17. X 5.39.1–60.
18. Sext. 5.11.1–24.
19. F. D. Logan, *Excommunication and the Secular Arm in medieval England* (Toronto, 1968).
20. DD at X 5.7.19.
21. E.g. A. Gauthier, *Roman Law and its Contribution to the Development of Canon Law* (Ottawa, 1996), 4–5.
22. J. Gaudemet, *La formation du droit séculier et du droit de l'église aux IVe et Ve siècles*, 2nd edn. (Paris, 1979), 216–30.
23. See *lex Ribuaria* c. 58 § 1, in *Lex Ribuaria et lex Francorum Chamavorum*, ed. R. Sohm (Hannover, 1883), 79.
24. P. Vinogradoff, *Roman Law in Medieval Europe*, revd. edn. (Cambridge, 1968), 11–41.
25. C. 12 q. 1 c. 7.
26. C. G. Fürst, 'Ecclesia vivit lege Romana?' *ZSS (Kanonistische Abteilung)* (1975): 27–30.
27. C. 1.6.1–3.
28. Nov. 83.1: 'secundum sacras et divinas regulas, quas etiam nostrae sequi non dedignantur leges'.

29. E.g. Letter (494) of Pope Gelasius to the bishops of Sicily approving application of the Roman law of prescription to possession of church property, in *Epistolae Romanorum pontificum*, ed. A. Thiel (Braunsberg, 1868), vol. 1, 381–82.
30. Gaudemet (n. 22), 227.
31. E.g. C. 8.38(39).2.
32. E.g. B. Ferme, *Introduction to the History of the Sources of Canon Law: The Ancient Law up to the* Decretum *of Gratian* (Montreal, 2007), 19–21.
33. W. Hartmann, *Kirche und Kirchenrecht um 900: Die Bedeutung der spätkarolingischen Zeit für Tradition und Innovation im kirchlichen Recht* (Hannover, 2008), 143–77.
34. See *Libri duo de synodalibus causis*, ed. F. G. A. Wasserschleben (Leipzig, 1840), 525.
35. *Anselmi episcopi Lucensis collection canonum*, lib. II, cc. 2–3, ed. F. Thaner (Innsbruck, 1915), 76.
36. Van Hove (n. 3), 239–40.
37. *Collectio canonum trium librorum*, ed. J. Motta (Vatican City, 2008), 375–76.
38. A. Winroth, *The Making of Gratian's Decretum* (Cambridge, 2000); C. Larrainzar, 'La formación del Decreto de Graciano por etapas', *ZSS* (*Kanonistische Abteilung*) 118 (2001): 5–83.
39. Dist. 12 cc. 6–7, taken from Inst. 1.2.9; C. 8.52(53).1; and see, generally, J. M. Viejo-Ximénez, 'La reception del deerecho Romano en el derecho canónico', *Anales de la Tradición Romanística*' 2 (2005), 139–69.
40. D. p. Dist. 10 c. 6.
41. C. 3 q. 7 c. 1, taken from D. 3.1.1.
42. C. 30 q. 3 c. 6, taken from D. 23.2.17.
43. C. 25 q. 2 cc. 15–16, taken from C. 1.19.3 and C. 1.19.7.
44. E.g. X 1.2.10.
45. X 5.33.28: 'occurrunt raro'.
46. O. Cassola, *La recezione del Diritto Civile nel Diritto Canonico*, 2nd edn. (Rome, 1969), 39–52.
47. See Gauthier (n. 21), 101–6.
48. C. 4.20.18.
49. X 2.21.1–11.
50. X 2.12.5.
51. D. 50.17.1–178 (*de diversis regulis iuris antiqui*). See Gauthier (n. 21), 107–17.
52. D. 22.6.6.
53. Reg. 13 in Sext, tit. *De regulis iuris.*
54. *Gl. ord.* ad id., v. *ignorantia facti.*
55. G. Dolezalek, *Scotland under Jus Commune* (Edinburgh, 2010), 3.
56. See M. Bellomo, *The Common Legal Past of Europe 1000–1800*, trans. L. Cochrane (Washington, D.C., 1995), xii; A. Lefebvre-Teillard, 'Le rôle des canonistes dans la formation d'un 'Droit Commun' romano-canonique', *Revue d'histoire des facultés de droit et de la culture juridique* 28 (2008): 215–26.
57. Vinogradoff (n. 24), 119–30.
58. X 3-30.1–35.
59. X 3.30.28, and *gl. ord.* ad id. v. *nisi cum onere.*
60. D. 18.1.67.
61. X 5.4.5.
62. D. 18.1.7 and *gl. ord.* ad id. v. *alieno arbitrio.*
63. C. 17 q. 4 c. 29.

64. D. 50.17.2.
65. *Gl. ord.* ad id v. *foemina.*
66. See, e.g., *gl. ord.* ad C. 3.1.14, v. *iudices*, citing X 2.28.61.
67. *Ordo iudiciarius*, Pt. I, tit. 6 § 8, in *Pillius, Tancredus, Gratia, Libri de iudiciorum ordine*, ed. F. C. Bergman (Göttingen, 1842), 114–23.
68. *De probationibus*, III, concl. 1232, no. 1 (Venice, 1593), 197.
69. Dec. 49 (1589), in Franciscus Mantica, *Decisiones Rotae Romanae* (Rome, 1619), 64–66.
70. Dec. 114 (1590), ibid. 140–41.
71. E.g. A. Wijffels, *Qui millies allegatur: les allégations du droit savant dans les dossiers du Grand Conseil de Malines (causes septentrionales, ca. 1460–1580)* (Leiden, 1985).
72. A version was ascribed to Bartolus, and is printed in Bartolus de Sassoferrato, *Commentaria*, IX (Rome, 1996), fol. 145v–49v, but the accuracy of the ascription is doubtful. See J. Portemer, *Recherches sur les 'Differentiae juris civilis et canonici' au temps du droit classique de l'Église* (Paris, 1946).
73. *De differentiis iuris canonici et civilis*, lim. 4 (1640).
74. *De differentiis inter ius canonicum et civile*, in TUI, vol. 1, fols. 197v–208.
75. F. Merzbacher, 'Die Parömie *Legista sine canonibus parum valet, canonista sine legibus nichil*', *Studia Gratiana* 13 (1967): 275–82.

20 Political Thought

Magnus Ryan

Roman law entered medieval political reflection in the late eleventh century as the law of the universal Roman empire, an organization foretold by Old Testament prophecy as the last empire to rule the world before Apocalypse and hallowed by Christ himself who had lived under the Caesars. It left the middle ages as a text beginning to radiate a different kind of universality: as a source of concepts and analytical categories relevant not merely to the history and contemporary structure of the empire, but to all societies. In this transformation – palpable, although far from complete, by the end of the period – Roman law was unshackled from the one universal society of the Roman empire and began to furnish the conceptual means to analyse and explain the relations between rulers and ruled in kingdoms and other polities.

1. Emperor and People: The *Lex Regia*

The *Corpus iuris civilis* tells a story about how the Roman empire ceased to be governed by the Roman people and changed its constitutional form, forever after to be ruled by emperors. This supposedly occurred when the people of Rome enacted a 'royal statute' or *lex regia* transferring to the new emperor all its powers of government. The notion that imperial powers had been created by one wholesale enactment was historically erroneous and probably reflects a confusion with the real laws passed at the accession of successive emperors according them a variety of specific exemptions and privileges. Nevertheless, it had become enshrined in Roman legal tradition by the time the compilers of the *Corpus iuris civilis* set to work in the early sixth century, and the early glossators of the twelfth century had no reason to doubt Justinian's account. The transfer of ruling powers by the Roman people to the emperor is mentioned at several prominent points in the text of the *Corpus iuris civilis* and was accordingly hard to overlook. In the title of the *Digest* on imperial constitutions the *lex regia* is mentioned by name to account for the claim that what has pleased the emperor has the force of law;[1] this passage is in turn paraphrased in an important section at the beginning of the *Institutes* on natural law, the law of nations, and civil law.[2] Elsewhere, in the constitution *Deo auctore*, Justinian himself cited the transfer of power by the Roman people as the reason he as emperor possessed the authority to make the entire *Corpus iuris civilis* into law.[3] According to these texts the Roman people had transferred all its *imperium* and *potestas* – in the constitution *Deo auctore* it is *ius* and *potestas* – to the emperor. The *lex regia* does not explain the origins of such governmental powers in themselves; it merely provides an account of how the imperial office was created and with what immediate effects; these passages do not even explain why the Roman people decided to bestow its powers of government on the emperor. The closest Roman law comes to explaining Rome's mutation into monarchy is an allusion to the senate's inability to rule over the provinces.[4] The references to the *lex regia* presented the glossators with a minor difficulty when read in conjunction with Justinian's description elsewhere of the empire as a gift from God to mankind, alongside the Church, because this implied that the empire had been founded by God rather than the Roman people; the eventual solution was that the Roman people had acted as God's instrument in establishing the imperial office, which accordingly was said to exist by God's authority and the people's ministry.[5]

The *lex regia* quickly achieved prominence in jurisprudence because it provided a solution to a problem about legislative power within the empire. *Code* 1.14.12 described the emperor as sole legislator, whereas D. 1.3.9 stated emphatically ('There is no doubt ... ') that the senate could still legislate. *Digest* 1.3.32 seemed to corroborate this second passage by explaining that laws were only binding because they expressed the people's consent; should the people express a contrary will by forming a custom contradicting a law, then that law would be abrogated.[6] The senate and the people on the one hand thus appeared to compete with the emperor on the other for the power to legislate, and the medieval interpreters of Roman law were thus confronted with a seeming contradiction in their source. The earliest known attempt at a resolution of this tension came from the most influential early teacher of Roman law in medieval Europe, Irnerius, according to whom the apparently discrepant texts referred to different periods in the history of Rome and were thus in harmony with one another. Commenting on D. 1.3.32, Irnerius explained:

> This applied in the times in which the people still had the power of laying down the law and so by the tacit consent of

> the people laws were abrogated. But nowadays, since this power has been transferred to the emperor, the disuse of a particular law by the people has no effect.[7]

For well over a century after intensive study of Roman law began, medieval civilians found no compelling reason to articulate a response to the *lex regia* except in relation to one organization: the Roman empire. The majority of the lawyers thought the transfer was irrevocable, partly because only this interpretation seemed to do full justice to the various declarations scattered throughout Roman law to the effect that the empire was from God; it was as if God had desired an empire and used the Roman people as His instrument to bring it into being. A brief review of the variations on this theme in what survives from twelfth-century jurisprudence reveals that Irnerius' fundamental assumption went largely unchallenged: for most of the twelfth century, lawyers followed him in maintaining that the *lex regia* had irrevocably shifted the monopoly of legislative power from the Roman people to the emperor. *Digest* 1.3.32, with its apparent endorsement of the contrary position to the effect that the people could abrogate a law by not applying it, was inevitably at the centre of debate. According to a school of thought which can be traced back to one of Irnerius' most influential pupils, Martinus Gosia (who died after 1158), the all-important passage did not allow the abrogation of an imperially sanctioned law by means of popular custom, but rather the abrogation of one written custom by a subsequent custom. On Martinus' interpretation, the expression *lex* in the *Digest* passage referred not to imperial law at all, but to written local custom which he called municipal law or *ius municipale*.[8] Martinus thus tried to resolve the tension between the ratification of a popular legislative power in D. 1.3.32 and the assertion of an imperial monopoly over legislation in C. 1.14.12 by re-orienting the former passage from the imperial to the municipal level, thereby safeguarding the imperial laws of the *Corpus iuris civilis* against all popular challenge and incidentally providing Justinianic authority for the formation of local custom in cities.[9] Placentinus followed him, underlining that the people had by the *lex regia* transferred to the emperor the power to make and abrogate law.[10] Several twelfth-century glossators thought the emperor stood in a ministerial relation to the people, with the result that his seemingly extensive powers – expressed most famously in D. 1.4.1: what has pleased the emperor has the force of law – were implicitly limited by his status as delegate, representative, or vicar of the people. However, the jurists who drew attention to this also emphasized that the Roman people had transferred all its legislative powers to the emperor.[11]

Unanimity on the irrevocability of the *lex regia* lasted until the late twelfth century and the jurisprudence of Johannes Bassianus, whose ideas were adopted by his pupil Azo, the most influential lawyer teaching at Bologna around 1200. Bassianus' solution addressed the apparent tension between those passages in Roman law attributing legislative power variously to the emperor and to the people. He argued that the emperor was superior to individuals within the Roman people, but not to the entire people taken as a corporate whole, a doctrine which would one day be summed up in five words: *princeps maior singulis minor universis*. Bassianus and Azo thus resolved the problem of apparently competing popular and imperial legislative capacities in the Roman law by turning the emperor into the sole legislator in a specific and highly qualified sense.[12] He was the only person who could legislate on his own as a single person, whereas the corporate people still had that power collectively and could therefore abrogate the emperor's laws and even revoke the powers granted him by the *lex regia*.[13] Accursius alluded to the distinction in his gloss to D. 1.3.9 and its assertion that the senate could make law. He noted that Johannes Bassianus had denied the senate the power to legislate on the grounds of the *lex regia*, and related the argument advanced by others to the effect that the Roman people and the senate could still legislate, since the apparent attribution of exclusive legislative power to the emperor at C. 1.14.12 meant that the emperor was the only person who could legislate on his own, and therefore only excluded other single persons from legislating. Accursius went on to say that the Roman people could revoke what it had granted and quoted an additional argument put forward by an older contemporary, Hugolinus, that the Roman people stood in the same relation to the emperor as a judge to his delegate.[14] Although the distinction between *singuli* and *universi* is not mentioned explicitly by Azo's great pupil in what would become the standard gloss to the *Corpus iuris civilis*, it is still very close to the surface in the gloss to D. 1.3.9, which is also where Accursius acknowledged the capacity of the Roman people to depose the emperor. However, at two further passages – D. 1.3.32 and C. 8.52(53).2 – where he might relevantly have mentioned it, Accursius omitted both the distinction itself and its consequence. The standard gloss therefore passed on to future generations of jurists a picture of a revocable *lex regia* as an explicit consequence of the corporate superiority of the Roman people over the emperor.

The jurisprudence of Odofredus, who was an exact Bolognese contemporary of Accursius and who died in 1265, relies heavily on the distinction. His principal treatment of the relationship between the Roman people and the emperor comes in his commentary to D. 1.3.1, where

Papinian defined law among other things as a communal directive and communal covenant of the commonwealth.[15] Significantly, Odofredus immediately understood this commonwealth to be that of Rome, as he explained that law was not what one Roman enacted, but what the Roman people enacted; later, in the same context, he referred to the commune of Rome.[16] Among the obvious objections to this definition of law, Odofredus listed the apparently enduring legislative power of the senate, as well as further texts attributing the same capacity to the praetorian prefect, the praetor, certain privileged legal experts authorized to give binding decisions, and the emperor, none of whom amounted to the Roman people. Here his answer is manifestly derived from the arguments of Bassianus, Azo, and Hugolinus but is more explicit than those of his predecessors and more expansive than the terse glosses of Accursius. All of the aforementioned figures legislated by the authority of the Roman people; the expression *solus princeps* should therefore be taken to exclude other single persons, not the people or senate. For the sake of thoroughness Odofredus also included the praetorian prefect and the praetor – single persons both – in the list, but added that such officials were not exceptions because they acted by the authority of the people. The *lex regia* therefore did not embody an abdication of power to the emperor – which, as Odofredus pointed out, was hardly surprising, since the law furnished other examples of jurisdiction which could be delegated without being permanently and irrevocably alienated. The *lex regia* was not even the first occasion in Roman history when the highest jurisdiction had changed hands. After all, the Romans had once expelled their kings.[17] To do this, Odofredus argued, they must have retained some vestigial powers even under the kingship; it should be no surprise if now, under the emperors, the people still had that same capacity to revoke its grant of legislative power.[18] Odofredus employed the same distinction between single persons and the collective to argue emphatically that the senate could still legislate despite the epithet of sole legislator attributed to the emperor.[19]

Several of the more influential French jurists accepted this framework of debate, with Jacques de Revigny adding the refinement that the people nowadays empowered to elect the emperor were the Germans, so they should be the ones to revoke the *lex regia* if need be.[20] As evidence that the people could never abdicate its powers irrevocably Jacques cited the removal of power from the Decemvirs mentioned in D. 1.2.2, an observation repeated to the same effect by Pierre de Belleperche.[21]

These examples could be multiplied but are sufficient to make a fundamental point. The glossators, when they attempted to disentangle such passages in the *Corpus iuris civilis*, did not believe they were confronting principles but the record of unique events which had created their own civilization, which as a result they could not regard with the detachment which is the hallmark of comparative or analogical method. Had the scholastic lawyers been as unencumbered by historical consciousness as is commonly asserted of scholastics in general, they would not have been so stretched between past and present. The institutional relevance of their texts was inescapable to them. This meant that they were doing more in the course of their exegesis than providing a twelfth-century translation as they applied the law to situations around them. The tension between institutional coordinates and abstraction is the most important characteristic of the medieval Roman-law mind; the stages by which this slackened in the course of the later middle ages constitute cardinal points in the way we plot change in the theory generated by Roman law in this period. Until it became possible to treat the texts of Roman law as abstract principles applicable to all polities, rather than as historical descriptions of the relationship between the emperor and the Roman people alone, Roman law jurisprudence would exhibit a powerful tension because the institutional rootedness of the texts in the real and enduring Roman empire lent urgency and immediacy to legal debate. With some rhetorical enhancement, urgency could become ferocity, and there is indeed a fervour about some twelfth-century civilian jurisprudence.

The phenomenon is magnificently illustrated by one of the most important texts to survive from the twelfth-century law schools: the anonymous treatise known as the 'Questions on the intricacies of law' or *Questiones de iuris subtilitatibus*.[22] The *Questiones* provide an eloquent and early testimony to the central role in much Roman law argument of historical time. The significance of the *Questiones* consists partly in the fact that they provide a narrative of the fortunes of the Roman law by reference to events which are not themselves mentioned in the *Corpus iuris civilis*. In the background is the demise of the empire under barbarian pressure and the consequent introduction of a plurality of tribal laws, all viewed from the exalted standpoint of the twelfth-century present when the Roman law enjoys full vigour once more. The validity of the barbarian laws is now extinct with their authors; if there is one empire now, there must be one law. The author regards the period since the barbarian invasions (or, possibly, the period since the collapse of Justinian's empire) as a dead time of undifferentiatedly illegitimate, fragmentary structures, irrelevant to legal science which is inextricably linked to the unity of mankind. The law is the corporate, collective manifestation of that *scientia* for which individual Roman authors were each separately famous in their distinct fields, and constitutes one of Rome's claims to universal hegemony now.[23] One or the other is inevitable: either the law is one since the empire is one, or, if there are many and various laws, there must be many kingdoms. Clearly, the author of the *Quaestiones* prefers the former. Law differs from the other arts because it has a necessary component of power (*potestas*), not merely knowledge (*auctoritas* or *scientia*).[24] This is where the *Questiones* introduce Rome's second claim to rule: divine approbation. Rome's power was not the outcome of tyrannical violence, for the Church, who established her principal seat there, would never have chosen a tyrannical or unjust power as her consort. If Scripture relates that it was within Caesar's authority to order by edict that a census be taken of all peoples, it must be legitimate for him to legislate for them too.[25] For this lawyer, then, the law of Rome's authority derived as much from the history of unrepeatable, ungeneralizable events as from its inherent reasonableness. This conviction lay so deep in the jurisprudence of the twelfth century that to our eyes it can be invisible, especially in the manuals and glosses which were not composed with the literary panache of the *Questiones*. But to lose sight of it renders much of what was to follow incomprehensible.

2. CUSTOM AND LAW

Twelfth-century efforts to extract from Justinian a coherent lesson on the locus of legislative power exhibit this time and again, with especial clarity in relation to how popular custom related to imperial law. A title in the *Code* devoted to 'What long-established custom is'[26] contains an excerpt from a constitution issued by Constantine the Great establishing that, although the force of long-observed custom and usage is not negligible, it can never overcome law or reason.[27] Constantine's words chimed with statements such as Ulpian's declaration in D. 1.4.1 that what pleased the prince had the force of law, and against Julian's assertion in D. 1.3.32.2 of a popular capacity to abrogate law by custom.[28] The solution which would command broad assent was provided by another pupil of Irnerius, Bulgarus, around the middle of the twelfth century. A custom observed by the entire Roman people abrogated a contrary law. A custom observed by a smaller community did not, but it was to be preferred in that locality without formally abrogating the contrary law, as long as the people of that community were aware of the existence of that law.[29] The specific derogated from the general, in other words. Where a people was ignorant that in its behaviour it was contradicting a law, no custom could arise and take the place of the law because error impedes consent, a necessary component of will (*voluntas*), without which law is nothing.[30] This resolution of the difficulty of clashing texts in the *Corpus iuris civilis* might appear to attribute to the entire Roman people a power to legislate superior to that of the emperor, and it is possible that this was Bulgarus' intention. However, Bulgarus' solution did not lead inevitably in this direction, because a generation later Johannes Bassianus, as reported by his pupil Azo, defined a universal custom as a custom observed by the Roman people *or the emperor*.[31] According to a further, anonymous, report, Bassianus' argument contained an additional element: custom overcame law unless the law concerned had been promulgated after the people committed its *imperium* to the emperor.[32] Bassianus appears to have transmitted two differing accounts to posterity, in one of which Irnerius' solution lived on. Bassianus' slightly older contemporary Albericus even specified that such a general custom *was* the custom of the emperor, who now took the place of the Roman people.[33] As this summary shows, in the twelfth-century theory of custom the fragment of Julian in D. 1.3.32 was interpreted as a commentary on the relations between the Roman people and the Roman emperor.

An opposing theory interpreted the passage as a reference to what happened at the level of cities within the Roman empire. Placentinus, who died in 1192, followed Irnerius in maintaining that the Roman people had transferred its legislative powers to the emperor by the *lex regia* and could no longer abrogate imperial law by forming a contrary custom.[34] His own solution to the conundrum was that the word 'law' (*lex*) in Julianus' dictum should be interpreted widely to mean custom as well as written law. For him, then, the passage meant that the people could by a new custom abrogate a preceding custom but not a written law, which was now the exclusive domain of the prince thanks to the *lex regia*.[35] It is noteworthy that this and Bulgarus' theory of locally specific custom allowed for the existence of peoples within the Roman people, which is already suggestive and was to become extremely important later on. For the moment it is important merely to register that the peoples concerned were all conceived as being within the Roman people, which therefore remained the all-encompassing unit presupposed by all contributors to these debates about custom and law. The reminder is salutary because scholars have occasionally interpreted early, seemingly definitive, statements by the glossators in a contrary sense. In the second volume of *A History of Mediaeval Political Theory in the West*, a book which still offers the most richly-illustrated English-language account of pre-fourteenth-century law-based political theory, the Carlyles quoted a fragment 'On equity' (*De aequitate*), inaccurately attributed to Irnerius, and a further authentic gloss by Irnerius to D. 1.3.1 as evidence that for Irnerius, a people was a corporation or *universitas*, in which capacity it commanded and legislated. They read these sources as expositions of a principle about 'the natural relation between a society and its members', a general principle which was then applied to the Roman people in the earliest surviving full-length work on Justinian's *Code*, the *Summa Trecensis*.[36] The *Summa Trecensis*, written a generation or so after Irnerius, does indeed focus entirely on the Roman people and the Roman emperor.[37] The first of these two opinions is not by Irnerius but emanates from the school of Martinus a generation later; the second is still thought to be Irnerian in inspiration. Misattributions apart, this entire manner of presenting the twelfth-century evidence is misleading. Neither passage mentions the people of a given city, still less the people of any imaginable city, as if it were already a general principle that the corporation of a city was its people and the legislative capacity in any *civitas* lodged in the people or its representative. In fact, the two opinions should be taken as referring to the Roman people and the Roman city, as the *Summa Trecensis* specifies. As Ulrich Meier observes in implicit correction of the Carlyles, to the glossators 'people' meant 'Roman people'.[38]

In the most theoretically challenging and politically tense scenario of a general custom of the entire Roman people abrogating a law passed by the emperor, the consent established by D. 1.3.32 as one of the poles of discussion tended to mutate from popular to imperial consent. This occurs in Johannes Bassianus' gloss to the effect that a general custom was as much the custom of the emperor as of the people, and Albericus' suggestion would fit very snugly with this. Crucially, however, for the shape of jurisprudence for generations and indeed centuries to come, Accursius embraced this solution which, enshrined in his *Glossa ordinaria*, became a central concept in jurisprudence. In his gloss to D. 1.3.32 and the claim made there that the only difference between laws and customs is their form – since the binding power of both arose from the consent of the people – he briefly referred to Irnerius' solution based on the *lex regia*, a solution which he also associated with Placentinus. But Accursius himself saw the solution in Bassianus' and Azo's distinction between general custom and the custom of a specific locality. Accursius explained the capacity of general custom to overcome law by reference to the emperor, who was deemed to have full knowledge of such a custom and therefore by not explicitly annulling it to ratify it implicitly. Whenever we seem to be spectators at a debate about disembodied, universal principles of political jurisprudence, as unspecified peoples take control of their destiny by exercising their respective collective wills, the glossators quickly reveal that they have only the Roman people in mind, and, behind the Roman people, the shadow of the emperor.

3. CHRIST'S EMPIRE

The Bassianus–Azo framework seems to have convinced most thirteenth-century jurists, but this broad consensus eventually cracked. It had always been vulnerable to an objection which had an impressive canon-law pedigree that no corporation – not even a corporate people – could act against or without its own head. Nicolaus de Matarellis made precisely this point in his commentary on D. 1.3.32.[39] A second trend, which apparently set in during the early fourteenth century, added another dimension to the notion of the revocable *lex regia* by as good as writing the people – whether Romans or Germans – out of the story completely. Cinus concluded his commentary on D. 1.3.9 by ascribing all of the power of the Roman people to the pope, who was alone able to depose the emperor, as he had already done in the case of Frederick II back in 1245. He had transferred the empire from the Greeks to the Germans and could, if he had good cause, give it to someone else or keep it for himself. Indeed, Cinus went on, if only he would: it would put an end to German barbarity in Italy.[40] The 'translation of empire' thesis seems to have made considerable headway among Romanists. Iacobus Butrigarius mentioned the pope's jurisdiction as a possibility without declaring his own position,[41] but Bartolus of Sassoferrato embraced it in arguing that the papal patrimony in central Italy did not constitute an exception to the putatively universal jurisdiction of the emperor.[42] The empire was willed by God (*Deo auctore* are the words with which Justinian initiated his directive to begin the *Corpus iuris civilis*), created by the Roman people, which by God's design had already won hegemony over the known world and in accordance with that same design transferred its powers to the emperor by the *lex regia*. The final confirmation of this arrangement came with Christ's recognition in His injunction 'Render to Caesar'. The prophecy of Daniel, which predicted a succession of world empires, was fulfilled when, with Christ's advent and recognition, the empire passed to him and via him to his vicar Peter, perpetually present in the person of each successive pope, as any hierocrat would explain. For Bartolus, the reason the empire must remain as it was presented in the *Corpus iuris* was that it had received divine approbation. Bartolus' sequential understanding of the relationship between the Roman people, the emperor, and finally Christ himself made of the *lex regia* something sacrosanct and irrevocable. Baldus de Ubaldis, Bartolus' most celebrated pupil who died in 1400, shared this view.[43] Baldus' pupil Paulus de Castro noted in his commentary on D. 1.3.32 that before Christ's advent the Roman people could revoke the *lex regia* and, with that law revoked, depose the emperor, since it could not impose a law upon itself from which it could not withdraw. However, Christ had transferred the Roman empire from the Roman people to the Church, with the result that the Roman empire 'has not remained except in name, and it is called the empire of Christ or the Church and only the pope can deprive the emperor, just as only the pope can confirm and crown him'.[44] It was only consistent that Paulus ended this particular set of comments with the words 'I conclude that nowadays the Roman people can do nothing in the empire.'

4. Kingdoms

Over a century before such arguments gained currency, however, the glossators routinely approached the *lex regia* in an exclusively Roman context. Whatever their conclusions about the relationship between the Roman emperor and the Roman people, they were not obviously applicable to other relationships of rule and subjection such as those between a king and his subjects. To repeat: the glossators did not routinely see in the *lex regia* an instance of a general principle at work, but Roman law's authoritative account of how the Roman republic had given way to the Roman empire. The Roman empire was universal. All smaller organizations such as kingdoms and city-states were accordingly within it. The prevailing conviction that the *lex regia* was revocable, which implied a strong endorsement of a residual popular authority over the ruler, applied to the whole but not necessarily to the parts.

The one episode in Azo's surviving jurisprudence which seems to challenge this interpretation turns out upon closer inspection to confirm it and is highly instructive in other respects. In a disputation on the handover by Philip Augustus, king of France, of his vassal Arthur of Brittany to king John of England – a legally contentious and for Arthur personally disastrous decision – Azo noted that Philip could do as he liked because 'nowadays, any [king] appears to possess the same power in his lands as the emperor'.[45] Azo's comment is famous among historians of Roman law because it convinced Francesco Calasso that Italian jurists possessed the mental agility to accommodate their jurisprudence to national kingdoms, the real forces in modern politics, and so recognized that the Roman empire was no longer the only body worthy of juristic discussion. Azo's *quaestio* thus appeared to furnish the decisive refutation of Francesco Ercole's opposing thesis that the Italian glossators of the thirteenth century were too conservative in outlook to depart so far from the letter of Justinian's law as to attribute the emperor's powers to kings, and so to contribute to what Ercole insisted was an originally French notion that a king – typically and originally the king of France – was emperor in his own kingdom.[46]

Azo's *quaestio* raises several questions. First, as Calasso noted, the force of Azo's formulation 'nowadays' is not obvious. Does it imply that at some earlier and unspecified point in history kings had not been free to do as they pleased because they were subject to the power of Rome? More importantly, Azo's legal justification for his assertion is perplexing because it is so perfunctory. He cited D. 1.4.1, to the effect that what has pleased the prince has force of law *because of the lex regia*, which might be taken to imply that Azo conceived of the king's power as the outcome of a grant or concession by his people.[47] Since his comment is not restricted to the king of France, moreover, this passage might even embody the first known use by a civilian of the *lex regia* outside the nexus of Roman people and Roman emperor to cover all monarchies, showing that as early as the first years of the thirteenth century the glossators already conceived the origins of the relationship between kings and their subjects in much the same way as the Roman law portrayed the creation of the Roman emperor by the Roman people, with all the consequences for kings that the revocable *lex regia* implied for the emperor. What did Azo mean? One superficially attractive hypothesis is that if kings became kings thanks to a mechanism akin to the *lex regia*, then every king's power became a revocable, delegated power in the same way and for the same reason that the emperor's power was subject to revocation by the Roman people. If so, Azo would then owe an explanation of how such a people came by its powers, a discussion which might helpfully include an analysis of the exact relationship between that people and the Roman people. It would also be pertinent to ask why a king's powers had to be *the same* as those of the emperor – would this not depend on the precise terms of the putative grant by his people?[48] Yet to ask such stringently consequential questions is to succumb to the danger of forcing an isolated passage. Azo's comment occurs in the course of a *quaestio*, a highly formalized genre of legal education in the early thirteenth century. A large part of the educational value of a *quaestio* consisted in its inclusion of arguments on both sides of the matter at issue. The objection which fatally undermines the hypothesis sketched above is that the claim is made as an argument supporting one side of this *quaestio*, whereas Azo favoured the opposite position. Since Azo's solution to the *quaestio* does not address the opposing case point by point, there is little we can say about this cryptic comment on which so much has been written.

Azo's famous *quaestio* therefore represents a false start as far as glossatorial meditation on royal power is concerned.[49] Two distinct accounts emerged in thirteenth-century jurisprudence, neither of which is genetically related to Azo's *quaestio*. In the course of a commentary on *Institutes* 4.6 (*De actionibus § Praeiudiciales*) the Burgundian jurist Johannes de Blanosco (Jean de Blanot), who had studied as well as taught for a while at Bologna,[50] asked whether the vassals of major nobles were *ipso facto* vassals of the king in whose kingdom they were, or of the emperor in the case where such nobles were directly subject to him. He answered in the negative – the traditional response to this technical question in the jurisprudence devoted to lords, vassals, and fiefs was that my vassal's vassal is not my own vassal – but went on to explain that although the vassals of such nobles were not in the king's *potestas* by any right of homage, they were still bound by the king's general jurisdiction in the kingdom.[51] Just as everything pertained to the emperor as far as jurisdiction was concerned in so far as he was lord of the world, so everything in the kingdom pertained to the king in administration.[52] The king therefore had *imperium* over everyone in his kingdom. Consequently, no baron of, say, the kingdom of France could oblige his vassals by virtue of their liege homage to him to take up arms against the king, for this would be to conspire in the death of a magistrate of the Roman people, one of several categories of treason defined by Roman law. Indeed, it would be to conspire directly against the emperor himself because the king of France was the emperor in his own kingdom, on the grounds that he recognized no superior in temporal matters.[53] Blanot's crucial step was therefore to claim that the king of France was not a representative of the emperor but the emperor himself within the confines of the kingdom of France. Non-recognition of a superior as a means of grounding royal power was almost certainly suggested to Blanot by the canon law,[54] rather than Azo's *quaestio*, which did not mention non-recognition but hinted instead and in the most oblique manner possible at a sort of French *lex regia*. However, Blanot's discussion contains a hint towards a Roman law explanation which goes beyond the argument from non-recognition of a superior. If called upon by the king of France to defend the kingdom against attack by the king of Germany, vassals of the Duke of Burgundy should assist the king, even if their duke demands their service in his own private war against the Duke of Lorraine. The distinction between the public good of the kingdom and the private good of a feudal lord practically seals the debate, but Blanot observed in addition that the king bore the administration of and issued orders in the name of the *patria* or kingdom – a turn of phrase which surely implies some priority of the kingdom over the king – which the vassals in question were bound by the law of nations to defend. His authority was D. 1.1.2, which mentioned 'religious duties towards God, or the duty to be obedient to one's parents and fatherland' as obligations arising from the *ius gentium*.[55] This discussion was further developed by Jacques de Revigny, who asked whether one's local *patria* took precedence over the communal *patria* of Rome, the head of the world.

The doctrine of non-recognition of a superior did not bring civilians any closer to a general set of reflections on the relationship between kings and their subjects; quite the opposite: it absolved lawyers from rendering a separate account of royal power in a given kingdom as the outcome of a specific transaction or negotiation between ruler and people. In fact, it explained nothing: not the origin nor the content nor the extent of royal powers in general or specific terms. Royal power simply appeared as an outcome of not recognizing the pre-existing authority of the emperor, and thus emerged as a geographically circumscribed splinter of imperial power. The powers of a king would on this reading be those of the emperor such that Roman law would provide the template for kingship. Kenneth Pennington is certainly right to suggest that in asking whether a king was *princeps*, thirteenth-century jurists were trying to ascertain whether he possessed the same powers of governance as the emperor.[56] However, evidence is very hard to find of Romanists who accepted that a king might be independent of the emperor *without* enjoying in his own kingdom the powers of the emperor.[57]

Two frustratingly brief comments by Jean de Blanot hint at currents of thought below the surface of jurisprudence, but do not provide answers to these questions. The second juristic account of royal power was – paradoxically – rooted in Roman law at the same time as implicitly undermining its authority.[58] *Digest* 1.1.5 (Hermogenian) stated that kingdoms were founded – *regna condita* – according to the law of nations (*ius gentium*), that part of natural law which related exclusively to human or rational nature. In the late thirteenth century, lawyers in the service of the Angevin kings of Sicily exploited this passage in order to argue that the Roman empire was illegitimate because it had been spread by violence at the expense of pre-existing kingdoms which were legitimately in existence thanks to the *ius gentium*.[59] A free king – so said the main author of this argument, Marinus de Caramanico – could pass laws for his subjects which contradicted Roman law, 'and no wonder because any people, of any municipality that is, or city, can make its own law . . . which municipal law is called the civil law, as if the specific law of that same city, as in *Digest* 1.1.9'.[60] Marinus did not explain how a text attributing such capacities to a people could benefit the king: his argument had the sole purpose of demonstrating that the king of Naples was not subject to the Roman emperor. What the Roman people had perpetrated on others it was now suffering itself: *quod fecit, passus est.*[61] As the tide of history turned, kingdoms were now reasserting their long-lost liberty against the decrepit and decaying empire such that – in a legal commonplace – 'the matter reverted to its original condition'.

In a splendidly manipulative passage Marinus concludes that his counter-argument to the usual claims of Roman universality is the more persuasive as it favours liberty, for people are thus restored to liberty and their proper nature.[62] All Marinus had in mind was that peoples who had been illegitimately subjected to the Roman people now returned to their 'liberty' under their own kings: his turn of phrase had no implications for the relationship between king and people.[63] Although his argument was in part a response to the description of *ius gentium* in D. 1.1.5, Marinus gave no account of how the kingdoms which had preceded the Roman empire had actually been established. Only fragmentary and partially contradictory evidence survives of what the other glossators thought about this, in the shape of their glosses to D. 1.1.5. Accursius observed that kingdoms had been founded by the single nations who elected their kings, a position which goes back at least to his teacher Azo,[64] but neither explored the relationship between such kingdoms, which were established under the *ius gentium*, and the empire.[65] Marinus also subverted Azo's claim that the Roman people had reserved or held back some jurisdiction when it established the emperor by means of the *lex regia*. In Marinus' Neapolitan re-setting of this argument, Azo's comment is used to explain how it is that the feudal lord of the kings of Naples – the pope – could still be said to retain some right in the kingdom which he had bestowed as a fief upon his vassal, the king, even though the king had thanks to that grant full exercise of jurisdiction.[66] A language of *dominium* in its proprietorial aspect pervades the rest of Marinus' commentary: the king owns the *universitas* of the kingdom, which is indeed a corporation but not of people: it is a corporation of goods and chattels. The king derives jurisdiction from his status as owner – jurisdiction coheres with the corporation which is the subject of the papal grant. Not even the corporate people of the twelfth-century glossators survives in Marinus' vision of the kingdom.

5. CITIES

Historical attention has focused less on the glossators' attempts to account for the existence and powers of kingdoms than on cities. Once again, the locus classicus is by Azo. The passage usually cited to prove that Azo endorsed the powers of cities occurs in book 3 title 13 of his *Summa codicis*, dedicated to the jurisdiction of judges and competence of courts. Explaining the concept of *merum imperium*, he rejected the opinion of some jurists that it pertained solely to the emperor; D. 5.1.1 strongly implied the contrary, while D. 1.18.6.8 explicitly gave it to provincial governors, so the emperor could not be the sole exponent of *merum imperium*. But this does not mean Azo thought cities had it: indeed, in the very next sentence he expressly denied that municipal magistrates possessed *merum imperium*. The emperor was still different: only he – in a formulation which is now familiar to us – could establish general equity, only he had full or the fullest jurisdiction and was the beneficiary of the *lex regia* (here called the *lex Hortensia* by Azo) by which the Roman people transferred all its *imperium* and *potestas* to him. Azo's point here was that other magistrates categorized by Roman law as 'sublime' had *merum imperium* too. His comments certainly prompt further questions; if the Roman people had transferred *all* its *imperium*, by what route did it reach these other officers too? He might have thought that a category of higher magistrates (defined in Roman law as 'sublime') held the right of the sword simply by right of office – *iure officii* – rather than by direct imperial grant, but this is to speculate uselessly, all the more so since Azo argued elsewhere that the Romans had maintained a residuum of authority which would allow them to depose the emperor. What matters in the present context is that Azo conceded nothing to cities which jurists had not already accorded them: he allowed that every municipal magistrate could establish law in his own city. The twelfth-century theory of custom had done no less. Azo's own resolution of the tension between the various passages we have already reviewed from the *Corpus iuris civilis* concerning the legislative capacity of emperor and people also turned on the distinction between the generally valid law of the emperor and local law. Cities are therefore not at the forefront of Azo's jurisprudence at this point. His argument requires that municipal magistrates possessed jurisdiction by operation of law – the Roman law of the Roman empire. He did not explain what the relationship was between such magistrates and the people they ruled. Azo's comments here are simply not part of any interesting story about cities; the theoretically heavy work in relation to civic or municipal powers was being done elsewhere.

Marinus de Caramanico had referred in passing to a passage of the *Digest* which allowed the people of any municipality or city to legislate for itself by creating its own civil law. This was D. 1.1.9, where the jurist Gaius famously declared that all peoples governed by laws and customs apply law which is partly their own and partly the law of all mankind – the latter being the law of nations or *ius gentium*, established by the natural reason common to all mankind. What each people legislates for itself is the law of that particular *civitas* and is known as its civil law. Even here, where Roman law spoke in the plural, at least one standard-setting jurist had interpreted the text in relation to the Roman people alone. A gloss to this passage in Azo's *apparatus* on the *Digestum vetus* predictably signalled a tension with C. 1.14.12 which made the emperor the sole legislator. Perhaps this second text was a correction of the first, but to claim that one text corrected another within the *Corpus iuris civilis* was always a tactic of last resort, and Azo's preferred solution was that the *Digest* passage referred to the period before the *lex regia* when the Roman people still possessed legislative capacity.[67] This comes as something of a surprise after Azo's espousal of Bassianus' notion that the emperor was the only *sole* legislator whereas the people possessed that power corporately; this entire chain of thought had been intended to counter precisely the argument advanced by Irnerius and latterly by Placentinus from the *lex regia*, an argument which strongly resembles the gloss now under examination. Attribution is not entirely secure, but the gloss turns up in too many manuscripts of Azo's *apparatus* to be ignored. Accursius thought differently: for him, Gaius in D. 1.1.9 only attributed general validity to the *ius gentium* as something which nature itself established between all people, in which sense it was not inconsistent with the general legislative capacity of the emperor. But the peoples Gaius allowed to legislate for themselves did so with local effect only, whereas the emperor could legislate with general effect for the entire empire. Accursius seems to have been thinking along the lines suggested by the jurisprudence he had inherited via Azo from the twelfth century on the relationship between custom and law, which, as we have seen, distinguished between the generally valid and the locally specific. For him, the force of D. 1.1.9 lay in its differentiation of local 'peoples' and the universal Roman empire; the peoples concerned were clearly part of the Roman people for Accursius, not outside it.[68] This interpretation of D. 1.1.9 was commonly (although not universally) accepted in the second half of the thirteenth century. Some influential jurists, such as Odofredus, certainly agreed with it.[69] Others seemingly did not: Jacobus de Arena, in a tantalizingly condensed passage, got far closer to Gaius' original intent in treating these peoples explicitly as free peoples (*populi liberi*) not subject to the Roman empire.[70] A third solution, much closer to the first, ran as follows: if D. 1.1.9 attributed local powers of legislation to peoples and then quickly switched to the vocabulary of cities, and if the contents of the *Corpus iuris civilis* enjoyed legal authority thanks to Justinian, its author, then the emperor himself emerged as the source of legislative authority in the cities.[71] It remained true that the emperor could withdraw that permission by a stroke of the pen.[72] The length and complexity of commentaries on D. 1.1.9 by the early fourteenth century should not obscure the fact that for most lawyers by about 1300, the people was the concept of principal significance when confronting the problems of the Italian cities,[73] and the explanation of the people's capacity to create its own civil law was rooted in the doctrine that D. 1.1.9 embodied an imperial concession.

Both ideas were at work in the juristic treatment of the Italian problem *par excellence*: exile, and the partisan diminution of civic rights. After the *popolo* of Florence had expelled the faction of the Burdones from its ranks by declaring them to be magnates and as such subject to a variety of legal disadvantages under the Ordinances of Justice, a set of anti-magnate statutes passed by the *popolo* between 1293 and 1295, Ricardus Malumbra defended the legality of the measure.[74] His opening point was a paraphrase of D. 1.1.9: all peoples ruled by laws and customs can make their own laws – the Florentines were a people and the law effecting the contested change in status of the Burdones was therefore valid. Whoever had the authority to legislate could grant that authority to another; in just such a way the emperor had permitted the peoples to legislate – this of course being backed up by a reference to D. 1.1.9 – so that the Florentine people was within its rights to delegate its authority to the representatives responsible for the recent alteration to statute. It remained the author of the statute passed by its representatives, just as Justinian remained the author of the *Corpus iuris civilis*, the compilation of which he had delegated to Tribonian and others.[75] Ricardus' consultation extracted the last consequence from the fact that the Florentines constituted a people empowered by D. 1.1.9. His opponent, Cino da Pistoia,[76] based his case on the formal insufficiencies in the technical terms of the delegation by the *popolo* to the Priors and the inadequacies in drafting of the resulting statute.[77] He could not well deny the *popolo*'s primary right to legislate since he was urging that thanks to such errors of footwork by the *popolo* and the Priors, the Ordinances of Justice should be upheld in their original rather than amended form.[78] Ricardus of course had to neutralize such objections but still founded a good part of his case on the mutability of civil law. *Digest* 1.3.32 derived law's power to bind from the people's will; if its will changed, a people could not be bound by the laws it had once promulgated; nor could the *princeps* be so bound: as D. 1.4.1 famously put it, he was *legibus solutus* – released from the laws.[79] This episode is so significant for two reasons. It demonstrates how robust the concept of the local-legislator people was even when, as Cino pointed out in the introduction to his consultation, the very word *populus* no longer preserved in common usage its strict legal meaning of the totality of the population such as to embrace magnates and commoners, but nowadays meant by the custom of almost all Italy only the commoners – that is, the *popolo*.[80] Florence acted, when it acted, as the Commune and People of Florence, just as Rome had acted as the Senate and People of Rome. Secondy, Ricardus applies the *lex regia* as a normative model to determine disputed points of law at the local level of a city. The Roman people had not excepted any pre-existing legislation from its grant of *imperium* and *potestas* to the new emperor; accordingly, the grant of *baylia* by the Florentine *popolo* to the reformers of the statutes should be interpreted expansively so as to include, and not except, the Ordinances of Justice.

It is clear, then, that cities understood as peoples were uncontroversially the beneficiaries of D. 1.1.9, which in turn was construed as an imperial concession of the authority to legislate. Under these postulates, a city could make and alter its laws, delegate its legislative power to committees responsible for drafting fresh legislation, and could not be bound by its own laws any more than Justinian himself. But such capacities really were only explicable under the postulate of imperial concession by means of D. 1.1.9: the logic came under pressure when for political reasons cities could not or would not readily accept the emperor as their superior. The jurist who addressed this problem in all its intractable modernity was Bartolus of Sassoferrato.[81] As we have seen, Bartolus shared the prevalent hierocracy of his colleagues and could not therefore avail himself of the Neapolitan argument by denying the legitimacy of the empire in the first place. He was also too honest to call the exercise of governmental power by cities in defiance of the empire by any other name than usurpation.[82] At least one jurist of the previous generation had argued that *merum imperium* was subject to prescription by certain people,[83] so it was not merely out of pedagogic thoroughness that Bartolus as a teacher had to devote column after column to the arguments pro and contra. Although Bartolus was prepared to discuss prescription as the potential source of a city's *merum imperium*, his deployment of the vocabulary of usurpation implicitly bars recourse to this mechanism. His final resolution of the problem was traditional in all its components but revolutionary in its ensemble. It was straightforward to build on the principle of non-recognition of a superior, which was by his time a crux in the juristic analysis of royal power. Cities which recognized no superior in temporal matters should be acknowledged as their own superiors – each would be emperor unto itself or *civitas sibi princeps*.[84] A second traditional quantity in the equation was Bartolus' insistence that usurping cities which had possessed *merum imperium* since time out of mind should be accorded the de facto right to do so. Juristic discussion of the kingdom of France in particular had exploited the vocabulary of de facto exercise of *merum imperium*, prompted no doubt by an originally canonistic stimulus.[85] Bartolus' masterstroke was to escape the legally rigorous juxtaposition which had characterized such debates in the thirteenth century – between the *de iure* as legitimate and the de facto as implicitly illegitimate – by according legitimacy to de facto claims to rule. Some such juristic periphrasis was a theoretical necessity: Bartolus' formulation preserved the empire whole and intact in the shape Christ had approved, for the emperor was still *de iure* lord over all; de facto exercise of power by others did not impinge upon his universal dominion. The notion had immense practical traction too. In situations, common enough in central and northern Italy, where neither contending party could cite irrefragable imperial or papal concession, competing claims could be adjudicated by reference to comparative not absolute strength of title. But the second revolutionary aspect of Bartolus' theory concerned the city itself. A city which recognized no superior became a free city, a term convertible – thanks in part to that same slide in vocabulary by Gaius from *populus* to *civitas* at D. 1.1.9 – with the expression 'free people'. The city or people became its own superior not merely via a felicitous and memorable stroke of Bartolus' pen: rather, it emerged as an abstraction capable of explaining and maintaining effective governance. Bartolus himself mentions two powerful examples. In such a city, who shall be the judge of appeals made from the court of the rector appointed by the city? The answer is the people itself, or the particular *ordo* in the city which appointed the rector, because the people or this particular echelon of it is alone superior to the people itself.[86] Again: an attempt to snatch power by a clique or would-be *signore* in a city which is itself already a usurper of the emperor's *merum imperium* could now be condemned as an offence against a public person, because it is an attempt to wrest the *res publica* from the *res publica* itself.[87] Language is under stress, but the point is nevertheless clear. Of course not every corporate organization could qualify as a people in the required sense. Bartolus prohibited corporations or *universitates* which were too small from effectively setting up on their own as autonomous governing and governed entities, and thus provided an empirical if not especially impressive juristic defence of the local lordships of free cities over smaller communities; freedom as an outcome of non-recognition was only intended to serve certain, large interests in Bartolus' jurisprudence.[88]

6. TOWARDS A GENERAL THEORY?

It is important to ask what distinguished Bartolus' deployment of the non-recognition argument from the way French jurists and others had used it in the course of the thirteenth century in their discussions of kingdoms. This is because of what was about to happen in Italian jurisprudence, in particular relating to Bartolus' most celebrated pupil, Baldus de Ubaldis. Baldus applied his master's logic not to free cities but to signorial regimes, pre-eminently that of the Visconti family, which at its broadest covered a substantial area of the old kingdom of Lombardy and was elevated by Wenzel, King of the Romans, to a duchy to be held in fief by Giangaleazzo Visconti in 1395. Whereas Bartolus' point of departure had been the observation that all over Italy cities exercised *merum imperium* without acknowledging the authority of the emperor, Baldus made practically the same observation of *signori* – whom Bartolus in conformity with Guelf propaganda had tended to characterize as tyrants – and reached a remarkably similar result in concluding that their claim to a fullness of power or *plenitudo potestatis* had de facto validity independently of imperial concession.[89]

Appraising the significance of Baldus' step comes down in large measure to what role is attributed to consent in Bartolus' original theory of non-recognition, and this is no easy question to settle. Bartolus' famous formulation of the free city is after all not a comment on the manner in which a city governs its inhabitants, but a mere expression of the fact that the city recognizes no superior in temporal matters. Although signorial regimes were in practice constrained by real political and not infrequently formal legalistic limitations of consent, their significance in Bartolus' theory is in their more reductive shape: quintessentially, a non-consensual rule. Modern scholars have suggested that Bartolus required the people constituting a city to be free in another sense entirely, as a pre-requisite of its successful non-recognition of a superior, as if the internal arrangements of such a city somehow softened the legal impact of its usurpation of *merum imperium*.[90] But this is probably both to ask and answer a question in terms that Bartolus would have found otiose. For legislation – certainly for the legislation of a city – to be effective it had to conform to a fundamental requirement: D. 1.3.32 stressed the centrality of the people's will in legislation, both in the strict sense and in the creation of custom. Cities had long been seen as local peoples by interpretation of D. 1.1.9 and hence as local legislators by imperial concession. Now they were legislators in their own right, admittedly in the counter-intuitive sense of Bartolus' de facto legitimacy. But this hardly altered the juristic DNA of customary and indeed all local law, which was the consent of the people. However, the example of Baldus' jurisprudence does demonstrate that once out of the bottle, the genie of de facto non-recognition of a superior was hard to discipline, because it could be applied to practically any regime which did not violate natural and divine law.

The question is significant because it reveals a suggestive contrast with the juristic analysis of royal power – and far more people lived under monarchs in the western middle ages than in city-states.[91] It was noted above that the thirteenth-century notion of the king who was emperor in his own kingdom as a consequence of his non-recognition of the emperor's superior authority left everything else about royal power unexplained. That included the requirement or otherwise of consent. Consent was comfortably circumvented by Marinus de Caramanico, a fact all the more noteworthy because his starting-point was the natural *ius gentium* legitimacy of kingdoms, whose genesis both Azo and the *Glossa ordinaria* had explained by reference to election. A markedly different story could have been told using the evidence from the canon lawyers in this respect. Henricus de Segusio, known by his cardinal's title simply as Hostiensis, noted in an off-hand way that if a king was emperor in his own kingdom, his power ought to reach him and be defined in scope by some such mechanism as the *lex regia*.[92] Even by 1400, the variety of political phenomena which the Roman-lawyers were called upon to analyse was not reducible to a universal set of legal formulae. There was no common denominator to articulate the relationship between rulers and ruled in such diverse organizations as the empire, kingdoms, territorial lordships, and autonomous cities. What made legal science valuable was its sensitivity to the particular. The vicissitudes of such fissile cities as Florence called forth some of the most sophisticated political analysis of the age from lawyers such as Cinus and Ricardus, whose opposing *consilia* on the Ordinances of Justice show a gritty respect for the realities of factionalism and the true, tortured contours of the legal landscape. Baldus was in the same tradition in stating that a gulf separated one type of polity from another, as he explained that a kingdom approximated more closely to *dominium* than any other form of government.[93] Despite the ubiquitous awareness amongst the lawyers that all governance was subject to natural and divine law, comments such as this by Baldus only did justice to the truth that not all temporal government was the same.

Change was in the air by the early fifteenth century. We saw that in his commentary on D. 1.3.9 Paulus de Castro repeated what was by then a standard opinion to the effect that the Roman people was now powerless to revoke the *lex regia* thanks to the advent of Christ. Most significantly, he argued elsewhere that in consequence of the fall of the Da Carrara dynasty and Padua's submission to Venice the city was no longer an independent unit capable of legislating for itself: 'The community of Padua has no jurisdiction, since it has transferred all its jurisdiction and *imperium* to the lordship of the Venetians, as in the *Digest*, 1.4.1'.[94] In Paulus' construction of events, the Paduans had mimicked the Romans by enacting their own *lex regia*. In handing themselves over to an external superior power they had effectively terminated the existence of their own city as an autonomous entity. The two positions encapsulate the ambivalent character of civilian jurisprudence at the end of the period under examination here. An orthodox reading of the *lex regia* as an irrevocable moment in Roman history which still underpinned the fundamental structure of Christendom in the here and now was accompanied in the jurisprudence of the same lawyer by a new kind of *lex regia*. If in the opinion of a standard-setting jurist like Paulus this 'little' *lex regia* could explain the creation and internal workings of a new hegemony such as Venice's terra firma lordship, then why not others too? There is every reason to believe that by the early fifteenth century Roman law was emerging from the restrictive hermeneutic imposed by the Roman empire into an institutionally neutral – and for that very reason generally applicable – body of ideas, capable of furnishing universal principles of political analysis.

NOTES

1. D. 1.4.1; Ulpian.
2. Inst. 1.2.6.
3. C. 1.17.1.7.
4. D. 1.2.2.11.
5. Accursius, *Volumen*, col. 41 [Nov. 6 = Auth. 1.6], gl. *imperium*.
6. Jul. D. 1.3.32.1: 'Ancient custom is not without reason observed as if it were law, and this is the law which is said to be established by mores. For since statutes themselves bind us for no other reason than that they have been accepted by the judgment of the people, certainly what the people has approved without any writing will bind all. For what does it matter whether the people declares its will by voting or by its very actions? Accordingly, it is absolutely right that statutes may be abrogated not only by vote of the legislator, but also by the tacit agreement of everyone expressed through

desuetude.' (Translation adapted from Watson ed. of *Digest.*) See also Accursius, *Digestum vetus*, col. 36 [D. 1.3.32], gl. *abrogentur.*

7. E. Cortese, *La norma giuridica. Spunti teoretici nel diritto comune classico*, 2 vols., (Milan, 1962–1964), vol. 2, 126 n. 55 for edition; A. Gouron, 'Coutume contre loi chez les premiers glossateurs', in *Renaissance du Pouvoir Législatif et Genèse de l'État*, ed. A. Gouron and A. Rigaudière (Montpellier, 1988), 117–30; A. Gouron, 'Non dixit, 'Ego sum consuetudo'', *ZSS* 74 (1988): 133–40.
8. E. Cortese, *Il problema della sovranità nel pensiero giuridico medioevale* (Rome, 1966), 96.
9. Cortese (n. 8), 96.
10. Cortese (n. 8), 97; Placentinus, *Summa codicis* 17 [1.14]; 416 [8.56]. Cortese (n. 7), vol. 2, 128 with n. 61, and 127 for the relationship between this notion and the argument advanced by Martinus.
11. Cortese (n. 8), 98–100; Cortese (n. 7), vol. 2, 174–75.
12. The phrase 'sole legislator' came from Justinian; see C. 1.14.12.4.
13. Azo, *Summa super codicem*, 9a; Azo, *Lectura super codicem*, 44; Cortese (n. 7), vol. 2, 175–76 and n. 14; Q. Skinner, 'The rediscovery of republican values', in Q. Skinner, *Visions of Politics* (Cambridge, 2002), vol. 2, 13–17.
14. Accursius, *Digestum vetus*, col. 30 [D. 1.3.9], gl. *Non ambigitur*, referring to Hugolinus de Presbiteriis, for whom see Cortese (n. 7), vol. 2, 131, 175, 183 n. 39 (on this gloss by Accursius).
15. D. 1.3.1.
16. Odofredus, *Lectura super digesto veteri*, fo. 10va [D. 1.3.1].
17. Not a new idea: cf. Azo, *Summa super codicem*, 9a.
18. Odofredus, *Lectura super digesto veteri*, fo. 10va-b [D. 1.3.1].
19. Odofredus, *Lectura super digesto veteri*, fo. 11va.
20. Iacobus de Ravanis, *Lectura super codice*, fo. 36 vb [C. 1.14.12].
21. Cortese (n. 7), vol. 2, 185 n. 45. I omit for reasons of space a detailed treatment of the French lawyer Johannes Faber, who represents something of an exception.
22. G. Zanetti, *Questiones de iuris subtilitatibus* (Florence, 1958); H. Lange, *Römisches Recht im Mittelalter. Vol. 1: Die Glossatoren* (Munich, 1997), 408–13; for the most plausible interpretation, see E. Cortese, *Il diritto nella storia medioevale. Vol. 2: Il basso medioevo* (Rome, 1995), vol. 2, 111–16; the last treatment in English: R. W. Carlyle and A. J. Carlyle, *A History of Mediaeval Political Thought in the West. Vol. 2: The Political Theory of the Roman Lawyers and the Canonists, from the Tenth Century to the Thirteenth Century;* vol. 6: *Political Theory from 1300 to 1600* (1909, 1936; repr. Edinburgh – London, 1970), vol. 2, 8–19; latest attempt at attribution in A. Gouron, 'Les 'Quaestiones de juris subtilitatibus': une œuvre du maître parisien Albéric', *Revue Historique* 618 (2001): 342–62.
23. B. Paradisi, 'Diritto canonico e tendenze di scuola nei glossatori da Irnerio ad Accursio', *Studi medievali* 6.2 (1965): 91; U. Niccolini, 'Leggendo le "Quaestiones de iuris subtilitatibus" ', *Jus* 28.1 (1981) esp. 30–47.
24. Zanetti (n. 22), 13 (para. 11): 'Law differs from the other sciences because only authority is required in the latter, whereas a legal judgment cannot subsist unless it is upheld both by the support of knowledge and power.' ('Distat ius a ceteris artibus illa quoque ratione, quod in illis quidem sola desideratur auctoritas, iuris autem censura non subsistit, nisi subnixa sit tam scientie quam potestatis aminiculo').
25. Zanetti (n. 22), 13, with reference to Luke 2.1.
26. Quae sit longa consuetudo: C. 8.52(53).2.

27. C. 8.52(53).2: 'The authority of long-established custom is not negligible, but it should not prevail to the point of overcoming reason or law.'
28. The following is based on Gouron (n. 7, both papers cited) and Cortese (n. 7), vol. 2, 102–46. The only resumé in English of some of the more important arguments is the concise if outdated A. J. Carlyle, 'The theory of the source of political authority, in the mediaeval civilians to the time of Accursius', in Mélanges Fitting vol. 1, 181–94. Aalen, repr. 1969.
29. Gouron (in Gouron and Rigaudière, n. 7), 120.
30. This in summary of the most important and ultimately successful position in a debate which had numerous etiolations, for which see Cortese (n. 7), vol. 2, 39–167 and 113 n. 29.
31. Azo, *Lectura super codicem*, 672 [C. 8.52(53).2].
32. Cortese (n. 7), vol. 2, 414.
33. For biographical details on Albericus see Lange (n. 22), 200–1; for the opinion itself that 'custom is either general, such as the custom of the Roman people, or rather of the emperor who stands in place and instead of the people, or it is special' (*consuetudo alia generalis, puta populi romani, immo principis qui optinet locum et vicem populi, alia specialis*), see Cortese (n. 7), vol. 2, 125 n. 53.
34. For biography, see Lange (n. 22), 207–9.
35. Cortese (n. 7), vol. 2, 128 with n. 61, and 127 for the relationship between this notion and the argument advanced in the previous generation by Placentinus' teacher Martinus.
36. Carlyle and Carlyle (n. 22), vol. 2, 57–8.
37. H. Fitting, *Summa codicis des Irnerius* (Berlin, 1894), 16 [1.14.3]; Carlyle and Carlyle (n. 22), vol. 2, 58 n. 1.
38. U. Meier, *Mensch und Bürger. Die Stadt im Denken spätmittelalterlicher Theologen, Philosophen und Juristen* (Munich, 1994), 138.
39. Ms. Stuttgart, WLB cod. jur. 123, fo. 12vb–19ra at 12vb: 'It is clear that the people and senate can do nothing relating to the governance of the empire without him [i.e., the emperor] because they constitute a corporation and he who belongs to a corporation can do nothing without consent or without its head.' (*patet quod populus et senatus quantum ad regimen imperii nichil facere potest sine eo [scil. imperatore] quia universitas et is qui pertinet ad universitatem nichil sine consensu sive capite facere potest ar. C. de decuri. l. ii* [C. 10.32.2] *et de ser. re. pu. ma.l. i. et ii.* [C. 7.9.1–2]). On Matarellis, who died in 1310, see M. Duynstee, 'An Unknown Fourteenth Century Lecture of the Orleans School: Jean Nicot on Book VI of the Code', in *TR* 60 (1992): 371–72.
40. Cinus at D. 1.3.9 in D. Maffei, *La 'Lectura super digesto veteri' di Cino da Pistoia. Studio sui mss Savigny 22 e Urb. Lat. 172*. Quaderni di Studi Senesi 10 (Milan, 1963), 56.
41. Iacobus Butrigarius 1963, fo. 1va, and discussion in C. N. S. Woolf, *Bartolus of Sassoferrato – His Position in the History of Medieval Political Thought* (Cambridge, 1913), 35–37.
42. M. Ryan, 'Bartolus of Sassoferrato and free cities', *Transactions of the Royal Historical Society*, 6th ser. 17 (2000): 75–76.
43. J. Canning, *The Political Thought of Baldus de Ubaldis* (Cambridge, 1987), 62; Baldus, *In primum, secundum et tertium Codicis libros commentaria*, fo. 66rb [C. 1.14.4]: 'Secondly, note that the emperor's authority depends from the *lex regia* which was promulgated by divine command'. (*Secundo no. quod authoritas Imperatoris pendet ex lege Regia quae*

fuit nutu divino promulgata). Baldus' comment here relates only to the *lex regia*, not to laws in general; cf. L. Mayali, 'Lex animata. Rationalisation du pouvoir politique et science juridique (XIIème–XIVème siècles)', in Gouron and Rigaudière (n. 7): 163. Baldus appears to have been thinking of Accursius' gloss at C. 1.14.4 and altering it.

44. Paulus Castrensis, *Pauli de Castro prima super digesto veteri*, fo. 10vb [D. 1.3.9]; see Carlyle and Carlyle (n. 22), vol. 6, 147; H. Morel, 'La place de la Lex regia dans l'histoire des idées politiques', in *Études offertes à Jean Macqueron*, ed. Y. Lobin (Aix-en-Provence, 1970), 547 n. 11.

45. The addition 'rex' is justified by the incipit of the *quaestio*, but the comment in K. Pennington, *The Prince and the Law. Sovereignty and Rights in the Western Legal Tradition 1200–1600* (Berkeley – Los Angeles, 1993), 35 n. 116 should nevertheless be noted; F. Calasso, *I glossatori e la teoria della sovranità*, 3rd ed., (Milan, 1957), 33–34; E. Landsberg, *Die quaestiones des Azo* (Freiburg, 1888), 86ff.

46. Calasso (n. 45), 22ff.; F. Ercole, 'L'Origine francese di una nota formola Bartoliana', *Archivio storico italiano*, 6th ser., 73 (1915): 241–94; F. Ercole, 'Sulla origine francese e le vicende in Italia della formola: "Rex superiorem non recognoscens est princeps in regno suo"', *Archivio storico italiano*, 7th ser., 16 (1931): 197–238.

47. The only other citation is D. 21.2.11 pr. The sequential reading of the separate *argumenta* of this text at Pennington (n. 45), 35 n. 116 is misguided.

48. Calasso (n. 45), 78; Pennington (n. 45), 31.

49. *Contra*: Calasso (n. 45), 35 who characterizes Azo's position as current doctrine at Bologna; Calasso's comment is true, however, of the canon lawyers there: see 31ff.

50. H. Lange and M. Kriechbaum, *Römisches Recht im Mittelalter. Vol. 2: Die Kommentatoren* (Munich, 2007), 461–68.

51. J. Acher, 'Notes sur le droit savant au moyen age', *Nouvelle Revue Historique de Droit Français et Étranger* 30 (1906): 125–78 is unusable; see Johannes de Blanosco, *De actionibus tractatus clarissimorum iurisconsultorum*, fo. 246rb; R. Feenstra, 'Jean de Blanot et la formule "Rex Francie in regno suo princeps est"', in *Études d'histoire du droit canonique dédiées à Gabrielle le Bras* (Paris, 1965), vol. 2, 890–91: 'general jurisdiction' is preferable to 'natural' (as opposed to Calasso (n. 45), 114), which also resolves the doubt expressed by M. Boulet-Sautel, 'Jean de Blanot et la conception du pouvoir royal au temps de Louis IX', in *Septième centenaire de la mort de Saint Louis: actes des colloques de Royaumont et de Paris*, ed. L. Carolus-Barré (Paris, 1976), 66.

52. For *dominium* as jurisdiction rather than in a proprietary sense, see Accursius, *Codicis Iustiniani ex repetita praelectione libri novem priores*, col. 1397 [C. 7.37.3], gl. *Omnia principis*; Canning (n. 43), 82; Pennington (n. 45), 16ff.

53. Feenstra (n. 51).

54. In lieu of a vast literature, see the fundamentals at Calasso (n. 45), 110ff.; 34ff. and K. Pennington, 'Law, legislative authority and theories of government, 1150–1300', in *The Cambridge History of Medieval Political Thought c.350–c.1450*, ed. J. H. Burns (Cambridge, 1988), 432–33.

55. Johannes de Blanosco (n. 51), fo. 246va; Boulet-Sautel (n. 51), 68 (without the Roman law reference); G. Post, 'Two Notes on Nationalism in the Middle Ages. I. Pugna pro patria', *Traditio* 9 (1953): 289–90.

56. Pennington (n. 45), 97.

57. Cf. Pennington (n. 45), 98 and n. 99, which must refer to pp. 99–110 and nn. 95 and 97.

58. Canning (n. 43), 68–70.

59. Calasso (n. 45), 125–162 and 179–205 for text.

60. Marinus de Caramanico in Calasso (n. 45), 180.
61. Calasso (n. 45), 197.
62. Calasso (n. 45), 198.
63. Cf. J. Canning, 'Ideas of the state in thirteenth and fourteenth-century commentators on Roman law', *Transactions of the Royal Historical Society*, 5th ser., 33 (1983): 7.
64. For Azo see mss BAV Vat. lat. 1408, fo. 3r [D. 1.1.5, gl. *regna condita*]: *a singulis gentibus que sibi reges elegerunt. az.*, also in Vat. lat. 2512 fo. 3r, Munich, BSB, Clm 14028 fo. 1rb and Bamberg, SB Jur. 11, fo. 3rb. See Accursius, *Digestum vetus*, col. 14 [D. 1.1.5], gl. *condita.*
65. I reserve a detailed discussion of the *provincia* in the works of the jurists for a separate study: see in the meantime Accursius, *Digestum vetus*, col. 86 [D. 1.18.3], gl. *praeses.*
66. Marinus de Caramanico in Calasso (n. 45), 195, citing Azo, *Summa codicis* 1.14. Cf. Pennington (n. 45), 103.
67. Azo, *Apparatus ad Digestum vetus*, D. 1.1.9, gl. *partim/proprio*: mss BAV 1408, fo. 3va; BAV Vat. lat. 2512, fo. 3rb; Munich BSB Clm. 14028, fo. 1rb, Bamberg SB Jur 11, fo. 3va: *C. de leg. et con. l. ult.* [C. 1.14.12; BAV 1408 adds: *contra. Solutio*] hec corrigitur per illam vel dicamus hanc non corrigi sed loqui secundum sua tempora hodie enim omne ius *quod* [Clm: omits] *populus habuit in imperatorem est translatum sed olim non habebat ut ff. de leg. et se. con. non ambigitur* [D. 1.1.9]. *az.* Only BAV 1408 is clear in attributing the gloss to Azo. Mss BAV 2512 and Munich give 'z' or something very similar, and ms Bamberg gives no siglum. In each case, however, the gloss pertains to the primary Azo stratum. There is no equivalent gloss in ms Munich BSB Clm 3887, fo. 1rb; Paris, BN lat. 4459 is illegible here owing to water damage.
68. Accursius, *Digestum vetus*, col. 16 [D. 1.1.9], gl. *suo proprio.*
69. Odofredus, *Lectura super digesto veteri*, fo. 8va [D. 1.3.9]; 15va [D. 1.3.32].
70. Iacobus de Arena, *Commentarii in universum ius civile*, fo. 63va [D. 1.1.9].
71. See, e.g., as an example Raynerius de Forlivio, *Repetitionum seu commentariorum in varia iurisconsultorum responsa volumen primum*, fo. 63vb [D. 1.1.9]: 'those subject to the emperor do this by the authority granted them by this law, therefore such things are legal' (*subditi imperatoris hoc faciunt authoritate imperatoris eis per hanc legem concessa. ergo sunt licita*). See also fo. 65ra: 'The solution is: I admit that peoples can do this by the authority of the emperor for as long he tolerates and suffers it: according to this law'. (*Solu[tio]. fateor populos hoc posse authoritate imperatoris quandiu tolerat et patitur: per hanc legem*).
72. Raynerius de Forlivio (n. 71), immediately following the passage above: 'but he nevertheless has the bridle in his hand, for by the most trivial law he can revoke that law [i.e., D. 1.1.9] and the statutes of the peoples'. (*sed tamen ipse habet frenum in manu, nam potest legem istam et populorum statuta una lege levissima revocare*).
73. M. Bellomo, *I fatti e il diritto. Tra le certezze e i dubbi dei giuristi medievali (secoli XIII–XIV)* (Rome, 2000), 450, n. 36.
74. Brief remarks in Bellomo (n. 73), 191, 286; M. Bellomo, *Quaestiones in iure civili disputatae. Didattici e prassi colta nel sistema del diritto comune fra duecento e trecento* (Rome, 2008), 300 for the *casus.*
75. Quoted here from ms. BAV Chigi E. VIII. 245, fo. 137va–138ra at 137va: 'So the Florentine *popolo* or those who represent the Florentine *popolo* could easily give the authority to legislate to the Piors and the Gonfaloniere, since they had previously been able to pass law, nor is the law passed by the aforementioned to be called the law of the Priors and the Gonfaloniere but the law of the Florentine *popolo* since "we rightly make all our own" etc.' (*bene ergo potuit populus florentinus seu illi qui representant*

populum florentinum quia pri[ius] l[egem] condere poterant prioribus et vesellifero conde[ndi] l[egis] auctoritatem prestare nec l[ex] q[ue] per predictos conditur lex priorum et veselliferi dicetur sed populi florentini cum omnia merito nostra facimus etc. ut C. de veteri iure et [sic] enucle. l. i. § sed neque [C. 1.17.1.6].)

76. Ms. BAV Chigi. E.VIII. 245, fo. 137ra-va. See Bellomo (n. 73), 450; Bellomo (n. 74), 299 for a partial edition.
77. See the marginalia published in Bellomo (n. 74), 300.
78. Ms. BAV Chigi E. VIII. 245, fo. 137ra, as an argument *contra* his own eventual position but which he does not challenge as a principle – only its execution in this case: 'it is clear that the statutes of the cities are civil laws as in D. 1.1.9. But civil laws can be altered, therefore [etc.]' (*certum est quod statuta civitatum sunt iura civilia ut l. omnes populi* [D. 1.1.9] *sed iura civilia mutari possunt ergo etc. ut insti. de iure na. § ult.* [Inst. 1.2 § 2]).
79. Ms. BAV Chigi E. VIII. 245, fo. 138ra: 'if the people wishes it is released from the laws . . . and the people annuls its own law as it wishes' (*populus si vult suis legibus solutus est ut ff. de leg. l. princeps* [D. 1.4.1] *et C. de le. l. dingna* [sic; C. 1.14.4] *et ipsam l[egem] suam populus pro suo libito extinguit ar. ff. ar. ff. [sic] de le. l. de quibus* [D. 1.32.2]).
80. See Bellomo (n. 74), 299; Ryan (n. 42), 80–82.
81. Meier (n. 38), 147–59; J. Canning 'Law, sovereignty and corporation theory, 1300–1450', in Burns (n. 54), 470–76; Ryan (n. 42).
82. Bartolus de Sassoferrato, *Bartoli a Sassoferrato in primam partem codicis commentaria*, fo. 49va [C. 2.3.28]: 'You know that generally the cities in Italy do not have *merum imperium* but have usurped it.' (*Scitis quod civitates communiter italie non habent merum imperium sed usurpaverunt*).
83. Iacobus de Belvisio, incipit: *Baro vel universitas in terris ecclesiae castrum sibi constituit*. See ms. BAV Chigi E. VIII. 245, fo. 102ra–103ra, solution to first question. This would still appear to exclude cities. For an analysis of Iacobus' argument from 'loci loicales' here, see Bellomo (n. 73), 586–93 and Bellomo (n. 74), 273 for an edition of the *casus*.
84. Examples in Woolf (n. 41), 155–59.
85. Calasso (n. 45), 31ff.; 77ff.
86. Bartolus de Sassoferrato, *Bartoli a Sassoferrato in secundam digesti novi partem commentaria*, fo. 208rb [D. 49.1.1]; Ryan (n. 42), 77 and n. 40.
87. Bartolus de Sassoferrato in D. Quaglioni, *Politica e diritto nel trecento italiano. Il 'De tyranno' di Bartolo da Sassoferrato (1314–1357)* (Florence, 1983), 138–39 [*De guelphis et gebellinis*, lines 149–151]; Ryan (n. 42), 83 and n. 55.
88. Bartolus de Sassoferrato in Quaglioni (n. 87), 168 [*De regimine civitatis*, lines 441–448]; Ryan (n. 42), 88.
89. Canning (n. 43), 221–27, esp. 224; Baldus, *Baldi Ubaldi Perusini . . . Consiliorum, sive responsorum volumen primum*, fo. 61vb; translation in Canning, 221–27; J. Black, *Absolutism in Renaissance Milan. Plenitude of Power under the Visconti and the Sforza 1329–1535* (Oxford, 2009), 63–67, esp. 66.
90. H. Walther, '*Regnum magis assimilatur dominio quam simplici regimini*. Zur Attraktivität der Monarchie in der politischen Theorie gelehrter Juristen des 15. Jahrhunderts', in *Sozialer Wandel im Mittelalter. Wahrnehmungsformen, Erklärungsmuster, Regelungsmechanismen*, ed. J. Miethke and K. Schreiner (Sigmaringen, 1994), 389.
91. Woolf (n. 41), 380 and Canning (n. 43), 97 for differing views on the magnitude of the step from royal to civic non-recognition, and Canning (n. 81), 470–71.

92. Hostiensis, *Summa aurea* (Venice, 1574), col. 1168 [3.39 n. 9], quoted by Calasso (n. 45), 78. Hostiensis disagreed with the application of the non-recognition principle anyway; see M. Boulet-Sautel, 'Le princeps de Guillaume Durand', *Études d'histoire du droit canonique dédiées à Gabriel Le Bras* (Paris, 1965), vol. 2, 809–10.
93. Walther (n. 90).
94. Paulus Castrensis, *Consiliorum sive responsorum . . . Pauli Castrensis volumen secundum*, cons. 230: *Sed communitas Paduae nullam habet iurisdictionem, cum omnem ipsius iurisdictionem et imperium transtulerit in dominium Venetorum l. i. in prin. ff. de consti. pecu.* [sic; D. 1.4.10].

21 Roman Law in the Modern World

Reinhard Zimmermann

1. Roman Law in Legal Practice*

> Three times the laws of the world were dictated by Rome, three times it bound the nations together in unity: first when the Roman people still stood in the fullness of their power, the unity of the *State*; secondly after the fall of that state, the unity of the *Church*; thirdly as a result of the reception of Roman law in the Middle Ages, the unity of the Law. The first was achieved by force of arms and compulsion, the latter two by the force of mind and reason.

These are the opening words of Rudolf von Jhering's *Geist des römischen Rechts auf den verschiedenen Stufen seiner Entwicklung* (1852–1865). And, indeed, Roman law was one of the elements of the culture of antiquity that left an enduring mark on contemporary Europe and beyond.

Of course, this is particularly conspicuous where the continuity of the development has not been disrupted or obscured by the intervention of the legislature. South Africa probably provides the best example in the modern world. Here Roman-Dutch law as imported by the settlers of the Dutch East India Company in the middle of the seventeenth century – that is, the early modern *ius commune* in its specifically Dutch variant – still applies today.[1] The courts in Cape Town, Blomfontein, and Pretoria therefore still occasionally rely on authors such as Voet and Vinnius, Van Bynkershoek, Grotius, and Ulrich Huber or even venture back directly to the Roman sources.[2] Within Europe, Roman law is still referred to, every now and again, in the Scottish courts. In spite of the Union of Crowns and Parliaments, Scotland retains an independent legal system which owes its civilian flavour mainly to the institutional writers of the seventeenth and eighteenth centuries.[3] As a result of having come under the influence of English law too, Scots law today presents the picture of a mixed jurisdiction;[4] together with South African law, it is the main modern exponent of this phenomenon that has remained uncodified.[5] In San Marino the *ius commune* still applies in its pure form, unaffected by a reception of English legal rules and doctrines. Professors from Italian faculties of law, appointed as judges of appeal, still today base their decisions ultimately on the *Corpus iuris civilis*.[6] By far the majority of the other civilian legal systems have codified their private law. Here the immediate practical relevance of Roman law is confined to the very rare occasions on which pre-unitarian law is still applicable, as in a decision of the German Federal Supreme Court of 1984 involving alluvions to an island situated in the river Mosel.[7]

But much more important, if less obvious, is the imprint that Roman law has left on modern codifications. For on a doctrinal level their draftsmen did not usually intend them to constitute a radical turning point. They aimed largely at setting out, incorporating, and consolidating 'the legal achievements of centuries',[8] as they had been processed and refined by generations of scholars. The codifications bore certain characteristics of a restatement and so they were immediately taken to provide a framework for the kind of scholarship of which they were themselves the product.[9]

2. Roman Law in the Modern Civil Codes

When we refer today in modern German law to claims for recovery of property, we distinguish between a claim based on ownership (*rei vindicatio*, *Vindikation*) and one based on unjustified enrichment (*condictio*, *Kondiktion*).[10] Where a possessor makes improvements to an object that does not belong to him and which he is not entitled to keep but has to return under a *rei vindicatio*, he may claim compensation from the owner. The relevant rules are laid down in §§ 994ff. of the German Civil Code (BGB); they are inspired by the Roman rules on the restitution of expenditure (*impensae*).[11] The most important unjustified enrichment claim, which is laid down in § 812 I 1, 1st alternative BGB, is often referred to as *condictio indebiti* (from *indebitum solutum* – that is, a payment that was not owed). § 812 I 2 BGB contains the *condictiones ob causam finitam* (the enrichment claim arising from the fact that the legal ground for a transfer has subsequently fallen away), and *causa data causa non secuta* (the enrichment claim for a cause that has failed to materialize).[12] In § 817,1 BGB we encounter the *condictio ob turpem vel iniustam causam* (the enrichment claim based on the recipient having acted illegally or immorally in receiving the transfer), which, however, can be excluded according to the maxim *in pari turpitudine melior est causa possidentis* (where both parties have acted illegally or immorally, the possessor is in a comparatively better position and therefore does not have to render restitution): § 817,2 BGB.[13] Here even the terminology still in use points to the Roman origins of modern private law.[14] The link is not always so obvious. The term 'delict' (*Delikt*) is derived from the Roman *delictum*; but the German word for contract (*Vertrag*, based on *sich vertragen*, meaning to make up, to be reconciled) was also formed on the model of the Latin term *pactum* (based on *pacisci*, to make peace),[15] as we find it in the edict of the Roman praetor (*pacta conventa . . . servabo*).[16] The famous provision on good faith in contract law (§ 242 BGB), as interpreted by the German courts from very soon after the BGB had entered into force, originates in the *exceptio doli*, as well as in the *bona fides* that governed the Roman consensual contracts.[17] A person is barred from exercising a contractual right if, by doing so, he contradicts his own previous behaviour (*venire contra factum proprium*), if he himself has not acted in accordance with contract (*tu quoque*), or if he claims something that he will subsequently have to return to the other party (*dolo agit qui petit, quod statim redditurus est*). We read these Roman legal maxims into § 242 BGB.[18] Sometimes the draftsmen of the BGB even received such maxims into the text of the BGB, although not in Latin. § 117 BGB on simulation (*plus valere quod agitur, quam quod simulate concipitur*) and § 305c II BGB (*interpretatio contra eum qui clarius loqui debuisset*, or *contra proferentem* rule)[19] provide examples. Systematic distinctions such as the one between contract and delict, between absolute and relative rights, and between the law of obligations and property law are inspired by Roman law. So are standard types of contract such as sale, exchange and donation, mandate, deposit and suretyship, and the distinction between loans for use (*Leihe*) and loans for consumption (*Darlehen*); general standards of liability such as the various forms of fault (*culpa, dolus, diligentia quam in suis*),[20] as well as specific instances of no-fault liability, such as the ones in § 536a BGB (liability of the lessor for defects in the object leased)[21] and §§ 701ff. BGB (innkeepers' liability);[22] as well as innumerable concepts, legal institutions, and individual rules: the invalidity of immoral contracts (*contra bonos mores*),[23] the special rules on delay on the part of the debtor (*mora debitoris*) and the creditor (*mora creditoris*),[24] the rights of termination and price reduction on account of delivery of a defective object (*actiones redhibitoria* and *quanti minoris*),[25] management of someone else's affairs without authority (*negotiorum gestio*),[26] and liability for damage done by animals.[27] These are just a few random examples that cannot do more than provide a cursory impression of the BGB's Roman impregnation and that have, moreover, been taken from only one specific area of private law: the law of obligations. Similar lists can be compiled for other areas, particularly property law and the law of succession.[28] The same can be said about the other continental codifications in Europe.[29] The French *Code civil* is in a number of respects even more Roman than the BGB:[30] in its rejection, in principle, of contracts in favour of third parties (art. 1121 *Code civil*, perpetuating the rule of *alteri stipulari nemo potest*);[31] in its insistence on certainty of price as a requirement for the validity of contracts of sale (art. 1591 *Code civil*, the modern version of the requirement of *pretium certum*);[32] in its rule that set-off operates 'de plein droit par la seule force de la loi, même à l'insu des débiteurs' (art. 1290 *Code civil*, which is supposed to be based on set-off *ipso iure* in Roman law);[33] and in its perpetuation of the systematic categories of contract, quasi-contract, delict, and quasi-delict.[34]

3. HOW ROMAN IS THE ROMAN LAW IN THE MODERN CIVIL CODES?

Misunderstandings, Different Layers of Tradition, Ambiguities

In all of these and in many other cases, our modern law and legal thinking have been moulded by Roman law. Yet hardly ever are the modern rules identical to Roman law (or with one another!).[35] Occasionally, the Roman model has even been turned on its head. Quasi-delict, as we see it today, was a systematic niche for a number of instances of extracontractual no-fault liability; these were kept apart from delictual liability, which depended upon fault.[36] For a long time, however, lawyers proceeded on the assumption that delictual liability was tantamount to intentional damage done to another, while quasi-delictual liability covered cases of negligence.[37] That misconception, which was caused by Justinian's attempt to reconceptualize the sources of classical law from the point of view of a generalized requirement of *culpa*, was shared by the draftsmen of the *Code civil*. But since liability for damage done negligently and damage done intentionally were placed on the same footing, the distinction between delictual and quasi-delictual liability had lost its significance. In addition, an appropriate place to accommodate the phenomenon of no-fault liability within the system of private law was now lacking.[38] Interpretation of the phrase 'ipso iure' in the sense of 'sine facto hominis' (that is, occurring automatically) was also based on a misunderstanding of the Roman sources. Originally, it had been intended to signify that set-off was not to be effected by the judge but that the plaintiff was forced 'by the law itself' to subtract the amount of the counterclaim from his own claim.[39] Moreover, the relevant sources merely concerned one specific type of set-off: the *agere cum compensatione* of the banker. Unlike modern law, Roman law did not recognize a uniform legal institution of set-off with standardized requirements: reflecting the 'actional' character of Roman law, four different types of set-off were distinguished.[40] With regard to *bonae fidei iudicia*, for example, set-off had to be pleaded. Justinian, too, in one of his constitutions stated that set-off must be declared;[41] and that statement was destined ultimately to shape the model of set-off that we find today in German law.[42]

Thus we are faced with a situation in which two completely different solutions to one and the same problem both find their origin in Roman law. It is not the only one. *Mora creditoris* (delay in accepting performance) provides another example, for both the concept that has found its way into the BGB (the creditor does not infringe a duty vis-à-vis his debtor and is not liable for damages but merely jeopardizes his own legal position in a number of respects) and the idea of *mora creditoris* constituting the mirror image of *mora debitoris* (and thus focusing on duty, fault, and damages) derive from Roman law.[43] Transfer of ownership as an 'abstract' legal act or as being based on a just cause (*iusta causa traditionis*) may also be mentioned.[44] It has even happened that two different solutions are based on one and the same fragment in the *Digest*. Gaius D. 19.2.25.7 is a case in point. Here someone who had contracted to transport columns was held to be responsible for damage done to the columns 'if they are damaged due to his own fault and/or the fault of those whom he used for the transport' (*si qua ipsius eorumque, quorum opera uteretur, culpa acciderit*). If *que* in *eorumque* is interpreted disjunctively,[45] the text provides a basis for a strict type of liability to be imposed on an entrepreneur for damage negligently caused by his employees. We find that solution today, so far as delictual liability is concerned, in art. 1384 *Code civil*.[46] Nineteenth-century German pandectists, on the other hand, understood the text to impose liability on the entrepreneur if he himself and those who had been employed by him had been at fault.[47] On that interpretation the text fitted in neatly with a precept very widely taken as axiomatic in contemporary scholarship, namely that extracontractual liability must be based on fault;[48] and it could be adduced in favour of the fault-based liability for the acts of others that we still find today in § 831 BGB.[49]

. . . *magis differat, quam avis a quadrupede*

Contracts can be formed *nudo consensu*, by mere informal agreement. This basic principle goes back to Roman law. And yet in Roman law it was valid only in certain situations; the general rule was that an informal agreement does not give rise to an action (*nuda pactio obligationem non parit*).[50] Agreements are to be observed (*pacta sunt servanda*) was a sentence that was formulated for the first time in the *Corpus iuris canonici*, the medieval collection of Canon law.[51] The development of contracts in favour of a third party, the law of agency, and the assignment of claims were for a long time impeded by the Roman idea of an obligation as a strictly personal legal bond between those who had concluded the contract.[52] At the same time, however, the *Corpus iuris civilis* contained a number of crucial points of departure for the eventual abandonment of this restrictive view.[53] One single, apparently innocuous text contained in the *Codex Iustiniani*[54] was to become the catalyst for the general *actio de in rem verso* (action for whatever has been used to enrich another person's property) of French law,[55] which, as such, is undoubtedly un-Roman. The *condictio indebiti* of modern German law, on the other hand, does have a model in Roman law, although one from which it differs considerably. Thus, for example, the Roman *condictio indebiti* lay for enrichment received rather than enrichment surviving;[56] also, it required a *mistaken* payment of something that was not owed. Two conflicting sources contained in the *Corpus iuris civilis* – one by Papinian,[57] the other attributed to the Emperors Diocletian and Maximian[58] – provided the main arguments in a centuries-old debate about the relevance, in this context, of an error of law.[59] In view of the recognition of *pacta sunt servanda*, the *condictio causa data causa non secuta* has largely lost its function; the *condictio ob turpem vel iniustam causam* has lost its completely.[60] As a result, the application of the *in pari turpitudine* rule has also become problematical.[61] Since the Roman *condictiones* in a way supplemented the fragmented Roman contract law,[62] recognition of the general concept of contract in the early modern period also paved the way towards a general enrichment action. This was pursued above all by Hugo Grotius,[63] the French *Cour de cassation*,[64] and Friedrich Carl von Savigny.[65] Each used different points of departure. Generalization of the liability for unjustified enrichment was in turn bound to affect the significance of the Roman rules on compensation for expenditure: if a person who had made improvements on an object belonging to someone else could avail himself of an enrichment claim, he no longer had to be protected by a special set of rules. The draftsmen of the BGB nonetheless decided to retain these special rules (§§ 994ff. BGB); but, by doing so, they had to turn their *ratio* on its head.[66] The decision to preserve the Roman rules under different auspices and within a changed doctrinal environment turned out to be distinctly unfortunate.[67] Delictual liability, too, was both modernized and generalized in medieval and early modern jurisprudence.[68] Again, it was possible to latch on to the successful attempts of Roman jurisprudence to convert a narrowly confined and strangely formulated enactment from the third century BC, the *lex Aquilia*, into a central pillar of the Roman law of delict.[69] Medieval and early modern lawyers continued to refer to 'Aquilian' liability, even though it had come to differ from its Roman origin 'more than a bird from a quadruped'.[70] That prompted Christian Thomasius in the early eighteenth century to 'tear off the Aquilian mask' from the action for damage done.[71] And yet modern delict is still based on concepts (particularly unlawfulness and fault) that originate in Roman law but cause considerable difficulties in view of the fact that the function of the modern law of delict differs from its Roman forebear.[72] The Roman law of sale was tailored exclusively for the sale of specific objects; the extension of its rules to the sale of objects described as being of a particular kind, or belonging to a particular class (unascertained goods), is due to one of many 'productive misunderstandings'[73] of the Roman sources by medieval jurisprudence.[74] That extension was a very progressive step, for the sale of unascertained goods was to become practically much more significant than the sale of individual objects. Yet at the same time a number of the rules of Roman sales law were hardly suitable for that type of transaction, above all the old rule that with the conclusion of the contract of sale, the risk passes to the buyer (*emptione perfecta periculum est emptoris*),[75] and the aedilician liability for latent defects.[76] The first of these problems was eventually resolved by the draftsmen of the BGB, who established a risk rule differing from Roman law (§ 446 BGB),[77] while the other, in spite of the compromise laid down in § 480 BGB (old version), essentially remained unsettled.[78]

4. Characteristics of Roman Law in Antiquity Essential for its Survival

Even these few examples illustrate a number of characteristics of Roman law that were to be essential for the development of the law in Europe:

(i) It constituted a highly developed jurisprudence, a specific branch of knowledge developed and sustained by lawyers. That was unique in the world of classical antiquity.

(ii) Closely related with it was what Fritz Schulz referred to as the isolation[79] of law vis-à-vis religion, morality, politics, and economics: the separation of law from non-law.

(iii) That, in turn, entailed a strong emphasis on private law (and civil procedure); criminal law and the administration of the state on the other hand appear to have been regarded by the Roman lawyers as not being subject to specifically legal criteria.

(iv) Roman private law was very largely 'lawyers' law' or 'Juristenrecht': it was not laid down in a systematic and comprehensive enactment, but was instead applied and developed by lawyers with great practical experience.[80]

(v) That explains, on the one hand, the great realism of Roman law and its focus on practical problems rather than abstract theory. On the other hand, it also explains the many controversies that tended to envelop the resolution of legal problems.

(vi) These controversies were an expression and a sign of the inherent dynamic of Roman law. It was constantly developing. Between Publius Mucius Scaevola (who was described as one of those who founded the civil law[81] and was consul in 133 BC) and Aemilius Papinianus (prefect of the praetorian guards from AD 205–212 and the most eminent lawyer of the late classical era), there was a period of more than 300 years in the course of which state and society, Roman legal culture, and Roman law were subject to fundamental change.

(vii) Reference just to 'Roman law' is therefore imprecise. Even the Roman law of classical antiquity constituted a tradition and was based on a discussion of legal problems spanning many generations of jurists. Here is a typical example:[82] In D. 24.3.66 pr. Justinian preserved a text by Javolenus[83] written at the turn from the early to the high classical period. It is taken from a work that constitutes a revision of the posthumous works of Marcus Antistius Labeo (a contemporary of Emperor Augustus)[84] and contains a rule according to which a husband is responsible for fault (*dolus* and *culpa*) with regard to property that he has received as a dowry. In support of that rule reference is made to the most prominent jurist of the pre-classical period, Servius Sulpicius Rufus.[85] Servius, in turn, had taken up the decision of a specific legal dispute by Publius Mucius Scaevola.[86] That dispute concerned the dowry of Licinnia, wife of Gaius Sempronius Gracchus, who had perished in the turmoils unleashed by the agrarian reforms masterminded by Gracchus.

(viii) Roman law, therefore, was extraordinarily complex. It was largely casuistic in nature. It was developed over many centuries and thus constituted a tradition. It was recorded in an abundant literature.[87] And it rested on two conceptually and historically separate foundations: the *ius civile* – that is, the traditional core of legal rules applying to a Roman citizen; and a *ius honorarium* – one might call it Equity – that had been introduced by the praetors in the public interest in order to assist, supplement, and correct the traditional civil law.[88]

(ix) Nonetheless, Roman law was not an impenetrable jungle of detail. The Roman jurists developed a large number of legal concepts, rules, and institutions, which they constantly attempted to coordinate, and intellectually to relate, to one other. They thus created a kind of 'open' system that combined consistency with a considerable degree of flexibility.[89] In the process, the Roman jurists were guided by a number of fundamental values, or principles, such as liberty, *bona fides*, *humanitas*, and the protection of acquired rights, particularly the right of ownership.[90]

(x) Another characteristic of Roman jurisprudence that contributed to making it such a fertile object of legal analysis was the fact that reasons for the decisions arrived at were either not given at all, or only hinted at.[91]

Roman case law is therefore particularly rich in tacit assumptions and presuppositions that can be, and have to be, unravelled by a process of interpretation. Again, an example may illustrate the point. In Marcianus D. 18.1.44 we find the following brief text: *Si duos quis servos emerit pariter uno pretio, quorum alter ante venditionem mortuus est, neque in vivo constat emptio*. Two slaves have been sold for one price. It subsequently turned out that, at the time when the contract was concluded, one of the slaves had already died. Its delivery could thus no longer be demanded, and the contract, as it stood, was invalid. The authors of the *ius commune* based that on the rule *impossibilium nulla obligatio* (there is no obligation concerning the impossible).[92] But can the purchaser request delivery of the second slave? Here we are faced with the problem of partial invalidity of legal transactions. From the time of the Glossators, the general rule was taken to be *utile per inutile non vitiatur*:[93] the 'useful' part of the transaction is not affected by the invalidity of part of it: it remains in force. That rule was taken from a fragment by Ulpian[94] who, however, had not intended to provide a general rule but had merely solved an individual case.

Marcianus' decision in D. 18.1.44 demonstrates that *utile per inutile non vitiatur* cannot have been recognized in Roman law as a general rule, for the contract is held to be invalid with regard to the second slave too. That may be related to the fact that the price for just one of the slaves was neither determined nor determinable with any degree of certainty. One of the requirements for the validity of a Roman contract of sale (*pretium certum*) was thus lacking.[95]

5. Roman Jurisprudence and Its Transmission

The emergence of a jurisprudence with these characteristics would hardly have been possible without the reception of Greek philosophy in republican Rome.[96] Of decisive importance, however, was the role of the legal expert in the application and development of law. In Greece itself that had been absent. Ancient Greek law had been, to put it very pointedly, a law without lawyers: legal disputes were decided by a number of laymen, appointed by drawing lots, who had to take their decision on the basis of oral proceedings, in the course of which parties were allocated a set time in which to argue their case, and the decision had to be given without any discussion or the possibility of asking questions, by secret ballot on the basis of a simple majority.[97] These were not fertile conditions for the establishment of a science of law or the flourishing of legal experts.

Decisive for the European significance of Roman law, moreover, was something that had been completely alien to classical Roman law: a comprehensive act of legislation by the Emperor Justinian. He ordered an enormous compilation of excerpts from the writings of the classical period to be produced (the *Digest*) which he then promulgated as law, together with a collection of previous imperial legislation and an introductory textbook. As is apparent from its Greek name (*pandectae*; hence pandectist legal science), the *Digest* was supposed to be comprehensive, which was also a rather un-Roman idea. 'May no lawyer dare to add commentaries to our work and spoil its brevity through his verbosity', Justinian decreed.[98] But that remained a naive and pious hope. Justinian could not prevent scholars from making a work of scholarship itself the object of scholarship. That was necessary, *inter alia*, because he had introduced an additional level of complexity into the body of legal sources: the texts to be compiled in the *Digest* were more than 300 years old, and Justinian had therefore ordered their revision and adaptation to contemporary conditions (this was the origin of the so-called interpolations); he had placed next to one another and invested with equal validity texts from completely different periods of

Roman legal development, and he had adopted into his compilation a variety of texts that reflected controversies among the Roman lawyers and that therefore hardly constituted the kind of material suitable for an act of legislation.

6. CHANGES IN THE PERCEPTION OF ROMAN LAW

The university is regarded as 'the European institution par excellence'.[99] It does not date back to classical antiquity but originated as a manifestation of the great occidental educational revolution towards the end of the twelfth century, first in Bologna, then in Paris, Oxford, and in an ever-increasing number of places in western, central, and southern Europe.[100] Law in Rome can be described as a jurisprudence without, however, having been an academic discipline taught at the university. But when in the high middle ages law was caught up in the educational revolution just mentioned, it was Roman law that lent itself like none of the other contemporary laws (with one exception closely linked to Roman law, namely Canon law) to scholastic analysis and hence to the type of scholarship appropriate to a university.[101] Roman legal texts therefore immediately occupied the central position in the study of the secular law. That applied to all universities founded on the model of Bologna throughout Europe, and it remained the case down to the era of codification – that is, in Germany until the end of the nineteenth century. Yet the approach towards the Roman texts was subject to considerable change.[102] Medieval jurisprudence predominantly regarded these texts as a logically consistent whole, and attempted to demonstrate how apparent divergences could be overcome. That way of proceeding provoked a reaction in the form of the legal humanism of the Renaissance period. The humanist lawyers were concerned, in the first place, to establish what the texts had originally been intended to mean by their ancient authors. That, essentially, marked the beginning of the history of legal history. But since the humanist lawyers took the Roman texts to embody not only a model of justice and fairness for classical antiquity, but also for contemporary society, they were confronted once again with the problem that some sources contradicted others, that there were questions to which they clearly did not provide an answer, and that some of the answers provided were obviously based on outdated ideas. These problems were tackled by the representatives of a school known programmatically as *usus modernus pandectarum* (modern usage of the *Digest*). Since they had gone through the humanist enlightenment, unlike the medieval lawyers they no longer regarded the texts of the *Corpus iuris civilis* as absolutely binding authority: one could generalize and further develop the ideas contained in them, critically examine them, or even declare them abrogated by disuse.[103]

At about the same time, another school of thought gained influence which also acknowledged that Roman law had many shortcomings and often merely hinted in the direction of what was just and fair: this school therefore endeavoured to bring out the fundamental truths hidden in the Roman texts by philosophical analysis: the late scholastic, and subsequently secular, Natural law. In the nineteenth century, legal scholarship in Germany was dominated by Savigny's Historical School, which, however, also had considerable appeal and influence in other European countries.[104] With the Historical School, an approach gained ascendancy that tended to look at Roman law from the point of view of contemporary law and so in a way made the analysis of historical texts once again serve present needs. The interpretation of the texts was largely inspired by the consideration of how they could be applied in modern practice. It was only the advent of the BGB that ultimately freed the 'Romanists' (that is, scholars dealing with the sources of Roman law) from the overwhelming weight of that concern and, in the process, converted them from legal doctrinalists into pure legal historians, studying Roman law as a manifestation of classical antiquity.[105]

7. ROMAN LAW AND *IUS COMMUNE*

In the broadest outline, this is the history of what is often called the second life of Roman law: its effect on European legal scholarship from the days of the 'reception'. Roman law became the foundation of the *ius commune*. That *ius commune* was a learned law, sustained by academic scholarship and study; it found its manifestation in a very large and essentially uniform body of literature across Europe; and it was based on a uniform university training in law.[106] But it was never on its own. The dualism of Empire and Church, and of Emperor and Pope, was reflected in the dualism of Roman law (that is, civil law) and Canon law, of secular and ecclesiastical courts, and of scholars studying Roman law (the legists) and Canon law (the canonists). At times, the jurisdiction of the ecclesiastical courts extended far into the core areas of private law.[107] There were jurisdictional shifts and conflicts that reflected the power politics between spiritual and secular rulers. But there were also far-reaching intellectual connections. Canon law was the law of the Roman Church, and it was largely based on Roman law; in turn, it exercised a considerable influence on the secular law.[108] The principle of *pacta sunt servanda* derives from Canon law,[109] as does the principle of restitution in kind.[110]

Apart from Roman law and Canon law, there was also feudal law which had, however, been incorporated through the *Libri feudorum* into the body of Roman law.[111] There were the systematic designs and the doctrines of the late scholastics in Spain[112] and, later, of the adherents of a rationalistic Natural law that were moulded by Roman law and, in turn, influenced the *ius commune*. There were customs (*consuetudines*), confined in their application to specific places and territories, which were recognized within the framework of the *ius commune* and subjected to scholarly analysis. There were the rules and customary laws – predominantly unwritten, but also sometimes laid down in writing – that had emerged, from about the twelfth century onwards, in fairs and trading centres across Europe, as well as in the harbour towns on the shores of the Mediterranean, the Atlantic Ocean, and the Baltic Sea.[113] Here, too, there was mutual influence with regard to Roman law and the Roman-Canon *ius commune*.

Above all, however, there was an enormous variety of territorial and local legal sources that, in theory, always enjoyed precedence before the courts. The *ius commune* was applicable only as a subsidiary source of law, yet practically it often gained the upper hand. According to early modern legal literature, there was even an established presumption (*fundata intentio*)[114] in favour of the application of the *ius commune*. But that presumption does not express the whole truth; for what actually happened in courtrooms across Europe was subject to considerable variation, and it could vary from place to place and from subject area to subject area. Even legal practice in the Holy Roman Empire of the German Nation, the heartland of the reception, can be said by way of summary to have been characterized by 'a legal pluralism hardly imaginable' today.[115] But it was a diversity within an overarching intellectual unity, and that intellectual unity was established by a legal training focusing everywhere in Europe on the body of the Roman legal sources. The unifying effect of the legal training was to become particularly evident, once again, in nineteenth-century Germany. Only in parts of Germany was the *ius commune* directly applicable. The remainder was subject to a range of special legal regimes, among them the Prussian code of 1794, the General Civil Code of Austria, the *Code civil*, the *Landrecht* of Baden (which, essentially, constituted a translation of the *Code civil*), and later also the Saxon Code of Private Law.[116] Nonetheless, it was the *ius commune* that provided the basis for interpreting and truly understanding these legal regimes,[117] and thus it claimed – and was, as a matter of course, granted – centre stage in the curricula of all German faculties of law.[118] The pandectist branch of the Historical School thus managed to create (or rather preserve) a distinctive cultural unity on the level of legal scholarship, enabling professors and students to move freely from Königsberg to Strasbourg, from Giessen to Vienna, or from Heidelberg to Leipzig.[119]

8. Roman Law and European Legal Tradition

The tension between unity and diversity is characteristic of European culture in general.[120] As will have become apparent by now, it is of central significance also for the European legal tradition.[121] That tradition was shaped by the *ius commune*, which in turn was largely based on Roman law. If one attempts to specify further features characterizing the European legal tradition in comparison with others in the world (that is, the chthonic, Talmudic, Islamic, Hindu, and East Asian),[122] the influence of Roman law can be shown in every instance. There is the element of writing.[123] One of the reasons why Roman law was so influential in medieval Europe is that it was a law that had been laid down in writing. It was *ratio scripta*. This is not only demonstrated by the process of reception itself, but also by the many endeavours to provide written documentation of customary laws prevailing in Europe from the end of the twelfth century (Glanvill and Bracton in England, the *coutumes* in France, the *fueros* in Spain, *Sachsenspiegel* and *Schwabenspiegel* in Germany). This remarkable development was inspired by the learned laws.[124]

Apart from that, Roman law was also for centuries regarded as *ratio scripta*: it was the model of a law that was reasonable – that is, in conformity with human reason. Roman law, therefore, was an expression of, and stimulated the quest for, a law that was rational and scholarly, intellectually coherent, and systematic.[125] At the same time, the specific nature of the Roman sources prevented that system from becoming inflexible and static. For European law has always been characterized by an inherent ability to develop. Or, in the words of Harold J. Berman: 'The concept of a . . . system of law depended for its vitality on the belief in the ongoing character of law, its capacity for growth over generations and centuries – a belief which is uniquely Western. The body of law only survives because it contains a built-in mechanism for organic change.'[126] European law is subject to constant adaptation; it is able to react to changed circumstances and new situations, and it has always displayed an extraordinary capacity for integration. Medieval Roman law was no longer the Roman law of classical antiquity, the *usus modernus pandectarum* no longer corresponded to the *usus medii aevi*, and pandectist legal doctrine was a far cry from the *usus modernus*. The development moved, to use a famous phrase coined by Rudolf von Jhering,[127] beyond Roman law by means of Roman law. In the days of the Roman republic and imperial Rome, legal experts had fashioned a Roman 'legal science'.[128] The medieval lawyers turned it into an academic discipline, a learned law that had to be studied at a university.

That is yet another characteristic of European law and also one that originates in Roman law. Law is a learned profession, and the application and development of the law is the task of learned jurists.[129] Closely related is the fact that law is an autonomous discipline and that as a result it is conceived as a system of rules that is separate, in principle, from other normative systems seeking to guide human conduct and to regulate society, such as religion.[130]

9. HOW EUROPEAN IS THE 'EUROPEAN' LEGAL TRADITION?

Modern European law still presents the image of an intriguing mixture of diversity and unity. Thus, the continental legal systems are usually subdivided into the Germanic and Romanistic legal families.[131] Moreover, a number of systems have to be located somewhere between these two legal families, particularly the Dutch and Italian ones. But even the systems belonging to the Germanic legal family display significant differences in style and substance. The Austrian and the German Civil Codes date from different periods of European legal development and are marked by different intellectual currents. Of the Swiss Civil Code it has been said that it received its characteristic mark 'largely from the special conditions of Switzerland and the traditions of that country's legal life'.[132] Nonetheless, it can hardly be disputed that all legal systems belonging to the Romanistic and Germanic legal families are sufficiently similar to describe them as different manifestations of one legal tradition.[133] The English term chosen for that tradition is 'civil law' (or 'civilian tradition'), which refers, historically, to Roman law.[134] But are we really entitled to speak of a European tradition? As far as the states of central and eastern Europe are concerned, the question probably has to be answered in the affirmative.[135] Up to the period of the World Wars of the twentieth century, they belonged to the cultural sphere of the *ius commune*. In some of them (most notably Hungary and Poland), the continued teaching of Roman law during the days of the rule of socialism maintained a connection with the west.[136] And since then we can see a process of re-integration 'by way of a renovation of private law guided by comparative scholarship'.[137] Lawyers in nineteenth-century Tsarist Russia had also availed themselves of the doctrines and methods of Roman law in order to cope with the social and legal challenges that traditional Russian law was unable adequately to deal with. Like lawyers in many other countries, they were particularly inspired by the legal development in Germany that was shaped by Savigny and the Historical School.[138] Turkey in 1926 took over Swiss private law and thus 'conclusively left the Islamic legal family'.[139] The Nordic legal systems are also predominantly regarded as part of the civilian tradition, in spite of having developed their own style in a number of respects.[140]

The central argument often advanced against the recognition of a genuinely European legal tradition is the existence of the English common law which, so it is said, has developed in noble isolation from Europe[141] and is therefore fundamentally different.[142] But the idea of the common law as an entirely autochthonous achievement of the English genius is a myth. In reality England was never completely cut off from continental legal culture; there was a constant intellectual contact that has left its imprint on English law.[143] Even in its origin it was an Anglo-Norman feudal law of a pattern typical of medieval Europe.[144] For many centuries, Latin and French remained the languages of English law. The Catholic Church brought its Canon law,[145] and international trade brought the *lex mercatoria*. In Oxford and Cambridge, two of the oldest European universities, Roman law was taught and studied on the model established in Bologna. From Scotland too Roman legal ideas filtered into English law; Scotland in the early modern period had become a far-flung province of the *ius commune* with particularly close relations to French and Dutch universities.[146] Modern English contract law has been decisively shaped by massive borrowings from authors such as Pothier, Domat, Grotius, Pufendorf, Burlamaqui, and Thibaut.[147] Of course, in many cases the inspiration provided by Roman law has led to entirely un-Roman results. But that was true also of the continental legal systems. Thus, in the best known of the cases concerning King Edward VII's coronation procession – which had to be postponed because the King had contracted peritonitis – we read: 'The real question in this case is the extent of the application in English law of the principle of the Roman law which has been adopted and acted on in many English decisions.'[148] The principle referred to is that of *debitor speciei liberatur casuali interitu rei* (the debtor is released from his obligation to perform when such performance becomes impossible and the impossibility is not attributable to his fault).[149] From about the middle of the nineteenth century onwards, the English courts had started to read that rule into the contractual agreement of the parties.[150] In the process they used a device also originating in Roman law: the implication of a tacit (resolutive) condition.[151] The foundations were thus laid for the doctrine of frustration of contract. Functionally, this corresponds to the continental doctrine of *clausula rebus sic stantibus*, which was also assembled with elements taken from Roman law, although as such it was unknown to Roman law.[152] But this is merely an example. Wherever one looks, one will find 'legal institutions, procedures, values, concepts and rules that English law shares with other Western legal systems'.[153] Hardly anything is sacred. Even the Magna Carta, 'the most basic statement of English customary law and constitutional principle', was partly shaped by influences coming from the *ius commune*.[154]

A person who does not merely confine his attention to the specific solutions to be found in the sources of Roman law, but also takes account of the flexibility of the civilian tradition and of its capacity for growth and productive assimilation, will be able to acknowledge that it has also shaped the English common law.[155] Of course, it is also marked (as are the continental systems) by countless peculiarities and idiosyncrasies. But it is clear today that these idiosyncrasies are increasingly being worn away, on both sides of the Channel. Basil Markesinis refers to a gradual convergence,[156] James Gordley to an outdated distinction between civil law and common law.[157] That applies on the level of substantive law as much as with regard to basic issues such as legal methodology.[158]

In addition, it must be kept in mind that many other parts of the world have been affected in one way or another by the European legal tradition. The United States inherited English common law,[159] as have most of the other territories once belonging to the British Empire. The Latin American countries received French, Spanish, Italian, and German law.[160] Japanese and (South) Korean law have been significantly shaped by German law;[161] Québec has to a large degree retained its French heritage;[162] Roman-Dutch law prevails in South Africa;[163] and so forth. If all this is taken into account, one may still say today, as Rudolf von Jhering did some 150 years ago:

> The historical significance and mission of Rome, in a nutshell, is to overcome the limitations of the principle of nationality through the idea of universality ... The special significance of Roman law for the modern world does not consist in the fact that, for some time, it was applied in practice as a source of law ... but that it has brought about an intellectual revolution which has decisively shaped our entire legal thinking. Roman

law has thus become, just as Christianity, a constituent cultural feature of the modern world.[164]

10. TEACHING AND RESEARCH IN ROMAN LAW

The codifications of continental Europe very largely brought to an end the 'second life' of Roman law, the story of its reception and transformation into a *ius commune*. In nineteenth-century Germany that *ius commune* experienced a last and dazzling flowering. German pandectist scholarship, as it had emerged in the wake of the Historical School, was influential throughout Europe and was accorded pride of place in the world of legal learning.[165] It was also in Germany that codification had particularly dramatic consequences for the scholarship of Roman law radiating, once again, across Europe,[166] for it could now devote its whole attention to antiquity itself and begin to understand the sources of Roman law in their historical context.[167] Otto Lenel reconstructed the praetorian edict on the basis of the fragments from the works of classical jurists contained in the *Digest* (*Das Edictum Perpetuum*, 1893). Lenel's other great work, the *Palingenesia Iuris Civilis* (1889), was a sustained attempt to recreate the classical law library as far as that was possible on the basis of the fragments that have come down to us. Ludwig Mitteis demonstrated the extent to which indigenous 'vulgar' legal conceptions, particularly of Hellenistic origin, remained alive in the eastern part of the Empire and he thus shattered the traditional understanding of a uniform – and uniformly Roman – legal order in imperial Rome (*Reichsrecht und Volksrecht in den östlichen Provinzen des römischen Kaiserreichs*, 1891).[168] Otto Gradenwitz and Fridolin Eisele were pioneers in the systematic search for interpolations. Fritz Schulz and Franz Wieacker set out to detect pre-Justinianic alterations of the classical texts. With West-Roman vulgar law, Ernst Levy unlocked the interface between ancient Roman law and medieval 'Germanic law'. Alongside private law and civil procedure, the history of criminal and constitutional law attracted increasing attention (Wolfgang Kunkel). Legal practice in the Roman provinces, as documented in a vast quantity of papyri, began to be scrutinized (Ludwig Mitteis, Ernst Rabel) and the horizon was broadened to include other ancient legal cultures (Josef Partsch, Fritz Pringsheim, Paul Koschaker).[169]

This very pronounced historicization of Roman law, with all its brilliant discoveries, and the simultaneous process of an 'emancipation . . . by thinking apart Roman and modern law',[170] also had a downside: legal scholarship was turned into a largely unhistorical intellectual enterprise; it lost its character as a 'historical science' (Savigny). The BGB was taken to constitute a comprehensive and closed system of legal rules. It constituted an autonomous interpretational space that was to be attributed sole, supreme, and unquestioned authority. All the energies of legal academics in the field of private law were channelled into the task of expounding the code and discussing court decisions based on its provisions. That in turn was to have dramatic consequences for the teaching of law. For it was the BGB that immediately acquired the central position in the law faculties' curricula throughout Germany.[171] Knowledge of Roman law was no longer of practical utility and thus its position within the law faculties was gradually weakened. Hardly any Romanist in Germany continued to teach Roman law in the pandectist tradition. Instead, the pronounced historicization of Roman law was also bound to shape its teaching, further contributing to the alienation between Roman law and modern law.[172] Sooner or later, the establishment of chairs for Roman law in law faculties was bound to be questioned. Roman law had, essentially, become a branch of the study of classical antiquity, employing methods of research entirely different from those of doctrinal scholarship in law. Similar developments and methodological debates have taken place in other countries in Europe. In only a few (Italy, Spain, partly also Austria) does Roman law remain reasonably well entrenched in the law curricula and the law faculties. In Germany and in the Netherlands the story is one of gradual decline, and the experience one of a deep-rooted sense of crisis.[173]

These developments, of course, are particularly paradoxical at a time which aspires to recreate a European private law or, at least, a European scholarship of private law.[174] We will have to overcome the nationalistic isolation of legal scholarship that is a consequence of tailoring law curricula around national codifications. Students will have to be made to see the fundamental connections and the European character of our legal culture. What could be better suited for this purpose – and for shaping the intellectual horizon of lawyers in Europe as European lawyers – than the study of the Roman foundations of the civilian tradition?

Notes

* Parts of this essay are based on my New Zealand Legal Research Foundation Lecture, published in *New Zealand LR* 2007: 341 and my entry 'Roman Law' in *Max Planck Encyclopedia of European Private Law*, ed. J. Basedow, K. J. Hopt, and R. Zimmermann (Oxford, 2012), 1487. This version dates from 2009.

1. R. Zimmermann, *Das römisch-holländische Recht in Südafrika* (Darmstadt, 1983). On 'classical' Roman-Dutch law, see R. Feenstra and R. Zimmermann, eds., *Das römisch-holländische Recht: Fortschritte des Zivilrechts im 17. und 18. Jahrhundert* (Berlin, 1992). On

the initial disintegration of the *ius commune* into Roman-Dutch, Roman-Scots, Roman-Hispanic law, etc., at the time of the *usus modernus*, see K. Luig, 'The Institutes of National Law in the Seventeenth and Eighteenth Centuries', *Juridical Review* 1972: 193.

2. R. Zimmermann, 'Roman Law in a Mixed Legal System: The South African Experience', in *The Civil Law Tradition in Scotland*, ed. R. Evans-Jones (Edinburgh, 1995), 41. Owing to English influence during the nineteenth century, South African law became a mixed system: R. Zimmermann and D. Visser, eds., *Southern Cross: Civil Law and Common Law in South Africa* (Oxford, 1996); R. Zimmermann, 'Gemeines Recht heute: Das Kreuz des Südens', in *Der praktische Nutzen der Rechtsgeschichte: Festschrift für Hans Hattenhauer*, ed. J. Eckert (Heidelberg, 2003), 601.
3. On the reception of Roman Law in Scotland, see P. Stein, 'The Influence of Roman Law on the Law of Scotland', *Juridical Review* 1963: 205 as well as the essays in Evans-Jones (n. 2), and D. Carey Miller and R. Zimmermann, eds., *The Civilian Tradition and Scots Law: Aberdeen Quincentenary Essays* (Berlin, 1997).
4. The historical development is traced in the essays in K. Reid and R. Zimmermann, eds., *A History of Private Law in Scotland*, 2 vols. (Oxford, 2000).
5. R. Zimmermann, D. Visser, and K. Reid, eds., *Mixed Legal Systems in Comparative Perspective: Property and Obligations in Scotland and South Africa* (Oxford, 2004); J. du Plessis, 'Comparative Law and the Study of Mixed Legal Systems', in *The Oxford Handbook of Comparative Law*, ed. M. Reimann and R. Zimmermann (Oxford, 2008), 477.
6. M. Reinkenhof, *Die Anwendung des ius commune in San Marino* (Berlin, 1997).
7. BGHZ 92: 326; cf. B. Kupisch, 'Eine Moselinsel, Kaiser Napoleon und das römische Recht', *Juristenzeitung* 1987: 1017. Cf. BGHZ 110: 148 (on riparian ownership).
8. B. Windscheid, 'Die geschichtliche Schule in der Rechtswissenschaft', in Windscheid, *Gesammelte Reden und Abhandlungen*, ed. P. Oertmann (Leipzig, 1904), 75.
9. See for Germany, H. H. Jakobs, *Wissenschaft und Gesetzgebung im bürgerlichen Recht nach der Rechtsquellenlehre des 19. Jahrhunderts* (Paderborn, 1983); U. Falk and H. Mohnhaupt, eds., *Das Bürgerliche Gesetzbuch und seine Richter* (Frankfurt, 2000). Cf. also Windscheid (n. 8), 75.
10. These terms are found even in short commentaries on the BGB such as by C. Berger in *Bürgerliches Gesetzbuch*, 14th edn. by O. Jauernig (Munich, 2011), § 985, n. 1; and *Vor* §§ 987–993, n. 3.
11. Following the model of Roman law, a distinction is drawn today between necessary, useful, and luxurious improvements (*impensae necessariae*, *utiles*, and *voluptuariae*); see, e.g., C. Berger (n. 10), *Vor* §§ 994–1003, n. 8 (the German Civil Code itself contains only provisions for the first two types of improvements).
12. Here also the Latin terms are to be found even in brief commentaries such as A. Stadler, in Jauernig (n. 10), § 812, nn. 13 and 14.
13. For a brief discussion in English of the German unjustified enrichment claims just mentioned, see R. Zimmermann, 'Unjustified Enrichment: The Modern Civilian Approach', *Oxford Journal of Legal Studies* 15 (1995): 403ff.
14. For the historical background, see R. Zimmermann, *The Law of Obligations: Roman Foundations of the Civilian Tradition* (Oxford, 1996), 857.
15. C. Wolff, *Grundsätze des Natur- und Völckerrechts* (Halle, 1754), § 438. For comment, see K.-P. Nanz, *Die Entstehung des allgemeinen Vertragsbegriffs im 16. bis 18. Jahrhundert* (Munich, 1985), 164.

16. Ulp. D. 2.14.7.7; see Zimmermann (n. 14), 508.
17. *Bona fides* was one of the driving forces for the development of Roman contract law: see S. Whittaker and R. Zimmermann, 'Good faith in European contract law: surveying the legal landscape', in R. Zimmermann and S. Whittaker, eds., *Good Faith in European Contract Law* (Cambridge, 2000), 16; M. Schermaier, 'Bona fides in Roman contract law', in Zimmermann and Whittaker, 63; R. Zimmermann, *Roman Law, Contemporary Law, European Law* (Oxford, 2001), 83. The most influential attempt to systematize the case law on § 242 BGB – F. Wieacker, *Zur rechtstheoretischen Präzisierung des § 242 BGB* (Tübingen, 1956) – was clearly inspired by Roman law.
18. Cf. H. P. Mansel, in Jauernig (n. 10), § 242, nn. 39, 47, and 48. For a brief discussion in English, see Zimmermann and Whittaker (n. 17), 22.
19. See Zimmermann (n. 14), 639; S. Vogenauer in *Historisch-kritischer Kommentar zum BGB*, ed. M. Schmoeckel, J. Rückert, and R. Zimmermann (Tübingen, 2007), vol. 2, §§ 305–310 (III), nn. 13ff.
20. See §§ 276f BGB; and M. Schermaier, in Schmoeckel et al. (n. 19), §§ 276–278.
21. See K. Luig, 'Zur Vorgeschichte der verschuldensunabhängigen Haftung des Vermieters für anfängliche Mängel nach § 538 BGB', in *Festschrift für Heinz Hübner*, ed. G. Baumgärtel et al. (Berlin – New York, 1984), 121; Zimmermann (n. 14), 367.
22. See R. Zimmermann, 'Die Geschichte der Gastwirtshaftung in Deutschland', in *Usus modernus pandectarum: Römisches Recht, Deutsches Recht und Naturrecht in der frühen Neuzeit: Festschrift für Klaus Luig*, ed. H.-P. Haferkamp and T. Repgen (Cologne – Weimar – Vienna, 2007), 271.
23. § 138 I BGB; see Zimmermann (n. 14), 713.
24. §§ 286ff. and 293ff. BGB; see Zimmermann (n. 14), 790, 817.
25. §§ 459ff. BGB of 1900; see Zimmermann (n. 14), 305. The rules were reformed in 2002: see R. Zimmermann, *The New German Law of Obligations: Historical and Comparative Perspectives* (Oxford, 2005), 79.
26. §§ 677ff. BGB; see Zimmermann (n. 14), 433.
27. § 833 BGB; see Zimmermann (n. 14), 1116.
28. On Roman law and the BGB, see M. Kaser, 'Der römische Anteil am deutschen bürgerlichen Recht', *Juristische Schulung* 1967: 337; R. Knütel, 'Römisches Recht und deutsches Bürgerliches Recht', in *Die Antike in der europäischen Gegenwart*, ed. W. Ludwig (Göttingen, 1993), 43; E. Picker, 'Zum Gegenwartswert des römischen Rechts', in *Das antike Rom in Europa*, ed. H. Bungert (Regensburg, 1985), 289. See also the table of Roman legal sources cited in the *travaux préparatoires* of the BGB, compiled by R. Knütel and M. Goetzmann in *Rechtsgeschichte und Privatrechtsdogmatik*, ed. R. Zimmermann, R. Knütel, and J. P. Meincke (Heidelberg, 1999), 679.
29. Up to and including the new Dutch Civil Code: H. Ankum, 'Römisches Recht im neuen niederländischen Bürgerlichen Gesetzbuch', in Zimmermann et al. (n. 28), 101. Generally, see A. Beck, 'Römisches Recht in unserer Rechtsordnung', in *Horizonte der Humanitas: Freundesgabe Walter Wili*, ed. G. Luck (Bern – Stuttgart, 1960), 120; R. Zimmermann, 'The Civil Law in European Codes', in Carey Miller and Zimmermann (n. 3), 259; A. Bürge, 'Das römische Recht als Grundlage für das Zivilrecht im künftigen Europa', in *Die Europäisierung der Rechtswissenschaft*, ed. F. Ranieri (Baden-Baden, 2002), 19.
30. See also J. Gordley, 'Myths of the French Civil Code', *American Journal of Comparative Law* 42 (1992): 459.

31. Zimmermann (n. 14), 45.
32. Zimmermann (n. 14), 253.
33. See text to n. 39, this chapter.
34. See book III title IV, chs. I and II of the *Code civil*. On the corresponding fourfold division of obligations in Justinian Inst. 3.13.2, see Zimmermann (n. 14), 14.
35. On illegality and unconscionability, see R. Zimmermann, 'The Civil Law in European Codes', in Carey Miller and Zimmermann (n. 3), 267.
36. See Zimmermann (n. 14), 16.
37. See, e.g., R. J. Pothier, *Traité des obligations*, in Pothier, *Traités de droit civil* (Paris, 1781), vol. 1, § 116.
38. See Zimmermann (n. 14), 1126.
39. P. Pichonnaz, *La compensation: Analyse historique et comparative des modes de compenser non conventionels* (Fribourg, 2001), 127; R. Zimmermann, in Schmoeckel et al. (n. 19), §§ 387–396, n. 6.
40. For details, see Pichonnaz (n. 39), 9; for an overview, M. Kaser, *Das römische Privatrecht*, 2nd edn. (Munich, 1971), vol. 1, 644; Zimmermann (n. 19), §§ 387–396, nn. 5ff.
41. C. 4.31.14.
42. For details, see Zimmermann (n. 19), §§ 387–396, nn. 11ff.
43. See Zimmermann (n. 14), 817.
44. See F. Ranieri, *Europäisches Obligationenrecht*, 3rd edn. (Vienna, 2009), 1045.
45. The majority view among modern Romanists: R. Knütel, 'Die Haftung für Hilfspersonen im römischen Recht', *ZSS* 100 (1983): 419ff.; Zimmermann (n. 14), 397; H. Wicke, *Respondeat Superior* (Berlin, 2000), 69.
46. See A. Watson, *Failures of the Legal Imagination* (Pennsylvania, 1988), 6, 15; K. Zweigert and H. Kötz, *Einführung in die Rechtsvergleichung*, 3rd edn. (Tübingen, 1996), 639.
47. See, e.g., B. Windscheid and T. Kipp, *Lehrbuch des Pandektenrechts*, 9th edn. (Frankfurt, 1906), § 401, 5.
48. See, e.g., H.-P. Benöhr, 'Die Entscheidung des BGB für das Verschuldensprinzip', *TR* 46 (1978): 1.
49. For the historical development, see H. H. Seiler, 'Die deliktische Gehilfenhaftung in historischer Sicht', *Juristenzeitung* 1967: 525; Zimmermann (n. 14), 1124.
50. Ulp. D. 2.14.7.4; Zimmermann (n. 14), 508.
51. More precisely, *pacta quantumcunque nuda servanda sunt*. For details, see Zimmermann (n. 14), 542; P. Landau, 'Pacta sunt servanda: Zu den kanonistischen Grundlagen der Privatautonomie', in *'Ins Wasser geworfen und Ozeane durchquert': Festschrift für Knut Wolfgang Nörr*, ed. M. Ascheri et al. (Cologne – Weimar – Vienna, 2003), 457.
52. Inst. 3.13 pr: *obligatio est iuris vinculum, quo necessitate adstringimur alicuius solvendae rei secundum nostrae civitatis iura*.
53. For the historical development, see Zimmermann (n. 14), 34, 45, and 58.
54. C. 4.26.7.3.
55. B. Kupisch, *Die Versionsklage* (Heidelberg, 1965); Zimmermann (n. 14), 878.
56. Unlike §§ 812ff. BGB, the Roman *condictio* did not focus on the entire patrimony of the enrichment debtor. The recipient was obliged to return the object received, and the content and fate of that obligation were governed by the general rules. On this and the further development, see W. Ernst, 'Werner Flumes Lehre von der ungerechtfertigten Bereicherung', in W. Flume, *Studien zur Lehre von der ungerechtfertigten Bereicherung* (Tübingen, 2003), 2.

57. Pap. D. 22.6.7.
58. C. 1.18.10.
59. Zimmermann (n. 14), 868.
60. For details, see Zimmermann (n. 14), 857.
61. Zimmermann (n. 14), 863.
62. B. Kupisch, *Ungerechtfertigte Bereicherung: geschichtliche Entwicklungen* (Heidelberg, 1987), 4; Zimmermann (n. 14), 841.
63. See R. Feenstra, 'Grotius' Doctrine of Unjust Enrichment as a Source of Obligation: Its Origin and Its Influence in Roman-Dutch Law', in *Unjust Enrichment: The Comparative Legal History of the Law of Restitution*, ed. E. J. H. Schrage, 2nd edn. (Berlin, 1999), 197; D. Visser, 'Das Recht der ungerechtfertigten Bereicherung', in Feenstra and Zimmermann (n. 1), 369.
64. See A. Bürge, 'Der Arrêt Boudier von 1892 vor dem Hintergrund der Entwicklung des französischen Bereicherungsrechts im 19. Jahrhundert', in *Festschrift für Hans Jürgen Sonnenberger*, ed. M. Coester, D. Martiny, and K. A. Prinz von Sachsen-Gessaphe (Munich, 2004), 3.
65. See N. Jansen, 'Die Korrektur grundloser Vermögensverschiebungen als Restitution? Zur Lehre von der ungerechtfertigten Bereicherung bei Savigny', *ZSS* 120 (2003): 106.
66. For details, see D. A. Verse, *Verwendungen im Eigentümer-Besitzer-Verhältnis: Eine kritische Betrachtung aus historisch-vergleichender Sicht* (Tübingen, 1999). Cf. Zimmermann (n. 17), 45.
67. The problems are analysed by Verse (n. 66), 1.
68. H. Kaufmann, *Rezeption und usus modernus der actio legis Aquiliae* (Cologne – Graz, 1958); H. Coing, *Europäisches Privatrecht* (Munich, 1985), vol. 1, 509; Zimmermann (n. 14), 1017; J. Schröder, 'Die zivilrechtliche Haftung für schuldhafte Schadenszufügungen im deutschen usus modernus', in *La responsabilità civile da atto illecito nella prospettiva storico-comparatistica*, ed. L. Vacca (Turin, 1995), 144.
69. For details, see Zimmermann (n. 14), 953.
70. *[A]ctio nostra, qua utimur, ab actione legis Aquiliae magis differat, quam avis a quadrupede*: C. Thomasius, *Larva Legis Aquiliae*, ed. and trans. M. Hewett (Oxford, 2000), § 1.
71. Thomasius (n. 70).
72. See N. Jansen, *Die Struktur des Haftungsrechts: Geschichte, Theorie und Dogmatik außervertraglicher Ansprüche auf Schadensersatz* (Tübingen, 2003).
73. This term was coined, at least for legal history, by H. R. Hoetink (who in turn took it from theological literature); see his 'Over het verstaan van vreemd recht' and 'Historische rechtsbeschouwing', in H. R. Hoetink, *Rechtsgeleerde opstellen* (Alphen, 1982), 34, 266.
74. M. Bauer, *Periculum Emptoris: Eine dogmengeschichtliche Untersuchung zur Gefahrtragung beim Kauf* (Berlin, 1998), 98; W. Ernst, 'Kurze Rechtsgeschichte des Gattungskaufs', *Zeitschrift für europäisches Privatrecht* 7 (1999): 612; Zimmermann (n. 25), 84.
75. Zimmermann (n. 14), 281.
76. Zimmermann (n. 14), 305.
77. Zimmermann (n. 14), 291.
78. Zimmermann (n. 25), 87.
79. F. Schulz, *Principles of Roman Law* (Oxford, 1936), 20.
80. See, e.g., the discussion by Bürge (n. 29), 21; A. Bürge, *Römisches Privatrecht* (Darmstadt, 1999), 17.

81. Pomp. D. 1.2.2.39.
82. Inspired by J. P. Meincke, *Juristenzeitung* 2006: 299.
83. On whom see W. Kunkel, *Herkunft und soziale Stellung der römischen Juristen*, 2nd edn. (Graz – Vienna – Cologne, 1967), 138.
84. W. Waldstein and J. M. Rainer, *Römische Rechtsgeschichte*, 10th edn. (Munich, 2005), 201; Kunkel (n. 83), 32.
85. On whom see Waldstein and Rainer (n. 84), 135; Kunkel (n. 83), 25.
86. On Publius Mucius Scaevola, see Waldstein and Rainer (n. 84), 133; Kunkel (n. 83), 12.
87. Justinian's compilers, in the sixth century, could still draw on 2,000 books (C. 1.17.2.1); the classical literature must have consisted of that number many times over: Waldstein and Rainer (n. 84), 199.
88. Pap. D. 1.1.7.1. See, generally, M. Kaser and R. Knütel, *Römisches Privatrecht*, 18th edn. (Munich, 2005), 19, 22.
89. Cf. also Waldstein and Rainer (n. 84), 196, and Kaser and Knütel (n. 88), 27 summarizing the prevailing view.
90. See, in particular, Schulz (n. 79), 140 (liberty), 189 (humanity), 223 (fidelity), and 239 (security in the sense of stability of acquired rights). On equity in Roman law, see P. Stein, 'Equitable Principles in Roman Law', in P. Stein, *The Character and Influence of the Roman Civil Law: Historical Essays* (London, 1988), 19.
91. Essential for the legitimacy of the jurists was their *auctoritas*, based on the knowledge acquired through their practical experience. On authority as a formative feature of Roman law, see Schulz (n. 79), 164 and, on the jurists, 183.
92. It is based on Cels. D. 50.17.185 but tended to be misunderstood, including by the draftsmen of the BGB: see § 306 BGB (old version). For details, see Zimmermann (n. 14), 686.
93. See Zimmermann (n. 14), 75.
94. Ulp. D. 45.1.1.5 *in fine*: ... *neque vitiatur utilis per hanc inutilem*.
95. H. H. Seiler, 'Utile per inutile non vitiatur: Zur Teilunwirksamkeit von Rechtsgeschäften im römischen Recht', in *Festschrift für Max Kaser*, ed. D. Medicus and H. H. Seiler (Munich, 1976), 130. On the requirement of a *pretium certum*, see Zimmermann (n. 14), 253.
96. For an overview, see Waldstein and Rainer (n. 84), 134. For further detail, F. Schulz, *History of Roman Legal Science* (Oxford, 1946), 38; F. Wieacker, *Römische Rechtsgeschichte* (Munich, 1988), vol. 1, 351, 618; M. Schermaier, *Materia* (Vienna – Cologne – Weimar, 1992), 35.
97. See, e.g., G. Thür, 'Recht im antiken Griechenland', in *Die Rechtskulturen der Antike*, ed. U. Manthe (Munich, 2003), 211.
98. C. 1.17.1.12; cf. C. 1.17.2.21.
99. W. Rüegg, 'Vorwort', in *Geschichte der Universität in Europa*, ed. W. Rüegg (Munich, 1993), vol. 1, 13.
100. See, e.g., M. Borgolte, *Europa entdeckt seine Vielfalt 1050–1250* (Stuttgart, 2002), 296; and the index and instructive maps in J. Verger, 'Grundlagen', in Rüegg (n. 99), vol. 1, 70.
101. The same was true already for the private law schools in Bologna in the second half of the eleventh and in the twelfth centuries, in particular for the school of Irnerius. On the significance of Irnerius, see F. Dorn in *Deutsche und Europäische Juristen aus neun Jahrhunderten*, ed. G. Kleinheyer and J. Schröder, 5th edn. (Heidelberg, 2008), 220.

102. For the detail, F. Wieacker, *A History of Private Law in Europe*, trans. T. Weir (Oxford, 1995); P. Koschaker, *Europa und das römische Recht*, 4th edn. (Munich – Berlin, 1966), 55ff.; P. Stein, *Roman Law in European History* (Cambridge, 1999); J. Gordley, 'Comparative Law and Legal History', in Reimann and Zimmermann (n. 5), 753ff.
103. Hence such books as Philibert Bugnyon, *Tractatus legum abrogatarum et inusitatarum in omnibus curiis, terris, jurisdictionibus, et dominiis regni Franciae* (1563) and Simon van Groenewegen van der Made, *Tractatus de legibus abrogatis et inusitatis in Hollandia vicinisque regionibus* (1649).
104. On the influence of the Historical School, see, e.g., J.-O. Sundell, 'German Influence on Swedish Private Law Doctrine 1870–1914', *Scandinavian Studies in Law* (1991): 237; J. H. A. Lokin, 'Het NBW en de pandektistiek', in *Historisch vooruitzicht. Opstellen over rechtsgeschiedenis en burgerlijk recht*, ed. M. E. Franke et al. (Arnhem, 1994), 125; R. Schulze, ed., *Deutsche Rechtswissenschaft und Staatslehre im Spiegel der italienischen Rechtskultur während der zweiten Hälfte des 19. Jahrhunderts* (Berlin, 1990); A. Bürge, *Das französische Privatrecht im 19. Jahrhundert: Zwischen Tradition und Pandektenwissenschaft, Liberalismus und Etatismus*, 2nd edn. (Frankfurt, 1995); A. Bürge, 'Ausstrahlungen der historischen Rechtsschule in Frankreich', *Zeitschrift für europäisches Privatrecht* 5 (1997): 643; W. Ogris, *Der Entwicklungsgang der österreichischen Privatrechtswissenschaft im 19. Jahrhundert* (Berlin, 1968); P. Caroni, 'Die Schweizer Romanistik im 19. Jahrhundert', *Zeitschrift für neuere Rechtsgeschichte* 16 (1994): 243; P. Stein, 'Legal Theory and the Reform of Legal Education in Mid-Nineteenth Century England', in Stein (n. 90), 238; A. Rodger, 'Scottish Advocates in the Nineteenth Century: The German Connection', *Law Quarterly Review* 110 (1994): 563ff.; J. Cairns, 'The Influence of the German Historical School in Early Nineteenth Century Edinburgh', *Syracuse Journal of International Law and Commerce* 20 (1994): 191.
105. See Section 10, this chapter.
106. See Coing (n. 68), 7; R. C. van Caenegem, *European Law in the Past and the Future* (Cambridge, 2002), 22 and 73.
107. In particular, matrimonial causes, probate, and promises affirmed by oath. For an overview, see W. Trusen, 'Die gelehrte Gerichtsbarkeit der Kirche', in *Handbuch der Quellen und Literatur der neueren europäischen Privatrechtsgeschichte*, ed. H. Coing vol. 1 (Munich, 1973), 483. For England, see R. Zimmermann, 'Der europäische Charakter des englischen Rechts: Historische Verbindungen zwischen civil law und common law', *Zeitschrift für europäisches Privatrecht* 1 (1993): 21.
108. Generally, on the influence of Canon law, see P. Landau, 'Der Einfluss des kanonischen Rechts auf die europäische Rechtskultur', in *Europäische Rechts- und Verfassungsgeschichte: Ergebnisse und Perspektiven der Forschung*, ed. R. Schulze (Berlin, 1991), 39; H. Scholler, ed., *Die Bedeutung des kanonischen Rechts für die Entwicklung einheitlicher Rechtsprinzipien* (Baden-Baden, 1996); H.-J. Becker, 'Spuren des kanonischen Rechts im Bürgerlichen Gesetzbuch', in Zimmermann et al. (n. 28), 159ff.
109. See text accompanying note 51, this chapter.
110. See U. Wolter, *Das Prinzip der Naturalrestitution nach § 249 BGB* (Berlin, 1985); N. Jansen, in Schmoeckel et al. (n. 19), §§ 249–253, 255, nn. 17ff.
111. See Coing (n. 68), 27, 352; cf. M. Mitterauer, *Warum Europa? Mittelalterliche Grundlagen eines Sonderwegs* (Munich, 2003), 109.
112. See, esp., J. Gordley, *The Philosophical Origins of Modern Contract Doctrine* (Oxford, 1991); J. Gordley, *Foundations of Private Law* (Oxford, 2006).

113. On the so-called *lex mercatoria* (law merchant), see Coing (n. 68), 519; H.J. Berman, *Law and Revolution: The Formation of the Western Legal Tradition* (Cambridge, Mass., 1983), 348; A. Cordes, 'Auf der Suche nach der Rechtswirklichkeit der mittelalterlichen Lex mercatoria', *ZSS (Germanistische Abteilung)* 118 (2001): 168; K.O. Scherner, 'Lex mercatoria – Realität, Geschichtsbild oder Vision?', *ZSS (Germanistische Abteilung)* 118 (2001): 148; K.O. Scherner, 'Goldschmidts Universum', in *'Ins Wasser geworfen und Ozeane durchquert': Festschrift für Knut Wolfgang Nörr*, ed. M. Ascheri et al. (Cologne – Weimar – Vienna, 2003), 859; and essays in V. Piergiovanni, ed., *From Lex Mercatoria to Commercial Law* (Berlin, 2005). Cf. for England, Zimmermann (n. 107), 29.
114. W. Wiegand, 'Zur Herkunft und Ausbreitung der Formel "habere fundatam intentionem"', in *Festschrift für Hermann Krause*, ed. S. Gagnér, H. Schlosser, and W. Wiegand (Cologne – Vienna, 1975), 126; Coing (n. 68), 132; K. Luig, 'Usus modernus', in *Handwörterbuch zur deutschen Rechtsgeschichte* (Berlin, 1998), vol. 5, cols. 628ff. Apart from that, sources of law that deviated from the *ius commune* had to be narrowly interpreted. See W. Trusen, 'Römisches und partikuläres Recht in der Rezeptionszeit', in *Festschrift für Heinrich Lange*, ed. K. Kuchinke (Munich, 1970), 108; H. Lange, 'Ius Commune und Statutarrecht in Christoph Besolds Consilia Tubigensia' in *Festschrift für Max Kaser*, ed. D. Medicus and H.H. Seiler (Munich, 1976), 646; R. Zimmermann, 'Statuta sunt stricte interpretanda, Statutes and the Common Law: A Continental Perspective', *Cambridge Law Journal* 56 (1997): 315.
115. The conclusion of P. Oestmann, *Rechtsvielfalt vor Gericht: Rechtsanwendung und Partikularrecht im Alten Reich* (Frankfurt, 2002), 681.
116. See, e.g., 'Anlage zur Denkschrift zum BGB', in B. Mugdan, ed., *Die gesammten Materialien zum Bürgerlichen Gesetzbuch für das Deutsche Reich* (Berlin, 1899), vol. 1, 844; and *Deutsche Rechts- und Gerichtskarte* (Kassel, 1896; new edn. by D. Klippel, 1996).
117. Thus, apart from still being directly applicable in parts of Germany, it also provided the underlying theory of private law wherever a codification had been enacted: see Koschaker (n. 102), 292.
118. For further references, see Zimmermann (n. 17), 2.
119. E. Friedberg, *Die künftige Gestaltung des deutschen Rechtsstudiums nach den Beschlüssen der Eisenacher Konferenz* (Leipzig, 1896), 7.
120. See, e.g., Borgolte (n. 100), 242ff.
121. See also, e.g., Berman (n. 113), 10.
122. See the division by P. Glenn, *Legal Traditions of the World*, 4th edn. (Oxford, 2010).
123. In contrast, the chthonic tradition is marked by its orality: see Glenn (n. 122), 64.
124. S. Gagnér, *Studien zur Ideengeschichte der Gesetzgebung* (Stockholm, 1960), 288.
125. H. Coing, 'Das Recht als Element der europäischen Kultur', *Historische Zeitschrift* 238 (1984): 7; F. Wieacker, 'Foundations of European Legal Culture', *American Journal of Comparative Law* 38 (1990): 25; P. Häberle, *Europäische Rechtskultur* (Frankfurt, 1997), 22.
126. Berman (n. 113), 9; Glenn (n. 122), 155.
127. R. von Jhering, *Geist des römischen Rechts auf den verschiedenen Stufen seiner Entwicklung*, 6th edn. (Leipzig, 1907), 14.
128. See Schulz (n. 96).
129. See Koschaker (n. 102), 164. For the Islamic tradition, see Glenn (n. 122), 187.
130. Coing (n. 125), 6; Wieacker (n. 125), 23.

131. Zweigert and Kötz (n. 46), 62.
132. Zweigert and Kötz (n. 46), 174. On the phenomenon of legal reception in Switzerland, see M. Immenhauser, 'Zur Rezeption der deutschen Schuldrechtsreform in der Schweiz', *recht* (2006): 1.
133. Glenn (n. 122), 133.
134. For the different meanings of the term 'civil law', see R. Zimmermann, in Carey Miller and Zimmermann (n. 3), 262.
135. For an overview, see Zweigert and Kötz (n. 46), 154; Z. Kühn, 'Comparative Law in Central and Eastern Europe', in Reimann and Zimmermann (n. 5), 215.
136. See, e.g., F. Mádl (then President of the Republic of Hungary), in *Aufbruch nach Europa*, ed. J. Basedow et al. (Tübingen, 2001), vii.
137. L. Vékás, 'Integration des östlichen Mitteleuropa im Wege rechtsvergleichender Zivilrechtserneuerung', *Zeitschrift für europäisches Privatrecht* 12 (2004): 454.
138. See, esp., M. Avenarius, *Rezeption des römischen Rechts in Rußland – Dmitrij Mejer, Nikolaj Djuvernua und Iosif Pokrovskij* (Göttingen, 2004); M. Avenarius 'Das russische Seminar für römisches Recht in Berlin (1887–1896)', *Zeitschrift für europäisches Privatrecht* 6 (1998): 893; M. Avenarius, 'Das pandektistische Rechtsstudium in St. Petersburg in den letzten Jahrzehnten der Zarenherrschaft', in *Deutsches Sachenrecht in polnischer Gerichtspraxis*, ed. W. Dajczak and H.-G. Knothe (Berlin, 2005), 51.
139. H. Schlosser, *Grundzüge der Neueren Privatrechtsgeschichte*, 10th edn. (Heidelberg, 2005), 214, who points out that this reception was neither extraordinary nor completely surprising. But cf. Zweigert and Kötz (n. 46), 175.
140. Zweigert and Kötz (n. 46), 271.
141. J. H. Baker, *An Introduction to English Legal History*, 3rd edn. (London, 1990), 35; in the 4th edn. (2002), the word 'noble' has been deleted.
142. See, e.g., K. Schurig, 'Europäisches Zivilrecht: Vielfalt oder Einerlei?', in *Festschrift für Bernhard Großfeld*, ed. U. Hüber und W. F. Ebke (Heidelberg, 1999), 1102; E. Bucher, 'Rechtsüberlieferung und heutiges Recht', *Zeitschrift für europäisches Privatrecht* 8 (2000): 409. Particularly pointedly, see P. Legrand, 'Legal Traditions in Western Europe: The Limits of Commonality', in *Transfrontier Mobility of Law*, ed. R. Jagtenberg, E. Örücü, and A. de Roo (The Hague, 1995), 63; P. Legrand, 'European Legal Systems are Not Converging', *International and Comparative Law Quarterly* 45 (1996): 52. Legrand refers to an unbridgeable epistemological chasm.
143. For what follows, see the essays in Stein (n. 90), 151, and Zimmermann (n. 107), 4. Also of interest in this context is the 'inner relationship' of (classical) Roman and English law: see F. Pringsheim, 'The Inner Relationship between English and Roman Law', *Cambridge Law Journal* 5 (1935): 347; P. Stein, 'Roman Law, Common Law, and Civil Law', *Tulane Law Review* 66 (1992): 1591; P. Stein, 'Logic and Experience in Roman and Common Law', in Stein (n. 90), 37.
144. R. C. van Caenegem, *The Birth of the English Common Law*, 2nd edn. (Cambridge, 1988).
145. R. H. Helmholz, *Canon Law and the Law of England* (London, 1987); R. H. Helmholz, *Roman Canon Law in Reformation England* (Cambridge, 1990); J. Martinez-Torrón, *Anglo-American Law and Canon Law: Canonical Roots of the Common Law Tradition* (Berlin, 1998).
146. On the civilian tradition in Scotland, see the references in nn. 3 and 4 above.
147. See, in particular, A. W. B. Simpson, 'Innovation in Nineteenth Century Contract Law', *Law Quarterly Review* 91 (1975): 247; Gordley (n. 112), 134; cf. D. Ibbetson, *A Historical Introduction to the Law of Obligations* (Oxford, 1999).

148. *Krell v Henry* [1903] 2 KB 740, 747 (CA).
149. See H. Dilcher, *Die Theorie der Leistungsstörungen bei Glossatoren, Kommentatoren und Kanonisten* (Frankfurt, 1960), 185.
150. *Taylor v Caldwell* (1863) 3 B & S 826; see, e.g., M. Rheinstein, *Die Struktur des vertraglichen Schuldverhältnisses im anglo-amerikanischen Recht* (Berlin – Leipzig, 1932), 173; G.H. Treitel, *Unmöglichkeit, 'Impracticability' and 'Frustration' im anglo-amerikanischen Recht* (Baden-Baden, 1991); M. Schmidt-Kessel, *Standards vertraglicher Haftung nach englischem Recht: Limits of Frustration* (Baden-Baden, 2003), 45.
151. See R. Zimmermann, '"Heard melodies are sweet, but those unheard are sweeter ... ": Conditio tacita, implied condition und die Fortbildung des europäischen Vertragsrechts', *Archiv für die civilistische Praxis* 193 (1993): 121. On implied terms in modern English contract law, see M. Schmidt-Kessel, 'Implied Term – auf der Suche nach dem Funktionsäquivalent', *Zeitschrift für vergleichende Rechtswissenschaft* 96 (1997): 101; W. Grobecker, *Implied Terms und Treu und Glauben: Vertragsergänzung im englischen Recht in rechtsvergleichender Perspektive* (Berlin, 1999).
152. See Zimmermann (n. 151), 134.
153. Berman (n. 113), 18.
154. R. H. Helmholz, 'Magna Carta and the *ius commune*', *University of Chicago Law Review* 66 (1999): 297, 371.
155. See, in particular, Berman (n. 113); Glenn (n. 122), 176. See also the studies by R. H. Helmholz, *The ius commune in England: Four Studies* (Oxford, 2001).
156. B. S. Markesinis, ed., *The Gradual Convergence: Foreign Ideas, Foreign Influences and English Law on the Eve of the 21st Century* (Oxford, 1994). Cf. R. C. van Caenegem, 'The Unification of European Law: a pipedream?' *European Review* 14 (2006): 33.
157. J. Gordley, 'Common law und civil law: eine überholte Unterscheidung', *Zeitschrift für europäisches Privatrecht* 1 (1993): 498.
158. S. Vogenauer, *Die Auslegung von Gesetzen in England und auf dem Kontinent*, 2 vols. (Tübingen, 2001) concludes that historically English law can be described as a province of the *ius commune* so far as statutory interpretation is concerned. A fundamental uniformity of approach in statutory interpretation can still be observed today: see Vogenauer, 1293; and S. Vogenauer, 'Zur Geschichte des Präjudizienrechts in England', *Zeitschrift für neuere Rechtsgeschichte* 28 (2006): 48. On the role of legal doctrine, see R. Goff, 'The Search for Principle', repr. in *The Search for Principle: Essays in Honour of Lord Goff of Chieveley*, ed. W. Swadling and G. Jones (New York, 1999), 313.
159. There was also some direct influence from civilian legal sources: P. Stein, 'The Attraction of the Civil Law in Post-Revolutionary America', in Stein (n. 90), 411; M. Reimann, *Historische Schule und Common Law* (Berlin, 1993); R. H. Helmholz, 'Use of the Civil Law in Post-Revolutionary American Jurisprudence', *Tulane Law Review* 66 (1992): 1649; M. H. Hoeflich, *Roman and Civil Law and the Development of Anglo-American Jurisprudence in the Nineteenth Century* (Athens, Georgia, 1997); M. H. Hoeflich, 'Translation and the Reception of Foreign Law in the Antebellum United States', *American Journal of Comparative Law* 50 (2002): 753.
160. E. Bucher, 'Zu Europa gehört auch Lateinamerika!' *Zeitschrift für europäisches Privatrecht* 12 (2004): 515; J. Kleinheisterkamp, 'Development of Comparative Law in Latin America', in Reimann and Zimmermann (n. 5), 261; J. Schmidt, *Zivilrechtskodifikation in Brasilien* (Tübingen, 2009), esp. chs. 1 and 7.
161. Z. Kitagawa, *Rezeption und Fortbildung des europäischen Zivilrechts in Japan* (Frankfurt – Berlin, 1970); Z. Kitagawa, 'Development of Comparative Law in East Asia', in

Reimann and Zimmermann (n. 5), 237; M. Rehbinder, Ju-Chan Sonn, eds., *Zur Rezeption des deutschen Rechts in Korea* (Baden-Baden, 1990).

162. M. McAuley, 'Québec', in *Mixed Jurisdictions Worldwide*, ed. V. V. Palmer, 2nd edn. (Cambridge, 2012), 329.

163. This chapter, n. 1.

164. Jhering (n. 127), 2.

165. This chapter, n. 104.

166. Partly, at least, as a result of the emigration of German Romanists during the Nazi regime: see P. Birks, 'Roman Law in Twentieth-Century Britain', and R. Zimmermann, 'Was Heimat hieß, nun heißt es Hölle', in *Jurists Uprooted: German-speaking Émigré Lawyers in Twentieth-century Britain*, ed. J. Beatson and R. Zimmermann (Oxford, 2004), 249 and 46 respectively.

167. For what follows, see Zimmermann (n. 17), 22; M. Rainer, 'Dieter Nörr e la romanistica tedesca', in *Dieter Nörr e la romanistica europea tra xx e xxi secolo*, ed. E. Stolfi (Turin, 2006), 7ff.

168. On Mitteis and the Mitteis school, see R. Zimmermann, ' "In der Schule von Ludwig Mitteis": Ernst Rabels rechtshistorische Ursprünge', *Rabels Zeitschrift* 65 (2001): 1.

169. On the challenges for Roman law scholarship today, see L. Capogrossi Colognesi and R. Knütel in Stolfi (n. 167), 77, 133.

170. E. I. Bekker, *Die Aktionen des römischen Privatrechts*, vol. 1 (Berlin, 1871), 2.

171. Zimmermann (n. 25), 14.

172. See also, for England, Birks (n. 166), 249, 260; for the Netherlands, see W. Zwalve, 'Teaching Roman Law in the Netherlands', *Zeitschrift für europäisches Privatrecht* 5 (1997): 393.

173. Zimmermann (n. 17), 44; Zwalve (n. 172).

174. R. Zimmermann, 'Comparative Law and the Europeanization of Private Law', in Reimann and Zimmermann (n. 5), 539; R. Zimmermann, 'Ius Commune and the Principles of European Contract Law: Contemporary Renewal of an Old Idea', in *European Contract Law*, ed. H. L. MacQueen and R. Zimmermann (Edinburgh, 2006), 1; R. Zimmermann, 'The Present State of European Private Law', *American Journal of Comparative Law* 57 (2009): 479.

Bibliography

I. Principal Roman Sources

This section lists only the principal sources of Roman law in their main modern editions, together with translations into English (if any).

Gaius, Institutes

(a) Editions

Gai Institutiones. Edited by E. Seckel and B. Kübler, Stuttgart, 1935.

Gai Institutiones. Editio minor. Edited by M. David. Leiden, 1948.

Gai Institutiones. Editio maior. Includes commentary. Books I and II, edited by M. David and H. L. W. Nelson; Leiden, 1954–68; Book III, edited by H. L. W. Nelson and U. Manthe; Berlin, 1992–2007; Book IV has yet to appear.

(b) Translations

Zulueta, F. de, editor. *The Institutes of Gaius*. Includes commentary. 2 vols. Oxford, 1946–53.

Gordon, W. M. and O. F. Robinson, editors. *The Institutes of Gaius*. London, 1988.

Codex Theodosianus

(a) Edition

Codex Theodosianus. Edited by T. Mommsen and P. Meyer. Berlin, 1962.

(b) Translation

Pharr, C. *The Theodosian Code and Novels and the Sirmondian Constitutions*. Princeton, 1952.

Corpus iuris civilis

(a) Editions

Corpus iuris civilis. Volume 1: *Institutiones*. Edited by P. Krueger; *Digesta. Editio minor*, edited by T. Mommsen and P. Krueger. Berlin, 1954.

Corpus iuris civilis. Volume 2: *Codex Iustinianus*. Edited by P. Krueger. Berlin, 1954.

Corpus iuris civilis. Volume 3: *Novellae*. Edited by R. Schoell and G. Kroll. Berlin, 1954.

Digesta. Editio maior. 2 vols. Edited by T. Mommsen. Berlin, 1868–70.

Codex Iustinianus. Editio maior. Edited by P. Krueger. Berlin, 1877.

(b) Translations

Thomas, J. A. C., editor. *The Institutes of Justinian.* Amsterdam, 1975.

Birks, P. and G. McLeod, editors. *Justinian's Institutes.* London, 1987.

Watson, A., editor. *The Digest of Justinian.* 4 vols. Philadelphia, 1985 (including the text of Mommsen's *editio maior*); 2 vols. Philadephia, 1997 (English translation only).

Basílica

Basilicorum libri LX. Series A: *Textus.* 8 volumes. Series B: *Scholia.* 9 volumes. Edited by H.J. Scheltema, D. Holwerda, and N. van der Wal. Groningen – The Hague, 1953–88.

II. Early Modern Authors

Accursius, *Volumen.* Lyon,1558.

Accursius, *Codicis Iustiniani ex repetita praelectione libri novem priores.* Lyon, 1560.

Accursius, *Digestum vetus. Pandectarum iuris civilis tomus primus.* Lyon, 1560.

Azo, *Azonis lectura super codicem. Hugolini apparatus in tres libros.* Corpus Glossatorum Juris Civilis III. Turin,1966.

Azo, *Azonis summa super codicem. Instituta. Extraordinaria.* Corpus Glossatorum Juris Civilis II. Turin, 1966.

Baldus de Ubaldis, *Baldi Ubaldi Perusini ... Consiliorum, sive responsorum volumen primum.* Venice, 1575.

Bartolus de Sassoferrato, *Bartoli a Sassoferrato in primam partem codicis commentaria.* Turin, 1574.

Bartolus de Sassoferrato, *Bartoli a Sassoferrato in secundam digesti novi partem commentaria.* Turin, 1574.

Bartolus de Sassoferrato, *De Guelphis et Gebellinis, De regimine civitatis* in Quaglioni, D., editor, *Politica e diritto nel trecento italiano.* Florence, 1983.

Iacobus de Arena, *Commentarii in universum ius civile.* Opera iuridica rariora XVI. Bologna, 1971.

Iacobus de Ravanis, *Lectura super codice.* Opera iuridica rariora I. Bologna, 1967.

Iohannes de Blanosco, *De actionibus tractatus clarissimorum ... iurisconsultorum* II. Lyon, 1596.

Marinus de Caramanico, *Proemium glossatoris in constitutiones regni Siciliae* in F. Calasso, I glossatori e la teoria della sovranità. 3rd edn. Milan, 1957, 179–205.

Odofredus de Denariis, *Lectura super digesto veteri.* Opera iuridica rariora II 1. Bologna, 1967.

Paulus Castrensis, *Pauli de Castro prima super digesto veteri.* Lyon, 1538.

Paulus Castrensis, *Consiliorum sive responsorum ... Pauli Castrensis volumen secundum.* Turin, 1580.

Placentinus, *Placentini summa codicis.* Turin, 1962.

Raynerius de Forlivio, *Repetitionum seu commentariorum in varia iurisconsultorum responsa volumen primum,* 63va–72ra. Lyon, 1553.

III. General Bibliography

Acher, J. 'Notes sur le droit savant au moyen âge'. *Nouvelle Revue Historique de Droit Français et Étranger* 30 (1906): 125–78.

Adams, J. N. *Bilingualism and the Latin Language.* Cambridge, 2003.

Adams, M. M. 'Universals in the early fourteenth century'. In *The Cambridge History of Later Medieval Philosophy*, edited by Norman Kretzmann, Anthony Kenny, and Jan Pinborg, 411–39. Cambridge, 1982.

Ahsmann, M. *Collegium und Kolleg: der juristische Unterricht an der Universität Leiden 1575–1630 unter besonderer Berücksichtigung der Disputationen*. Frankfurt, 2000.

Albanese, B. 'La nozione del 'furtum' nell'elaborazione dei giuristi romani'. *Jus* 5 (1958) 315–26.

Albanese, B. 'Sulla responsabilità del *dominus sciens* per i delitti del servo'. *BIDR* 70 (1967): 119–86.

Albanese, B. *Scritti Giuridici*, vol. 1. Palermo, 1991.

Albertario, E. 'Di alcuni riferimenti al matrimonio e al possesso in Sant'Agostino'. *Rivista di Filosofia Neo-scolastica*. Supplement to vol. 23 (1931): 367–76.

Alföldy, G. *Fasti Hispanienses*. Wiesbaden, 1969.

Allison, J. E. and J. D. Cloud, 'The *lex Iulia Maiestatis*'. *Latomus* 21 (1962): 711–31.

Amelotti, M. *Il testamento romano*. Florence, 1966.

Amelotti, M. *Le costituzioni giustinianee nei papiri e nelle epigrafi*, 2nd edn. Milan, 1985.

Ando, C. *The Matter of the Gods: Religion and the Roman Empire*. Berkeley, 2008.

Andreau, J. *La vie financière dans le monde romain. Les métiers de manieurs d'argent (IVe siècle av. J.-C.–IIIe siècle ap. J.-C.)*. Rome, 1987.

Andreau, J. *Banking and Business in the Roman World*. Cambridge, 1999.

Andreau, J. 'Registers, Account-Books, and Written Documents in the *de Frumento*'. In Sicilia nutrix plebis Romanae. *Rhetoric, Law, and Taxation in Cicero's Verrines*, edited by J. R. W. Prag, 81–92. London, 2007.

Angelini, P. 'The Code of Dušan 1349–1354'. *TR* 80 (2012): 77–93.

Ankum, J. A. Review of M. Kaser, *Das römische Privatrecht*, 2nd edn. by Max Kaser. *Nederlands Juristenblad* 1972, 138.

Ankum, J. A. 'Stenen voor brood'. *Ars Aequi* 42 (1993): 459–63.

Ankum, J. A. 'Römisches Recht im neuen niederländischen Bürgerlichen Gesetzbuch'. In *Rechtsgeschichte und Privatrechtsdogmatik*, edited by R. Zimmermann, R. Knütel, and J. P. Meincke, 101–15. Heidelberg, 1999.

Ankum, J. A. 'Some aspects of maritime loans in old-Greek and in Roman law'. In *Mélanges I. Triantaphyllopoulos*, edited by I. Velissaropoulou-Karakosta, 293–306. Komotini, 2000.

Ankum, J. A. and E. Pool. '*Rem in bonis meis esse and rem in bonis meam esse*: Traces of the Development of Roman Double Ownership'. In *New Perspectives in the Roman Law of Property*, edited by P. Birks, 5–42. Oxford, 1989.

Arangio-Ruiz, V. *Cours de droit romain: les actions*. Naples, 1935.

Arangio-Ruiz, V. 'Il processo di Iusta'. *La Parola del Passato* 3 (1948): 129–51.

Arangio-Ruiz, V. 'Nuove osservazioni sul processo di Giusta'. *La Parola del Passato* (1951): 116–23.

Arangio-Ruiz, V. 'Nuovi aspetti del processo romano in un 'fascicolo' ercolanense'. In *Atti del Congresso Internazionale del Diritto Processuale Civile* (1953), 166–204.

Arangio-Ruiz, V. 'Testi e documenti'. *BIDR* 61 (1958): 293–310.

Arangio-Ruiz, V. 'Lo "status" di Venidio Ennico ercolanense'. In *Droits de l'antiquité et sociologie juridique. Mélanges Lévy-Bruhl*, 9–24. Paris, 1959.

Arangio-Ruiz, V. and G. Pugliese Carratelli. 'Tabulae Herculanenses'. *La Parola del Passato* 1 (1946): 379–85; 3 (1948): 165–84; 8 (1953): 455–63; 9 (1954): 54–74; 10 (1955): 448–77; 16 (1961): 66–73.

Archi, G. G. 'L'aspetto funzionale del "dominium" romano'. *BIDR* 61 (1958): 61–79.

Archi, G. G. 'Il concetto della proprietà nei diritti del mondo antico'. *RIDA* 6 (1959): 229–49.

Ariño, B. Díaz, *Epigrafía Latina Republicana de España*. Barcelona, 2008.

Arjava, A. *Women and Law in Late Antiquity*. Oxford, 1998.

Armstrong, L. and J. Kirshner, *The Politics of Law in Late Medieval and Renaissance Italy. Essays in Honor of Lauro Martines*. Toronto, 2011.

Atzeri, L. *Gesta senatus Romani de Theodosiano publicando. Il Codice Teodosiano e la sua diffusione ufficiale in Occidente*. Berlin, 2008.

Aubert, J.-J. 'Workshop managers'. In *The Inscribed Economy. Production and Distribution in the Roman Empire in the Light of* instrumentum domesticum, edited by W. V. Harris, 171–89. Ann Arbor, 1993.

Aubert, J.-J. *Business Managers in Ancient Rome. A Social and Economic Study of Institores, 200 BC–AD 250*. Leiden – New York – Cologne, 1994.

Aubert, J.-J. 'La gestion des *collegia*: aspects juridiques, économiques et sociaux'. *CCG* 10 (1999): 49–69.

Aubert, J.-J. 'Les *institores* et le commerce maritime dans l'empire romain'. *Topoi* 9 (1999): 145–64.

Aubert, J.-J. 'En guise d'introduction: contrats publics et cahiers des charges'. In *Tâches publiques et entreprise privée*, edited by J.-J. Aubert, 1–25. Neuchâtel – Geneva, 2003.

Aubert, J.-J. 'The republican economy and Roman law: regulation, promotion, or reflection?'. In *The Cambridge Companion to the Roman Republic*, edited by H. I. Flower, 160–78. Cambridge, 2004.

Aubert, J.-J. 'Corpse disposal in the Roman colony of Puteoli: public concern and private enterprise'. In *Noctes Campanae. Studi di storia antica ed archeologia dell'Italia preromana e romana in memoria di Martin W. Frederiksen*, edited by W. V. Harris and E. Lo Cascio, 141–57. Naples, 2005.

Aubert, J.-J. 'L'estampillage des briques et des tuiles: une explication juridique fondée sur une approche globale'. In *Interpretare i bolli laterizi di Roma e della Valle del Tevere: Produzione, storia economica e topografia*, edited by C. Bruun, 53–59. Rome, 2005.

Aubert, J.-J. 'Dealing with the abyss: the nature and purpose of the Rhodian sea-law on jettison (*Lex Rhodia de iactu*, D 14.2) and the making of Justinian's *Digest*'. In *Beyond Dogmatics. Law and Society in the Roman World*, edited by J. W. Cairns and P. du Plessis, 157–72. Edinburgh, 2007.

Aubert, J.-J. 'L'économie romaine et le droit de la représentation indirecte sous la République romaine'. In *Fides, Humanitas, Ius. Studii in onore di Luigi Labruna*, edited by C. Cascione and C. Masi Doria, 215–30. Naples, 2007.

Aubert, J.-J. 'Productive investment in agriculture: *instrumentum fundi* and *peculium* in the later Roman Republic'. In *Agricoltura e scambi*, edited by J. Carlsen and E. Lo Cascio. Bari, 2009.

Aubert, J.-J. 'Productive investment in agriculture: *instrumentum fundi* and *peculium* in the later Roman Republic'. In *Agricoltura e scambi nell'Italia tardo-repubblicana*, edited by J. Carlsen and E. Lo Cascio, 167–85. Bari, 2010.

Aubert, J.-J. 'Vitia animi: tares mentales, psychologiques, caractérielles et intellectuelles des esclaves en droit romain'. In *I diritti degli altri in Grecia e a Roma*, edited by A. Maffi and L. Gagliardi, 236–48. Sankt Augustin, 2011.

Aubert, J.-J. '*Dumtaxat de peculio*: what's in a *peculium* or the extent of the principal's liability'. In *New Frontiers: Law and Society in the Roman World*, edited by P. du Plessis, 192–206. Edinburgh, 2013.

Aubert, J.-J. and G. Raepsaet, 'Un mandat inscrit sur une sigillée argonnaise à Liberchies-Geminiacum'. In *L'Antiquité classique* 80 (2011): 139–56.

Aucouturier, V. *Qu'est-ce que l'intentionalité?* Paris, 2012.

Ausbüttel, F. M. *Die Verwaltung der Städte und Provinzen im spätantiken Italien*. Frankfurt – Bern – New York – Paris, 1988.

Avenarius, M. 'Das russische Seminar für römisches Recht in Berlin (1887–1896)'. *Zeitschrift für europäisches Privatrecht* 6 (1998): 893–908.

Avenarius, M. *Rezeption des römischen Rechts in Rußland – Dmitrij Mejer, Nikolaj Djuvernua und Iosif Pokrovskij*. Göttingen, 2004.

Avenarius, M. 'Das pandektistische Rechtsstudium in St. Petersburg in den letzten Jahrzehnten der Zarenherrschaft'. In *Deutsches Sachenrecht in polnischer Gerichtspraxis*, edited by W. Dajczak and H.-G. Knothe, 51–75. Berlin, 2005.

Bablitz, L. *Actors and Audience in the Roman Courtroom*. New York, 2007.

Babusiaux, U. *Papinians Quaestiones. Zur rhetorischen Methode eines spätklassischen Juristen*. Munich, 2011.

Bader, K. S. 'Beseler, Gerhard Friedrich von'. In *Neue Deutsche Biographie*, vol. 2, 175. 1955. URL: http://www.deutsche-biographie.de/pnd116154012.html.

Badoud, N. *La lex Rhodia de iactu*. Forthcoming.

Bagnall, R. W. 'Monks and property: rhetoric, law, and patronage in the Apophthegmata Patrum and the papyri'. *Greek, Roman and Byzantine Studies* 42 (2001): 7–24.

Baker, J. H. *An Introduction to English Legal History*, 4th edn. London, 2002.

Bardenhewer, O. *Geschichte der altkirchlichen Literatur*. Freiburg, 1902–1932, reissued 2007.

Barone-Adesi, G. *Ricerche sui Corpora Normativi dell' Impero Romano*, vol. 1. Turin, 1998.

Barnes, T. D. *Constantine and Eusebius*. Cambridge, Mass., 1981.

Barnes, T. D. *Early Christian Historiography and Roman History*. Tübingen, 2010.

Bartoletti Colombi, A. M. *Novellae, pars Latina. (Legum Iustiniani imperatoris vocabularium.)* 10 vols. Milan, 1977–79.

Bartoletti Colombi, A. M. *Novellae, pars Graeca. (Legum Iustiniani imperatoris vocabularium.)* 7 vols. Milan, 1984–89.

Barton, J. 'Roman Law in England'. *Ius Romanum Medii Aevi* part V.13a. Milan,1971.

Bassano, M. '*Dominus domini mei dixit*'. *Enseignement du droit et construction d'une identité autour des juristes et de la science juridique au studium d'Orléans (1230–1320)*. (Thesis, University of Paris II, 2008), Leiden, 2013.

Bauer, M. *Periculum Emptoris: Eine dogmengeschichtliche Untersuchung zur Gefahrtragung beim Kauf*. Berlin, 1998.

Bauman, R. *Lawyers and Politics in the Early Roman Empire*. Munich, 1989.

Beaucamp, J. 'L'histoire du droit byzantin face à la papyrologie juridique. Bilan et perspectives'. *Fontes Minores* 11 (2005): 5–55.

Beck, A. 'Römisches Recht in unserer Rechtsordnung'. In *Horizonte der Humanitas: Freundesgabe Walter Wili*, edited by G. Luck, 120–33. Bern – Stuttgart, 1960.

Beck, A. *Römisches Recht bei Tertullian und Cyprian. Eine Studie zur frühen Kirchenrechtgeschichte*, 2nd edn. Aalen, 1967.

Becker, H.-J. 'Spuren des kanonischen Rechts im Bürgerlichen Gesetzbuch'. In *Rechtsgeschichte und Privatrechtsdogmatik*, edited by R. Zimmermann, R. Knütel, and J. P. Meincke, 159–69. Heidelberg, 1999.

Behrends, O. *Die römische Geschworenenverfassung*. Göttingen, 1970.

Behrends, O. *Institut und Prinzip. Siedlungsgeschichtliche Grundlagen, philosophische Einflüsse und das Fortwirken der beiden republikanischen Konzeptionen in den kaiserzeitlichen*

Rechtsschulen. Ausgewählte Aufsätze, edited by M. Avenarius, R. Meyer-Pritzl, and C. Möller, 2 vols. Göttingen, 2004.

Bekker, E. I. *Die Aktionen des römischen Privatrechts*, vol. 1. Berlin, 1871.

Bellomo, M. 'Federico II, lo "Studium" a Napoli e il diritto comune nel "Regnum"'. *Rivista internazionale di diritto comune* 2 (1991): 135–15.

Bellomo, M. *The Common Legal Past of Europe 1000–1800*, translated by L. Cochrane. Washington, D.C., 1995.

Bellomo, M. *I fatti e il diritto. Tra le certezze e i dubbi dei giuristi medievali (secoli XIII–XIV)*. Rome, 2000.

Bellomo, M. *Quaestiones in iure civili disputatae. Didattici e prassi colta nel sistema del diritto comune fra duecento e trecento*. Rome, 2008.

Beltrán Lloris, F. 'An irrigation decree from Roman Spain: *the Lex rivi hiberiensis*'. *JRS* 96 (2006): 147–97.

Benda-Beckmann vón, F. and K. von Benda-Beckmann. 'The dynamics of change and continuity in plural legal orders'. *Journal of Legal Pluralism and Unofficial law* 53–54 (2006): 1–44.

Benöhr, H.-P. 'Die Entscheidung des BGB für das Verschuldensprinzip'. *TR* 46 (1978): 1–31.

Bergh, G. C. J. J. van den. *The Life and Work of Gerard Noodt, 1647–1725: Dutch Legal Scholarship between Humanism and Enlightenment*. Oxford, 1988.

Bergh, G. C. J. J. van den. *Die hollandische elegante Schule: ein Beitrag zur Geschichte von Humanismus und Rechtswissenschaft in den Niederlanden 1500–1800*. Frankfurt, 2002.

Berkowitz, B. A. *Execution and Invention: Death Penalty Discourse in Early Rabbinic and Christian Cultures*. Oxford, 2006.

Berman, H. J. *Law and Revolution: The Formation of the Western Legal Tradition*. Cambridge, Mass., 1983.

Bertoldi, F. *La lex Iulia iudiciorum privatorum*. Turin, 2003.

Bertrand-Dagenbach, C., A. Chauvot, M. Matter, and J.-M. Salamito, editors. *Carcer. Prison et Privation de Liberté dans l'antiquité classique: Actes du colloque de Strasbourg (5 et 6 décembre 1997)*. Paris, 1999.

Bezemer, K. *What Jacques Saw: Thirteenth Century France through the Eyes of Jacques de Révigny Professor of Law at Orléans*. Frankfurt, 1997.

Bezemer, K. *Pierre de Belleperche: Portrait of a Legal Puritan*. Frankfurt, 2005.

Bianchi, P. *Iura-Leges. Un'Apparente Questione Terminologica della Tarda Antichità. Storiografia e Storia*. Milan, 2007.

Bianchini, M. 'Diritto commerciale nel diritto romano'. In *Digesto delle Discipline privatistiche. Sezione commerciale IV*, 320–33. Torino, 1989.

Bianchini, M. 'Attività commerciali fra privato e pubblico in età imperiale'. In *Fides, Humanitas, Ius. Studii in onore di Luigi Labruna*, edited by C. Cascione and C. Masi Doria, 423–38. Naples, 2007.

Biener, F. *Geschichte der Novellen Justinians*. Berlin, 1824, reprinted 1970.

Biondi, B. *Il Diritto Romano Cristiano*, 3 vols. Milan, 1952–54.

Birks, P. 'From *Legis Actio* to *Formula*'. *The Irish Jurist* (n.s.) 4 (1969): 356–67.

Birks, P. 'A Note on the Development of Furtum'. *Irish Jurist* 8 (1973): 349–55.

Birks, P. 'New light on the Roman legal system: the appointment of judges'. *Cambridge Law Journal* 47 (1988): 36–60.

Birks, P. 'Definition and division: a meditation on institutes 3.13'. In *The Classification of Obligations*, edited by P. Birks, 1–35. Oxford, 1997.

Birks, P. 'Roman law in twentieth-century Britain'. In *Jurists Uprooted: German-speaking Émigré Lawyers in Twentieth-century Britain*, edited by J. Beatson and R. Zimmermann, 249–68. Oxford, 2004.

Birks, P., A. Rodger, and J. S. Richardson. 'Further aspects of the *Tabula Contrebiensis*'. *JRS* 74 (1984): 45–73.

Biscardi, A. Actio pecuniae traiecticiae. *Contributo alla dottrina delle clausole penali*, 2nd edn. Turin, 1974.

Blaas, P. B. M., *Henk Hoetink 1900–1963, een intellectuele bibliografie*. Hilversum, 2010.

Black, J. *Absolutism in Renaissance Milan. Plenitude of Power under the Visconti and the Sforza 1329–1535*. Oxford, 2009.

Bleicken, J. 'Ursprung und Bedeutung des Provokationsrechtes'. *ZSS* 76 (1959): 324–77.

Bleicken, J. *Senatsgericht und Kaisergericht*. Göttingen, 1962.

Bleicken, J. *Verfassungs- und Sozialgeschichte des Römischen Kaiserreiches*, 3rd edn. 2 vols. Paderborn – Munich – Vienna – Zurich, 1989–1994.

Böcking, E. *Gai Institutionum Commentarii Quattuor*. Leipzig, 1855.

Borgolte, M. *Europa entdeckt seine Vielfalt 1050–1250*. Stuttgart, 2002.

Borkowski, A. and P. du Plessis. *Textbook on Roman Law*, 3rd edn. Oxford, 2005.

Bowman, A. K., R. S. O. Tomlin, and K. A. Worp, '*Emptio Bovis Frisica*: the "Frisian Ox Sale" Reconsidered'. *JRS* 99 (2009) 156–70.

Boyer, L. 'La fonction sociale des legs d'après la jurisprudence classique'. *RHD* 43 (1965) 333–408.

Brandis, C. 'Dacia'. In *RE IV* (1901), cols. 1973–74.

Brennan, T. C. *The Praetorship in the Roman Republic*. Oxford, 2000.

Briguglio, F. *Gai codex rescriptus in Bibliotheca Capitulari Ecclesiae Cathedralis Veronensis*. Florence, 2012.

Briguglio, F. *Il Codice Veronese in trasparenza. Genesi e formazione del testo delle Istituzioni di Gaio*. Bologna, 2012.

Browning, R. *Medieval and Modern Greek*, 2nd edn. Cambridge, 1983.

Brundage, J. A. *The Medieval Origins of the Legal Profession*. Chicago, 2008.

Bruno Siola, R. B., S. Giglio, and S. Lazzarini, editors. *Auctores latini e graeci tardae aetatis (saec. IV–VI a.D) quorum scripta ad propositum opus utilia videntur*. Milan, 1985; 2nd revd. edn. by G. M. Facchetti, 2000.

Brunt, P. A. 'Procuratorial jurisdiction'. In P. A. Brunt, *Roman Imperial Themes*, 163–87. Oxford, 1990.

Bucher, E. 'Rechtsüberlieferung und heutiges Recht'. *Zeitschrift für europäisches Privatrecht* 8 (2000): 394–543.

Bucher, E. 'Zu Europa gehört auch Lateinamerika!' *Zeitschrift für europäisches Privatrecht* 12 (2004): 515–47.

Buckland, W. W. *The Roman Law of Slavery*. Cambridge, 1908.

Buckland, W. W. *A Text-Book of Roman Law*, 3rd edn. revd. by P. Stein. Cambridge, 1963.

Büll, R. and E. Moser, 'Wachs'. In *RE* Suppl. 13 (1973), cols. 1366–72.

Bugnyon, P. *Tractatus legum abrogatarum et inusitatarum in omnibus curiis, terris, jurisdictionibus, et dominiis regni Franciae* (1563).

Bund, E. 'Otto Lenel'. In: *Deutsche Biographie*, vol. 14, 204–5. Munich, 1985.

Bürge, A. *Das französische Privatrecht im 19. Jahrhundert: Zwischen Tradition und Pandektenwissenschaft, Liberalismus und Etatismus*, 2nd edn. Frankfurt, 1995.

Bürge, A. 'Zum Edikt *De edendo*'. *ZSS* 112 (1995): 1–50.

Bürge, A. 'Ausstrahlungen der historischen Rechtsschule in Frankreich'. *Zeitschrift für europäisches Privatrecht* 5 (1997): 643–53.

Bürge, A. 'Der Text als Problem des Kontextes'. *ZSS* 115 (1998): 150–60.

Bürge, A. *Römisches Privatrecht*. Darmstadt, 1999.

Bürge, A. 'Das römische Recht als Grundlage für das Zivilrecht im künftigen Europa'. In *Die Europäisierung der Rechtswissenschaft*, edited by F. Ranieri, 19–40. Baden-Baden, 2002.

Bürge, A. 'Der Arrêt Boudier von 1892 vor dem Hintergrund der Entwicklung des französischen Bereicherungsrechts im 19. Jahrhundert'. In *Festschrift für Hans Jürgen Sonnenberger*, edited by M. Coester, D. Martiny, and K. A. Prinz von Sachsen-Gessaphe, 3–21. Munich, 2004.

Burgmann, L., editor. *Ecloga. Das Gesetzbuch Leons III. und Konstantinos' V.* Frankfurt, 1983.

Burgmann, L. 'Ansinnen an byzantinische Rechtshistoriker. II: "Do we need a new history of Byzantine law"?' *Rechtshistorisches Journal* 10 (1991): 198–200.

Burgmann, L. 'Lexeis rhomaïkai. Lateinische Wörter in byzantinischen Rechtstexten'. In *Lexicographica byzantina*, edited by W. Hörandner and E. Trapp, 61–79. Vienna, 1991.

Burgmann, L. 'Reformation oder Restauration? Zum Ehegüterrecht der Ecloga'. In *Eherecht und Familiengut in Antike und Mittelalter*, edited by D. Simon, 29–42. Munich, 1992.

Burgmann, L., M. T. Fögen, A. Schminck, and D. Simon. *Repertorium der Handschriften des byzantinischen Rechts. Teil 1: Die Handschriften des weltlichen Rechts (Nr. 1 327)*. Frankfurt, 1995.

Burgmann, L. and H. Kaufhold. *Bibliographie zur Rezeption des byzantinischen Rechts im alten Rußland sowie zur Geschichte des armenischen und georgischen Rechts*. Frankfurt, 1992.

Burgmann, L. and S. Troianos. 'Appendix Eclogae'. *Fontes Minores* 3 (1979): 24–125.

Burgmann, L. and S. Troianos. 'Nomos Mosaïkos'. *Fontes Minores* 3 (1979): 126–67.

Burton, G. P. 'Proconsuls, assizes and the administration of justice under the empire'. *JRS* 65 (1975): 92–106.

Buti, I. 'La "cognitio extra ordinem": da Augusto a Diocleziano'. *ANRW* vol. 2.14 (1982): 29–59.

Buti, I. *Il 'praetor' e le formalità introduttive del processo formulare*. Naples, 1984.

Cadoppi, I. 'Sul lessico giuridico nell'Apologeticum di Tertulliano'. *Acme* 49 (1996): 153–65.

Caenegem, R. C. van. 'Le droit romain en Belgique'. *Ius Romanum Medii Aevi* part V.5b. Milan, 1966.

Caenegem, R. C. van. *History of European Civil Procedure*. (International Encyclopedia of Comparative Law, volume 16.2). Tübingen, 1987.

Caenegem, R. C. van. *The Birth of the English Common Law*, 2nd edn. Cambridge, 1988.

Caenegem, R. C. van. *European Law in the Past and the Future: Unity and Diversity over Two Millennia*. Cambridge, 2002.

Caenegem, R. C. van. 'The unification of European law: a pipedream?' *European Review* 14 (2006): 33–48.

Cairns, J. 'The influence of the German historical school in early nineteenth century Edinburgh'. *Syracuse Journal of International Law and Commerce* 20 (1994): 191–203.

Calasso, F. *I glossatori e la teoria della sovranità*, 3rd edn. Milan, 1957.

Cameron, A. *The Last Pagans of Rome*. Oxford, 2010.

Camodeca, G. 'Riedizione del trittico ercolanense TH 77+78+80+53+92 del 26 gennaio 69'. *Cronache Ercolanensi* 24 (1994): 137–46.

Camodeca, G. 'La ricostruzione dell'élite municipale ercolanese degli anni 50–70'. *CCG* 7 (1996): 172–91.

Camodeca, G., *Tabulae Pompeianae Sulpiciorum. Edizione critica dell'archivio puteolano dei Sulpicii*, 2 vols. Rome, 1999.

Camodeca, G. 'Per un primo aggiornamento all'edizione dell'archivio dei Sulpicii'. *CCG* 11 (2000): 175–79.

Camodeca, G. 'Per una reedizione dell'archivio ercolanense di L. Venidius Ennychus'. *Cronache ercolanensi* 32 (2002): 257–80.

Camodeca, G. 'Altri considerazioni sull'archivio dei Sulpicii e sull'edificio pompeiano di Moregine'. In *Moregine*, edited by V. Scarano Ussani, 23–41. Naples, 2005.

Camodeca, G. 'Dittici e trittici nella documentazione campana (8 a.C.–79 d.C.)'. In *Eburnea diptycha. I dittici d'avorio tra Antichità e Medioevo*, edited by M. David, 81–109. Bari, 2007.

Camodeca, G. 'L'evoluzione della forma dei documenti giuridici romani alla luce della prassi campana'. In Fides humanitas ius. *Studii in onore di Luigi Labruna*, edited by C. Cascione and C. M Doria, 617–37. Naples, 2007.

Campbell, B. *The Writings of the Roman Land Surveyors: Introduction, Text, Translation and Commentary*. London, 2000.

Canellis, A. *Supplique aux Empereurs*. (Sources Chrétiennes vol. 504). Paris, 2006.

Caner, D. *Wandering Begging Monks. Spiritual Authority and the Promotion of Monasticism in Late Antiquity*. Berkeley and Los Angeles, 2002.

Cannata, C. A. *Profilo istituzionale del processo privato romano*. Turin, 1982/89.

Cannata, C. A. 'Qui prior vindicaverat: la posizione delle parti nella 'legis actio sacramento in rem'. In *Mélanges Felix Wubbe*, edited by J. A. Ankum, R. Feenstra, J. E. Spruit, C. A. Cannata, Y. Le Roy, and P. Weimar, 83–96. Fribourg, 1993.

Canning, J. *The Political Thought of Baldus de Ubaldis*. Cambridge, 1987.

Canning, J. 'Law, sovereignty and corporation theory, 1300–1450'. In *The Cambridge History of Medieval Political Thought c.350–c.1450*, edited by J. H. Burns, 454–76. Cambridge, 1988.

Capogrossi Colognesi, L. 'Per la storia della proprietà romana'. *Labeo* 18 (1972): 373–98.

Capogrossi Colognesi, L. 'La proprietà in Roma dalla fine del sistema patriarcale alla fioritura dell'ordinamento schiavistico'. In *La Terra in Roma antica: forme di proprietà e rapporti produttivi*, edited by L. Capogrossi Colognesi, vol. 1, 135–69. Rome, 1981.

Capogrossi Colognesi, L. 'Dominium e possessio nell'Italia Romana'. In *La proprietà e le proprietà*, edited by E. Cortese, 141–82. Milan, 1988.

Capogrossi Colognesi, L. 'Ius commercii, conubium, civitas sine suffragio. Le origini del diritto internazionale privato e la romanizzazione delle comunità latino-campane'. In *Le strade del potere*, edited by A. Corbino, 3–64. Catania, 1994.

Capogrossi Colognesi, L. 'Dieter Nörr e le sfide poste alla romanistica contemporanea'. In *Dieter Nörr e la romanistica europea tra xx e xxi secolo*, edited by E. Stolfi, 77–111. Turin, 2006.

Caqueray, G. F. M. de. *Explications des passages de droit privé contenus dans l'œuvre de Cicéron*. Paris, 1857; reprinted Aalen, 1969.

Cardascia, G. 'La portée primitive de la loi Aquilia'. In *Daube Noster: Essays in Legal History for David Daube*, edited by A. Watson, 53–75. Edinburgh, 1974.

Carey Miller, D. and R. Zimmermann, editors. *The Civilian Tradition and Scots Law: Aberdeen Quincentenary Essays*. Berlin, 1997.

Carlyle, A. J. 'The theory of the source of political authority, in the mediaeval civilians to the time of Accursius'. In *Mélanges Fitting* vol. 1, 181–94. Aalen, reprinted 1969.

Carlyle, R. W. and A. J. Carlyle. *A History of Mediaeval Political Thought in the West. Vol. 2: The Political Theory of the Roman Lawyers and the Canonists, from the Tenth Century to the Thirteenth Century; Vol. 6: Political Theory from 1300 to 1600*. Edinburgh – London, reprinted 1970.

Caroni, P. 'Die Schweizer Romanistik im 19. Jahrhundert'. *Zeitschrift für neuere Rechtsgeschichte* 16 (1994): 243–71.

Carusi, Z. B. 'Diritto romano e patristica'. In *Studi giuridici in onore di Carlo Fadda*, vol. 2, 71–97. Naples, 1906.

Cascione, C. *Tresviri capitales. Storia di una magistratura minore*. Naples, 1999.

Cassola, O. *La recezione del Diritto Civile nel Diritto Canonico*, 2nd edn. Rome, 1969.

Casson L. 'New light on maritime loans: P. Vindob. G. 19792 (= *SB* VI 9571)'. In *Studies in Roman Law in Memory of A. Arthur Schiller*, edited by R. S. Bagnall and W. V. Harris, 11–17. Leiden – New York, 1986.

Casson L. 'New light on maritime loans: P. Vindob. G 40822', *ZPE* 84 (1990): 195–206.

Cerami, P. and A. Petrucci. *Diritto commerciale romano. Profilo storico*, 3rd edn. Turin, 2010.

Cervenca, G. *Il Processo privato romano: le fonti*. Bologna, 1983.

Champaud, C. *Le droit des affaires*, 5th edn. Paris, 1994.

Champlin, E. *Final Judgments*. Princeton, 1991.

Chêne, C. *L'enseignement du droit français en pays de droit écrit (1679–1793)*. Geneva, 1982.

Chevreau, E. 'La lex Rhodia de iactu: un exemple de la réception d'une institution étrangère dans le droit romain'. *TR* 73 (2005): 67–80.

Chiusi, T. J. *Contributo allo studio dell'editto 'de tributoria actione'*. Rome, 1993.

Chiusi, T. J. *Die actio de in rem verso im römischen Recht*. Munich, 2001.

Chorus, J. M. J. 'Romeins recht op de Zuidpool en elders'. In *Coniectanea iuris Romani*, edited by J. E. Spruit, 139–149. Zwolle, 1974.

Churruca, J. de. 'Un rescrit de Caracalla utilisé par Ulpien et interprété par Saint Augustin'. In *Collatio Iuris Romani. Études Dédieés à Hans Ankum*, edited by R. Feenstra, A. S. Hartkamp, J. E. Spruit, P. J. Sijpesteijn, and L. C. Winkel, vol. 1, 71–80. Amsterdam, 1995.

Churruca, J. de. 'Le commerce comme élément de civilisation dans la *Géographie* de Strabon'. *RIDA* 48 (2001): 41–56.

Clauss, M. *Der magister officiorum in der Spätantike (4.-6. Jahrhundert): Das Amt und sein Einfluss auf die kaiserliche Politik*. Munich, 1980.

Cloud, J. D. '*Parricidium* from the *lex Numae* to the *lex Pompeia de parricidiis*'. *ZSS* 88 (1971): 1–66.

Cloud, J. D. 'The constitution and criminal law'. *CAH* vol. 9, 491–530, 2nd edn. Cambridge, 1994.

Coarelli, F. 'I luoghi del processo'. In *La repressione criminale nella Roma repubblicana fra norma e persuasione*, edited by B. Santalucia, 3–13. Pavia, 2009.

Cogliolo, P. *Gli istituti commerciali nel diritto romano. Corso compilato dall'Avv. E. Finzi e dallo studente G.G. Traverso, Anno accademico 1921–1922*. Genova, 1922.

Cohen, E. E. *Ancient Athenian Maritime Courts*. Princeton, 1973.

Cohen, E. E. (2005) 'Commercial law'. In *The Cambridge Companion to Ancient Greek Law*, edited by M. Gagarin and D. Cohen, 290–302. Cambridge, 2005.

Coing, H. *Handbuch der Quellen und Literatur der neueren europäischen Privatrechtsgeschichte. I: Mittelalter (1100–1500).* Munich, 1973.

Coing, H. 'Das Recht als Element der europäischen Kultur'. *Historische Zeitschrift* 238 (1984): 1–15.

Coing, H. *Europäisches Privatrecht*, vol. 1. Munich, 1985.

Collinet, P. *Histoire de l'école de droit de Beyrouth*. Paris, 1925.

Connolly, S. *Lives behind the Laws. The World of the Codex Hermogenianus*. Bloomington, 2010.

Conrat, M. *Die Epitome Exactis regibus*. Berlin, 1884.

Conrat, M. *Geschichte der Quellen und Literatur des römischen Rechts im früheren Mittelalter*. Leipzig, 1891 (reprinted Aalen, 1963).

Conte, E. *Tres Libri codicis. La ricomparsa del testo e l'esegesi scolastica prima di Accursio*. Frankfurt, 1990.

Conte, E. and S. Menzinger, *La Summa Trium Librorum di Rolando da Lucca (1195–1234): Fisco, Politica, Scientia iuris*. Rome, 2012.

Coppola Bisazza, G. *Lo iussum domini e la sostituzione negoziale nell'esperienza romana*. Milan, 2003.

Corbett, P. E. *The Roman Law of Marriage*. Oxford, 1930.

Corcoran, S. *The Empire of the Tetrarchs. Imperial Pronouncements and Government AD 284–324*, revd. edn. Oxford, 2000.

Corcoran, S. 'The publication of laws in the era of the tetrarchs'. In *Diokletian und die Tetrarchie*, edited by A. Demandt, A. Goltz and H. Schlange-Schöningen, 56–73. Berlin, 2004.

Corcoran, S. 'The tetrarchy. Policy and image as reflected in imperial pronouncements'. In *Die Tetrarchie. Ein neues Regierungssystem und seine mediale Präsentation*, edited by D. Boschung and W. Eck, 31–61. Wiesbaden, 2006.

Corcoran, S. 'Two tales, two cities: Antinoopolis and Nottingham'. In *Wolf Liebeschuetz Reflected: Essays Presented by Colleagues, Friends, and Pupils*, edited by J. Drinkwater and B. Salway, 193–209. London, 2007.

Corcoran, S. 'Justinian and his two codes. Revisiting P. Oxy. 1814'. *JJP* 38 (2008): 73–111.

Corcoran, S. 'After Krüger: observations on some additional or revised Justinian Code headings and subscripts'. *ZSS* 126 (2009): 423–39.

Corcoran, S. 'Anastasius, Justinian, and the pagans: a tale of two law codes and a Papyrus'. *Journal of Late Antiquity* 2 (2009): 183–208.

Corcoran, S. 'New subscripts for old rescripts: the Vallicelliana fragments of Justinian Code Book VII'. *ZSS* 126 (2009): 401–22.

Corcoran, S. 'The novus codex and the codex repetitae praelectionis: Justinian and his codex'. In: *Figures d'empire, fragments de mémoire: pouvoirs et identités dans le monde romain impérial (IIe s. av. n. è.–VIe s. de n. è.)*, edited by S. Benoist, A. Dagues-Gagey, and C. Hoët-van Cauwenberge, 425–44. Villeneuve d'Ascg, 2011.

Corcoran, S. and B. Salway, 'A lost law-code rediscovered? The Fragmenta Londinensia anteiustiniana'. *ZSS* 127 (2009): 677–78.

Corcoran, S. and B. Salway, 'Fragmenta londinensia anteiustiniana: preliminary observations'. *Roman Legal Tradition* 8 (2012): 63–83.

Cordes, A. 'Auf der Suche nach der Rechtswirklichkeit der mittelalterlichen Lex mercatoria'. *ZSS (Germanistische Abteilung)* 118 (2001): 168–84.

Coriat, J.-P. 'La palingénesie des constitutions impériales. Histoire d'un projet et méthode pour le recueil de la législation du principat'. *Mélanges de l'Ecole française de Rome, Antiquité* 101 (1989): 873–923.

Coriat, J.-P. *Le Prince Législateur*. Rome, 1997.
Cortese, E. *La norma giuridica. Spunti teoretici nel diritto comune classico*, 2 vols. Milan, 1962–64.
Cortese, E. *Il problema della sovranità nel pensiero giuridico medioevale*. Rome, 1966.
Cortese, E. 'Legisti, canonisti e feudisti: la formazione di un ceto medioevale'. In *Università e Società nei secoli XII–XVI*, 195–281. Pistoia, 1982.
Cortese, E. *Il rinascimento giuridico medioevale*. Rome, 1992.
Cortese, E. *Il diritto nella storia medioevale, II. Il basso medioevo*. Rome, 1995.
Coskun, A. 'Der Praefect Maximinus, der Jude Isaak und der Strafprozeß gegen Bischof Damasus von Rom'. *Jahrbuch für Antike und Christentum* 46 [2003] (2005): 17–44.
Costa, E. *Il diritto privato romano nelle comedie di Plauto*. Turin, 1890; reprinted Rome, 1968.
Costa, E. *Il diritto privato romano nelle comedie di Terenzio*. Turin, 1890; reprinted Rome, 1970.
Costa, E. *Cicerone giureconsulto*. Bologna, 1927; reprinted Rome, 1964.
Costa, P. *Iurisdictio. Semantica del potere politica nella pubblicistica medievale, 1100–1433*, 2nd edn. Milan, 2002.
Cottier, M., M. H. Crawford, C. V. Crowther, J. L. Ferrary, B. M. Levick, O. Salomies, and M. Wörrle, editors. *The Customs Law of Asia*. Oxford, 2008.
Cotton, H. 'The guardianship of Jesus, son of Babatha: Roman and local law in the province of Arabia'. *JRS* 83 (1993): 94–108.
Courtois, C., L. Leschi, C. Perrat, and C. Saumagne, *Les tablettes Albertini: actes privés de l'époque vandale*. Paris, 1952.
Crawford, M. 'Aut sacrom aut poublicom'. In *New Perspectives in the Roman Law of Property*, edited by P. Birks, 93–98. Oxford, 1989.
Crawford, M. H. and F. Beltrán Lloris, 'The Lex rivi Hiberiensis.' *JRS* 103 (2013): 233.
Crifò, G. 'Isolierung e valutazione giuridica'. In *Diritto e letteratura*, edited by F. Spantigati, 30–36. Milan, 2006.
Crook, J. A. *Law and Life of Rome*. London, 1967; reprinted Ithaca NY, 1984.
Crook, J. A. '*Patria potestas*'. *CQ* 17 (1967): 113–22.
Crook, J. A. 'Intestacy in Roman society'. *Proceedings of the Cambridge Philological Society* 19 (1973): 38–44.
Crook, J. A. 'Three hundred and six stakes'. In *Quaestiones iuris*, edited by U. Manthe and C. Krampe, 77–81. Berlin, 2000.
Crook, J. A. 'The development of Roman private law'. In *CAH* vol. 9, 531–64, 2nd edn. Cambridge, 1994.
Crook, J. A. *Legal Advocacy in the Roman World*. Ithaca NY, 1995.
Cuiacius, J. *Opera Omnia*, Frankfurt, 1623.
Cuneo, P. O. *La Legislazione di Costantino II, Costanzo II e Costante (337–361)*. Milan, 1997.
D'Arms, J. H. *Commerce and Social Standing in Ancient Rome*. Cambridge, Mass., 1981.
Daube, D. 'On the Third Chapter of the Lex Aquilia'. *Law Quarterly Review* 52 (1936): 253–68.
Daube, D. 'On the use of the term *damnum*'. In *Studi Solazzi*, 93–156. Naples, 1948.
Daube, D. 'The peregrine praetor'. *JRS* 41 (1951): 66–70.
Daube, D. 'The preponderance of intestacy at Rome'. *Tulane Law Review* 39 (1965): 253–62.
Daube, D. *Roman Law, Linguistic, Social and Philosophical Aspects*. Edinburgh, 1969.
David, J.-M. *Le patronat judiciaire au dernier siècle de la république romaine*. Rome, 1992.
Degrassi, A. *I fasti consolari dell'impero romano*. Rome, 1952.

Delmaire, R. *Largesses sacrées et res privata: L'aerarium impérial et son administration du IVe au VIe siècle*. Rome, 1989.

Delmaire, R. *Les institutions du Bas-Empire Romain de Constantin à Justinien. Vol. 1: Les institutions civiles palatines*. Paris, 1995.

Demandt, A. *Antike Staatsformen. Eine vergleichrende Verfassungsgeschichte der Alten Welt*. Berlin, 1995.

Demandt, A. *Die Spätantike. Römische Geschichte von Diocletian bis Justinian, 284–565 n. Chr*. 2nd edn. Munich, 2008.

Desanti, L. Restitutionis post mortem onus. *I fedecommessi di restituirsi dopo la morte dell'onerato*. Milan, 2003.

Dihle, A. *Theory of the Will in Classical Antiquity*. Berkeley, 1981.

Dilcher, H. *Die Theorie der Leistungsstörungen bei Glossatoren, Kommentatoren und Kanonisten*. Frankfurt, 1960.

Diliberto, O. 'La satira e il diritto, una nuova lettura di Horat., *sat.* 1.3.115–117'. *Annali del Seminario Giuridico dell'Università di Palermo* 55 (2012): 385–402.

Dilke, O. *The Roman Land Surveyors: An Introduction to the Agrimensores*. Newton Abbot, 1971.

Diósdi, G. *Ownership in Ancient and Preclassical Roman Law*. Budapest, 1970.

Dolezalek, G. *Repertorium manuscriptorum veterum Codicis Iustiniani*, 2 vols. Frankfurt, 1985.

Dolezalek, G. *Scotland under Jus Commune*. Edinburgh, 2010.

Dolezalek, G. and L. Mayali, *Repertorium manuscriptorum Codicis Justiniani*. Frankfurt, 1985.

Dölger, F. and J. Karayannopoulos. *Byzantinische Urkundenlehre*. Munich, 1968.

Domingo, R. *Estudios sobre el primer título del edicto pretorio*. Santiago de Compostela, 1993.

Donadio, N. '*Iudicium domesticum – riprovazione sociale e persecuzione pubblica di atti commessi da sottoposti alla patria potestas*'. *Index* 40 (2012): 175–95.

Dorn, F. 'Irnerius'. In *Deutsche und Europäische Juristen aus neun Jahrhunderten*, edited by G. Kleinheyer and J. Schröder, 220, 5th edn. Heidelberg, 2008.

Dovere, E. *Ius Principale e catholica lex (secolo V)*. Naples, 1999.

Drecoll, C. *Die Liturgien im römischen Kaiserreich des 3. und 4. Jahrhunderts*. Stuttgart, 1997.

Duff, A. M. *Freedmen in the Early Roman Empire*. Cambridge, 1958.

Duynstee, M. 'An unknown fourteenth century lecture of the Orleans school: Jean Nicot on book VI of the Code'. *TR* 60 (1992): 363–76.

Eck. W., A. Caballos, and F. Fernandez. *Das senatus consultum de Cn. Pisone patre*. Munich, 1996.

Eger, O. 'Rechtswörter und Rechtsbilder in den paulinischen Briefen'. *Zeitschrift fur die neutestamentliche Wissenschaft* 18 (1918): 84–108.

Ehrenberg, V. and A. H. M. Jones, *Documents illustrating the Reigns of Augustus and Tiberius*, 2nd edn. Oxford, 1976.

Elia, O. 'La domus marittima delle tabulae ceratae nel suburbio di Pompei'. *Bolletino d'Arte* 46 (1961): 200–11.

Elm, S. 'A programmatic Life: Gregory of Nazianzus' Orations 42 and 43 and the Constantinopolitan Elites'. *Arethusa* 33 (2000): 411–27.

Eno, R. *Saint Augustine, Letters. Volume 6 (1*–29*)*. Washington, D.C., 1989.

Ercole, F. 'L'origine francese di una nota formola Bartoliana'. *Archivio storico italiano* (6th series) 73 (1915): 241–94.

Ercole, F. 'Sulla origine francese e le vicende in Italia della formola: "Rex superiorem non recognoscens est princeps in regno suo"'. *Archivio storico italiano* (7th series) 16 (1931): 197–238.

Ernst, W. 'Kurze Rechtsgeschichte des Gattungskaufs'. *Zeitschrift für europäisches Privatrecht* 7 (1999): 583–641.

Ernst, W. 'Werner Flumes Lehre von der ungerechtfertigten Bereicherung'. In W. Flume, *Studien zur Lehre von der ungerechtfertigten Bereicherung*, 1–24. Tübingen, 2003.

Evans, J. A. *The Emperor Justinian and the Byzantine Empire*. Westport, 2005.

Evans Grubb, J. *Law and Family in Late Antiquity*. Oxford, 1995.

Evans Grubb, J. *Women and the Law in the Roman Empire: A Sourcebook on Marriage, Divorce and Widowhood*. London, 2002.

Evans-Jones, R. and G. MacCormack. '*Iusta causa traditionis*'. In *New Perspectives in the Roman Law of Property*, edited by P. Birks, 99–109. Oxford, 1989.

Fabrot, C. A., editor. *Ton Basilikon biblia LX*, 7 vols. Paris, 1647.

Fadda, C. *Istituti commerciali del diritto romano. Lezioni dettate nella R. Università di Napoli nell'anno scolastico 1902–1903*. Naples, 1903; reprinted with a note by L. Bove, 1987.

Falchi, G. L. 'L'influenza della patristica sulla politica legislativa de nuptiis degli imperatori romani dei secoli IV e V'. *Augustinianum* 50 (2010): 351–407.

Falk, U. and H. Mohnhaupt, editors. *Das Bürgerliche Gesetzbuch und seine Richter*. Frankfurt, 2000.

Fanizza, L. *L'amministrazione della giustizia nel principato*. Rome, 1999.

Feenstra, R. 'Jean de Blanot et la formule "Rex Francie in regno suo princeps est" '. In *Études d'histoire du droit canonique dédiées à Gabriel Le Bras*, vol. 2, 885–95. Paris, 1965.

Feenstra, R. '*Dominium* and *ius in re aliena*: the origins of a civil law distinction'. In *New Perspectives in the Roman Law of Property*, edited by P. Birks, 111–22. Oxford, 1989.

Feenstra, R. 'Law'. In *The Legacy of Rome: A New Appraisal*, edited by R. Jenkyns, 399–420. Oxford, 1992.

Feenstra, R. 'Grotius' doctrine of unjust enrichment as a source of obligation: its origin and its influence in Roman-Dutch law'. In *Unjust Enrichment: The Comparative Legal History of the Law of Restitution*, edited by E. J. H. Schrage, 197–236, 2nd edn. Berlin, 1999.

Feenstra, R. and C. J. D. Waal. *Seventeenth-Century Leyden Law Professors and Their Influence on the Development of the Civil Law: A Study of Bronchorst, Vinnius and Voet*. Amsterdam, 1975.

Feenstra, R. and R. Zimmermann, editors. *Das römisch-holländische Recht: Fortschritte des Zivilrechts im 17. und 18. Jahrhundert*. Berlin, 1992.

Feissel, D. 'Pétitions aux Empereurs et formes du rescrit dans les sources documentaries du IVe au Vie siècle'. In *La Pétition à Byzance*, edited by D. Feissel and J. Gascou. Paris, 2004.

Feissel, D. 'Les actes de l'État impérial dans l'epigraphie tardive (324–610): Prolégomènes à un inventaire'. In *Selbstdarstellung und Kommunikation. Die Veröffentlichung staatlicher Urkunden auf Stein und Bronze in der römischen Welt. Internationales Kolloquium an der Kommission für Alte Geschichte und Epigraphik in München (1. bis 3. Juli 2006)*, edited by R. Haensch, 97–128. Munich, 2009.

Felice, F. 'Su le idee giuridiche contenute nei libri V e VI delle Istituzioni di Lattanzio'. *Rivista internazionale di scienze sociali e discipline ausiliarie* 5 (1894): 581–58.

Ferenczy, E. 'Die römisch-punischen Verträge und die Protohistorie des *commercium*'. *RIDA* 16 (1969): 259–82.

Ferme, B. *Introduction to the History of the Sources of Canon Law: The Ancient Law up to the Decretum of Gratian*. Montreal, 2007.

Ferrini, C. 'Le cognizioni giuridiche di Lattanzio, Arnobio e Minucio Felice'. *Memorie dell'Accademia delle Scienze di Modena* (series 2) 10 (1894): 195–210.

Fitting, H. *Summa codicis des Irnerius*. Berlin, 1894.

Fögen, M. T. 'Gesetz und Gesetzgebung in Byzanz. Versuch einer Funktionsanalyse'. *Ius Commune* 14 (1987): 137–58.

Fogliani, T. G. *T. C. Cipriano. Contributo alla ricerca di riferimenti legali in testi extragiuridici del III sec. d.c.* Modena, 1928.

Földi, A. 'Eine alternative Annäherungsweise: Gedanken zum Problem des Handelsrechts in der römischen Welt'. *RIDA* 48 (2001): 65–90.

Fraher, R. 'The theoretical justification for the new criminal law of the High Middle Ages: *Rei publicae interest, ne crimina remaneant impunita*'. *University of Illinois Law Review* (1984): 577–95.

Frakes, R. M. *Compiling the Collatio Legum Mosaicarum et Romanarum in Late Antiquity*. Oxford, 2011.

France, J. Quadragesima Galliarum. *L'organisation douanière des provinces alpestres, gauloises et germaniques de l'empire romain*. Rome, 2001.

Frede, M. 'John of Damascus on human action, the will and human freedom'. In *Byzantine Philosophy and Its Ancient Sources*, edited by K. Ierodiakonou, 63–96. Oxford, 2006.

Friedberg, E. *Die künftige Gestaltung des deutschen Rechtsstudiums nach den Beschlüssen der Eisenacher Konferenz*. Leipzig, 1896.

Frier, B. W. 'Roman law and the wine trade: the problem of "vinegar" sold as wine'. *ZSS* 100 (1983): 257–95.

Frier, B. W. *The Rise of the Roman Jurists*. Princeton, 1985.

Frier, B. W. 'Finding a place for law in the High Empire: Tacitus, Dialogus 39.1–4'. In *Spaces of Justice in the Roman World*, edited by W. V. Harris and F. de Angelis, 67–87. Leiden, 2010.

Frier, B. W. and D. Kehoe. 'Law and economic institutions'. In *The Cambridge Economic History of the Greco-Roman World*, edited by I. Morris, R. Saller, and W. Scheidel, 113–43. Cambridge, 2013.

Frier, B. W. and T. A. J. McGinn. *A Casebook on Roman Family Law*. New York, 2003.

Fürst, C. G. 'Ecclesia vivit lege Romana?' *ZSS (Kanonistische Abteilung)* (1975): 17–36.

Gagnér, S. *Studien zur Ideengeschichte der Gesetzgebung*. Stockholm, 1960.

Galanter, M. 'Justice in many rooms: courts, private ordering, and indigenous law'. *Journal of Legal Pluralism and Unofficial Law* 19 (1981): 1–30.

Gallagher, C. *Church Law and Church Order in Rome and Byzantium: A Comparative Study*. Aldershot, 2002.

Gardner, J. F. *Women in Roman Law and Society*. London, 1986.

Gardner, J. F. *Family and Familia in Roman Law and Life*. Oxford, 1998.

Gardner, J. F. and T. Wiedemann. *The Roman Household: A Sourcebook*. London, 1991.

Garnsey, P. 'Adultery trials and the survival of the *quaestiones* in the Severan age'. *JRS* 57 (1967): 56–60.

Garnsey, P. *Social Status and Legal Privilege in the Roman Empire*. Oxford, 1970.

Garnsey, P. *Thinking about Property: From Antiquity to the Age of Revolution*. Cambridge, 2007.

Garnsey, P. and C. Humfress. *The Evolution of the Late Antique World*. Cambridge 2001.

Garofalo, L. *La persecuzione dello stellionato in diritto romano*. Padua, 1992.

Gaudemet, J. *Le droit romain dans la littérature chrétienne occidentale du III au V siècle*. Milan, 1978.

Gaudemet, J. *La formation du droit séculier et du droit de l'église aux IVe et Ve siècles*, 2nd edn. Paris, 1979.

Gaudemet, J. *Institutions de l'Antiquité*, 2nd edn. Paris, 1982.

Gaudemet, J. 'L'Apport du Droit Romain à la Patristique Latine du IVe Siècle'. *Miscellanea Historiae Ecclesiasticae*, vol. 6, 165–81. Brussels, 1983.

Gaurier, D. *Le droit maritime romain*. Rennes, 2004.

Gauthier, A. *Roman Law and Its Contribution to the Development of Canon Law*. Ottawa, 1996.

Gauthier, R. 'Introduction'. In *L'Ethique à Nicomaque*, edited by R. A. Gauthier and J. Y. Jolif, I-1, 2nd edn. Louvain – Paris, 1970.

Gerkens, J.-F. 'Chronique de la 55e session de la Société internationale Fernand de Visscher pour l'histoire des droits de l'Antiquité à Rotterdam (18 au 22 septembre 2001)'. *RIDA* 50 (2003): 489–516.

Germino, E. 'La legislazione dell'imperatore Giuliano: primi appunti per una palingenesi'. *Antiquité Tardive* 17 (2009): 159–74.

Giachi, C. 'Storia dell'editto e struttura del processo in età pre-adrianea. Un'ipotesi di lavoro'. In *Atti del Convegno Processo civile e processo penale nell'esperienza giuridica del mondo antico in memoria di Arnaldo Biscardi, Siena, Certosa di Pontignano, 13–15 dicembre 2001*. *Rivista di diritto romano* (2001): http://www.ledonline.it/rivistadirittoromano/attipontignano.html (12/01/09).

Giachi, C. *Studi su Sesto Pedio. La tradizione, l'editto*. Milan, 2005.

Giardina, A. *Aspetti della burocrazia nel Basso Impero*. Rome, 1977.

Gigante, M. *Νόμος Βασιλεύς*. Naples, 1993.

Giglio, S. *Il tardo impero d'Occidente e il suo senato*. Naples, 1990.

Giliberti, G. 'Dominium caesaris'. *Index* 24 (1996): 199–228.

Giodice Sabbatelli, V. *La tutela giuridica dei fedecommessi fra Augusto e Vespasiano*. Bari, 1993.

Giodice Sabbatelli, V. *Fideicommissorum persecutio: contributo allo studio delle cognizioni straordinarie*. Bari, 2001.

Giomaro, M. 'Ulpiano e le 'stipulationes praetoriae'. In *Studi in onore di Arnaldo Biscardi*, vol. 4, 413–40. Milan, 1983.

Giomaro, A. *Il Codex repetitae praelectionis. Contributi allo studio dello schema delle raccolte normative da Teodosio a Giustiniano*. Mursia, 2001.

Giordanengo, G. *Le droit féodal dans les pays de droit écrit. L'exemple de la Provence et du Dauphiné, XIIè-début XIVè siècle*. Rome, 1988.

Giordanengo, G. 'Le pouvoir legislatif du roi de France, (XIe–XIIIe siecles) Travaux recents et hypothèses de recherche'. *Bibliothèque de l'Ecole des Chartes* 147 (1989): 283–310.

Giordanengo, G. 'Le roi de France et la loi. 1137–1285'. In *Colendo Iustitiam et Iura Condendo. Federico II legislatore del regno di Sicilia nell'Europa del Duecento*, edited by A. Romano, 345–95. Rome, 1997.

Giordanengo, G. '*Jus commune* et droit commun en France du XIIIe au XVe siècle'. In *Droit romain, ius civile et droit français*, edited by J. Krynen, 219–47. Toulouse, 1999.

Giordano, C. 'Su alcune tavolette cerate dell'agro Murecine'. *RAAN* 41 (1966): 107–21.

Giordano, C. 'Nuove tavolette cerate pompeiane'. *RAAN* 45 (1970): 211–25.

Giordano, C. 'Nuove tavolette cerate pompeiane'. *RAAN* 46 (1971): 183–95.

Giordano, C. 'Quarto contributo alle tavolette cerate pompeiane'. *RAAN* 47 (1972): 311–16.

Giovanni, L. de. *Istituzioni scienza giuridica codici nel mondo tardo-antico. Alle radici di una nuova storia*. Rome, 2007.

Girardet, K. M. 'Trier 385. Der Prozess gegen die Priszillianer'. *Chiron* 4 (1974): 577–608.

Girardet, K. M. *Kaisergericht und Bischofsgericht. Studien zu den Anfängen des Donatistenstreites (313–315) und zum Prozeß des Athanasius (328–346).* Bonn, 1975.

Girardet, K. M. *Kaisertum, Religionspolitik und das Recht von Staat und Kirche in der Spätantike.* Bonn, 2009.

Glenn, P. *Legal Traditions of the World*, 3rd edn. Oxford, 2007.

Gluckman, M. *Politics, Law and Ritual in Tribal Society.* Oxford, 1965.

Goff, R. 'The search for principle'. In *The Search for Principle: Essays in Honour of Lord Goff of Chieveley*, edited by W. Swadling and G. Jones, 313–30. New York, 1999.

Gordley, J. *The Philosophical Origins of Modern Contract Doctrine.* Oxford, 1991.

Gordley, J. 'Common law und civil law: eine überholte Unterscheidung'. *Zeitschrift für europäisches Privatrecht* 1 (1993): 498–518.

Gordley, J. 'Myths of the French Civil Code'. *American Journal of Comparative Law* 42 (1994): 459–505.

Gordley, J. *Foundations of Private Law.* Oxford, 2006.

Gordley, J. 'Comparative law and legal history'. In *The Oxford Handbook of Comparative Law*, edited by M. Reimann and R. Zimmermann, 753–73. Oxford, 2008.

Gómez-Iglesias, A. 'Lex Irnitana *cap. 91*: lis iudici damni sit'. *SDHI* 72 (2006): 465–505.

González, J. 'The lex Irnitana: a new Flavian municipal law'. *JRS* 76 (1986): 147–243.

Goode, R. *Commercial Law*, 3rd edn. London, 2004.

Gordon, W. and O. Robinson. *The Institutes of Gaius.* London, 1988.

Gouron, A. 'Diffusion des Consulats Méridionaux et Expansion du droit romain aux XIIe et XIIIe siècles'. *Bibliothèque de l'Ecole des Chartes* (1963): 26–76.

Gouron, A. 'La science juridique française aux XIe e XIIe siècles: diffusion du droit de Justinien et influences canoniques jusqu'à Gratien'. *Ius Romanum Medii Aevi* part I.4d-e. Milan, 1978.

Gouron, A. *La science du droit dans le Midi de la France au Moyen Age.* London, 1984.

Gouron, A. 'Coutume contre loi chez les premiers glossateurs'. In *Renaissance du Pouvoir Législatif et Genèse de l'État.* (Publications de la Société D'Histoire du Droit et des Institutions des Anciens Pays de Droit Écrit.) vol. 4, 117–30. Montpellier, 1988.

Gouron, A. 'Non dixit, "Ego sum consuetudo"'. *ZSS* 74 (1988): 133–40.

Gouron, A. 'Un assaut en deux vagues: la diffusion du droit romain'. In *L'Europe du XIIème siècle, El Dret Comù i Catalunya*, edited by A. Iglesia Ferreiros, 47–63. Barcelona, 1991.

Gouron, A. 'Les "Quaestiones de juris subtilitatibus": une œuvre du maître parisien Albéric'. *Revue Historique* 618 (2001): 342–62.

Gouron, A., G. Giordanengo, and J. Dufour. 'L'attrait des *leges*: note sur la lettre d'un moine victorin (vers 1124–1127)'. *SDHI* 45 (1979): 504–29.

Gradenwitz, O. *Interpolationen in den Pandekten.* Berlin, 1887.

Graumann, T. '"Reading" the first council of Ephesus 431'. In *Chalcedon in Context. Church Councils 400–700*, edited by R. Price and M. Whitby, 27–44. Liverpool, 2009.

Greenidge, A. H. J. *The Legal Procedure of Cicero's Time.* Oxford, 1901.

Griffin, M. 'The tribune C. Cornelius'. *JRS* 63 (1973): 196–213.

Grobecker, W. *Implied Terms und Treu und Glauben: Vertragsergänzung im englischen Recht in rechtsvergleichender Perspektive.* Berlin, 1999.

Groenewegen van der Made, S. van. *Tractatus de legibus abrogatis et inusitatis in Hollandia vicinisque regionibus.* 1649.

Gröschler, P. *Actiones in factum. Eine Untersuchung zur Klage-Neuschöpfung im nichtvertraglichen Bereich.* Berlin, 2002.

Grossi, P. *L'europa del diritto*. Rome, 2007.

Grosso, G. *I legati nel diritto romano*. Turin, 1966.

Grusková, J. and B. H. Stolte. 'Zwei neue Basiliken-Handschriften in der Österreichischen Nationalbibliothek. I: Paläographisch-kodikologische Analyse; II: Rechtshistorische Analyse. Mit 30 Tafeln'. In *Quellen zur byzantinischen Rechtspraxis. Aspekte der Textüberlieferung, Paläographie und Diplomatik. Akten des internationalen Symposiums Wien, 5.–7.11. 2007*, edited by C. Gastgeber, 107–82. Vienna, 2010.

Gualandi, G. *Legislazione imperiale e giurisprudenza*, 2 vols. Milan, 1963.

Guarino, A. 'La formazione dell'editto perpetuo'. *ANRW* 2.13 (1980): 62–102.

Guenther, O., editor. *Epistolae Imperatorum Pontificum Aliorum Inde ab a. CCCLXVII usque DLIII datae Avellana Quae Dicitur Collectio*. (Corpus Scriptorum Ecclesiasticorum Latinorum, vol. 35.) Prague – Vienna – Leipzig, 1895.

Guinot, J.-N. and F. Richard. editors. *Empire Chrétien et Église aux IVe et Ve siècles. Intégration ou 'concordat'? Le Témoignage du Code Théodosien*. Lyon, 2008.

Häberle, P. *Europäische Rechtskultur*. Frankfurt, 1997.

Hackl, K. *Praeiudicium im klassischen römischen Recht*. Salzburg, 1975.

Harries, J. *Law and Empire in Late Antiquity*. Cambridge, 1999.

Harries, J. *Cicero and the Jurists: From Citizens' Law to the Lawful State*. London, 2006.

Harries, J. 'Tertullianus & Son?' In *A Wandering Galilean: Essays in Honour of Seán Freyne*, edited by Z. Rodgers, M. Daly-Denton, and A. F. Fitzpatrick-McKinley. Leiden, 2009.

Harries, J. and I. Wood, editors. *The Theodosian Code: Studies in the Imperial Law of Late Antiquity*, 2nd edn. London, 2010.

Harris, W. V. 'Roman governments and commerce, 300 B.C.–A.D. 300'. In *Mercanti e politica nel mondo antico*, edited by C. Zaccagnini, 275–305. Rome, 2003.

Hartmann, W. *Kirche und Kirchenrecht um 900: Die Bedeutung der spätkarolingischen Zeit für Tradition und Innovation im kirchlichen Recht*. Hannover, 2008.

Heggelbacher, O. *Vom römischen zum christlichen Recht. Juristische Elemente in den Schriften des sogenanntes Ambrosiaster*. Freiburg, 1959.

Heimbach, C. G. E., E. C. Ferrini, G. Mercati, and K. E. Zachariae von Lingenthal, editors. *Basilicorum libri LX*, 6 vols. & 2 suppls. Leipzig, 1833–97.

Helmholz, R. H. *Canon Law and the Law of England*. London, 1987.

Helmholz, R. H. *Roman Canon Law in Reformation England*. Cambridge, 1990.

Helmholz, R. H. 'Use of the Civil Law in Post-Revolutionary American Jurisprudence'. *Tulane Law Review* 66 (1992): 1649–84.

Helmholz, R. H. 'Magna Carta and the ius commune'. *University of Chicago Law Review* 66 (1999): 297–371.

Helmholz, R. H. *The ius commune in England: Four Studies*. Oxford, 2001.

Henriot, E. *Les poètes juristes*. Paris, 1858; reprinted Aalen, 1970.

Henriot, E. *Moeurs juridiques et judiciaires de l'ancienne Rome d'après les poètes latins*. Paris, 1858; reprinted Aalen, 1970.

Herrmann-Otto, E. *Ecclesia in re publica. Die Entwicklung der Kirche von pseudo-staatlicher zu staatlich inkorporierter Existenz*. Frankfurt, 1980.

Hezser, C. 'Roman Law and Rabbinic Legal Composition'. In *The Cambridge Companion to The Talmud and Rabbinic Literature*, edited by C. E. Fonrobert and M. S. Jaffee, 144–63. Cambridge, 2007.

Hill, M. *Ecclesiastical Law*, 2nd edn. London, 2001.

Hirschfeld, O. *Die kaiserlichen Verwaltungsbeamten bis auf Diokletian*. Berlin, 1905 (4th edn., 1975).

Hoeflich, M. H. *Roman and Civil Law and the Development of Anglo-American Jurisprudence in the Nineteenth Century* (Athens, Georgia, 1997).
Hoeflich, M. H. 'Translation and the Reception of Foreign Law in the Antebellum United States'. *American Journal of Comparative Law* 50 (2002): 753–75.
Hoetink, H. R. *De achtergrond van het Romeinse recht.* Haarlem, 1935; French translation: 'L'arrière-plan du droit romain'. In H. R. Hoetink, *Opera Selecta*, 73–108. Zutphen, 1986.
Hoetink, H. R. 'The origin of the dual mode in Roman procedure'. *Seminar* 5 (1947): 16–30.
Hoetink, H. R. *Rechtsgeleerde opstellen.* Alphen, 1982.
Hoffmann, A. *Kirchliche Strukturen und römisches Recht bei Cyprian von Karthago.* Paderborn, 2000.
Honoré, T. *Gaius.* Oxford, 1962.
Honoré, T. *Tribonian.* London, 1978.
Honoré, T. *Emperors and Lawyers*, 2nd edn. Oxford, 1994.
Honoré, T. *Law in the Crisis of Empire, 379–455 AD.* Oxford, 1998.
Honoré, T. *Justinian's Digest. Character and Compilation.* Oxford, 2010.
Hopkins, K. *Death and Renewal.* Cambridge, 1983.
Hove, A. van. *Prolegomena ad codicem iuris canonici.* Mechelen – Rome, 1945.
Hoz Montoya, J. de la. 'Neron y el impuesto sobre la venta de esclavos'. *SDHI* 74 (2008): 367–95.
Humbert, M. *Le remariage à Rome: Étude d'histoire juridique et sociale.* Milan, 1972.
Humbert, M. 'Il valore semantico e giuridico di vsvs nelle Dodici Tavole'. In *Le Dodici Tavole. Dai Decemviri agli Umanisti*, edited by M. Humbert, 377–400. Pavia, 2005.
Humfress, C. 'Law and legal practice in the age of Justinian'. In *The Cambridge Companion to the Age of Justinian*, edited by M. Maas, 161–84. Cambridge, 2005.
Humfress, C. *Orthodoxy and the Courts.* Oxford, 2007.
Humfress, C. 'Bishops and law courts in Late Antiquity. How (Not) to make sense of the legal evidence'. *Journal of Early Christian Studies* 19 (2011): 375–400.
Hunger, H. *Die Textüberlieferung der antiken Literatur und der Bibel*, edited by O. Stegmüller, 2nd edn. Munich, 1988.
Hunter, D. G. and S. A. Harvey, editors. *The Oxford Handbook of Early Christian Studies.* Oxford, 2008.
Huvelin, P. *Etudes d'histoire du droit commercial romain (Histoire externe – Droit maritime).* Paris, 1929.
Ibbetson, D. 'The danger of definition: contrectatio and appropriation'. In *The Roman Law Tradition*, edited by A. D. E. Lewis and D. Ibbetson, 54–72. Cambridge, 1994.
Ibbetson, D. *A Historical Introduction to the Law of Obligations.* Oxford, 1999.
Immenhauser, M. 'Zur Rezeption der deutschen Schuldrechtsreform in der Schweiz', *recht* (2006): 1–16.
Impallomeni, G. *L'editto degli edili curuli.* Padua, 1955.
Impallomeni, G. *Le manomissioni mortis causa: studi sulle fonti autoritative romane.* Padua, 1963.
Indra, M. *Status Quaestio. Studien zum Freiheitsprozess im klassischen römischen Recht.* Berlin, 2011.
Jacques, J. *Le privilège de liberté. Politique impériale et autonomie municipale dans les cités de l'Occident romain (161–244).* Paris – Rome, 1984.
Jakab, E. 'Vertragspraxis und Bankgeschäfte im antiken Puteoli: *TPSulp* 48 neu interpretiert'. In Pistoi dia tèn technèn. *Bankers, Loans and Archives in the Ancient World.*

Studies in Honour of Raymond Bogaert, edited by K. Verboven, K. Vandorpe, and V. Chankowski, 321–44. Leuven, 2008.

Jakobs, H. H. *Wissenschaft und Gesetzgebung im bürgerlichen Recht nach der Rechtsquellenlehre des 19. Jahrhunderts*. Paderborn, 1983.

Jansen, N. 'Die Korrektur grundloser Vermögensverschiebungen als Restitution? Zur Lehre von der ungerechtfertigten Bereicherung bei Savigny'. *ZSS* 120 (2003): 106–62.

Jansen, N. *Die Struktur des Haftungsrechts: Geschichte, Theorie und Dogmatik außervertraglicher Ansprüche auf Schadensersatz*. Tübingen, 2003.

Jauernig, O., editor. *Bürgerliches Gesetzbuch*, 14th edn. Munich, 2011.

Jenkins, T. *The Life of Property*. New York, 2010.

Jhering, R. von. *Geist des römischen Rechts auf den verschiedenen Stufen seiner Entwicklung*, 6th edn. Leipzig, 1907.

Johnston, D. 'Three thoughts on Roman private law and the lex Irnitana'. *JRS* 77 (1987): 62–77.

Johnston, D. *The Roman Law of Trusts*. Oxford, 1988.

Johnston, D. *Roman Law in Context*. Cambridge, 1999.

Jokisch, B. *Islamic Imperial Law. Harun-Al-Rashid's Codification Project*. Berlin – New York, 2007.

Jolowicz, H. F. 'The original scope of the lex Aquilia and the question of damages'. *Law Quarterly Review* 38 (1922): 221–30.

Jolowicz, H. F. *Digest XLVII, 2, De Furtis*. Cambridge, 1940.

Jolowicz, H. F. 'The judex and the arbitral principle'. *RIDA* 2 (1949): 477–92.

Jolowicz, H. F. *Historical Introduction to the Study of Roman Law*, 2nd edn. Cambridge, 1954.

Jolowicz, H. F. and B. Nicholas. *Historical Introduction to the Study of Roman Law*, 3rd edn. Cambridge, 1972.

Jones, A. H. M. *The Later Roman Empire 284–602*, 3 vols. Oxford, 1964.

Jones, A. H. M. 'Imperial and senatorial jurisdiction in the early Principate'. In A. H. M. Jones, *Studies in Roman Government and Law*. Oxford, 1968.

Jones, D. *The Bankers of Puteoli. Finance, Trade and Industry in the Roman World*. Stroud, 2006.

Jones Hall, L. *Roman Berytos, Beirut in Late Antiquity*. London – New York, 2004.

Jongmann, W. *The Economy and Society of Pompeii*. Amsterdam, 1991.

Jörs, P. 'Codex Iustinianus'. In *RE* IV.1 (1900), cols. 167–70.

Kaiser, W. 'Digestenentstehung und Digestenüberlieferung'. *ZSS* 108 (1991): 330–50.

Kaiser, W. 'Digesten (Überlieferung)'. In *Der Neue Pauly*, vol. 13, cols. 845–52. Stuttgart – Weimar 1999.

Kaiser, W. 'Schreiber und Korrektoren des Codex Florentinus'. *ZSS* 118 (2001): 133–219.

Kaiser, W. *Die Epitome Iuliani. Beiträge zum römischen Recht im frühen Mittelalter und zum byzantinischen Rechtsunterricht* (Studien zur Europäischen Rechtsgeschichte 175). Frankfurt, 2004.

Kaiser, W. 'Nachvergleichungen von Novellen- und Codexzitaten in einer frühmittelalterlichen Sammlung mit Exzerpten aus dem Register Gregors d. Gr. (Reg. 13, 49 [50])'. *ZSS* 125 (2008): 603–44.

Kaiser, W. 'Abhilfe für gescheiterte Gesetze. Zur Novelle Justinians vom 1. Mai 538'. In *Die Bedeutung der Rechtsdogmatik für die Rechtsentwicklung. Ein japanisch-deutsches Symposium*, edited by R. Stürner, 65–88. Tübingen, 2010.

Kaiser, W. 'Ein unbekanntes Zitat von Institutiones Iustiniani 3, 6 pr.–8 in einer Abhandlung des Hrabanus Maurus zum Ehehindernis der Verwandtschaft'. In

Festschrift für Rolf Knütel zum 70. Geburtstag, edited by H. Altmeppen, I. Reichard, and M. Schermaier, 513–57. Heidelberg, 2010.

Kaiser, W. 'Zum Zeitpunkt des Inkrafttretens von Kaisergesetzen unter Justinian'. *ZSS* 127 (2010): 172–201.

Kaiser, W. 'Besserlesungen in den Vulgathandschriften gegenüber Codex Florentinus und Basiliken? Zur Genuinität der erneuten Inskription vor D. 3, 5, 30, 3 (Pap. 2 resp.) in den Handschriften des Digestum vetus'. In *Römische Jurisprudenz. Dogmatik, Überlieferung, Rezeption. Festschrift für Detlef Liebs zum 75. Geburtstag*, edited by K. H. Muscheler, 293–319. Berlin, 2011.

Kaiser, W. 'Zur äußeren Gestalt der Novellen Justinians'. In *Introduzione al diritto bizantino. Da Giustiniano ai Basilici*, edited by J. H. A. Lokin and B. H. Stolte, 159–73. Pavia, 2011.

Kaiser, W. 'Zur Ausfertigung justinianischer Novellen an staatliche und kirchliche Würdenträger'. In *Novellae constitutiones. L'ultima legislazione di giustiniano tra oriente e occidente, da Triboniano a Savigny. Atti del Convegno Internazionale Teramo, 30–31 ottobre 2009*, edited by L. LoSchiavo, G. Mancini and C. Vano, 25–58. Naples, 2011.

Kaiser, W. 'Zur Textkritik von D. 19, 1, 30, 1 (Africanus, 8 quaest.)'. In *Africani quaestiones: Studien zur Geschichte und Dogmatik des Privatrechts*, edited by J. Harke, 53–72. Berlin – Heidelberg, 2011.

Kaiser, W. 'Die Zweisprachigkeit reichsweiter Novellen unter Justinian. Studien zu den Novellen Justinians (I)'. *ZSS* 129 (2012): 392–474.

Kaiser, W. 'Unterschiede zwischen griechischen und lateinischen Ausfertigungen von Novellen am Beispiel des Gesetzes vom 1. Juni 535 über Darlehen an Bauern. Studien zu den Novellen Justinians (II)'. *ZSS* 129 (2012): 475–500.

Kaiser, W. 'Zu den Initia lateinischer Novellen im Breviarium novellarum des Theodorus. Studien zu den Novellen Justinians (III)'. *ZSS* 129 (2012): 501–21.

Kaiser, W. 'Spätantike Rechtstexte in agrimensorischen Sammlungen'. *ZSS* 130 (2013): 273–347.

Kantorowicz, E. 'The sovereignty of the artist. A note on legal maxims and Renaissance theories of art'. *In De Artibus Opuscula XL. Essays in Honor of Erwin Panofsky*, 267–79. New York, 1961 (reprinted in *Selected Studies*, 352–65. New York, 1965).

Kantorowicz, H. and W. Buckland. *Studies in the Glossators of the Roman Law*. Cambridge, 1939, reprinted with addenda and corrigenda, Aalen, 1969.

Karayannopoulos, J. *Das Finanzwesen des frühbyzantinischen Staates*. Munich, 1958.

Karlowa, O. *Römische Rechtsgeschichte*. Leipzig, 1885.

Kaser, M. 'Vom Begriff des *commercium*'. In *Studi in onore di V. Arangio-Ruiz*, vol. 2, 131–67. Naples, 1953.

Kaser, M. 'Die lex Aebutia'. In *Studi in memoria di Emilio Albertario*, 25–59. Milan, 1953.

Kaser, M. *Eigentum und Besitz im älteren römischen Recht*, 2nd edn. Cologne, 1956.

Kaser, M. 'Gradenwitz, Otto'. In *Neue Deutsche Biographie*, vol. 6, 702–3. 1964 and : http://www.deutsche-biographie.de/pnd116807229.html.

Kaser, M. 'Der römische Anteil am deutschen bürgerlichen Recht'. *Juristische Schulung* 1967: 337–44.

Kaser, M. 'The changing face of Roman jurisdiction'. *Irish Jurist* (n.s.) 2 (1967): 129–43.

Kaser, M. 'Nuovi studi sul processo civile Romano'. *Labeo* 15 (1969): 190–98.

Kaser, M. *Das römische Privatrecht*, 2 vols., 2nd edn. Munich, 1971–75.

Kaser, M. *Zur Methodologie der römischen Rechtsquellenforschung*. Vienna, 1972.

Kaser, M. 'Zum Ursprung des geteilten römischen Zivilprozessverfahrens'. In M. Kaser, *Ausgewählten Schriften*, vol. 2, 385–409. Naples, 1976.

Kaser, M. 'Über "relatives Eigentum" im altrömischen Recht'. *ZSS* 102 (1985): 1–39.
Kaser, M. 'Ein Jahrhundert Interpolationenforschung an den römischen Rechtsquellen'. In M. Kaser, *Römische Rechtsquellen und angewandte Juristenmethode*, 112–54. Vienna – Cologne, 1986.
Kaser, M. 'Altrömische Eigentum und usucapio'. *ZSS* 105 (1988): 122–64.
Kaser, M. *Das römische Zivilprozessrecht*, 2nd edn. by K. Hackl. Munich, 1996.
Kaser, M. *Römisches Privatrecht*, 17th edn. by R. Knütel. Munich, 2003; 18th edn., 2005.
Kaufmann, H. *Rezeption und usus modernus der actio legis Aquiliae*. Cologne – Graz, 1958.
Kazhdan, A. 'Do we need a new history of Byzantine law?' *Jahrbuch der Österreichischen Byzantinistik* 39 (1989): 1–28.
Kazhdan, A., editor. *Oxford Dictionary of Byzantium*. Oxford, 1991.
Kelly, B. *Petitions, Litigation, and Social Control in Roman Egypt*. Oxford, 2011.
Kelly, D., A. Holmes, and R. Hayward, *Business Law*, 5th edn. Abingdon – New York, 2005.
Kelly, G. P. *A History of Exile under the Roman Republic*. Cambridge, 2006.
Kelly, J. M. Princeps Iudex. *Eine Untersuchung zu der Begrundung der kaiserlichen Gerichtsbarkeit*. Weimar, 1957.
Kelly, J. M. *Roman Litigation*. Oxford, 1966.
Kelly, J. M. *Studies in the Civil Judicature of the Roman Republic*. Oxford, 1976.
Kenny, A. *Aristotle's Theory of the Will*. Oxford, 1980.
Kensky, M. Z. *Trying Man, Trying God. The Divine Courtroom in Early Jewish and Christian Literature*. Tübingen, 2010.
Kipp. T. 'Contumacia'. In *RE* vol. 4, col. 1165 (1901).
Kitagawa, Z. *Rezeption und Fortbildung des europäischen Zivilrechts in Japan*. Frankfurt – Berlin, 1970.
Kitagawa, Z. 'Development of Comparative Law in East Asia'. In *The Oxford Handbook of Comparative Law*, edited by M. Reimann and R. Zimmermann, 237–60. Oxford, 2008.
Kleinheisterkamp, J. 'Development of comparative law in Latin America'. In *The Oxford Handbook of Comparative Law*, edited by M. Reimann and R. Zimmermann, 261–301. Oxford, 2008.
Knütel, R. 'Die Haftung für Hilfspersonen im römischen Recht'. *ZSS* 100 (1983): 340–443.
Knütel, R. 'Römisches Recht und deutsches Bürgerliches Recht'. In *Die Antike in der europäischen Gegenwart*, edited by W. Ludwig, 43–70. Göttingen, 1993.
Knütel, R. '"Nicht leichter, aber um so reizvoller" – Zum methodologischen Vermächtnis von Max Kaser'. *ZSS* 115 (1998): 33–65.
Knütel, R. 'I compiti della romanistica nel nostro tempo'. In *Dieter Nörr e la romanistica europea tra xx e xxi secolo*, edited by E. Stolfi, 133–52. Turin, 2006.
Knütel, R. and M. Goetzmann. 'Register der in den Materialien zum BGB zitierten römischen Rechtsquellen'. in *Rechtsgeschichte und Privatrechtsdogmatik*, edited by R. Zimmermann, R. Knütel, and J. P. Meincke, 679–84. Heidelberg, 1999.
Koschaker, P. *Europa und das römische Recht*, 4th edn. Munich – Berlin, 1966.
Krause, J.-U. *Gefängnisse im römischen Reich*. Stuttgart, 1996.
Krause, J.-U. 'Prisons et crimes dans l'Empire romain'. In *Carcer. Prison et Privation de Liberté dans l'antiquité classique: Actes du colloque de Strasbourg (5 et 6 décembre 1997)*, edited by C. Bertrand-Dagenbach, A. Chauvot, M. Matter, and J.-M. Salamito, 118–28. Paris, 1999.

Kremer, D. 'Trattato internazionale e legge delle Dodici Tavole'. In *Le Dodici Tavole. Dai Decemviri agli Umanisti*, edited by M. Humbert, 191–207. Pavia, 2005.

Krüger, P. *Geschichte der Quellen und Litteratur des römischen Rechts*, 2nd edn. Munich – Leipzig, 1912.

Krynen, J. *L'empire du roi. Idées et croyances politiques en France. XIIè–XVème siècle*. Paris, 1993.

Kübler, B. 'Rechtsunterricht'. In *RE* vol. IA.1, cols. 394–405 (1914).

Kübler, B. *Geschichte des römischen Rechts*, 2nd edn. Leipzig, 1925.

Kudlien, F. '*Mutator* und *permutatio* als finanz- und handelstechnische Termini'. *Münstersche Beiträge zur Antiken Handelsgeschichte* 20.1 (2001): 48–54.

Kühn, Z. 'Comparative Law in Central and Eastern Europe'. In *The Oxford Handbook of Comparative Law*, edited by M. Reimann and R. Zimmermann, 215–36. Oxford, 2008.

Kunkel, W. *Untersuchungen zur Entwicklung des römischen Kriminalverfahrens in vorsullanischer Zeit*. Munich, 1962.

Kunkel, W. '*Quaestio*'. In *RE* vol. 24, cols. 720–68 (1963).

Kunkel, W. *Herkunft und soziale Stellung der römischen Juristen*, 2nd edn. Graz – Vienna – Cologne, 1967.

Kupisch, B. *Die Versionsklage*. Heidelberg, 1965.

Kupisch, B. *In integrum restitutio und vindicatio utilis bei Eigentumsübertragungen im klassischen römischen Recht*. Berlin, 1974.

Kupisch, B. 'Eine Moselinsel, Kaiser Napoleon und das römische Recht'. *Juristenzeitung* 1987: 1017–20.

Kupisch, B. *Ungerechtfertigte Bereicherung: geschichtliche Entwicklungen*. Heidelberg, 1987.

Labruna, L. 'Il diritto mercantile dei Romani e l'espansionismo'. In *Le strade del potere*, edited by A. Corbino, 115–37. Catania, 1994.

Lafon, X. 'Les îles de la mer Tyrrhénienne: entre palais et prisons sous les Julio-Claudiens'. In *Carcer. Prison et Privation de Liberté dans l'antiquité classique: Actes du colloque de Strasbourg (5 et 6 décembre 1997)*, edited by C. Bertrand-Dagenbach, A. Chauvot, M. Matter, and J.-M. Salamito,149–61. Paris, 1999.

Lamberti, F. *Tabulae Irnitanae: municipalità e 'ius Romanorum'*. Naples, 1993.

Lancel, S. *Actes de la Conférence de Carthage en 411*. (Sources Chrétiennes vols. 194, 195, 224, and 373). Paris, 1972–91.

Landau, P. 'Der Einfluss des kanonischen Rechts auf die europäische Rechtskultur'. In *Europäische Rechts- und Verfassungsgeschichte: Ergebnisse und Perspektiven der Forschung*, edited by R. Schulze, 39–57. Berlin, 1991.

Landau, P. 'Pacta sunt servanda: Zu den kanonistischen Grundlagen der Privatautonomie'. In *'Ins Wasser geworfen und Ozeane durchquert': Festschrift für Knut Wolfgang Nörr*, edited by M. Ascheri, F. Ebel, M. Heckel, A. Padoa-Schioppa, W. Pöggeler, F. Ranieri, and W. Rütter, 457–74. Cologne – Weimar – Vienna, 2003.

Landau, P. 'The origins of legal science in England in the twelfth century: Lincoln, Oxford and the career of Vacarius'. In *Readers, Texts and Compilers in the Earlier Middle Ages. Studies in Honour of Linda Fowler-Magerl*, edited by M. Brett and K. Cushing, 165–82. Aldershot – Burlington, 2009.

Landi, A. 'Ricerche sull'onomastica delle tabelle dell'agro Murecine'. *Atti dell'Accademia Pontaniana* 29 (1980): 193–97.

Landsberg, E. *Die quaestiones des Azo*. Freiburg, 1888.

Lanfranchi, F. *Il diritto nei retori romani*. Milan, 1938.

Lange, H. 'Ius Commune und Statutarrecht in Christoph Besolds Consilia Tubigensia'. In *Festschrift für Max Kaser*, edited by D. Medicus and H. H. Seiler, 637–56. Munich, 1976.

Lange, H. *Römisches Recht im Mittelalter. I. Die Glossatoren*. Munich, 1997.

Lange, H. and M. Kriechbaum. *Römisches Recht im Mittelalter. II. Die Kommentatoren*. Munich, 2007.

Laniado, A. *Recherches sur les notables municipaux dans l'empire protobyzantin*. Paris, 2002.

Lardone, F. G. 'Roman law in the works of St. Augustine'. *Georgetown Law Journal* (1956): 435–56.

Larrainzar, C. 'La formación del Decreto de Graciano por etapas'. *ZSS (Kanonistische Abteilung)* 118 (2001): 5–83.

Le Bras, G. 'Le droit romain au service de la domination pontificale'. *RHDFE* 27 (1949): 377–98.

Leder, S., editor. *Die arabische Ecloga. Das vierte Buch der Kanones der Könige aus der Sammlung des Makarios*. Frankfurt, 1985.

Leesen, T. *Gaius Meets Cicero: Law and Rhetoric in the School Controversies*. Leiden, 2010.

Lefebvre-Teillard, A. 'Le rôle des canonistes dans la formation d'un 'droit commun' romano-canonique'. *Revue d'histoire des facultés de droit et de la culture juridique* 28 (2008): 215–16.

Legeais, D. *Droit commercial et des affaires*, 15th edn. Paris, 2003.

Legrand, P. 'Legal traditions in Western Europe: the limits of commonality'. In *Transfrontier Mobility of Law*, edited by R. Jagtenberg, E. Örücü, and A. de Roo, 63–84. The Hague, 1995.

Legrand, P. 'European legal systems are not converging'. *International and Comparative Law Quarterly* 45 (1996): 52–81.

Lehoux, D. *What Did the Roman Know? An Inquiry into Science and Worldmaking*. Chicago, 2012.

Leitner, P. 'Die plautinischen Komödien als Quellen des römischen Rechts'. In *Diritto e teatro in Grecia e a Roma*, edited by E. Cantarella and L. Gagliardi, 69–92, Milan, 2007.

Lemerle, P., N. Oikonomides, and J. Lefort, editors. *Archives de l'Athos*. Paris, 1937.

Lenel, O. *Palingenesia Iuris Civilis*, 2 vols. Leipzig, 1889.

Lenel, O. *Das Edictum Perpetuum*, 3rd edn. Leipzig, 1927.

Levy, E. *West Roman Vulgar Law*. Philadelphia, 1951.

Lewis, N. *On Government and Law in Roman Egypt*. Atlanta, 1995.

Lewis, N., Y. Yadin, and J. C. Greenfield. *The Documents from the Bar Kochba Perod in the Cave of Letters. Greek Papyri, Aramaic and Nabataean Signatures and Subscriptions*. Jerusalem, 1989.

Lieberman, S. 'Roman legal institutions in early Rabbinics and in the Acta Martyrum'. *Jewish Quarterly Review* 35 (1944): 1–57.

Liebeschuetz, J. H. W. G. 'Berytos'. In *RAC* suppl. 1 cols. 1027–42 (2001).

Liebeschuetz, J. H. W. G. *Decline and Fall of the Roman City*. Oxford, 2001.

Liebs, D. 'Ulpiani Opinionum libri VI'. *TR* 41 (1973): 279–310.

Liebs, D. 'Römische Provinzialjurisprudenz'. *ANRW* 2.15: 288–362 (1976).

Liebs, D. 'The History of the Roman *Condictio* up to Justinian'. In *The Legal Mind: Essays for Tony Honoré*, edited by N. MacCormick and P. Birks, 163–83. Oxford, 1986.

Liebs, D. *Die Jurisprudenz im spätantiken Italien (260–640 n. Chr.)*. Berlin, 1987.

Liebs, D. 'Recht und Rechtsliteratur'. In *Restauration und Erneuerung. Die lateinische Literatur von 284 bis 374 n. Chr.*, edited by H. Herzog, 55–73. Munich, 1989.

Liebs, D. 'Jurisprudenz'. In *Die Literatur des Umbruchs. Von der römischen zur christlichen Literatur 117 n. Chr. bis 284 n. Chr.*, edited by K. Sallmann, 83–217. Munich, 1997.

Liebs, D. 'Roman Law'. In *CAH* vol. 14, 240–41 (2000).

Liebs, D. *Römische Jurisprudenz in Gallien (2. bis 8. Jahrhundert)*. Berlin, 2002.

Liebs, D. *Römische Jurisprudenz in Africa mit Studien zu den pseudopaulinischen Sentenzen*, 2nd edn. Berlin, 2005.

Liebs, D. *Vor den Richtern Roms. Berühmte Prozesse der Antike*. Munich, 2007.

Liebs, D. 'Esoterische römische Rechtsliteratur vor Justinian'. In *Akten des 36. Deutschen Rechtshistorikertages, Halle an der Saale, 10.–14.* September *2006*, edited by R. Lieberwirt and H. Lück, 40–79. Baden-Baden, 2008.

Liebs, D. 'Juristenausbildung in der Spätantike'. In *Juristenausbildung in Europa zwischen Tradition und Reform*, edited by C. Baldus, T. Finkenauer, T. Rüfner, 31–45. Tübingen, 2008.

Liebs, D. *Hofjuristen der römischen Kaiser bis Justinian*. Munich, 2010.

Liebs, D. 'Connolly, *Lives behind the Laws*'. *ZSS* 129 (2012): 711–24.

Lintott, A. '*Provocatio*. From the struggle of the orders to the principate'. *ANRW* 1.2: 226–67 (1972).

Lintott, A. 'The *leges de repetundis* and associate measures under the Republic'. *ZSS* 98 (1981): 162–212.

Lintott, A. 'Le procès devant les recuperatores d'après les données épigraphiques jusqu'au règne d'Auguste'. *RHDFE* 68 (1990): 1–11.

Lintott, A. *Judicial Reform and Land Reform in the Roman Republic*. Cambridge, 1992.

Lintott, A. *Imperium Romanum: Politics and Administration*. London, 1993.

Lintott, A. *The Constitution of the Roman Republic*. Oxford, 1999.

Lintott, A. *Violence in Republican Rome*, 2nd edn. Oxford, 1999.

Lintott, A. '*Delator* and *index*: informers and accusers at Rome from the republic to the early principate'. *Accordia Research Papers* 9 (2001–3): 105–22.

Lintott, A. 'Legal procedure in Cicero's time'. In *Cicero the Advocate*, edited by J. Powell and J. Paterson, 61–78. Oxford, 2004.

Lintott, A. *Cicero as Evidence: A Historian's Companion*. Oxford, 2008.

Lintott, A. '*Provocatio* e *iudicium populi* dopo Kunkel'. In *La repressione criminale nella Roma repubblicana fra norma e persuasione*, edited by B. Santalucia, 15–24. Pavia, 2009.

Litewski, W. 'Römisches Seedarlehen'. *Iura* 24 (1973): 112–83.

Litewski, W. *Der römisch-kanonische Zivilprozess nach den älteren ordines iudiciarii*. Krakow, 1999.

Lo Cascio, E. 'The early Roman empire: the state and the economy'. In *The Cambridge Economic History of the Greco-Roman World*, edited by I. Morris, R. Saller, and W. Scheidel, 619–47. Cambridge, 2007.

Logan, F. D. *Excommunication and the Secular Arm in Medieval England*. Toronto, 1968.

Lokin, J. H. A. 'Het NBW en de pandektistiek'. In *Historisch vooruitzicht. Opstellen over rechtsgeschiedenis en burgerlijk recht*, edited by M. E. Franke, 125–39. Arnhem, 1994.

Lokin, J. H. A. 'The end of an epoch. Epilegomena to a century of interpolation Criticism'. In *Collatio Iuris Romani. Etudes dédiées à Hans Ankum*, edited by R. Feenstra, 261–73. Amsterdam, 1995.

Lokin, J. H. A., R. Meijering, B. H. Stolte, and N. van der Wal. *Theophili Antecessoris Paraphrasis Institutionum*. With a translation by A. F. Murison. Groningen, 2010.

Lomas, K. 'Italy during the Roman Republic: 338–31 BC'. In *The Cambridge Companion to the Roman Republic*, edited by H. Flower, 199–224. Cambridge, 2004.

LoSchiavo, L. 'Il codex graecus e le origini del Liber authenticorum. Due contributi alla storia dell'Authenticum'. *ZSS* 127 (2010): 115–71.

LoSchiavo, L. 'La riscoperta dell'Authenticum e la prima esegesi die Glossatori'. In *Novellae constitutiones. L'ultima legislazione di Giustiniano tra oriente e occidente, da Triboniano a Savigny. Atti del Convegno Internazionale Teramo, 30–31 ottobre 2009*, edited by L. LoSchiavo, G. Mancini, and C. Vano, 111–39. Napoli, 2011.

Lounghis, T., B. Blysidu, and S Lampakes. *Regesten der Kaiserurkunden des oströmischen Reiches von 476 bis 565* (Quellen und Studien zur Geschichte Zyperns, 52). Nicosia, 2005.

Lovato A. *Il carcere nel diritto penale romano (dai Severi a Giustiniano)*. Bari, 1994.

Lowe, E. A. *Codices Latini Antiquiores*, vols. 1–11 and suppl. Oxford, 1934–1971 (2nd edn. of vol. 2, 1972).

Lucas, F.-X. *Le droit des affaires*. Paris, 2005.

Luchetti, G. *Nuove ricerche sulle Istituzioni di Giustiniano*. Milan, 2004.

Luig, K. 'The institutes of national law in the seventeenth and eighteenth centuries'. *Juridical Review* 1972: 193–226.

Luig, K. 'Zur Vorgeschichte der verschuldensunabhängigen Haftung des Vermieters für anfängliche Mängel nach § 538 BGB'. In *Festschrift für Heinz Hübner*, edited by G. Baumgärtel, 121–44. Berlin – New York, 1984.

Luig, K. 'Usus modernus'. In *Handwörterbuch zur deutschen Rechtsgeschichte*, vol. 5, col. 628. Berlin, 1998.

Luzzatto, G. *Procedura civile romana*, 3 vols. Bologna, 1945–48.

Lyon, E. 'Le droit chez Isidore de Péluse'. *Etudes d'histoire juridique offertes à Paul Girard*, vol. 2, 209–22. Paris, 1912–13.

McAuley, M. 'Québec'. In *Mixed Jurisdictions Worldwide*, edited by V. Palmer, 354–80, 2nd edn. Cambridge, 2012.

MacCormack, G. 'Roman and African Litigation'. *TR* 39 (1971): 221–55.

MacCormack, G. 'The liability of the judge'. In *ANRW*, vol. II.14, 3–28. Berlin, 1982.

MacCoull, L. S. B. 'Apa Abraham: Testament of Apa Abraham, Bishop of Hermonthis, for the Monastery of St. Phoibammon near Thebes, Egypt'. In *Byzantine Monastic Foundation Documents*, edited by J. P. Thomas, 51–58. Washington, D.C., 2000.

Maas, M. *The Cambridge Companion to the Age of Justinian*. Cambridge, 2005.

Macino, F. *Sulle tracce delle Istituzioni di Giustiniano nell'alto medioevo. I manoscritti dal VI al XII secolo*. Vatican City, 2008.

Mádl F. 'Geleitwort'. In *Aufbruch nach Europa*, edited by J. Basedow, vii–x. Tübingen, 2001.

Maffei, D. *La 'Lectura super digesto veteri' di Cino da Pistoia. Studio sui mss Savigny 22 e Urb. Lat. 172*. (Quaderni di Studi Senesi 10.) Milan, 1963.

Maffei, D. *Gli inizi dell'umanesimo giuridico*. Milan, 1964.

Maffei, D. *La donazione di Costantino nei giuristi medievali*. Milan, 1964.

Maganzani, L. *Pubblicani e debitori d'imposta. Ricerche sul titolo edittale de publicanis*. Turin, 2002.

Maganzani, L. 'L'editto provinciale alla luce delle *Verrine*: profili strutturali, criteri applicative'. In *La Sicile de Cicéron. Lectures des Verrines*, edited by J. Dubouloz and S. Pittia, 127–46. Besançon, 2007.

Magie, D. *Roman Rule in Asia Minor*. Princeton, 1950.

Magnou-Nortier, É. *Le Code Théodosien, Livre XVI et sa Réception au Moyen Âge*. Paris, 2002.

Maier, J.-L., editor. *Le Dossier du Donatisme*, 2 vols. Berlin, 1987–89.

Maine, H. *Ancient Law*, 8th edn. London, 1880.

Malanima, P. 'Progresso o stabilità? Il mercato nelle economie preindustriali'. *Studi storici* 50 (2009): 5–23.

Mantello, A. '*De iurisconsultorum philosophia*, spunti e riflessioni sulla giurisprudenza nel primo principato'. *SDHI* 67 (2001): 1–57.

Manthe, U. *Das senatus consultum Pegasianum*. Berlin, 1989.

Manthe, U. 'Wurde die Collatio vom Ambrosiaster Isaak geschrieben?' In *Festschrift für Rolf Knütel zum 70. Geburtstag*, edited by H. Altmeppen, I. Reichard, and M. Schermaier, 737–54. Heidelberg, 2010.

Mantovani, D. *Digesto e masse Bluhmiane*. Milan, 1987.

Mantovani, D. 'Sulla competenza penale del *praefectus urbi* attraverso il *liber singularis* di Ulpiano'. In *Idee vecchie e nuove sul diritto criminale romano*, edited by A. Burdese, 171–223. Padua, 1988.

Mantovani, D. 'Le masse bluhmiane sono tre'. *Seminarios Complutenses de derecho romano* (1993): 87–119.

Mantovani, D. *Le formule del processo privato romano: per la didattica delle Istituzioni di diritto romano*, 2nd edn. Padua, 1999.

Mantovani, D. 'L'édit comme code'. In *La codification des lois dans l'Antiquité. Actes du colloque de Strasbourg, 27–29 novembre 1997*, edited by E. Lévy, 257–72. Paris, 2000.

Mantovani, D. 'La "diei diffissio" nella "lex Irnitana"'. In *Iuris Vincula: Studi in onore di Mario Talamanca*, vol. 5, 13–72. Naples, 2001.

Maran, G. de. *Discours politique de l'établissement et conservation des lois et de la justice*. Toulouse, 1628.

Markesinis, B. S., editor. *The Gradual Convergence: Foreign Ideas, Foreign Influences and English Law on the Eve of the 21st Century*. Oxford, 1994.

Marotta, V. *Ulpiano e l'Impero II: Studi sui libri de officio proconsulis e la loro fortuna tardoantica*. Naples, 2004.

Marquardt, J. *Römische Staatsverwaltung*, 1st edn. Leipzig, 1873–78; 2nd edn. 1884–85, reprinted 1952.

Marshall, A. J. 'The structure of Cicero's edict'. *AJP* 85 (1964): 185–89.

Marshall, A. J. 'Governors on the move'. *Phoenix* 20 (1966): 231–46.

Martens, J. W. *One God. One Law. Philo of Alexandria on the Mosaic and Greco-Roman Law*. Boston, 2003.

Martinez-Torrón, J. *Anglo-American Law and Canon Law: Canonical Roots of the Common Law Tradition*. Berlin, 1998.

Martino, F. de. *Storia della costituzione romana*. Naples, 1975.

Massmann, H. F. *Libellus aurarius*. Leipzig, 1840.

Matthews, J. *Laying down the Law: A Study of the Theodosian Code*. New Haven, 2000.

Mayali, L. '*Lex animata*. Rationalisation du pouvoir politique et science juridique (XIIè-XIVè siècles)'. In *Renaissance du pouvoir législatif et genèse de l'Etat*, edited by A. Gouron and A. Rigaudière, 155–64. Montpellier, 1988.

Mayali, L. 'Mythes et réalités de la renaissance juridique au douzième siècle'. In *El dret comù i Catalunya* III, edited by A. Iglesias Ferreirós and A. Gouron, 187–202. Barcelona, 1993.

Mayer-Maly, T. '*Commercium*'. *TR* 71 (2003): 1–6.

Meier, M. *Das andere Zeitalter Justinians. Kontingenzerfahrung und Kontingenz-bewältigung im 6. Jahrhundert n. Chr.* Göttingen, 2003.

Meier, M., editor. *Justinian*. Darmstadt, 2011.

Meier, U. *Mensch und Bürger. Die Stadt im Denken spätmittelalterlicher Theologen, Philosophen und Juristen*. Munich, 1994.

Meijers, E. M. 'Het feilloze deel van ons Burgerlijk Wetboek [The infallible part of the Civil Code]' *Weekblad voor Privaatrecht, Notariaat en Registratie* 3031 (1928); also in E. M. Meijers, *Verzamelde Privaatrechtelijke Opstellen*. I, 93–98. Leiden, 1954.

Meincke, J. P. 'Corpus Iuris Civilis vol. IV'. *Juristenzeitung* 2006: 299–300.

Merryman, J. H. *The Civil Law Tradition. An Introduction to the Legal Systems of Western Europe and Latin America*, 2nd edn. Stanford, 1985.

Merzbacher, F. 'Die Parömie *Legista sine canonibus parum valet, canonista sine legibus nihil*'. *Studia Gratiana* 13 (1967): 275–82.

Metzger, E. *A New Outline of the Roman Civil Trial*. Oxford, 1997.

Metzger, E. *A Companion to Justinian's Institutes*. Ithaca NY, 1998, reprinted 2002.

Metzger, E. 'Roman Judges, Case Law, and Principles of Procedure'. *Law and History Review* 22 (2004): 243–75.

Metzger, E. *Litigation in Roman Law*. Oxford, 2005.

Metzger, E. 'Absent parties and bloody-minded judges'. In *Mapping the Law: Essays in Memory of Peter Birks*, edited by A. Burrows and A. Rodger, 455–73. Oxford, 2006.

Metzger, E. 'Lawsuits in Context'. In *Beyond Dogmatics: Law and Society in the Roman World*, edited by J. Cairns and P. du Plessis, 187–205. Edinburgh, 2007.

Metzger, E. 'Formula'. In *Oxford International Encyclopaedia of Legal History*, edited by S. N. Katz. New York, 2009.

Metzger, E. 'Lex Irnitana'. In *Oxford International Encyclopaedia of Legal History*, edited by S. N. Katz. New York, 2009.

Metzger, E. 'Having an audience with the magistrate'. In *Spaces of Justice in the Roman World*, edited by W. V. Harris and F. de Angelis, 27–41. Leiden, 2010.

Metzger, E. 'Remedy of prohibition against Roman judges in civil trial'. In *Judges and Judging: Proceedings of the Eighteenth British Legal History Conference*, edited by P. Brand and J. Getzler, 177–91. Cambridge, 2012.

Metzger, E. 'Agree to disagree: local jurisdiction in the *lex Irnitana*'. In *Judge and Jurist: Essays in Memory of Lord Rodger of Earlsferry*, edited by A. Burrows, D. Johnston, and R. Zimmermann, 207–25. Oxford, 2013.

Meyer, E. A. 'Diplomatics, law and Romanisation in the documents from the Judaean desert'. In *Beyond Dogmatics: Law and Society in the Roman World*, edited by J. W. Cairns and P. du Plessis, 53–82. Edinburgh, 2007.

Meyer, E. A. *Legitimacy and Law in the Roman World: Tabulae in Roman Belief and Practice*. Cambridge, 2004.

Meylan, P. '*Permutatio rerum*'. In *Ius et lex. Festgabe zum 70. Geburtstag von M. Gutzwiller*, 45–64. Basel, 1959, reprinted 1977.

Mezey, N. 'Law as Culture'. *Yale Journal of Law and the Humanities* 13 (2001): 35–67.

Miceli, M. *Sulla struttura formulare delle actiones adiecticiae qualitatis*. Turin, 2001.

Millar, F. 'Paul of Samosata, Zenobia and Aurelian: the church, local culture and political allegiance in third century Syria'. *JRS* 61 (1971): 1–17.

Millar, F. *The Emperor in the Roman World*. London, 1977.

Millar, F. *A Greek Roman Empire. Power and Belief under Theodosius II (408–450)*. Berkeley and Los Angeles, 2006.

Millar, F. 'Un dossier d'accusation déposé auprès du praeses de Syrie seconde pour transmission à Justin Ier'. *Antiquité Tardive* 18 (2010): 231–42.

Minaud, G. *Les gens de commerce et le droit à Rome*. Aix-en-Provence, 2011.

Mitteis, L. *Reichsrecht und Volksrecht in den östlichen Provinzen des römischen Kaiserreichs*. Leipzig, 1891.

Mitterauer, M. *Warum Europa? Mittelalterliche Grundlagen eines Sonderwegs*. Munich, 2003.

Modrzejewski, J. 'Grégoire le Thaumaturge et le droit romain. À propos d'une édition récente'. *RHDFE* 49 (1971): 321–22.

Mölk, U., editor. *Literatur und Recht. Literarische Rechtsfälle von der Antike bis in die Gegenwart*. Göttingen, 1996.

Mommsen, T. *Römisches Strafrecht*. Leipzig, 1899.

Mommsen, T. 'Die pompeianischen Quittungstafeln des L. Caecilius Iucundus'. In T. Mommsen, *Gesammelte Schriften*, vol. 3, 221–74. Berlin, 1907, reprinted 1965.

Morel, H. 'La place de la Lex regia dans l'histoire des idées politiques'. In *Études offertes à Jean Macqueron*, edited by Y. Lobin, 545–55. Aix-en-Provence, 1970.

Mugdan, B., editor. *Die gesammten Materialien zum Bürgerlichen Gesetzbuch für das Deutsche Reich*. Berlin, 1899.

Müller-Ehlen, M. *Hereditatis petitio*. Cologne – Weimar – Vienna, 1998.

Murison, A. F. 'The law in the Latin poets'. In *Atti del Congresso Internazionale di Diritto Romano Roma* II, 609–39. Pavia, 1935.

Nanz, K.-P. *Die Entstehung des allgemeinen Vertragsbegriffs im 16. bis 18. Jahrhundert*. Munich, 1985.

Nasti, F. *Papyrus Hauniensis de legatis et fideicommissis. Pars prior (PHaun. III 45 recto + CPL 73 A e B recto)*. Naples, 2010.

Nelson, H. L. W. *Überlieferung, Aufbau und Stil von Gai Institutiones*. Leiden, 1981.

Neri, C. 'Ci sono testimonianze giuridiche nelle fonti monastiche?' *AARC* 15 (2005): 107–17.

Niccolini, U. 'Leggendo le "Quaestiones de iuris subtilitatibus" '. *Jus* 28 (1981): 27–119.

Nicholas, B. 'Theophilus and Contrectatio'. In *Studies in Justinian's Institutes*, edited by P. Stein and A. D. E. Lewis, 118–24. London, 1983.

Nicosia, G. *Il processo privato romano: corso di diritto romano*. Turin, 1986.

Nippel, W. *Public Order in Ancient Rome*. Cambridge, 1995.

Noailles, P. *Les collections de novelles de l'empereur Justinian. Vol. 1: Origine et formation sous Justinien. Vol. 2: La collection grecque des 168 novelles*. Paris, 1912–14.

Nonnoi, D. 'Sant'Agostino e il diritto romano'. *Rivista Italiana per le Scienze Giuridiche* 12 (1934): 531–622.

Nörr, D. 'The xenokritai in Babatha's archive'. *Israel Law Review* 29 (1995): 83–94.

Nörr, D. 'Zu den Xenokriten (Rekuperatoren) in der römischen Provinzialgerichtsbarkeit'. In *Lokale Autonomie und römische Ordnungsmacht in den kaiserzeitlichen Provinzen vom 1. bis 3. Jahrhundert*, edited by W. Eck, 257–301. Munich, 1999.

Nörr, D. 'PSI VII 743r fr. e: Fragment einer römischen Prozeßformel? Bemerkungen zum vorhadrianischen Edikt und zu den Hermeneumata Pseudodositheana'. *ZSS* 117 (2000): 179–215.

Nörr, D. 'Der Jurist im Kreis der Intellektuellen: Mitspieler oder Außenseiter?' In *Festschrift Max Kaser*, edited by D. Medicus and H. H. Seiler, 57–90. Munich, 1976; also in D. Nörr, *Historiae Iuris Antiqui*, 951–84. Goldbach, 2003.

Nörr, D. *Historiae Iuris Antiqui. Gesammelte Schriften*, edited by T. J. Chiusi, W. Kaiser, and H.-D. Spengler, 3 vols. Goldbach, 2003.

Nörr, D. 'Osservazioni in tema di terminologia giuridica predecemvirale e di ius mercatorum mediterraneo: il primo trattato cartaginese-romano'. In *Le Dodici Tavole. Dai Decemviri agli Umanisti*, edited by M. Humbert, 147–89. Pavia, 2005.

Nörr, D. 'Prozessuales (und mehr) in der Lex Rivi Hiberiensis'. *ZSS* 125 (2008): 108–88.

Nörr, D. 'P. Haun III 45 und der verlorene Traktat Modestins zum Vermächtnisrecht'. *ZSS* 127 (2009): 53–114.

Nörr, D. 'Zur Formel der *actio legis Aquiliae*'. In *Festschrift für Rolf Knütel zum 70. Geburtstag*, edited by H. Altmeppen, I. Reichard, and M. Schermaier, 833–48. Heidelberg, 2009.

Nörr, D. *Schriften 2001–2010*. Madrid – Barcelona – Buenos Aires, 2012.

Nörr, K. W. *Romanisch-kanonisches Prozessrecht: Erkenntnisverfahren erster Instanz in civilibus*. Heidelberg, 2012.

North, D. *Structure and Change in Economic History*. New York – London, 1981.

North, D. *Institutions, Institutional Change and Economic Performance*. Cambridge, 1991.

North, D. and R. P. Thomas. *The Rise of the Western World: A New Economic History*. Cambridge, 1973.

Nuyens, F. J. C. J. *Ontwikkelingsmomenten in de zielkunde van Aristoteles*. Nijmegen – Utrecht, 1939; French version: *L'evolution de la psychologie d'Aristote*. Louvain, 1948.

Obolensky, D. *The Byzantine Commonwealth. Eastern Europe 500–1453*. London, 1971.

Oestmann, P. *Rechtsvielfalt vor Gericht: Rechtsanwendung und Partikularrecht im Alten Reich*. Frankfurt, 2002.

Ogris, W. *Der Entwicklungsgang der österreichischen Privatrechtswissenschaft im 19. Jahrhundert*. Berlin, 1968.

Osler, D. *Bibliographica iuridica*, 6 vols. Frankfurt, 2000–9.

Ourliac, P. 'Une statue de Justinien en Rouergue, vers 1140'. In P. Ourliac, *Les pays de Garonne vers l'an mil. La société et le droit*, 167–71. Toulouse, 1993.

Oven, J. C. van. *Leerboek van Romeinsch Privaatrecht*, 3rd edn. Leiden, 1948.

Pagano, M. 'L'edificio dell'agro Murecine a Pompeii'. *RAAN* 58 (1983): 325–61.

Palazzini Finetti, L. *Storia della ricerca delle interpolazioni nel Corpus Iuris Giustinianeo*. Milan, 1953.

Palazzolo, N. 'Sulla *lex Cornelia de edictis*'. *Labeo* 37 (1991): 242–45.

Papagianni, E. 'Un témoin de la réalité juridique byzantine: la jurisprudence patriarcale au XIVe siècle'. *Fontes Minores* 11 (2005): 213–27.

Paradisi, B. 'Diritto canonico e tendenze di scuola nei glossatori da Irnerio ad Accursio'. *Studi medievali* 6 (1965): 1–133.

Patsch, C. 'Breuci'. In *RE* 3, col. 831 (1897).

Peachin, M. Iudex vice Caesaris. *Deputy Emperors and the Administration of Justice During the Principate*. Stuttgart, 1996.

Pellecchi, L. *Per una lettura giuridica della 'Rudens' di Plauto*. Faenza, 2012.

Pennington, K. 'Law, legislative authority and theories of government, 1150–1300'. In *The Cambridge History of Medieval Political Thought c.350–c.1450*, edited by J. H. Burns, 424–53, Cambridge, 1988.

Pennington, K. *The Prince and the Law. Sovereignty and Rights in the Western Legal Tradition 1200–1600*. Berkeley – Los Angeles, 1993.

Peppe, L. 'Note sull'editto di Cicerone in Cilicia'. *Labeo* 37 (1991): 14–93.

Pergami, F. *La legislazione di Valentiniano e Valente (364–375)*. Milan, 1993.

Pesaresi, R. *Studi sul processo penale in età repubblicana*. Naples, 2005.

Petra, G. de. *Le tavolette cerate di Pompei*. Naples, 1876.

Petrucci, A. Mensam exercere. *Studi sull'impresa finanziaria romana (II secolo a.C.–metà del III secolo d.C.)*. Naples, 1991.

Petrucci, A. *Profili giuridici delle attività e dell'organizzazione delle banche romane*. Turin, 2002.

Pfister, L. 'Connan (Connanus), François'. In *Dictionnaire historique des juristes français, XIIᵉ–XXᵉ siècle*, edited by P. Arabeyre, Jean-Louis Halpérin, and Jacques Krynen, 199–200. Paris, 2007.

Pfister, L. 'Doneau (Donellus), Hugues'. In *Dictionnaire historique des juristes français, XIIᵉ–XXᵉ siècle*, edited by P. Arabeyre, Jean-Louis Halpérin, and Jacques Krynen, 256–58. Paris, 2007.

Pharr, C. *The Theodosian Code and Novels and the Sirmondian Constitutions. A Translation with Commentary, Glossary and Bibliography*. Princeton, 1952.

Piccinelli, F. *Studi e ricerche intorno alla definizione 'dominium est ius utendi et abutendi re sua quatenus iuris ratio patitur'*. Naples, 1980.

Pichonnaz, P. *La compensation: Analyse historique et comparative des modes de compenser non conventionels*. Fribourg, 2001.

Picker, E. 'Zum Gegenwartswert des Römischen Rechts'. In *Das antike Rom in Europa*, edited by H. Bungert, 289–316. Regensburg, 1985.

Pieler, P. E. 'Byzantinische Rechtsliteratur'. In *Die hochsprachliche profane Literatur der Byzantiner*, edited by H. Hunger, 341–480. Munich, 1978.

Pieler, P. E. 'Anakatharsis ton palaion nomon und makedonische Renaissance'. *Subseciva Groningana* 3 (1995): 61–78.

Piergiovanni, V., editor. *From Lex Mercatoria to Commercial Law*. Berlin, 2005.

Pinna Parpaglia, P. *Per una interpretazione della 'lex Cornelia de edictis praetorum' del 67 A.C.* Sassari, 1987.

Pinna Parpaglia, P. '*Lex Cornelia de edictis*, mutui feneratizi, certezza del diritto'. *Labeo* 38 (1992): 372–78.

Platschek, J. *Studien zu Ciceros Rede für P. Quinctius*. Munich, 2005.

Plessis, J. du. 'Comparative Law and the Study of Mixed Legal Systems'. In *The Oxford Handbook of Comparative Law*, edited by M. Reimann and R. Zimmermann, 477–512. Oxford, 2008.

Pölönen, J. 'The case for a sociology of Roman law'. In *Law and Sociology*, edited by M. Freeman, 398–408. Oxford, 2005.

Portemer, J. *Recherches sur les 'Differentiae juris civilis et canonici' au temps du droit classique de l'Église*. Paris, 1946.

Porto, A. di. *Impresa collettiva e schiavo 'manager' in Roma antica (II sec. a.C.–II sec. d.C.)*. Milan, 1984.

Porto, A. di. 'Il diritto commerciale romano. Una "zona d'ombra" nella storiografia romanistica e nelle riflessioni storico-comparative dei commercialisti'. In *Nozione, formazione e interpretazione del diritto dall'età romana alle esperienze moderne. Ricerche dedicate al Prof. Filippo Gallo*, edited by M. Marrone, vol. 3, 413–52. Naples, 1997.

Post, G. 'Ratio publicae utilitatis, ratio status and 'reason of state', 100–1300'. In G. Post, *Studies in Medieval Legal Thought: Public Law and the State*, 241–309. Princeton, 1964.

Post, G. 'Status regni: lestat du roialme in the statute of York 1322'. In G. Post, *Studies in Medieval Legal Thought: Public Law and the State*, 310–32. Princeton, 1964.

Pothier, R. J. *Traité des obligations*. In R. J. Pothier, *Traités de droit civil*. Paris, 1781.

Powell J. and J. Paterson. 'Introduction'. In *Cicero the Advocate*, edited by J. Powell and J. Paterson, 10–18. Oxford, 2004.

Prévost, X. *Jacques Cujas (1522–1590). Le droit à l'épreuve de l'humanisme*. Paris – Geneva, 2014.

Price, R. *The Acts of the Council of Constantinople of 553 with Related Texts on the Three Chapters Controversy*. Liverpool, 2009.

Price, R. and M. Gaddis. *The Acts of the Council of Chalcedon I–III*. Liverpool, 2005.

Pringsheim, F. 'The Inner Relationship between English and Roman Law'. *Cambridge Law Journal* 5 (1935): 347–65.

Pringsheim, F. 'The origin of the "lex Aquilia"'. In *Mélanges Levy-Bruhl*, 233–44. Paris, 1959.

Prinzing, G., editor. *Demetrii Chomateni Ponemata diaphora*. Berlin – New York, 2002.

Pugliese, G. *Il processo civile romano*. Milan, 1963.

Pugliese, G. 'Riflessioni sull'editto di Cicerone in Cilicia'. In *Synteleia V. Arangio-Ruiz*, vol. 2, 972–96. Naples, 1964.

Puglisi, G. 'Giustizia criminale e persecuzioni antieretiche (Priscilliano e Ursino, Ambrogio e Damaso). *Siculorum Gymnasium* 43 (1990): 91–137.

Pugsley, D. 'The Aedilician edict'. In *Daube Noster. Essays in Legal History for David Daube*, edited by A. Watson, 253–64. Edinburgh – London, 1974.

Quaglioni, D. *Politica e diritto nel trecento italiano. Il 'De tyranno' di Bartolo da Sassoferrato (1314–1357)*. Florence, 1983.

Radding, C. and A. Ciaralli. *The Corpus iuris in the Middle Ages. Manuscripts and Transmission from the Sixth Century to the Juristic Revival*. Leiden – Boston, 2007.

Rainer, J. M. 'Zum Ursprung der extraordinaria cognitio'. In *Roman Law as Formative of Modern Legal Systems*, edited by J. Sondel, 69–74. Krakow, 2003.

Rainer, J. M. 'Dieter Nörr e la romanistica tedesca'. In *Dieter Nörr e la romanistica europea tra xx e xxi secolo*, edited by E. Stolfi, 7–19. Turin, 2006.

Ramsey, J. T. 'Mark Antony's judicial reform and its revival under the Triumvirs'. *JRS* 95 (2005): 20–37.

Randazzo, S. 'Doppio grado di giurisdizione e potere politico nel primo secolo dell'impero'. In *Roman Law as Formative of Modern Legal Systems. Studies in Honour of Wiesław Litewski*, edited by J. Sondel, J. Reszczyński, and P. Ściślicki, vol. 2, 75–94. Krakow, 2003.

Ranieri, F. *Europäisches Obligationenrecht*, 3rd edn. Vienna, 2009.

Rawson, B., editor. *The Family in Ancient Rome: New Perspectives*. London, 1986, reprinted Ithaca NY, 1993.

Rawson, B., editor. *Marriage, Divorce and Children in Ancient Rome*. Oxford, 1991.

Rawson, B. and P. Weaver, editors. *The Roman Family in Italy: Status, Sentiment and Space*. Oxford, 1997.

Reduzzi-Merola, F. 'Ventes d'esclaves sur les marchés de Campanie'. In *Routes et marchés d'esclaves. 26e colloque du GIREA*, 321–25. Besançon, 2001.

Rehbinder, M. and Ju-Chan Sonn, editors. *Zur Rezeption des deutschen Rechts in Korea*. Baden-Baden, 1990.

Reid, K. and R. Zimmermann, editors. *A History of Private Law in Scotland*, 2 vols. Oxford, 2000.

Reimann, M. *Historische Schule und Common Law*. Berlin, 1993.

Reinkenhof, M. *Die Anwendung des ius commune in San Marino*. Berlin, 1997.

Rhalles, G. A. and M. Potles, editors. *Syntagma ton theion kai hieron kanonon*, 6 vols. Athens, 1852–59.

Rheinstein, M. *Die Struktur des vertraglichen Schuldverhältnisses im anglo-amerikanischen Recht*. Berlin – Leipzig, 1932.

Richardson, J. S. 'The *Tabula Contrebiensis*: Roman law in Spain in the early first century BC'. *JRS 73* (1983): 33–41.

Richardson, J. S. *The Romans in Spain*. Oxford, 1996.
Richardson, J. S. *The Language of Empire: Rome and the Idea of Empire from the Third Century BC to the Second Century AD*. Cambridge, 2008.
Rilinger, R. *Humiliores – Honestiores*. Munich, 1988.
Ristuccia, N. J. 'Law and legal documents in the Sermons of Peter Chrysologus'. *Journal of Late Antiquity* 4 (2011): 124–56.
Rivière, Y. 'Détention préventive, mise à l'épreuve et démonstration de la preuve (Ier–IIIe siècles ap. J.-C.). In *Carcer. Prison et Privation de Liberté dans l'antiquité classique: Actes du colloque de Strasbourg (5 et 6 décembre 1997)*, edited by C. Bertrand-Dagenbach, A. Chauvot, M. Matter, and J.-M. Salamito, 57–73. Paris, 1999.
Rivière, Y. *Les délateurs sous l'empire romain*. Rome, 2002.
Rivière, Y. 'L'Italie, les îles et le continent; recherches sur l'exil et l'administration du territoire impérial (Ier–IIIe siècles)'. *Entretiens Fondation Hardt* 54 (2008): 261–310.
Roberti, M. 'Contributo allo studio delle relazioni fra diritto romano e patristica tratto dall'esame delle fonti Agostiniane'. *Rivista di Filosofia neo-scolastica*. Suppl. to vol. 23 (1931): 305–66.
Robinson, O. 'Justinian's institutional classification and the class of quasi-delict'. *Journal of Legal History* 19 (1998): 245–50.
Robinson, O. 'The 'iudex qui litem suam fecerit' explained'. *ZSS* 116 (1999): 195–99.
Robinson, O. 'Gaius and the class of quasi-delict'. In *Iuris Vincula: Studi in onore di Mario Talamanca*, vol. 7, 120–28. Naples, 2001.
Robinson, O. 'Justinian and the compilers' view of the *iudex qui litem suam fecerit*'. In *Status Familiae*, edited by H.-G. Knothe and J. Kohler, 389–96. Munich, 2001.
Rodger, A. *Owners and Neighbours in Roman Law*. Oxford, 1972.
Rodger, A. 'Scottish advocates in the nineteenth century: The German connection'. *Law Quarterly Review* 110 (1994): 563–91.
Rodger, A. F. 'The palingenesia of the commentaries relating to the lex Aquilia'. *ZSS* 124 (2007): 145–97.
Röhle, R. 'Neue Lesarten zum Text des Codex Florentinus'. *ZSS* 122 (2005): 62–90.
Romeijn, P. *Specimen juridicum inaugurale exhibens loca nonnulla ex Plautii comoediis jure civili illustrata*. Deventer, 1836.
Rostovtzeff, M. *Gesellschaft und Wirtschaft im römischen Kaiserreich*. Leipzig, 1929, reprinted Aalen, 1985.
Rotondi, G. *Leges publicae populi romani*. Milano, 1912.
Rotondi, G. 'Indice dei richiami al diritto nei testi extragiuridici latini dei secoli IV-VII'. In *Scritti Giuridici*, edited by V. Arangio-Ruiz and P. de Francisci, vol. 1, 490–582. Milan, 1922.
Rougé, J. *Recherches sur l'organisation du commerce maritime en Méditerranée sous l'empire romain*. Paris, 1966.
Rougé, J., R. Delmaire, and F. Richard, editors. *Les Lois Religieuses des Empereurs Romains de Constantin à Théodose II. Volume I: Code Théodosien XVI*. (Sources Chrétiennes, vol. 497). Paris, 2005.
Rougé, J., R. Delmaire, O. Huck, F. Richard, and L. Guichard, editors. *Les Lois Religieuses des Empereurs Romains de Constantin à Théodose II. Vol. II: Code Théodosien I-XV, Code Justinien, Constitutions Sirmondiennes*. (Sources Chrétiennes, vol. 531). Paris, 2009.
Rowe, G. 'Trimalchio's World'. *Scripta Classica Israelica* 20 (2001): 225–45.
Rüegg, W. 'Vorwort'. In *Geschichte der Universität in Europa*, edited by W. Rüegg, vol. 1, 13. Munich, 1993.

Ruelle, A. and M. Berlingin, editors. *Le droit romain d'hier à aujourd'hui. Collationes et oblationes. Liber amicorum en l'honneur du professeur Gilbert Hanard*. Brussels, 2009.

Russo Ruggeri, C. *Studi sulle quinquaginta decisiones*. Milan, 1999.

Rutledge, S. H. *Imperial Inquisitions: Prosecutors and Informants from Tiberius to Domitian*. London – New York, 2001.

Ryan, M. 'Bartolus of Sassoferrato and free cities'. *Transactions of the Royal Historical Society* (6th series) (2000): 65–89.

Saller, R. *Personal Patronage under the Early Empire*. Cambridge, 1982.

Saller, R. *Patriarchy, Property and Death in the Roman Family*. Cambridge, 1994.

Salvo, L. de. *I corpora naviculariorum: economia privata e pubblici servizi nell'impero romano*. Messina, 1992.

Santalucia, B. *L'opera di Gai 'ad edictum praetoris urbani'*. Milan, 1975.

Santalucia, B. *Diritto e processo penale nell'antica Roma*, 2nd edn. Milan, 1998.

Santalucia, B., editor. *La repressione criminale nella Roma repubblicana fra norma e persuasione*. Pavia, 2009.

Sargenti, M. and R. B. Bruno Siola. *Normativa Imperiale e Diritto Romano negli Scritti di S. Ambrogio*. Milan, 1991.

Sarris, P. *Economy and Society in the Age of Justinian*. Cambridge, 2006.

Sbordone, F. 'Nuovo contributo alle tavolette cerate pompeiane'. *RAAN* 46 (1971): 173–82.

Sbordone, F. 'Operazioni di mutuo del 48 d.C'. *RAAN* 47 (1972): 307–10.

Sbordone, F. 'Preambolo per'edizione critica delle tavolette cerate di Pompeii'. *RAAN* 51 (1976): 145–67.

Sbordone, F. 'Frustula Pompeiana'. *RAAN* 53 (1978): 249–69.

Sbordone, F. and C. Giordano. 'Dittico Greco-latino dell'agro Murecine'. *RAAN* 43 (1968): 3–12.

Sbriccoli, M. *L'interpretazione dello statuto. Contributo allo studio della funzione dei giuristi nell'età comunale*. Milan, 1969.

Scafuro, A. *The Forensic Stage: Settling Disputes in Graeco-Roman New Comedy*. Cambridge, 1997.

Schauenburg, K. 'Zur "Porticus der Triklinen" am Pagus maritimus bei Pompeji'. *Gymnasium* 69 (1962): 521–29.

Scheltema, H. J. 'Subseciva XI. Das Authenticum'. *TR* 31 (1963): 275–79.

Scheltema, H. J. *L'enseignement de droit des antécesseurs*. Leiden, 1970.

Scheltema, H. J. 'Das Kommentarverbot Justinians'. *TR* 45 (1977): 307–31.

Scheltema, H. J. and N. van der Wal, editors. *Opera minora ad iuris historiam pertinentia*. Groningen, 2004.

Schermaier, M. *Materia*. Vienna – Cologne – Weimar, 1992.

Schermaier, M. 'Bona fides in Roman contract law'. In *Good Faith in European Contract Law*, edited by R. Zimmermann and S. Whittaker, 63–92. Cambridge, 2000.

Scherner, K. O. 'Lex mercatoria – Realität, Geschichtsbild oder Vision?' *ZSS (Germanistische Abteilung)* 118 (2001): 148–67.

Scherner, K. O. 'Goldschmidts Universum'. In *'Ins Wasser geworfen und Ozeane durchquert': Festschrift für Knut Wolfgang Nörr*, edited by M. Ascheri, 859. Cologne – Weimar – Vienna, 2003.

Schiavone, A. *Nascita della giurisprudenza: cultura aristocratica e pensiero giuridico nella Roma tardo-repubblicana*. Rome, 1976.

Schiavone, A. *The Invention of Law in the West*. Translated by J. Carden and A. Shugaar. Cambridge, Mass., 2012.

Schiller, A. A. *Roman Law: Mechanisms of Development*. The Hague, 1978.
Schindler, K. H. *Justinians Haltung zur Klassik, Versuch einer Darstellung an Hand seiner Kontroversen entscheidenden Konstitutionen*. Cologne – Graz, 1966.
Schleppinkhoff, A. M. M. Actio quod iussu. *Die Geheissklage (und ihre Bedeutung für die Entwicklung des Stellvertretungsgedanken im 19. Jahrhundert*. Dissertation: Cologne, 1996.
Schlosser, H. *Grundzüge der neueren Privatrechtsgeschichte*, 10th edn. Heidelberg, 2005.
Schmidt, J. *Zivilrechtskodifikation in Brasilien*. Tübingen, 2009.
Schmidt-Kessel, M. 'Implied Term – auf der Suche nach dem Funktionsäquivalent'. *Zeitschrift für vergleichende Rechtswissenschaft* 96 (1997): 101–55.
Schmidt-Kessel, M. *Standards vertraglicher Haftung nach englischem Recht: Limits of Frustration*. Baden-Baden, 2003.
Schmoeckel, M., J. Rückert, and R. Zimmermann, editors. *Historisch-kritischer Kommentar zum BGB*. Tübingen, 2007.
Scholler, H., editor. *Die Bedeutung des kanonischen Rechts für die Entwicklung einheitlicher Rechtsprinzipien*. Baden-Baden, 1996.
Schröder, J. 'Die zivilrechtliche Haftung für schuldhafte Schadenszufügungen im deutschen usus modernus'. In *La responsabilità civile da atto illecito nella prospettiva storico-comparatistica*, edited by L. Vacca, 144–67. Turin, 1995.
Schulz, F. *Principles of Roman Law*. Oxford, 1936.
Schulz, F. *History of Roman Legal Science*. Oxford, 1946.
Schulz, F. *Classical Roman Law*. Oxford, 1954.
Schulze, R., editor. *Deutsche Rechtswissenschaft und Staatslehre im Spiegel der italienischen Rechtskultur während der zweiten Hälfte des 19. Jahrhunderts*. Berlin, 1990.
Schulze, W. *Zur Geschichte Lateinischer Eigennamen*, 2nd edn. Berlin, 1966.
Schurig, K. 'Europäisches Zivilrecht: Vielfalt oder Einerlei?' In *Festschrift für Bernhard Großfeld*, edited by U. Hüber und W. F. Ebke, 1089–111. Heidelberg, 1999.
Schuster, S. *Das Seedarlehen in den Gerichtsreden des Demosthenes: mit einem Ausblick auf die weitere historische Entwicklung des Rechtsinstitutes: dáneion nautikón, fenus nauticum und Bodmerei*. Berlin, 2005.
Seeck, O. *Regesten der Kaiser und Päpste für die Jahre 311 bis 476 n. Chr.* Stuttgart, 1919.
Seider, R. *Paläographie der lateinischen Papyri. Vol. 2.2: Juristische und christliche Texte*. Stuttgart, 1981.
Seidl, E. *Römische Rechtsgeschichte und Römisches Zivilprozessrecht*. Cologne, 1962.
Seiler, H. H. 'Die deliktische Gehilfenhaftung in historischer Sicht'. *Juristenzeitung* 1967: 525–29.
Seiler, H. H. 'Utile per inutile non vitiatur: Zur Teilunwirksamkeit von Rechtsgeschäften im römischen Recht'. In *Festschrift für Max Kaser*, edited by D. Medicus and H. H. Seiler, 127. Munich, 1976.
Serrao, F. *La 'iurisdictio' del pretore peregrino*. Milan, 1954.
Serrao, F. *Impresa e responsabilità a Roma nell'età commerciale: forme giuridiche di un'economia-mondo*. Ospedaletto, 1989.
Serrao, F. 'Impresa, mercato, diritto. Riflessioni minime'. In *Mercati permanenti e mercati periodici nel mondo romano. Atti degli incontri capresi di storia dell'economia antica (Capri 13–15 ottobre 1997)*, edited by E. Lo Cascio, 31–67. Bari, 2000.
Shaw, B. D. 'Judicial nightmares and Christian memory'. *Journal of Early Christian Studies* 11 (2003): 533–63.
Sherk, R. *Roman Documents from the Greek East*. Baltimore, 1969.

Sherwin-White, A. N. *Roman Society and Roman Law in the New Testament*. Oxford, 1963.

Sider, R. D. *Ancient Rhetoric and the Art of Tertullian*. Oxford, 1971.

Siems, H. 'Codex Theodosianus'. In *Reallexikon der germanischen Altertumskunde*, vol. 5, cols. 47–52.

Silli, P. *Testi Costantiniani nelle Fonti Letterarie*. Milan, 1987.

Silver, M. 'Roman economic growth and living standards: perceptions versus evidence'. *Ancient Society* 37 (2007): 191–252.

Simon, D. 'Aus dem Codexunterricht des Thalelaios. C. Interpolationsberichte'. *RIDA* 16 (1969): 283–308.

Simon, D. *Untersuchungen zum justinianischen Zivilprozeß*. Munich, 1969.

Simon, D. 'Aus dem Codexunterricht des Thalelaios. B. Die Heroen'. *ZSS* 87 (1970): 315–94.

Simon, D. *Rechtsfindung am byzantinischen Reichsgericht*. Frankfurt, 1973.

Simon, D. 'Das Ehegüterrecht der Pira. Ein systematischer Versuch'. *Fontes Minores* 7 (1986): 193–238.

Simon, D. 'Das Novellenexemplar des Athanasios'. *Fontes minores* 7 (1986): 117–40.

Simon, D. 'Die animusbesessene Spätzeit'. *Rechtshistorisches Journal* 14 (1995): 253–80.

Simpson, A. W. B. 'Innovation in nineteenth century contract law'. *Law Quarterly Review* 91 (1975): 247–78.

Sirks, A. J. B. *Food for Rome*. Amsterdam, 1991.

Sirks, A. J. B. 'Sailing in the off-season with reduced financial risk'. In Speculum iuris. *Roman Law as a Reflection of Social and Economic Life in Antiquity*, edited by J.-J. Aubert and A. J. B. Sirks, 134–50. Ann Arbor, 2002.

Sirks, A. J. B. *The Theodosian Code. A Study*. Friedrichsdorf, 2007.

Sirks, A. J. B. 'The delictual origin, penal nature and reipersecutory object of the actio damni iniuriae legis Aquiliae'. *TR* 77 (2009): 303–53.

Sirks, A. J. B. 'The slave who was slain twice: causality and the lex Aquilia (Iul. 38 *dig.* D. 9, 2, 51)'. *TR* 79 (2011): 313–51.

Sirks, A. J. B. 'Furtum and manus / potestas'. *TR* 81 (2013): 465–506.

Sirks, A. J. B. 'Noxa caput sequitur'. *TR* 81 (2013): 81–108.

Sirks, A. J. B. 'Law, commerce and finance in the Roman empire'. In *Trade, Commerce and the State in the Roman World*, edited by A. I. Wilson and A. K. Bowman (Oxford, forthcoming).

Sirks, A. J. B., P. Sijpestein, and K. A. Worp, editors. *Ein frühbyzantinisches Szenario für die Amtswechslung in der Sitonie: Die griechischen Papyri aus Pommersfelden (PPG) mit einem Anhang über die Pommersfeldener Digestenfragmente und die Überlieferungsgeschichte der Digesten*. Munich, 1996.

Skinner, Q. 'The rediscovery of republican values'. In *Visions of Politics*, edited by Q. Skinner, vol. 2, 10–38. Cambridge, 2002.

Smith, A. *Lectures on Jurisprudence*, edited by R. Meek, D. Raphael, and P. Stein. Oxford, 1978).

Soetermeer, F. *Utrumque ius in peciis: die Produktion juristischer Bücher an italienischen und französischen Universitäten des 13. und 14. Jahrhunderts*. Translated by G. Hillner. Frankfurt, 2002.

Spangenberg, E. *Einleitung in das roemisch-justinianeische Rechtsbuch oder Corpus iuris civilis Romani*. Hannover, 1817; reprinted Aalen, 1970.

Speciale, G. 'Garnerius Theutonicus' Nuove fonti su Irnerio e i quattro dottori'. *Rivista internazionale di diritto comune* 2 (1991): 123–33.

Speciale, G. *La memoria del diritto comune: sulle tracce d'uso del Codex di Giustiniano (secoli XII–XV)*. Rome, 1994.

Spengler, H.-D. *Studien zur interrogatio in iure*. Munich, 1994.

Sperandio, M. U. *Codex Gregorianus. Origini e vicende*. Naples, 2005.

Ššapov, J. N. and L. Burgmann, editors. *Die slavische Ecloga*. Frankfurt, 2011.

Stanojević, O. *Gaius Noster – Plaidoyer pour Gaius*. Amsterdam, 1989.

Stefania, P. *Religio e Ius Romanum nell'epistolario di Leone Magno*. Milan, 2002.

Stein, P. 'The influence of Roman law on the law of Scotland'. *Juridical Review* 1963: 205–45.

Stein, P. 'Roman law in Scotland'. *Ius Romanum Medii Aevi*, part V.13b. Milan, 1968.

Stein, P. 'Equitable principles in Roman law'. In P. Stein, *The Character and Influence of the Roman Civil Law: Historical Essays*, 19–36. London, 1988.

Stein, P. 'Legal theory and the reform of legal education in mid-nineteenth century England'. In P. Stein, *The Character and Influence of the Roman Civil Law: Historical Essays*, 231–50. London, 1988.

Stein, P. 'Logic and experience in Roman and Common law'. In P. Stein, *The Character and Influence of the Roman Civil Law: Historical Essays*, 37–51. London, 1988.

Stein, P. 'The attraction of the civil law in post-revolutionary America'. In P. Stein, *The Character and Influence of the Roman Civil Law: Historical Essays*, 411–42. London, 1988.

Stein, P. ''Equitable' Remedies for the Protection of Property'. In *New Perspectives in the Roman Law of Property: Essays for Barry Nicholas*, edited by P. Birks, 185–94. Oxford, 1989.

Stein, P. 'Roman law, Common law, and Civil law'. *Tulane Law Review* 66 (1992): 1591–603.

Stein, P. *Roman Law in European History*. Cambridge, 1999.

Stein, P. and F. de Zulueta. *The Teaching of Roman Law in England Around 1200*. London, 1990.

Steinwenter, A. *Studien zum römischen Versäumnisverfahren*. Munich, 1914.

Steinwenter, A. 'Der Einfluss des römischen Rechtes auf den antiken kanonischen Prozess'. In *Congresso Internationale di Diritto Romano*, vol. 2, 227–41. Rome, 1935.

Stelling-Michaud, S. 'La diffusion du droit romain en Suisse: étudiants suisses à l'étranger et leur activité professionnelle ultérieure'. *Ius Romanum Medii Aevi*, part V.12b. Milan, 1977.

Stelzer, W. Deutsches Archiv für Erforschung des Mittelalters, *Monumenta Germaniae Historica*, 34 (1978): 123–65.

Stolte, B. H. 'Finium regundorum and the Agrimensores'. *Subseciva Groningana* 5 (1992) 61–76.

Stolte, B. H. 'Not new but novel. Notes on the historiography of Byzantine law'. *Byzantine and Modern Greek Studies* 22 (1998): 264–79.

Stolte, B. H. 'Some thoughts on the early history of the Digest text. Appendix: Ms. Naples IV. A. 8 foll. 36–39 rescr'. *Subseciva Groningana* 6 (1999): 103–19.

Stolte, B. H. 'Is Byzantine law Roman law?' *Acta Byzantina Fennica* 2 (n.s.) (2003–4): 111–26.

Stolte, B. H. 'Balancing Byzantine law'. *Fontes Minores* 11 (2005): 57–75.

Stolte, B. H. 'A crisis of jurisprudence? the end of legal writing in the classical tradition'. In *Crises and Roman Empire. Proceedings of the Seventh Workshop of the International*

Network Impact of Empire (Nijmegen, June 20–24, 2006), edited by O. Hekster, G. de Kleijn, and D. Slootjes, 355–66. Leiden, 2007.

Stolte, B. H. 'Justice: legal literature'. In *The Oxford Handbook of Byzantine Studies*, edited by E. Jeffreys, 691–98. Oxford, 2008.

Stolte, B. H. 'Zwei neue Basilikenhandschriften in der Wiener Nationalbibliothek II: Rechtshistorische Analyse'. In *Quellen zur byzantinischen Rechtspraxis. Aspekte der Textüberlieferung, Paläographie und Diplomatik. Akten des internationalen Symposiums, Wien, 5.–7.11.2007*, edited by C. Gastgeber, 139–51. Vienna, 2010.

Stolte, B. H. 'The value of the Byzantine tradition for textual criticism of the Corpus Iuris Civilis. 'Graeca leguntur''. In *Introduzione al diritto bizantino*, edited by J. H. A. Lokin and B. H. Stolte, 667–80. Pavia, 2011.

Stolte, B. H. 'The Byzantine law of obligations'. In *Obligations in Roman Law. Past, Present and Future*, edited by T. A. J. McGinn, 320–33. Ann Arbor, 2012.

Stroux, J. *Summum ius summa iniuria*. Leipzig, 1926.

Sundell, J.-O. 'German influence on Swedish private law doctrine 1870–1914'. *Scandinavian Studies in Law* (1991): 236–68.

Talamanca, M. 'Lo schema genus – species nelle sistematiche dei giuristi romani'. In *La filosofia greca e il diritto romano, II*. Rome, 1977.

Talamanca, M. *Istituzioni di diritto romano*. Milan, 1990.

Talbert, R. J. A. *The Senate of Imperial Rome*. Princeton, 1984.

Tchernia, A. 'Le *plebiscitum Claudianum*'. In *Vocabulaire et expression de l'économie dans le monde antique*, edited by J. Andreau and V. Chankowski, 253–78. Bordeaux, 2007.

Tellegen, J. W. *The Roman Law of Succession in the Letters of Pliny the Younger I*. Zutphen, 1982.

Tellegen-Couperus, O. *A Short History of Roman Law*. London, 1993.

Tellegen-Couperus, O. 'Introduction'. In *Quintilian and the Law: The Art of Persuasion and Politics*, edited by O. Tellegen-Couperus, 12–17. Leuven, 2003.

Terpstra, T. 'Roman law, transaction costs and the Roman economy: evidence from the Sulpicii archive'. In *Pistoi dia tèn technèn. Bankers, Loans and Archives in the Ancient World. Studies in Honour of Raymond Bogaert*, edited by K. Verboven, K. Vandorpe, and V. Chankowski, 345–69. Leuven, 2008.

Thomas, J. A. C. 'Contrectatio, complicity and furtum'. *Iura* 13 (1962): 69–88.

Thomas, J. A. C. *Textbook of Roman Law*. Amsterdam, 1976.

Thomasius, C. *Larva Legis Aquiliae*, edited and translated by M. Hewett. Oxford, 2000.

Thür, G. 'Recht im antiken Griechenland'. In *Die Rechtskulturen der Antike*, edited by U. Manthe, 191–238. Munich, 2003.

Tisset, P. 'Mythes et réalités du droit romain'. In *Etudes d'histoire du droit privé offertes à P. Petot*, 553–60. Paris, 1959.

Tomulescu, C. S. 'La valeur juridique de l'Histoire de Tite-Live'. *Labeo* 21 (1975): 295–321.

Tomulescu, C. S. 'Observations sur la terminologie juridique de Plaute'. In *Sodalitas. Scritti in onore di Antonio Guarino*, edited by V. Giuffre, vol. 6, 2771–81. Naples, 1984.

Torelli, M. *Typology and Structure of Roman Historical Reliefs*. Ann Arbor, 1982.

Tort-Martorell, C. *Tradicion textual del Codex Iustinianus. Un estudio del libro 2*. Frankfurt, 1989.

Treggiari, S. *Roman Freedmen during the Late Republic*. Oxford, 1969.

Treggiari, S. *Roman Marriage: Iusti Coniuges from the Time of Cicero to the Time of Ulpian*. Oxford, 1991.

Treitel, G. H. *Unmöglichkeit, 'Impracticability' and 'Frustration' im anglo-amerikanischen Recht.* Baden-Baden, 1991.

Triantaphyllopoulos, J. '*Cantar le leggi.* ' *Atti dell'Accademia Mediterranea delle Scienze.* Anno I, Vol. I, Supplemento I, 27–34. Catania, 1983.

Troianos, S. 'Die Collectio Ambrosiana'. *Fontes minores* 2 (1977): 30–48.

Troianos, S. 'Von der Hexabiblos zu den Basiliken'. *Subseciva Groningana* 3 (1989): 127–41.

Troianos, S. *Oi peges tou buzantinou dikaiou*, 3rd augmented edn. Athens-Komotini, 2011.

Troje, H. E. *Graeca leguntur: die Aneignung des byzantinischen Rechts und der Entstehung eines humanistischen Corpus iuris civilis in der Jurisprudenz des 16. Jahrhunderts.* Cologne – Vienna, 1971.

Troje, H. E. *Humanistische Jurisprudenz. Studien zur europäischen Rechtswissenschaft unter dem Einfluß des Humanismus.* Goldbach, 1993.

Troje, H. E. 'Zur Historia Pandectarum: Vorläufer der Editio Taurelliana'. In *Festschrift für Rolf Knütel zum 70. Geburtstag*, edited by H. Altmeppen, I. Reichard, and M. Schermaier, 1301–24. Heidelberg, 2010.

Troje, H. E. *Crisis digestorum. Studien zur historia pandectarum.* Frankfurt, 2011.

Trusen, W. 'Römisches und partikuläres Recht in der Rezeptionszeit'. In *Festschrift für Heinrich Lange*, edited by K. Kuchinke, 91–120. Munich, 1970.

Trusen, W. 'Die gelehrte Gerichtsbarkeit der Kirche'. In *Handbuch der Quellen und Literatur der neueren europäischen Privatrechtsgeschichte*, edited by H. Coing, vol. 1, 467–504. Munich, 1973.

Tuori, K. *Ancient Roman Lawyers and Modern Legal Ideals. Studies on the Impact of Contemporary Concerns in the Interpretation of Ancient Roman Legal History.* Frankfurt, 2007.

Tuori, K. 'A Place for Jurists in the Spaces of Justice?' In *Spaces of Justice in the Roman World*, edited by W. V. Harris and F. de Angelis, 43–65. Leiden, 2010.

Turelli, G. '*'Res incorporales'* e beni immateriali: categorie affini, ma non congruenti'. *Teoria e Storia del Diritto Privato* (2012): 1–17.

Turpin, W. 'Formula, *cognitio*, and Proceedings *extra ordinem*'. *RIDA* 46 (1999): 499–574.

Tzadua, Abba. P., translator, and P. L. Strauss, editor. *The Fetha Nagast. The Law of the Kings*, 2nd edn. Durham, NC, 2009; 1st edn. Addis Ababa, 1968.

Uhalde, K. *Expectations of Justice in the Age of Augustine.* Philadelphia, 2007.

Ullmann, W. 'The medieval interpretation of Frederick I's authentic *Habita*'. In W. Ullmann, *Scholarship and Politics in the Middle Ages.* London, 1978.

Vacca, L. 'Il c[osí]. d[etto]. Duplex dominium e l'actio publiciana'. In *La proprietà e le proprietà*, edited by E. Cortese, 39–74. Milan, 1988.

Vallejo, J. *Ruda equidad, ley consumada: concepcion de la potestad normativa (1250–1350).* Madrid, 1992.

Varvaro, M. 'Manu(m) conserere e omnibus verbis vindicare (Gellius 20.10.7)'. In *Le dodici tavole: dai decemviri agli umanisti*, edited by M. Humbert, 267–309. Pavia, 2005.

Vékás, L. 'Integration des östlichen Mitteleuropa im Wege rechtsvergleichender Zivilrechtserneuerung'. *Zeitschrift für europäisches Privatrecht* 12 (2004): 454–76.

Venturini, C. 'La repressione degli abusi dei magistrati romani ai danni delle popolazioni soggette fino alla *lex Calpurnia* del 149 a.c'. *BIDR* 72 (1969): 19–87.

Verger, J. 'Grundlagen'. In *Geschichte der Universität in Europa*, edited by W. Rüegg, vol. 1, 49–78. Munich, 1993.

Verse, D. A. *Verwendungen im Eigentümer-Besitzer-Verhältnis: Eine kritische Betrachtung aus historisch-vergleichender Sicht.* Tübingen, 1999.

Vessey, M. 'The origins of the Collectio Sirmondiana: a new look at the evidence'. In *The Theodosian Code: Studies in the Imperial Law of Late Antiquity*, edited by J. Harries and I. Wood, 178–99, 2nd edn. London, 2010.

Viejo-Ximénez, J. M. 'La reception del derecho romano en el derecho canónico'. *Anales de la Tradición Romanística* 2 (2005): 139–69.

Vincenti, U. *Categorie del diritto romano*, 2nd edn. Naples, 2008.

Vinogradoff, P. *Roman Law in Medieval Europe*. Cambridge, 1968.

Violardo, G. *Il pensiero giuridico di San Girolamo*. Milan, 1937.

Visscher, F. de. 'Les fantaisies formulaires de Verres'. *Revue d'Etudes Latines* 33 (1956): 136–39; reprinted in F. de Visscher, *Etudes de droit romain*, vol. 3, 425–28.

Visser, D. 'Das Recht der ungerechtfertigten Bereicherung'. In *Das römisch-holländische Recht: Fortschritte des Zivilrechts im 17. und 18. Jahrhundert*, edited by R. Feenstra and R. Zimmermann, 369–428. Berlin, 1992.

Voci, P. *Diritto ereditario romano*, 2 vols. Florence, 1963, 1967.

Vogenauer, S. *Die Auslegung von Gesetzen in England und auf dem Kontinent*, 2 vols. Tübingen, 2001.

Vogenauer, S. 'Zur Geschichte des Präjudizienrechts in England'. *Zeitschrift für neuere Rechtsgeschichte* 28 (2006): 48–78.

Volterra, E. 'Considerazioni teologico-giuridiche di Asterio di Amasea'. *Rivista italiana per le scienze giuridiche* n.s. 4 (1929): 3–10.

Wacke, A. 'Lothar Anton Alfred Pernice'. In *Neue Deutsche Biographie*, vol. 20, 194–95. Berlin, 2001.

Wal, N. van der. *Manuale Novellarum Justiniani. Aperçu systématique du contenu des novelles de Justinien*. Groningen – Amsterdam, 1964; 2nd edn., 1998.

Wal, N. van der. 'Die Schreibweise der dem Lateinischen entlehnten Fachworten in der frühbyzantinischen Juristensprache'. *Scriptorium* 37 (1983): 29–53.

Wal, N. van der and J. H. A. Lokin. *Delineatio iuris graeci-romani. Les sources du droit byzantin de 300 à 1453*. Groningen, 1985.

Waldstein, W. and J. M. Rainer. *Römische Rechtsgeschichte*, 10th edn. Munich, 2005.

Wallinga, T. 'Honoré, Justinian's Digest'. *Edinburgh Law Review* 16 (2012): 119–22.

Walther, H. '*Regnum magis assimilatur dominio quam simplici regimini*. Zur Attraktivität der Monarchie in der politischen Theorie gelehrter Juristen des 15. Jahrhunderts'. In *Sozialer Wandel im Mittelalter. Wahrnehmungsformen, Erklärungsmuster, Regelungsmechanismen*, edited by J. Miethke and K. Schreiner, 383–99. Sigmaringen, 1994.

Watson, W. A. J. 'Contrectatio as an essential of furtum'. *Law Quarterly Review* 77 (1961): 526–32.

Watson, A. *The Law of Property in the Later Roman Republic*. Oxford, 1968.

Watson, A. *Law Making in the Later Roman Republic*. Oxford, 1974.

Watson, A. *Roman Slave Law*. Baltimore, 1987.

Watson, A. *Failures of the Legal Imagination*. Pennsylvania, 1988.

Watson, A. *International Law in Archaic Rome: War and Religion*. Baltimore, 1993.

Weimar, P. 'Die legistische Literatur der Glossatorenzeit'. In *Handbuch der Quellen und Literatur zur neueren europäischen Privatrechtsgeschichte I. Mittelalter*, edited by H. Coing, 129–260. Munich, 1973.

Weiss, E. '*Recitatio* und *responsum* im römischen Provinzialprozeß, ein Beitrag zum Gerichtsgebrauch'. *ZSS* 33 (1912): 212–39.

Weiss, E. 'Peregrinische Manzipationsakte'. *ZSS* 37 (1916): 136–76.

Wenger, L. 'Um die Zukunft des römischen Rechts'. In *Festschrift Fritz Schulz*, vol. 2, 364–86. Weimar, 1951.

Wenger, L. *Die Quellen des römischen Rechts*. Vienna, 1953.

Wesener, G. 'Ius possessionis'. In *Festschrift für Max Kaser zum 70. Geburtsdag*, edited by D. Medicus and H. H. Seiler, 159–78. Munich, 1976.

Westbrook, R. 'The nature and origin of the twelve tables'. *ZSS* 105 (1988): 74–121.

Wetzler, C. *Rechtsstaat und Absolutismus. Überlegungen zur Verfassung des spätantiken Kaiserreichs anhand von CJ 1.14.8*. Berlin, 1997.

Whittaker, S. and R. Zimmermann, 'Good faith in European contract law: surveying the legal landscape'. In R. Zimmermann and S. Whittaker, editors, *Good Faith in European Contract Law*, 7–62. Cambridge, 2000.

Wicke, H. *Respondeat Superior*. Berlin, 2000.

Wieacker, F. *Zur rechtstheoretischen Präzisierung des § 242 BGB*. Tübingen, 1956.

Wieacker, F. *Textstufen klassischer Juristen*. Göttingen, 1959, reprinted 1975.

Wieacker, F. *Römische Rechtsgeschichte*, vol. 1. Munich, 1988.

Wieacker, F. 'Foundations of European Legal Culture'. *American Journal of Comparative Law* 38 (1990): 1–29.

Wieacker, F. *A History of Private Law in Europe*. Translated by T. Weir. Oxford, 1995.

Wiegand, W. 'Zur Herkunft und Ausbreitung der Formel 'habere fundatam intentionem''. In *Festschrift für Hermann Krause*, edited by S. Gagnér, H. Schlosser, and W. Wiegand, 126–87. Cologne – Vienna, 1975.

Wijffels, A. *Qui millies allegatur: les allégations du droit savant dans les dossiers du Grand Conseil de Malines (causes septentrionales, ca. 1460–1580)*. Leiden, 1985.

Windscheid, B. 'Die geschichtliche Schule in der Rechtswissenschaft'. In B. Windscheid, *Gesammelte Reden und Abhandlungen*, edited by P. Oertmann, 66–80. Leipzig, 1904.

Windscheid, B. and T. Kipp. *Lehrbuch des Pandektenrechts*, 9th edn. Frankfurt, 1906.

Winkel, L. 'Die stoische οἰκείωσις-Lehre und Ulpians Definition der Gerechtigkeit'. *ZSS* 105 (1988): 669–79.

Winkel, L. 'Das sokratische Paradoxon 'οὐδεὶς ἑκὼν ἐξαμαρτάνει' und strafrechtliche Zurechnung im Lichte der neueren Literatur'. In *Symposion VI. Beiträge zur griechischen und hellenistischen Rechtsgeschichte*, 109–17. Vienna – Cologne, 1989.

Winkel, L. 'Einige Bemerkungen über *ius naturale* und *ius gentium*'. In *Ars boni et aequi. Festschrift für Wolfgang Waldstein*, edited by M. J. Schermaier and Z. Végh, 443–49. Stuttgart, 1993.

Winkel, L. 'Rechtsgeschiedenis en integratie van de rechtswetenschap'. In *Geïntegreerde rechtswetenschap*, edited by R. Foqué, 207–20. Arnhem, 1994.

Winkel, L. 'Le droit romain et la philosophie grecque, quelques problèmes de méthode'. *TR* 65 (1997): 373–84.

Winkel, L. 'Cujas (Cujacius), Jacques'. In *Dictionnaire historique des juristes français, XIIe–XXe siècle*, edited by P. Arabeyre, Jean-Louis Halpérin, and Jacques Krynen, 220–22. Paris, 2007.

Winkel, L. 'Inst. Iust. 4,4 pr.: Kübler et Daube sur les mots ἀδικία (adikia) et ἀδίκημα (adikèma), ἁμαρτία (hamartia) et ἁμαρτῆμα (hamartèma)'. In *Fides, humanitas, ius: Studii in onore di Luigi Labruna*, edited by C. Cascione and C. M. Doria, vol. 8, 5927–934. Naples, 2007.

Winkel, L. Review of W. J. Zwalve, *Hoofdstukken uit de geschiedenis van het Europees Privaatrecht. I: Inleiding en zakenrecht*. In *Zeitschrift für europäisches Privatrecht* 16 (2008): 435–37.

Winkel, L. 'Some thoughts on the *formulae ficticiae* of citizenship in Gaius, 4.37: a form of reception?' In *Judge and Jurist. Essays in Memory of Lord Rodger of Earlsferry*, edited by A. Burrows, D. Johnston, and R. Zimmermann, 299–308. Oxford, 2013.

Winroth, A. *The Making of Gratian's Decretum*. Cambridge, 2000.

Witte, J. and F. Alexander, editors. *Christianity and Law: An Introduction*. Cambridge, 2008.

Woess, F. von. *Das römische Erbrecht und die Erbanwärter*. Berlin, 1911.

Wolf, J. G. 'Die Kondiktionen des C. Sulpicius Cinnamus'. *SDHI* 45 (1979): 142–77.

Wolf, J. G. 'Das sogenannte Ladungsvadimonium'. In *Satura Roberto Feenstra oblata*, edited by J. A. Ankum, J. E. Spruit, and F. B. J. Wubbe, 59–69. Fribourg, 1985.

Wolf, J. G. 'Die Streitbeilegung zwischen L. Faenius Eumenes und C. Sulpicius Faustus'. In *Studi in onore di Cesare Sanfilippo*, vol. 6, 769–88. Milan, 1985.

Wolf, J. G. 'Die Naulotike des Menelaos – Seedarlehen oder Seefrachtvertrag?' In *Iuris vincula: Studi in onore di Mario Talamanca*, 421–63. Naples, 2001.

Wolf, J. G. 'Intertium – und kein Ende?' *BIDR* 39 (2001): 1–36.

Wolf, J. G. Review of G. Camodeca, *Tabulae Pompeianae Sulpiciorum. Edizione critica dell'archivio puteolano dei Sulpicii*. *SZ* 118 (2001): 73–132.

Wolf, J. G. ''Vadimonium' in Ciceros Rede pro Quinctio'. *SDHI* 74 (2008): 79–97.

Wolf, J. G. *Aus dem neuen pompeianischen Urkundenfund: Gesammelte Aufsätze*. Berlin, 2010.

Wolf, J. G. 'Eine Eidesdelation und eine Eidesleistung'. In *Festschrift für Rolf Knütel*, edited by H. Altmeppen, I. Reichard, and M. Schermaier, 1459–68. Heidelberg, 2010.

Wolf, J. G. 'Eine Empfangserklärung aus Herculaneum'. In *Studi in onore di Antonio Metro*, edited by C. Russo Ruggeri, 491–501. Milan, 2010.

Wolf, J. G. *Neue Rechtsurkunden aus Pompeji: Tabulae Pompeianae Novae*. Darmstadt, 2010.

Wolf, J. G. and J. A. Crook. *Rechtsurkunden in Vulgärlatein*. Heidelberg, 1989.

Wolff, C. *Grundsätze des Natur- und Völckerrechts*. Halle, 1754.

Wolff, H. J. 'Ulpian XVIII ad edictum in Collatio and Digest and the problem of postclassical editions of classical works'. In *Scritti Ferrini*, vol. 4, 64–90. Milan, 1949.

Wolff, H. J. *Das Problem der Konkurrenz von Rechtsordnungen in der Antike*. Heidelberg, 1979.

Wolff, H. J. *Das Recht der griechischen Papyri Ägyptens*, vol. 1. Munich, 2002.

Wolter, U. *Das Prinzip der Naturalrestitution nach § 249 BGB*. Berlin, 1985.

Wood, I. 'Administration, Law and Culture in Merovingian Gaul'. In *From Roman Provinces to Medieval Kingdoms*, edited by T. Noble, 358–75. Abingdon, 2006.

Woolf, C. N. S. *Bartolus of Sassoferrato – His Position in the History of Medieval Political Thought*. Cambridge, 1913.

Yoshiko Reed, A. '"Jewish Christianity" as counter-history? The apostolic past in Eusebius' Ecclesiastical History and the Pseudo-Clementine Homilies'. In *Antiquity in Antiquity: Jewish and Christian Pasts in the Greco-Roman World*, edited by G. Gardner and K. L. Osterloh, 173–216. Tübingen, 2008.

Zachariä von Lingenthal, K. E. *Geschichte des griechisch-römischen Rechts*, 3rd edn., 1892; reprinted Aalen, 1955.

Zanetti, G. *Questiones de iuris subtilitatibus*. Florence, 1958.

Zangemeister, C. 'Tabulae ceratae Pompeis repertae annis MDCCCLXXV et MDCCCLXXXVII'. In *CIL* IV suppl. I no. 3340 I-CLIII. (1898).

Zanon, G. *Indicazioni di metodo giuridico dalla Consultatio veteris cuiusdam iurisconsulti*, 2nd edn. Naples, 2009.

Zimmermann, R. *Das römisch-holländische Recht in Südafrika*. Darmstadt, 1983.

Zimmermann, R. 'Der europäische Charakter des englischen Rechts: Historische Verbindungen zwischen civil law und common law'. *Zeitschrift für europäisches Privatrecht* 1 (1993): 4–51.

Zimmermann, R. '"Heard melodies are sweet, but those unheard are sweeter . . .": Conditio tacita, implied condition und die Fortbildung des europäischen Vertragsrechts'. *Archiv für die civilistische Praxis* 193 (1993): 121–73.

Zimmermann, R. 'Rechtsvergelijking, rechtsgeschiedenis en ius commune'. *Ars Aequi* 43 (1994): 276–83.

Zimmermann, R. 'Roman law in a mixed legal system: the South African experience'. In *The Civil Law Tradition in Scotland*, edited by R. Evans-Jones, 41–78. Edinburgh, 1995.

Zimmermann, R. 'Unjustified enrichment: the modern civilian approach'. *Oxford Journal of Legal Studies* 15 (1995): 403–29.

Zimmermann, R. *The Law of Obligations: Roman Foundations of the Civilian Tradition*. 1990; reprinted Oxford, 1996.

Zimmermann, R. 'Statuta sunt stricte interpretanda. Statutes and the common law: a continental perspective'. *Cambridge Law Journal* 56 (1997): 315–28.

Zimmermann, R. 'The civil law in European codes'. In *The Civilian Tradition and Scots Law: Aberdeen Quincentenary Essays*, edited by D. Carey Miller and R. Zimmermann, 259–93. Berlin, 1997.

Zimmermann, R. '"In der Schule von Ludwig Mitteis": Ernst Rabels rechtshistorische Ursprünge'. *Rabels Zeitschrift* 65 (2001): 1–38.

Zimmermann, R. *Roman Law, Contemporary Law, European Law*. Oxford, 2001.

Zimmermann, R. 'Gemeines Recht heute: Das Kreuz des Südens'. In *Der praktische Nutzen der Rechtsgeschichte: Festschrift für Hans Hattenhauer*, edited by J. Eckert, 601–27. Heidelberg, 2003.

Zimmermann, R. 'Was Heimat hieß, nun heißt es Hölle'. In *Jurists Uprooted: German-speaking Émigré Lawyers in Twentieth-Century Britain*, edited by J. Beatson and R. Zimmermann, 1–71. Oxford, 2004.

Zimmermann, R. *The New German Law of Obligations: Historical and Comparative Perspectives*. Oxford, 2005.

Zimmermann, R. 'Ius Commune and the principles of European contract law: contemporary renewal of an old idea'. In *European Contract Law*, edited by H. L. MacQueen and R. Zimmermann, 1–42. Edinburgh, 2006.

Zimmermann, R. 'Die Geschichte der Gastwirtshaftung in Deutschland'. In *Usus modernus pandectarum: Römisches Recht, Deutsches Recht und Naturrecht in der frühen Neuzeit: Festschrift für Klaus Luig*, edited by H.-P. Haferkamp and T. Repgen, 271–339. Cologne – Weimar – Vienna, 2007.

Zimmermann, R. 'Comparative law and the Europeanization of private law'. In *The Oxford Handbook of Comparative Law*, edited by M. Reimann and R. Zimmermann, 539–78. Oxford, 2008.

Zimmermann, R. 'The present state of European private law'. *American Journal of Comparative Law* 57 (2009): 479–512.

Zimmermann, R. and D. Visser, editors. *Southern Cross: Civil Law and Common Law in South Africa*. Oxford, 1996.

Zimmermann, R., D. Visser, and K. Reid, editors. *Mixed Legal Systems in Comparative Perspective: Property and Obligations in Scotland and South Africa*. Oxford, 2004.

Zocco-Rosa, A. *Imp. Iustiniani institutionum palingenesia*, 2 vols. Catania, 1908, 1911.

Zwalve, W.J. 'De toekomst van het Romeinse recht', *Ars Aequi* 42 (1993): 455–59.
Zwalve, W. 'Teaching Roman law in the Netherlands'. *Zeitschrift für europäisches Privatrecht* 5 (1997): 393–404.
Zwalve W.J. *Hoofdstukken uit de geschiedenis van het Europees Privaatrecht. I: Inleiding en zakenrecht.* Deventer, 2006.
Zwalve, W.J. and A.J.B. Sirks. *Grundzüge der europäischen Privatrechtsgeschichte. Einführung und Sachenrecht.* Cologne – Weimar – Vienna, 2012.
Zweigert, K. and H. Kötz. *Einführung in die Rechtsvergleichung*, 3rd edn. Tübingen, 1996.

Index

Printed in Great Britain
by Amazon

86101758R00315